The Economy of Saudi Arabia
in the 21st Century

MIDDLE EAST POLITICAL ECONOMY SERIES

The Middle East Political Economy Series is devoted to the publication of theoretically informed, analytically rigorous, and empirically grounded work on concerns critical to the economics and politics of the MENA region. These include energy, investment, finance, debt, employment, agriculture, and industry. The series welcomes original contributions on seminal topics such as structural transformation, policy reform, economic diversification, environmental sustainability, labour economics, demographic transitions, regional integration, the dynamics of inequality, business–government relations, and the management of economic crises. It also offers a scholarly platform for exploring issues of private entrepreneurship, technological innovation, gender equality, human welfare, civil society, the challenges of urbanization, the rule of law, the changing role of the state, and the effects of globalization. The series embraces a multidisciplinary approach to political economy, and it seeks to attract a new generation of scholars, students, and practitioners in enriching discourse on the region's development and prospects.

Series Editors

Don Babai, Harvard University and John Sfakianakis, University of Cambridge

The Economy of Saudi Arabia in the 21st Century

Realities and Prospects

Edited by

John Sfakianakis

OXFORD
UNIVERSITY PRESS

OXFORD
UNIVERSITY PRESS

Great Clarendon Street, Oxford, OX2 6DP,
United Kingdom

Oxford University Press is a department of the University of Oxford.
It furthers the University's objective of excellence in research, scholarship,
and education by publishing worldwide. Oxford is a registered trade mark of
Oxford University Press in the UK and in certain other countries

Published in the United States of America by Oxford University Press
198 Madison Avenue, New York, NY 10016, United States of America

British Library Cataloguing in Publication Data

Data available

Library of Congress Control Number: 2024906942

ISBN 9780198863878

DOI: 10.1093/oso/9780198863878.001.0001

Printed and bound by
CPI Group (UK) Ltd, Croydon, CR0 4YY

Links to third party websites are provided by Oxford in good faith and
for information only. Oxford disclaims any responsibility for the materials
contained in any third party website referenced in this work.

Acknowledgements

As with all books of this nature, the best ideas come through experience, and Saudi Arabia has been my life and work for almost two decades. Several conversations with my long-trusted friend, Don Babai at Harvard, convinced me this project had traction to enlighten readers. At the time, a monograph was prohibitive (but will follow in suit in earnest), while an edited volume was easier. I regret I did not listen to Don who argued for a single-authored book as the edited volume required convincing the publisher and twelve contributors. At times, some contributors became impossibly difficult and managing their vicissitudes was a learning experience. Convincing an academic publisher was equally taxing and, again, Don's experience helped tremendously as he read many versions of redrafted proposals. His attention to meticulous editorial rigour was at times unnerving, yet invigorating. Adam Swallow at Oxford University Press was a breath of fresh air as he understood what I was proposing and trying to accomplish. He was enlightening and always encouraging. A huge supporter has been Zafiris Tzannatos, who embraced the proposal and added several suggestions. I have come to learn a lot from his candour and demeanour. He is a true mentor and a scholar.

Soliciting contributors was not easy as some refused and others became fussy throughout the process. Some did not want to appear in the same volume as other authors. The likes and dislikes of academia are often trivial. One requested an unlimited amount of space and freedom to write anything without editorial suggestions or restrictions. Then, prior to the pandemic, my long-time mentor, Roger Owen, passed away and, as the project was facing difficulties, I became more convinced of the need to proceed. Roger was a huge influence on my thinking as a young doctoral student in the study of the region's economics, politics, and history, and I felt the need to contribute something. Roger was despondent that my doctoral work remained unpublished, due largely to my languor and preoccupation with other things in life.

However, little did I know that the pandemic would unleash a flurry of panic among the contributors. One fell seriously ill and had to undergo treatment. He was an intellectual soulmate while sojourning Oxford, and initiated a small monthly gathering among a group of Gulf experts. The pandemic forced another contributor to bail out and required a new author to step in.

And a third contributor, who faced long Covid and major surgery, was unable to write but was always there in support of the project.

After eighteen years living and working in Saudi Arabia, my respect and appreciation for the country and its people is immense. This, however, is a volume intended neither to praise nor to bash, but to offer a balanced view of the changes the Kingdom has undergone. Nor is it meant to be a sensationalist account of what has transpired as journalists are better suited to write such an account in a world that reads less and thinks less still. Economic reform is all about change, good and bad, as well as bold decisions. Much of the thinking was done while I was an international fellow at the Said Business School at the University of Oxford. Moving to Cambridge was not easy as my appointment at Pembroke College, Cambridge, and my subsequent affiliation with the Judge Business School became tedious during the pandemic. A special thanks goes to Lord Chris Smith, Master of Pembroke College, and deep gratitude to Geoffrey Edwards. I was the only scholar of the University of Cambridge residing in Oxford for the longest of times. Passing every other day in front of Roger's old office at Oxford's Centre for Middle Eastern studies, however, brought good memories of the collection of old tutors who had shaped my thinking over the years: Fred Halliday, P. J. Vatikiotis, and last but not least, Charles Tripp. Their contemporaries and I face a long road to fill their shoes.

I am indebted to all my contributors who offered their time and effort to see the completion of this volume. Vicki Sunter displayed great editorial support at Oxford University Press, with her colleagues who encouraged this project from its outset.

Over the years, my deep friendship with the founder and chairman of the Gulf Research Center (GRC), Abdulaziz Sager, has been tremendous. He has been a man of inspiration over the last twenty years. He would refer to me as 'John Saudi', which was humbling but also respectful of my love for the country and its people. The GRC is the best independent think tank the region has produced, and my affiliation has been tumultuously stimulating. It all began in 2002 in Montecatini, when Giacomo Luciani and I were lunching over a nice Florentine steak along with Imco Brouwer, who introduced me to Abdulaziz Sager. Within the GRC, Christian Koch, Oskar Ziemelis, Ahmed Sager, and Mohammed Sager were invaluable intellectual partners. In Saudi Arabia, I have been supported over the years by too many to list individually, but above all and everyone else stands my beloved brotherly intellectual companion, Ibrahim Abdul Haliq. His friendship I cherish like the winter months one longs for as the simmering heat arrives in Riyadh. His fortitude and modest demeanour are unique. Lastly, my dearest brotherly friend John Saracakis has always been there for me. Although not an academic, John's admiration and respect for scholastic endeavours is rare. I am grateful to Dr Mohammed (Abu Abdulaziz) for his invaluable support all these years. He is, indeed, an honest and pure man. Also, my good friend William Gianopulos was excellent in providing encouragement. My final gratitude goes to my wife, Antonia, and my children, Anastasia and Ioannis-Alexandros.

This volume is dedicated to my mother. Her support and her unwavering respect for the Arab world and its language steered and stimulated me to study the region. Her deep respect, love, and longing for Saudi Arabia stand above all others. Her trips to Riyadh were memorable, as were the friendships she cultivated over the years with Saudis.

Contents

List of Contributors

Aisha Al-Sarihi is a Research Fellow on the Political Economy of Climate and Environment at the National University of Singapore's Middle East Institute and a non-resident fellow at Chatham House, the Middle East Council on Global Affairs, and the Arab Gulf States Institute in Washington. Her other areas of research include geopolitics, policy, and governance of energy, climate, and environment, with a focus on the Middle East and Southeast Asia. She has authored several publications, including articles in *Environmental Policy and Governance*, *Renewable Energy*, and *Climate Policy*. Her research has been featured in international media outlets including Reuters, Associated Press, and Arab News, among many others. She holds a Ph.D. from the Centre for Environmental Policy at Imperial College London.

Jumana Alaref is an Economist at the World Bank. She has been working on social protection and jobs for over nine years in both the South Asia and Middle East and North Africa (MENA) regions. Her work focuses on improving human development outcomes through strengthening social safety nets, improving female employment, investing in skills development and active labour market programmes, and overall system strengthening using the latest research and original analysis to inform policy. In South Asia, Jumana focuses on supporting countries in building a delivery system for the provision of employment support services, as well as enhancing their analytical and informational capacity through the establishment of Labour Market Information Systems. Jumana has also worked on the development of national labour market strategies in both Saudi Arabia and Kuwait. Jumana's work includes using original research and primary data collection to inform policy making. She has co-led impact evaluations of labour market programmes in Lebanon and Tunisia. Jumana holds a Master's degree in public policy from the University of Chicago.

Nabil Ben Ltaifa is a Senior Economist currently working as the lead desk on Bosnia and Herzegovina in the European Department of the International Monetary Fund (IMF). He was the senior desk on Saudi Arabia from September 2015 to October 2020. He holds a Ph.D. in international economics from the University of Wisconsin and a Master's in Economics from the University of Illinois. He has been Fund staff since 1999, and prior to joining the IMF, he was staff of the Institute of the Arab Monetary Fund (in Abu Dhabi), teaching courses in macroeconomic policy and analysis from 1994. At the IMF, Mr Ben Ltaifa has had extensive experience working on programme and non-programme countries in Europe, the Middle East, and Central Asia, as well as in the Africa region. Further to his country work, Mr Ben Ltaifa also participated in several capacity development missions to IMF member countries.

Tim Callen is a Visiting Fellow at the Arab Gulf States Institute in Washington. He is a former Assistant Director in the Middle East and Central Asia department at the IMF. He served as the IMF's mission chief for Saudi Arabia and as the chief of the Gulf Cooperation Council (GCC) countries' division from 2012 to 2021. He was responsible for the IMF's engagement with the government of Saudi Arabia and for the institution's research and publications on the country. He also led the IMF's research programme on the GCC region. From 2021 to 2022, he served as special advisor to the Executive Director for Saudi Arabia on the IMF's Executive Board. Callen joined the IMF in 1993 and also worked in the Asia and Pacific, Communications, and Research departments. Before joining the IMF, he worked in the Economic Departments at the Bank of England and the Reserve Bank of Australia and at Hambros Bank. He holds a Bachelor's degree in economics from the University of Essex and a Master's in economics from the University of Warwick.

Kristin Diwan is a Senior Resident Scholar at the Arab Gulf States Institute in Washington and Visiting Professorial Lecturer at George Washington University. She works at the intersection of comparative politics and international relations with an emphasis on social movements. Her current projects concern generational change, nationalism, and the evolution of Islamism in the Arab Gulf states. Her articles have appeared in both academic and policy journals such as *International Affairs* and *Foreign Affairs*, and her commentary in prominent media such as the *New York Times*, *Financial Times*, and *Washington Post*. She holds a Ph.D. in

government from Harvard University.

Dr Bassam Fattouh is the Director of the Oxford Institute for Energy Studies (OIES) and Professor at the School of Oriental and African Studies (SOAS). He has published a variety of articles on energy policy, the international oil pricing system, OPEC behavior, the energy transition, and the economies of oil producing countries. Dr Fattouh served as a member of an independent expert group established to provide recommendations to the 12th International Energy Forum (IEF) Ministerial Meeting in Cancun (29–31 March 2010) for strengthening the architecture of the producer-consumer dialogue through the IEF and reducing energy market volatility. He is the recipient of the 2018 OPEC Award for Research. He acts as an advisor to a number of governments and companies.

Larry Fallin is currently a Managing Director for the Berkeley Research Group (BRG). He has been working in the Kingdom of Saudi Arabia since 1979. He has advised several ministries over the years with a focus on technology introduction and labour force development and economics. In 2019 he was the lead author on a definitive study of the suitability of a minimum wage system for Saudi Arabia. Larry holds a degree in economic statistics from the University of Hawaii, Manoa.

Steffen Hertog is Associate Professor of Comparative Politics at the London School of Economics and Political Science. He is a comparative political economist with particular focus on the Middle East and has worked with a wide range of organizations on economic development issues in the MENA region.

His most recent book is *Locked Out of Development: Insiders and Outsiders in Arab Capitalism* (Cambridge University Press, 2022).

Giacomo Luciani teaches at the Paris School of International Affairs, Sciences Po. From 2008 to 2023 he also taught at the Geneva Graduate Institute of International and Development Studies, and in 2010–13 he was Global Scholar at Princeton University. His work has focused on the political economy of the Middle East and North Africa. With Hazem Beblawi, he edited a book on *The Rentier State* (1987), which is frequently cited as one of the origins of the concept. His latest edited publications include *Combining Economic and Political Development: The Experience of MENA* (Brill, 2017) and *When Can Oil Economies Be Deemed Sustainable?* (Palgrave, 2020), co-edited with Tom Moerenhout.

Neil Quilliam is an energy policy, geopolitics, and foreign affairs specialist. He is an Associate Fellow at Chatham House, where he served as a Senior Research Fellow for a decade. Neil is also Research Director at SRMG Think. He previously served as senior MENA energy adviser at the Foreign, Commonwealth Development Office (FCDO), senior MENA analyst at Control Risks, London, and senior programme officer at the United Nations University, Amman. Neil completed his Ph.D. in international relations at the University of Durham.

John Sfakianakis is the Chief Economist of the Gulf Research Center and a Trustee of its foundation in Cambridge and Geneva. He is a Director at the Middle East Policy Initiative, a Cambridge-based think tank. He is a Fellow at the Judge Business School at the University of

Cambridge and the Royal Institute of International Affairs (Chatham House). Previously he held senior positions in the Middle East for the Ashmore Group, HSBC, Credit Agricole, Bain & Company, SNB, ARCH EM Partners, and MASIC. He is the co-editor of the Middle East Political Economy series for Oxford University Press.

Mark C. Thompson is Senior Research Fellow and Head of the Socioeconomics Program at the King Faisal Center for Research and Islamic Studies in Riyadh. His books include *Saudi Arabia and the Path to Political Change: National Dialogue and Civil Society* (Bloomsbury, IB Tauris, 2014), *Being Young, Male and Saudi: Identity and Politics in a Globalized Kingdom* (Cambridge University Press, 2019), and *Youth Issues and Everyday Life in Saudi Arabia* (Cambridge University Press, 2025). Mark is also the co-editor with Neil Quilliam of *Policymaking in the GCC: State, Citizens and Institutions* (Bloomsbury, IB Tauris, 2017), *Governance and Domestic Policy Making in Saudi Arabia: Transforming Society, Economics, Politics, and Culture* (Bloomsbury, IB Tauris, 2022), and *Saudi Youth: Policies and Processes* (Springer 2024).

Zafiris Tzannatos is an economist and currently a Senior Fellow at the Jordan Strategy Forum, and the Lebanese Center for Policy Studies in Lebanon where he was previously Professor and Chair of the Economics Department at the American University of Beirut. He previously held senior positions at the World Bank, the International Labour Organization, and the United Nations Development Program, and worked with governments of industrialized, transition, emerging, developing, fragile, and in-conflict countries across all continents. His research has been on development strategy, labour, education, skills development, gender, child labour, broader social policy, and, more recently, on post-2010 developments in the Arab region and the EuroMed.

Karen E. Young is a political economist focusing on the Gulf states and the intersection of energy, finance, and security. She is a Senior Research Scholar at the Columbia University Center on Global Energy Policy. She was founding director of the Program on Economics and Energy at the Middle East Institute. She is the author of two books: *The Economic Statecraft of the Gulf Arab States: Deploying Aid, Investment and Development across MENAP* (Bloomsbury, IB Tauris, 2022) and *The Political Economy of Energy, Finance and Security in the United Arab Emirates:*

Between the Majilis and the Market (Palgrave Macmillan, 2014).

Rodney Wilson has researched on economic development in the Gulf States and wider Islamic world for over five decades. He was the founder of the Islamic finance programme at Durham University in the UK where he continues to be an Emeritus Professor. Previously he was a Visiting Professor at the Qatar Faculty of Islamic Studies and the International Centre for Education in Islamic Finance, Kuala Lumpur. Professor Wilson was awarded a prize in Islamic banking by the Jeddah-based Islamic Development Bank in recognition of his academic work on the subject. He has written twelve books and over forty articles during his long academic career, and has supervised thirty doctoral students, including ten from Saudi Arabia.

Introduction

The Epoch of Reform

John Sfakianakis

Saudi Arabia is an important oil producer and its contribution to the world economy has been significant due to global dependence on traditional energy sources. It has also invested globally over several decades and influenced the transmission and pricing of assets worldwide. By employing many migrant workers, it has enabled substantial amounts of remittances to flow into the labour-sending countries, thereby increasing their families' welfare and enabling higher rates of investment in those countries.

The chapters collected in this book analyse the trajectory of the Saudi economy and the reforms introduced after King Salman and his son, Crown Prince Mohammed bin Salman, took the helm of the country in 2015. Reform efforts prior to 2015 pale in comparison to what ensued during the first eight years of the Salman era. The reforms included in and spearheaded under Vision 2030, which was introduced in 2016, can be considered revolutionary for a country that had spoken about diversification of the economy and the Saudization of employment for several decades but had little to show for it until the 2010s.

The reforms undertaken are important not only for the sustainability and prosperity of Saudi Arabia but as a roadmap for other oil- and natural resource-based economies. The Saudi experiment is a novel one in depth, breadth, and timeframe. Only a few countries can be cited as examples of successful diversification away from natural resources—Mexico, Malaysia, and Indonesia in the case of oil, and Chile, in the case of copper.[1] Mexico's location has been essential to its success in manufacturing as the United States of America (USA) is its biggest beneficiary and main investor. Malaysia's diversification, like that of Indonesia, kickstarted when its oil revenues fell

---

[1] T. Callen, R. Cherif, F. Hasanov, A. Hegazy, and P. Khandelwal, *'Economic Diversification in the GCC: The Past, the Present, and the Future', Institute for Capacity Development and Middle East and Central Asia Department* (Washington DC: International Monetary Fund, 2014).

John Sfakianakis, *Introduction*. In: *The Economy of Saudi Arabia in the 21st Century*. Edited by: John Sfakianakis, Oxford University Press. © John Sfakianakis (2024). DOI: 10.1093/oso/9780198863878.003.0001

substantially and was aided by foreign direct investment (FDI). Chile's governance structure and business-friendly environment paved the way for complex exports that were not linked to its natural resource base.[2] It is certainly the case that diversification is arduous, location and timing are important, it needs to be pursued consistently over time, and, in the case of energy-rich economies, the stop–go cycles associated with fluctuations in the price of oil need to be avoided.

The scale of Saudi Arabia's envisaged transformation is monumental especially given the fast-paced changes brought to the country's socio-economic map. Regardless of whether Vision 2030 is too ambitious in several of its targets, it has set a clear course of action and is calling upon all the institutions of the state and society to gear up and cooperate towards achieving a common goal. The Vision has introduced a fundamental policy shift in response to low oil prices, which started tumbling in mid-2014. Diversifying the economy, creating jobs for nationals in the private sector, and implementing a gradual, but noteworthy, fiscal consolidation programme are key priorities. Vision 2030 was borne of a realization that the old system was defunct and that something needed to be done to address deep-seated structural challenges. The pillars that had supported the monarchy for decades—religion, business, and the royal family—have been shaken and new rules have been put in place. Economists examine output and outcomes as well as intended and unintended consequences. Diversification is a moving target and has been used in every public document in Saudi Arabia since the early 1970s. From that point on, the vernacular was replete with the use of the term 'diversification'. However, world economic history is full of examples of diversification failures rather than successes. Hence, Saudi Arabia started with a handicap, needing to chart its own course of trials and errors. It will be nearly impossible for Saudi Arabia in a very short period to move from dependency on oil to complete diversification. Oil and its derived products will continue to play a role, and it remains to be seen what sectors and products will rise to challenge its prominence.

The reforms have been bold, far-reaching, and fast (at times, hastened). The then deputy Crown Prince was quick to announce in April 2016 that 'the Saudi addiction to oil had disturbed the development of many sectors in past years' and 'the Kingdom can live in 2020 without any dependence on oil'.[3] The statement was true in that oil rents had resulted in an economy habituated by vested interests, weak competition, low productivity, and a multi-segmented

---

[2] G. Salinas, 'Chile: A Role Model of Export Diversification Policies', IMF Working Paper 2021/148 (2021).
[3] https://www.bbc.com/news/world-middle-east-36131391.

labour market along the lines of nationals versus migrants, public versus private sector workers, and women versus men. The structure of the private sector was rent seeking, oligopolistic, and at times collusive. Given the relatively low capacity of the civil service to produce elaborate economic and fiscal plans in the past, the task was delegated to management consultants. This approach also absolved the bureaucracy from internal admonition as foreign consultants were perceived to be autonomous and neutral, although their interests and time horizon diverted from those of the Kingdom, at times to the detriment of the country.

Saudi Arabia required a total makeover, which was long overdue. The National Transformation Plan (NTP) introduced in 2016 is the first document outlining the economic agenda associated with the Vision. It lays out 178 strategic objectives with over 340 targets and benchmarks for 24 ministries, all to be achieved by 2020. Since then, several ministries merged or have been restructured to support the reforms. A significant challenge was to meet the aspirations of a young and growing population. Generating about 4.5 million jobs for nationals entering the labour force through 2030 is an overarching challenge. The 1.7 million jobs created for Saudis as a result of the oil rise from 2003 to 2013 were largely employed in the public sector. Job creation had to slow in the coming years as nearly half of the country's budget was being expended on the wage bill. The NTP set an objective of reducing civil service employment by 20 per cent by 2020, which has still yet to be realized. Creating jobs in the private sector has always been key, but the sector has been overly reliant on cheap foreign labour since the 1970s. Addressing the employment challenge for young people was central to creating the power base needed to carry out Crown Prince Mohammed's bold economic reform agenda. Saudi Arabia's football player buying spree has involved more than simply sports, public relations, soft power, and the diversification of the Kingdom's economy: a reform agenda appealing to the country's youth and its sense of national identity are arguably essential motivating factors.

The reforms were announced while the economy was entering a difficult phase, as the fiscal deficit had widened significantly in 2015 despite a sizeable reduction in spending. A deficit of 15.9 per cent of gross domestic product (GDP) was recorded in 2015, rising from 3.4 per cent in 2014. The government deferred massive payments to contractors, which had been accumulating because of the project work undertaken during the oil boom years, and also delayed some wage payments. Funding the deficit was carried out by tapping into reserve deposits and domestic borrowing from institutional investors, mainly local banks. As one would expect, the current account moved into a deficit of more than 8 per cent of GDP in 2015 as oil revenues fell. Within a year, the foreign assets of the Saudi Arabian Monetary Authority (SAMA) declined by $154 billion as there was pressure on the riyal in the forward market and local banks were stopped from selling option contracts to foreign exchange forwards. In an environment where liquidity was being curtailed as banks had to purchase government bonds, Saudi Interbank Interest Rates moved much higher and the spread to US rates widened, which led to higher local borrowing costs for all. Bank credit, which traditionally constituted a key channel of transmission from oil prices to the real economy in Saudi Arabia, started entering an unstable phase. Private sector credit was kept artificially high by contractors having to fill the gap caused by the government's arrears. In a climate of falling growth and general economic unease, two major credit-rating agencies (Fitch and Moody's) started downgrading Saudi Arabia.

Revenue and expenditure reforms were instrumental for the new Saudi Arabia. Energy and water reform had been discussed for years but had long been considered a taboo political subject. The fear of social unrest especially after the 2011 Arab revolts was a red line for King Abdullah and his government. However, higher energy and water prices were introduced in late 2015, ranging from 10 to 134 per cent, generating revenues of around $8 billion for Aramco in 2016. The government's decision to implement the first round of energy reforms was abrupt, despite criticism from the International Monetary Fund, yet effective. Its impact on inflation in later months was felt by society generally, but despite people's initial negative reaction, they adjusted their consumption and accepted the higher fuel costs. As energy prices increased in the ensuing years (another 80 per cent increase in the price of gasoline and electricity for households, and a 195 per cent increase in the price of diesel), the reforms would be seen as successful, as consumption of energy and water declined and revenues increased. Saudi Arabia established an automatic pricing formula which had already been introduced in Oman and the United Arab Emirates (UAE). Strengthening non-oil revenues became a central pillar of the reform agenda and in 2016 the introduction of a value added tax (VAT) was announced for 2018. Excise taxes on tobacco and sugary drinks were announced for 2017 and a tax on undeveloped land was also introduced. An expatriate levy was introduced in July 2017, phased in through to 2020. The levy, which became highly unpopular with the private sector, witnessed a fourfold increase for companies whose foreign labour exceeded their number of Saudi employees, and a twofold increase for companies in which expats did not exceed nationals (which until then had not been paying a levy). The levy included dependants. A host of other initiatives were introduced in 2017, such as visa fees, municipal fees, road fines, and various other fees. From 2019 to 2022, non-oil tax revenue doubled to reach 10.6 per cent of GDP which is noteworthy for a country that had negligeable revenues from taxes but still below the G20 average.

Non-oil tax revenue has doubled over the past four years to reach 10.6 per cent of GDP and 14 per cent of non-oil GDP in 2022, still below the G20 average, while the tax gap with Saudi Arabia's estimated tax capacity reduced to around 10 per cent of non-oil GDP in 2022 (from 15 per cent in 2019).

On the expenditure side, the government initiated a steadfast policy to contain public spending. The Bureau of Spending Rationalization was established in 2017 to work with government ministries and other bodies to review spending and procurement practices. However, as the government was trying to rationalize its spending, it was also establishing a myriad of new government bodies. Over the medium term and in a low-oil-price environment, it remains to be seen if the new entities will be willing to reduce Saudi staff numbers.

Reforms were introduced to improve the business environment by increasing local investment and FDI. The target for FDI by 2030 was set at 5.7 per cent, rising from 1.2 per cent in 2016. FDI inflows, having been historically volatile, had slowed significantly since 2010 and this was another wake-up call that something had to be done. The business environment was anachronistic, slow, and replete with vested interests. From 2016 to 2017 a series of structural reforms were enacted. Starting a business in Saudi Arabia used to take fifteen days whereas in the UAE it only took a few hours. Access to credit was for the privileged few and name lending was widespread. Saudi Arabia was scoring poorly in the index for legal rights for borrowers and lenders. Trading across borders was cumbersome; Saudi Arabia required ninety hours to complete clearance procedures, compared to two hours for advanced countries. The time taken to clear imports and exports through local ports was reduced from eighteen days to one day. Commercial courts were dysfunctional, enforcing contracts was time-consuming, and limited recourse was available for settling matters outside of the court system. A series of new laws were introduced, including an updated competition law, a commercial mortgage law, an insolvency law, and a franchise law, as well as a new bankruptcy law (2018). A new Saudi arbitration centre was established that enabled the settling of commercial disputes outside of the court system. Construction permits were expedited and could now be acquired in sixteen days instead of more than 110 previously. Finally, on the capital markets front, restrictions on investment in the equity market by qualified foreign investors were relaxed, a much-desired T+2 settlement system was activated, and a parallel equity market for smaller companies (Nomu) was established.

As energy became more expensive for households and a 5 per cent VAT was enacted in 2018, it became obvious that some sort of cash transfer had to be done. Inflation was on the rise and citizens were beginning to voice increased concerns on social media. The Citizens' Account took two years to formulate (2017–18), as it was required to check the more than 14 million people who had registered to receive the handout. In April 2018, some 3.7 million households received a cash transfer (83 per cent of all those registered), of which 57 per cent received a full compensation that averaged $249 per month.

Governance and corruption have preoccupied students of Saudi Arabia for decades. The events that transpired in the Ritz-Carlton Hotel, Riyadh, in November 2017—where elite businessmen, senior royals, senior ministers, officials, and other professionals were arrested on corruption charges—brought the governance debate to the fore. The arrests had several consequences. First, they were a clear demonstration of power to all those who were in doubt, particularly to members of the royal family and businessmen who might have thought they were above the law. This had an enormous appeal to the less endowed members of society. The new top-down Saudi Arabia that was under construction permitted other sources of power. Second, this was also a way to increase the revenue stream of the state by attaining wealth from those who had abused their public office or abused the system for personal gain. The Public Investment Fund (PIF), which was the main recipient of the newly sequestrated assets, as well as the Ministry of Finance benefited from the new sources of wealth in both the public and private domains. The PIF's assets increased in size, which was in line with the aspirations of Vision 2030 for it to become the largest sovereign wealth fund in the world. Third, it compelled the private sector to work with the state but more importantly to follow the state, principally the PIF, in its direction of investment. Fourth, international investors would be welcomed, but the close networks developed over decades with the private sector would have to be revised and recalibrated as the state became, at times, the partner and co-investor of private sector companies. It also permitted foreign investors to differentiate their local partners into two categories: those businessmen who had been detained at the Ritz-Carlton or who still faced the reprimand of the state and settlement; and those who did not. Those who did not were the clear winners from this campaign and were preferred by international businesses. Finally, corruption and the enforcement power of the anti-corruption commission made everyone obsessed with the abuse of power and misuse of funds, from the bottom all the way to the top of most state entities. Pre-2017, anecdotes of excessive commission fees and abuse of power by businessmen were endemic. Businessmen and state officials are warier now of the massive prowling that went on in previous periods. Business–state relations have been reconfigured since 2018. The state has become more autonomous and powerful, as the private sector has become more subdued and subservient to the dictates of the political economy.

Saudi Arabia had never been known for its fiscal transparency. For the first time, in 2018 it published a pre-budget statement. The budget statement had been one of the best-kept secrets as regards its synthesis and content. For decades, the budget statement was meant to mislead than guide its readers. In the same year, the publication of financial data by Aramco in its bond prospectus was a big step forward, and this was followed by the publication of a myriad of support documents in preparation of its initial public offering (IPO) in 2020. Aramco was the blackest of black horses in Saudi Arabia and became a quite transparent national oil company in a matter of two and a half years. The PIF seems to be following a similar path. When compared to other sovereign funds, disclosure practices of the PIF are beginning to appear anything but negligible. In 2022, as a result of its first bond issue, for the first time the PIF announced its financial performance for the year 2021. This helped assuage sceptics about its transparency and governance.[4] Spending and withdrawals were becoming more transparent, as is already the case with the sovereign funds of Azerbaijan, Kazakhstan, Mexico, and even Russia, which pass through the national budget.

In terms of financials, however, accounting and spending largely remain off budget especially when relating to mega projects. At this stage of Saudi Arabia's economic development—where all decisions come from the very top—everything that is sovereign-fund related also remains off budget and largely unaccounted for within the strictures of the country's financial ecosystem. Perhaps adjustments will be made when more lessons are learned, and governance and accountability will increase by necessity as with Aramco's IPO and PIF's bond. Russia as well as the central Asian republics are not known for their accountability, but sets of rules and oversight have been put in place by the state and are monitored by the state. The borrowing and investment decisions of the PIF are more frequently discussed by the Finance Committee at the royal court. Aramco's IPO, regardless of whether it was subscribed by local investors, was a highly regarded institution in terms of efficiency, capacity, and technical prowess. Going public, albeit only in

---

[4] https://www.ft.com/content/16bab8f8-0311-4409-bed1-21ea46e0650b.

Saudi Arabia, made it known to the wider international investor community. The PIF was until 2015 an institution operating under the authority of the Ministry of Finance and the minister was its chairman. It was a far more personalized institution, and its general structure was often critiqued post 2015 as personalized and patrimonial, which fitted with its special-purpose mandate. Over the coming years it will be interesting to observe if the breadth of its portfolio will encourage a different modus operandi with greater embedded autonomy.

Saudi Arabia responded to the COVID-19 pandemic quickly and effectively. From a health protection perspective, the pandemic in Saudi Arabia was contained due to early measures. At the peak of the pandemic in June 2020, daily infection rates were at almost 5,000 while countries with similar populations were clocking above 100,000. In March 2020, SAMA introduced programmes to support the private sector. Total support amounted to 6.5 per cent of non-oil GDP, which was among the lowest in the G20 and was perhaps preparing for an economic slowdown because of falling oil prices— Brent averaged $42 per barrel from $66 in 2019. As a result, the fiscal deficit widened to 11.1 per cent, which was the highest since 2016.

Flooding the market with billions of Saudi riyals has been a trait of Saudi economic policy for decades. However, after 2015, each time a project was announced it was bigger than the previous one. In 2021, the government announced a National Investment Strategy (NIS) to boost investment. The NIS goal of $3.3 trillion of domestic investment by 2030 would be sourced from the PIF, Aramco, Sabic, large private firms, and by attracting FDI. The NIS's target is equal to the total net assets of the public sector or 407 per cent of 2021 GDP. The NIS set an FDI target of more than $100 billion annually by 2030. Reaching this target would require more than doubling the size of the economy. Historically, FDI was principally invested in the oil and gas sector and seldom in the non-oil economy. One of the highest recorded FDI years was 2021 when inflows totalled $19.3 billion, of which the bulk came from Aramco selling a $12.4 billion stake in an oil pipeline entity to foreign investors. In 2022, FDI amounted to $32.5 billion, revised from the about $8 billion figure that had been published previously. The updated figure was a result of a new framework methodology for publishing FDI data in Saudi Arabia which was adopted in late 2023.

The macroeconomic implications of the NIS will have to be assessed continually, especially through market tests of large-scale projects and the role of the public and private sectors. So far, defined entry and exit parameters for the state in the economy and for private sector participation have failed to be set. Although the PIF's board, in 2021, committed to a five-year exit strategy from its investments in domestic firms and sectors—a tall order with its current structure and assets—economic conditions, prevailing incentives, and the structure of the exit will be important determining factors. The role of the private sector in the economy is paramount, but its prospects must be carefully calibrated. There has been a clear redistribution of wealth and an implicit dividend paid since 2017 by the private sector, whether in the form of the Ritz-Carlton settlement or its participation in the Aramco public listing. Other IPOs, such as the $80 billion Neom listing, would certainly ensue as the state would have to diversify its leverage options as the balance sheet of the sovereign fund expands and its liabilities increase.[5] Over-reliance on the country's stock market should be balanced and avoid crowding out the private sector's ability to deepen its presence in capital markets and draw funding. Another way of raising cash was through asset transfers between different state entities. In 2020, the PIF sold its 70 per cent ownership of Sabic to Aramco for $69 billion. The liabilities were transferred but the cash from the equity stake was deployed by the PIF with an implied risk-adjusted return implication which had not been present before.

The state's dependence on the value of oil resources is still very high: if we account for the net assets of the public sector—excluding central government assets—Aramco represented 69 per cent in 2022. If the net value of oil resources declines, the domestic economy will have to generate alternative new sources of wealth sufficient to cover multiple demands and the mega projects promoted by the state, in addition to taking public several partially state-owned firms and private companies.

The call for the private sector and banks to participate in many of these projects will continue. These demands will have to be balanced with the private sector's growth and employment targets. The private sector's is required to make a 65 per cent contribution to the country's GDP in 2030, up from 40 per cent in 2016. After seven years of reforms, by 2023 the private sector's contribution to GDP was around 44 per cent from 40 per cent in 2016, while the government's share in the country's output was increasing year after year. Moreover, if the public sector balance sheet, which includes both the PIF and the National Development Fund—currently recorded as contributing entities of non-oil activities—are accounted differently, the private sector's contribution would be much lower. The private sector is being called on to invest

---

[5] King Abdullah Economic City in Rabigh was also listed in 2006 but failed to meet its targets promulgated in 2005. The city had attracted limited investment and had failed to become a hub for logistics and manufacturing, intended to employ 1 million people and house 2 million residents, respectively. By 2018, the city had a population of only 7,000. https://www.ft.com/content/ae48574c-58e6-11e8-bdb7-f6677d2e1ce8.

in the country's manufacturing sector, which over the last two decades has contributed on average a respectable 10 per cent of the country's GDP. In 2019, the National Industrial Development and Logistics Program (NIDLP) published a 500-page plan which 'illustrates the country's willingness to think big', aiming to attract $453 billion in investment and create 1.6 million jobs by 2030.[6]

Besides increasing the role of the private sector in the economy, it is expected that by 2030 non-oil exports will rise from 16 per cent to 50 per cent of GDP. Industrial policy will be channelled through the Saudi Industrial Development Fund, which provides credit to private sector entities, and also the PIF, but will include several other enablers: the Local Content and Private Sector Development Unit; the National Industrial Clusters Development Program; the Saudi Exports Development Authority; the National Committee for RDI; the King Abdulaziz City for Science and Technology; and the Saudi Authority for Industrial Cities and Technology Zones. The aim is to build local supply chains based on a local procurement policy and implementation of import substitution. The four sectors covered by the NIDLP are industry, energy, mining, and logistics. Within industry it has identified several target segments: equipment and machinery; renewable energy supplies; and pharmaceuticals and medical supplies. Some sectors are bound to fail and others to succeed, but picking winners and directing capital will be a process determined by the destination of products. Simply put, import substitution can work for some products and industries. However, neither is the domestic market vast, nor will the misallocation of resources and rent seeking be contained if products are limited to the local economy. An export focus and increasing the value and sophistication of products should create higher wages and greater employment for Saudis over the long term. And even if there is a domestic market, localization becomes a challenge in certain highly protected fields such as military industries. Saudi Arabia is the third largest importer of military equipment in the world and aims to localize 50 per cent of military expenditure by 2030. Despite having the market, developing local capacity in a high-tech and intellectual-property-heavy global ecosystem in such a short period of time remains a massive challenge. Even partial success, however, will help change the need for outgoing capital to fund the military's build-up in an ever-changing geopolitical map.

Its role in the economy being omnipresent, a strong state should be able to intervene in support of domestic firms by enhancing their sophistication

---

[6] https://www.sidf.gov.sa/en/Documents/SIDF%20final%20by%20page%20300820.pdf.

and export orientation through competition. The challenge for Saudi Arabia is not only to get the sectors right but also to create jobs for Saudis, who have traditionally commanded high salaries and opted not to be employed in industry. And what is happening outside the country's borders is equally and probably more important than what is happening inside: automation. Although the debate about automation and job creation has been discussed since the industrial revolution, Saudi Arabia is at a critical juncture. On the one hand, it will have to develop more complex products for the export market, and on the other hand, it must make sure that while it is delivering high-value goods, it is creating high-skill and high-wage jobs for nationals. Saudi Arabia has no choice but to push ahead with its industrial policy, prioritizing and learning from its errors in a far more competitive world.

Saudi Arabia has awakened at a time when huge structural shifts are taking place beyond its borders. Climate change, the need for a reduction in carbon emissions, and the emergence of a powerful discourse on renewable energy are formidable challenges. The country's ability to transform its economy fast will depend not only on the changes it undergoes domestically but also on how quickly the rest of the world transforms and how Saudi Arabia competes with it. Over the last twenty years, the economy's reliance on revenue from oil fell from 80 per cent of its GDP to 50 per cent by 2021, and the proportion of exports accounted for by oil fell from 90 per cent to 70 per cent during the same period. These accomplishments are quite respectable for Saudi Arabia, but it is important to remember that the regional context is also very important in terms of competition as it has a direct effect on investors' appetites and the attractiveness of business. In this context, the other members of the Gulf Cooperation Council also witnessed measurable declines in their oil dependence: oil revenues fell from 80 per cent to 60 per cent, while oil exports declined from 80 per cent to 60 per cent over the last twenty years. Since 2016, however, Saudi Arabia has made noticeable progress in terms of the oil sector's contribution both to revenues and to exports, surpassing all of its regional peers except the UAE.[7]

The privatization programme of Saudi Arabia was launched in 2017 with more than 160 projects in sixteen sectors for private sector participation (mostly through public–private partnerships) or asset sales. The Private Sector Participation Laws passed in 2021 set out the regulatory framework for the privatization process while exempting privatizations from the employment requirements of state-owned organizations. Privatization is a test of the willingness of the private sector, both foreign and local, to participate,

---

[7] https://economicdiversification.com/?country_gedi=saudi-arabia.

but also a test of the actual market value of these firms. Governments typically over-promise and over-value the firms undergoing privatization. The process also reveals the way in which privatization sales are financed and the proportionality of debt and equity. In Saudi Arabia, the corporate system has relied on debt to fund its expansion and thus far many of the privatizations have been carried out on a higher proportion of leverage than equity. An important part of the corporate sector in Saudi Arabia is not listed and little is known about its performance or leverage. The performance of the corporate sector is arguably linked to oil prices, government contracts, bank lending, and sentiment. In 2015, net income for listed companies shrank by 25 per cent as oil prices negatively impacted the economy. The fate of privatization will be determined by a host of factors including the regulatory environment and the appetite to provide affordable credit in a rising cost of capital scenario. Moreover, the role the private sector in the economy depends on its ability to raise capital from local banks and its ability to participate in many of the projects spearheaded by the PIF. The role of the PIF is to provide seed money in sectors the private sector has limited footprint and a high barrier to entry such as the electric vehicle sector which Saudi Arabia is on truck to having three different manufacturing brands, Lucent, Ceer and Hyundai.

How the proceeds of privatization are used, and whether this utilization is productive, is equally important. Again, it remains to be seen how the role of the state in the economy unfolds. Privatization is attempting to pull the state out of the economy while the PIF's domineering role is still having a crowding-out effect on the private sector. The role of the PIF is to subject itself continually to meticulous risk-adjusted assessments and cost–benefit analysis with a view to involving the private sector. However, there could be a more subtle intra-state rowding out taking place. This is mostly an unintended consequence of the extreme competition between different state entities with competing mandates, although some within the state bureaucracy justify it as a way of having a pattern of 'creative destruction'. For example, the urban area of Neom is vying to attract investors, more foreign than local, due to its sheer economic size and its primacy status. Despite the volatility the country is encountering in attracting foreign investment, the incentives offered to encourage businesses to set up operations in Neom are superior to those of any other entity. The other entities are therefore trying to gain certain exclusivities on labour, capital, and taxation, or to become Special Economic Zones, which could lead to investor confusion and eventually impact job creation opportunities for nationals.

Saudi Arabia's regional economic assertiveness was evidenced with its announcement in 2021 that it would allow foreign firms until the end of 2023 to set up headquarters in the country or risk losing out on government contracts. The target is for some 480 companies to move to Riyadh by 2030, which places the country in direct competition with the UAE, which is the regional business hub. To achieve this target, Saudi Arabia would have to compete aggressively with the UAE around regulations, taxes, lifestyle, connectivity, as well as operational costs and a skilled foreign workforce. Saudi Arabia is using its fiscal power to enter the same sectors the UAE has become known for over the years. It intends to spend $147 billion to become the air and sea logistical hub of the region and another $1 trillion over the next decade to attract 55 million foreign tourists annually by 2030. The UAE attracts around 25 million tourists annually, of whom 15 million visit Dubai. By 2025, Dubai aims to increase its tourism intake to 25 million. There can only be one regional business and finance hub in the Gulf and the wider Middle East, and it remains to be seen if first-mover advantage makes the difference and if the investment Saudi Arabia is making brings lasting intergenerational returns. There might also be a price to be paid for making monumental changes in a country with such deeply ingrained structural inefficiencies. The changes that are being introduced in the economy and society are monumental regardless of whether the Kingdom becomes the regional hub. However, although Saudi Arabia might never become *the* destination, it could become *a* destination—far more than it used to be before. Another intangible would be that it provides its local population with a common goal and aspiration that makes society more ambitious and eventually more actively productive. And perhaps as economists we should allow some slack in measuring the successes and failures of an economy perennially seen as anachronistic and dependent on oil. Perhaps for an economy that was so entitled, embedded in oil rents, and socially behind the times, the only way to reform at all was to place these wild bets that have shaken society and business out of their archaic moulds.

In the age of decarbonization, Saudi Arabia finds itself in a precarious situation. There are unique centrifugal forces that will change energy markets. Oil will still be needed as the pace of decarbonization remains unclear and its impact is 'dirtier' than its appearance, but still structural changes in the global energy market have commenced and are gaining in strength. The energy crisis resulting from the war in Ukraine could have lasting repercussions for the country's geopolitical standing. The green recovery will impact the demand drivers of all oil importers, especially those in Asia. China's path to a renewables future will have a structural effect on the demand for oil.

Another factor of change is Saudi Arabia itself and the demands of its population for economic prosperity. The demographic make-up will change over the next two decades and the youth dividend will decline. The reliance on oil for completing many of the country's mega projects is substantial. The economic bets Saudi Arabia is making are many times more than the size of its economy and only time will tell if the investment is accruing a return or being intergenerationally dissipated.

One thing for certain is that the balance sheet of the state is more exposed to all kinds of projects whose sustainability and, by extension, credibility will be brought into question by an oil price shock. In many ways, Saudi Arabia cannot afford an oil price shock of the scale and longevity of the one from 2015 to 2020. And the costlier many of these projects become with time, as many of their technologies remain nascent, so will the expenses of the economy increase. The number of commitments Saudi Arabia has rendered domestically necessitate an oil price close to $100 per barrel. Equally important, Saudi Arabia's foreign economic bilateral commitments are estimated at $200–250 billion, which is equal to a year's worth of oil export revenues at around $75 per barrel and 10 million barrels capacity. Since 2016, Saudi Arabia has also embarked on a more assertive foreign policy. Bilateral economic relations have often become more targeted and disciplined, which is a definite positive. Gone are the days of gifts and grants to regional Arab economies. A wiser direct investment approach has been established during the Salman era. Acquiring publicly listed assets as a way of helping struggling economies has been a more prudent approach, as these are tangible investments with a revenue stream. Conditionality to foreign economic aid was first adopted by the UAE in 2014 for its aid to Egypt and has been pursued by Saudi Arabia during the Salman reign.

Besides the country's regional and global assertiveness via its oil policy, Saudi Arabia is far more visible today, as a country, than seven years ago as the world is observing all the changes it has undertaken. Its economic performance, its dealings with the USA and the world via its oil policy, and its relations with Asia, Russia, and China will define it. Saudi Arabia sought the world's attention and it gained it, but not without scrutiny, doubt, and criticism. Its future place in the global arena will be determined, in large part, by its economic reform agenda and its degree of success. It remains to be seen if Saudi Arabia's deployment of soft power alongside other forms of persuasion is successful in reaching the right trade agreements, joining new clubs, and winning new friends. Striking the right balance between grabbing investors' attention and countering their incredulity is not easy. Many of the mega projects currently under way are receiving notoriety or critical scrutiny which could lead to foreign investors deciding against Saudi Arabia as an investment destination. Attracting foreign high-skilled talent is not easy in the post-pandemic era of remote work and reduced mobility. And Saudi Arabia is not alone in trying to attract foreign talent; so is its next-door neighbour, the UAE. The Kingdom's domestic politics have been revolutionized and large segments of its population have been embedded in its Vision while others have been alienated. The inclusion of young people has been accomplished through jobs and higher wage entitlements. Youth unemployment fell from 32 per cent in 2020 to 16 per cent in 2022, while female participation in the labour force exceeded the 30 per cent target under Vision 2030, reaching 36 per cent in 2022. Average wages for Saudis are just below the $3,000 mark, foreigners are at $1,040, and an average government salary pays double that of a private sector salary. In an economy of high oil prices, this would be less challenging, but in a declining oil environment it can create not only fiscal worries but also productivity lags and inefficiencies. Saudi Arabia has long remained politically stable, even if the wider region is comprised of failed or semi-failed states such as Yemen, Syria, Libya, Iraq, and Lebanon. Saudi Arabia has attracted a host of pontificators whose proclamations of the imminent collapse of the country are grossly exaggerated and structurally unfounded. Saudi Arabia is a very different country since Crown Prince Mohammed enacted far-reaching and irreversible social and economic reforms that have significantly enhanced women's professional and social opportunities, introduced an entertainment and tourism industry, and enacted bold economic reforms. All in all, the Crown Prince is positioning Saudi Arabia as a major power in a new multipolar world order with greater strategic autonomy.

The Dawn of a New Era?

Reform is all about managing the change in structures of the economy to achieve an advantage for future generations while minimizing errors. It is evident that the ambitious reforms initiated since 2016 represent a break with the past in contemporary Saudi Arabia. What are the long-term prospects of these reforms? How will they transform the economy of Saudi Arabia? How credible are they? How likely are they to endure? What obstacles will they need to overcome? The following twelve chapters aim to address these and related questions. With reforms come many challenges, both intended and unintended. All the authors address the accomplishments of the reforms of the last few years but also analyse the myriad of obstacles that lie ahead.

Saudi Arabia's economic future will depend on its ability to admit to its short-comings and address them in an effective way. The pandemic overly delayed this volume's publication, but it also provided more time to assess the reform period post-2016. The pandemic forced three authors to bail out, two due to serious illness, and their chapters to be reapportioned. A chapter on the study of industry was omitted as its author also fell ill due to long Covid. One of the most daunting tasks for the volume was to keep up with a flurry of announcements and changes which made it difficult for contributors to manage resubmissions; hence, at times some chapters could appear dated. However, this is an academic endeavour that attempts to examine and evaluate the first few years of Saudi Arabia's reforms and the challenges that lie ahead. Predicting the future of any economy is as good as trying to predict the weather beyond a span of a week, but there are certain elements that are worth highlighting for policy-makers, economists, and the wider academic community studying oil-dependent economies. A monograph on the economy will follow in due course, examining state–business relations.

In Chapter 1, John Sfakianakis and Zafiris Tzannatos discuss the key development policy instrument in Saudi Arabia of the last fifty years: the five-year development plans. They argue that Saudi Arabia has both a roadmap and, unlike any other time in its economic history, the political will to press ahead. So far, the evidence points to an impressive array of changes brought to the country in a very short period. The speed with which Saudi Arabia has transformed is remarkable. The state has a critical role to play in ensuring transparency and competition in the economy, and incubating and abetting new industries and sectors, keeping the objective of Saudization in mind. The pre-2016 projects that have followed a stop–go trajectory and that have called for bailouts from the state coffers provide several lessons for the future. Still, even if they are fully successful, a question for the mega projects remains: that is, whether they will give sufficient impetus to transform Saudi Arabia into a post-oil economy over a reasonable time horizon, so that the new social contract is supportable by ordinary Saudis and therefore viable. A critical factor for ongoing and future policies will be the price of oil, as Saudi Arabia is still as reliant on it as the main source of export and fiscal revenues as ever. The role of the private sector is fundamental if it is to contribute to 65 per cent of the country's GDP by 2030 and by extension become the main generator of employment opportunities. Sfakianakis and Tzannatos posit that it remains to be seen how the state will change its current leading role and how the private sector will react, evolve, and prosper.

Oil is always a complicated subject to examine and easily the one that is dated the soonest. In Chapter 2, Bassam Fattouh takes the view that oil will continue to be the cornerstone of Saudi Arabia's political economy and its international relations. He makes the point that the role of oil in shaping Saudi's political and economic future will become more important as the transformations in the Saudi economy and global oil market continue, although its contribution to the future trajectory of the Kingdom will take different forms from in the past. Fattouh argues that diversifying away from oil and reducing the role of the oil sector in the Kingdom's future development path is not only unrealistic but also, at a strategic and policy level, suboptimal. He believes that Saudi Arabia should continue to leverage its core sector by enhancing its competitiveness through improving efficiency, promoting greater integration, and decarbonizing oil production and products. Doom-and-gloom predictions infer that Saudi Arabia will emerge as a definite loser in the transition, with increasing risk of economic collapse and an inability to navigate through the transformations in global energy markets, and that its geopolitical importance and role in energy markets are destined only to decline. To say the least, these predictions are rather simplistic, Fattouh points out. They ignore the Kingdom's core strengths and strategic choices, and tend to assume a fast, uniform, and smooth energy transition across the globe. Transformations in global energy markets are already shaping Saudi choices, but the choices that the Kingdom makes will also influence the energy landscape.

Nabil Ben Ltaifa and Tim Callen, in Chapter 3, explain the substantial progress Saudi Arabia has made with respect to fiscal reforms. The non-oil revenues base has been broadened, domestic energy prices raised, expenditure management strengthened, fiscal transparency improved, and the institutional basis and analysis of fiscal policy strengthened. The authors highlight that key challenges remain, of which oil price volatility is of prime importance. Ensuring fiscal sustainability in the medium to long term means that efforts to raise new sources of revenue, contain government spending and improve its efficiency, and strengthen the overall management of government finances, assets, and liabilities will need to continue. Ltaifa and Callen assert that getting the pace of fiscal adjustment right will be critical. Too rapid an adjustment will stall growth, while too slow will expose the fiscal position to the vicissitudes of oil prices. Moreover, a more effective tax system is required. The authors argue that revenue reforms should introduce a progressive tax system with income and property taxes supplemented by excises on high-end consumption goods. Strengthening the medium-term orientation of the budget process and reducing the procyclicality of fiscal policy are essential. A very important point raised by Ltaifa and Callen is the need for transparency in numerous extra-budgetary institutions and state-owned enterprises which remain outside the budget process, such as the PIF.

According to Rodney Wilson, writing in Chapter 4, Saudi Arabia has a highly developed financial system which has long served the Kingdom well. The banking system follows international best practice with provisions to ensure there is sufficient liquidity and appropriate capital adequacy. There is sound independent financial reporting and investors have confidence in SAMA and the Capital Markets Authority as regulators, as well as in the banking and insurance institutions. Government debt is modest and mostly held by the financial institutions in Saudi Arabia, and little debt is held by foreign banks or investment companies, including hedge funds. Wilson makes the point that, as the economy continues to diversify, there will be new opportunities for the financial sector, not least in insurance provision where the market is underdeveloped. The financial sector has enjoyed, as he says, considerable success in developing Islamic financial products that are sound and have proven public appeal. Saudi Arabia is a leader in the world of Islamic finance. However, Wilson highlights that there are challenges at the microeconomic level for banks. Another issue is the likely consolidation in the banking sector with more mergers and acquisitions in an already overbanked ecosystem. Wilson argues that the banking sector remains focused on rent seeking and rent extraction, but the problem is that there is less and less rent to extract.

A topic of great interest especially regarding Saudi Arabia since 2016 is the specific mechanics and characteristics of state capitalism. Saudi state capitalism is distinct from the examples of China, East Asia, and South America. It is personalistic, argues Karen Young in Chapter 5, and driven by the aspirations of Crown Prince Mohammed bin Salman. Diversification efforts tend to repeat old patterns of state-led interventions in the economy, despite some real efforts at liberalization in financial markets and expansion of investment and ownership opportunity. Young argues that there may be an opportunity for significant foreign investment in tourism within the Kingdom, but it will most certainly be in partnership with state entities. Where other state-led development agendas have tried to create ecosystems guided by state industrial policy, those ecosystems usually deployed investments in human capital and an array of supporting institutions from universities to business groups to multiple supporting ministries, while the Saudi case seems to rely on the PIF for its diversification and revenue-generation plans. The PIF dominates the new Saudi state capitalism. Young demonstrates how the state intervenes in the economy—through the stock market and the PIF—and argues that its appetite for risk may create distinct social and political effects in the future.

However, competing in areas where the state is also in business, or acting as an investor competitor to the state when it has the PIF and its mandate to acquire domestic opportunities aggressively, is a significant challenge. Young makes the case that there cannot be fund similar to the PIF, but in private hands and with the assets and political leverage of the PIF. Even an external investment fund will choose to partner the PIF rather than bid against it. Outside investors have not been attracted to invest in Saudi Arabia and, as Young asserts, it 'has become evidence that something is not working in the Kingdom's plans for economic liberalization and diversification; it is the best evidence of a distorted market'.

In Chapter 6, Zafiris Tzannatos and John Sfakianakis examine the functioning and outcomes of the labour market in the context of the development model Saudi Arabia has pursued from 1974 to the early 2020s. They note the historical failure of policies to provide decent employment to Saudis outside the public sector, to increase productivity, and to accelerate economic growth despite massive revenues from the oil sector. The reasons for these less than satisfactory outcomes can be associated politically with a social contract that has been based on an authoritarian bargain between the political leaders and the citizens, and economically with the patronage of the private sector in a way that its proceeds have mainly been appropriated by the establishment's elite. Both have resulted in the poor use of oil revenues. Tzannatos and Sfakianakis find that the end result has been problematic for both principal sectors of the labour market. On the one hand, the public sector lacks *fiscal* discipline by acting as the employer of last resort. On the other hand, the private sector lacks *domestic market* discipline as the migration policy allows employers to hire workers at the low levels of wages that prevail in the sending countries. Public sector employment has not been a vehicle for providing valuable goods and services but has served as a mechanism for redistributing the national patrimony. This political and economic configuration, combined with an excessive reliance on low-wage migrant labour, has had a direct adverse effect on the employment outcomes for nationals. Vision 2030 aims to address these areas, among others, by eliminating corruption, energizing the economy through the private sector, and reducing the number of migrants and increasing the employment of nationals.

Social protection is a difficult subject as its mired in political sensitivities in Saudi Arabia but requires technical, in-country expertise and access to data. In Chapter 7, Jumana Alaref contends that social protection has long been embedded in the fabric of the social contract that has historically provided seemingly generous subsidies and support to the wider population, in line with its Islamic foundations. While the Saudi government frequently discloses the amount dedicated to new and existing social protection programmes, it does not readily release statistics related to the number of people within the Kingdom in need of this financial support. According to official figures, Alaref says, 4.5 per cent live in extreme poverty, but this number probably underestimates the Saudi poverty threshold. Other reports estimate that 12 per cent of the population live under the threshold, and according to the number of beneficiaries of the Citizen's Account, over 30 per cent need and are eligible for financial assistance. Alaref aptly argues that, ultimately, it is important to remember that moving away from state dependence requires the development of an elaborate support system and the creation of a network, rather than a net, that empowers the population to develop the capacity to generate the income necessary to live, at minimum, a 'decent life'. The social safety net system under Vision 2030 has shifted the narrative away from support towards independence and self-sufficiency. This is a recalibration of the social contract to which many have been accustomed since the establishment of the contemporary Saudi state. Shifting away from this well-established system must be seen by everyone in the ecosystem as a process that necessitates collaboration and transparency, and one requiring compromises that will inevitably result in discomfort and contradictions.

Exploring the extent to which the natural environment, climate change, and the sustainability of natural resources are addressed by Saudi Arabia's economic development is timely. Aisha Al-Sarihi argues, in Chapter 8, that the early stages of environmental protection were mainly focused on enhancing agricultural production and water management. Economic advancement, increasing standards of living, and low prices of electricity, water, and fuel resulted in unintended consequences of unsustainable patterns of energy consumption, making the Kingdom not only affected by the impacts of climate change but a contributor to it, as one of the world's top emitters of carbon emissions on a per capita basis. Al-Sarihi argues that an effective alignment of environmental sustainability and climate change in Saudi Arabia is still hindered by a low data and information profile; fragmentation of leadership; weaknesses in implementing environmental protection regulations; absence of a climate action plan; and fragmentated environmental and climate-related policies and efforts. Furthermore, she reveals that a tangible alignment between economic development and environmental and climate change requires enhancement of human, technical, and financial resources. The Kingdom has in place the institutional architecture, Al-Sarihi says, which is in principle conducive to environmental protection, with twenty-two environmental regulations covering a range of environmental issues such as agriculture, water, biodiversity, marine environment, and air quality. Importantly, such environmental issues have been made an integral part of Vision 2030 and its operationalization plan, the National Transformation Program of 2020. The NTP dedicated fifty-seven programmes and initiatives to enhance the sustainability of water, food, biodiversity, urban spaces, and marine environments, while aiming to reduce all types of environmental pollution, waste, and desertification. Yet Al-Sarihi concludes that despite the ongoing efforts, the Kingdom still performs below the world average in terms of air quality, pollution emissions, biodiversity and habitats, water resources, and climate action, and faces substantial challenges in implementing its environment- and climate-related Sustainable Development Goals.

One of the most fascinating sectors, which merits its own chapter, is entertainment and tourism. Billions of dollars are being continually spent in the hope that it will assist the country's diversification efforts. Kristin Diwan and Larry Fallin, in Chapter 9, address how the Saudi leadership under the direction of Crown Prince Mohammed bin Salman is pressing ahead in tourism, arts, and entertainment. Indeed, Diwan and Fallin argue, many of these weaknesses, such as lack of previous experience, cultural change and existing regional competition, are simultaneously targets for change in the Kingdom's blueprint for socio-economic reform. Diwan and Fallin say, it is difficult to discern if these social and cultural changes are needed in the pursuit of this line of economic diversification, or if these industries have been selected for their service to the end of sociocultural opening and land development. Clearly the new leadership is embracing the opportunity to leave its mark on the Kingdom through remaking law, culture, vast landscapes, and Saudi Arabia's orientation in the world. This is a younger and more globally oriented Kingdom, and tourism, accompanied by new entertainment and creative ventures, is central to its new national presentation. The promise of these new industries is built from their previous neglect; both non-religious tourism and entertainment were discouraged under Saudi Arabia's earlier religious-sanctioned order. Diwan and Fallin argue that the risks come in the huge investments being made in tourism, especially in a time of rising economic competition. Every state in the Gulf is making a similar move to diversify into tourism, and it is unclear whether these offerings will be complementary. According to Diwan and Fallin, the appeal of Saudi Arabia is unproven apart from in religious tourism. Will foreign visitors appreciate the novelty of the Kingdom newly opening to visitors and offering unique heritage and archaeological sites beyond those offered in neighbouring countries? Or will the sociocultural barriers and still-deficient infrastructure deter them? Tourism within the Kingdom also faces risks from the security environment. It is not coincidental that Saudi Arabia's increased interest in Red Sea security, including the establishment of a Red Sea Council, has expanded alongside planned tourist and urban investments along that coastline.

The institutional changes brought about since 2016, as well as 'repurposing ministries', are an important highlight of the reforms. Mark Thompson and Neil Quilliam, in Chapter 10, discuss the pathway followed by the chief architect of the reforms, Crown Prince Mohammed bin Salman, and his trusted inner circle in not only changing the Kingdom's institutional infrastructure, but also developing its capacity by drawing on Saudi Arabia's youth dividend. At the same time, they address the thorny issue of foreign management consultancies and the role they have played in the Kingdom's transition, which has often divided opinion within Saudi Arabia. The authors make the point that foreign management consultancies continue to play a dominant role in the implementation of Vision 2030 and are given a higher priority than Saudi management consultancies. They argue that this has led to a culture of dependency, especially among senior decision-makers, many of whom continue to rely upon external advice. As such, the contribution that foreign management consultancies now offer is finely balanced between help and hindrance with an increasing tendency towards the latter. Thompson and Quilliam make the point that repurposing key ministries and creating new agencies have been positive developments, but that they remain largely unproductive and redundant, as the newly established and reconfigured institutions and agencies coexist with their predecessors and, in many cases, pursue overlapping mandates. In fact, the problems arising from this situation are all too familiar in the Kingdom's longstanding institutions. They include an intense competition for resources among peer institutions: not only financial but also in terms of securing time and access to the Kingdom's most senior leaders. The authors note that the implementation of the Vision is overly dependent upon a small pool of trusted individuals, all of whom are overburdened with multiple portfolios and, more ominously, in constant danger of being dismissed.

Steffen Hertog, in Chapter 11, argues that the old Saudi social contract is eroding and, with it, the old growth model based on state spending and state employment. At the same time, the social opening of the country is compensating for the erosion of the older system. Nevertheless, the new era has yet to bring about new private economic activities as the economy continues to rely on fiscal stimulus from the state, government employment, and low labour costs through the employment of migrant workers. Economic diversification is hard and takes a long time under the best circumstances. The adjustment process may not be completed by 2030 and much pain could be inflicted along the way, with living standards dropping. Vision 2030 has focused more on large projects than on addressing structural constraints to economic development—although, in the end, it will very likely be these constraints which determine the Kingdom's growth and diversification trajectory. Hertog assesses that many of the Vision's components are being deployed only slowly, not only because of limited buy-in by the stakeholders but also because they are in tension with the structural foundations of the established social contract and growth model. He proposes some reorientation of rent sharing towards market-conforming welfare mechanisms rather than simply dismantling the old social contract through a reactive policy of austerity.

The challenges facing the post-oil economy are discussed at length in Chapter 12 by Giacomo Luciani, the author of the seminal work on the rentier state in the 1980s. Luciani argues that in a decarbonizing world, major oil- and gas-producing countries may successfully adapt their economies after undertaking massive investment, but it remains to be seen if the necessary policies will be implemented. While the future price of oil and its impact on revenues often receives considerable attention, the added cost of eliminating carbon emissions that oil states will have to bear is neglected. Luciani emphasizes that diversification begins with the fiscal foundations of the state. Government budgets need to be adapted to revenues that will likely be both lower in absolute terms and different in terms of their composition, with oil revenues playing a reduced role. This will lead to a transformation of the state and alter its rentier nature. Other changes may involve a broader political participation and reduced regional rivalries, giving rise to regional economic integration. The first seven years of Saudi Arabia's economic reforms have been undoubtedly astounding. Yet it remains to be seen how quickly these reform be enough to catapult the Kingdom to a post-oil future whilst maintaining real incomes for nationals over time.

PART 1
STOCK TAKING

1

The Entropic Growth of the GCC Economies

Will Saudi Arabia Be Different in the Future?

John Sfakianakis and Zafiris Tzannatos

Introduction

The key development policy instrument used in Saudi Arabia in the last fifty years has been the successive five-year development plans. The First Plan was introduced in 1970 and the last one (the Tenth Plan) covered the period between 2015 and 2019, during which Vision 2030 was introduced. All ten plans have set targets that have rarely been achieved but it might be premature to forecast a similar fate for the Vision.

The following sections in this chapter, first, provide a stylized summary of what the plans envisaged; second, discuss their outcomes, focusing on investment and how the economy has grown over the last few decades, both in comparison to the other members of the Gulf Cooperation Council (GCC) and globally; and third, consider what can be expected of Vision 2030.

The Plans

The five-year development plans, prepared by the Ministry of Economy and Planning, each summarized what had been achieved by the previous plan, assessed the situation as it applied to the first year of the upcoming plan, set desirable targets, and prescribed economic, social, and institutional policies to achieve the selected targets. Prominent among those targets were those that would attract investment, encourage private sector development, and increase the role of nationals in the labour market while reducing the number of migrant workers. How the plans treated labour issues is discussed in

John Sfakianakis and Zafiris Tzannatos, *The Entropic Growth of the GCC Economies*. In: *The Economy of Saudi Arabia in the 21st Century*. Edited by: John Sfakianakis, Oxford University Press. © John Sfakianakis and Zafiris Tzannatos (2024). DOI: 10.1093/oso/9780198863878.003.0002

more detail in Chapter 6 and the discussion below focuses more on macro, industrial, and private sector issues.

The First Development Plan (1970–5) was drafted prior to the sudden and substantial increase in the price of oil in 1973. However, it was no less inclusive or ambitious than those that followed, with a major exception. The government was expected to play a significant role. Accordingly, the First Plan aimed at 'the rapid transformation into a more advanced nation by focusing on the provision of infrastructure and basic government services such as water supply and electricity generation.[1]

The Second Development Plan (1975–80) was prepared after the increase in oil prices, government revenues having increased sixteen-fold since the previous plan (from SAR6 billion in 1970 to SAR93 billion in 1975).[2] It was during the Second Plan that the size of state started multiplying. Perhaps the Second Plan was the most defining one for the course Saudi Arabia has since followed. It sowed the seeds for an authoritarian bargain and private sector patronage in a way that would serve the interest of a relatively small number of Saudi sponsors at the expense of a large number of Saudi job-seekers, as the limited administrative capacity and expertise to manage a largely illiterate society

> led to uncontrolled, patronage-based bureaucratic sprawl centered on the Saudi royal family. … [T]op-level ministerial officials and princes (often one and the same) became the heads of autonomous bureaucratic fiefdoms. Like other rentier states, the Saudi regime coopted society by offering generous social benefits in exchange for political quiescence, discouraging the formation of civil society.[3]

The Third Development Plan (1980–5) was prepared when oil prices had peaked at the end of the 1970s and government revenues had increased further to SAR320 billion by 1980, an increase of more than 5,000 per cent since 1970.[4] It reflected the optimism that came with this situation, but following the collapse of oil prices in 1981, there have since been budget surpluses in only thirteen years.[5]

---

[1] https://www.mof.gov.sa/en/about/OldStratigy/First%20Development%20Plan%20-%20Chapter%201%20-%20Introduction-%D9%85%D8%AF%D9%85%D8%AC.pdf.

[2] Saudi Arabia Monetary Agency (SAMA), *Annual Report* (1981).

[3] S. Hertog, *Princes, Brokers, and Bureaucrats: Oil and the State in Saudi Arabia* (New York: Cornell University Press, 2010).

[4] SAMA Annual Report 1981, p. 12, and I. M. Al-Awaji, 'Bureaucracy and Society in Saudi Arabia', p. 86.

[5] https://journals.sagepub.com/doi/full/10.1177/0046958020984682 and IMF Article IV consultations (2020).

The declining ability of public revenues to support the government's economic and social objectives led the Fourth Development Plan (1985–90) to refer to the need for 'restructuring the economy with the private sector playing a leading role'. Accordingly, the Fourth Plan and also its two successors, the Fifth Development Plan (1990–4) and the Sixth Development Plan (1995–9), noted the decline in productivity, and encouraged private sector participation in areas where the government had traditionally provided services, such as public utilities and transportation. The Seventh Plan (2000–4) was the last one to be completed during the period of low oil prices and allocated substantial amounts for the development of small and medium-sized enterprises (SMEs) compared to previous efforts that had focused on large organizations.

The Eighth Development Plan (2004–9) benefited from a substantial increase in the price of oil, which reached $97/barrel in 2008. Yet the average annual gross domestic product (GDP) growth of 3.5 per cent during the Eighth Plan fell below projections by nearly 25 per cent. And despite the thirty-year experience of previous plans, the targets set by the Ninth Development Plan (2009–14) proved, again, to be optimistic. The Tenth Development Plan (2015–19) was superseded by Vision 2030, which is discussed in the final section of this chapter.

In all, the development plans have taken an increasingly technocratic perspective and moved away from rigid planning methodologies towards more market-oriented ones. However, they have generally been aspirational and failed to create the necessary momentum for a less oil-dependent and diversified economy: 'The Saudi government has made great efforts to diversify the sources of income since the first plan of 1970–1975, but so far [till 2015] such efforts have been unsuccessful.'[6] The performance of Saudi Arabia over time is suggestive of a lack of dynamism that has haunted the economy since the 1970s, as discussed below.

Initiatives Related or Additional to the Plans

While the development plans set the broad priorities for Saudi Arabia, there have also been specific initiatives aiming to implement visionary projects; some included in Vision 2030 are discussed later in this chapter.

---

[6] B. A. Albassam, 'Economic Diversification in Saudi Arabia: Myth or Reality?', *Resources Policy* 44 (2015), pp. 112–17, doi: 10.1016/j.resourpol.2015.02.005. See also T. Fadaak, 'Poverty in the Kingdom of Saudi Arabia: An Exploratory Study of Poverty and Female-Headed Households in Jeddah City', *Social Policy and Administration* 44, no. 6 (2010), pp. 689–707, doi: 10.1111/j.1467-9515.2010.00738.x.

This has not been uncommon among the GCC states; in fact, such initiatives have been rather dominant in most of them, initially in the United Arab Emirates (UAE), especially Dubai, and more recently in Qatar. Usually labelled mega (or, at the time, 'trophy') projects, such high-profile public works have been conceived during periods of high oil revenues, though at times their implementation has been lagging either because the price of oil has declined or because implementation has been delayed due to the projects' size and demanding logistics. The common thread among them is that they have been justified on the premise of diversifying the economy and reducing the dependency on oil revenues and the volatility that comes with it.

In the case of Saudi Arabia, a noteworthy project was King Abdullah Economic City (KAEC, discussed in more detail below), announced in 2005 and subsequently listed on the local stock market in 2006.[7] In the latter year, when oil prices were peaking after the long hiatus since the early 1980s, the creation of several more cities was announced. These included Hail Economic City, Madinah Knowledge City (which was also publicly listed in 2010), Tabuk Economic City, Eastern Economic City, and in 2007 Jazan Economic City. Altogether these new cities were expected to bring in $80 billion worth of foreign investment and to create 1 million jobs in the next ten to twenty years. However, outcomes fell short of expectations. The Hail, Tabuk, and Eastern Economic Cities never started. Madinah became a much smaller real-estate project. In Jazan, a refinery was constructed by Saudi Aramco, but it proved to be less functional than expected in the absence of adequate pipeline connectivity to receive crude oil. Few jobs were created, which went mainly to low-paid expatriates who worked in the manufacturing sites or service areas. Despite having benefited from nearly a decade of high oil prices since the mid-2000s, Saudi Arabia was unable to sustain the spending required for these economic cities.

Another project was the Public Pension Fund's King Abdullah Financial District (KAFD) in 2006. Following an earlier initiative by Dubai (the creation of the Dubai International Financial Center in 2004), the idea was to attract major local and international banks and become a regional financial hub—effectively in direct competition with Dubai. Though KAFD was eventually opened in 2022, comprising eighty-three buildings and sixty-one towers (roughly four times the size of the London's Canary Wharf), the project was plagued with delays and cost overruns. The Public Investment Fund (PIF) became its new $10 billion landlord and saviour in 2018.[8] Still,

---

[7] 'Saudi Arabia's Sleepy City Offers Prince a Cautionary Tale', *Financial Times* (27 May 2018).
[8] https://www.reuters.com/article/us-saudi-economy-finance-exclusive-idUSKBN1I41YK.

most of the tenants have been local ones including the headquarters of the PIF, several government entities, and a few financial institutions including the Capital Market Authority and Saudi Arabia's largest state-owned bank, Saudi National Bank, which is owned by the PIF. Overall, KAFD had limited success in becoming a regional financial hub or a preferred site for international firms.[9]

Returning to KAEC, the project aimed to create a new city with an eventual resident population of 2 million by 2020, which would feature several leisure activities, including golf. The city, situated at the crossroads of major shipping lanes on the Red Sea coast, would generate revenue for its port, jobs for its citizens, and inward investment. The Saudi Arabian General Investment Authority (renamed and upgraded to the Ministry of Investments in 2020) envisaged that KAEC would become a significant manufacturing and logistics hub. Foreign companies were expected to join, enticed by a port that would rival all those in the Red Sea and beyond, including Jeddah Islamic Port. The demand for its services could lead to sizeable job creation. Members of the Jeddah private sector who were supportive of the endeavour came up with several incentives, including offering affordable land for firms to move at least part of their business.

As of 2023, however, only around 30 per cent of the physical area of KAEC has been developed, which includes the Crown Prince Mohammed bin Salman College, the Industrial Valley, King Abdullah Port, and the Royal Greens Golf and Country Club. Overall, the project did not meet its targets for several reasons. The scale and costs of the project were beyond the fiscal capacity of the government, even with the support of private developers. KAEC has been unable to rival the industrial zones of Jeddah, Riyadh, Jebel Ali, and others. Some industries have moved into KAEC, such as Mars, and in 2022 the luxury electric vehicle maker, Lucid Group (majority owned by the PIF) announced that it would set up a $3.4 billion plant in KAEC, producing up to 150,000 electric vehicles per year.[10] Generally, however, local businesses have been reluctant to relocate over the years. Tourism activity also did not take off. The equity collected from the initial public offering (IPO) dried up and the city had to reach out to the state for financing, while many decision-makers remained unsupportive. In 2022, the PIF became a 25 per cent shareholder in KAEC, which should provide a much-needed financial lifeline. As of 2022, however, its population was estimated at only around 10,000–15,000—not all of whom are permanent residents.

[9] https://www.bloomberg.com/news/articles/2016-04-19/saudi-10-billion-financial-district-missing-one-thing-banks; https://www.meed.com/riyadh-to-salvage-economic-cities-and-financial-district/.
[10] https://www.arabnews.com/node/2051066/business-economy.

There are significant differences between KAEC and a more recent city project called Neom, the brainchild of Crown Prince Mohammed bin Salman. KAEC and Neom share two common features. First, both aim to wean Saudi Arabia away from its dependence on oil. Second, both to some extent reflect the Dubai approach summarized in the phrase 'build it and they'll come.'[11] However, although KAEC largely failed to diversify the country's sources of revenue and subsequently became dependent on state funding for its survival, Neom is different in the sense that it reflects the rising aspirations of Saudi Arabia's Vision 2030 and expects that funding will not be an issue. KAEC is the size of Washington DC; Neom is a dozen times bigger, approximately the size of Belgium. KAEC is 127 kilometres from Jeddah, but Neom's closest city, Tabuk, is some 215 kilometres away. KAEC's initial budget was $27 billion,[12] though it had reached $100 billion by 2015.[13] Neom was initially budgeted at $500 billion,[14] but its costs are estimated to have surpassed $1 trillion by 2022—including 'The Line', a transport service stretching 170 kilometres whose building cost alone may reach $200 billion.[15] The Line aims to build twin skyscrapers about 500 metres tall. Neom is intending to include a ski resort and swimming lanes for commuters.[16] In addition to its residential and manufacturing centre, Neom is expected to be a zero-carbon city. Neom also wants to become a hub for producing hydrogen for fuel-cell vehicles.[17]

Neom is not the only post-2016 project. A parallel initiative is the Diriyah Gate in the city of Ad-Diriyah, on the outskirts of Riyadh, which is the ancestral home of the royal family, founded in the fifteenth century and declared the capital of the first Saudi state in 1744. The plan is to turn the wider location into a tourism, culture, and entertainment destination, with thirty-eight

---

[11] This approach produced elusive results in the case of KAEC and it remains to be seen how close to Dubai (and Abu Dhabi) Neom can come. For example, although Dubai was simply a desert outpost city before its transformation, it had an established history of trade with many of its neighbours and connectivity with the subcontinent, central Asia and Iran, as well as a rather diverse ethnic composition and an open-door policy. Dubai started much before Saudi Arabia when there was little competition in the region and more recently has not shied away from attracting those sanctioned out of other parts of the world and allowing them to establish second homes in the UAE, along with the rise of Abu Dhabi. https://www.ft.com/content/4d169d0c-4be4-11e9-8b7f-d49067e0f50d.

[12] https://www.files.ethz.ch/isn/142863/Special%20Report%20on%20Future%20Economic%20Cities%20of%20Saudi%20Arabia%20-%2005.2007.pdf.

[13] https://www.pri.org/stories/2015-03-20/saudi-arabia-plans-100-billion-mega-city-help-end-its-oil-dependence.

[14] https://www.reuters.com/article/us-saudi-economy-reserves-idINKBN2352TM.

[15] During the 2015–17 oil slump, nominal GDP was around $645–80 billion, although after oil prices jumped to above $70 per barrel, GDP increased to $817 billion.

[16] https://www.bloomberg.com/news/newsletters/2022-07-15/bloomberg-big-take-inside-mbs-s-smart-city-neom.

[17] https://www.reuters.com/article/us-saudi-neom-project/saudi-crown-prince-launches-zero-carbon-city-in-neom-business-zone-idUSKBN29F0L8.

hotels, twelve museums, and a golf course built around a UNESCO world heritage site. Its costs, initially estimated at $20 billion, have reached $50 billion. Another initiative is the Red Sea Project and Amaala, which are discussed at length in Chapter 9. In short, this project will house seventy-five luxury hotels and more than 2,000 luxury residential properties at an estimated cost of $16 billion (in 2022), to be financed by the PIF and debt financing from local banks.

In summary, Vision 2030 can benefit from Saudi Arabia's experience of ambitious projects in view of their fiscal implications and their wider aims of diversifying the economy. Before this is discussed, the next section traces the development of the Saudi economy in comparison to other GCC countries, the world economy, and a frontier oil economy, namely Norway.

Benchmarking Saudi Arabia: Slow Growth in the GCC

Output growth, a significant determinant of employment creation, has historically been slow in Saudi Arabia. The way oil revenues have been used has deprived the economy of diversification. Moreover, output growth in Saudi Arabia has been highly variable. Finally, pursuing the policy of fixed exchange rates in combination with the effects of Dutch disease has prevented the economy from achieving external equilibrium. Currency overvaluation has been exercising upward pressure on the prices of non-tradables such as services, local production, and real estate—all associated with a greater use of migrant labour, thus reducing the employment opportunities for nationals.[18] Although Saudi Arabia is not very different in this respect from the other GCC economies, all of which have been affected by the 'oil curse', its economic growth has lagged behind them—and has lagged even more by comparison to the rest of the world.

In 1970, per capita income in Saudi Arabia was 15 per cent above the world average ($921 in Saudi Arabia compared to $804 in the world as a whole). By 1981, the difference had increased to approximately 700 per cent in favour of Saudi Arabia (nearly $18,000 in Saudi Arabia compared to just over $2,500 in the world). By 2019, the difference had dwindled to 200 per cent ($23,000 compared to $11,500). Since the 1970s, per capita income in Saudi Arabia has increased by less than 60 per cent of the world average and nearly that little compared to the Middle East and North Africa (MENA) region, including

---

[18] I. Diwan, 'Fiscal Sustainability, the Labor Market, and Growth in Saudi Arabia', in G. Luciani and T. Moerenhout (eds.), *When Can Oil Economies Be Deemed Sustainable?* (London: Palgrave Macmillan, 2020).

all Arab countries.[19] Alternatively put, the per capita income in high-income countries, the world, MENA, and the other Arab countries increased by between 2.3 times and 2.7 more than in Saudi Arabia (Figure 1.1).

Saudi Arabia has not done well even in comparison to its neighbours. It has lagged the other GCC economies in terms of real per capita GDP growth. In each decade since the 1980s, its annual growth rate has been lower than the average rate in the other five Gulf countries. The difference was most pronounced in the 1980s and 1990s when the difference was more than 2 percentage points.[20] Between 1968 and 1981 the nominal per capita income in Saudi Arabia had increased twenty-fold (Figure 1.2). It took another thirty years for the level of income to reach 1981 levels, even in nominal terms. Since then, the increase has been lower than those in all other GCC economies with the exception of the UAE, which has a much larger migrant population in proportional terms. The two economies that have fared best in the last forty years are Oman and Bahrain—both are less dependent on oil than the other four GCC countries.[21]

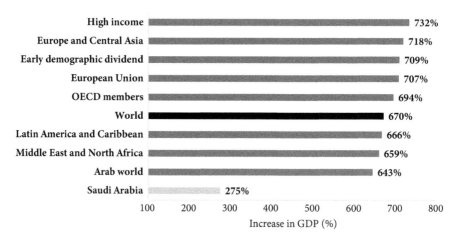

Figure 1.1 Increase in GDP (%) in Saudi Arabia and selected world regions, 1970s to 2010s

Note: 1970s = average 1974–8; 2010s = average 2015–19

Source: World Bank, *World Development Indicators*.

[19] The MENA region includes Iran and excludes several of the twenty-two Arab countries, mainly in sub-Saharan Africa.

[20] The respective annual rates for Saudi Arabia and the other five GCC economies have been −0.6 vs. 1.6 (1980–9), 2.7 vs. 5.2 (1990–9), 5 vs. 5.8 (2000–9), and 4.8 vs. 4.6 (2000–15). World Bank, *World Development Indicators*.

[21] Some of the variation between the GCC countries is due to the changing share of the migrant population, an issue that is discussed later on.

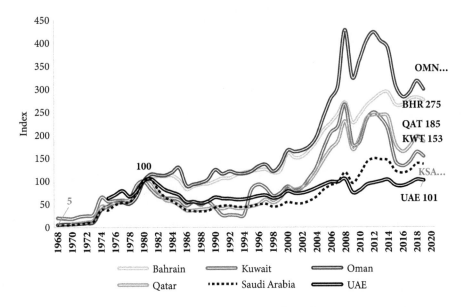

Figure 1.2 GDP growth in the GCC, 1968–2019 (current US$, index 1980 = 100)

Note: No data for Kuwait 1992–4 (its GDP is assumed to have increased at the average rate of increase of the remaining GCC countries during these years).

Source: World Bank, *World Development Indicators*.

Saudi Arabia is different from the other GCC economies with respect to three characteristics. First, it has the highest share of nationals in the population and therefore faces more pressure to spend domestically on social and employment programmes for political reasons. In Saudi Arabia, public expenditures as a share of GDP have been higher than those in other GCC countries. They peaked in 1987 at 58 per cent of GDP and have generally been about 10 per cent higher than the average shares of public expenditure in the GCC.[22]

Second and relatedly, Saudi Arabia has increasingly assumed for itself the role of a regional peacekeeper. Providing 'a good security system' has been a principal objective along with 'sustaining high religious values and improving the economy and standard of living'[23]. While military spending as a percentage of GDP was equal to the world average at around 6 per cent in the early 1960s, it has since increased significantly and averaged 10 per cent in the 2010s, compared to around 2 per cent in the rest of the world (Figure 1.3).

[22] I. Diwan and T. Akin, 'Fifty Years of Fiscal Policy in the Arab Region', Economic Research Forum Working Paper 914 (May 2015).
[23] K. M. Khuthaila, *Saudi Arabia's development: a dependency theory perspective*. New York: Syracuse University (1984), quoted from A. Alghamedi, 'Enhancing employment opportunities in the Saudi Arabian private sector', Los Angeles: Pepperepperdine University Theses and Dissertations. 752 (2016). p. 21 at https://digitalcommons.pepperdine.edu/etd/752, p. 21.

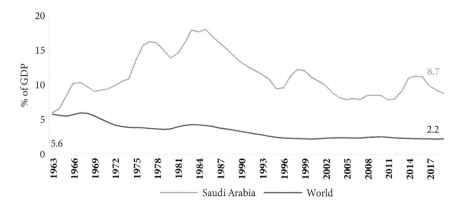

Figure 1.3 Military expenditure, 1963–2018 (% of GDP)

Note: Five-year moving average.

Source: World Bank, *World Development Indicators*.

Third, although the GCC countries share many common characteristics, Saudi Arabia differs from the others in intensity. For example, Figure 1.4 shows the relationship between 'voice and accountability'[24] and economic growth until the Arab Uprisings.[25]

All Arab countries are located in the south-west quadrant in terms of voice and accountability. Of the six Arab countries with the lowest score on accountability and voice, five experienced political instability during the 2010s, ranging from protests (Tunisia and Egypt) to outright civil war (Libya, Syria, and Yemen). The only exception among this group of countries was Saudi Arabia, which had the lowest voice and accountability with the exception of Libya. Saudi Arabia seems to have managed to contain the unrest partly because it introduced a wide range of economic and social protection measures including, among others, increases in public sector employment, wages, benefits, and pensions.[26]

---

[24] The Kaufmann–Kraay–Zoido Lobaton index (KKZ) takes into account freedom of expression, freedom of association, and free media as well as the perceptions of citizens regarding the extent to which they are able to participate in selecting their government. See D. Kaufmann, A. Kraay, and P. Zoido, *Governance Matters* (August 1999) at https://ssrn.com/abstract=188568.

[25] This period is chosen to avoid complications that arose from the Arab Uprisings that started in 2011. It should, however, be noted that since 1990 Saudi Arabia has grown at an annual rate of 3.1 per cent against a population growth of 2.6 per cent. This has resulted in an annual increase in average per capita incomes of only 0.5 per cent.

[26] After the Arab Uprisings, Saudi Arabia raised the monthly minimum wage for government employees by nearly 20 per cent (SAR3,000/$800) and for teachers working in the private sector to (SAR5,000/1,333); increased the minimum pension of retired civil servants (to SAR4,000/$1,067); and created 60,000 military jobs in the Interior Ministry, 500 jobs to assist the Ministry of Trade and Industry in monitoring the job market, and 300 more jobs in the administration of scientific research. It also introduced an unemployment assistance scheme for the first time, expanded training, and increased spending on infrastructure (ILO/UNDP), Rethinking Economic Growth: Towards Productive and Inclusive Arab Societies.

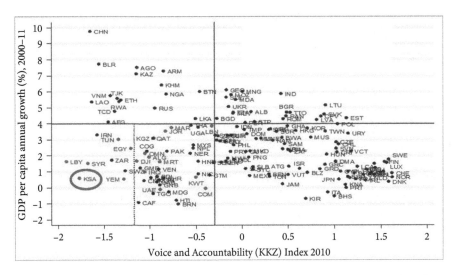

Figure 1.4 Economic growth, voice, and accountability have been low in Saudi Arabia

Note: KSA = Kingdom of Saudi Arabia.

Source: ILO/UNDP, 2012.

An Economic and Political Comparison with the Frontier

Researchers have used many ways to probe the reasons for the sluggish macroeconomic performance of Saudi Arabia and to measure the gap in comparison to other countries. Several explanations have been offered, including in this volume. Rather than attempting to summarize them, the discussion below adopts the rather common comparison between Saudi Arabia and Norway, but in a more heuristic approach than previous studies.[27] It focuses on the impact of oil on the macro economy with added reference to the labour market as a proxy for developments in the social sectors.

Saudi Arabia and Norway share several common economic characteristics. Agricultural production is minimal in both countries. Both countries are oil producers. From an employment perspective, the services sector is dominant. In the last fifty years, their per capita incomes have increased remarkably by the same amount—almost thirty-fold in nominal terms (Figure 1.5). In fact, during most of this period the increase in incomes has been well correlated with the price of oil. The share of household consumption in GDP is similar

Beirut: ILO Regional Office for the Arab States, 2012, at https://www.ilo.org/wcmsp5/groups/public/---arabstates/---ro-beirut/documents/publication/wcms_208346.pdf.

[27] See the collection of papers in G. Luciani and T. Moerenhout (eds.), When Can Oil Economies Be Deemed Sustainable? (2021). Palgrave Macmillan, especially papers by I. Diwan, Fiscal Sustainability, the Labour Market and Growth in Saudi Arabia, and J. Beutel, Economic Diversification and Sustainable Development of the GCC, at https://link.springer.com/book/10.1007/978-981-15-5728-6.

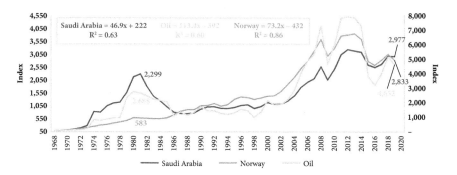

Figure 1.5 Oil prices (right axis) and GDP growth in Saudi Arabia and Norway, 1968–2019 (current US$, index 1968 = 100)

Sources: GDP: World Bank, *World Development Indicators*; oil annual prices: World Bank commodity price data.

in the two countries (46 per cent in Norway and 43 per cent in Saudi Arabia) as also are their respective shares of government consumption (24 per cent and 26 per cent).[28]

The initial difference in the growth trajectory between Norway and Saudi Arabia during the 1970s can be attributed to the former's belated participation in the oil boom of that decade. Norway's first licensing round was announced in 1965, its first discovery of oil was in 1967, and production started only in 1971.[29] Predictably, as oil production grew slowly at first and reached 20 per cent of GDP only in 2000, a share that has been relatively stable since. Its oil economy currently contributes 46 per cent to exports and 26 per cent to government revenues.[30] In the case of Saudi Arabia, the corresponding contribution to the economy and exports is roughly double (43 per cent of GDP in 2023, and 79.5 per cent of exports in 2022), and to government revenues is more than double (67 per cent in 2022).[31] Thus, Saudi Arabia is more dependent on oil, has remained more exposed to fluctuations in oil prices, and has been less able to weather the impact of volatile oil prices through macroeconomic management.

[28] J. Beutel, 'Economic Diversification and Sustinable Development of the GCC', in G. Luciani and T. Moerenhout (eds.), *When Can Oil Economies Be Deemed Sustainable?* (Palgrave Macmillan, 2021) at https://link.springer.com/book/10.1007/978-981-15-5728-6

[29] Ministry of Petroleum and Energy and the Norwegian Petroleum Directorate, 'Norwegian Petroleum: The Petroleum History' (Norsk olje og gass, 2020), https://www.norskpetroleum.no/en/framework/norways-petroleum-history/#:~:text=The%20first%20exploration%20well%20was,shelf%20was%20Balder%20in%201967.&text=This%20was%20when%20Norway's%20success,started%20on%2015%20June%201971.

[30] T Statistics Norway (National Accounts) and Ministry of Finance (The National Budget 2021).

[31] 'Saudi Arabia's Oh So Green Bond Offering', *Financial Times*, https://www.ft.com/content/dc463877-9c07-45f2-9c0a-0bdd998b2e15.

Following the oil price hike in the 1970s, the per capita income in Saudi Arabia peaked in 1981, almost in line with the increase in the international price of oil. Its incomes fell quickly by the mid-1980s, however, and have since moved more or less in line with those of Norway. Despite the country capitalizing heavily on the oil price hike during the 1970s, a linear regression applied to the period between 1968 and 2019 suggests that nominal per capita incomes in Saudi Arabia have increased annually by $47 compared to $73 in Norway (see Figures 1.5 and 1.6). In terms of annual rate of growth, per capita incomes increased by 0.7 per cent in Saudi Arabia. The rate was less than half of that for the world (1.6 per cent), and only one-third that of Norway (2.2 per cent). Although oil is an important component of economic activity in both countries, the increase in incomes in Norway has been steadier and less affected by fluctuations in the price of oil over time: the regression's coefficient of determination (R^2) for Norway is 0.86. By comparison, the coefficient of determination for Saudi Arabia (0.63) is almost equal to that for the oil price (0.6) (Figure 1.5).

Narrowing this long historical perspective, the two countries initially had the same level of total GDP at just below $120 billion in 1990, which tripled to approximately $300 billion by 2005 (when oil prices started increasing for the first time since the 1980s). During this period the share of agriculture fell by 2 percentage points in both countries while the share of industrial production (including oil) increased by the same amount (i.e. by approximately 20 per cent) (Table 1.1). One can hardly get a better fit at this aggregate level in a comparative economics context.

Figure 1.6   Real per capita income, 1968–2019 (index 100 = 1968)

Source: World Bank, *World Development Indicators*.

Table 1.1 GDP and employment distribution in Saudi Arabia and Norway, 1990 and 2005

Output	GDP ($bn)		Share of GDP by sector					
			Agriculture		Industry		Services	
	1990	2005	1990	2005	1990	2005	1990	2005
Norway	116	296	4%	2%	36%	43%	61%	55%
Saudi Arabia	117	310	6%	4%	49%	59%	46%	37%
% of male employment								
Norway				5%		32%		63%
Saudi Arabia				5%		24%		71%
% of female employment								
Norway				2%		8%		90%
Saudi Arabia				1%		1%		98%

Note: Figures subject to rounding.
Source: World Bank, *World Development Indicators*.

Despite these similarities, there were significant differences in the underlying employment structures of the two economies. During the period under consideration only around 450,000 of Norway's resident population (less than 10 per cent) were migrants, including children born in Norway to immigrant parents, compared to 7 million in Saudi Arabia (around 30 per cent), most of whom were workers.[32]

The services sector in Norway employs far fewer workers, both male and female, as a percentage of the employed population compared to Saudi Arabia. Yet the services sector accounts for a far greater share of GDP in Norway than in Saudi Arabia. These two statistics considered together imply that service workers in Norway are much more productive than those in Saudi Arabia, where the industrial sector employs fewer workers and has a higher share of GDP—yet another sign that the oil sector, with its downstream activities and exports, is dominant. Finally, with respect to labour issues, the unemployment rate in Norway was around one-quarter of that in Saudi Arabia in the mid-2000s (around 2–3 per cent in Norway versus 10 per cent or more in Saudi Arabia). This difference is even more startling when it is considered that in Norway the female labour force participation rate of 75 per

[32] At the time Norway had a population of 4.6 million compared to 24 million in Saudi Arabia. Since 2005, the population of Saudi Arabia has increased by 10 million (43 per cent) compared to 700,000 (16 per cent) in Norway. For the record, in 1960 the population size of the two countries was broadly the same: 3.6 million in Norway and 4.1 million in Saudi Arabia. Today the population in Saudi Arabia is sixfold that of Norway (34 million compared to 5.4 million).

cent is at near parity with the male one. In Saudi Arabia, the female-to-male rate was lower than 20 per cent in 2005.[33]

Finally, the two countries differ significantly with respect to political arrangements, though both are monarchies. Norway is a constitutional monarchy with the King of Norway being the head of state in a parliamentary system of government headed by an elected Prime Minister. The monarch's duties are strictly representative and ceremonial, serving as official diplomatic representation abroad and as a symbol of the country's unity. The executive powers are exercised by the Prime Minister, while legislative power is vested with both the government and a Parliament elected on the basis of proportional representation. According to the Democracy Index, Norway is the world's most democratic country and has been in the top position for several years.[34] Norway is also the country with the highest value for the index of voice and accountability shown in Figure 1.4, although annual per capita income growth averaged about the same in Norway and Saudi Arabia at approximately 1 per cent in the first decade of the twenty-first century.[35]

In Saudi Arabia, the King combines executive and judicial functions with legislation based on royal decrees (until 2022 the King held the post of Prime Minister, but now the Crown Prince holds that role). The political system revolves around the royal family controlling several government posts, including key ministries and regional governorships. If not politically motivated, the arrest of princes, government ministers, and business people accused of corruption in 2017 lends support to the belief that power structures exist which appropriate the country's wealth—something that Vision 2030 aims to address.

Looking at the composition of output, it has been argued that Saudi Arabia compares well with Norway in terms of economic diversification, and it has even been claimed that in some areas the relevant metrics exceed those of Norway.[36] Saudi Arabia is said to be within 95 per cent of Norway regarding the effects on the economy of an increase in domestic production of a specific branch of economic activity (the Leontief Inverse Matrix). This has been interpreted as an indication that 'Saudi Arabia has reached an international level of industrial diversification'.[37] However, if imported intermediate inputs

[33] International Labour Organization, ILOSTAT database. Data retrieved 21 June 2020.
[34] The Democracy Index is compiled by the Economist Intelligence Unit (EIU) and ranks 166 countries in terms of their state of democracy. See https://en.wikipedia.org/wiki/Democracy_Index.
[35] This period is chosen to avoid complications that arose from the global financial crisis in 2008 and the Arab Uprisings that started in 2011.
[36] J. Beutel, 'Economic Diversification and Sustainable Development of GCC Countries', in Luciani and Moerenhout, *When Can Oil Economies Be Deemed Sustainable?*
[37] Ibid., pp. 121–2.

are included, the level of diversification in Saudi Arabia decreases to 86 per cent of that in Norway. In fact, the shares of intermediates in total output are significantly lower in Saudi Arabia than in Norway (31 vs. 46 per cent of output), as are the shares of imported intermediates (5 vs. 10 per cent). Still, it has been claimed that inter-industry differences are 'not strikingly high' and that 'by 2011, Saudi Arabia almost reached the diversity level of Norway ... a considerable achievement of the Saudi development policy'.[38] Moreover, in terms of sustainable development, Saudi Arabia

> has significant net incomes from abroad, low allocations for consumption of fixed capital, moderate allocation for natural resource depletion and the highest allocations for education expenditures of the GCC countries. Since 2005, adjusted net savings are in the range of 20–30 per cent of GNI [gross national income]. This level is an achievement as it even exceeded the corresponding level of Norway.[39]

In contrast to these findings that Saudi Arabia is catching up with, if not exceeding, Norway in terms of sustainable development, its progress has been slow in regard to the depletion of natural resources and environmental pollution. Norway has made important strides towards the green economy despite the costs associated with it. CO_2 emissions per capita were the same at around 11,500 metric tons per capita in both countries in 1989/90. They have since been reduced to less than 8,000 metric tons per capita in Norway but increased to 17,000 metric tons per capita in Saudi Arabia.[40] Electric car registrations in Norway rose from 20 per cent in 2017 to more than 50 per cent of all new registrations in 2020, rising to 75 per cent when plug-in hybrids are included.[41] In the last thirty years, domestic energy consumption in Saudi Arabia has increased by more than population growth and, in most years, by more than GDP growth.[42] Significant causes of the growth in energy consumption are low-quality insulation, poor equipment maintenance, and an abundance of oversized vehicles, resulting in per capita energy consumption in Saudi Arabia being 1.5 times the average of the world's high-income countries. The heavy reliance of domestic consumption on oil may significantly

---

[38] Ibid., p. 130.
[39] Ibid., p. 149.
[40] Word Bank, https://data.worldbank.org/indicator/EN.ATM.CO2E.PC?locations=SA-NO. The latest date for which information is available is 2016.
[41] Norwegian Road Federation, https://ofv.no/bilsalget/bilsalget-i-desember-2020. Norway imposes hefty vehicle import duties and car registration taxes, making cars significantly more expensive than in most other countries, but it waives these duties for electric vehicles.
[42] E. Azar and M. A. Raouf, *Sustainability in the Gulf: Challenges and Opportunities* (Abingdon: Routledge, 2017).

compromise Saudi Arabia's future capacity to export hydrocarbons and its fiscal potential.[43]

In addition to diversification and sustainability issues, the issues of who appropriates the proceeds of production, especially oil revenues, and how wealth is distributed have implications for the citizenry. According to one source (Bloomberg), the Al Saud family is the fourth richest family in the world with net wealth of $95 billion derived from no specific company, unlike the three richer families who are identified with Walmart, Mars, and Koch Industries.[44] Relatedly, Norway produces only around 2 million barrels of oil per day, but its sovereign wealth fund (the Government Pension Fund Global, also known as the Oil Fund) had amassed more than $1.3 trillion by 2023.[45] In contrast, the equivalent fund (the Public Investment Fund, PIF) in Saudi Arabia was founded in 1971—although for the first five decades since its inception it was predominantly a passive investor in local firms in contrast to Norway's Fund which is mandated never to invest in its economy. For much of its life, the PIF's assets never surpassed above $150 billion whilst hardly liquid, at most times. During these first five decades, it was the assets of the Central Bank (SAMA)—which effectively became responsible for making overseas investments—that reached $724 billion in 2014 despite the fact that daily production in Saudi Arabia is around six times more than that of Norway.[46] It was only in 2015, that PIF effectively became the country's sovereign fund with a renewed mandate to invest inside and outside the country and by 2023 its assets under management had reached 66 per cent of the country's economy of which majority of its assets were held within its borders. In Norway, the sovereign wealth fund is restricted in depleting its capital, but it can use its returns to fund the stabilization and growth needs of the economy for the benefit of future generations.

By comparison, the sovereign fund in Saudi Arabia has not published a charter or whether any restrictions apply to it. The International Monetary Fund (IMF) has highlighted in its annual Article IV reviews of the country

[43] P. Stevens and G. Lahn, *Burning Oil to Keep Cool: The Hidden Energy Crisis in Saudi Arabia* (London: Chatham House, 2011).
[44] The net worth of the three richest families in the world is $215 billion for the Walton family (Walmart), $120 billion for the Mars family (Mars), and $110 billion for the Koch family (Koch Industries). https://www.bloomberg.com/features/richest-families-in-the-world/. Another source claims that Saudi Arabia's ruling royal family has a net worth of about $1.4 trillion across the nearly 15,000 royal family members. https://www.trtworld.com/middle-east/saudi-royal-family-s-1-4-trillion-wealth-and-lavish-spending-36040.
[45] Oil production in Norway declined significantly between 2001 to 2013, from 3.4 million barrels per day to 1.8 million and has since oscillated around 2 million barrels. https://www.statista.com/statistics/265186/oil-production-in-norway-in-barrels-per-day/.
[46] Saudi Arabia's oil production from 1998 to 2019 averaged around 11.8 million barrels of oil daily. https://www.statista.com/statistics/265190/oil-production-in-saudi-arabia-in-barrels-per-day/.

that oversight of the sovereign fund and its off-budget activities is needed.[47] In 2021, the PIF announced its annual local investment targets of $40 billion until 2025.[48] In 2022, in preparation for issuing a debut green bond, the PIF announced a 25 per cent shareholder return for 2021 which was in line with that of investors in the S&P 500 Index: that is, 27 per cent.[49] It remains to be seen how the PIF's investment commitments will fare in a period of lower oil revenue. The IMF warned in 2020 that the region's, including Saudi Arabia financial wealth could be depleted by 2034.[50]

The PIF missed its investment target of $40 billion in 2021, investing only $22 billion, although 2021 was the year with the lowest budget deficit at 2.3 per cent since the advent of Vision 2030.[51]

Finally, government spending in Saudi Arabia has been rather erratic and reactive. It increased precipitously following the oil bonanza of the 1970s and also after the Arab Uprisings (Figure 1.7). Part of Saudi spending is payments

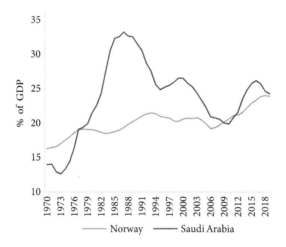

Figure 1.7 General government final consumption expenditure, 1970–2019 (% of GDP)

Note: Five-year moving average.
Source: World Bank, *World Development Indicators*.

[47] Saudi Arabia, Article IV Consultation, 2018. IMF Country Report No. 18/263, p. 27.
[48] https://www.reuters.com/article/saudi-crownprince-pif-int-idUSKBN27S2WZ.
[49] https://www.ft.com/content/16bab8f8-0311-4409-bed1-21ea46e0650b. According to the prospectus, the annual average return of the PIF was 12 per cent between 2017 and 2020.
[50] Fiscal sustainability will require significant consolidation in the coming years. Its speed is an intergenerational choice. Fully preserving current wealth will require large upfront fiscal adjustments. More gradual efforts would ease the short-term adjustment burden but at the expense of resources available to future generations. https://www.imf.org/-/media/Files/Publications/DP/2020/English/FOFSGCCEA.ashx.
[51] https://www.reuters.com/markets/funds/saudi-austere-budget-outsources-spending-pif-leaves-room-debt-2021-12-13/.

made to public sector employees, who are mostly nationals. The monthly average wage for Saudi workers was SAR10.238 in 2018 with considerable differences across sectors. It was SAR11.198 in the public sector, SAR7.339 in the private sector, SAR4.750 in non-profit organizations, and SAR16.257 in international and regional agencies.[52] The resulting average wage for Saudi workers is 142 per cent of GDP. This compares to an average salary in Norway that is only 87 per cent of GDP. Even compared to other GCC countries, the government wage bill in Saudi Arabia is high, reaching 12 per cent of GDP on average between 2005 and 2016, compared to 3 per cent in the UAE, 5 per cent in Qatar, around 9 per cent in Oman and Bahrain, and just over 10 per cent in Kuwait.[53] As for military spending, although it is located in a different region, Norway has reduced its budget from 3.5 per cent of GDP in the 1960s to 1.6 per cent by 2019, which is a fraction of what Saudi Arabia spends, while Norway spends a commendable over 1 per cent of its GDP on overseas development assistance.[54]

In conclusion, the Saudi Arabian rents from oil have not been used in the most productive way. Saudi Arabia has performed less well than the other GCC economies where, as in other resource-abundant countries, political stability has been a challenging goal for their authoritarian elites.[55] It has also performed markedly less well compared to Norway. The use of oil revenues and excessive public sector employment as a means of wealth distribution has led to unsustainable public spending and has distorted the macro economy. This, in combination with a migration policy that supports a rentier private sector, has adversely affected productivity, economic growth, and the labour market. Overall, Saudi Arabia is facing what even Western democracies are subjected to: that is, political elites and organized groups representing economic interests which can exercise substantial independent impacts on government policy. Ordinary citizens and their mass-based interest groups have little, and at times no, independent influence. Such an environment gives rise to 'elite domination' or 'biased pluralism' where elections do not matter much for the majority of citizens.[56]

---

[52] The figures include the basic salary plus allowances, bonuses, and overtime. General Authority for Statistics, https://www.stats.gov.sa/en/news/292.

[53] IMF, 'Regional Economic Outlook: Middle East, North Africa, Afghanistan, and Pakistan' (2018), https://www.imf.org/en/Publications/~/media/E7F9D70809DF41A8A55D8046A13480F0.ashx.

[54] https://donortracker.org/country/norway, p.24.

[55] I. Elbadawi, 'Thresholds Matters: Resource Abundance, Development and Democratic Transitions in the Arab World', in I. Diwan and A. Galal (eds.), *The Middle East in Times of Transition* (London: Palgrave Macmillan), p. 86.

[56] M. Gilens and B. I. Page, 'Testing Theories of American Politics: Elites, Interest Groups, and Average Citizens', *Perspectives on Politics* 12, no. 3 (2014), pp. 564–81.

These are issues that Vision 2030 aims to address by eliminating corruption, energizing the private sector, increasing the role of nationals in the labour market, and reducing the dependency of citizens on state benefits. The Vision's accomplishments by 2030 will be conditioned on domestic and international developments until that date, and the following section reviews its course during the first seven years (2016–23) after it was adopted.

Vision 2030

Vision 2030 was announced in 2016 and coincided with the beginning of the Tenth Development Plan (2015–19). The plan expected an annual average economic growth rate of 5 per cent and the share of the private sector in GDP to increase from 45 per cent in 2014 to 51 per cent in 2019.[57] The Vision set up even more ambitious targets, both institutional and numerical. Both seem to be challenging, if judged by the evolution of real per capita incomes since the mid-2010s (Figure 1.8), which have recently been affected by external developments such as changes in the international price of oil and the onset of the COVID-19 pandemic.

Institutionally, Vision 2030 included legal, structural, economic, social, and cultural reforms, although there do not seem to be any political reforms on the horizon.[58] Progress has been made in the sense that the programmes set out in the Vision have been established and most have been posted

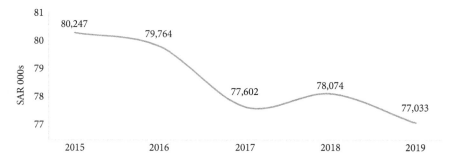

Figure 1.8 Real per capita GDP, 2015–19 (SAR)

Source: World Bank.

[57] http://g20.org.tr/wp-content/uploads/2014/12/g20_comprehensive_growth_strategy_saudi_arabia.pdf.

[58] Jane Kinninmont, 'Vision 2030 and Saudi Arabia's Social Contract', Chatham House (July 2017), https://www.chathamhouse.org/sites/default/files/publications/research/2017-07-20-vision-2030-saudi-kinninmont.pdf.

online, although little information has so far been made public to assess their evolution.[59] However, the institutional challenge in achieving the many targets included in the Vision (more than 300) is daunting. The Vision envisages that coordination towards the achievement of these targets will cut across as many as twenty-five ministries and agencies that will oversee more than 150 planned initial public offerings.[60] Much will depend on the oversight authority of the Crown Prince and his ability to reduce corruption in a 'society where family, tribal, and regional ties are stronger than the nebulous conception of state identity'[61]—a society characterized by 'a kin-based social structure coexisting with a modernizing technocratic elite and a cosmopolitan business class, yielding a multiplicity of informal relationships' and giving rise to opportunism and 'norms that are not bound by procedural rules.'[62] In addition, some of the gains achieved in several social and labour market areas may work against themselves. For example, the religious police are reported to have now been consigned to desk duties, and this raises the prospect that at some point citizens' demands may get ahead of how far the leaders are prepared to go.[63] Moreover, it remains to be seen how society responds to the state's role vis-à-vis religion and identity even in an environment where the young are the main constituents and supporters of Vision 2030.

Numerically, Vision 2030 expects to double GDP and reach US$1.3 trillion by 2030, making Saudi Arabia the fifteenth largest economy in the world. This would require a consistent annual rate of economic growth of more than 7 per cent. However, even as the economy never averaged anything close to 7 per cent real growth rates - except 8.7 per cent in 2022 - it seems that Saudi Arabia's GDP is not too far from reaching its goal as in 2022 it surpassed the $1.1 trillion mark. Much of the growth in the economy size was due to two essential factors that worked in its favour: a 17 per cent increase in oil exports and 40 per cent rise in the average price of Saudi crude exports.

The Vision also expects that the share of SMEs in GDP will increase from 20 to 35 per cent. This would require the SME sector to grow by an annual rate of more than 10 per cent. The contribution of the not-for-profit profit sector to GDP is expected to reach 5 per cent by 2030 (from 1 per cent in the mid-2010s). If this sector's contribution to GDP by 2030 is added to the

[59] https://www.atlanticcouncil.org/wp-content/uploads/2020/06/Assessing-Saudi-Vision-2030-A-2020-review.pdf.

[60] R. Bhatia, 'Assessment of the National Transformation Program (NTP)', Gulf International Bank (June 2016), https://www.gib.com/sites/default/files/ntp_ebook_-_website_1.pdf.

[61] H. Khashan, 'Saudi Arabia's Flawed "Vision 2030"', *Middle East Quarterly* 44, no. 1.

[62] Hertog, *Princes, Brokers, and Bureaucrats*, p. 54.

[63] https://edition.cnn.com/travel/article/saudi-arabia-fun-tourists/index.html.

expected growth of the private sector, it reduces the oil sector's share of GDP by half, from 60 per cent to 30 per cent.[64] Reaching a 50 per cent share of non-oil exports in GDP from 16 per cent would require an increase of 17 per cent annually. All this would require the private sector to sustain an annual growth rate of more than 9 per cent through 2030.[65]

What is more certain is that Saudi Arabia needs high rates of investment. However, they may be slow to come. For example, plans by the PIF to invest $70 billion annually in domestic projects started with only $15.5 billion in 2019 and $22 billion in 2021, a little more than half of what was expected. This is despite the fact that in 2020 the PIF received $40 billion from the reserves of the Saudi Arabian Monetary Authority to take advantage of the dip in international stock markets by investing in various blue-chip corporations.[66] Reaching the target would require using a mixture of the PIF's own equity, loans, and bonds which may not be forthcoming in a lower oil price environment. In January 2021, the PIF announced that it planned to make an additional contribution to non-oil GDP of SAR1.2 trillion ($320 billion).[67] Aramco's ambitious In-Kingdom Total Value Added programme, initiated in 2015 and supported by investments from twenty-five countries, had attracted an estimated capital expenditure of only $6.5 billion by 2019.[68]

While the above numerical review of Vision 2030's broad targets may not be exact, it suggests that achieving the Vision's goals constitutes a radical

---

[64] Council of Economic and Development Affairs of Saudi Arabia, 'Saudi Vision 2030' (April 2016); A. Amirat and M. Zaidi, 'Estimating GDP Growth in Saudi Arabia under the Government's Vision 2030: A Knowledge-Based Economy Approach', *Journal of the Knowledge Economy* 11, no. 3, pp. 1145–70, doi: 10.1007/s13132-019-00596-2; http://vision2030.gov.sa/en (accessed 16 November 2016).

[65] A promising development is the private sector reforms that have been introduced in line with the Vision 2030, encompassing a variety of legal and structural reforms. In 2018 and 2019, Saudi Arabia introduced eight reforms in the areas measured by the World Bank's *Doing Business* report, something that ranked it as the top global performer. In terms of specific reforms, it overhauled the previous insolvency framework and strengthened minority investor protections; established a one-stop shop for company registration procedures; made issuing construction permits easier by launching an online platform; streamlined getting electricity connections; strengthened access to credit; introduced a value added tax; reduced red tape for trading across borders; reduced the paid-in minimum capital requirement as a percentage of per capita income to zero; and eliminated the requirement for married women to provide additional documents when applying for a national identity card. http://documents1.worldbank.org/curated/en/688761571934946384/pdf/Doing-Business-2020-Comparing-Business-Regulation-in-190-Economies.pdf. The two areas in which there were no reforms were 'registering property' and 'paying taxes'.

[66] https://www.reuters.com/article/us-saudi-economy-reserves-idINKBN2352TM.

[67] The investments are to cover sectors such as real-estate development, infrastructure, tourism, hospitality, entertainment, transportation, recycling, renewable energy and some unspecified others. https://english.aawsat.com/home/article/2768136/pif-seeks-invest-66-bln-annually-new-saudi-projects.

[68] https://www.oxfordenergy.org/wpcms/wp-content/uploads/2021/01/Saudi-Oil-Policy-Continuity-and-Change-in-the-Era-of-the-Energy-Transtion-WPM-81.pdf; D. Olawuyi, Local content and procurement requirements in oil and gas contracts: Regional trends in the Middle East and North Africa'. MEP 18. Oxford: Oxford Institute for Energy Studies, 2017 at https://www.oxfordenergy.org/wpcms/wp-content/uploads/2017/11/Local-content-and-procurementrequirements-in-oil-and-gas-contracts-regional-trends-in-the-Middle-East-and-North-Africa-MEP18.pdf.

divergence from past trends of investment, output growth, share of the private sector, and exports. Policy coherence and consistent implementation remain to be seen. Much will also depend on the global demand for Saudi oil and the international price of oil, which it is thought needs to stay consistently above $80 per barrel for the Kingdom to balance its fiscal accounts (Figure 1.9). If we account for many of the off-budget PIF projects, such as Neom, then fiscal balance is achievable above a $105 per barrel of oil.

If Saudi Arabia plays the role of the price leader in the oil market and cuts production, this will lower its exports and the revenues upon which much of domestic economic development depends. Even if oil prices increase and stay at a high level, they can make shale production profitable and Iran's reaction unpredictable. In the meantime, the rest of the world is moving ahead with greening their economies, which could have dire implications for Saudi Arabia's main export commodity. Thus, the benefits from oil could be compromised. It remains to be seen whether the planned mega projects will be completed, at least on time, and whether payments of social benefits and grants to compensate citizens for the reforms included in the Vision can proceed without aggravating the fiscal situation.[69]

One level below this aggregate macro picture lie the challenges facing the structural transformation and the drive for diversification. Modern production is based on supply chains that spread across the globe and take

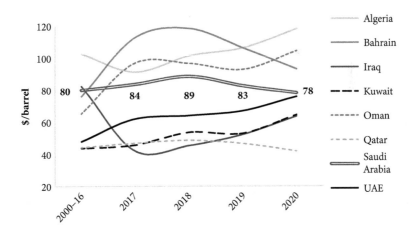

Figure 1.9 Fiscal breakeven price of oil, Arab countries, 2000–20 ($/barrel)
Source: IMF.

[69] See vision2030.gov.sa/sites/default/files/attachments/BB2020_EN.pdf. Saudi Arabia had the highest fiscal allocation to energy subsidies, estimated to amount to 10 per cent of GDP, among the oil producers, and not only in the GCC included in the study by the IMF: *Energy Subsidy Reform: Lessons and Implications* (Washington DC: International Monetary Fund, 2013).

time to establish. It requires the creation of interconnected networks among companies that are codependent and move at the same pace with the same level of efficiency, reliability, and affordability. Historically, Saudi Arabia has periodically met the last requirement, namely affordability, depending on the price of oil. Moreover, Saudi Arabia is a late comer to the globalization game with respect both to the agile 'tiger' economies and to the giant BRICS (Brazil, Russia, India, China, and South Africa). The economies in these two groups of countries took off when labour costs were low. With a high-cost national labour force, Saudi Arabia cannot compete in low-end goods with China, Vietnam, India, and Bangladesh, or against the more sophisticated economies of Brazil and Turkey. Neither does Saudi Arabia have the population size of these countries, which can draw on sufficient numbers of qualified workers from the outset. Nor does it have the small landscape of city-states of its neighbours, which constitutes an advantage for developing infrastructure points located in close proximity.

In the year Vision 2030 was announced, the IMF's assessment was that Saudi Arabia was facing the risk of running out of foreign reserves to fund imports given the rate of deficit spending, to the point that it had already concluded by then that the Vision was likely to fail.[70] The fact that the Vision is silent on political reforms raises the prospect that there might be unpredictable policy reversals, delaying progress towards its targets under a business-as-usual scenario. As seen in other Middle Eastern countries, data can presented to suit policy outcomes but the discourse can change with times especially if exogenous factors imply greater change than expected.

The process of planning in a post-2016 Saudi Arabia revolves around the Strategic Management Office (SMO) and the Council of Economic and Development Affairs, both at the royal court.[71] Prior to 2016, the Ministry of Economy and Planning was mandated to produce the development plans, although it had limited implementation capacity and oversight over other ministries and government agencies.

Summarizing the overall development experience of Saudi Arabia since the 1970s, one can say that Saudi Arabia has experienced 'entropic economic growth'—to borrow a term from physics that is nevertheless also used by economists. Entropy is a measure of a system's thermal energy that is unavailable for doing useful work and represents the degree of the system's disorder, leading to processes that are irreversible or impossible, aside from

---

[70] I. Leclerc, 'Saudi Arabia's Vision 2030 Is Going to Fail' (16 May 2016), https://www.theodysseyonline.com/saudi-arabias-vision-2030-is-going-to-fail.

[71] From 2015 to 2017 the main responsibility for economic planning rested with the Ministry of Economy and Planning, and it was only after 2018/19 that the SMO became responsible.

the requirement of not violating the conservation of energy. If one replaces (1) 'thermal' energy by 'oil energy', (2) 'processes' by 'ten development plans that have largely failed to halt and reverse the model established in the 1970s', and (3) 'the requirement of not violating the conservation of energy' by the 'the requirement of not violating citizens' rights for too long', the 'irreversible or impossible' may or may not hold true in the future, even if Vision 2030 is successfully implemented.

Concluding Remarks

Although the historical experience of Saudi Arabia with its five-year plans and specific projects suggests that more could have been achieved, a major difference between these plans and Vision 2030 is the institutional arrangements that have been introduced since 2016, which point towards a different role for the state and its relations with the private sector, particularly as it addresses corruption.

In the past, the operations of the private sector were widely considered to be opaque. Many businesses generated wealth because of their ties to officials. During the 2000s, and the decade that ensued—which was among the longest high-priced oil eras of the last two decades—the perception existed that the established public and private insiders were the largest beneficiaries of prosperity. This ended abruptly with the Ritz-Carlton affair in 2017, which aimed to break the pattern of abuse of the state. In this new Saudi Arabia, the state is the lead investor—through the PIF—and the private sector is an investor and sometimes a co-investor. Vision 2030 anticipates the private sector to be a 65 per cent contributor to the country's GDP and by extension the main generator of employment opportunities. It remains to be seen how the state will change its current leading role and how the private sector will react, evolve, and prosper.

Today Saudi Arabia has a roadmap and, unlike any other time in its economic history, the political will to press ahead. So far, the evidence points to an impressive array of changes brought to a country in a very short period. The speed with which Saudi Arabia has transformed has aroused attention ranging from admiration to criticism. A critical factor for the effects of ongoing and future policies will be the price of oil, as Saudi Arabia is still so heavily reliant on it as the main source of its export and fiscal revenues.

The state has a critical role to play in ensuring transparency and competition in the economy, and incubating and abetting new industries and sectors, keeping the objective of Saudization in mind. The latter, as Chapter 6 argues, would require that the state is not the employer of last resort but hires and rewards based on merit—not merely nationality. The pre-2016 projects, which have followed a stop–go, at times chaotic, trajectory requiring bailouts from the state coffers, provide several lessons for the future. Still, even if they are fully successful, a question for the mega projects remains: that is, whether there will be sufficient impetus to transform Saudi Arabia into a post-oil economy over a reasonable time horizon, so that the new social contract is supported by ordinary Saudis, and therefore viable. Adding to the complexity is the progress and pace of the world's economy decarbonization and climate change impetus advances which will unavoidably impact Saudi Arabia. Hence, not only will Saudi Arabia have to get it right domestically but it also needs to reform quickly enough whilst the world does not shift away from hydrocarbons too fast by the time Saudi Arabia is able to discover additional sources of income other than oil.

2

Saudi Oil Policy

Continuity and Change in the Era of the Energy Transition

Bassam Fattouh

Introduction

The crucial position that Saudi Arabia has in global oil markets cannot be overstated.[1] In 2019, its proven crude oil reserves stood at 297.6 billion barrels, representing 17 per cent of the world's total.[2] In the same year Saudi Arabia produced 11.8 million barrels per day (mb/d) of crude, blended, and unblended condensates, and natural gas liquids.[3] The country produces a wide array of crudes, ranging from Arab Super Light (American Petroleum Institute [API] gravity > 40° and sulphur content < 0.5 per cent) all the way to Arabian Heavy (API gravity < 29° and sulphur content > 2.9 per cent). Despite rising domestic demand in the past few decades, Saudi Arabia exports the bulk of its crude production and thus has a dominant position in international trade: exports averaged around 7.2 mb/d in 2019.[4] It is the only country that has an official policy of maintaining spare capacity that can be utilized within a relatively short time at a low cost. Saudi Arabia's reserves are also among the cheapest in the world to find, develop, and produce. In 2019, Saudi Aramco's average upstream lifting cost was estimated at $2.8 per barrel of oil equivalent (boe) produced.[5] The wedge between international oil prices and production costs generates high rents for the Kingdom. In 2018 and 2019, Saudi Aramco's income (before taxes) stood at $212.7 billion and $177.8 billion respectively.[6]

---

[1] The research for this chapter was undertaken as part of the UK Energy Research Centre research programme. It was funded by the UK Research and Innovation Energy Programme under grant number EP/S029575/1.

[2] *BP Statistical Review of World Energy*, 69th edn. (London: BP, 2020). Saudi Arabia's official numbers are slightly lower at 266.7 billion barrels.

[3] Ibid.

[4] Ibid.

[5] Saudi Aramco, *Annual Report* (2019).

[6] In 2019, Saudi Aramco's net income was more than $88 billion. Ibid.

Bassam Fattouh, *Saudi Oil Policy*. In: *The Economy of Saudi Arabia in the 21st Century*. Edited by: John Sfakianakis, Oxford University Press. © Bassam Fattouh (2024). DOI: 10.1093/oso/9780198863878.003.0003

In contrast to some neighbouring countries and other members of the Organization of the Petroleum Exporting Countries (OPEC), such as Iran, Iraq, Libya, and Venezuela, Saudi Arabia has not experienced conflict or political instability and has not been subject to international sanctions. It has thus been able to invest heavily in its energy sector and integrate the upstream sector with refining and downstream assets, both in the Kingdom and overseas. In 2019, Saudi Aramco's gross refining capacity stood at 6.4 mb/d, while its gross chemical production capacity stood at 46.1 million tonnes.[7] In the same year, Saudi Aramco's downstream operations consumed 38 per cent of its crude oil production.[8] The oil and gas sectors are also heavily integrated, given the large volumes of associated gas produced. Saudi Aramco has been investing heavily in developing its non-associated and shale gas reserves, thereby increasing the flexibility of its oil policy.[9]

Saudi Arabia also has a dominant position in OPEC and historically the organization's key decisions have been shaped by the Kingdom, either those related to cutting output to balance the market or those increasing output to offset output disruption within OPEC and elsewhere. Although Saudi Arabia's output has not been impacted by political or military shocks (notwithstanding the September 2019 attacks on Saudi Aramco facilities, which disrupted output only temporarily), it has nonetheless been highly variable,[10] reflecting the Kingdom's flexibility to increase and decrease output in response to shocks.

Given its size and large margins, the oil sector also plays a key role in the Saudi economy. Despite efforts to diversify its revenue base over the past few decades, oil revenues still accounted for an average of 86 per cent of total government revenues during 2012–15, while non-oil revenues averaged less than 5 per cent of gross domestic product (GDP).[11] Recently the government has diversified its sources of income, for instance by introducing a value added tax (VAT), excise taxes, fees on expatriate workers, and other fees and taxes. These helped increase non-oil revenues to around 8 per cent of GDP[12] and reduced the share of oil revenues to 64 per cent and 67.5 per cent of total government revenue in 2018 and 2019 (General Authority of Statistics). Despite

[7] Ibid.
[8] Ibid.
[9] B. Fattouh and R. Shabaneh, 'The Future of Gas in Saudi Arabia's Transition', in J. P. Stern (ed.), *The Future of Gas in the Gulf: Continuity and Change* (Oxford: Oxford Institute for Energy Studies, 2019), pp. 85–113.
[10] A. Nakov and G. Nuño, 'Saudi Arabia and the Oil Market', *Economic Journal* 132, no. 12 (2013), pp. 1333–62.
[11] IMF, 'Saudi Arabia: Selected Issues', Middle East and Central Asia Department (Washington, DC: International Monetary Fund, 2019).
[12] Ibid.

these new revenue sources, the government remains reliant on oil revenues for its current and capital spending, many components of which—such as public wages—remain rigid[13] and therefore difficult to adjust downwards during economic downturns. In addition, government spending is a key driver of growth in non-oil and private sector activity through infrastructure investment, public sector wage bills, and social transfers.[14]

All the aforementioned features have shaped Saudi oil policy choices and its relations with other producers over the years. The main purpose of this chapter is to analyse a range of these policy choices and oil relations, their determinants, and the evolving role of the oil sector in the context of an energy transition, the speed of which remains highly uncertain and its impact across the globe is highly uneven.[15]

How Is Saudi Arabia's Oil Policy Characterized in the Literature?

Given its core position in the oil market, many studies have modelled Saudi Arabia as the dominant producer, with the other producers (both OPEC and non-OPEC) acting as a competitive fringe.[16] As the dominant producer, Saudi Arabia sets its output in anticipation of the reaction of the fringe and maximizes its profits based on the residual demand. In particular, Saudi Arabia produces less oil than its capacity given the oil price, allowing it to charge a mark-up over its marginal cost.[17]

Despite this prevalent view of Saudi Arabia in the literature, the empirical evidence has not been supportive of the 'dominant producer' model. For instance, J. L. Smith finds no evidence in support of a dominant producer

[13] N. T. Tamirisa and C. Duenwald, *Public Wage Bills in the Middle East and Central Asia* (Washington, DC: International Monetary Fund, 2018).

[14] M. A. Fouejieu, S. Rodriguez, and M. S. Shahid, 'Fiscal Adjustment in the Gulf Countries: Less Costly than Previously Thought' (Washington, DC: International Monetary Fund, 2018), doi: 10.5089/9781484361573.001. M. Al-Moneef and F. Hasanov, 'Fiscal Multipliers for Saudi Arabia Revisited', KAPSARC Discussion Paper (Riyadh: KAPSARC, 2020).

[15] B. Fattouh, R. Poudineh, and R. West, 'The Rise of Renewables and Energy Transition: What Adaptation Strategy Exists for Oil Companies and Oil-Exporting Countries?', *Energy Transit* 3 (2019), pp. 45–58, doi: 10.1007/s41825-019-00013-x.

[16] R. Mabro, 'Can OPEC Hold the Line?', in *OPEC and the World Oil Market: The Genesis of the 1986 Price Crisis* (Oxford: Oxford Institute for Energy Studies, 1975); S. Salant, 'Exhaustible Resources and Industrial Structure: A Nash–Cournot Approach to the World Oil Market', *Journal of Political Economy* 84, no. 5 (1976), pp. 1079–93; Nakov and Nuño, 'Saudi Arabia and the Oil Market'; R. Golombek, A. A. Irarrazabal, and L. Ma, 'OPEC's Market Power: An Empirical Dominant Firm Model for the Oil Market', *Energy Economics* 70 (2018), pp. 98–115. For a more extensive literature review, see B. Fattouh and L. Mahadeva, 'OPEC: What Difference Has It Made?', *Annual Review of Resource Economics* 5 (2013), pp. 427–43.

[17] Nakov and Nuño, 'Saudi Arabia and the Oil Market'

and concludes that 'if Saudi Arabia ... has assumed the role of Stackelberg leader, dominant firm, or swing producer, it must not have been pursued with enough vigour and continuity, either before or after the quota system was adopted, to have left a discernible pattern in the data.'[18]

Griffin and Nielson find evidence that rather than acting as a dominant or a swing producer, Saudi Arabia opted for a tit-for-tat strategy that punishes members for producing above their quotas and rewards those that comply.[19] They identify three strategies used by Saudi Arabia: the Cournot strategy, the swing producer strategy, and the tit-for-tat strategy.[20] As long as Saudi Arabia earns more than Cournot profits, it will be willing to tolerate deviations from the quota and at times it may act as a swing producer to earn profits in excess of the Cournot equilibrium level. However, if cheating becomes flagrant, Saudi Arabia will punish the 'cheaters' by increasing its output until every producer is reduced to Cournot profits.

The above suggests that Saudi Arabia's and, more broadly, OPEC's pricing power is not constant over time.[21] Geroski et al. find that collusion is rarely perfect, and some producers may change their behaviour in response to a rival's previous actions. Their empirical results show that varying-behaviour models tend to outperform constant-conduct models.[22] Almoguera et al. identify multiple switches between collusive and non-cooperative behaviour during the 1974–2004 period. They find that although there were periods in which oil prices were higher due to collusion among OPEC members, overall OPEC has not been effective in systematically raising prices above Cournot competition levels.[23] Using quarterly data from 1986 to 2016, Golombek et al. also find that while OPEC exerts market power, this power tends to vary over time.[24]

---

[18] J. L. Smith, 'Inscrutable OPEC? Behavioral Tests of the Cartel Hypothesis', *Energy Journal* 26, no. 1 (2005), pp. 51–82.

[19] J. M. Griffin and W. S. Nielson, 'The 1985–86 Price Collapse and Afterwards: What Does Game Theory Add?', *Economic Inquiry* 17 (1994), pp. 543–61.

[20] In the standard Cournot strategy, each producer takes the output of the other producers as given and equates the marginal cost with the marginal revenue. In Griffin and Nielson's analysis, the Cournot equilibrium sets the floor for the level of profits that Saudi Arabia can achieve if other strategies fail. In the swing producer regime, Saudi Arabia adjusts its production in response to other OPEC members producing above their quotas (i.e. cheating), and hence one would expect to see stable prices in this regime. In the tit-for-tat strategy, Saudi Arabia punishes other OPEC members for producing above the quota and matches their cheating, barrel by barrel, resulting in greater price variation than in the swing producer regime.

[21] P. A. Geroski, A. M. Ulph, and D. T. Ulph, 'A Model of the Crude Oil Market in which Market Conduct Varies', *Economic Journal* 97 (1987), pp. 77–86; P. Almoguera, C. Douglas, and A. M. Herrera, 'Testing for the Cartel in OPEC: Noncooperative Collusion or Just Non-cooperative?', *Oxford Review of Economic Policy* 27, no. 1 (2011), pp. 144–68.

[22] Geroski et al., 'A Model of the Crude Oil Market'.

[23] Almoguera et al., 'Testing for the Cartel in OPEC'.

[24] Golombek et al., 'OPEC's Market Power'.

More recent studies also show that Saudi Arabia's oil policy should not be analysed in isolation from the evolution of global oil market dynamics, such as the entry of United States (US) shale with its short-term investment cycle, low capital intensity, and higher responsiveness to price signals.[25] Some argue that the entry of US shale has complicated both OPEC's and Saudi Arabia's management of the market, rendering the option to shift to a high-volume strategy more attractive under certain conditions. Using a static game under uncertainty, Fattouh et al. show that without sufficient knowledge about how elastic US shale is, it was rational for Saudi Arabia to test the resilience of US shale and not cut output in 2014.[26] The large size of the market imbalance in the fourth quarter of 2014, the difficulty of reaching an agreement with OPEC and non-OPEC producers to cut output, its unwillingness to act unilaterally to balance the market, and its belief that it can withstand lower oil prices for longer as a result of its accumulation of large foreign reserves also contributed to Saudi Arabia's decision in 2014. Behar and Ritz show that pursuing a high-volume strategy becomes the dominant strategy when global oil demand growth is slower, US shale oil production is higher, cohesiveness within OPEC is low, and output in other non-OPEC countries is higher.[27]

Ansari tests various market setups and finds that all of them fail to explain the price fall in 2014–16, which declined beyond perfect competition outcomes, concluding that the shift in Saudi policy could have been an attempt to defend market share and test the resilience of US shale.[28] Similarly, Berk and Çam find that although oligopolistic market structures fit the market outcomes before 2014, they fail to explain the low oil prices during 2015 and 2016, which were closer to levels generated by a competitive market, supporting the view that the market has shifted to a more competitive structure.[29]

In addition to these market factors, Saudi oil policy is fundamentally rooted in and shaped by salient features of its economic structures. One of the key factors that has a direct influence on oil policy is the Kingdom's

[25] B. Fattouh and A. Sen, 'Saudi Arabia Oil Policy: More than Meets the Eye?', MEP 13 (Oxford: Oxford Institute for Energy Studies, 2015); B. Fattouh, 'Adjustment in the Oil Market: Structural, Cyclical or Both', OIES Energy Comment (Oxford: Oxford Institute for Energy Studies, 2016).
[26] B. Fattouh, R. Poudineh, and A. Sen, 'The Dynamics of the Revenue Maximization–Market Share Trade-Off: Saudi Arabia's Oil Policy in the 2014–15 Price Fall', *Oxford Review of Economic Policy* 32, no. 2 (2016), pp. 223–40.
[27] A. Behar and R. A. Ritz, 'OPEC vs US Shale: Analyzing the Shift to a Market-Share Strategy', *Energy Economics* 63 (2017), pp. 185–98.
[28] D. Ansari, 'OPEC, Saudi Arabia, and the Shale Revolution: Insights from Equilibrium Modelling and Oil Politics', *Energy Policy* 111 (2017), pp. 166–78.
[29] I. Berk and E. Çam, 'The Shift in Global Crude Oil Market Structure: A Model-Based Analysis of the Period 2013–2017', *Energy Policy* 142, issue C (2020), https://www.sciencedirect.com/science/article/abs/pii/S0301421520302391.

dependency on oil revenues. The government also continues to play a central role in the country's development path through its capital expenditure and revenue spending, which remain a key engine behind the growth of its non-oil economy and the private sector.[30] Given the central role the oil sector continues to play in the Saudi economy, the objective of optimizing oil revenues will always rank high in any output decision and acts as a constraint on oil policy choices.[31]

Early models of OPEC behaviour approached this objective of revenue maximization from the point of view of a 'wealth-maximizing rational monopolist'.[32] However,

> in practice, … the revenue maximization objective which theory postulates and core producers would dearly like to achieve is not credible. [Instead, producers have to] become content with a second best: to obtain through the pricing policy more revenues than would have accrued under a competitive market structure. This may be much better than nothing but is likely to be very different from the optimum.[33]

It is in the context of second best, trade-offs, dynamic behaviour, and economic constraints that this chapter analyses Saudi oil policy.

Saudi Oil Relations and the Expansion from OPEC to OPEC+

In face of a negative demand shock (such as the COVID-19 crisis) or positive supply shock (US shale), Saudi Arabia can coordinate its oil production policy with other producers under the umbrella of OPEC to boost its oil revenues. All OPEC members recognize the fact that in the face of ex-ante excess supply due to overproduction and/or a negative demand shock, reliance on price or market mechanisms to correct the market imbalance and clear the resulting large build-up in inventories is a lengthy and painful process as revenues fall sharply. Cooperation on the output front to restrict supplies is the most effective way to reverse the price decline and balance the market. There is rarely disagreement on this general principle. But disagreements usually

---

[30] Al-Moneef and Hasanov (2020).
[31] Fattouh and Sen, 'Saudi Arabia Oil Policy'.
[32] R. S. Pindyck, 'Gains to Producers from the Cartelization of Exhaustible Resources', *Review of Economics and Statistics 60* (1978), pp. 238–51.
[33] R. Mabro, 'OPEC and the Price of Oil', *Energy Journal 13*, no. 2 (1991), pp. 1–17.

arise over which countries should shoulder the burden of the cut. It has long been the case that non-OPEC countries leave it to OPEC to implement cuts. In turn, many within OPEC would like to leave it to Saudi Arabia to shoulder the burden.[34]

However, following the experience of the price collapse in 1985, nobody can realistically expect Saudi Arabia to balance the market unliterally. At that time, Saudi Arabia's attempts to defend the marker price resulted in a huge loss of market share and revenues: the Kingdom reduced its production from 10.2 mb/d in 1980 to 3.6 mb/d in 1985 while prices continued to fall. This episode still shapes Saudi oil policy to this day.

Over the years, through its announcements and actions, Saudi Arabia has insisted on the principle that any cut should be implemented collectively with other producers. In addition, with OPEC's market share declining over time, the principle of collective cuts has extended to non-OPEC producers, particularly to big producers such as Russia. In fact, this has been the main motivation behind the Declaration of Cooperation which saw OPEC countries coordinate with non-OPEC oil producing countries and the conclusion of the Charter of Cooperation in 2019 (this group is usually referred to as OPEC+).[35]

The cooperation between Russia and OPEC followed a series of failed attempts.[36] In the 1997–8 oil price crisis, OPEC called for production restraint from non-OPEC producers, and while Russia promised a reduction in output, it increased its exports by 400,000 barrels per day (b/d). In 2001, following the attacks on the World Trade Center in New York and as the global economy took a downturn, oil prices fell sharply. OPEC offered an output cut of 1.5 mb/d if non-OPEC countries implemented a 500,000 b/d cut. Russia promised a 30,000 b/d reduction, increasing its offer to 50,000 b/d, but ultimately delivered no reduction at all. During the financial crisis in 2008–9, Russia attended three consecutive OPEC meetings as an observer, encouraging production cuts from OPEC but without promising any cuts itself. While Russia claimed it had cut output and exports during 2009, its overseas sales increased by 700,000 b/d.[37] The real breakthrough came only in December 2016 with the Declaration of Cooperation (DoC) between OPEC

[34] R. Mabro, 'The Oil Price Crisis of 1998', Working Paper SP10 (Oxford: Oxford Institute for Energy Studies, 1998).
[35] A. Economou and B. Fattouh, '5+1 Key Facts about the OPEC Declaration of Cooperation', OIES Energy Comment (Oxford: Oxford Institute for Energy Studies, 2018).
[36] J. Henderson and B. Fattouh, 'Russia and OPEC: Uneasy Partners', OIES Energy Comment (Oxford: Oxford Institute for Energy Studies, 2016).
[37] Ibid.

and non-OPEC members[38] that constituted an unprecedented milestone in Russia–Saudi oil relations.[39] The DoC occurred against a background of a sharp and extended period of oil price falls between 2014 and 2016 as oil exporters competed for market share.

Reaching agreements to cut output with a diverse and heterogeneous group of producers has always been challenging, and it has become increasingly so with the larger number of producers under the OPEC+ umbrella. Various studies show that the cost of negotiating agreements is large when there is asymmetry between parties, as there is no focal point for them to select as an equilibrium.[40] Agreements may also take a long time to conclude due to bargaining problems.[41] These could concern the timing of the cut, its size, the allocation of the cut among individual members, and the timing of exiting the agreement. This became evident during the break-up of the OPEC+ agreement in March 2020. The negative demand shock due to COVID-19 brought to the fore the differences in perspectives between the biggest OPEC+ producers—Saudi Arabia and Russia—on the size of the cut and its timing. The inability to reach an agreement caused a shift in policy towards maximizing market share and, in the face of demand contraction, put severe pressure on oil prices and the oil market infrastructure, eroding revenues for all producers.[42]

But even if producers do agree on the optimal size of the collective cut,[43] how to distribute the burden of the cut across individual members remains a key challenge. The current quota system used by OPEC does not have 'formal' rules for allocation and this may give rise to a sense of unfairness among some of the producers, affecting their incentive to comply with their quotas.[44]

[38] The larger group is often referred to as OPEC+.

[39] Economou and Fattouh, '5+1 Key Facts'. The unprecedented conformity levels achieved by the OPEC+ producers, led by Saudi Arabia and Russia, surprised the market and proved that both producers were committed to bringing the market into balance.

[40] R. Thomadsen and K. E. Rhee, 'Costly Collusion in Differentiated Industries', *Marketing Science* 26, no. 5 (2007), pp. 660–5.

[41] K. Hyndman, 'Disagreement in Bargaining: An Empirical Analysis of OPEC', *International Journal of Industrial Organization* 26, no. 3 (2008), pp. 811–28.

[42] Saudi Arabia recognized the extent of the impact of the virus on demand early on and pushed for implementing a deeper cut in production. Russia, on the other hand, showed strong resistance to deepening the cut and was not willing to implement even a small reduction. This reflects Russia's fundamentally different perspective on the crisis and other players' behaviour. Either Russia did not appreciate the scale of the shock, or it did not see any value in deepening the cut given the size of the shock and amidst concerns that US shale producers could increase output to compensate for it. Russia would also have benefited from free-riding on OPEC's decision, if OPEC had gone ahead and unilaterally implemented its proposed deeper cut.

[43] Empirical evidence suggests that this may not be the case. Berk and Çam, 'The Shift in Global Crude Oil Market Structure', show that planned OPEC+ cuts in 2017 should have been much larger and that by cutting deeper, OPEC+ would have fully exerted market power.

[44] J. Gault, C. Spierer, J.-L. Bertholet, and B. Karbassioun, 'How Does OPEC Allocate Quotas?', *Journal of Energy Finance and Development* 4, no. 2 (1999), pp. 137–48.

This is especially true when the required cuts are large, as OPEC members with small levels of production find it difficult to reduce their production on a pro-rata basis, the system adopted by OPEC over the years. But setting alternative formal rules to distribute the burden of the collective cut is not feasible as there are many criteria that could be used. For instance, from a pure efficiency point of view, OPEC members with high production costs should cut production first and then be compensated by financial transfers from low-cost producers.[45] OPEC, however, does not have a system to determine the size of transfer or the mechanisms to implement such transfer schemes. Other criteria for allocating production quotas, such as the size of reserves, population size, fiscal buffers, and level of development, all suffer from their own limitations as each country will choose the criterion or set of criteria that suits it best. The bargaining process of selecting relevant criteria itself could constitute an additional source of disagreement, with the outcome depending on the relative negotiating power of the different countries. One of the key innovations in the 35th OPEC and non-OPEC Minstrial Meeting in June 2023 was the introduction of independent assessments of OPEC+ countries' upstream capacities. In the past, each country used to declare its production capacity without any independent verification or assessment. For many countries, the declared capacities usually came at a much higher levels than the actual levels because countries wanted to negotiate higher output quotas. In the new agreement, all OPEC+ countries will go through an assessment process by independent bodies to completed by the end of June 2024. These independent assessments should help OPEC+ decide on more realistic production targets for individual countries.

Agreements to distribute output cuts across individual members are often reached, usually following a lengthy and tough bargaining process and a prolonged period of low oil prices. As Mabro notes, OPEC members' ability to 'compromise to reach agreement should not be underestimated. It is founded on the belief that all members, including the largest producers, would be worse off without OPEC.'[46] Hyndman shows that the larger the shock (positive or negative), the more likely it is for OPEC to reach an agreement.[47]

Reaching an agreement does not imply the end of the process. An additional challenge is to verify and ensure that member countries abide by the agreed individual quotas. Since individual member countries have no

[45] J. S. Bain, 'Output Quotas in Imperfect Cartels', *Quarterly Journal of Economics* 62, no. 4 (1948), pp. 617–22.
[46] Mabro, 'The Oil Price Crisis of 1998'.
[47] Hyndman, 'Disagreement in Bargaining'.

incentive to reveal the true level of their production, OPEC members and more recently non-OPEC countries participating in the DoC rely on 'secondary sources' to monitor compliance.[48] This mechanism is imperfect, as secondary sources use different methodologies and definitions and cannot observe domestic refinery runs to reach accurate production numbers. Nevertheless, reliance on sources other than direct reporting by participating countries helps resolve the credibility problem.

But even if OPEC+ is able to verify non-compliance, it has no formal enforcement mechanism to ensure that producers abide by their quotas.[49] Since agreements extend over multiple months or even years, ensuring compliance over an extended period of time is challenging. The incentive for each individual country to comply with the agreement results from comparing the short-run gain from deviating from the agreement (which is the difference between deviation profit and collusive profit) and the cost or losses resulting from a collapse of the agreement and the resulting fall in oil prices. These trade-offs are not constant over time, especially if some producers believe that deviations from the agreement will not be detected immediately.

The ability of Saudi Arabia to increase its supply at short notice, and its willingness to shift policy if there is no agreement on collective cuts and/or if compliance falls to unacceptable levels, increases the cost of non-compliance for all producers. In effect, these shifts in conduct are needed to enforce discipline in the absence of formal enforcement mechanisms. In contrast to Stigler, who considers a price war to be a signal of the collapse of collusion,[50] insights from game theory suggest that in the absence of a formal disciplinary mechanism, collusion could still work if implicit threats force members to abide by the agreed quotas. In the work of Porter and Green, 'price wars' represent the equilibrium outcome of a dynamic non-cooperative game and are the solution to the problems of imperfect information that plague OPEC. They are also a credible means of communicating and signalling to other players—hence price wars can be strategic and tactical in nature.[51]

---

[48] At the December 2019 meeting, non-OPEC members in OPEC+ were allowed to exclude condensate from the production data they submit, but agreed in return to use secondary sources rather than direct communication to assess compliance with targets.

[49] W. L. Kohl, 'OPEC Behaviour, 1998–2001', *Quarterly Review of Economics and Finance* 42, no. 2 (2002), pp. 209–33; G. D. Libecap and J. L. Smith, 'Political Constraints on Government Cartelization: The Case of Oil Production Regulation in Texas and Saudi Arabia', in P. Grossman (ed.), *How Cartels Endure and How They Fail: Studies of Industrial Collusion* (Cheltenham: Edward Elgar, 2004).

[50] G. J. Stigler, 'A Theory of Oligopoly', *Journal of Political Economy* 72, no. 1 (1964), pp. 44–61.

[51] R. H. Porter, 'A Study of Cartel Stability: The Joint Executive Committee, 1880–1886', *Bell Journal of Economics* 14, no. 2 (1983), pp. 301–14; R. H. Porter, 'Optimal Cartel Trigger Price Strategies', *Journal of Economic Theory* 29 no. 2 (1983), pp. 313–18; E. Green and R. Porter, 'Noncooperative Collusion under Imperfect Price Information', *Econometrica* 52, no. 1 (1984), pp. 87–100.

Saudi Arabia's decision not to adjust its output to balance the market in 2014–16 and its decision in March 2020 to increase output following the break-up of the OPEC+ agreement provide support to this view. The severity of the price fall in April 2020 had the effect of focusing the minds of the world's largest producers. Unlike the 1997–8 and the 2014–16 price cycles, when it took several months to reach an agreement to cut output, producers' response was much faster during the COVID-19 shock—within weeks, OPEC+ was able to reach an agreement to implement a historic cut of 9.7 mb/d.[52]

Sustaining cooperation when prices are recovering is also essential for the success of an agreement, as an early or late exit reduces the net gains from cooperation. Since countries participating in OPEC+ have different budgetary requirements, fiscal stabilization schemes, oil industry structures, and perceptions about the resilience of US shale, they have different trigger points for the 'desired exit' and thus there may be disagreement on the optimal timing of easing the cut.

In short, in pursuing collective cuts with other producers, there is always the risk that: (1) no agreement can be reached; and/or (2) an agreement can be reached only after a long period of inaction or shift in conduct, which could result in a dramatic fall in oil prices and rise in inventories; and/or (3) an agreement can be reached with a cut that is lower than the optimal size; and/or (4) there is unequal sharing of the burden of adjustment; and/or (5) producers do not abide by their quotas; and/or (6) the timing of exit from the agreement is suboptimal. All these factors limit the potential net gains that could be achieved from cooperation.

If the net gains associated with cooperation become very small or highly uncertain, Saudi Arabia can choose to adopt a high volume or market share strategy for tactical reasons or as a permanent strategy. The Kingdom is in an advantageous position to implement such a strategy: it has the capacity to increase output in a short period of time and it has a very well-developed infrastructure to market its crude and compete in any region. As a long-term strategy, the Kingdom can increase its investment and the size of its productive capacity and capture a larger share of the market (see the next section).

---

[52] Without the United States of America (USA), an agreement would eventually have been reached, but it would have taken several months. Thus, US pressure did accelerate the process of reaching an agreement. Given their strategic alliance, the fact that the Kingdom is sensitive to US interests should not come as a surprise. What is new in this relationship is the USA's dual role: in a low-price environment it acts as a producer and prefers a higher oil price; and in a high-price environment it acts as a consumer and prefers a lower oil price.

However, this strategy risks a fall in total oil revenues in the short term because the higher revenue due to the increase in market share may not compensate for the loss of revenues due to the lower oil price resulting from higher production. Low oil prices may not result in the immediate shut-in of oil production in high-cost producers and/or induce a strong recovery in oil demand. In addition, for a market share strategy to work, it requires that prices stay lower for long enough to affect expectations and alter the behaviour of high-cost producers and their financial backers. Sustaining such a policy for a prolonged period, beyond achieving some short-term strategic objectives, may not be feasible given Saudi Arabia's high reliance on oil revenues.[53] Pursuing a market share strategy also results in the accumulation of stocks that may take months or even years to clear.

There may be opportunities for Saudi Arabia to increase its share without undermining revenues. Such a strategy could succeed in specific contexts: for instance, in a world of growing demand, declining or stagnating non-OPEC supply, output from other producers being disrupted, or a combination of these circumstances. Thus, the timing of implementation of such shifts in strategy and the ability to act proactively are key to capturing these opportunities. For instance, the transformation of the supply curve as a result of the lack of appetite for financing hydrocarbon projects could present Saudi Arabia with an opportunity to increase production without jeopardizing revenues.[54] If the demand proves to be stronger than expected by some of the current projections, and if the US supply/non-OPEC supply response turns out to be weaker than in previous cycles due to lack of investment and investors' lack of appetite to finance oil projects, then Saudi Arabia may find itself able to increase production and capture market share by substituting for production losses elsewhere. Revenues from higher production and exports may compensate partially or fully for lost revenue due to the lower oil prices needed to keep US shale growth in check.

In short, Saudi Arabia recognizes that there are net gains available from pursuing collective cuts with other producers. But the size of these gains is shaped by market conditions, internal cohesion within OPEC, cooperation from non-OPEC producers, and the nature of the shocks, among other factors. If these gains become small or uncertain, Saudi Arabia has shown willingness to shift policy towards market share. Thus, Saudi Arabia's

---

[53] Mabro, 'The Oil Price Crisis of 1998'.
[54] B. Fattouh and A. Economou, 'Is the Worst of the Oil Crisis Behind Us?', OIES Energy Comment (Oxford: Oxford Institute for Energy Studies, 2020).

output policy is not constant, and it continues to shift depending on market conditions and the behaviour of other producers.

Capacity Expansion and Monetization Strategy

Short-term strategies cannot be isolated from medium- and long-term issues, particularly those of investment in new productive capacity, the size of spare capacity, and monetization of reserves.

Given Saudi Arabia's large oil reserve base, relatively low development costs, stable investment environment, and competent national oil company that has a strong record of executing mega projects, there are no technical, financial, or geopolitical barriers that would prevent the Kingdom from increasing its productive capacity above the stated current level of 12.5 mb/d (including the neutral zone). The investment cycle, however, is longer than for US shale, and plans to expand capacity beyond current levels would take time to implement and require heavy investment, not only in the upstream sector, but also in calibrating the entire system, including increasing the capacity of gas-processing plants and building storage facilities, pipelines, and terminals.[55]

Thus, the decision to expand productive capacity and how fast is primarily a strategic one and will be determined by views on the future demand for Saudi crude. This is due not only to the wide uncertainty regarding the speed of the energy transition and its impact on growth in global oil demand, but also to uncertainty about how the energy transition will impact the financing of hydrocarbon projects, the growth in oil supply outside Saudi Arabia, the shift in portfolios of international oil companies, and the fragility of some oil exporters and their ability to increase productive capacity in a more challenging environment. Decisions are also shaped by internal factors, particularly the expected growth in Saudi domestic energy demand, which in turn is closely tied to a wide range of policies including energy pricing reform, energy efficiency measures, and increases in the share of gas and renewables in the power mix.

[55] For instance, Saudi Arabia decided in 2004 gradually to increase its sustainable productive capacity from 11 mb/d to 12.5 mb/d and completed the expansion by approximately 2010. This involved the development of mega projects including the Haradah Increment III (0.3 mb/d), the Abu Hadriya, Fadhili, the Khursaniya Project (0.5 mb/d), Khurais (1.2 mb/d), the Shaybah Increment (0.3 mb/d), and Nuayyim (0.1 mb/d). During this period, the gross additions amounted to around 2.35 mb/d, with 0.8 mb/d of this earmarked to make up for declining rates in mature fields. Of the new capacity additions, 1.1 mb/d was Arab Light quality, while the rest consisted of Arab Extra and Arab Super Light crudes.

Many are of the view that large reserve holders should focus on monetizing their reserves as quickly as possible so as not to be left with stranded assets. However, a rapid monetization strategy in the face of slower demand growth due to the transition may result in a sharp decline in oil prices and oil revenues, and thus could act as a constraint on a high investment–high output policy.[56]

Were Saudi Arabia's economy highly diversified and its government finances less reliant on oil revenues, adopting a rapid monetization strategy would become more feasible given its status as one of the world's lowest-cost producers. However, this constraint could become less binding over time if Saudi Arabia is successful in implementing deep economic transformations. Factors such as the speed of the energy transition could also result in a more competitive oil market[57]. The higher output strategy could result in higher revenues for Saudi Arabia in the long run if some existing producers fail to adjust their economies to a sharp decline in oil revenues, causing them serious economic, social, and political repercussions that prevent these countries from expanding or even maintaining oil productive capacity. In other words, the calculus for Saudi Arabia on shifting to a high volume–high market share strategy could change over time, and therefore a gradual shift away from the current strategy represents a strategic choice that should not be dismissed in the medium to long term.[58]

Spare Capacity When Prospects for Demand Remain Highly Uncertain

Upstream investment is also linked to the optimal size of spare capacity. Decisions on optimal sustainable production capacity and spare capacity involve a trade-off. On the one hand, productive capacity should not be so large that Saudi Arabia ends up with spare capacity that is costly to maintain and could adversely affect the Kingdom's long-term revenues by putting downward pressure on prices. Moreover, as Saudi Arabia increases its productive capacity, cutting production becomes more challenging, as no producer wants to operate well below its maximum sustainable productive capacity.

On the other hand, spare capacity should not be so small that Saudi Arabia loses control of the market on the upside and risks higher and more volatile

---

[56] Moreover, fast monetization of oil reserves that does not take into account demand growth can result in stranded assets if investments in new capacity end up being underutilized.

[57] Ibid.

[58] The picture is much more complex as the decision involves not only whether to increase productive capacity or not, but also, as important, the timing of the implementation of any particular strategy.

prices undermining demand growth. Given the Kingdom's large oil reserve base, ensuring a stable oil market has been a key long-term policy objective. Historical evidence shows that OPEC spare capacity (largely concentrated in Saudi Arabia) has had a smoothing effect on global oil price movements, with prices under the counterfactual scenario in which there is no spare capacity exhibiting much sharper cycles both on the upside and the downside and higher volatility relative to the actual observed.[59] On a yearly basis, Fattouh and Economou find that price volatility under the counterfactual scenario would have been higher by 15.5 per cent because, in the absence of a buffer, even small shocks could induce higher price volatility.[60] The ability to ramp up production also serves as a mechanism to enforce discipline within OPEC. Finally, spare capacity allows the Kingdom to offer additional supplies during disruptions, when prices are usually high, boosting its revenues and its geopolitical standing. By utilizing its spare capacity, Saudi Aramco generated an estimated $35.5 billion of additional revenues from 2013 to 2018.[61]

The issue of maintaining spare capacity has become more complex in the context of the energy transition. If the energy transition has the effect of increasing the probability of supply shocks and their size and/or causes a slowdown in supply growth outside Saudi Arabia, the demand for Saudi crude could still rise and, in the absence of new investments, spare capacity would erode over time. The question is then whether Saudi Arabia should aim to increase its productive capacity and maintain spare capacity even in a world where oil demand is declining. If, by contrast, the demand for Saudi crude does fall over time, then Saudi Arabia may end up with larger spare capacity. In this case, should Saudi Arabia adopt a strategy to reduce its productive capacity or should it instead utilize all its spare capacity and pursue a faster monetization strategy? Thus, the size of spare capacity depends on a number of factors including Saudi Arabia's strategic choices. If market management is the preferred strategy, then availability of spare capacity is

---

[59] B. Fattouh and A. Economou, 'OPEC at 60: The World with and without OPEC', presented at the OPEC Technical Workshop on OPEC at 60: Contributions to the Global Economy and Energy Market (23 June 2020), https://www.oxfordenergy.org/wpcms/wp-content/uploads/2020/06/OPEC-at-60-The-World-With-and-Without-OPEC.pdf; A. Pierru, J. L. Smith, and T. Zamrik, 'OPEC's Impact on Oil Price Volatility: The Role of Spare Capacity', *Energy Journal* 39, no. 2 (2018), pp. 103–22. For instance, Fattouh and Economou find that in a world without OPEC spare capacity, the price would have risen by $110 per barrel (b), from $51.6/b in 2010 to $161.7/b in 2012, compared to $30.7/b in the actual world. In 2012, the Brent price would have been $39/b higher than actually observed. On the other hand, in weak markets where OPEC had to cut output to balance the market, the oil price would have stayed lower for longer. For instance, following the 2008–9 oil price collapse, in the absence of OPEC cuts prices would have remained in the $50–60/b range until early 2011, compared to the actual swift price recovery to above $80/b by the second half of 2009.

[60] Fattouh and Economou, 'OPEC at 60'.

[61] Saudi Aramco, *Saudi Arabian Oil Company (Saudi Aramco) Prospectus* (2018), https://www.aramco.com/-/media/images/investors/saudi-aramco-prospectus-en.pdf.

essential, especially if supply becomes more inelastic during the transition. If there is a shift in policy towards market share, then spare capacity becomes less important and the available spare capacity could be utilized in advancing such a strategy.

Until recently, Saudi Arabia's stated official policy has been to maintain its productive capacity of 12.5 mb/d. While it continued to develop and expand new fields, they did not represent net additions, but instead changed the quality mix of the Kingdom's production. In 2020, Saudi Aramco announced that it had received a directive from the Ministry of Energy to increase maximum sustainable capacity from 12 mb/d to 13 mb/d. Overall, the Kingdom is poised to increase its production capacity to 13.3–13.4 mb/d by the end of 2026/early 2027. This indicates that Saudi Arabia still expects an increase in demand for its crude as supplies from outside the Kingdom fall, or it wishes to retain enough spare capacity for its effective management of the market, or both. However, the relatively modest proposed increase in productive capacity, and the flexibility in the time frame, show that in this environment where prospects for global oil demand have become more uncertain, the option to wait has increased in value.

The Oil Sector, Diversification, and the Energy Transition

There has been considerable discussion about the transition strategies that oil-exporting countries should adopt to mitigate the adverse effects and risks of disruptive trends in the energy sector. Most of these strategies focus on economic diversification.[62] Diversification reduces the variance of return in an uncertain environment by spreading risk, for instance by creating new sectors other than oil and gas.[63] But oil-exporting countries face real challenges in achieving a meaningful diversification strategy. This is because diversification is only successful if it offers risk reduction by pooling uncorrelated income streams: for instance, by creating new sectors or new sources of taxation. If these countries diversify into sectors where inputs rely on energy infrastructure, they may not achieve sufficient risk reduction. Conversely, if they diversify into substantively different areas that have little in common with their current primary industry, they run the risk of failing to establish viable non-resource export sectors.[64] Furthermore, achieving

---

[62] R. Cherif and F. Hasanov, 'Soaring of the Gulf Falcons: Diversification in the GCC Oil Exporters in Seven Propositions', IMF Working Paper 14–177 (Washington, DC: International Monetary Fund, 2014).

[63] R. Poudineh and B. Fattouh, 'Diversification Strategy under Deep Uncertainty for MENA Oil Exporting Countries', OIES Energy Insight 69 (Oxford: Oxford Institute for Energy Studies, 2020), https://www.oxfordenergy.org/wpcms/wp-content/uploads/2020/05/Diversification-Strategy-Under-Deep-Uncertainty-for-MENA-Oil-Exporting-Countries-Insight-69.pdf.

[64] Ibid.

diversification requires building human capital and improving the education system, as well as extensive reforms to improve the business environment, transparency, and economic governance, and introducing taxation, which requires developing the administrative capabilities of the state.[65] It also calls for the streamlining of procedures, reducing excess monopoly rents in non-tradable sectors, and removing barriers to private-sector participation.[66] There is uncertainty about how rapidly such economic and institutional reforms can be implemented, and how effective they will be in diversifying the sources of government income.

Thus, to expect Saudi Arabia to diversify away from the oil sector, which constitutes its core competitive advantage, and for this strategic sector to play a lesser role in the transition process is not only unrealistic but also sub-optimal, as the Kingdom will be limiting its risk reduction strategies and abandoning a core strength and an important source of revenues. After all, the oil sector remains very profitable and enjoys higher margins than any new industries/sectors that the government aims to establish. Furthermore, the sector could contribute to the overall diversification strategy.[67] By lever-aging the energy sector and its income, the government could also finance the creation of new sectors and ease the pain of reforms, increasing the chances of success by introducing targeted compensatory measures to shield the most affected households and sectors.

Therefore, *in addition* to diversification, which is needed to enhance fiscal diversification, Saudi Arabia should pursue a conservative bet-hedging strat-egy,[68] the essence of which is reflected in the old saying that 'a bird in the hand is worth two in the bush'. The core of a conservative bet-hedging strat-egy is to enhance the competitiveness of the energy sector and increase its resilience against potential risks of disruption due to the energy transition. This could be achieved by adopting a set of measures that includes:

- lowering production costs and increasing oil and gas production effi-ciency so that Saudi Arabia can compete in any price environment and maintain healthy margins;
- reducing the carbon footprint of oil and gas production to enhance competitiveness;

[65] G. Luciani, 'Framing the Economic Sustainability of Oil Economies', in G. Luciani and T. Moeren-hout (eds.), *When Can Oil Economies Be Deemed Sustainable? The Political Economy of the Middle East* (Singapore: Palgrave Macmillan, 2021), pp. 349–365, doi: 10.1007/978-981-15-5728-6_2.
[66] Hvidt, 'Economic Diversification in GCC Countries'.
[67] B. Fattouh and A. Sen, 'Economic Diversification in Arab Oil-Exporting Countries in the Context of Peak Oil and the Energy Transition', in G. Luciani and T. Moerenhout (eds.), *When Can Oil Economies Be Deemed Sustainable? The Political Economy of the Middle East* (Singapore: Palgrave Macmillan, 2021), pp. 212–236, doi: 10.1007/978-981-15-5728-6_5.
[68] Poudineh and Fattouh, 'Diversification Strategy under Deep Uncertainty'.

- improving the efficiency of domestic energy use and optimizing the energy mix to maximize the country's oil export potential;
- shifting the portfolio towards petrochemicals and non-combustible uses of oil; and
- decarbonizing final petroleum products to sustain long-term demand for the Kingdom's core products as the transition towards decarbonized sources of energy accelerates.

Competing in a Low Oil Price Environment

As the energy transition advances, it could result in a shift to a more competitive market structure and lower margins.[69] Saudi Arabia already has some of the lowest costs of oil production in the world: the average upstream lifting cost is estimated at $2.8/boe produced, enabling the Kingdom to compete in a low-price environment. In a more competitive environment, Saudi Arabia must maintain and enhance its ability to compete by improving the efficiency of its operations, reducing production costs, and maintaining its status as a reliable supplier so that it can compete in any region. The well-developed infrastructure of pipelines, storage, and refining facilities both inside and outside the Kingdom, and marketing departments in key consuming centres, are all additional sources of comparative advantage.

Reducing the Carbon Footprint of Oil and Gas Production

But cost is not the only area in which the Kingdom can compete. Saudi Arabia has one of the lowest carbon intensities of oil and gas production,[70] and in a world of potentially rising carbon prices and carbon border taxes, this could provide a key additional source of competitive advantage. Its lower carbon intensity is due in part to the nature of its reserve base but also to the country's heavy investment in infrastructure over the years, such as the establishment of the Master Gas System (MGS), which resulted in a massive reduction in the routine flaring of gas.[71] Due to its small number of extremely large and productive fields, the Kingdom has very low gas flaring rates per barrel and low

---

[69] Dale and Fattouh, 'Peak Oil Demand and Long Run Oil Prices'.
[70] M. S. Masnadi, H. M. El-Houjeiri, D. Schunack, Y. Li, S. O. Roberts, S. Przesmitzki, A. R. Brandt, and M. Wang, 'Well-to-Refinery Emissions and Net-Energy Analysis of China's Crude-Oil Supply', *Nature Energy* 3, no. 3 (2018), p. 220, doi: 10.1038/s41560-018-0090-7.
[71] Ibid.; M. Al-Suwailem, 'Saudi Arabia's Gas Flaring Mitigation Experience', KAPSARC Commentary (Riyadh: KAPSARC, 2020).

water volume per unit of oil produced, and less energy is used for separation, treatment, and reinjection. All these factors contribute to the lower carbon intensity of its production. This is in contrast, for instance, to the extraction and processing of heavy oils in Venezuela and oil sands in Canada, which are characterized as very energy and carbon intensive.

One area in which Saudi Arabia performs particularly well is gas flaring, where Saudi Aramco has been implementing major projects to mitigate routine gas flaring across its oil and gas value chain. These include revisions to its standards and the use of innovative technologies and flare gas recovery systems in its gas oil separator plants and crude- and gas-processing complexes.[72] According to Saudi Aramco, flaring intensity remains at less than 1 per cent of total gas production. According to World Bank data, Saudi Arabia has one of the lowest gas flaring rates per barrel of oil produced. In 2019, Saudi Arabia joined the World Bank initiative to reduce gas flaring to zero by 2030.[73] Saudi Aramco's methane emissions are also among the lowest in the industry, with a 2018 methane intensity of 0.06 per cent.

Optimizing the Domestic Energy Mix

One of the notable features of Saudi Arabia over the last few decades has been the rapid increase in electricity demand driven by multiple factors, including high population growth, robust economic performance, improvements in standards of living, and harsh weather conditions. Limited gas supplies, gas infrastructure constraints, and long lead times to develop alternatives such as renewables and nuclear energy mean that Saudi Arabia continues to burn large volumes of liquids, primarily heavy fuel oil and crude oil, to meet electricity demand. Optimizing the energy mix would increase the Kingdom's core competitive advantage by freeing crude and products for export in the most cost-effective way, as compared, for instance, to increasing exports by increasing productive capacity through investment. This could be achieved through multiple routes, such as enhancing efficiency, reforming domestic energy prices, increasing the domestic use of gas and renewables in the power sector to displace liquids,[74] and investing in the necessary infrastructure such

---

[72] Al-Suwailem, 'Saudi Arabia's Gas Flaring Mitigation Experience'.
[73] Non-routine flaring is an important safety feature of oil- and gas-producing and processing facilities. It provides a safe and effective means of burning gas during a plant emergency, such as a valve leak, a purge, or a terrorist attack.
[74] J. Blazquez, M. Galeotti, B. Manzano, A. Pierru, and S. Pradhan, 'Analyzing the Effects of Saudi Arabia's Economic Reforms Using a Dynamic Stochastic General Equilibrium Model', KAPSARC Discussion Paper (Riyadh: KAPSARC, 2020).

as expanding the MGS and improving the robustness of the grid to enable the entry of these new sources. Saudi Arabia has made progress in all these areas.

In terms of efficiency, the government has been introducing tougher energy efficiency standards.[75] Efforts to promote a nationwide energy efficiency programme in the Kingdom started as early as 2003 with the launch of the National Energy Efficiency Program. In 2010, following a royal decree, the Council of Ministers transformed the programme into a permanent and broader energy efficiency programme, renaming it the Saudi Energy Efficiency Center. It was mandated to develop the country's energy efficiency policies, regulations, and rules, and to support their implementation. An inter-agency project called the Saudi Energy Efficiency Program was created to improve energy efficiency primarily in three major sectors: industry, buildings (residential, commercial, and government), and transport, which account for 90 per cent of energy consumption in Saudi Arabia. In the industrial sector, the program has focused its efforts on enforcing energy efficiency targets in three of its largest subsectors: petrochemicals, cement, and steel. Improving the efficiency of the Saudi power sector has also been a priority. Saudi Arabia's power generation capacity is largely dominated by steam and gas turbines. Subsidized fuel for power plants and low electricity tariffs discouraged investment in the past, but recent price reforms and policies have started a push towards a more efficient power system. There has been a gradual progression towards combined-cycle power plants. In addition, some of the steam power plants have been retrofitted with supercritical boilers to improve efficiency.[76]

Saudi Arabia has also been reforming its energy prices, particularly transport fuels. Following decades of very low gasoline prices, the government introduced two waves of major price increases, the first in December 2015 and the second in January 2018, which saw prices of Premium 95-octane gasoline increase from SAR0.60 per litre to SAR2.04 per litre, more than a threefold increase, albeit from a low base. Since the start of 2019, the government has also been adjusting gasoline prices on a quarterly basis depending on changes in international oil prices.[77] The impact on gasoline demand is already visible. After growing by an average of 6.3 per cent annually between 2002 and 2015, gasoline consumption has slowed markedly, contracting by 6.4 per cent between 2017 and 2018.[78] Although this decline cannot be

---

[75] Fattouh and Shabaneh, 'The Future of Gas in Saudi Arabia's Transition'.
[76] Ibid.
[77] M. Al-Dubyan and A. Gasim, 'Gasoline Price Reform in Saudi Arabia', KAPSARC Commentary (Riyadh: KAPSARC, 2019).
[78] Ibid.

attributed solely to gasoline price increases, energy price reform played the most important role by far.[79]

But reform has not been limited to transport fuels. Historically, the government has provided electricity at highly subsidized prices. Low tariff rates encouraged the inefficient use of electricity and did not cover the costs of electricity production, despite the government providing fuels for the power sector at subsidized prices. In 2015, the government raised prices for fuels used in the power sector—diesel, crude oil, heavy fuel oil, and methane. The increases ranged from 67 per cent for methane to 225 per cent for diesel. Even before these feedstock price hikes, the Saudi Electricity Company was making losses. To offset part of these increased costs and rationalize electricity demand, the government raised electricity tariffs. The government's ultimate objective is to increase tariffs to levels that reflect 'the production cost based on fuel prices, assuming ideal efficiency'.

These new electricity prices, although low by international standards, are expected to rationalize growth in electricity demand.[80] Between 2015 and 2018, residential electricity consumption in Saudi Arabia started to flatten, eventually falling from a peak of 144 TWh in 2015 to 130 TWh in 2018, with factors such as energy price reform and improved energy efficiency accounting for the decline.[81] In 2019, for the first time since data have been collected, electricity consumption dropped by 3.5 per cent year-on-year.[82]

The Saudi government also revised its natural gas prices in 2016, raising the price of ethane (the main feedstock used in the petrochemical industry) to $1.75 per million British thermal units (mmBtu), an increase of 133 per cent, and the price of methane (used mainly in the power sector) to $1.25/mmBtu, an increase of 67 per cent. The Fiscal Balance Programme 2017–20, launched in December 2016, aims for 'a targeted and gradual transition' of the gas price to 'a linked reference price with an applied price ceiling' by 2020/1. The 'gradual transition' and 'ceiling' reflect the government's effort

[79] M. Al-Dubyan and A. Gasim, 'Energy Price Reform in Saudi Arabia: Modeling the Economic and Environmental Impact and Understanding the Demand Responses', KAPSARC Discussion Paper (Riyadh: KAPSARC, 2020). Al-Dubyan and Gasim find that price reform accounts for 1.9 billion litres of the 2.2 billion litre annual decrease, while for residential electricity, higher prices contributed 9.1 terawatt hours (TWh) of the 13.0 TWh annual decline in 2018.

[80] While the cash handouts disbursed through the newly established cash transfer scheme (the Citizen's Account) will help alleviate some of the pain for lower-income households, the allowances have not been large enough to cover increases in the cost of other fuels such as gasoline, the indirect costs of energy price increases, and the introduction of VAT. The impact of higher electricity prices on demand is already being felt.

[81] M. Al-Dubyan and A. Gasim, 'What Happened to Residential Electricity Consumption in Saudi Arabia between 2015 and 2018?', KAPSARC Commentary (Riyadh: KAPSARC, 2020).

[82] S. Soummane, 'Saudi Electricity Demand Drops for the First Time on Record', KAPSARC Data Insight (Riyadh: KAPSARC, 2020).

to try to strike a balance between reforming gas prices and keeping energy and petrochemical industries competitive, as they remain at the heart of the Kingdom's industrialization strategy.[83]

The government has ambitious plans to reduce liquid burn in the power sector by increasing the share of natural gas and renewables in the power generation mix. Saudi Aramco has been investing heavily in developing its domestic gas reserves, and the new increments of gas supplies have reduced the volume and share of crude burn in power generation and moderated the sharp swings in crude burn.[84] The Kingdom's oil and gas policies are highly integrated. A key objective of gas policy has been to develop domestic gas reserves to replace crude oil in the power mix and develop non-associated gas reserves. This in large part explains the recent focus on developing unconventional gas such as the Jafurah field[85] and offshore non-associated gas reserves, which not only are needed to meet the current ambitious targets, but will also increase the Kingdom's flexibility in conducting its oil policy.[86]

In addition to natural gas, the Kingdom has ambitious plans to increase the share of renewables in the power mix, with the aim of renewables accounting for up to 50 per cent of power generation capacity by 2030 depending on economic growth. In locations where it is uneconomical to deliver gas because of lack of infrastructure, renewables can fill the gap, although this requires building energy storage systems and battery storage to overcome intermittency issues. Despite the great potential of renewable resources in Saudi Arabia, especially for solar energy, only 92 megawatts of renewable capacity were recorded in 2017, equating to 0.1 per cent of existing capacity.[87] But since then, there has been a rise in activity with more than 3.3 gigawatts (GW) of projects being tendered and some projects already under construction. Initially Saudi Arabia targeted 9.5 GW of renewable energy capacity by 2023. The current targets have almost reverted back to the original plan drawn up by King Abdullah City for Atomic and Renewable Energy, the lead organization at the time that was established to oversee development of alternative energy in 2013, which called for 54 GW of renewable capacity by

---

[83] Fattouh and Shabaneh, 'The Future of Gas in Saudi Arabia's Transition'.

[84] EIA, 'Saudi Arabia Used Less Crude Oil for Power Generation in 2018' (Washington, DC: US Energy Information Administration, 2019), https://www.eia.gov/todayinenergy/detail.php?id=39693.

[85] Gas reserves in Jafurah are estimated at 200 trillion cubic feet of raw gas with output estimated to reach around 2.2 billion cubic feet per day of sales gas by 2036, with an associated 425 million cubic feet per day of ethane. The field would also produce some 550,000 barrels per day of gas liquids and condensates. See Reuters, 'Saudi Aramco Launches Largest Shale Gas Development Outside US' (24 February 2020), https://www.reuters.com/article/us-saudi-shale-gas/saudi-aramco-launches-largest-shale-gas-development-outside-u-s-idUKKCN20I29A?edition-redirect=uk.

[86] Fattouh and Shabaneh, 'The Future of Gas in Saudi Arabia's Transition'.

[87] IRENA, 'Renewable Capacity Statistics 2018' (Abu Dhabi: International Renewable Energy Agency, 2018), http://irena.org/publications/2018/Mar/Renewable-Capacity-Statistics-2018.

2032. The new plan drafted under the National Renewable Energy Program, however, includes more detail and clarity in terms of technology, locations, and a roadmap for development. The lead organization of energy mix is the Ministry of Energy (in collaboration with other concerned entities in the ecosystem). A Supreme Committee for Energy Mix Affairs and Enabling Renewable Energy was also established to endorse renewables plans and provide support to achieve them.

All these measures would contribute towards Saudi Arabia meeting its nationally determined contribution (NDC) under the Paris Agreement.[88] Saudi Arabia communicated its intended NDC in November 2015, which subsequently became the Kingdom's first NDC after the agreement was ratified on 3 November 2016. The Kingdom aims to achieve mitigation co-benefits by avoiding up to 130 million tonnes of CO_2 equivalent per annum by 2030 through economic diversification policies and adaptation measures.

Extending the Value Chain

A core strategy in Saudi Arabia's efforts to diversify its economy has been to capture more value added across the hydrocarbon value chain. It has done this through vertical integration into refining and petrochemicals, and finished products manufactured in industrial parks that attract private sector and foreign direct investment. In addition, Saudi Aramco has developed a non-metallic programme to create new innovative materials from hydrocarbon and polymers, to replace conventional material like cement, steel, aluminium, and glass in key sectors such as oil and gas, automotives, building and construction, packaging, and renewables.[89] The move towards non-combustible uses of oil such as petrochemicals is expected to offer a degree of hedging against the possibility of a drop in oil demand, and to create new industries and jobs.[90] The Saudi petrochemical sector has established itself as one of the main pillars of the economy, in large part through heavy

[88] D. Wogan, E. Carey, and D. Cooke, 'Policy Pathways to Meet Saudi Arabia's Contribution to the Paris Agreement', KAPSARC Discussion Paper (Riyadh: KAPSARC, 2019). Wogan et al. find that by rationalizing costs of fuel inputs, Saudi Arabia could achieve large CO_2 emission reductions while providing a net economic benefit to its economy. Specifically, their results show that fully deregulating fuel prices achieves CO_2 emission reductions of 1.2 billion tonnes cumulative through to 2030. In such a scenario, electricity demand would be met by natural gas-fired combined-cycle gas turbines (64 per cent) and solar photovoltaic generation (20 per cent).

[89] See Saudi Aramco website, Non Metallic Solutions, https://www.aramco.com/en/creating-value/technology-development/in-house-developed-technologies/nonmetallic-solutions#.

[90] IEA, 'The Future of Petrochemicals: Towards More Sustainable Plastics and Fertilisers' (Paris: International Energy Agency, 2018), https://webstore.iea.org/download/direct/2310?fileName=The_Future_of_Petrochemicals.pdf.

government investment in new industrial cities and the MGS, encouraging investor participation, supporting joint ventures with foreign companies for new petrochemical projects, and providing cheap feedstock. But the traditional model based on cheap ethane and producing basic petrochemicals seems to have reached its limits in terms of development goals and offering a hedge for the Kingdom. Instead, Saudi Arabia needs to move towards more speciality products, accelerate the shift of its feedstocks towards liquids such as crude and naphtha, and invest in new technologies of production and recycling. Part of this strategy is to invest in technologies that could convert 70–80 per cent of crude intake into chemicals.[91]

Decarbonizing Final Products through the Circular Carbon Economy

A key part of a conservative bet-hedging strategy is to decarbonize products and sustain the continued use of fossil fuels by replacing oil exports with new energy carriers that are clean and can be produced using existing oil and gas infrastructure. There is wide recognition in Saudi Arabia that this is essential to ensure the long-term viability of its oil industry. A key concept advanced by the Kingdom has been that of the Circular Carbon Economy (CCE), in which emissions of carbon from all sectors are managed in a way that allows the carbon to move in a closed-loop system.[92] Under the Saudi Group of 20 (G20) presidency, the G20 energy ministers endorsed the CCE approach and its '4Rs' framework (reduce, reuse, recycle, and remove) as a 'holistic, integrated, inclusive, and pragmatic approach to managing emissions that can be applied reflecting countries' priorities and circumstances.'[93] The CCE approach requires enabling policies that incentivize investment and continuous improvement in technologies such as carbon capture, utilization, and storage (CCUS), human capital, engineering and design, patenting laws, and

---

[91] Reuters, 'Saudi Aramco Signs Crude-to-Chemicals Technology Agreement' (18 January 2018), https://mobile.reuters.com/article/amp/idUSKBN1F727B. Saudi Aramco and Saudi Basic Industries Corporation have recently announced that they would re-evaluate their crude-oil-to-chemicals project in Yanbu.

[92] A. Al-Khuwaiter and Y. Al-Mufti, 'An Alternative Energy Transition Pathway Enabled by the Oil and Gas Industry', Oxford Energy Forum 121 (2020), pp. 14–19.

[93] G20, 'G20 Energy Ministers Meeting Communique' (27–8 September 2020), https://g20.org/en/media/Documents/G20SS_Energy%20Ministerial%20Communique.pdf. Saudi Arabia's role in climate change negotiations has often been described as 'obstructionist': Joanna Depledge, 'Striving for No: Saudi Arabia in the Climate Change Regime', Global Environmental Politics 8, no. 4 (2008), pp. 9–35. Promoting CCE represents a different strategy that emphasizes 'managing emissions', while taking into account a 'country's priorities and circumstances', and encourages all possible climate mitigation options.

expertise in trade laws. It remains to be seen how successful the Kingdom will be in its decarbonization efforts through the CCE approach, but recent initiatives indicate that Saudi Arabia is accelerating its work to decarbonize its products. One such initiative is the world's first shipment of 40 tonnes of blue ammonia from Saudi Aramco to Japan.[94] This remains a one-off shipment to test the concept and additional investment will be needed to make the project economically viable. But it shows that for Saudi Arabia, hydrogen and CCUS represent key opportunities for decarbonization and constitute the cornerstones of the CCE.[95] In 2021, Saudi Arabia pledged to cut its carbon emissions to net zero by 2060.

Conservative Bet-Hedging Strategy: Costs and Limitations

The return on a conservative bet-hedging strategy is lower than the current default strategy of exporting oil and gas, given the costs involved in decarbonization and the potentially lower margins in the new low-carbon businesses. But such a strategy lowers the risk profile and improves the resilience of a key sector of the economy.[96] Policy-makers need to realize that while decarbonization polices such as the CCE approach come at a cost, and thus lower the overall return from existing assets, they also reduce the risk of disruption to their energy sectors and economies in the long term. The availability of cheap-to-extract oil enables Saudi Arabia to absorb the added cost of decarbonization as a form of internal carbon tax. Moreover, this strategy is less complex to implement given its close relationship with the existing hydrocarbon business, and it enables countries to build on their core strengths. Currently, many decarbonization technologies such as CCUS remain costly, but this means there is significant room for cost efficiency gains that could be exploited. During the transition era, which is highly uneven across the globe and the speed of which is highly uncertain, Saudi Arabia can still export oil and benefit from the rents generated, while at the same time improving the return on decarbonized products.

[94] J. Ingram, 'Saudi Arabia Ships "Blue Ammonia" to Japan in World First', *MEES* 63, no. 40 (2020), pp. 7–9. The ammonia was produced from hydrogen from hydrocarbons with the associated CO_2 captured and utilized by Saudi Aramco.

[95] In a recent interview, chief executive of Saudi Aramco, Amin Nasser, said that 'hydrogen is among the long-term business opportunities that we are expending a lot of R&D money on ... crude-to-hydrogen and gas-to-hydrogen are definitely opportunities that we are interested in'.

[96] Poudineh and Fattouh, 'Diversification Strategy under Deep Uncertainty'.

Nevertheless, this strategy of investing to increase the resilience of the energy sector suffers from some drawbacks. First, the cost of decarbonizing final products remains highly uncertain, and although decarbonization costs are expected to decline, this depends on the large-scale deployment of certain technologies such as CCUS and hydrogen. This deployment in turn depends on the policy framework, the ability to develop business models that ensure that costs are shared between producers, consumers, and various parts of the supply chain, and well-designed policies that allow supply-side technologies to be part of the solution.[97] This requires a proactive approach and international coordination and cooperation.

Second, the energy industry is capital intensive and does not generate enough jobs for the hundreds of thousands entering the Saudi labour market each year. It is not sufficient for the energy sector to generate a return and improve its resilience; the oil sector has to contribute to economic diversification by creating new sectors and jobs. By extending the value chain and moving away from basic products, Saudi Arabia can create new industries that generate not only more jobs, but different types of jobs, including those in the service sector, such as trading, marketing and sales, procurement, and logistics, as well as support services such as accounting, finance, and human resource management.[98]

In this respect, the Local Content Requirements that give priority to nationals in employment opportunities, domestic companies in contract opportunities, and locally produced goods and services will only increase in importance. The objectives of such policies are to create a level playing field for local industries, create jobs for locals, and enhance the transfer of technology and technical expertise and skills.[99] Saudi Aramco has one of the most ambitious localization plans in the region with its In-Kingdom Total Value Add programme, launched in 2015. The main objective of the programme is to maximize the impact of the company's capital expenditure on the local economy, generating growth, new industries, and employment.[100]

[97] P. Zakkour and W. Heidug, 'Supply-Side Climate Policy for Crude Oil Producers: Exploring Policy Pathways for Decarbonizing Fossil Fuels', KAPSARC Discussion Paper (Riyadh: KAPSARC, 2020).
[98] M. Hvidt, 'Economic Diversification and Job Creation in the Arab Gulf Countries: Applying a Value Chain Perspective', in G. Luciani and T. Moerenhout (eds.), *When Can Oil Economies Be Deemed Sustainable? The Political Economy of the Middle East* (Singapore: Palgrave Macmillan, 2021), pp. 281–300, doi: 10.1007/978-981-15-5728-6_11.
[99] D. Olawuyi, 'Local Content and Procurement Requirements in Oil and Gas Contracts: Regional Trends in the Middle East and North Africa', MEP 18 (Oxford: Oxford Institute for Energy Studies, 2017), https://www.oxfordenergy.org/wpcms/wp-content/uploads/2017/11/Local-content-and-procurement-requirements-in-oil-and-gas-contracts-regional-trends-in-the-Middle-East-and-North-Africa-MEP-18.pdf.
[100] So far, the In-Kingdom Total Value Add programme has attracted 468 investments from 25 countries with an estimated capital expenditure of $6.5 billion, resulting in 44 industrial facilities completed to date

The extent to which the energy sector can play a role in diversification also depends on the wider structural reforms. The inefficient economic structures and policies surrounding the energy sector have not only constituted barriers to meaningful diversification, but also limited the energy sector's contribution to broader and deeper diversification. The recent energy pricing, labour market, and fiscal reforms will act as additional enablers to the transition of the Saudi energy system, enhance its diversification role, and provide greater flexibility in terms of oil policy.

Conclusion

Oil will continue to be the cornerstone of Saudi Arabia's political economy and its international relations. In the era of energy transition, and as Saudi Arabia implements its Vision 2030, many are of the view that the oil sector's contribution to the Kingdom's future development path and international relations will become less important over time, with some having already moved to analysing Saudi Arabia beyond oil.[101] This view is premature: the role of oil in shaping the Kingdom's political and economic future will become more important as the transformations in the Saudi economy and global oil market continue, although its contribution to the future trajectory of the Kingdom will take different forms from the past.

Thus, in addition to economic and fiscal diversification, Saudi Arabia should adopt policies to increase the resilience of its oil sector. Diversifying away from oil and reducing the role of the oil sector in the Kingdom's future development path is not only unrealistic but also, at a strategic and policy level, suboptimal. Saudi Arabia should continue to leverage its core sector by enhancing its competitiveness through improving efficiency, promoting greater integration, and reducing the carbon footprint of its oil activities. It should equally use the rents generated to ease the pain of structural reforms needed to place the economy on a more sustainable path, and leverage the scale of the oil sector to create meaningful backward and forward linkages to the rest of the economy.

Saudi Arabia is very well positioned to implement such strategies and is in a strong position to mitigate the potentially disruptive impacts on its energy

and another 64 facilities under construction. In terms of localization, Saudi Aramco's procurement spent in the Kingdom rose from 35 per cent in 2015 to 56 per cent in 2019.

[101] McKinsey Global Institute, 'Saudi Arabia beyond Oil: The Investment and Productivity Transformation' (New York: McKinsey Global Institute, 2015).

sector and economy. This strength is reflected in the level of development of its energy sector, its high degree of integration, its core comparative advantage as the lowest-cost and least carbon-intensive producer, the potential to assume a leading position in the development of renewables and low carbon technologies such as CCUS and hydrogen, its highly capable national oil company, and a stable environment over many years which has ensured continued investment in the energy sector.

3

Fiscal Policy

The Past, the Present, and the Future

Nabil Ben Ltaifa and Tim Callen

Introduction

Fiscal policy is the main vehicle through which revenues from the sale of oil reach the domestic economy.[1] The government receives royalties, income taxes, and dividends from Aramco, the national oil company. These revenues together with more limited, though rising, non-oil revenues help finance spending on wages of government employees, who make up a large share of working Saudi nationals, purchases of goods and services, and investments in capital projects. Government spending has averaged 60 per cent of non-oil GDP over the past decade and is a key driver of growth in the non-oil economy.

Government spending has supported rapid economic development in Saudi Arabia over the past fifty to sixty years. The country has seen huge gains in human development indicators, rising per capita incomes, and the establishment of good-quality infrastructure. As well as being the key policy for driving economic and social development over the medium and long term, fiscal policy is the main macroeconomic policy instrument available to the government for managing aggregate demand in the short term, given that the longstanding exchange rate peg to the United States (US) dollar means that monetary policy largely follows that of the US Federal Reserve. Lastly, by determining the balance between spending and saving, fiscal policy determines the allocation of the non-renewable oil revenues across generations.

[1] The authors acknowledge research support from Tian Zhang. The authors were in the Middle East and Central Asia Department at the International Monetary Fund (IMF) at the time of writing. The views expressed herein are those of the authors and should not be attributed to the IMF, its Executive Board, or its management.

Nabil Ben Ltaifa and Tim Callen, *Fiscal Policy*. In: *The Economy of Saudi Arabia in the 21st Century*. Edited by: John Sfakianakis, Oxford University Press. © Nabil Ben Ltaifa and Tim Callen (2024). DOI: 10.1093/oso/9780198863878.003.0004

Oil revenues have provided huge benefits to the Saudi Arabian economy, although the reliance of the budget on oil revenues also has drawbacks. Periods of high oil prices create pressures for the government to spend. But increased spending raises fiscal vulnerabilities which are more clearly exposed only when oil prices fall. Spending then needs to be cut back, and this adjustment has usually been focused on capital rather than current spending, and current spending tends to be more rigid and harder to reverse. Fiscal policy is procyclical with respect to the oil price—adding to the strength of the upswing and contributing to the extent of the downswing. The 1980s and 1990s, when oil prices were depressed, saw weak growth and a large build-up in public debt to over 100 per cent of gross domestic product (GDP). The decline in oil prices in 2014 and in early 2020 as COVID-19 struck the world economy put pressure on the fiscal position. Non-oil growth has been weaker in recent years than in the decade up to 2014, although it has rebounded since the pandemic.

Recognizing the challenges posed by the reliance on volatile oil revenues and intent on doing more to support private sector development and diversification, the government has embarked on wide-ranging fiscal reforms as part of its broader economic and social reform initiatives under Vision 2030. The reforms have put in place a modern budget process and fiscal framework, begun to diversify sources of revenue away from oil, taken some steps to improve the efficiency of government spending, supported a deeper analysis of the impact of fiscal policy on the economy, and put in place a modern debt management framework.

At the time of writing in early 2022, much has been achieved in a short period of time. That Saudi Arabia would have introduced a value added tax (VAT), raised domestic gasoline prices, and be regularly publishing fiscal information would have been unthinkable to most observers at the beginning of 2015. The government deserves credit for the fiscal reforms it has implemented. Nevertheless, the journey is ongoing, and there is further to travel. Procyclical fiscal policy has not yet been fully tamed and a large government wage bill continues to constrain fiscal policy flexibility. Further, the energy price reforms need to be completed, and fiscal transparency, while improved, lags behind what would be expected from a country of Saudi Arabia's global stature.

This chapter looks at fiscal policy in Saudi Arabia in a historic context, including the relationship between fiscal policy and non-oil growth, to help understand why fundamental fiscal reform was needed. It then discusses the reforms through the period to the end of 2021 and concludes by highlighting key unfinished items on the fiscal reform agenda that still need the authorities' attention.

Fiscal Policy in Saudi Arabia—A Long-Term Perspective

Oil revenues accounted for an average of 83 per cent of total government revenues in the two decades to 2014.[2] Given the wide swings in oil prices and production, government revenues have been very volatile, reaching highs of 75 per cent of GDP in the mid-1970s and lows of 15 per cent of GDP in the 1980s and 1990s (Figure 3.1). Prior to 2017, non-oil revenues were limited and mainly comprised *zakat* (see below), customs duties, a profits tax on foreign companies, and multiple fees and fines. Specifically:

- Foreign companies are subject to a corporate income tax of 20 per cent, and a 20 per cent capital gains tax is applied to the disposal by a non-resident of shares in a resident company. Some tax relief and incentives apply, which lower the effective tax rate.
- National companies pay an obligatory annual *zakat* contribution at a 2.5 per cent rate of net worth in support of charitable causes (*zakat* proceeds are collected by the tax authorities and then redistributed in the form of social benefits as part of the budget).
- Customs duties are imposed on imports from outside the Gulf Cooperation Council (GCC). A Common External Tariff has been imposed on imports into the GCC since January 2003. The standard customs duty

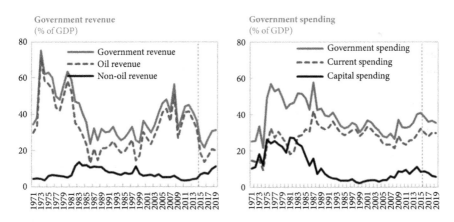

Figure 3.1 Government revenue and spending, 1971–2019 (% of GDP)
Note: Fiscal data for 1990 and 1991 are interpolated given data absence.
Sources: Country authorities; IMF staff calculations.

---

[2] In its longer-term analysis, the chapter uses data up until 2019 to abstract from the impact of COVID-19 (2020) and the recovery from it (2021), which significantly affected growth and fiscal outcomes in these years.

rate on non-GCC products was set at 5 per cent (this changed when Saudi Arabia increased a range of custom duties in June 2020).

- Companies operating in the oil and gas sectors are subject to a different and more complex tax structure.

Since mid-2017, various excises on products seen as harmful to health and a VAT (at 5 per cent initially, increased to 15 per cent in July 2020) have been introduced. Further, the levy on expatriate workers (which previously did not go to the government budget) has been increased and a new levy on their dependants enacted. There are no taxes on wage income for nationals and non-nationals, nor taxes on property income for nationals.

Until recently, the government has forgone most of the revenue it could have received (through Aramco) from the sales of energy products in the domestic market because of the very low prices in place (revenues would have been well below what could be earned if these products were exported). While for many countries, energy subsidies take the form of an explicit expenditure in the budget, in Saudi Arabia they are implicit and take the form of forgone revenues.

On the expenditure side, current and capital spending accounted for a broadly equal share of total spending in the 1970s as the government focused on developing the infrastructure of the country and the size of government employment remained relatively contained. However, with the decline in oil revenues in the 1980s, capital spending was cut back significantly and almost all government outlays went on current spending. With the oil price boom in the 2000s, capital spending once again picked up but it remained lower as a share of total spending than in the 1970s. Within current spending, employee compensation is by far the largest component. While data limitations (data start in 2010) do not permit a full analysis, employee compensation has accounted for 40–50 per cent of government spending over the past decade (Figure 3.2).

The history of the fiscal balance in Saudi Arabia can be broadly (although not perfectly) divided into four periods—two of 'high' oil prices and two of 'low' oil prices (Figure 3.3).[3] Specifically, these periods are: (1) a period of fiscal surpluses in the early 1970s to the early 1980s when oil prices jumped during the 1973 oil embargo and the 1979 Iranian revolution; (2) sustained fiscal deficits from the mid-1980s to the mid-2000s when oil prices were depressed by new sources of supply and relatively slow growth in global

[3] The average real oil price during 1970–2019 was $58 a barrel. High oil prices are defined as being above and low oil prices below this average.

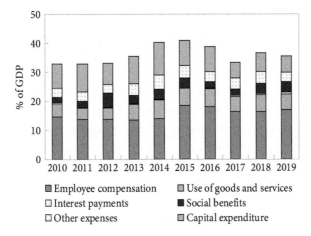

Figure 3.2 Composition of government spending,
2010–19 (% of GDP)

Sources: Country authorities; IMF staff calculations.

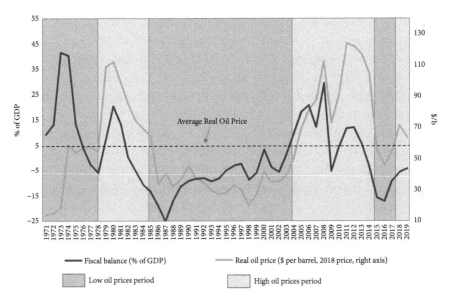

Figure 3.3 Real oil prices and the fiscal balance, 1971–19

Note: High/low price periods are defined based on whether the real oil price is above/below the
period average, which is $58 per barrel at 2018 prices.
Source: County authorities; and IMF staff calculations.

oil demand; (3) large fiscal surpluses from the mid-2000s to 2014 when the
strong growth in oil demand, particularly from China, drove oil prices higher
(temporarily interrupted by the global financial crisis); and (4) from 2015 to
2021 when lower oil prices resulted in renewed and sustained fiscal deficits.

Swings in oil prices are not, however, the whole story. Expenditure policy has played an important role. While the growth of government spending is generally contained in the early years of oil price booms (relative to the increase in revenues), it becomes increasingly hard to contain as oil boom continues. Spending tends to respond with a lag to changes in revenues. For example, during 1973–4, government revenues grew by 155 per cent a year on average while spending growth was about one-half this rate. During 1975–7, though, spending growth averaged close to 60 per cent a year while revenues grew by 8 per cent. Similarly, from 2003 to 2008, revenues grew on average by around 30 per cent a year while spending grew at about half this rate. Then, between 2008 and 2014, revenues declined slightly (although oil prices remained high, they did not increase), while spending growth averaged 14 per cent a year.

Another feature of fiscal policy has been the consistent over- or under-execution of the budget depending on within-year developments in oil revenues (Figure 3.4). Specifically, in years where oil revenues turn out to be higher than assumed in the budget, spending typically exceeds budget (usually with a surge towards the end of the year). Similarly, if oil revenues fall below budget, expenditure is typically also contained under budget. This tendency further added to the unpredictability of fiscal policy with projects either accelerated or delayed from year to year depending on oil price developments.

As a result of the volatility of oil revenues and the lagged response of spending to changes in oil revenues, the fiscal balance has been very volatile. This volatility has been much higher than in other G20 countries. For example, a budget surplus of 30 per cent of GDP was recorded in 2007, but this turned

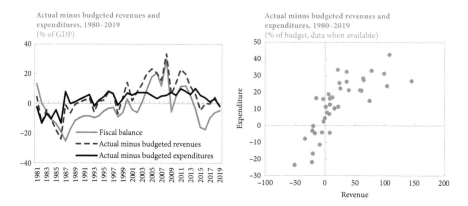

Figure 3.4 Government revenue and expenditures relative to budget, 1980–2019

Sources: Country authorities; IMF staff calculations.

into a deficit of 5.4 per cent of GDP in 2008 as the global financial crisis hit oil prices and expenditure continued to grow, before returning to a surplus of over 11 per cent of GDP in 2010 as oil prices recovered.

Central government net financial assets (CGNFA)—defined as central government deposits at the central bank less gross debt—are built up during 'good' times and run down during 'bad' times (Figure 3.5). The CGNFA-to-GDP ratio increased substantially during the 1970s due to the very large fiscal surpluses that were run early in the decade, but after close to twenty years of fiscal deficits, these assets were exhausted and government debt rose to over 100 per cent of GDP in the late 1990s. Debt was reduced to close to zero and financial assets were rebuilt during the years to 2014, and Saudi Arabia entered the oil price slump in 2014 with a CGNFA ratio of around 50 per cent of GDP. By the end of 2019, the CGNFA had declined to −5 per cent of GDP.

Government spending plays a key role in driving growth in the non-oil sector in Saudi Arabia (Figure 3.6). This is because a large proportion of Saudi Arabian nationals work for the government (and broader public sector) and many businesses are reliant on government contracts. When government spending growth was weak in the 1990s, non-oil growth averaged 3 per cent a year, while during the oil price boom from 2004 to 2013, average annual non-oil growth was 7.7 per cent. Fouejieu et al. report strong and significant contemporaneous and one-year lagged correlations between real non-oil GDP and real government spending growth.[4]

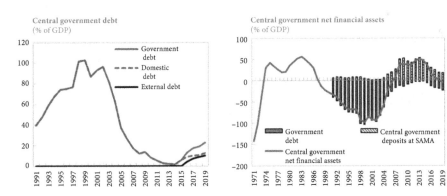

Figure 3.5 Central government debt, 1991–2019, and net financial assets, 1971–2019 (% of GDP)

Sources: Country authorities; IMF staff calculations.

---

[4] A. Fouejieu, S. Rodrigues, and S. Shahid, 'Fiscal Adjustment in the Gulf Countries: Less Costly than Previously Thought', IMF Working Paper WP/18/133 (Washington, DC: International Monetary Fund, 2018).

Real non-oil GDP and government spending growth (%)

Volatility of real non-oil GDP and real government spending growth (standard deviation of annual growth)

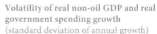
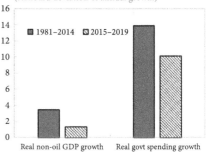

Figure 3.6 Growth and volatility of non-oil GDP and government spending, 1981–2019

Sources: Country authorities; IMF staff calculations.

Nevertheless, the structure of the Saudi economy means that much of the government's spending 'leaks' out through imports, expatriate worker remittances, and spending on foreign services, particularly travel and tourism. These leakages mean that while government spending is a very important driver of non-oil growth, it is not an efficient driver in that a lot of spending is needed to generate additional growth.

Several studies have looked at the relationship between government spending and non-oil growth in Saudi Arabia and more broadly in the GCC. They calculate the 'fiscal multiplier': that is, the amount of additional GDP that is generated by (say) SAR1 of additional government spending. The IMF reports that such studies tend to find current and capital spending multipliers in the range of 0.2–0.5 in the short term. In the longer term, the current spending multiplier is found to be around 0.5 and the capital spending multiplier in the range of 0.6–1.1.[5] At the GCC level, there is also some evidence that expenditure multipliers have declined since 2011 when government spending increased sharply in the wake of the Arab Spring.[6] Given the limited history of domestic taxation, however, it is not yet possible to estimate a revenue multiplier for Saudi Arabia.

[5] IMF, 'How Can Growth Friendlier Expenditure-Based Fiscal Adjustment Be Achieved in the GCC?', Annual GCC Meeting of Ministers of Finance and Central Bank Governors (Washington, DC: International Monetary Fund). These estimates are averages over the whole sample period. There is international evidence that fiscal multipliers are larger during recessions. These multipliers appear to be lower than in advanced countries but not necessarily out of line with emerging market countries: see, for example, N. Batini, L. Eyraud, L. Forni, and A. Weber, 'Fiscal Multipliers: Size, Determinants, and Use in Macroeconomic Projections', IMF Technical Notes and Manuals (Washington, DC: International Monetary Fund, 2014).

[6] Fouejieu et al., 'Fiscal Adjustment in the Gulf Countries'.

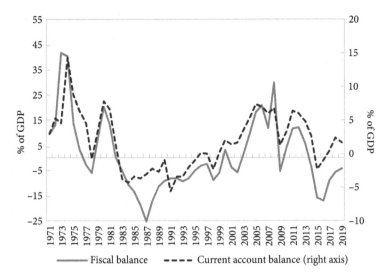

Figure 3.7 Fiscal and current account balances, 1971–2019 (% of GDP)

Sources: Country authorities; IMF staff calculations.

Fiscal and current account balances are highly correlated in Saudi Arabia (Figure 3.7). Fiscal revenues/exports are both highly dependent on oil revenues and government spending is import intensive both directly and indirectly through the employment of expatriate labour in companies fulfilling government contracts and providing services to government workers.

In sum, fiscal policy has successfully supported economic development in Saudi Arabia, but over time two related weaknesses have persisted. First, the reliance of the budget on oil revenues and second the control of spending during extended periods of high oil prices. At their core, the reforms discussed in the next section are designed to address these weaknesses.

Fiscal Reforms, 2015–2021

Fiscal reforms constitute one of the main pillars of Vision 2030. The Fiscal Balance Program (FBP) was launched in December 2016 as one of the first of the Vision Realization Programs developed to implement the objectives of Vision 2030. FBP 2016[7] targeted achieving budget balance by 2020 and committed the government to strengthening fiscal governance, increasing

---

[7] There have been so far two vintages of the FBP. FBP 2016 accompanied the 2016 Budget and the FBP Update 2018 was issued with the 2018 Budget. Ministry of Finance, 'Fiscal Balance Program, Balanced Budget 2020' (Riyadh: Ministry of Finance, 2016); Ministry of Finance, 'Fiscal Balance Program Update' (Riyadh: Ministry of Finance, 2018).

non-oil revenues, reforming domestic energy prices, and improving the efficiency of spending on programmes and projects. It also aimed to contribute to improving social outcomes—better targeting of the social welfare system, for example—and making the Saudi economy more competitive.

Since 2016, the targets and objectives in the FBP have been updated to incorporate key macroeconomic and fiscal developments, progress with reforms, as well as the new challenges that have emerged. The FBP Updates of 2018 and 2019 incorporated a more gradual implementation path for the energy price increases previously identified and a slower pace of the overall fiscal adjustment. The target date for balancing the budget was moved to 2023 from 2020. This target was eventually replaced in the 2020 Budget with a more conceptual target of achieving fiscal sustainability. The 2021 Budget once again projected broad fiscal balance in 2023.

Fiscal adjustment was under way in the aftermath of the 2014 oil price decline and before the FBP was published. Initially, adjustment was mainly achieved through reductions in capital spending and one-off non-oil revenue initiatives. Over time, however, sustainable non-oil revenue sources have been put in place (see below) and the balance of adjustment has become tilted towards raising non-oil revenues rather than reducing spending.

Between 2014 and 2019, oil revenues (excluding those raised from domestic energy price reforms) declined by nearly 14 per cent of GDP. Non-oil revenues increased by 6.7 per cent of GDP, revenues from domestic energy price reforms contributed an additional 1.6 per cent of GDP to revenues, while capital spending was reduced by 5.6 per cent of GDP (Table 3.1). Current spending increased by about 1 per cent of GDP, although more than half of this increase was due to higher interest costs as debt increased. While the overall fiscal deficit increased by nearly 1 per cent of GDP between 2014 and 2019, the non-exported oil primary deficit as a share of GDP declined by nearly 13½ percentage points, a considerable fiscal effort by any account.

The reforms that have been implemented so far are very important for ensuring the continued sustainability of Saudi Arabia's fiscal position in an environment where oil revenues are likely to stay much lower than in the decade to 2014. Indeed, on reasonable projections of oil prices over the next five years (based on futures markets), Saudi Arabia should be able to reduce its fiscal deficit and broadly stabilize its CGNFA ratio at a level that would be the envy of most countries. However, that may not be enough, depending both on the longer-term outlook for the global oil market and the weight that policy-makers put on saving some of the current oil wealth for future generations.

Table 3.1 Fiscal adjustment in Saudi Arabia, 2014–19 (% of GDP)

	2014	2019	Change
Revenues	36.7	31.2	−5.5
Oil	32.2	20.0	−12.2
o/w domestic energy price reforms	0.0	1.6	1.6
Non-oil	4.5	11.2	6.7
o/w investment income	0.6	0.7	0.1
Expenditures	40.2	35.6	−4.6
Current	29.0	29.9	1.0
o/w interest costs	0.1	0.7	0.6
Capital	11.3	5.7	−5.6
Fiscal balance	−3.5	−4.5	−0.9
Memo items:			
Non-exported oil primary balance	−36.2	−22.8	13.4
Contribution from:			
Non-exported oil primary revenues			8.2
Primary current expenditures			−0.4
Capital expenditures			5.6

Source: Author estimates based on Ministry of Finance data.

Oil resources are also exhaustible: that is, once extracted, they cannot be replaced (although, of course, the size of oil reserves in a country is uncertain, both because they may not all have been discovered and because new technological innovations may mean that previously inaccessible reserves can now be extracted). But the exhaustible nature of oil raises the question of whether the proceeds from its sale should be spent by current generations or should in part be saved for use by future generations. This has led to analysis that looks at what it would take to stabilize government net wealth (defined as financial and the value of oil in the ground),[8] or what wealth level would be required to achieve some equitable income flow from the oil wealth across generations (the so-called Permanent Income Hypothesis).[9] While these approaches differ in specifics, they both suggest that fiscal adjustment in Saudi Arabia may need to continue.

---

[8] See, for example, T. Mirzoev, L. Zhu, Y. Yang, A. Pescatori, and A. Matsumoto, 'The Future of Oil and Fiscal Sustainability in the GCC Region', IMF Department Paper 20/01 (Washington, DC: International Monetary Fund, 2020).
[9] See T. Mirzoev and L. Zhu, 'Rethinking Fiscal Policy in Oil Exporting Countries', IMF Working Paper 19/108 (Washington, DC: International Monetary Fund, 2019).

Revenue Reforms

Non-oil revenue and domestic energy price reforms have led the fiscal reform efforts.[10] The focus has been on introducing a VAT and a number of excises on harmful products, raising a previously introduced levy on expatriate workers and extending it to their dependants, and raising domestic energy prices. An assortment of fees and fines have also been introduced. One aim of the reforms is to introduce a modern tax system that is broadly based and efficient. Another is to begin to reduce the excessive domestic consumption of energy products.

The main non-oil revenue reforms are estimated to have raised additional revenues of 6 per cent of GDP in 2019 (Figure 3.8), with the rest of the increase in non-oil revenues shown in Table 3.1 coming from higher yields on existing sources of revenue. The VAT, expatriate levy, and energy price reforms accounted for 34, 25, and 34 per cent of this increase, respectively. The recent increase in the VAT rate (see below) will see the VAT make an even stronger contribution to revenue generation once the economy recovers from the effects of COVID-19.

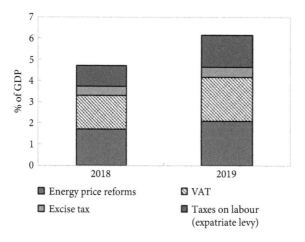

Figure 3.8 Revenues from new measures, 2018–19 (% of GDP)

Sources: Country authorities; IMF staff calculations.

---

[10] For a more detailed discussion of non-oil revenue reforms, see IMF, 'Saudi Arabia, 2017 Article IV Consultation—Press Release and Staff Report', IMF Country Report 17/316 (Washington, DC: International Monetary Fund), pp. 8–9; IMF, 'Saudi Arabia, Selected Issues', IMF Country Report 19/291 (Washington, DC: International Monetary Fund, 2019), pp. 21–9.

To support the tax reforms, the Department of Zakat has been transformed into a modern tax administration—renamed the General Authority of Zakat and Tax (GAZT)—that is independent of the Ministry of Finance (MoF). GAZT is governed by an Executive Board, has the Minister of Finance as the chairman of the board, and is headed by a Governor, who is also a board member.

Value Added Tax

The introduction of the VAT was a landmark achievement. The main parameters of the VAT were defined in a common legal framework agreed by all GCC countries in 2016, with the agreement coming into effect after ratification by two member countries (Saudi Arabia and the United Arab Emirates, UAE)—as required by the agreement—in 2017. Saudi Arabia approved and published its VAT law in July 2017 and related implementing regulations followed in September of the same year. A VAT at a 5 per cent rate was introduced on 1 January 2018 with the registration threshold for the first year set at SAR1 million ($267,000). This threshold was reduced to the level defined in the GCC agreement of SAR375,000 ($100,000) on 1 January 2019. At the time of its introduction, the VAT rate was low and the registration threshold high by international standards (Figure 3.9).

The VAT has performed well. Its successful introduction was helped by the application of a low VAT rate and the limited exemptions and zero-rated items adopted. Further, the concentration of registration efforts on large taxpayers in the initial phase helped secure a large portion of the VAT revenue base early on. On-time filings of large taxpayers (representing over 85 per cent of the tax base) averaged over 99 per cent and those for small and medium taxpayers were around 85 per cent in 2018. In the second year of implementation (2019), VAT revenues reached over 2 per cent of GDP and the c-efficiency ratio was around 65 per cent, in line with top-performing countries. The government raised the VAT rate to 15 per cent on 1 July 2020 as part of a package of measures to mitigate the budgetary impact of the COVID-19 crisis.

Excise Taxes

The GCC Agreement on Excise Taxes was signed in May 2017 and established a common legal framework for the implementation of excise taxes in the region. It focused on a few goods deemed harmful to human health and/or the environment. Saudi Arabia started in the second half of 2017 imposing excises on tobacco and energy drinks (at a 100 per cent rate) and carbonated drinks (50 per cent rate). In May 2019, the Excise Tax Implementing Regulations were amended to expand the application of the excise tax

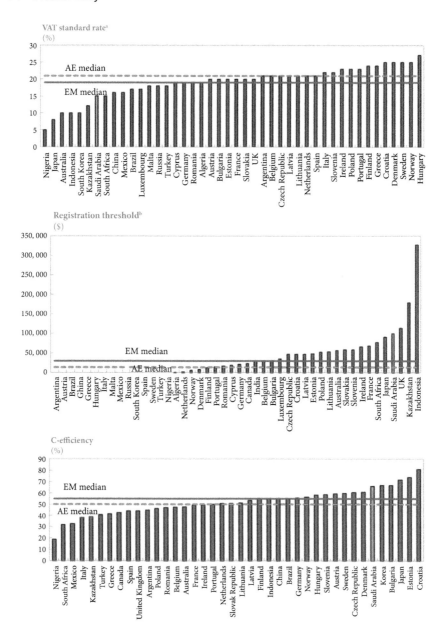

Figure 3.9 Key features of the VAT

Notes: [a] For Saudi Arabia, rate as of 1 July 2020. [b] Converted to $ at 2018 average exchange rates. AE = advanced economies; EM = emerging markets.
Sources: Country authorities; IMF staff calculations.

base to 'sugar sweetened beverages' (at a 50 per cent rate), electronic devices and equipment for smoking (100 per cent), and liquids used by the latter (100 per cent). Revenues from excises reached 0.5 per cent of GDP in 2019. These revenues are high by international standards, reflecting the high rates applied, but would be expected to decline over time as awareness about the health risks of consuming these products increases.

Levy on Expatriate Workers and Their Dependants

A levy on expatriate workers was introduced in 2011 with the objective of supporting the development and employment of Saudi workers. The initial levy was SAR200 a month per expatriate employee in companies where expatriate employees outnumbered Saudi employees. The revenues were used to cover the cost of various labour market and training programmes implemented by the Human Resources Development Fund.

FBP 2016 expanded the scope and size of the levy. It introduced a schedule for increasing the levy starting in 2018 through to 2020, as well as a new levy on dependants. The levy on expatriate workers was set to increase over the three-year period to SAR700 for companies where the number of expatriate workers was equal to the number of Saudi workers and to SAR800 for companies where expatriate workers exceeded the number if Saudi workers (Table 3.2).

The fees on dependants were started in July 2017 at a rate of SAR100 a month per person and are set to rise to SAR400 per month this year. Revenue from the expatriate levy has been substantial—1 per cent of GDP in 2018 rising to 1.5 per cent of GDP in 2019.

The expatriate levy policy has, however, run into some challenges. The increased cost burden has led to a substantial decline in expatriate workers—as well as their families—which has negatively impacted non-oil growth. To mitigate some of these adverse effects the government offered in 2019 to reimburse some of the fees to companies that had a number of Saudi

Table 3.2 Expatriate levy (monthly payments, SAR)

	Levy on dependants of expatriates (July onwards)	Levy where no. of expatriates equal to no. of Saudis in a company (January onwards)	Levy where more expatriates than Saudis in a company (January onwards)
2017	100		
2018	200	300	400
2019	300	500	600
2020	400	700	800

Source: Ministry of Finance.

employees higher or equal to their number of expatriates. Further, fees on expatriate workers employed in the industrial sector have been waived since 1 October 2019 as part of a national strategy to develop the industrial sector.

Energy (and Water) Price Reforms

A first round of energy price reforms took place in December 2015.[11] Gasoline, diesel, gas, and electricity prices were increased by between 10 and 134 per cent. Water prices were also increased, but they ran into problems because of issues with the metering infrastructure and were suspended. FBP 2016 laid out a roadmap for the phased increase in energy prices over the following years, 2017–20. By 2020, all product prices—for both households and non-households—were to be increased to their respective reference prices. However, as part of the decision to slow the pace of fiscal consolidation, the FBP Update 2018 extended the energy price reform timeline to 2025.

A second round of energy price reforms was implemented on 1 January 2018. Gasoline prices were increased further and the consumer subsidy on Octane 95 was effectively eliminated. Electricity prices were also raised, and the pricing tiers simplified. The tariffs reflected the average supply cost of electricity, but still contained a consumer subsidy because the electricity company receives fuel inputs at a subsidized price. During 2019 and 2020, the subsidy on Octane 91 gasoline was eliminated and gasoline prices were linked to movements in export prices through monthly indexation (Figure 3.10). This indexation, however, was suspended in mid-2021.

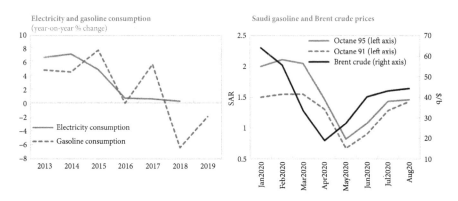

Figure 3.10 Energy consumption, 2013–19, and gasoline prices, 2020

Sources: Country authorities; Argaam; IMF staff calculations.

[11] For a more detailed discussion of energy price reforms, see IMF, 'Saudi Arabia, 2017 Article IV Consultation', p. 9, and IMF, 'Saudi Arabia, 2018 Article IV Consultation—Press Release and Staff Report', IMF Country Report 18/263 (Washington, DC: International Monetary Fund, 2018), pp. 60–7.

Higher energy prices appear to be having an impact on domestic energy consumption. Per capita consumption of electricity and gasoline have declined since 2015. While slower non-oil growth has also contributed, the new pricing environment is having an impact on consumption levels.

Expenditure Policy and Reforms

FBP 2016 recognized the need to contain government expenditures as part of the fiscal adjustment effort and set ambitious objectives that targeted a slowdown in the annual growth of nominal expenditures to zero by 2020. Yet, while significant reductions in spending, particularly on the capital side, were initially made, once oil prices started rising, the spending envelope expanded again. In 2020, spending in nominal terms was only just below its peak level in 2014. The demands of the COVID-19 shock understandably put renewed upward pressure on spending in 2020, although this abated in 2021. The 2022 budget again projected a lower medium-term expenditure path, signalling renewed commitment to containing spending.

Most of the expenditure adjustment since 2015 has been the result of a reduction in capital spending. Overall spending has grown at an average annual rate of 1.4 per cent, driven by growth in current expenditures (3 per cent a year), while capital expenditures have contracted by 5.3 per

Table 3.3 GCC countries—expenditure developments, 2014–19

	Saudi Arabia	Qatar	UAE	Kuwait	Oman	Bahrain
	% change, 2014–19					
Total expenditure	−7	−14	−4	5	−12	35
Current expenses	8	−21	−6	6	−6	36
Net acquisition of non-financial assets	−47	−1	23	−4	−35	25
	Change between 2014 and 2019 (% of non-oil GDP)					
Total expenditure	−18.3	−17.2	−9.5	−22.8	−24.2	1.4
Current expenses	−6.9	−14.0	−9.7	−19.3	−14.5	1.6
Net acquisition of non-financial assets	−11.4	−3.2	0.2	−3.5	−9.8	−0.2
	Change between 2014 and 2019 (% of GDP)					
Total expenditure	−4.6	0.2	−2.6	8.5	−3.2	4.7
Current expenses	1.0	−1.6	−3.1	8.0	0.0	4.4
Net acquisition of non-financial assets	−5.6	1.9	0.5	0.4	−3.1	0.3

Sources: Country authorities and IMF staff calculations.

cent annually. The growth in current expenditures was led by the wage bill (2.6 per cent a year) and spending on social benefits (28 per cent a year). The shares of current expenditures and the wage bill in total expenditures increased from 72 per cent and 35 per cent in 2015 to 84 per cent and 48 per cent, respectively, in 2019.

While the results vary with the metric used (change in nominal terms, change in percentage of non-oil GDP, change in percentage of GDP), the broad picture is that the size of the expenditure adjustment in Saudi Arabia since 2014 has been broadly similar to other GCC countries (Table 3.3 and Figure 3.11). The adjustment, however, has relied more on reducing capital spending than in other GCC countries, where there has been a greater focus on reducing current expenditures. Compared with the Organization for Economic Cooperation and Development (OECD) and emerging market (EM) countries, expenditure adjustment during the period has been much more sizeable, which is unsurprising given that these countries have not experienced the size of revenue shock that Saudi Arabia and the other GCC countries have (Figure 3.12). Compared to other Middle East and North Africa (MENA) oil exporters,[12] the adjustment in the GCC has been less, although the disparate nature of the countries in this group reduces the usefulness of this comparison.

A broader comparison indicates that government spending is in line with the EM average and well below the OECD average as a percentage of GDP,

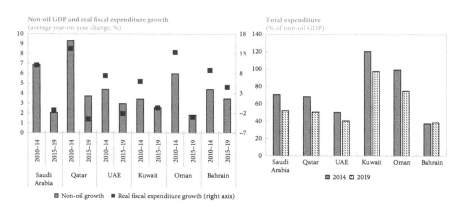

Figure 3.11 GCC expenditure developments, 2014–19

Sources: Country authorities; IMF staff calculations.

---

[12] Other MENA oil exporters are Algeria, Iran, Iraq, Yemen, and Libya.

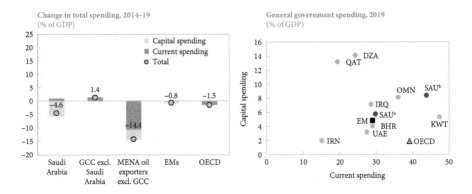

Figure 3.12 Saudi Arabia versus global comparators, 2014–19

Note: In the left panel, simple average is shown for GCC excluding Saudi Arabia and MENA oil exporters excluding GCC. In the right panel, SAU[a] is measured by GDP, and SAU[b] is measured by non-oil GDP.

Sources: Country authorities; IMF staff calculations.

but is well above both of these comparators as a share of non-oil GDP.[13] In terms of the composition of spending, it is striking how high the share of wage bill and capital spending is in Saudi Arabia (Figure 3.13).

The Bureau of Spending Rationalization, later renamed the Center for Spending Efficiency (CSR), was created in 2016 to identify opportunities for savings in both capital and operational expenditures of key line ministries. It has focused on the efficiency with which public resources are being procured

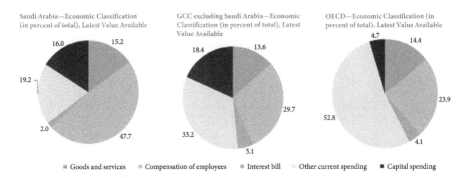

Figure 3.13 Economic classification of Saudi Arabia versus global comparators, latest available (% of total)

Sources: Country authorities; IMF staff calculations.

[13] Arguments can be made for both comparators (share of total and non-oil GDP). On balance, IMF staff believe the comparator to non-oil GDP is more appropriate given that government spending is almost entirely directed at the non-oil economy and that there are longer-term uncertainties about the potential output and revenues from the oil sector.

and utilized, including revisiting the rationale for projects that were in the capital expenditure pipeline, introducing more stringent assessments of new projects, and revamping public procurement processes including through standardizing procurement on common-use items, formulating standard procurement templates, and promoting development objectives (including local content and promotion of small and medium enterprises). A new public procurement law has been introduced.

Initial efforts to reduce government expenditures in 2015–16 led to the sizeable accumulation of payment arrears to contractors and consequent pressure on private sector finances. The emergence of these arrears empha-sized the need for the MoF to strengthen the system of expenditure commit-ment and control (which it has done with the introduction of Etimad—see below).

Wage Bill

The government wage bill is high (Figure 3.14). It averaged around 47 per cent of total expenditures and 25 per cent of non-oil GDP during 2015–19. Efforts to contain the wage bill have so far had limited suc-cess. Of the three saving measures introduced in 2016—shifting from the Islamic to Gregorian calendar for monthly wage payments (thus saving the thirteenth-month wage payment every three years), removing the annual

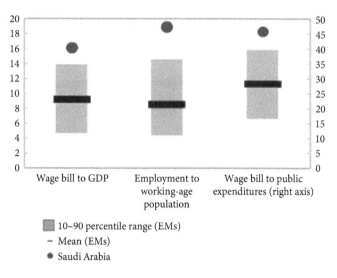

Figure 3.14 Benchmarking of the wage bill and employment, 2018 or latest available (%)

Sources: Country authorities; IMF staff calculations.

step pay increase, and cutting employee allowances and bonuses—the latter was reversed relatively quickly. Furthermore, in January 2018, a royal decree introduced Cost of Living Allowances (COLA) for a broad range of Saudi nationals including government employees, initially for one year but later extended into 2019 and the first half of 2020. These payments were removed in June 2020.

During the period since 2015, the government has limited the growth in the size of the civil service workforce to 2 per cent. However, at the same time the government has also employed more people outside the civil service structure as it has sought to introduce new talent into government ministries and agencies to give impetus to the Vision 2030 reforms. Further, significant employment in the military and security services is paid for from the central budget, and information on how the number of employees in these services has evolved is not available. Nevertheless, estimates of employment of Saudi nationals in the government sector suggest it is high as a share of total national employment.

Capital Expenditures

Saudi Arabia has good-quality public infrastructure but appears to have spent more on average than other countries to achieve this (Figure 3.15). While the reduction in capital spending in recent years has reduced its share of GDP to around 6 per cent, there still appears to be room for improving the efficiency of capital expenditures while preserving high-quality infrastructure (the further reduction in capital spending outlined in the 2021 budget would bring spending into line with that in other countries with similar

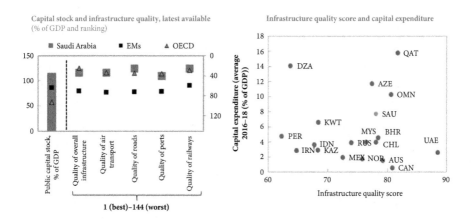

Figure 3.15 Capital spending and quality of infrastructure

Source: IMF FAD Expenditure Assessment Tool.

infrastructure quality). In this regard, reforms led by the CSR to improve expenditure planning, prioritization, and project selection play an important role, as do government reforms aimed at leveraging private sector capital and investments via privatization and public–private partnerships (PPPs) which are beginning to pick up pace. It is essential that an effective legal and regulatory framework and sufficient management capacity are in place to help control risks and contingencies that the government may incur as a result of PPP operations.

Social Assistance and the Citizen's Account

Saudi Arabia has an extensive social assistance system that covers a wide range of beneficiaries through multiple schemes. These include standard non-contributory cash transfers or in-kind benefits programmes—including the income guarantee programme, social care programmes for orphans and people with disabilities, the national school programme (Takaful), support for charities, and the social housing programme.

Against this backdrop, a review of social assistance programmes has been undertaken with the aim of improving the targeting of the social safety net and generating savings for the budget. The current benefit system is fragmented and poorly targeted, with different programmes managed by different government entities and benefits targeted to whole groups such as widows or retirees rather than being based on need.

The Citizen's Account (CA) programme, a cash transfer programme designed to compensate low- and middle-income Saudi households for the cost of the reforms, was launched in December 2017 ahead of the introduction of the VAT and the second round of energy price increases. It aims to protect the purchasing power of Saudis from the higher retail prices that resulted from the VAT, energy prices, and the expatriate levy reforms. Registration to the CA was open to all Saudi households, and eligibility was assessed against three criteria—household composition, residency registration, and citizenship. The benchmark compensation level was calibrated on fair energy and food consumption levels of representative households. The monthly cash transfer decrease in line with household income. The CA programme covers more Saudis than any other social support programme in place.

The budgetary cost of the CA is around 1 per cent of GDP. During 2020, the average number of beneficiaries declined from over 12 million in the six months to June, to around 10.7 million in July as reforms were introduced to enhance the targeting of the programme and ensure that the eligibility criteria were more effectively enforced.

Sectoral Spending

Spending inefficiencies are evident in some sectors. For example, in the education sector, student performance does not match spending levels (Figure 3.16). This suggests that efficiency gains could be realized through better resource allocation while raising the quality of education services. Reforms to improve the efficiency of education spending will cut across and be informed by measures already discussed, particularly as employment levels in the education sector are probably higher than needed for effective service delivery.

Reforms of the Fiscal Framework and Institutions

Saudi Arabia has made important progress in strengthening its fiscal framework. Reforms have focused on strengthening fiscal institutions, improving fiscal transparency, and enhancing the budget process. While ongoing reforms have led to tangible progress in improving budget preparation, reporting, and monitoring, reforms of budget execution have lagged, and budget outturns continue to reflect weaknesses in fiscal management.

Reforms to strengthen budget institutions have focused on enhancing fiscal policy analysis and the budget process. The main actors in charge of budget preparation and execution at the MoF are the Budget and the Treasury Deputyships. The former oversees budget preparation and implementation, and the latter, accounting and processing payments. With the onset of reforms, the MoF created new supporting units that have matured over time

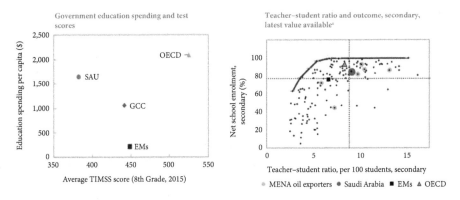

Figure 3.16 Education spending and outcomes

Note: [a] Teacher–student ratio means the number of teachers per 100 students.
Sources: IMF FAD Expenditure Assessment Tool; World Bank; World Health Organization, HALE data; EPD pension database.

becoming deputyships or national centres and playing key roles in fiscal policy analysis and/or management.

For example, the Macro Fiscal Policy Deputyship (MFPD) was established as the Macro Fiscal Policy Unit in 2016 and takes the lead role in economic and fiscal policy analysis. Its mandate focuses on improving budget monitoring and reporting, enhancing fiscal policy analysis, and developing a Medium-Term Fiscal Framework (MTFF). Over time the MFPD has also taken the lead in improving fiscal transparency and data quality and in producing scenario analysis and assessing fiscal risks.

Progress has been made in enhancing fiscal transparency, albeit coming from an exceptionally low base. The MoF published FBP 2016, outlining for the first time its medium-term fiscal strategy, and it has been publishing updates since within or separately from Budget Statements. Further, Budget Statements since 2018 have presented medium-term fiscal projections and a qualitative discussion of some risks to the outlook. Other new fiscal publications include the Pre-Budget Statement and the Citizens' Budget. The MoF has also published quarterly budget performance reports since 2017 and published End-of-Year Budget Reports in early 2018 and 2019 (for the 2017 and 2018 fiscal years). Fiscal data are now published in accordance with the IMF's *Government Finance Statistics Manual* (2014).

One of the objectives is to improve Saudi Arabia's score in the Open Budget Index. The score increased from 1 (out of 100) in the 2017 report to 18 in the 2019 report, ranking Saudi Arabia 99th out of 117 countries covered. This indicates that progress has been made, but there is significant scope for further gains. Opportunities for further reforms include more detailed reporting of fiscal execution, fiscal risk analysis, publication of audited financial statements of the central government (then to be expanded to extra-budgetary funds and corporations), and wider public participation in the budget process.

Reforms to improve budget preparation and develop the MTFF started with preparation of the 2016 Budget. The use of a top-down and bottom-up approach in budget discussions/negotiations started with the preparation of the 2018 Budget. The MFPD, working closely with the FBP team in the MoF, have taken the lead in developing medium-term macroeconomic and fiscal projections, and fiscal targets have been constantly reviewed (and updated) to reflect ongoing macroeconomic developments and fiscal policy adjustments. Ongoing work to develop the MTFF continues, including to develop different fiscal policy scenarios and to strengthen fiscal risk assessments and analysis.

The MoF launched in 2018 a digital platform, Etimad, to improve the expenditure management process. Etimad aims to better link the various stages of the expenditure management process from budget allocation through to final payment, increasing transparency and improving the monitoring of spending, unifying financial service procedures, ensuring timeliness of payment, and enabling broader access to public tenders.

Fiscal Financing

At the time of the decline in oil prices in 2014, the government had not issued new debt for many years. Consequently, there was no system in place for modern debt management. While the government could use its large deposits at the Saudi Arabian Monetary Authority to finance the fiscal deficit that emerged in 2015, it realized that it would also need to begin issuing debt again and established the Debt Management Office (DMO) within the MoF in 2016 to do this.

The DMO has developed a national debt management framework and manages borrowing operations. Its key responsibilities encompass developing and implementing the Annual Borrowing Plan, developing the Medium-Term Debt Strategy, and managing borrowing operations and guarantees to support the Kingdom's public financing. The DMO later became the National Debt Management Center (NDMC) to reflect its importance within the government structure. The government initially set out a goal of keeping government debt below 30 per cent of GDP and this was raised to 50 per cent of GDP in early 2020.

Borrowing has comprised both international and domestic issuances, traditional and *sukuk*, and loans from international banks. At the end of 2019, total government debt stood at 23 per cent of GDP, with 55 per cent issued domestically and 45 per cent internationally.

The NDMC has focused on developing the domestic government debt market. Reforms have included the establishment of a primary dealer system, the issuance of instruments with longer maturities (a forty-year *sukuk* has been issued), the listing of all government debt on the Tadawul, issuance in smaller denominations to attract retail investors, and allowing foreign investors to buy domestically issued government debt. Liquidity in the government debt market increased substantially during 2020.

The NDMC is coordinating the issuance of international debt by other government-related borrowers to ensure the market does not become oversupplied. Further, led by the MFPD, and in coordination with the NDMC and the Public Investment Fund (PIF), a broader asset–liability management framework for the public sector is being developed with the aim of ensuring that investment and borrowing decisions of the public sector are well coordinated and that the full risk and return profile of public sector financial assets and liabilities is understood.

Medium- to Long-Term Fiscal Targets

Gauging the necessary size of fiscal adjustment over the medium to long term is not easy in an oil-exporting country such as Saudi Arabia where most revenues still come from exhaustible natural resources, where the balance sheet is strong, but where future trends are likely to see a gradual move to reduce the growth in the global consumption of oil. Traditional metrics for judging fiscal sustainability through stabilization of public debt at or below a threshold deemed sustainable provide information for an oil-exporting country but do not tell the whole story.

Remaining Challenges and Next Steps

Saudi Arabia has made substantial progress with its fiscal reforms. The non-oil revenue base has been broadened, domestic energy prices raised, expenditure management strengthened, the Citizen's Account programme introduced, fiscal transparency improved, and the institutional basis and analysis of fiscal policy strengthened.

Looking forward, key challenges remain. Saudi Arabia is likely to record a fiscal surplus in 2022 given the path of oil prices expected by financial markets. This will be a turnaround from the 2015–21 period. Nevertheless, the experience of the past decade has indicated that the only thing that is guaranteed is that the oil price will remain volatile. Fiscal policy needs to be conducted in a way that accounts for such likely volatility. Ensuring fiscal sustainability in the medium to longer term means that efforts to raise new sources of revenue, contain government spending and improve its efficiency, and strengthen the overall management of government finances and assets and liabilities will need to continue. At the same time, getting the pace of fiscal adjustment right will be critical. Too rapid an adjustment will stall growth; too slow an adjustment will unnecessarily expose the fiscal position to risks from a sharp and sudden reversal of oil prices in the future.

Non-oil revenue reforms will need to continue to reduce budgetary dependence on oil. The tripling of the VAT rate to 15 per cent will bring considerable additional revenues once private consumption has fully recovered from the pandemic. The increase in the VAT rate has brought Saudi Arabia more in line with other countries in the region and EMs but has taken it out of line with other GCC countries where the VAT rate is 5 per cent or VAT has not yet been introduced. The differences in VAT rates raise risks of revenue leakages which will need to be carefully monitored.

Other aspects of the tax system remain underdeveloped. While ultimately the revenue-raising needs of the government will be determined by the desired size of government spending, decisions on the financial saving goals, and the expected path of oil revenues, the absence of a personal income tax and limited taxation of real estate is striking. Revenue reforms should seek to introduce a progressive tax system with income and property taxes supplemented by excises on high-end consumption goods. On the corporate side, an evaluation of the effective tax incidence on domestic companies (subject to *zakat*) and foreign companies (subject to corporate income tax) would be useful.

Energy price reforms have advanced substantially on the household side, but less so on the corporate side where businesses structured around the availability of cheap energy inputs will be particularly challenged to remain viable with higher input costs. Further, water price reforms—with a large share of water generated through desalination which benefits from cheap energy inputs—are an area that still needs to be tackled. These reforms need to be completed, but businesses should receive temporary and transparent support during a predetermined and announced adjustment period, provided they are expected to remain viable in the post-adjustment higher price environment.

Improving the composition of budgetary spending and its efficiency is another difficult challenge. The government wage bill has remained untouched during the reform period. The removal of the COLA in 2020 was a helpful first step, but a more comprehensive rationalization of employment levels and streamlining of wage benefits, including for government employees outside the civil service structure, will be crucial to containing the growth of the wage bill. This should be based on a full review of the staffing needs of ministries and agencies to ensure they have adequate staff for efficient service provision, but not excess employment. The government should no longer be the employer of first and last resort. Rather the focus should be on efficient service delivery. Wage scales should be reviewed to ensure they do not disincentivize private sector employment, while ensuring that the government is able to attract the skills it needs. This is likely to require some steepening of the pay curve with lower-skilled employees paid less than at present and higher-skilled ones more. Lastly, allowances should be reviewed to ensure they are meeting clear and current needs.

More broadly, a public expenditure review would help benchmark spending against international comparators. Spending on both education and infrastructure appears to be high given needs/outcomes, and a more granular understanding of the main components of this spending would help guide reforms. Moreover, a more integrated public investment plan, clear cost–benefit analysis, and stricter project prioritization would increase spending efficiency in this area.

Protecting the less well-off against the costs of reforms is critical. The challenge is to boost support to those in need while streamlining the fragmented social safety net in place. The Citizen's Account is an important initiative that has helped cushion the effects of the reforms on households, and recent efforts to target this support better are welcome. As reforms continue, the CA should be used to channel support to those in need rather than the broader and more ad hoc support provided in early 2018 through the cost-of-living allowances.

Strengthening the medium-term orientation of the budget process and reducing the procyclicality of fiscal policy is essential. An annual spending envelope that is consistent with a budget target that excludes oil revenues, and which is anchored in a sustainable MTFF could contribute to reducing the procyclicality of government spending and in turn encourage more sustained private sector investment and non-oil growth. This will need to be supported by further improvements in budget execution, spending controls, and accountability. Disclosure and transparency practices should also be brought in line with international standards.

Lastly, the central government is only one part of the public sector. Numerous extra-budgetary institutions and state-owned enterprises (SOEs) remain outside the budget process with the risk that fiscal spending migrates outside the central budget. Over time, the coverage of fiscal data should be expanded to include extra-budgetary funds and SOEs. This will give a fuller assessment of the impact of the public sector on the economy and how public resources are being utilized. Ultimately, the objective should be to develop a consolidated set of public sector accounts including a balance sheet. The importance of this is growing as the role of the PIF, in particular, expands.

4

Monetary Policy, Banking, and the Financial System

Rodney Wilson

Introduction

There have been significant recent changes in monetary and banking policy in Saudi Arabia, which contrast with the continuity of the last seven decades when the main focus was on financial stability. Under the Saudi Central Bank Law of 2020, the Saudi Arabian Monetary Authority (SAMA) was renamed the Saudi Central Bank to align its nomenclature with international norms, but within the Kingdom it will continue to be designated as SAMA, the name which has also been retained in this chapter. It remains to be seen whether the new policy remit, which includes SAMA promoting economic growth, is a step forwards or backwards. Growth brings economic benefits, and may be a political imperative for Saudi Arabia, but it can also result in instability and social disruption. This chapter examines monetary policy and the financial sector, including banking, capital markets, and insurance. How far are the financial institutions equipped to facilitate the attainment of the Kingdom's Vision 2030 goals? Saudi Arabia is moving into an era when both the state and private sector are rent seeking and economic power is shifting, but in what direction?

Rather than competing over rent extraction, the state seems to support a greater role for the private sector in a diversifying economy. Can the existing financial infrastructure accommodate these changes, or is more fundamental reform needed? Is the allocation of funding by the banks determined by customer demand, or is the government trying to influence who and what gets financed? There has been some blurring of responsibilities between SAMA and the Ministry of Finance. Looking forwards, how independent will the central bank be in practice and has it been strengthened or weakened by the reorganization of 2020?

Rodney Wilson, *Monetary Policy, Banking, and the Financial System*. In: *The Economy of Saudi Arabia in the 21st Century.* Edited by: John Sfakianakis, Oxford University Press. © Rodney Wilson (2024).
DOI: 10.1093/oso/9780198863878.003.0005

Stabilization

The aim of monetary and banking policy over the last seven decades in Saudi Arabia has been to ensure economic stability. SAMA has been very conservative and rightly cautious ever since its establishment in 1952.[1] This approach has undoubtedly enhanced confidence, both domestically and internationally, in the Kingdom's financial institutions.[2] The major challenge throughout the period has been that domestic economic activity has been dependent on oil production and international oil prices, neither of which the government can fully control despite the Kingdom's aspirations to be a swing producer.[3] SAMA has, however, successfully mitigated the effects of external shocks on the domestic economy and has acquired extensive experience in neutralizing monetary inflows and outflows.[4]

The significance of the Saudi Central Bank Law of 2020 is the clarification of SAMA's regulatory role and responsibilities. Most important is the affirmation of SAMA's independence in determining monetary policy and choosing what instruments to use. The emphasis in the new law continues to be on financial stability, but, as indicated in the introduction, the remit of SAMA now explicitly includes supporting economic growth to achieve the Vision 2030 objectives.[5]

Central banks do not normally have mandates to promote economic growth, as this could conflict with the objective of price stability. It is unclear how SAMA will promote economic growth, and what policy instruments could be used. The Deputy Governor, Ayman Alsayari, stated in an interview that financial innovation could foster higher growth, but the evidence of this in the empirical literature is mixed, and during recessions it might actually weaken the banks.[6] A precondition is having a pool of entrepreneurial talent, as is the case in many Asian countries, with the entrepreneurs rather

[1] M. Al-Jasser and A. Banafe, 'Monetary Policy Instruments and Procedures in Saudi Arabia', Bank for International Settlements Policy Paper 5 (1999), pp. 203–17.

[2] M. A. Ramady, 'Evolving Banking Regulation and Supervision: A Case Study of the Saudi Arabian Monetary Agency (SAMA)', *International Journal of Islamic and Middle Eastern Finance and Management* 2, no. 3 (2009), pp. 235–50.

[3] A. Al-Hamidy, 'Monetary Policy in Saudi Arabia', Bank for International Settlements Policy Paper 57 (2011), pp. 301–5.

[4] A. Banafe and R. Macleod, *The Saudi Arabian Monetary Agency, 1952–2016: Central Bank of Oil* (New York: Springer, 2017).

[5] M. Martin and A. Abu Omar, 'Saudi Arabia Broadens Central Bank's Mandate to Promote Economic Growth', Bloomberg (26 November 2020).

[6] T. Beck, T. Chen, C. Lin, and F. M. Song, 'Financial Innovation: The Bright and the Dark Sides', *Journal of Banking and Finance* 72 (2016), pp. 28–51.

than the banks taking the initiative. There is evidence that Saudi Arabia has indigenous entrepreneurial talent, but its further cultivation will take time, and 2030 is possibly too soon.[7]

SAMA never has a specific inflation target, nor is there any growth target. This is fortunate as it cannot therefore be blamed for missing targets. Nevertheless there are concerns that the reputation of SAMA has been undermined by recent developments and the increasing centralization of power in the Kingdom. The independence of SAMA is achieved by its being directly accountable to the King, rather than to the Finance Ministry or the Ministry of Economy and Planning. Economic and financial power appeared to be in a state of flux between 2020–2022 with the Minister of Finance, Mohammed Al-Jaadan, also serving as the acting Minister of Economy and Planning. In 2022, Faisal Alibrahim was appointed Minister of Economy and Planning. How SAMA fits into this structure is unclear, and uncertainty deters investment, which was 50 per cent less than anticipated in 2019. The weakness of SAMA was revealed in March and April 2020 when it was ordered to transfer SAR150 billion of its foreign exchange reserves to the Kingdom's Public Investment Fund (PIF). This funding was supposed to be to help restart the economy following the COVID-19 pandemic, with the aim according to Al-Jadaan being to promote economic diversification, increase local content, and support the growth of the private sector in line with Vision 2030. Before disbursement, Al-Jadaan argued, the funds could earn a return rather than being held as liquid assets by SAMA with no return. The likelihood of SAMA having the funds returned is zero, as their use will save on general government spending which is increasingly financed by borrowing. SAMA performed competently in managing the Kingdom's reserves over many decades. With the downgrading of SAMA's role and much of the responsibility now in the hands of the PIF, which has less experience, it remains to be seen how well the substantial funds are managed.

SAMA serves as the regulator of the banking system in the Kingdom, which has proved remarkably stable as a result of the strict monitoring of financial risks, particularly by focusing on liquidity and capital adequacy, in line with international best practice in implementing the Basel protocols of the Bank for International Settlements (BIS).[8] This will be discussed in more detail

---

[7] M. R. Khan, 'Mapping the Entrepreneurship Ecosystem of Saudi Arabia', *World Journal of Entrepreneurship, Management and Sustainable Development* 9, no. 1 (2013), pp. 28–54.

[8] A. Y. Saif-Alyousf, A. Saha, and R. Md-Rus, 'Profitability of Saudi Commercial Banks: A Comparative Evaluation between Domestic and Foreign Banks Using Capital Adequacy, Asset Quality, Management

in this chapter.[9] The structure and durability of the banking sector will be reviewed, with a focus on the two largest institutions, Al-Ahli Bank, also designated the National Commercial Bank, and the Al Rajhi Group, the largest Islamic bank in the world in terms of assets.

Given the size and complexity of the economy of Saudi Arabia and the development of its financial markets, it is appropriate that a separate institution, the Capital Market Authority (CMA), has been established to oversee corporate issuance and stock market trading. Its role will also be discussed in detail. There is great interest in the Saudi Arabian stock market, the Tadāwul, among both domestic and international investors. There have been several significant privatizations, including that of the Saudi Basic Industries Corporation (SABIC) and Saudi Aramco, the oil producing company. The Tadāwul is the ninth largest stock market in the world in terms of market capitalization and the largest in the Middle East with 204 publicly listed companies.

Monetary Policy and Inflation

The major objective of monetary policy is to stabilize inflation at a low level, although as already indicated, there is no formal target rate. SAMA has considerable discretion, but monetary policy is much influenced by the fiscal stance of the Ministry of Finance. Ultimately, it is fiscal policy which is autonomous and monetary policy which has to be accommodating. In other words, fiscal policy determines monetary policy but not vice versa. From a monetary perspective the emphasis on controlling inflation is to ensure that investors, both local and foreign, have confidence in the riyal. Equally important, if not more so, is the need to shield local consumers from the effects of inflation and ensure that their purchasing power is maintained rather than being eaten away by higher prices.

In practice, although inflation has been relatively low by regional standards, it has been quite variable, rising to a peak of almost 10 per cent in the aftermath of the global financial crisis in 2008.[10] In recent years, inflation has been lower; indeed it moved into negative territory in 2017, with prices declining by 0.84 per cent. Subsequently, inflation jumped to 6.2 per cent in 2020 due to value added tax tripling in order to raise government

Quality, Earning Ability and Liquidity Parameters', *International Journal of Economics and Financial Issues* 7, no. 2 (2017), pp. 477–84.

[9] A. Polat and H. Al-Khalaf, 'What Determines Capital Adequacy in the Banking System of the Kingdom of Saudi Arabia? A Panel Data Analysis of Tadawul Banks', *Journal of Applied Finance and Banking* 4, no. 5 (2014), pp. 27–43.

[10] M. A. Ramady, 'External and Internal Determinants of Inflation: A Case Study of Saudi Arabia', *Middle East Journal of Economics and Finance* 2, no. 1–2 (2009), pp. 25–38.

revenue and reduce the fiscal deficit. This was a one-off tax increase, however, with inflation soon declining again. The more important question is:
what drives inflation in the Kingdom, demand pressures or supply-side constraints? The answer is both, and this means that the longer-term outlook for
inflation is less favourable than in the past.[11] There are some positive factors, especially the fixed exchange rate with the United States (US) dollar
and the open trading regime. The former helps prevent imported inflation
as if the riyal were not pegged it would be likely to depreciate, increasing
import prices in terms of local currency. The free trade regime with no tariffs
on imported goods ensures that this is not a contributor to inflation. Rather
than relying on tariffs as a source of revenue, Saudi Arabia has adopted the
advice of the International Monetary Fund (IMF) which favours value added
taxation.

Inflation in the Kingdom comes from two main sources, distribution
margins and property prices.[12] The policy of replacing expatriate workers
with Saudi nationals helps create job opportunities and is an economic
and political imperative. As in many other economies, high unemployment among school and university leavers aspiring to join the workforce
inevitable fuels social tensions. Many Saudi nationals are employed in the
public sector, but because it cannot absorb increasing numbers, the Ministry of Labour is encouraging the private sector to recruit local citizens.
However, to make these jobs more attractive, the minimum wage for local
citizens is twice as high as that for migrant workers. Inevitably these additional labour costs have to be passed on to customers, hence rising consumer
price inflation.

Residential and commercial property prices declined from their peak in
2014, with the index falling from 100 to stabilize around 80 in 2019. Expatriates leaving the Kingdom accounted for much of the decline in the rental
market. However, given the government's aim of increasing the percentage
of local nationals owning property from 50 per cent in 2018 to over 70
per cent by the end of the National Transformation Program and National
Vision 2030, this will undoubtedly result in property price increases.[13] In
Saudi Arabia, as everywhere else, housing is seen as not only a family need,

---

[11] A. M. Osman, A. O. Ahmed, M. N. Eltahir, A. S. Mohamed, O. S. Shidwan, and M. Ghada, 'Investigating the Causes of Inflation in Saudi Arabia: An Application of the Autoregressive Distributed Lag (ARDL)
Model', *International Journal of Applied Engineering Research* 14, no. 21 (2019), pp. 3980–6.
[12] D. Obaid, T. Johnston, and N. M. Khanfar, 'Monetary Policy and the House Price Index: A VAR
Analysis for Saudi Arabia', *Journal of Business Studies Quarterly* 10, no. 1 (2020), pp. 12–21.
[13] E. Mulliner and M. Algrnas, 'Preferences for Housing Attributes in Saudi Arabia: A Comparison
between Consumers' and Property Practitioners' Views', *Cities* 83 (2018), pp. 152–64.

but an investment in the future.[14] However, if prices are falling it is a poor investment. Therefore, moderately rising property prices are beneficial for the market, and hence are not likely to result in SAMA applying the monetary brakes.

Instruments of Monetary Policy

The most important operational instruments of monetary policy in Saudi Arabia are the commercial bank deposits with SAMA. These are governed by Article 7 of the Banking Control Law of 1966 which ensures that commercial banks have adequate liquidity. The default provision is for the banks' statutory deposit with SAMA to be 15 per cent of its deposit liabilities, with variation between 10 and 17.5 per cent permitted. There is, in other words, not a fixed liquidity ratio under the law; rather SAMA can ask the banks to increase or reduce their deposits according to its monetary stance. If, for instance, SAMA wishes to dampen inflation, it will ask the banks to increase their liquid deposits, resulting in the banks having less funding to make available to their customers. This in turn reduces demand in the economy and curtails inflationary pressures. If, alternatively, SAMA wants to stimulate the economy through a monetary expansion, the banks reduce their deposits and make increased funding available to their customers.

It should be noted that SAMA has considerable flexibility to vary what is appropriate for each bank, which depends on the bank's financial circumstances and not only on the monetary stance of SAMA.[15] The processes of monetary expansion and contraction involve informal consultations, although in the last instance the banks must take the action demanded by SAMA as regulator of the banking system. Under the Banking Control Law of 1966, in addition to the statutory reserve requirement banks are obliged to maintain a further liquid reserve of 15 per cent in the form of cash, gold, and assets convertible into cash within a period of thirty days. This can be raised to 20 per cent if SAMA has liquidity concerns. Article 7 was maintained in the revised Banking Control Law of 2008, which did not affect the substance of the earlier law but introduced higher penalties for non-compliance.

The major innovation in monetary instruments in Saudi Arabia was the introduction of repurchase agreements (repos) to facilitate government

---

[14] K. I. Batayneh and A. M. Al-Malki, 'The Relationship between House Prices and Stock Prices in Saudi Arabia: An Empirical Analysis', *International Journal of Economics and Finance* 7, no. 2 (2015), pp. 156–67.
[15] Banafe and Macleod, 'The Saudi Arabian Monetary Agency'.

borrowing from 1986. Most were in the form of reverse repos, a short-term agreement to purchase securities in order to sell them back at a slightly higher price. Repos and reverse repos are used for short-term borrowing and lending, often overnight. SAMA, like other central banks, uses reverse repos to add to the money supply via open market operations.[16] Note the repo rate is the percentage which the commercial banks pay to SAMA for borrowing and the reverse repo rate is the percentage cost of funds obtained by SAMA from the commercial banks. Repos and reverse repos are used extensively by the Federal Reserve in the United States of America (USA) and by central banks in Europe, China and Japan, but they are less used in the Middle East. The Saudi Arabian repo rate fell to 0.5 per cent in April 2020, which was substantially below the US dollar rate, prompting outward financial flows. These reduced the Saudi Arabian government's ability to borrow and subsequently repos were temporally withdrawn.

From the perspective of Saudi Arabian banks, the attraction of repos is that they provide a return, even if it is modest.[17] Repos have the same liquidity characteristics as funds parked overnight with SAMA that do not provide a return. If sukuk—Shari'ah-compliant, asset-backed securities—were allowed to be used for statutory reserves, or more likely as part of the additional liquid assets held by Saudi Arabian banks, this could result in higher returns. Such a possibility would be welcomed by Islamic financial institutions in the Kingdom. In Bahrain, this innovation has been adopted, but in Saudi Arabia there is a reluctance to follow, largely because sukuk are regarded as carrying more risk than repos or reverse repos. Sukuk are becoming more popular as capital market investments, but the main buyers are investment companies and private investors. The development of sukuk issuance will be discussed later in the chapter.

Although SAMA was founded in 1952 as a state institution, it has sought to maintain independence from government, partly by emphasizing its technocratic credentials and highly apolitical remit. The Ministry of Finance determines fiscal policy, but SAMA enjoys a considerable amount of autonomy on monetary policy, including on risk management in the banking sector. It is operationally independent and is viewed by the ministries as being technocratic. The governor will usually be consulted on financial issues but does not determine government spending allocations, which are the responsibility of the Ministry of Finance. Overall the institutional set-up is regarded as being fit for purpose, and having served the Kingdom well. Resistance to

---

[16] K. Miyajima, 'What Influences Bank Lending in Saudi Arabia?', *Islamic Economic Studies* 27, no. 2 (2020), pp. 125–51.

[17] Al-Jasser and Banafe, 'Monetary Policy Instruments and Procedures in Saudi Arabia'.

change which threatens to politicize financial decision making is likely to be considerable, as the present system is safeguarded by appropriate checks and balances.

The Merits of Fixed Exchange Rates

Confidence in the Saudi Arabian riyal is maintained by having a fixed exchange rate with the US dollar.[18] The exchange rate has been fixed since June 1986 at SAR3.75 to the dollar.[19] Prior to this the riyal was pegged to the Special Drawing Right (SDR), the IMF's unit of account, based on a basket of currencies, but with the US dollar having the most weight as the currency of the world's largest economy. The SDR remains the unit of account for the Jeddah-based Islamic Development Bank (IsDB), being designated as an Islamic dinar. It is unlikely that Saudi Arabia would revert to an SDR peg, as the currency weights do not reflect the Kingdom's trade and investment. When it was first created, the price of the SDR was denominated in gold, which was supported by many in Saudi Arabia given the use of gold historically. Saudi Arabia continued to use the SDR after it was re-denominated in terms of leading international currencies. However, in the current SDR basket the US dollar accounts for 42 per cent, the euro 31 per cent, the Chinese yuan 11 per cent, and the Japanese yen and the United Kingdom pound 8 per cent each. As Saudi Arabia's trade with Europe and European investment have declined relatively, an SDR peg would no longer reflect economic reality. China has become the Kingdom's major trading partner for exports and imports. India is also important, but the rupee is not included in the SDR basket.

There are three main factors supporting the currency peg with the US dollar, the first being that oil prices and revenues are dollar-denominated.[20] Of the major oil-exporting nations, only Russia and Iran denominate oil sales in euro, but this is largely due to political considerations regarding relations with the USA, not least sanctions. This does not apply in the case of Saudi Arabia as the USA is perceived as being an ally of the Kingdom. Secondly, countries such as China and India are not pressing to internationalize their currencies and are content, for the moment at least, to use dollars for

[18] E. A. Aleisa and S. Diboo̧glu, 'Sources of Real Exchange Rate Movements in Saudi Arabia', *Journal of Economics and Finance* 26, no. 1 (2002), pp. 101–10.

[19] A. Al-Hamidy and A. Banafe, 'Foreign Exchange Intervention in Saudi Arabia', Bank for International Settlements Paper 73 (2013), pp. 301–6.

[20] I. Althumairi, 'Fixed Exchange Rate or Flexible Exchange Rate for Saudi Arabia: Optimal Solution of CGE Model', *International Journal of Basic and Applied Sciences* 1, no. 2 (2012), pp. 67–87.

trade and investment. Third, neighbouring countries, notably Kuwait, which have tried alternative currency arrangements do not appear to have gained much, if anything. The Kuwaiti dinar has been valued against a basket of currencies which supposedly reflect Kuwait's trade and investment flows. In practice, these change frequently, but it is not clear if the currency weights are also changed as this information is not disclosed by the Central Bank of Kuwait. It seems probable that they remain unchanged in order not to upset investor confidence or cause instability. Given this experience, it is unclear what the advantage would be for Saudi Arabia in following Kuwait's example.

The limitation of Saudi Arabia's fixed currency peg is that no devaluation is possible to correct foreign trade or balance of payments deficits. Monetary policy options are inevitably more limited given the currency constraints.[21] Instead, to achieve a deficit reduction the solution is to attempt to raise the price of oil in international markets. Saudi Arabia has more influence on oil prices than other members of the Organization of Petroleum Exporting Countries given the scale of its output, but increases in oil prices can only be achieved by curtailing production, which is self-defeating as potential revenue gains from rising prices are, at least partially, wiped out by falling production.[22] If instead the Kingdom devalued, this would increase revenue denominated in riyals. The trade balance could improve, as although there would be higher prices for imported goods, these would not wholly offset the local currency gains from export earnings. The budgetary deficit could also be reduced, as with higher riyal-denominated government revenue this could cover a greater proportion of government spending.

Despite these advantages, a change of policy abandoning the fixed riyal–dollar exchange rate is unlikely because of two major negative consequences. First, the consumer price index would inevitably rise with imported inflation as local distributors had to pay more for foreign supplies. Inflation is becoming a more politically sensitive issue in the Kingdom and therefore government caution over a policy change which would inevitably result in rising prices is likely. Secondly, there are no controls over capital movements into and out of the Kingdom and therefore local and foreign investors have a free choice of where they deploy their funds. If a devaluation of the riyal were anticipated, investors would hold off from committing themselves to investments denominated in local currency. There would be the danger of a loss of

---

[21] H. E. Abouwafia and M. J. Chambers, 'Monetary Policy, Exchange Rates and Stock Prices in the Middle East Region', *International Review of Financial Analysis* 37 (2015), pp. 14–28.

[22] M. Suliman, T. Hassen, and M. Abid, 'The Impacts of Oil Price on Exchange Rates: Evidence from Saudi Arabia', *Energy Exploration and Exploitation* 38, no. 5 (2020), pp. 2037–58.

confidence, resulting in investors closing down or reducing their deposits in riyal-denominated accounts and switching to US dollar bank accounts.[23]

Devaluation would, of course, signal a change of exchange rate policy. It would create a precedent for further downward moves in the riyal–dollar rate. There are other options, however, which might be seen as more attractive, as they would be less likely to be regarded as signs of economic weakness or vulnerability. Instead of having a one-off devaluation, or a series of devaluations, an exchange policy reform might involve a move from fixed to floating rates. These could be described as market determined and publicized as a move to a more liberal exchange rate regime. The world's major currencies, including the US dollar, have been floating since the breakdown of the Bretton Woods system in 1971. Fixed currency regimes have mainly prevailed in former colonies that wished to continue trade and investment links cemented in the colonial era. Saudi Arabia never had such relationships, and its continuation with the dollar peg can be seen as the exception rather than the norm. Furthermore, a floating rate should not be regarded as a sign of economic weakness. With floating there is always the possibility of appreciation as well as depreciation. A rise in the riyal–dollar exchange rate could reduce the riyal cost of energy supplies denominated in dollars. This could be beneficial for the local petrochemical industry.

In the short or even medium term, it is unlikely, however, that domestic circumstances will bring about a policy shift with respect to exchange rates. More probable is change in the longer term. In particular, one significant change would be to have oil prices cited in the currencies of the major oil-exporting countries including Saudi Arabia, with the riyal as a unit of account. It might also become a store of value, but this will depend on the growth of capital markets in the Kingdom and their accessibility to foreign investors. In a multi-currency world, rather than one where a single currency is dominant, the economy of Saudi Arabia is sufficiently large to make the riyal a significant currency for international transactions, especially for crude oil, refined products, gas, and petrochemicals. Vision 2030 contains no discussion of currency issues, but perhaps that should change given the emphasis on being open for business and investing for the long term. Vision 2030 identifies the Kingdom as being at the crossroads of three continents: Asia, Europe, and Africa. Perhaps the currency usage should reflect this in the longer term rather than being tied to a more distant currency, the dollar, especially as economic transactions with the USA are declining relatively.

---

[23] M. Abdelaziz, G. Chortareas, and A. Cipollini, 'Stock Prices, Exchange Rates and Oil: Evidence from Middle East Oil-Exporting Countries', Topics in Middle Eastern and North African Economies, Quinlan School of Business, Loyola University, *Chicago eCommons* 10 (2008), pp. 1–27.

Development of Retail Banking Services

Saudi Arabia has twenty-four licensed banks which are regulated by SAMA, the largest being the National Commercial Bank, usually referred to in Arabic as Al-Ahli Bank. The bank has 7.5 million customers, 434 branches, and over 8,000 staff. Al-Ahli Bank was incorporated in 1953 in Jeddah, where it is still headquartered.[24] With incorporation the interests of the Bin Mahfouz and Kaki families were merged, these being the owners of the largest money-changing establishments where pilgrims to Mecca exchanged currency. As the Kingdom's economy grew with increasing oil revenues, many migrant workers came to Saudi Arabia, initially mainly from Arab countries, but later from South Asia. These migrants transferred most of their earnings to their families in their countries of origin, with Al-Ahli Bank providing a reliable and efficient service arranging the transfers from the 1950s onwards. As more Saudi Arabian citizens moved into formal employment, often with the government, they needed bank accounts for everyday transactions. Over time, as elsewhere, employees were paid by having their salaries credited to their bank accounts rather than being paid in cash. By the 1960s most Al-Ahli customers were local nationals whose financial needs were growing and becoming more sophisticated.[25] This encouraged the development of transactions services, including direct debits, standing orders, debit and credit cards, and more recently a wide range of electronic services. These were delivered initially through the web using personal computers and then, from 2016, through smartphone apps. The transactions services offered by the banks in Saudi Arabia are state of the art, being user friendly, convenient, and, most importantly, secure. Much of the information technology (IT) development has been outsourced to specialist companies with considerable experience worldwide in ensuring that systems are robust.

Until the 1990s, most Saudi Arabian families spent within their means and were reluctant to take on household debt. Banking operations were comparatively simple, with salaries being credited to clients' accounts each month, followed by a series of payments which reduced the account balances to almost zero, but not into negative territory. Overdrafts could be arranged for non-recurrent expenditures, such as on family weddings, but the banks and their clients regarded such finance as temporary, and exit routes back to credit balance were agreed before the finance could be made available.

---

[24] M. I. Allahham, 'Impact of Capital Structure on the Financial Performance of the Al-Ahli Bank in Saudi Arabia', *International Journal of Marketing and Technology* 5, no. 11 (2015), pp. 56–69.

[25] D. Martín-Consuegra, A. Molina, and Á. Esteban, 'Market Driving in Retail Banking: An Empirical Investigation in Saudi Arabia', *International Journal of Bank Marketing* 26, no. 4 (2008), pp. 260–74.

Negotiating overdraft facilities for modest amounts can be time-consuming, especially as it usually involves risk assessment. Such personalized treatment is also costly, but generates only limited revenue for the banks. As a consequence, banks in Saudi Arabia, in common with those elsewhere, have developed standardized financing facilities that can be marketed to many clients, with at most minor legal contractual variations to cater for clients with different financial circumstances.[26] For consumer finance, Al-Ahli Bank has focused on two areas: vehicle finance and housing mortgages. The vehicle finance is short term, covering both new and used car purchases. It is covered by a leasing contract with the client paying half of the purchase price on the date of the contract and repaying the bank the remaining half after two years. Under the leasing contract, the client pays rent to the bank for the use of the vehicle, which is how the bank generates its profit. In 2020, the cost of the finance under the 50/50 programme was 12.3 per cent per annum plus an arrangement fee of 1 per cent.

Home ownership continues to rise and, as already indicated, a major goal of the Vision 2030 strategy is for 70 per cent of Saudi Arabian citizens to own their own homes. Given the demography of the Kingdom, with a high proportion of young people forming new families, the demand for housing is increasing by more than 5 per cent per annum in terms of volume. The government subsidizes affordable housing projects through the Real Estate Development Fund, but property purchasers at all income levels look to the banks for mortgages. Al-Ahli Bank is the leading provider of residential finance in the Kingdom, covering up to 90 per cent of the value of the property being purchased, or 70 per cent for those who already have residential finance but are moving home. The value of the financing is up to SAR7 million, which therefore includes luxury property in desirable locations. Financing may be part of a package, as Al-Ahli Bank administers finance for the less affluent by the Real Estate Development Fund, the limit under this scheme being SAR400,000. The bank also offers a two-in-one scheme providing housing finance together with liquid funding, which many applicants use for furniture and other household goods. Some housing developers offer discounts or cash incentives for purchasers who complete before a specified date to stimulate interest. Al-Ahli Bank administers these incentives on behalf of the developers, making the transaction seamless for the client.

Al-Ahli Bank provides different levels of services depending on the fees paid by the customers and their income levels. There is a choice of type of credit card and special platinum and gold accounts, branded *wessam*, for the

---

[26] A. S. Alshetwi, 'Study on the Marketing Strategies of NCB in Saudi Arabia', *Global Journal of Management and Business Studies* 3, no. 2 (2013), pp. 75–80.

most affluent. In selected branches, there are well-appointed offices exclusively for *wessam* account holders, where the range of financial products the customer might find useful is discussed. The aim is to adopt international best practice on private banking and provide it to Saudi Arabian citizens. Targeted marketing, which can be enabled through customer segregation, is much more cost effective. The merger in 2021 of Al-Ahli Bank with Samba, the former Saudi American Bank, will considerably enhance private banking services.[27] Samba, which used to be part owned by Citibank, has a much higher proportion of high-net-worth customers than other banks in the Kingdom. The prospect of Al-Ahli Bank taking over these customers was one of the key factors behind the merger.

Competition in the Banking Sector

As already mentioned, Al-Ahli Bank was granted a banking licence by SAMA in 1953, the year after SAMA was established. Although there were numerous money changers in the Kingdom, they were not allowed to accept deposits. Al-Ahli Bank therefore had a monopoly of formal financial business, although most of its business originated in Jeddah where it was based. To serve the political capital, Riyadh Bank was awarded a licence in 1957, but because it and Al-Ahli Bank were focused on different geographical areas there was little competition between the two banks initially. It was from the 1960s onwards that both banks opened branches throughout the Kingdom, with a duopoly replacing the monopolies. However, given the rapidly growing economy, with oil production rising significantly, SAMA became increasingly of the view that a more diversified banking system was needed.[28] Foreign banks were seeking licences to enter the Kingdom, not least because they wanted to serve the increasing number of expatriates working in Saudi Arabia. US expatriates working for Aramco, the Arabian American Oil Company, wanted to use their own banks to conduct financial business. After much lobbying, in 1955 SAMA permitted Citibank to open a branch in Eastern Province, the centre for the oil industry. A precedent had already been set when Saudi British Bank was granted a licence in 1978, with the British minority share being purchased by HSBC in 1992 when the bank, originally based in Hong Kong, was seeking to diversify its business internationally.

---

[27] M. Ben-Jadeed and A. Molina, 'The Emergence and Evolution of E-banking in Saudi Arabia: The Case of Samba Financial Group', *Frontiers of e-Business Research* 1 (2004), pp. 90–106.
[28] J. Al-Suhaimi, 'Consolidation, Competition, Foreign Presence and Systemic Stability in the Saudi Banking Industry', Bank for International Settlements Background Paper 4 (2001), pp. 128–32.

Initially the foreign banks in Saudi Arabia were very restricted as they were not permitted to open more than a single branch. Hence Saudi British Bank was confined to Riyadh and Citibank to Damman. It was only in 1980 that a new policy was introduced by the Saudi Arabian government and implemented by SAMA. This provided for the foreign banks to list on the Saudi Arabian stock market and recapitalize, with local investors taking a majority ownership stake, usually 60 per cent. Once under majority local ownership, the banks were allowed to open branches and establish a nationwide presence if that was their goal. The aim of SAMA was to make the banking sector more competitive, while drawing on the strengths of their minority shareholders.[29] The assumption was that nationality was a factor differentiating styles and expertise in banking. Many countries were represented, with not only Samba and Saudi British Bank, but Banque Saudi Fransi and Saudi Hollandi Bank. The Amman-based Arab Bank was also a beneficiary of this change of policy, but with this exception the list of banks was Europe- and USA-focused. The criticism was that with trade and financial flows from both Europe and the USA declining relatively, and links with China and South Asia increasing in importance, it would have been desirable to have more eastern representation. Admittedly, HSBC was involved through Saudi British Bank, but its ethos is more British than Chinese; indeed HSBC carries a lot of baggage given its recent history and policy choices, which limits its attractiveness from a Chinese perspective.

The most recent policy initiative, in 2006, was to encourage investment banks to establish a presence in the Kingdom as their skills and expertise could help the development of the local capital markets. The policy has enjoyed some success with BNP Paribas, Deutsche Bank, EFG Hermes, JPMorgan, Merrill Lynch, and Morgan Stanley all opening offices in Riyadh. As the field is rather crowded, this may be the most competitive sector for the provision of banking services. Winning mandates for advisory work on activities such as mergers and acquisitions has proved very challenging, and as the opening up in this area was quickly followed by the global financial crisis, there was banking overcapacity in Riyadh. Nevertheless, for institutions prepared to take a long-term view, there is considerable potential in the Saudi Arabian market. Given the substantial number of high-net-worth families in the Kingdom, it is not surprising that private banking and wealth management are highly developed, with institutions such as Al-Ahli Bank and Samba being especially active in this area.

[29] R. B. Sharma and N. A. M. Senan, 'A Study on Effectiveness of Internal Control Systems in Selected Banks in Saudi Arabia', *Asian Journal of Managerial Science* 8, no. 1 (2019), pp. 41–7.

The investment banks which have entered the Kingdom all provide wealth management services, resulting in increased competition, but most of the business remains with the established banks. Wealth management and investment advisory institutions fall within the remit of the CMA rather than SAMA with respect to regulation. This is appropriate given the specialized nature of their activity.

Banking Regulation

SAMA was created in order to provide effective bank regulation to ensure the stability of the financial system. The major vulnerability has been and remains the financial impact of oil price changes, which are often unexpected.[30] Inevitably there have been banking crises, but the government has recapitalized the banks involved, which have included both the Riyadh Bank and Al-Ahli Bank. The later faced major difficulties in 1989 when, as a result of falling oil prices, construction activity declined and many contractors were unable to meet their financial commitments to the bank. Al-Ahli Bank had to write off some of the debts and make provision for this from its capital. However, the crisis soon passed. There have been no bank failures in Saudi Arabia and confidence in the institutions, including SAMA as regulator, remains high. The global financial crisis of 2007–8 had virtually no impact on the banking sector in Saudi Arabia as it had much less international exposure than the banks in the United Arab Emirates (UAE).[31] The COVID-19 pandemic has fortunately had a relatively limited effect on the Kingdom, although the restrictions on Hajj have had a severe negative impact on business in Jeddah, Mecca, and Madinah with the loss in 2020 being over SAR40 billon.

The current structure of the banking system and the position of the leading players are a reflection of past licensing policies more than of market forces. As already indicated, there are twenty-four licensed banks in the Kingdom, of varying size and capability. The issue is whether the market structure is optimal for the needs of the Kingdom, or whether more licences should be granted. However, rather than waiting for applicants, SAMA could play a more active role in encouraging new potential entrants, particularly from China, India, and Pakistan, as well as African countries, especially given the Vision 2030 objective of having closer economic and financial linkages with

---

[30] Ramady, 'Evolving Banking Regulation and Supervision'.
[31] A. Al-Hamidy, 'The Global Financial Crisis: Impact on Saudi Arabia', Bank for International Settlements Paper 54 (2010), pp. 347–57.

these regions. There have been some positive moves by SAMA, notably the award of a licence to the Bank of China in 2020.

The Saudi Arabian market could be described as rather fragmented, with a need for mergers and acquisitions to increase the size of the banks. This would enable the banks to benefit from economies of scope, by widening their range of product offerings, and economies of scale, by spreading costs over a larger number of customers. For example, with IT investment there are high fixed costs but low variable costs. The costs of serving 5 million clients are only marginally more than those of serving 50,000 customers. The largest proposed merger in the banking history of the Kingdom was submitted to SAMA for approval in 2021.[32] This involves Al-Ahli Bank, already the largest bank in Saudi Arabia, merging with Samba. If approved, which is likely, the two institutions will keep their distinctive branding initially. The deal is being financed by the issuance of new shares worth SAR57.4 billion that will be allocated to Samba shareholders in exchange for their existing shares. In many respects, the deal is a takeover rather than a merger. However, there are clear benefits as Samba has more high-net-worth clients, while Al-Ahli has existing resources that will help cater for their needs without incurring large expenditures. Both banks have overseas affiliates: Samba in Dubai, Doha, and Pakistan, where it has thirty-seven branches; and Al-Ahli Bank in Turkey, where it owns two-thirds of the capital of Turkiye Finans Katilim Bankasi which has 286 branches throughout the republic. The merged bank will have assets exceeding SAR840 billion and a combined equity base of SAR120 billion. Its earnings are the highest in the Middle East and North Africa (MENA) region, but in terms of capital, the accepted measure of bank size, it will be the third largest MENA bank after the Qatar National Group and First Abu Dhabi Bank. Recent years have seen several significant bank mergers in the MENA region, including the merger of Saudi British Bank with Al Awwal Bank to create the third largest bank in the Kingdom. SAMA appears to let the market evolve as bank shareholders wish, without imposing regulatory directives. It is clear that its priority is not to maintain as many banks as possible in the interest of competition, but rather to approve mergers which bring scale advantages, notably the widening and strengthening of the financial services offered.

Both Al-Ahli Bank and Al Rajhi started as family businesses with informal governance structures. SAMA as regulator encouraged both institutions to list on the stock market as this would result in greater transparency

[32] F. Kane, 'NCB–Samba Merger to Create National Champion in Banking', *Arab News* (21 November 2020).

and increase their capital, although there were mixed feelings within the controlling families over listing, which would inevitably result in a loss of control. This has indeed been the case, although the rise in the value of their shareholdings after listing arguably more than compensated for their reduced influence. In the case of foreign banks such as Saudi American and Saudi British, they had to agree in return for their licences to take on board founder shareholders, all of whom were from wealthy business families. As the shares increased in value considerably, their wealth also increased substantially. This is all history, however, and since the 1980s standards of corporate governance have improved significantly and are in line with international best practice. Minutes are taken of formal meetings and there are remuneration committees which report to the board of directors of each bank. SAMA is highly regarded as an independent regulator, and directors and senior executive know that they or their relatives cannot get funding on advantageous terms. Financing applications have to be considered objectively and so-called name lending is not approved of by SAMA.

Regulations on liquidity and capital adequacy in Saudi Arabia comply with the Basel accords which were agreed by the Group of Twenty leading economies (G20), of which the Kingdom is an active member. SAMA works closely with the BIS and has ensured that all banks in Saudi Arabia comply with the provisions of Basel III on liquidity and capital adequacy which were adopted in the aftermath of the global financial crisis.[33] Compliance ensures banks have confidence in the institutions they are dealing with in terms of payments, interbank transactions, and capital market instruments. All banks in Saudi Arabia have sufficient unencumbered high-quality liquid assets to cover stress scenarios lasting thirty days. Work on capital adequacy is ongoing at the BIS, especially in terms of types of capital to mitigate risk and the standards that should be applied to different types of bank. All of the banks in Saudi Arabia have compliance departments that analyse their ever-changing exposure so that risks can be properly identified. Most of the banks in the Kingdom have relatively straightforward transactions and financing practices, and their compliance officers work closely with SAMA. The smaller banks with fewer compliance officers get technological assistance from SAMA, which attempts to standardize the systems in the Kingdom.

The resolution of disputes between the banks and their customers is an important responsibility of SAMA. Most of the disputes have arisen when

[33] M. I. Allahham, 'Impact of Capital Structure on Bank Financial Performance of Al-Ahli Bank in Saudi Arabia', *International Letters of Social and Humanistic Sciences* 60 (2015), pp. 10–16.

customers breach their contractual obligations by failing to make repayments, this being particularly prevalent in the construction sector because of cyclical movements in the prices paid for commercial real estate. There have been conflicts over late payment penalties, which are normal in commercial law but which many believe conflict with *Shari'ah* law, as such penalties constitute *riba* and are contrary to the principles of Islamic law, which stresses leniency towards debtors. Islamic courts do not deal with commercial disputes, which are often complex; hence there was ambiguity over how these cases should be dealt with. The banks urged SAMA to take the initiative, and as a consequence it established the Committee for the Settlement of Banking Disputes.[34] This has become the arbitrator and is now referred to in many financial contracts. Defaulters who claim that the banks are not adhering to *Shari'ah* law with their payment demands do not have any possibility of success, as the contracts are all approved by the *Shari'ah* boards of each bank. Therefore claims that the contracts are defective imply challenging the judgement of the *Shari'ah* scholars. Not only are the defaulters in breach of contract, but they are attempting to undermine the *fatwa* of the *Shari'ah* board.

SME and Business Finance

As already mentioned, in Saudi Arabia the focus has been on retail banking rather than business support. This means in practice that the banks are supporting consumer finance: in other words, demand in the economy rather than supply. Business finance enhances supply capacity in the economy, which is created through funding for production and investment, not least in infrastructure. Financing demand should not be viewed as being at the expense of supply; it is not a zero-sum game. Rather a balance is needed, as without demand there will be underutilization of capital and unwanted spare capacity. The financing of family vehicle purchases and housing mortgages is viewed as low risk, especially if the salaries of the beneficiaries are credited to their bank accounts. In contrast, the supply-side funding is higher risk as business receipts and earnings may vary considerably, with, in the case of Saudi Arabia, these being related to oil prices and production.[35]

[34] Z. S. Al-Herbish, 'Jurisdiction over Banking Disputes in Saudi Arabia', *Arab Law Quarterly* 25 (2011), pp. 221–8.
[35] A. Alrashidi and O. Bakeel, 'The Impact of Operational Risk Management on the Financial Development and Economic Growth: A Case Study of Saudi SME Companies', *European Journal of Business and Management* 4, no. 5 (2012), pp. 15–21.

Who is financed is also an issue in the Kingdom, with most consumer finance going to Saudi Arabian citizens rather than migrants and expatriates. In contrast, although the finance of small and medium-sized enterprises (SMEs) is managed by Saudi Arabian business owners, expansion often results in an increase in the employment of migrants. There are increasing numbers of sectors in the economy reserved exclusively for local citizens, but creating employment for local nationals is often a challenge, and migrants still predominate in most small manufacturing and construction businesses. As migrants repatriate a substantial proportion of their income, this represents a leakage for the Kingdom's economy. In contrast, spending on vehicles and housing generates multipliers which stimulate local activity. Even though most of the vehicles are imported, they are serviced and maintained in Saudi Arabia.

Vision 2030 stresses the importance of SME financing for the diversification of the economy. Al-Ahli is the leading bank participating in the *kafala* programme, sponsored by the Ministry of Finance with government funds disbursed through the Saudi Industrial Development Fund (SIDF). Going beyond finance, Al-Ahli Bank runs seminars and workshops for the owners and managers of SMEs and provides professional advice on what it believes is the most appropriate form of financing. Rather than a 'one size fits all approach' Al-Ahli Bank attempts to identify and provide financial solutions tailored to what is optimal for a particular SME given its existing financial resources. Leaders of SMEs are invited to give presentations on their business plans, with specialists from the Al-Ahli Bank and the SIDF providing critical, but helpful, feedback.

Significant government funding been used to establish new agencies to aid SMEs, notably Monsha'at, which reimburses the tax paid by SMEs during their first three years of operations. It also provides top-up funding to complement bank finance. The PIF, for its part, invested SAR4 billion into a fund for SMEs, and in 2019 established Jada Investment to provide private equity and venture capital for SMEs.

It remains to seen whether this proliferation of institutions will actually help SMEs. The record to date is disappointing, with SMEs contributing around 20 per cent of GDP—much lower than in the UAE, where SMEs account for 53 per cent of GDP.[36] Owners of SMEs complain that it is difficult to obtain funding from the banks despite all the subsidies from government agencies. Their complaints are supported by an analysis of the data in the banks' financial reports. For example, in the financial statements of Al Rajhi

---

[36] M. Thompson, 'Saudi Arabia's Vision for SMEs', *Gulf Monitor* (14 April 2020).

Bank the amount of mortgage finance for residential property increased from SAR32 billion in 2018 to SAR55 billion in 2019. In comparison, the finance allocated by Al Rajhi Bank to SMEs in 2019 was SAR2.6 billion, indicating that they were a low priority. The problems go deeper, however, with Saudi Arabia's position in the Global Entrepreneurship Index falling. In the Ease of Doing Business World Bank ranking for MENA, the Kingdom is not only behind the UAE and Bahrain, as might be expected, but also below Morocco.

All of the usual financial services are available for businesses in Saudi Arabia, the major difference being the increasing recourse to Islamic finance, which will be discussed in the next section. Specialist areas include project finance advisory services, real-estate finance, and acquisition funding, as well as the issuance of asset-based securities with the option of selling the future cash flow of receivables.[37] Trade finance remains important, but much of it is now structured using *Shari'ah*-compliant financial instruments. Al-Ahli Bank has a syndications and placements unit that can arrange, structure, and distribute credit products. Local and international brokerage services are offered as well as advice on initial public offers (IPOs) where companies are seeking a stock market listing.

Islamic Banking and Finance

As Saudi Arabia is the heartland of Islam, with the two holiest shrines, it is to be expected that Islamic banking and finance should be well developed in the Kingdom; and indeed it is. Obedience to *Shari'ah* teaching is spiritually motivated and idealistic, but SAMA and the Jeddah-based IsDB have played a major role in translating the noble goals of *Shari'ah* into practical financial solutions. Unlike Iran, which passed laws compelling everyone to use Islamic financial products, in Saudi Arabia the use of Islamic finance is a matter of client choice. Customers want to conduct their banking and financial in accordance with Islamic principles not only because they are Muslims, but because the products offered meet their needs and are competitively priced.

There are many excellent guides to Islamic banking and finance, which has become a global industry, with a significant presence in both Muslim-majority and minority countries. The interested reader can consult these guides, including a comprehensive guide to Islamic finance in Saudi Arabia, and no attempt is made here to examine the products in detail.[38] The key

[37] A. Rafiki, 'Determinants of SME Growth: An Empirical Study in Saudi Arabia', *International Journal of Organizational Analysis* 28, no. 1 (2020), pp. 205–25.
[38] Islamic Development Bank, *Islamic Finance in Saudi Arabia: Leading the Way to Vision 2030* (Jeddah: Islamic Research and Training Institute, 2020).

principle of Islamic finance is the prohibition of *riba*, which stakeholders in the Islamic finance industry equate with interest dealings. These are seen as unjust and exploitative, with risks loaded onto the client rather than being shared by the financial institution. Instead of charging and paying interest for borrowing, most Islamic finance involves profit sharing with the buying and selling of assets; or leasing contracts with the payment of rent. These have design characteristics that make them acceptable from an Islamic perspective, and all Islamic financial institutions have *Shari'ah* boards, as part of their governance structures, that must approve the products prior to their being marketed.

It should be noted that the IsDB is a multinational institution, and although its establishment was a Saudi Arabian initiative and it is based in Jeddah, it is not part of the Kingdom's financial system. Its funding originally came from the governments of the fifty-seven Muslim-majority states comprising the Organization for Islamic Cooperation (OIC), with Saudi Arabia providing 23.5 per cent of the paid-up capital, Libya 9.43 per cent, and Iran, the third largest subscriber, 8.25 per cent. Since 2005, almost SAR94 billion has been raised through *sukuk* issuance. The IsDB has an exemplary repayments record and is rated AAA by Standard and Poor's (S&P), Moody's, and Fitch. It can be regarded as a World Bank for OIC member states and it avoids getting involved in their internal politics. Originally, much of its funding was to enable poor Muslim states to continue importing oil at the grossly inflated prices after 1974, but in recent years most of its funding has involved project finance, often in partnership with local agencies. Much of the financing benefits African states, identified as one of three geographical elements in Saudi Arabia's Vision 2030. All IsDB financing is *Shari'ah* compliant and it has taken a leadership role in propagating Islamic finance worldwide.

To appreciate the significance of Islamic banking and finance and the scope of the business, it is informative to look at Al Rajhi Bank as a case study, as it is the second largest bank in the Kingdom and the largest Islamic bank in the world in terms of asset holdings.[39] It was licensed to operate as a bank in 1957, as previously it had been a money-changing business serving pilgrims on Hajj as well as migrant workers through handling their remittances. In addition, by the 1950s Al Rajhi was also accepting deposits and providing funding: in other words, increasingly operating as a bank. As a consequence, SAMA, and indeed the Al Rajhi family which owned the business, felt the time had come to apply for a banking licence. The family's major concern was

---

[39] F. A. Al Dugaishem and M. J. Khawaja, 'Customer Satisfaction with Islamic Banks: A Case Study of Al Rajhi Bank', *Tazkia Islamic Finance and Business Review* 11, no. 1 (2018), pp. 57–80.

that SAMA should understand the structures of the Islamic financial products being offered, and that it could not pay interest to depositors or charge
interest on financing; nor could it engage in lending or borrowing.

SAMA rose to the challenge and its being a regulated financial institution increased confidence in Al Rajhi, which thrived as a result. By 2020, Al
Rajhi's total assets were SAR384 billion and its net profits SAR11.3 billion. It
had 544 branches throughout the Kingdom as well as 5,215 automated teller
machines in both branches and shopping centres. It has the largest customer
base in the Kingdom with over 9 million accounts, more than Al-Ahli Bank,
but the clients of the latter are on average more affluent, hence the higher
value of Al-Ahli's assets. Al Rajhi, like the other banks in the Kingdom, is a
listed company on the Saudi Arabian stock market, and it is required to make
the same disclosures to its shareholders as the other banks.[40] It is important
to note that Al Rajhi is involved in the same financing as the other banks,
with much of its financing being for mortgages on residential properties and
vehicle purchases. In other words, it is not what is financed that is any different, but rather the instruments used for the financing, with, as already
mentioned, trading contracts where profits are shared or leasing contracts
involving rental payments and receipts.

Al Rajhi has sought in recent years to expand and diversify its business,
both domestically and overseas. Like the other banks in Saudi Arabia which
have established overseas affiliates, the focus has been on getting to know the
market in a particular country rather than attempting to establish subsidiaries
globally. In the case of Al Rajhi, the target market is Malaysia, where it opened
its first branch in 2006. By 2020, Al Rajhi had sixteen branches throughout
the country providing mostly retail financial services, taking the products and
instruments developed in Saudi Arabia to a different part of the world.[41] As
already mentioned, other Saudi Arabian banks have also expanded overseas,
notably Samba in Pakistan and Al-Ahli Bank in Turkey. There are, of course,
closer ties between the Kingdom and Pakistan, given the substantial numbers of expatriates from the subcontinent working in the Kingdom. Malaysia,
being more affluent and smaller in terms of population size, has few of its citizens living and working in Saudi Arabia. Rather it is best known to Saudis
as a tourist destination. From a Saudi banking perspective, an attraction of
Malaysia has been its stable currency, in contrast to Turkey which has a long

---

[40] A. M. Alwehabie, 'Criteria for Measuring the Efficiency and Effectiveness of Human Resources Management Strategy and Its Relation to Institutional Performance at Al Rajhi Bank at Al Qassim in Saudi
Arabia from the Employees' Point of View', *International Journal of Business and Management* 12, no. 10
(2017), pp. 111–20.
[41] A. A. E. Mohammed and N. Kim-Soon, 'Characteristics of GCC Islamic Bank Investment in Malaysia',
European Journal of Scientific Research 140, no. 4 (2016), pp. 448–57.

history of devaluations and inflation, eroding the value of investments over time if they are measured against the US dollar and Saudi Arabian riyal.

Islamic finance often involves investment in equity rather than the debt finance associated with lending and borrowing. In the case of Al Rajhi, it has turned itself into a group involved in investments in a wide range of sectors, some quite removed from banking. Al Rajhi is not the first Islamic institution to follow such a path, as from the 1980s Kuwait Finance House invested in, and managed, car showrooms. It also took over the ownership of Kuwait's largest shopping centre, having financed its construction. In the case of Al Rajhi Holdings, it has acquired the Sky Centre in Jeddah and established real-estate and marketing subsidiaries as well as purchasing Delta Express, a delivery firm, and Gulf Pack, a packaging business. It has its own car rental business, Farnas, and owns the Kabria, Shami, and Ramesses restaurant chains as well as the Food Manufacturing Group (FMG). Since its inception, Al Rajhi has provided services for Hajj and Umrah, but it has now branched out into the wider market for tourism by establishing a travel agency business.

Regulating such a diverse conglomerate poses challenges, as in the unlikely event of some of the businesses being declared bankrupt there could be adverse implications for the banking subsidiary. Al Rajhi Bank is, of course, regulated by SAMA and meets its capital and liquidity requirements. The other subsidiaries are subject to company law as well as the need for timeliness and transparency in financial reporting. However, they are not classified as banks and there is less stakeholder protection. Tighter regulatory requirements would certainly add to business costs and could even result in the subsidiaries being less competitive than their rivals. It is unlikely, therefore, that there would be much support for regulatory reform, but the issue remains to be addressed.

The Stock Market and Fund Management

Saudi Arabia has a large and sophisticated stock market which, as already indicated, is the ninth largest in the world with 204 companies listed. As there are over 1 million investors in the Kingdom there is scope for many more private equity companies to be listed, if and when the owners believe more capital injections would help build their business.[42] Most of the investment is by private citizens rather than institutions, but the latter are gaining

[42] M. Z. Rehman, M. N. Khan, and I. Khokhar, 'Investigating Liquidity-Profitability Relationship: Evidence from Companies Listed in Saudi Stock Exchange (Tadawul)', *Journal of Applied Finance and Banking* 5, no. 3 (2015), pp. 159–73.

ground because of the growth of managed funds. Investors have mostly benefited from capital gains, but as with other stock markets there have also been periods of crisis and reversal, most notably during 'black Monday' in 2006. Speculation had caused a market bubble the previous year, with many investors borrowing from banks to finance share purchases. When the market collapsed, many leading investors could not repay their bank loans and were technically bankrupt. Fortunately, strong family bonds meant that most managed to raise sufficient finance to muddle through. The crisis did not reflect well on the banks, however, as it revealed inadequate risk appraisal and the danger of lending by name. Working within cultural norms may be safer for the banks than being confrontational towards their customers.

Privatizations have helped expand the market, notably the listing of the petrochemical company SABIC[43] and Saudi Aramco, the Kingdom's number one company and the world's largest oil producer.[44] Utility companies such as Saudi Electric account for a significant portion of market value, as do telecommunication companies such as Mobily and Zain. The latter is a Kuwaiti company with a cross-listing on the Tadāwul; it has mobile phone, fibre and data management businesses throughout the Middle East and Africa, serving almost 50 million customers. All banks in the Kingdom are listed on the Tadāwul, with their value accounting for around one-quarter of the total market value. All of the banks with capital market divisions or affiliates are members of the Tadāwul, enabling them to provide investment services. In addition, there are independent investment companies which are members, including Jadwa Investment.

The Tadāwul was established in 2007 as a joint stock company whose remit was to manage all capital market transactions in the Kingdom. Rather than having SAMA as regulator, it was felt that a more specialist institution in line with international best practice was required. Hence at the same time as the Tadāwul was launched, the CMA was established as its regulator. The aim was not to protect investors financially, but to ensure that they had access to the information relevant for their decision making. The CMA ensures that financial information is disclosed in an accurate and timely manner, and all financial reports are required to be signed off by independent auditors. Furthermore, there should be a level playing field for investors, and insider trading is a criminal offence. Investors who believe they have been victims

[43] H. J. M. Alotaibi, 'An Assessment of the Connection of Elements in a Strategic Plan: A Case Study of Sabic', *International Journal of Advanced Research in Management and Social Sciences* 4, no. 10 (2015), pp. 19–36.
[44] K. Mehrez, L. Hamid, A. Medabesh, and G. Nesreen, 'Saudi Aramco's IPO: The Motivational Factors Involved in the Purchase of Saudi Aramco Shares', *Journal of Business and Retail Management Research* 15, no. 1 (2020), pp. 59–68.

of fraud can and should lodge an official complaint with the CMA, which is empowered to investigate the matter. The CMA has an excellent reputation as a robust institution, serving the investment community well, in line with international best practice.

There has been considerable public interest in capital markets in Saudi Arabia, as a high proportion of domestic savings are invested either directly in company stock, or indirectly through mutual funds. This is partly because there is little personal saving deposited into bank accounts. Retail clients have their salaries deposited each month, but any surpluses after expenses are covered simply remain in their transactions accounts, which pay no return. Savings accounts never took off in Saudi Arabia, as these pay interest to depositors. The wider public regard these payments as *riba*, which is of course prohibited in Islamic law as already discussed. Not only do customers not want savings accounts, but banks are unwilling to promote them, as this would result in much public criticism. Customers, however, saw no reason why they should let the banks be custodians of their finances while paying nothing for the balances held, not least as the banks used the funds for financing their clients. This funding earned a return, but this was not shared with the depositors.

Although these practices suited the banks, which were very profitable given the zero cost of their funding, the lack of returns was seen as unfair by their customers. To rectify this situation in 1980 Al-Ahli Bank took the strategic decision to promote mutual funds as an alternative to savings accounts.[45] Initially there was no *Shariah* oversight as the bank did not have a *Shariah* board, but as support for a reform of governance grew, Al-Ahli Bank appointed its own board following the example of Dubai Islamic Bank. Since then, all Al-Ahli funds have to be approved and monitored by their *Shariah* board. The mutual funds can only invest in activities accepted as being *halal*, with *haram* investment prohibited.

Al-Ahli Bank is the world's largest provider of Islamic mutual funds, which include four index funds, six regional funds, three thematic funds, three money market funds, a fixed income fund, two actively managed trade funds and five multi-asset funds, as well as a real estate investment trust. In other words, there is an array of funds to cater for different categories of investor according to their appetite for risk and the amount they have to invest. The funds are either riyal- or dollar-denominated, which makes no difference given the fixed exchange rate. They are all liquid, and holdings can be sold

[45] H. Merdad, M. K. Hassan, and M. Khawaja, 'Does Faith Matter in Mutual Funds Investing? Evidence from Saudi Arabia', *Emerging Markets Finance and Trade* 52, no. 4 (2016), pp. 938–60.

at any time. The equity funds should be regarded as long-term investments as they have yielded positive returns over ten years but, in some cases, losses over shorter periods. The index funds have performed well and have lower management charges. The Health Care fund and the Saudi equity fund have generated high returns, but some of the wider Gulf Cooperation Council (GCC) funds have proved disappointing, as have the real-estate funds. The multi-asset funds are low risk but the returns have been modest. Management fees for the actively traded funds are 1.75 per cent per annum, which is relatively high by international standards.[46]

Al Rajhi Capital is the second largest mutual fund provider in Saudi Arabia. Its management charges are also 1.75 per cent per annum for its Saudi Equity Fund and the returns are comparable with similar funds managed by Al-Ahli Bank. Al Rajhi's range of funds offered is similar to Al-Ahli, but there are no thematic funds and hence no health care offering. Its multi-asset funds are categorized as conservative, balanced, and growth. The other major mutual fund provider in Saudi Arabia is Jadwa, an investment company established in Riyadh in 2006. Not being a bank, it has fewer opportunities to cross-sell to clients, but being focused on investment it has been able to recruit a highly specialist team. In addition to investment in mutual funds, Jadwa also offers private equity investment opportunities for families of high net worth, with SAR5.4 billion invested in ten companies by 2020. There has been an excellent performance for some of the nineteen mutual funds offered, with its Saudi Equity B fund rising by 381 per cent over the period from 2007 until 2020. The yield on some of the funds exceeds 14 per cent per annum, a spectacular result.

The government has underwritten the market in recent years to maintain confidence and ensure politically powerful investors are less exposed to losses. Downward market movements have been constrained by end-of-the-day trading by government agencies, but not surprisingly given experiences elsewhere, such intervention has been costly but usually ineffective. The combined resources of SAMA and the PIF are far behind those in the Chinese, UAE, and Norwegian funds. Furthermore, SAMA has to hold safe assets such as short-dated *sukuk* rather than equity, so it is reluctant to see its funding used for unsustainable stock market intervention. The PIF was set up to invest in overseas assets, and obviously the more resources it puts into the Tadāwul, the less it has for foreign investment. The inclusion of the Tadāwul

---

[46] H. Merdad, M. K. Hassan, and Y. Alhenawi, 'Islamic versus Conventional Mutual Funds Performance in Saudi Arabia: A Case Study', *Journal of King Abdulaziz University: Islamic Economics* 362, no. 3061 (2010), pp. 1–75.

in the MSCI Emerging Market Index was regarded as a considerable achievement in Riyadh, but Saudi Arabian stock only accounts for 2.7 per cent of the total.

A major aim of Vision 2030 was the privatization of state-owned enterprises, the most ambitious being the IPO of Aramco, the national oil company. The government envisaged this would be the largest privatization with the proceeds used to promote economic diversification. It was originally planned that a listing would be sought in major international financial markets, including London and New York. However, international investors were less enthusiastic, noting the decline of oil prices and production, as well as political risks because of the Kingdom's involvement in Yemen's civil war and the threat from Iran. Originally scheduled for 2016, the plans were seriously delayed, and when eventually the IPO was approved in 2019 it was limited to the Tadāwul and only a small proportion of the stock was sold.

Sukuk Instruments for Debt Management

The banks and investment companies in Saudi Arabia also offer *sukuk* funds to their clients. These are fixed-income investment instruments for a specified period with the investors receiving their funds back in full on maturity providing there has been no default.[47] In the case of Saudi Arabia, there has yet to be a *sukuk* default, hence investors have never lost their capital, but there have been defaults elsewhere, notably in Kuwait and Malaysia, so investors should not be complacent about their exposure to risk. However, unlike equities whose prices change from day to day and even hour to hour, the price of a *sukuk* only rises if it is paying more income than new *sukuk* issuance, and only falls if it is paying less. The price at maturity converges with the initial offer price. In practice, *sukuk* prices in Riyadh seldom change as these securities are held to maturity rather than being traded in the secondary market.

In terms of financial characteristics, a *sukuk* is identical to a bond. The income is, however, not regarded as interest, and indeed it is not interest; instead it is derived from either the rent or a profit share which the investor receives from the user of the asset being financed. All *sukuk* are asset backed, which is a *Shari'ah* requirement. Bonds are simply instruments to securitize debt which can be used for any purpose. In contrast, *sukuk* involve investing in a specific asset used for a purpose which must be approved by a *Shari'ah*

---

[47] A. Alshamrani, 'Sukuk Issuance and Its Regulatory Framework in Saudi Arabia', *Journal of Islamic Banking and Finance* 2, no. 1 (2014), pp. 305–33.

board and fully disclosed to the investors. Arguably there is more certainty and less risk with *sukuk* because of their greater transparency. The nearest conventional instrument is a covered bond, which is also asset backed, but the assets are only held so that investors can sell the bond in the event of a default. They have no interest in the asset or what the income from the asset actually represents.

The Al-Ahli Sukuk Fund was launched in 2010 with the period to maturity being ten years. It is highly liquid and can be redeemed within three days. The management fee is 0.75 per cent, well below the fee for equity fund investments. The cumulative return over the ten-year period was 26.18 per cent, rather low but better than holding cash. The minimum investment was SAR375,000, a modest amount which provided an investment opportunity in *sukuk* which was quite affordable for most Saudi Arabian investors. Jadwa Investment has launched four global *sukuk* funds, the first in 2007, a second in 2018, and two in 2020 as interest in this type of investment picked up. The fund launched in 2007 has yielded a cumulative return of 38.48 per cent over the period to 2020.

The *sukuk* funds invest in corporate rather than sovereign *sukuk* and are similar to corporate bond funds. Returns are higher but the risks are also greater than with sovereign *sukuk* which have government guarantees.[48] In practice, Saudi Arabian *sukuk* are managed cautiously. The Jadwa Global Sukuk funds are more regional than global, with 36.5 per cent of the holdings in the UAE, 34.2 per cent at home in Saudi Arabia, and 8.1 per cent in Bahrain. Some investment has been allocated to *sukuk* issued in Indonesia, Turkey, Pakistan, and Oman, but the relative shares are small. As the worldwide *sukuk* market grows, there will undoubtedly be opportunities for Saudi Arabian investors to widen their horizons. However, exchange rate considerations are likely to result in caution among investors from Riyadh. Turkey, for example, has vibrant manufacturing and services sectors which already have some experience of *sukuk* issuance. The presence of Al-Ahli Bank in Turkey means that Saudi Arabian institutions are well placed to participate in the Turkish debt market. What discourages investment is the instability of the Turkish lira, with rapid depreciations and high inflation, which lowers the value of any investment. Businesses in Turkey could, of course, issue *sukuk* denominated in US dollars or euro, but if their revenues are mainly in local currency, payment prospects would be problematic and the securities have the risk of becoming junk *sukuk*.

---

[48] A. Echchabi, H. A. Aziz, and U. Idriss, 'Does *Sukuk* Financing Promote Economic Growth? An Emphasis on the Major Issuing Countries', *Turkish Journal of Islamic Economics* 3, no. 2 (2016), pp. 63–73.

Most of the corporate *sukuk* in Saudi Arabia has been issued by companies in which the government has a major ownership stake, but these are classified as corporate debt instruments rather than sovereign debt.[49] Nevertheless, investors in Saudi Arabia, including the banks themselves, are willing and able to hold government debt. This is a minimal risk investment, as S&P, the independent global rating agency, awarded Saudi Arabia an A-A-2 rate in 2020, with the economic outlook seen as stable. This favourable debt rating is comparable to those of the world's leading economies. Although the oil price and production levels have been lower than the Kingdom's government envisaged, and the COVID-19 pandemic has resulted in additional expenditure, the amount of sovereign debt is manageable. The debt increased from a very low level of 1.6 per cent of GDP in 2014 to 22.8 per cent of GDP in 2019, and is forecast to peak at around 25 per cent of GDP in 2025. This compares with a level of 136.4 per cent in the USA and 156.9 per cent in Italy according to data from the Organization for Economic Cooperation and Development. Saudi Arabia can easily cut spending without exacerbating unemployment by making expatriates and migrant labourers redundant while maintaining employment for local citizens. Furthermore, oil revenue cuts simply result in deferred revenue because, with carbon neutrality years away, the medium-term prospects for oil production and revenue remain encouraging. It can be argued that Saudi Arabia has too little rather than too much sovereign debt.

Insurance Provision

The insurance industry remains underdeveloped in Saudi Arabia, but business has increased over the last decade and is expected to rise further in the next five years.[50] The companies are both local affiliates of major international insurance companies and Saudi Arabian banks which have diversified into insurance. The largest company is BUPA Arabia, an affiliate of London-based BUPA, with a turnover of SAR10.4 billion in 2019, followed by Tawuniya, a local company. Al Rajhi Takaful, the insurance subsidiary of this Islamic bank, is ranked third with a turnover of SAR2.4 billion. AXA Cooperative is in fifth position, and Saudi Franzi Bank, with an Allianz franchise and branding, has risen to become the seventieth largest insurance provider in the market. Insurance business is regulated by SAMA, which has

---

[49] M. Nagano, 'Who Issues *Sukuk* and When? An Analysis of the Determinants of Islamic Bond Issuance', *Review of Financial Economics* 31 (2016), pp. 45–55.

[50] S. N. NuHtay, M. Hamat, W. Z. W. Ismail, and S. A. Salman, '*Takaful* (Islamic Insurance): Historical, Shari'ah and Operational Perspectives', *International Business Management* 9, no. 1 (2015), pp. 65–9.

licensed thirty-three insurance operators, but over 90 per cent of the business is undertaken by the ten largest operators. The market is fragmented at the bottom end, and to strengthen resources SAMA has increased the capital requirements for insurance providers. This is expected to result in mergers and acquisitions.

The largest business segment is health insurance for both expatriates and Saudi citizens, although all citizens are entitled to the basic state provision. Vehicle insurance is mandatory, but not very profitable given the high level of accident claims in the country. The most rapidly expanding insurance sector is family *takaful*, which is a *Shari'ah*-compliant alternative to mortgage protection or endowment insurance. The rise in residential mortgages, with an increasing proportion of Saudi Arabian citizens wanting their own home, explains much of the interest in family *takaful*. The cover of these insurance policies ensures that if the mortgage holder dies or becomes seriously ill and unfit to continue working, the amount of the mortgage remaining is paid off by the insurance provider and the family can continue living in their home without any further payments being made. Often family *takaful* is bundled with a savings plan in which the mortgage holder is provided with a lump sum or monthly income stream when the mortgage matures. In other words, the mortgage holder benefits from having what amounts to an additional pension. The bundle is, however, more costly with higher monthly premiums.

A *takaful* contract implies a mutual guarantee, which may affect how insurance services are organized.[51] In Saudi Arabia, there was some discussion of *takaful* being provided through cooperatives in which the policy holders were the stakeholders rather than having separate shareholders whose interests might conflict with those of the insured. High payouts to policy holders could reduce dividends paid to shareholders and potentially reduce the share price of the insurance company. To avoid exploitation of the policy holders by the shareholders, a separate *takaful* fund is created, with either an agreed management fee paid from the fund, or a profit share. The management fee approach is usually applied to health and vehicle insurance policies which are renewable annually, and the profit-sharing approach is applied to mortgage protection where the contracts may be for twenty years or longer.

The organization of *takaful* provision and the contracts offered are certainly distinctive from those with conventional insurance, and are often more complex. As with Islamic banking, the range of products offered covers

---

[51] M. Sadeghi, 'The Evolution of Islamic Insurance-*Takaful*: A Literature Survey', *Insurance Markets and Companies: Analyses and Actuarial Computations* 1, no. 2 (2010), pp. 100–7.

the same areas as its conventional counterparts. In other words, as already observed, but worth stressing, the difference lies in how the financial services, including both banking and insurance, are distributed rather than in what is provided.

Future Challenges

Saudi Arabia has a highly developed financial system which serves the Kingdom well. The regulation follows international best practice with provisions to ensure there is sufficient liquidity and appropriate capital adequacy. There is sound independent financial reporting and investors have confidence in SAMA and the CMA as regulators, as well as in the banking and insurance institutions themselves. Most encouragingly, many Saudi Arabian citizens aspire to work in finance, which, apart from government ministries, has become the sector employing most local citizens.[52] Saudi Arabians now account for over 95 per cent of the workforce.[53] Many women are employed in the sector, usually in sexually segregated offices which the women themselves prefer. Women are not confined to back-office jobs, however, as all of the large banks have women's branches run by women for women.[54]

Looking ahead, the macroeconomic situation is favourable, as government debt is modest and mostly held by the financial institutions in the Kingdom and Saudi Arabian citizens. Little debt is held by foreign banks or investment companies, including hedge funds. As the economy continues to diversify, there will be new opportunities for the financial sector, not least in insurance provision where the market is underdeveloped. The financial sector has enjoyed considerable success in developing Islamic financial products that are operationally sound and have proven public appeal. The Kingdom is a leader in the world of Islamic finance.

All of this is extremely positive, but at the microeconomic level there are challenges for the banks. Further consolidation is likely in the banking sector with more mergers and acquisitions. As elsewhere, IT is transforming banking, and the Kingdom's IT infrastructure compares favourably with the most

[52] A. Aamir, K. Jehanzeb, A. Rasheed, and O. M. Malik, 'Compensation Methods and Employees Motivation (with Reference to Employees of National Commercial Bank, Riyadh)', *International Journal of Human Resource Studies* 2, no. 3 (2012), pp. 221–30.

[53] N. Fawzi and S. Almarshed, 'HRM Context: Saudi Culture, *Wasta* and Employee Recruitment: A Post-Positivist Methodological Approach—The Case of Saudi Arabia', *Journal of Human Resources Management and Labour Studies* 1, no. 2 (2013), pp. 25–38.

[54] M. Parveen, 'Enhancement of Managerial and Leadership Role of Saudi Woman [sic] in the Banking Industry: An Exploratory Study on Different Banks in Jeddah—Kingdom of Saudi Arabia', *International Journal of Advanced Research in Management and Social Sciences* 3, no. 9 (2014), pp. 141–54.

advanced globally.[55] Good websites and customer friendly apps are crucial for success.[56] It is, however, evident that although the local demographics are favourable, many expatriates are leaving or have already left the Kingdom, reducing the demand for banking services. Furthermore, the Kingdom is overbanked, with too many small branches which are often far from busy. There have yet to be significant branch closures, but these are inevitable and will involve staff redundancies. As the layoffs will mostly involve Saudi Arabian citizens, this is going to be a sensitive issue which will be difficult to address. The King Abdullah Financial District in Riyadh has failed to attract much interest from financial institutions and investors. It is being relaunched as yet another housing project, but with units which are too small for most Saudi Arabian families. In the end, however, it is human capital that matters more than the physical infrastructure, in finance as in other fields. There is much financial expertise in Riyadh and Jeddah, and in the long term this is what matters most.

Despite the successes of banking and the financial sector, the future outlook is becoming more challenging. Moody's reduced its ratings for the banks to negative following the cuts announced in government spending in the 2020 Budget. It is anticipated that the cutbacks will have adverse consequences for the non-oil sector, with the commercial and residential property markets, in which the banks are heavily involved, being hardest hit. The expenditure cutbacks reflect a fiscal squeeze, resulting from oil revenues being lower than anticipated, combined with higher health spending arising from COVID-19. The latter is arguably a one-off expenditure, but the continuing overdependence on oil is concerning, throwing doubt on the extent to which the Kingdom can be regarded as a post-rentier state. Arguably, the banks remain focused on rent seeking and rent extraction, the problem being that there is less and less rent to extract.

---

[55] W. Al-Ghaith, L. Sanzogni, and K. Sandhu, 'Factors Influencing the Adoption and Usage of Online Services in Saudi Arabia', *Electronic Journal of Information Systems in Developing Countries* 40, no. 1 (2010), pp. 1–32.

[56] R. Alabdan, 'The Adoption of Online Banking with Saudi Arabian Banks: A Saudi Female Perspective', *Journal of Internet Banking and Commerce* (2017): 1–18.

5

Saudi State Capitalism

Karen E. Young

Introduction

Can a capitalist economy be state controlled? How might a state presence
or dominance in a domestic economy be deleterious or beneficial to economic growth? Twenty-first century capitalism has some strange variations,
including the rise of authoritarian capitalism and the growth of state-owned
or state-related firms and investment vehicles that operate within a global
market system. China's rise, with its 'developmental state with predatory
admixtures', has been an example to other developing economies of a hybrid
model in which different ownership structures of firms might coexist and
receive state support through private and government-owned financial institutions and targeted industrial policies.[1] This grey area of hybrid state assets
includes companies, sovereign wealth funds (SWFs), and tradeable assets
that serve the interests and operate at the direction of states—usually the kind
of states that have concentrated power structures and undemocratic forms of
governance. Tools of state capitalism can be extremely effective as tools of
economic statecraft abroad.[2]

The effects on the domestic economies of these entities can be stifling to
competition and defeating to those who do not enjoy access to their revenue
streams. But state-owned investment funds and entities can also be engines
of growth and a force for domestic investment. State-led growth has had
some historical success, most notably in the East Asian 'miracle', and in those
locales where a form of business corporatism unified a growing industrial

[1] W. Ritt and G. Redding, 'China: Authoritarian Capitalism' in W. Ritt and G. Redding (eds.), *The Oxford Handbook of Asian Business Systems* (Oxford: Oxford University Press, 2018), pp. 11–32, at p. 4.
[2] K. E. Young, 'A New Politics of GCC Economic Statecraft: The Case of UAE Aid and Financial Intervention in Egypt', *Journal of Arabian Studies* 7, no. 1 (2017), pp. 113–36, doi: 10.1080/21534764.2017.1316051.

Karen E. Young, *Saudi State Capitalism*. In: *The Economy of Saudi Arabia in the 21st Century*. Edited by: John Sfakianakis, Oxford University Press. © Karen E. Young (2024). DOI: 10.1093/oso/9780198863878.003.0006

sector with government policy objectives for growth, as the example of Brazilian corporatism in a nascent aerospace sector demonstrated.[3]

This chapter seeks to contribute to the debate and literature on state-led growth with an examination of the Saudi case, particularly the aggressive reliance on state investment and state direction of the economy under the Vision 2030 initiative and leadership of Crown Prince Mohamed bin Salman since 2016.[4] The current variant of Saudi state capitalism is indeed distinct from its Chinese contemporary and its earlier East Asian and South American predecessors. Saudi state capitalism is more personalistic, driven by the aspirations and at the direction of its new leadership under Crown Prince Mohamed bin Salman. And it focuses less on creating an ecosystem of state-owned entities and bureaucracy designed to meld business and public sector interests, instead funnelling state development policy and resources through limited channels, mainly the country's SWF, the Public Investment Fund (PIF). State-led development in Saudi Arabia is also very much funded by a singular source of natural resource revenue, controlled entirely by the state, despite a much-lauded but hardly impactful effort to partially privatize the national oil company. The outcome is that Saudi state capitalism is by its very personalistic and top-down nature less strategic than the developmental state models current in China, or those we have seen historically in other regions.

It is argued here that the Saudi state developmental model relies on some old structural features and some predatory new ones. The old structural features are related to the nature of an oil-dependent national economy, fed by revenues from a state-owned oil company. The historical institutional model of the Saudi economy is bifurcated in its pre-oil structures namely strong social institutions, and its post-oil discovery structures, which align with the creation of the modern Saudi state and its ruling family, the Al Saud. As historian Alexei Vassiliev has argued, 'a market economy was introduced from the outside into a feudal-tribal society that was not prepared for such a transformation and lacked the necessary personnel, state and public institutions and legal system'.[5] Capitalism came quickly to Saudi Arabia and implanted on top of existing social institutions formed over centuries to privilege kinship, relationships, and ideas about tribute and social ledgers of debt

[3] World Bank, 'The East Asian Miracle: Economic Growth and Public Policy' (Oxford: Oxford University Press, 1993), http://documents1.worldbank.org/curated/en/975081468244550798/pdf/multi-page.pdf; D. Limoeiro and B. R. Schneider, 'State-Led Innovation: SOEs, Institutional Fragmentation, and Policy Making in Brazil', MIT Industrial Performance Center Working Paper (2017), https://ipc.mit.edu/sites/default/files/2019-01/17-004.pdf.

[4] K. Wolff and S. Grand, 'Assessing Saudi Vision 2030: A 2020 Review', Atlantic Council Research Report (2020), https://www.atlanticcouncil.org/in-depth-research-reports/report/assessing-saudi-vision-2030-a-2020-review/.

[5] A. Vassiliev, The History of Saudi Arabia (London: Saqi Books, 2000).

and responsibility. These social institutions may in some ways retain value and excuse what Western capitalism would consider insider information and trading and the return of business favours—in other words, widespread corruption. As Douglas North's foundational work on institutional change in economies showed, the norms and patterns of behaviour within societies shape how economic institutions form and their pathways of change.[6] Social norms and systems of order (including kinship, tribal identity, and ideas about tribute and reciprocity) are not static in Saudi Arabia or any other state, but they can exist and transform along with the imposition of new rules on economic and political life.

In his book *State, Society and Economy in Saudi Arabia*, Tim Niblock clearly outlines how political institutional development in Saudi Arabia has flowed from development of the national oil industry under the direct authority of the monarch.[7] The sequential and, as he argues, slow development of government institutions has been matched by the enduring role of social institutions—the norms and patterns of behaviour and relationships that structure both political and economic life. As Niblock describes in the introduction to his volume, 'the forces of modernism and traditionalism ... far from being in conflict—have often served common purposes and proved mutually supportive'.[8] Therefore, the political economy of Saudi Arabia exists as a pattern of interaction between certain social institutions, including the monarchy, and the specific historical development of political institutions of government that were largely created as by-products of an oil industry. The Saudi state, per se, has managed capitalism and the growth of economic institutions in the country, but social institutions, many of whose origins predate the state, also inform how business is conducted in the Kingdom. Steffen Hertog's work on the relationship between ministries and the bureaucracy of the state, the business community, and members of the ruling family has detailed the design and functionality of Saudi capitalism, including his concept of 'segmented clientelism'.[9] The events of 2015 and the rise of Crown Prince Mohamed bin Salman mark a kind of critical juncture in the history and institutionalization of the Saudi economy, as existing patterns of economic behaviour in contracting from the state, the primacy of Aramco, and the proliferation of bureaucracy and ministries as positions of tribute and

[6] D. North, *Institutions, Institutional Change, and Economic Performance* (Cambridge: Cambridge University Press, 1990).
[7] T. Niblock, 'Introduction', in T. Niblock (ed.), State, Society and Economy in Saudi Arabia (London: Routledge, ebook 2015; 1st edn. 1982), pp. 11–22.
[8] Ibid., p. 13.
[9] S. Hertog, *Princes, Brokers, and Bureaucrats: Oil and the State in Saudi Arabia* (Ithaca: Cornell University Press, 2010), p. 137.

power sharing began to centralize around the ambitions and new preferred institutions of the Crown Prince. Therefore, Saudi state capitalism is not necessarily new, but it does seem to have taken a significant turn in recent years. The new Saudi state capitalism is perhaps more centralized, less bureaucratic or power-sharing by nature, and tests the resilience of the very social institutions and norms that have facilitated the introduction of oil-backed capital economic institutions since the mid-twentieth century.

The new features of Saudi state capitalism include the politicization and manipulation of the PIF, the Saudi SWF, and a determined national economic agenda that privileges state ownership of firms, rewards 'unicorn' success stories of private firms with an influx of state funding or equity stakes, and trades ownership stakes in semi-private entities like a fungible budget line. The outcome is a market that is dominated by state activity, which has the effect of paralysing outside investment that fears the reach (and predation) of the state. The foreign policy agenda of the Saudi state has also made difficult its own inward foreign investment goals. While the Vision 2030 agenda offers some timely upgrades to the Saudi regulatory environment, including expansion of equities ownership rights for foreigners and more clearly delineated bankruptcy proceedings for firms, the Vision ultimately gives the Saudi state (and the personal brand of the Crown Prince) ownership of the development agenda. And rather than increasing the power of citizen investors and entrepreneurs, the development agenda often serves to strengthen the hand of the state, and the ideas and projects of the Crown Prince within the economy.

While the focus of economic transformation has been closely linked with the persona of the young leadership, the successes and early winds of the transformation are often better associated with more technocratic aspects of the Saudi government. These early wins include increasing female labour participation, expanding access to credit, especially in mortgages, and a fiscal discipline in streamlining some ministry spending, including on subsidies and the military. The contours of Saudi Arabia's new economic policies are sometimes difficult to identify. Riyadh, for one, remains highly dependent on oil. Net oil and gas exports were 70.1 per cent of the country's total exports in 2020. Simultaneously, however, overall exports constituted just 26 per cent of gross domestic product (GDP)—a sign of Saudi Arabia's potential as the Gulf's largest domestic consumer market. Oil and gas revenue is also shrinking as a percentage of the government's overall budget, down from 64 per cent in 2016 to just 52.8 per cent in 2020.[10] And even in the hyper-cycle of high

[10] K. E. Young, 'The MBS Economy', *Foreign Affairs* (27 January 2022), https://www.foreignaffairs.com/articles/saudi-arabia/2022-01-27/mbs-economy.

oil prices predicated on the Russian invasion of Ukraine in February 2022, the Saudi government has not committed to major fiscal policy changes to release the spending taps.

The COVID-19 pandemic, moreover, spurred the government to identify novel ways of generating revenue and spending less. In response to the collapse of oil prices in the spring of 2020 and a longer-term global transition away from fossil fuels, Saudi decision-makers realized that they needed to turn the economy in a new direction. As part of this effort, Riyadh increased a new value added tax (VAT) from 5 per cent to 15 per cent in the summer of 2020, boosting non-oil revenues by more than 30 per cent over the first nine months of 2021. Taxes on goods and services now account for about SAR70 billion, or around half of all oil income. Government spending on major infrastructure projects, by contrast, has contracted dramatically.

The Saudi private sector is also expanding, albeit from a weak base. After shrinking for seven consecutive quarters, the economy finally began to grow again in the second quarter of 2021, with GDP up by 1.5 per cent. Private sector growth outside the oil sector also rose by 7.5 per cent in the first half of 2021. Government attempts to shift social services such as health care and education into the private sector account for part of this expansion. Saudis now pay more out-of-pocket for health care than most of their peers in the Gulf states; the government covers about 60 per cent of health care spending, according to 2018 data from the World Bank, a relatively low proportion by Gulf standards.[11]

The government's belt tightening also extends to public sector and military expenditures. Despite the pandemic, spending on public sector wages declined from a high of nearly SAR510 billion by the end of 2019 to about SAR490 billion by the end of 2021. Military spending, for its part, decreased from SAR540 billion in 2019 to SAR440 billion at the end of 2021. Recent high-level efforts to wind down the war in Yemen also have a fiscal rationale.

Separately, women are beginning to take on new roles in the labour market—improving access to economic mobility across the country. Some 25 per cent of Saudi women now work, compared with 15 per cent in 2018. A similar trend exists among other demographics, with the labour force participation rate among 20- to 24-year-old men now at 55 per cent, compared to 40 per cent in 2018. And although unemployment among job-seekers is still high—around 11 per cent—more Saudis are looking for work now than before the Vision 2030 reforms. These numbers are partly the

---

[11] R. Gatti, D. Lederman, R. Y. Fan, A. Hatefi, H. Nguyen, A. Sautmann, J. M. Sax, C. A. Wood, 'Overconfident : How Economic and Health Fault Lines Left the Middle East and North Africa Ill-Prepared to Face COVID-19', MENA Economic Update (Washington, DC: World Bank, 2021).

result of government efforts to replace foreign workers with Saudi nationals, with certain jobs—such as those in retail—reserved for citizens only. Coupled with the pandemic, such workforce development programmes have largely succeeded. Since early 2020, 600,000 foreign workers have left the Kingdom.

Finally, with the government's urging, Saudis are now borrowing money to meet their lifestyle expectations rather than expecting the state to pay. One of Vision 2030's objectives, after all, was to expand access to mortgages and develop a more accessible financial services sector by encouraging citizens to invest domestically and increasing the number of firms listed on the local stock exchange. Saudis have seized the opportunity. Saudi banks sold a record SAR46.7 billion of new mortgages in the first quarter of 2021, up from SAR31.2 billion in the previous year. The United States (US) credit rating agency S&P Global Ratings, moreover, expects the Saudi mortgage market to increase by 30 per cent annually between 2021 and 2023.[12] This progress, however, is somewhat in spite of continued government intervention in the Saudi economy. Where there is an opportunity for borrowing and easing restrictions on labour markets, we see people jumping at the chance. However, where there are limitations, these are often caused by the parallel financial interests of the state.

This chapter examines four case studies of the heavy state intervention in the Saudi economy. These cases are interlinked, as they fit together into an ecosystem of financial regulations and institutions that aid the dominance of the state at the expense of the private sector of the Saudi economy. First, the Saudi domestic stock market, the Tadāwul, is examined together with recent regulatory changes to expand ownership opportunity and internationalization of the exchange. The findings suggest that despite efforts such as index inclusion for institutional investors abroad, the exchange remains dominated by domestic trades, largely driven by state investor activity and incentives. Secondly, the chapter tackles the shifting role of the PIF, and the government's efforts to feed it with capital intended for both domestic investment and outward acquisition, meant to create new revenue from investment as well as introducing a kind of rebranding of the soft power of Saudi wealth deployed abroad. Thirdly, the chapter addresses the problem of 'captured unicorns', or the dilemma of successful private firms that find themselves the target of state envy and state investment. The example of ACWA Power, an independent utility company, is instructive. Fourthly, the chapter examines the problem of foreign direct investment (FDI) in Saudi Arabia, why it is a discrete objective of Vision 2030, and why the Kingdom has struggled to see

---

[12] S&P Global (2021), https://www.spglobal.com/marketintelligence/en/news-insights/latest-news-headlines/saudi-arabia-s-fannie-mae-to-boost-portfolio-issue-mortgage-backed-securities-64480064.

a rebound in capital inflows. The insistence on attracting FDI for tourism, for example, has been met with some interest, but is largely countered by the state's dominance in tourism opportunity development. Externalities like the COVID-19 pandemic and Saudi foreign policy crises have only deepened the FDI challenge.

In Saudi Arabia, the government has always been in business. With its foundational asset of oil reserves, the state has justified its intervention in the economy and its dominance over political and associational life since 1932.[13] But the Saudi state is not just the arbiter of the domestic oil industry; the state holds a preponderance of ownership in firms across several economic sectors, a dominant stake in the largest firms in the domestic stock market, a significant stake in financial institutions and the position of key source of private bank deposits, and an ability to create winners in the private firms which it favours and often takes over. State–business networks and favouritism towards elites and members of the ruling family have dominated the Saudi economy for decades. The Vision 2030 agenda and leadership of Mohamed bin Salman in fact made a public effort to detangle some of these networks and corrupt practices, but the Crown Prince has failed to institute a new level playing field in which new firms and independent actors might compete with state-related entities.[14] In fact, the continuing efforts to detangle corruption and connected contracting between ruling family members, elites, and the state have only served to deter private entities (and wealthy Saudi business owners) from proximity to the state's economic interests.[15] In some respects, Saudi Arabia has a history of both crony capitalism and state capitalism.[16] What dominates the Saudi economic sphere now is the omnipresence not just of the state, but of specific government instruments, particularly with the rise of the PIF and the specific ideas about growth and development held by the empowered and central figure of new leadership, Mohamed bin Salman.

The Saudi Stock Market

The Saudi stock market, the Tadāwul, has traditionally been a sleepy domain within the Saudi economy. Officially launched in 2007, the joint stock company is a securities exchange regulated by the Capital Market Authority

---

[13] Hertog, *Princes, Brokers, and Bureaucrats.*

[14] K. E. Young, 'Corruption Purge Overshadows Stalled Reality of Saudi Economy', Lawfare (16 November 2017), https://www.lawfareblog.com/corruption-purge-overshadows-stalled-reality-saudi-economy.

[15] S. Kerr, 'Saudi Arabia Sacks Two Senior Royals as Part of Corruption Purge', *Financial Times* (1 September 2020), https://www.ft.com/content/1ab1ee54-2efd-48c7-ac2e-523c3a572028.

[16] I. Diwan, A. Malik, and I. Atiyas (eds.), *Crony Capitalism in the Middle East: Business and Politics from Liberalization to the Arab Spring* (Oxford: Oxford University Press, 2019).

(CMA). In 2015, the exchange opened to qualified foreign investors, and in 2019 it began to allow the listing of foreign firms. Interestingly, the exchange itself is fully owned by the PIF, which is 'fully subscribed' to the 120 million shares of the Tadāwul. In turn, the Tadāwul is the 100 per cent owner of Muqassa and Edaa, a security-clearing centre and a securities depository centre, respectively.[17]

While the exchange is fully owned by the state SWF, the PIF, it is also dominated by firms that are partially owned by the government. The most actively traded firms and those with the largest value are congregated in a few sectors: oil (most recently with the addition of a partial Saudi Aramco listing, discussed in more detail below), banking, petrochemicals, and health care. Who trades on the Saudi stock market has been limited largely to local investors and government institutional investors, until very recently.

The Tadāwul began loosening its restrictions on foreign investors in 2015 when it opened trading to Qualified Foreign Investor (QFI) applicants, which were required to be financial institutions located in a CMA-approved jurisdiction and to have assets in excess of $5 billion. That asset requirement was quickly pared down, first to $3 billion in 2016, then to $1 billion in 2017, and finally to $500 million in January 2018. A requirement that QFIs have a minimum of five years' investment experience was also removed from the rules at the beginning of 2018.[18] This rapid loosening of terms indicates how important foreign inflows have become to Vision 2030 and how difficult it has proven to attract foreign portfolio investment. Moreover, the regulator, the CMA, has delegated to custodian banks its authority to certify if an investor meets the conditions for QFI status.[19]

Despite these measures, under way since 2015, and the Vision 2030 programme announced in 2016, the efforts to increase the participation of foreign investors in the Tadāwul, and to encourage institutional investors and more passive investment funds to enter the market, have been met with a muted response. Even with the important designation of 'emerging market' status in three leading indices (MSCI, S&P Dow Jones, and FTSE Russell), the share of foreign ownership in Saudi-listed firms remains around 3.2 per cent, excluding strategic stakes, which is low compared with emerging market

[17] Saudi Stock Exchange, 'Tadawul Annual Report 2019' (2019), https://www.tadawul.com.sa/wps/wcm/connect/728038d0-b0ab-48bd-9a4a-989394921120/Tadawul±AR±2019±%28English%29.pdf?MOD=AJPERES&CONVERT_TO=url&CACHEID=ROOTWORKSPACE-728038d0-b0ab-48bd-9a4a-989394921120-nc5DIoO.
[18] Ibid., p. 6.
[19] Deutsche Securities Saudi Arabia, 'Saudi Arabia Gets Hotter' (Frankfurt: Deutsche Bank, 2018), https://cib.db.com/insights-and-initiatives/flow/securities-services/saudi-arabia-gets-hotter.htm.

peers.[20] The number of QFIs investing in firms listed on the Tadāwul, according to the exchange's 2019 end of year report, was 1,800, up from 500 in 2018.[21] The ability to classify Saudi-listed firms as having 'emerging market' status in key indices means that more and more investors globally may find that their portfolios include some holdings of Saudi-listed firms, but for the near term, the expected inflows from index inclusion have not been dramatic.

Index inclusion has been a trend across the Gulf Arab states in the last few years, with Saudi Arabia and Kuwait joining Egypt, the United Arab Emirates (UAE), and Qatar in the MSCI EM index in 2019.[22] At the same time, Saudi Arabia, Qatar, the UAE, Bahrain, and Kuwait joined Oman in the JPMorgan Emerging Market government bond index.[23] Kuwait was classified as having 'secondary emerging' status in 2018 in FTSE's Russell index, and Saudi Arabia was included in March 2019.[24] While the objective is sound to attract all kinds of investment, from passive portfolio investment in equities to finding a broader investor audience for Gulf sovereign debt, there is some inherent risk in relying on index inclusion to do the work of creating an environment that welcomes outside investment. The risk is that further economic reform would make it easier for more firms to form and operate, and then listing on the local exchange becomes secondary to the appeal of one major offering, such as the prize of Aramco, or one signal or indicator of external investor interest.

And that seems to be what has occurred in the year or two since index inclusion. Access to international debt capital markets may be encouraging governments to finance their deficits with international debt issuance, while doing little to spur more organic growth in local private companies. While Saudi Arabia and other regional governments have done some groundwork in order to achieve index inclusion, by regulating their capital markets and exchanges, the harder structural reforms of opening up the economy and

---

[20] S. Shamma, 'The "Halo Effect" of Saudi Arabia's Emerging Markets Arrival', Franklin Resources (11 June 2019), https://www.franklintempleton.ca/en-ca/investor/commentary-details?contentPath=en-ca/blog-posts/beyond-bulls-and-bears/the-halo-effect-of-saudi-arabias-emerging-markets-arrival.

[21] Saudi Stock Exchange, 'Tadawul Annual Report 2019', p. 8.

[22] MSCI, 'MSCI Emerging Markets Index' (2020), https://www.msci.com/documents/10199/c0db0a48-01f2-4ba9-ad01-226fd5678111; M. Rashad, 'Saudi Stock Exchange Now Full MSCI Member, But Market Euphoria May Fade', Reuters (29 August 2019), https://www.reuters.com/article/us-saudi-exchange-inclusion/saudi-stock-exchange-now-full-msci-member-but-market-euphoria-may-fade-idUSKCN1VJ1VM.

[23] D. Barbuscia, 'Saudi Arabia, Four Other Gulf States to Enter Key JP Morgan Bond Indexes', Reuters (26 September 2018), https://www.reuters.com/article/us-gulf-bonds-jpmorgan/saudi-arabia-four-other-gulf-states-to-enter-key-jp-morgan-bond-indexes-idUSKCN1M61HZ.

[24] N. Turak, 'Saudi Arabia's Stock Exchange Makes Its Debut on Global Emerging Markets Indexes', CNBC Markets (18 March 2019), https://www.cnbc.com/2019/03/18/saudi-arabias-tadawul-joins-global-emerging-markets-indexes.html.

creating a level playing field for business are far from accomplished.[25] Index-linked capital flows also have some discriminatory preferences, not always linked to finding or rewarding the most dynamic growth markets.

Instead of rewarding diversification efforts, index inclusion may have the effect of leaving some behind. Inflows to Dubai, a beacon of economic openness in the region, were relatively flat between 2017 and 2019, while neighbours seen as safe havens, or at least as low-hanging fruit, often received more. Kuwait and Egypt have seen a greater inflow of foreign capital. Saudi Arabia has been subject to intense capital inflow variability, which some attribute to the 2017 corruption purge and the backlash over the murder of Jamal Khashoggi.[26] In the first few months of index inclusion, however, between March and September 2019, EPFR data (a private database of fund flows) shows that flows to Saudi equity funds rose sharply, taking in over $1 billion in a single week in that period, then declining.[27]

Between October 2017 and October 2018, Kuwait received more than $700 million in net foreign inflows, more than any previous year, according to research by EFG-Hermes SAE. This was led by passive inflows from FTSE trackers. Other reasons for increased investment were a low debt-to-GDP ratio, a national budget that breaks even at a low price for oil, a government programme to increase infrastructure investment, and (compared to some of its neighbours) a problem-free foreign policy environment. The inflows into Egypt are also related to resource revenues (specifically, the development of natural gas production for export), improved tourism, and the sheer size of the consumer market. For investors, the inclusion of resource-rich Gulf Arab states in emerging market indexes will increase their vulnerability to fluctuations in energy prices. Sovereign debt from countries of the Gulf Cooperation Council (GCC) has been surging among emerging market issuance, with analysts at the Kuwait Financial Centre (Markaz) expecting GCC sovereign debt issuance to surpass the 2019 total issuance of over $100 billion in 2020.[28] In effect, index inclusion of emerging market debt has been more influential in Gulf economic policy choices than in equity index inclusion. The result

[25] K. E. Young, 'Arab States Should Beware of Indexes Bearing Easy Money', Bloomberg (22 January 2019), https://www.bloomberg.com/opinion/articles/2019-01-22/arab-states-should-beware-of-indices-bearing-easy-money?sref=euelgVQS.

[26] S. Algethami and A. Narayanan, 'Saudi Purge Puts Investments at Risk as Uncertainty Lingers', Bloomberg (29 January 2018), https://www.bloomberg.com/news/articles/2018-01-29/saudi-corruption-purge-risks-investments-as-uncertainty-lingers?sref=euelgVQS.

[27] 'EPFR Global Fund Flows', Macrobond, https://www.macrobond.com/epfr-global-fund-flows/; S. Baronyan, 'Quants Corner', Financial Intelligence (24 September 2019), https://financialintelligence.informa.com/resources/product-content/quants-corner-epfr-saudi-oil-facility-attack-and-fund-flows.

[28] G. Platt, 'GCC's Borrowing Binge', Global Finance (28 July 2020), https://www.gfmag.com/magazine/julyaugust-2020/gccs-borrowing-binge.

for the private business community in Saudi Arabia, and arguably across the GCC, is that the state has been better positioned to access capital for debt issuance than firms have been able to access capital through equity.

As a transition to a discussion of the PIF, it is worthwhile to examine which Saudi-listed firms have the PIF as an investor shareholder. Figure 5.1 illustrates the broad sectoral stakes the PIF holds in Saudi-listed firms. In some respects, this was the initial intention of the fund—to be a source of local investment for key industries. The PIF has developed its role and is now dominant as an outward investor as well as a local investor. PIF holdings in Saudi firms correlate with the largest entities on the Tadāwul. At the top, the PIF holds roughly $37 billion worth of shares in the Saudi Telecom Company (STC), $13.6 billion in the dominant local bank NCB, and an $8.1 billion stake in Maaden, the Saudi mining giant.[29] But the PIF's holdings of firms

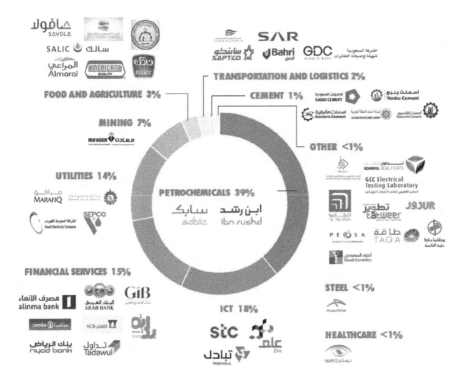

Figure 5.1 PIF assets—Saudi holdings
Sources: PIF, JPMorgan.

---

[29] K. E. Young, 'Economic Diversification in the Wake of Covid-19 in Saudi Arabia', in *Report MED2020: Navigating the Pandemic* (Rome: Italian Institute of Strategic Studies, 2020).

listed on the Tadāwul are most concentrated in just three sectors: information and communications technology (ICT), petrochemicals, and financial institutions. In these three sectors, we find that 39 per cent of the PIF's Saudi holdings are in petrochemicals, mostly in Saudi Basic Industries Corporation (SABIC; more on this below), 18 per cent are in ICT, namely in the Saudi Telecom Company (STC), and 15 per cent are in domestic banks like the NCB, Riyad Bank, Samba, Arab Bank, and the Tadāwul itself, as a financial institution.

Feeding the Public Investment Fund

The Saudi SWF, the PIF, is the central player in the story of 21st-century Saudi state capitalism. But Aramco, the national oil company, has an important role as well, particularly as the early arbiter of the design of the Saudi economy and its persistent reliance on oil revenues to feed government expenditure, and to trickle down in the form of contracting and related spending across the broader economy. In this sense, the reliance on government spending and contracting has shaped the culture of economic activity in Saudi Arabia. Economists call this 'pro-cyclical spending': when oil revenues are high, government spending increases and stimulates economic activity throughout the economy. Government deposits in local banks expand lending and commercial activities, and government procurement dominates which firms find such opportunities. There is an expectation that the government has a responsibility to drive investment decisions and then fund them. And, in a way, the PIF is like a new version of oil, a new source of revenue generation for the state and a director of how and where domestic economic activity should move. The shift from oil to investments as a generator of wealth and rents is part of the diversification effort planned under Vision 2030, relying on the PIF as a central government force to unify and direct the projects meant to create new employment opportunities outside of the public sector and oil production. The PIF is intended to be an engine of growth, sustained by the returns on its investments, but also acting as a director of domestic economic activity. The notion of diversification is somewhat ironic in centralizing authority and economic power within the state, or specific entities of the state.

But there are limits to how far economic diversification may be expected to reach.[30] Unfortunately, the global structural pressures of plentiful oil supply (much of it due to technology advances and the efficiency of US shale

---

[30] Ibid.

production), an expected plateau of oil demand from 2035 onwards, and the need for government stimulus to shield the economy from the COVID-19 pandemic all make that shift more precarious.[31] The recent reliance on foreign reserves and savings built up when oil prices were high, in the 'magic decade' between 2003 and 2014, is unlikely to be replaced in the near term, exposing the government to future fiscal vulnerability and possible currency devaluation.[32] Just evaluating the drawdowns of foreign reserves from the Saudi Arabian Monetary Authority (SAMA) between June 2014 and June 2020, foreign currency reserves declined from SAR2,800 billion ($746 billion) to SAR1,700 billion ($453.2 billion); meanwhile, government deposits at SAMA declined from SAR1,600 billion ($426.5 billion) to SAR1,000 billion ($266.6 billion) over the same six-year period, according to data reported by SAMA and Riyad Capital.[33]

While global demand for energy is expected to increase, global oil demand is expected to plateau or decline over the next twenty years.[34] In the same period, Saudi pension systems will be grossly underfunded, the Kingdom's public health and education systems will be overburdened, and social safety nets for the chronically unemployed and underemployed will all compete with the fiscal burden of debt service.[35] The current 'youth bulge' will not be replaced by a similar-sized young population once they reach their fifties and edge towards retirement. Even with substantial increases in taxation through the new 15 per cent VAT rate and possible imposition of further fees and even personal income tax, more expensive, ageing citizens will be a larger demographic than the next generation of Saudi workers.

The sectors which were showing promise in diversification, such as tourism, hospitality, and entertainment, also tend to have been those most sensitive to the effects of the COVID-19 pandemic. The development of these sectors represents a significant shift in the Saudi economy and in its society. Religious tourism already represents an important source of non-oil revenue to the Saudi economy, but even a substantial increase in tourism

[31] S. Dale and B. Fattouh, 'Peak Oil Demand and Long-Run Prices', BP Oil (January 2018), https://www.bp.com/en/global/corporate/energy-economics/spencer-dale-group-chief-economist/peak-oil-demand-and-long-run-oil-prices.html.

[32] A. Chopra, 'Saudis Reel from Austerity Drive after Oil-Rich "Magic Decade"', Barron's (14 May 2020), https://www.barrons.com/news/saudis-reel-from-austerity-drive-after-oil-rich-magic-decade-01589507705.

[33] H. P. Huber, 'Saudi Economic Chartbook, 3rd Quarter 2020', Riyad Capital (June 2020).

[34] 'Energy Outlook 2020', BP Oil (14 September 2020), https://www.bp.com/en/global/corporate/energy-economics/energy-outlook.html.

[35] K. Boehmer, 'The Looming Pension Crisis Part II: Government Pension Plans', Mackenzie Investments (2019), https://www.mackenzieinvestments.com/content/dam/mackenzie/en/2019/06/wp-the-looming-pension-crisis-part2-en.pdf.

to archaeological and urban locations has had a limited economic impact.[36] COVID-19 will not last for ever and Saudi tourism will rebound. For domestic tourism, the demand will depend on how Saudi citizens and consumers are able to increase their discretionary spending, which is difficult for the reasons mentioned above, along with rising Saudi consumer debt. In terms of attracting international tourists and developing world-class resorts, the Red Sea Development Corporation, an entity owned by the PIF, faces strong regional competition and requires capital investment that will only drain state resources further; its activities also anger local residents who are displaced and unlikely to reap the economic benefits of the government-owned projects.[37]

The PIF has divided its portfolio or assets under management into distinct domestic and international categories. The logic is to drive and determine the location, sector, and pace of domestic investment and economic growth, while at the same time making significant investments abroad across a number of high-profile and somewhat more speculative placements, especially in technology. These are categorized as 'international strategic investments' and account for about $100 billion of the reported $320 billion assets under management (in mid-2020), with the aspiration to reach $400 billion by the end of 2020 (see Table 5.1).[38] The largest of these external strategic investments is a stake of $45 billion in the Softbank Vision Fund.[39] There are similar co-investments in larger private funds and SWFs, including a $20 billion stake in the Blackstone Infrastructure Fund and a $10 billion co-investment with the Russian Direct Investment Fund.[40] Other high-profile stakes have included a $3.5 billion investment in Uber and a $1 billion stake in both Virgin Galactic (which Virgin Chairman, Richard Branson, has since

---

[36] O. C. Diaz, 'Tourism to Contribute $70bn to Saudi Arabian Economy in 2019', Arab News (29 April 2019), https://www.arabnews.com/node/1489416/business-economy.

[37] Red Sea Development Company, https://www.theredsea.sa/en; R. Michaelson, '"It's Being Built on Our Blood": The True Cost of Saudi Arabia's $500bn Megacity', The Guardian (4 May 2020), https:// www.theguardian.com/global-development/2020/may/04/its-being-built-on-our-blood-the-true-cost- of-saudi-arabia-5bn-mega-city-neom.

[38] A. England, 'Cash-Rich Gulf Funds Hunt for Bargains as Asset Prices Plunge', Financial Times (16 April 2020), https://www.ft.com/content/3facc407-200f-4e7c-9914-79b4baece119; Public Investment Fund, 'Public Investment Fund to Increase Assets under Management to over $400 Billion by 2020' (24 October 2017), https://www.pif.gov.sa/en/MediaCenter/Pages/NewsDetails.aspx?NewsID=32.

[39] I. A. Hamilton, 'Saudi Arabia Is Reportedly Talking to SoftBank about Pouring Billions into Its Second Vision Fund', Business Insider (28 October 2019), https://www.businessinsider.com/saudi-arabia- reportedly-considers-investing-in-softbank-vision-fund-2-2019-10.

[40] G. Tan, 'How Blackstone Landed $20 Billion from Saudis for New Fund', Bloomberg (21 October 2018), https://www.bloomberg.com/news/articles/2018-10-22/how-blackstone-landed-20-billion-from- saudis-for-infrastructure; Russian Direct Investment Fund, 'Saudi Arabia to Invest Record $10bn in Russia' (6 July 2015), https://rdif.ru/Eng_fullNews/1481/.

Table 5.1 Selected PIF assets under management, 2020

International strategic investments	$bn
Softbank Vision Fund	45
Blackstone Infrastructure Fund	20
Egyptian Investment Fund	16
Jordan Investment Fund	
Russian Direct Investment Fund	10
French private equity	
Uber	3.5
Virgin Galactic	1
Lucid	1
International diversified pool	**$bn**
US holdings	9.9
Eni	0.3

declined after the murder of Jamal Khashoggi) and Lucid, an electric car maker.[41]

On the domestic side, the PIF has invested in a number of large infrastructure and tourism development initiatives, which are central to the Vision 2030 agenda. These include so-called 'giga projects' Neom, Quiddiya, and along the Red Sea coast, massive state development projects designed to modernize the Saudi economy and capitalize on untouched tourism and entertainment markets in the Kingdom. Traditional infrastructure in airports and urban development in the holy city of Mecca are also to receive a boost from the PIF.

More traditionally, the PIF (like other SWFs globally) maintains a strong position in US equity markets (Table 5.2). Along with holdings of US Treasuries, the PIF's position as an investor in US-listed companies is substantial, though not often discussed in matters of US foreign policy and the Saudi–US bilateral relationship.

The central role of the PIF in Saudi state capitalism is a factor both in its financial preponderance within the Saudi economy (and the efforts to which the state goes to direct money to its own projects), and also in its rhetorical

[41] M. Isaac and M. J. de la Merced, 'Uber Turns to Saudi Arabia for $3.5 Billion Cash Infusion', *New York Times* (1 June 2016), https://www.nytimes.com/2016/06/02/technology/uber-investment-saudi-arabia.html; L. Grush, 'Richard Branson Suspends Saudi Arabia's Investment in Space Ventures over Missing Journalist', The Verge (13 October 2018), https://www.theverge.com/2018/10/13/17967954/virgin-galactic-richard-branson-saudi-arabia-jamal-khashoggi; Lucid Motors, 'Lucid Motors Closes $1BN+ Investment from the Public Investment Fund of Saudi Arabia' (3 April 2019), https://www.lucidmotors.com/media-room/lucid-motors-closes-1bn-investment-public-investment-fund-saudi-arabia/.

Table 5.2 PIF SEC declared US holdings

Name of issuer	Value ($000)	Shares
Automatic Data Processing	78,454	574,000
Bank of America Corp.	487,569	22,966,034
Berkshire Hathaway Inc.	78,434	429,000
Boeing Co.	713,677	4,785,281
Bookings Holdings Inc.	78,029	58,000
BP PLC	827,751	33,938,127
Broadcom Inc.	76,583	323,000
Canadian Natural Resources Ltd	408,129	30,120,239
Carnival Corp.	456,856	34,689,148
Cisco Systems Inc.	490,881	12,487,436
Citigroup Inc.	521,979	12,392,668
Disney Walt Co.	495,802	5,132,522
Facebook Inc.	521,859	3,128,653
International Business Machines	77,651	700,000
Live Nation Entertainment	416,119	9,153,521
Marriott International Inc. New	513,931	6,869,816
Pfizer Inc.	78,524	2,405,755
Qualcomm Inc.	77,798	1,150,000
Royal Dutch Shell PLC	483,643	13,861,948
Starbucks Corp.	77,573	1,180,000
Suncor Energy Inc. New	481,072	30,447,579
Total S.A.	222,336	5,970,364
Uber Technologies Inc.	2,033,708	72,840,541
Union PAC Corp.	78,841	559,000

Sources: PIF, JPMorgan.

and political influence on Saudi economic life.[42] As a concept, rentierism has dominated socio-political analysis of the Gulf oil-exporting states. In essence, the theory is that the distribution of rents from natural resources allows political space for authoritarian control, making the population more passive and compliant to the state's dominance across social, economic, and political life.[43] Rentier theory has its weaknesses, but it also deserves an examination in relation to the changing nature of the PIF in Saudi political and economic life, especially given the wide opening of Saudi society under the leadership of Mohamed bin Salman and his attempts to 'normalize' the country.[44]

The concept of rentierism is deeply entangled with understandings of state formation and state–society relations in the Arab Gulf states. But it is not just

---

[42] Portions of this section are reprinted with permission from Karen E. Young, 'Sovereign Risk: Gulf Sovereign Wealth Funds as Engines of Growth and Political Resource', *British Journal of Middle Eastern Studies* 47, no. 1 (2020), pp. 96–116, doi: 10.1080/13530194.2020.1714866.

[43] Ibid.

[44] B. Hubbard, 'MBS: The Rise of a Saudi Prince', *New York Times* (21 March 2020), https://www.nytimes.com/2020/03/21/world/middleeast/mohammed-bin-salman-saudi-arabia.html.

about oil; rentierism and 'late rentierism' are investigations into the political consequences of ownership and the sharing of everything from resources and public employment to electricity and foreign investments. This 'sharing' reflects the tension between state and society—what citizens expect from their governments in terms of social services, job provision, and confidence in the rents of natural resources saved for future growth, and in return how the state expects citizens to conform or behave in their demands for political representation and intervention. The core assumption in the literature on rentierism has been somewhat deterministic of the economic power of the state in eliminating representation demands.[45] However, this conception has not gone unchallenged. Examinations by scholars like Gwen Okruhlik and the late Kiren Aziz Chaudhry have noted how financial inflows from resources can be contested in local politics, how resources can drive and create opposition politics, and how the influx of wealth creates its own social and political effects locally.[46]

It should come as no surprise that the idea of shared ownership of resource wealth might be contested, especially at a time of changing understandings of what states can dedicate in their fiscal policy towards the public sector wage bill, mounting defence spending, regional aid, and outwardly placed investment partnerships. One thing is certain in the period of oil price volatility from late 2014 to the present: governments are more experimental in their fiscal policy and more open to shifting responsibilities to both the private sector and their citizens for the provision of social services, while expecting some fees and taxes in return. The decline in oil prices in late 2014 precipitated a torrent of fiscal policy changes across the Gulf Arab states. These reforms covered sensitive issues such as labour market reform; financial sector liberalization; the introduction of consumption and land taxes; and the removal or reduction of subsidies on electricity, water, and fuel.[47]

As a result, it is reasonable to expect some reconfiguration of state–society relations in the Gulf states. Yet there are few signs of public unrest or protest, even with higher costs of living and limited availability of public sector jobs. This muted reaction is a puzzle, at least as a short-term observation. We can also identify how states are proactively anticipating citizen concern, and calibrating reform efforts to buffer or pre-empt discontent. But

---

[45] H. Beblawi and G. Luciani, *The Rentier State: National, State and Integration in the Arab World* (London: Croom Helm, 1987).

[46] G. Okruhlik, 'Rentier Wealth, Unruly Law, and the Rise of the Opposition', *Comparative Politics* 31, no. 3 (1999), pp. 295–315; K. A. Chaudhry, *The Price of Wealth: Economies and Institutions in the Middle East* (Ithaca: Cornell University Press, 1997).

[47] K. E. Young, 'Experiments in Fiscal Governance: The Economic Reform Agenda in the GCC', Rice University's Baker Institute for Public Policy (6 September 2018), https://www.bakerinstitute.org/media/files/research-document/34dcc305/bi-brief-090618-cme-carnegie-young.pdf.

the shifts under way are structural, and society—both citizens and foreign residents—will likely take some time to absorb the impact fully.

In effect, what we have witnessed since late 2014 is a new period of policy experimentation in which the 'end' of a diversified economy, less reliant on oil exports, has justified the 'means' of achieving a radical break in the system of social welfare, changing employment preferences and practices, and establishing a new role for the state in prescribing an agenda for growth. The notion that there is a distinction between private wealth and public wealth becomes relevant. But since the private wealth of citizens often operates in the same spaces and markets as their shared wealth, citizens have a new information flow about the governance and deployment of resource rents. SWFs, as the mechanism to transform oil and gas wealth into financial assets deployed globally in the equity markets of New York and London, in assets of real estate and private equity investments in new technology firms in Silicon Valley, become measurable and quantifiable and can be evaluated by the metrics of an investor—a citizen investor.

SWFs are based upon the shared rents from oil (really, any natural resource) production, but as they have evolved they are also becoming transformative in new national development strategies. These SWFs now veer from traditional practices of safeguarding wealth, to more experimental and high-risk strategies that claim to be able to diversify national economies away from oil dependency, while also promising high returns. The moment of late rentierism is now heightening questions of ownership, of the state's role as guardian or steward of society's wealth. SWFs are also now more closely linked to individual leadership and 'visions' of economic development. They project a collective agreement about how future growth should be achieved, yet their decision making is a hybrid of corporatized investment banking mixed with the will of select leadership. In some ways, SWFs are even more absent of the collective decision making of citizens than traditional political institutions of the region. In Saudi Arabia, as elsewhere, the SWF has become highly personalistic and closely linked to the individual vision and preoccupations of a new generation of leadership. The purpose of the SWF is to function like an inter-generational savings account, a collective nest egg of society that is held and managed by the state.

SWFs in the Gulf states are thus developing some distinctive characteristics, reflective of the 'visions' of their leaders for national economic development. SWFs and their management can tell us about how leadership in these states prioritizes (or minimizes) local economic growth and domestic constituencies (citizens and foreign residents). They tell us how Gulf governments view international partnerships as targets of state investment initiatives. They tell us a lot about the appetite for risk, not just in the language of investments, but also in how leaders take liberties with the savings of their citizens. Even more broadly, the ideas of collective wealth embodied in the SWF can serve as a barometer of state–society relations, defined by how leaders and governments view their responsibility for taking care of and increasing national wealth. These choices also demonstrate how leadership perceives a time horizon for meeting development goals. For example, a certain level of risk is invited by prioritizing the short-term goal of job creation for nationals by accelerating both domestic and external investments in new firms that promise to provide local operations, including investments focused on new technology. A willingness to borrow signals that an SWF is more of an active investment fund, or a hedge fund, than a safe deposit for shared wealth. Here we see the emerging characteristics of the Saudi SWF, the PIF. It is borrowing, selling off existing stakes in state firms, taking a short-term view of returns, and willing to engage in partnerships with foreign funds.[48] A higher risk tolerance of an SWF towards investments can be an indication of the state's perception of threats to its domestic legitimacy—perform and deliver now, or risk unrest and an unsatisfied population at home.

The PIF strategy towards other state-related entities is especially telling. The predatory nature of PIF acquisitions and sell-offs to enable further acquisitions reflects the fund's insulation from normal political debate, consensus, or process. The PIF can simply demand that other state-related entities accommodate its need for funding and its ideas about how to raise capital. SABIC, a major chemical producer, is a key example. The state required funding for the PIF, so Aramco purchased the PIF's 70 per cent stake in SABIC, the Saudi petrochemical giant, at a cost of nearly $70 billion.[49] The Aramco purchase of SABIC shares enabled the PIF to further its own acquisition spree and domestic development projects in an act of government accounting gymnastics.[50]

There is a logic to the PIF's intervention and domineering over other state entities. If the PIF is the master of Saudi Arabia's future, then the traditional engines of growth in oil and petrochemicals are now at the service of its

---

[48] Algethami and Narayanan, 'Saudi Purge Puts Investments at Risk'; A. Narayanan and D. Nair, 'Citi and Goldman to Advise on Mega Saudi Aramco-Sabic Deal', Bloomberg (10 September 2018), https://www.bloomberg.com/news/articles/2018-09-10/citi-goldman-said-to-advise-on-mega-saudi-aramco-sabic-deal; S. Hariharan, 'Saudi Arabia PIF-Backed SoftBank Vision Fund Closes US$93 Billion in Funding', Entrepreneur (23 May 2017), https://www.entrepreneur.com/article/294681.

[49] A. Chopra and O. Hassan, 'Saudi Aramco Deal Throws IPO Further into Doubt', Yahoo! News (31 July 2018), https://www.yahoo.com/news/saudi-aramco-deal-throws-ipo-further-doubt-102841260.html.

[50] K. E. Young, 'Spending to Grow in Saudi Arabia', Arab Gulf States Institute in Washington (10 August 2018), https://agsiw.org/spending-grow-saudi-arabia/.

hybrid diversification strategy. That strategy is to build Saudi expertise in the energy sector into a global energy giant, with more streamlined production from crude oil to refined petroleum to petrochemicals and plastics. The PIF will control this transition, including how to monetize the traditional revenue streams from entities like Aramco. Therefore, the sale of PIF shares of SABIC is intertwined with the Aramco public offering and new efforts to monetize Aramco's assets. In December 2020, Aramco announced plans to sell off pipelines and subsidiaries to raise approximately $10 billion.[51]

The hybrid diversification strategy is an attempt to rebuild revenue streams by investment, with an understanding that oil revenue generation has lost its singular power to drive the Saudi economy. Saudi reserve assets increased from less than $30 billion in 2003 to over $750 billion by early 2015, according to SAMA.[52] Such a jump is not likely to happen again. Saudi reserves are built on oil revenues. Oil prices recovered from their lows of under $30/barrel in 2016 thanks to collaboration between the Organization of Petroleum Exporting Countries (OPEC), Russia, and Mexico, but the shale revolution, electric vehicles, energy efficiency, and a long-term declining demand curve suggest that lower oil prices are here for good. The COVID-19 pandemic has also made that clear. But more importantly, Saudi Arabia has little else with which to fund growth.

Diversification from energy resource dependency is now understood as the development of full-scale energy production into petrochemicals. For Saudi Arabia, the future is plastic and its market is eastward in Asia.[53] And while there is good reason to see the future of global growth in the emerging middle-class consumer market of Asia, we should not see oil as a sustainable source of revenue, even when it is processed into new chemicals and products. As technology advances, it will change the way that we both consume and create all kinds of single-use plastic and more durable products.

Both consumer tastes and regulation will impact the demand for petroleum-based products in the future, certainly in developed economies, but also in emerging markets. Major international oil companies accept this reality. The 2019 *BP Energy Outlook* suggests that the overall growth in energy demand from emerging markets is being offset by declines in energy

---

[51] N. Parasie, A. Narayanan, D. Nair, and M. Martin, 'Aramco Hires Moelis to Raise Billions from Asset Sales', Bloomberg (10 December 2020), https://www.bloomberg.com/news/articles/2020-12-10/aramco-is-said-to-hire-moelis-to-raise-billions-from-asset-sales?srnd=premium-middle-east&sref=euelgVQS.

[52] Saudi Central Bank, 'Monthly Bulletin' (October 2020), https://www.sama.gov.sa/en-us/economicreports/pages/monthlystatistics.aspx.

[53] K. E. Young, 'The Gulf's Eastward Turn: The Logic of Gulf–China Economic Ties', American Enterprise Institute (14 February 2019), https://www.aei.org/research-products/report/the-gulfs-eastward-turn-the-logic-of-gulf-china-economic-ties/.

intensity.[54] Improvements in efficiency and the use of technology will allow global GDP to double by 2040, but energy consumption is set to increase by only a third. This is the new law of diminishing returns if you are an energy exporter.

Therefore, the Saudi economy, along with all other energy-dependent export economies, has a problem. It has massive fiscal commitments both at home and abroad. It has a diminishing source of revenue and a diminishing pool of wealth to draw upon in its foreign reserve assets. Its SWF, the PIF, is responsible for generating returns on investment, but it is capitalized with debt and taking on increasingly risky assets, a departure from traditional government fund strategies that are meant to preserve public shared wealth.[55]

The PIF took out an $11 billion bank loan late in 2018, another in 2019, and pushed Aramco to issue a bond to buy out its shares of SABIC.[56] The PIF sought an additional $7 billion commercial loan to expand its purchasing power in December 2020. Aramco issued an $8 billion bond just a month earlier in November 2020.[57] The state's strategy is to borrow itself into revenue generation, leveraging the assets of the national oil company and privileging the investment strategy of the PIF in the hope of obtaining future returns. The assets of the PIF have doubled in value since 2016, as the acquisition spree has grown faster than the fund's earnings. According to research by Bloomberg, JPMorgan, and national authorities, the composition of PIF assets is also shifting considerably.

In 2016, the PIF had roughly $150 billion in assets, composed of holdings in major state-linked companies such as SABIC, Maaden, Al Marai, Saudi Telecom, and Alinma, and few foreign assets. By 2018, the PIF had nearly $300 billion in assets, of which about 10 per cent, or $30 billion, were foreign assets, up from about $11 billion in 2017, made possible by an injection from SAMA and the Ministry of Finance in late 2016. This injection may also account for the increased amount of capital outflows as the PIF invests

[54] BP Oil, 'Energy Outlook 2019' (14 February 2019), https://www.bp.com/en/global/corporate/news-and-insights/press-releases/bp-energy-outlook-2019.html.

[55] K. E. Young, 'What's Yours Is Mine: Gulf Sovereign Wealth Funds as a Barometer of State–Society Relations', Project on Middle East Political Science (31 January 2019), https://www.aei.org/articles/whats-yours-is-mine-gulf-sovereign-wealth-funds-as-a-barometer-of-state-society-relations/.

[56] D. Afanasieva, 'Saudi Sovereign Fund PIF Raises $11 Billion Loan: Source', Reuters (24 August 2018), https://www.reuters.com/article/us-saudi-aramco-ipo-loan/saudi-sovereign-fund-pif-raises-11-billion-loan-source-idUSKCN1L90WK; A. Narayanan, J. Poh, and M. Martin, 'Saudi Wealth Fund Said to Seek Bridge Loan of Up to $8 Billion', Bloomberg (12 April 2019), https://www.bloomberg.com/news/articles/2019-04-12/saudi-wealth-fund-said-to-seek-bridge-loan-of-up-to-8-billion; 'Aramco Plans $10 Billion Bond Issue to Finance SABIC Acquisition', Seeking Alpha (16 January 2019), https://seekingalpha.com/article/4233669-aramco-plans-10-billion-bond-issue-to-finance-sabic-acquisition.

[57] M. Martin, N. I. Ismail, D. C. Mutua, and S. Maki, 'World's Biggest Oil Firm Saudi Aramco Raises $8 Billion Bond', Bloomberg (17 November 2020). https://www.bloomberg.com/news/articles/2020-11-17/world-s-biggest-oil-firm-saudi-aramco-kicks-off-jumbo-bond-sale?sref=euelgVQS.

in companies abroad, either in equities or by direct investments. The strong preference for technology investments, from Uber to Magic Leap, indicates some sector leanings probably driven by a top decision-maker rather than financial managers.[58]

As an example of the new focus on technology investment, the PIF is a major partner in the SoftBank Vision Fund, an investment fund focused on new technology. The Vision Fund is part of the larger company SoftBank, which is a telecommunications provider and investor. SoftBank's operating profit jumped by nearly 50 per cent in 2018, including a profit of JPY245 billion (about $2.21 billion) in the Vision Fund, specifically.[59] The Vision Fund is the brainchild of Masayoshi Son, the head of SoftBank, who in 2017 convinced Saudi Arabia (through its PIF) to partner him, along with Apple Inc. and other backers, to pool nearly $100 billion to deploy in robotics, artificial intelligence, e-commerce, ride-sharing, satellites, and future technology companies.[60] The Vision Fund (or the first fund of two planned) had a rather rocky debut, with its performance in early 2020 posting significant losses. At the end of fiscal 2019, SoftBank Group reported that the Vision Fund held eighty-eight investments that had lost $75 billion. By the end of 2020, performance improved somewhat on the back of the pandemic tech rebound.[61] The experience so far, however, has clearly demonstrated the risk and volatility of technology sector investing, especially for a fund largely composed of government, and therefore citizens', investments.

The PIF is not just a passive investor, however. Much of Vision 2030—the ambitious economic and social plan to diversify Saudi Arabia's economy, jump-start its private sector, and create jobs for young people—relies on the PIF as an orchestrator of economic growth. In fact, the PIF is so central to the government's growth strategy that finding resources to feed the PIF has become a national economic priority. The initial public offering (IPO) of a small stake in the state-owned oil giant Aramco was intended to provide funds to the PIF for its broader national economic growth strategy. That strategy now looks somewhat unwieldy, given that the IPO ended up as the

---

[58] E. Brown and G. Bensinger, 'Saudi Money Flows into Silicon Valley—and with It Qualms', *Wall Street Journal* (16 October 2018), https://www.wsj.com/articles/saudi-backlash-threatens-u-s-startups-1539707574; A. Strange, 'Magic Leap Confirms Massive New $461 Million Investment from Saudi Investors and Others', Next Reality (7 March 2018), https://magic-leap.reality.news/news/magic-leap-confirms-massive-new-461-million-investment-from-saudi-investors-others-0183311/.
[59] P. Alpeyev, 'SoftBank Is Starting to Look a Lot Like a Private Equity Firm', Bloomberg (6 August 2018), https://www.bloomberg.com/news/articles/2018-08-06/softbank-profit-jumps-on-boost-from-arm-vision-fund-gains.
[60] Young, 'Spending to Grow in Saudi Arabia'.
[61] A. Wilhelm, 'How SoftBank's Vision Fund Turned Losses into Gold This Summer', Tech Crunch (12 November 2020), https://techcrunch.com/2020/11/12/how-softbanks-vision-fund-turned-losses-into-gold-this-summer/.

sale of a very small stake in the national oil company and was only listed on the domestic exchange, the Tadāwul.[62]

Furthermore, Aramco has found itself not only pillaged for the PIF, but more directly used as a foreign economic policy tool by the state and its young leadership. For example, in the oil price war of March 2020, as the COVID-19 pandemic hit oil demand in China and the OPEC+ agreement in place since December 2016 began to wobble, the Crown Prince made a calculated decision to flood international oil markets with Saudi supply.[63] The Saudi political directive made it very clear that despite the IPO and the Kingdom's extreme fiscal vulnerability to low oil prices, the national oil company remained the domain of the ruler, or his uniquely empowered deputy.

Aramco as a company was doing just fine; it did not need to raise capital through a public offering. Its success was the result of its singular purpose and simple business model—to produce and export oil to generate revenue for the state. The IPO was never about raising capital for the company, but rather to fund the enormous spending requirements of the state. As a result, Aramco moved closer to its new strategy of becoming a major international oil contender with capacities in upstream, production, refining, petrochemical production, and the natural gas business. This too was a synergy of government political alignment with its key customers in the East, a diversification strategy from its core area of revenue generation to energy products of all kinds, and a continued dependency between the state and its core economic resource. The rate that the government takes from Aramco's earnings was reduced from 85 to 50 per cent, and the company made a number of changes in its legal structures to make it more attractive to new shareholders, publishing a corporate charter and providing more details on reserves and financials as part of a bond prospectus.[64] Changing the legal structure into a joint stock company in early 2018 was a first step to putting Aramco into position for even a local offering.[65] A listing on the local exchange, the Tadāwul,

[62] K. Kelly and S. Reed, 'How Aramco's Huge IPO Fell Short of Saudi Prince's Wish', *New York Times* (6 December 2019), https://www.nytimes.com/2019/12/06/business/energy-environment/saudi-aramco-ipo.html.

[63] M. Martin and A. DiPaola, 'Crown Prince's Oil War Looms over First Aramco Results since IPO', BNN Bloomberg (13 March 2020), https://www.bnnbloomberg.ca/crown-prince-s-oil-war-looms-over-first-aramco-results-since-ipo-1.1405343.

[64] P. Cornell, 'Saudi Aramco Bond Offering: What Does It Say about the Kingdom and Oil Markets?', Atlantic Council (23 April 2019), https://www.atlanticcouncil.org/blogs/energysource/saudi-aramco-bond-offering-what-does-it-say-about-the-kingdom-and-oil-markets/; Saudi Aramco, 'Global Medium Term Note Programme' (1 April 2019), https://www.rns-pdf.londonstockexchange.com/rns/6727U_1-2019-4-1.pdf.

[65] R. El Gamal and A. El Yaakoubi, 'Saudi Arabia Converts Aramco into Joint-Stock Company ahead of Historic IPO', Reuters (4 January 2018), https://www.reuters.com/article/us-saudi-aramco-saudi-arabia-converts-aramco-into-joint-stock-company-ahead-of-historic-ipo-idUSKBN1EU09O.

looked to be simple on paper but was overwhelming for the small market. Aramco's market cap surpassed the entire market cap of companies listed on the exchange.[66] The Aramco IPO can be summarized in this way: it was a political decision deemed necessary to satisfy the ambition and development agenda of the Crown Prince, spearheaded by the PIF.[67]

There is little public discussion in Saudi Arabia of how government-funded investment strategy works for the benefit of citizens. Of course, in Saudi Arabia citizens are not active shareholders of the PIF, but rather beneficiaries of the government's largesse. The government remains the largest employer and source of economic activity in the country.[68] Its domination of the economy continues, including efforts of the PIF to spend, or invest, its way to growth. But the PIF has been so active and so very public in its new investment strategy that citizens cannot help but be aware of the change in direction, and the mounting responsibility of this fund for national economic development. So, in effect, the PIF is an arm of fiscal policy more broadly in Saudi Arabia, virtually a parallel government institution with enormous responsibility and flexibility in using its shared resources. Its new choices should generate returns, just like any other investment, but some investments will be winners and others will be disappointments. In fact, many of the choices the PIF makes now will determine what resources exist for domestic investment many years in the future, when oil revenue and foreign reserves have dwindled.

Captured Unicorns

The Aramco IPO was a big deal, but it should not have been.[69] The gap between the expectation and the outcome of the 'world's biggest IPO' only underscores the region's failure to incubate and nurture new business giants. Aramco is a large and successful state-owned monopoly, forced to sell off shares to citizens and friends of the government to provide resources for the

[66] F. Pacheco, 'Aramco's Giant Profit Dwarfs Earnings of 163 Saudi Stocks', Bloomberg (1 April 2019), https://www.bloomberg.com/news/articles/2019-04-01/aramco-s-giant-profit-dwarfs-joint-earnings-of-163-saudi-stocks.

[67] K. E. Young, 'Saudi Arabia Selling the Aramco IPO, Yet Again', Al-Monitor (20 August 2019), https://www.al-monitor.com/pulse/originals/2019/08/saudi-arabia-selling-aramco-ipo.html#ixzz6fxpBO7vh.

[68] Harvard Kennedy School, 'The Labor Market in Saudi Arabia: Background, Areas of Progress, and Insights for the Future' (2019), https://epod.cid.harvard.edu/sites/default/files/2019-08/EPD_Report_Digital.pdf.

[69] K. E. Young, 'Where Are the Other IPOs in the Mideast?', Al-Monitor (13 November 2019), https://www.al-monitor.com/pulse/originals/2019/11/ipo-aramco-middle-east-saudi-arabia-business.html#ixzz6fxuheSaQ.

state.[70] However, it does not inhabit a regulatory environment or rules-based economy that can make it a global, investor-owned, publicly traded powerhouse. Aramco is clearly owned by the state; but how do smaller, more entrepreneurial firms fare in the Saudi ecosystem?

Across the Middle East, the volume of IPOs is low. Part of the reason is that it is difficult for businesses to grow. Most people in the private sector end up working in small businesses. Researchers at the World Bank have found that small-scale activities provide the majority of jobs in the Middle East and North Africa (MENA), with some variation across countries.[71] Employment in microbusinesses with fewer than five employees dominates the private sector in Egypt and the West Bank and Gaza, reaching almost 60 per cent. It is significantly lower in Jordan (40 per cent) and Tunisia (37 per cent), and the lowest in Turkey (34 per cent). The share of jobs in establishments with at least 1,000 employees is below 10 per cent in all five countries. In high-income countries, larger firms are more likely to employ a large portion of the workforce and to train and promote employees. The World Bank study on 'Jobs or Privileges' compared firms' growth in MENA to that in the United States of America, where 48 per cent of all employees work in firms with more than 10,000 employees.[72] As many medium and larger firms in the Middle East become part of a cycle of elite 'state capture', they tend not to continue growing, productivity slows down, and there is little reason for meritocracy in promotion.[73]

IPOs in the Middle East fall into three categories: toxic and inefficient state-owned assets; amalgamations of real-estate holdings (often via real-estate investment trusts) that do little to boost economic productivity; and the rare unicorn of a real business, which may also be partially or fully government owned.[74] Aramco is the latter. For investors in the Middle East, there are slim pickings. Aramco's listing drives home the reality that citizen investors have limited investment opportunities, and many are crowded out by their governments.

[70] D. Nair and M. Martin, 'Aramco Taps Saudi Billionaires for Major IPO Orders', Bloomberg, 7 November (2019), https://www.bloomberg.com/news/articles/2019-11-07/aramco-taps-billionaire-olayans-prince-alwaleed-for-ipo-orders.

[71] M. Schiffbauer, A. Sy, S. Hussain, H. Sahnoun, and P. Keefer, 'Jobs or Privileges: Unleashing the Employment Potential of the Middle East and North Africa' (Washington, DC: World Bank, 2015), https://openknowledge.worldbank.org/handle/10986/20591.

[72] Ibid.

[73] T. C. Wittes, 'Want to Stabilize the Middle East? Start with Governance', Brookings (22 November 2016), https://www.brookings.edu/blog/markaz/2016/11/22/want-to-stabilize-the-middle-east-start-with-governance/.

[74] PwC, 'Emergence of Real Estate Investment Trust (REIT) in the Middle East' (2017), https://www.pwc.com/m1/en/publications/emergence-real-estate-investment-trust.html.

Citizens from Saudi Arabia to Egypt are encouraged to buy shares in government-owned entities that they should probably be given, not sold. Egypt saw a flurry of pre-IPO activity because the government has come under pressure from the International Monetary Fund (IMF) to sell off state-owned assets, mostly owned by its military, to demonstrate its commitment to a more open economy and secure a further IMF funding package in 2020.[75] Egyptian officials aim to sell off stakes in over twenty firms across a range of sectors, from petrochemicals to finance and real estate, with hopes of raising close to $5 billion.[76] Saudi Arabia is likely to move into a similar pattern, not to secure an IMF package, but to raise capital for broader development goals, particularly during the recovery from the terrible economic performance of 2020 following the oil price collapse and the COVID-19 pandemic, which derailed many of the tourism and FDI goals of the Kingdom. There are signs of increasing listings and IPOs of firms in Saudi Arabia, some of state-owned assets, and other private entities in more promising areas of growth, especially in health care.[77]

A survey of IPOs across MENA by the consultancy EY found sixty-nine IPOs from the first quarter of 2017 to the third quarter of 2019, just nine of which were in 2019.[78] The year 2019 was slow, with fits and starts, and the volume of capital raised is even more disappointing. While the second quarter of 2019 had the highest level of quarterly proceeds raised in more than two years, at just over $2.6 billion, the third quarter of 2019 saw just $190 million in issues raised in MENA. There can be wide variation in the size and quantity of listings from quarter to quarter as in any regional market, but the MENA region can be especially volatile. Globally, in the third quarter of 2019, there were 256 IPOs, raising $40.2 billion. While analysing one quarter of activity gives more of a snapshot indicator (one big issue can skew the data widely), it demonstrates the low and inconsistent volume that the Middle East generates.

There are unicorns in the Middle East, but even they are subject to the appreciative gaze of the state. Consider ACWA Power as an example. Formed

[75] V. Furness, 'Egypt Hopes to Secure New IMF Agreement by March, Says Finance Minister', Euromoney (25 October 2019), https://www.euromoney.com/article/b1hr139z1htyq4/egypt-hopes-to-secure-new-imf-agreement-by-march-says-finance-minister.

[76] M. Magdy, 'Aramco IPO Becomes Factor in Timing of Egypt's Own Share Offers', Bloomberg (31 October 2019), https://www.bloomberg.com/news/articles/2019-10-31/aramco-ipo-becomes-factor-in-timing-of-egypt-s-own-share-offers.

[77] C. Mellow, 'There's Another Pipeline for IPOs Beyond Wall Street. It's Saudi Arabia. Really', Barron's (11 December 2020), https://www.barrons.com/articles/theres-another-pipeline-for-ipos-beyond-wall-street-its-saudi-arabia-really-51607706526.

[78] EY, 'When Will the Economy Catch Up with the Capital Markets?' (Q3, 2020), https://assets.ey.com/content/dam/ey-sites/ey-com/en_gl/topics/growth/ey-global-ipo-trends-2020-q3-final-v1.pdf.

in 2004, ACWA Power is now the largest developer of power and desalination projects in MENA, with a specialization in renewable and solar projects. ACWA's management has frequently talked about an IPO of the company, but the listing has been delayed as the company has taken on more private investors, most notably the PIF.[79]

The PIF has gradually increased its ownership stake (initially 12 per cent, then 25 per cent, 40 per cent, and 50 per cent in late 2020) in ACWA since 2017, as opportunities for investment in renewable energy in both Saudi Arabia and the GCC have expanded with respective national renewable energy targets.[80] As the Chief Executive of ACWA said in an interview with MEED, 'They [the PIF] bring the ability to invest as co-investors in some of the larger projects we do.'[81] Those larger projects include Saudi government contracts, which now also benefit the PIF as investor and owner. The Saudi government will profit from its equity stake when the firm does list publicly, but the opportunity for private investors will be halved.

There are some successful IPO stories, notably in areas where the provision of state services is poor or in need of reform. For example, the listing of the private school provider Ataa Educational Company on the Saudi Tadāwul in the third quarter of 2019 raised $93 million.[82] The company provides K-12 education in Saudi Arabia, something the state also does but which it hopes to do less, so that citizens can pay out-of-pocket and the demands on fiscal outlays for education spending might decrease.

The problem of captured unicorns, and the rarity of new business listings in general, is the challenge of competing in areas where the state is also in business, or acting as an investor-competitor to the state when the latter has the PIF and its mandate to acquire domestic opportunities aggressively. There can be no similar fund in private hands that has the assets and political leverage of the PIF. Even external investment funds will choose to partner with the PIF rather than bid against it.

[79] P. Dey, 'ACWA Power to Reveal IPO Plans "Soon"', Argaam (24 March 2019), https://www.argaam.com/en/article/articledetail/id/600644.
[80] Acwa Power, 'Public Investment Fund Acquires Significant Stake in Acwa Power' (4 July 2018), https://www.acwapower.com/news/public-investment-fund-acquires-significant-stake-in-acwa-power/; M. Martin and D. Nair, 'Saudi Wealth Fund Increases ACWA Stake to 50% Ahead of IPO', Bloomberg (19 November 2020), https://www.bloomberg.com/news/articles/2020-11-19/saudi-wealth-fund-said-near-deal-to-boost-acwa-stake-before-ipo.
[81] A. Roscoe, 'Leading the Transition to Renewable Energy', MEED (24 October 2019), https://www.meed.com/leading-transition-renewable-energy/.
[82] 'Saudi Private School Operator Ataa Educational Jumps 10% in Riyadh Trading Debut', Arabian Business (31 July 2019), https://www.arabianbusiness.com/education/425076-saudi-private-school-operator-ataa-educational-jumps-10-in-riyadh-trading-debut.

The Problem of Foreign Direct Investment

The assets of the state, including its SWF, its national oil company, and the financial institutions it dominates to regulate the market, are all examples of the supply side of Saudi state capitalism. Saudi Arabia's inability to attract FDI demonstrates the demand side of the problem of state capitalism. Although Saudi economic statecraft has some significant leverage in the political economy of the wider region, and the PIF has demonstrated its ability to gobble up equity stakes in technology firms and funds worldwide, the real power of a domestic economy is judged by its ability to attract capital. The lack of outside investors has become evidence that something is not working in the Kingdom's plans for economic liberalization and diversification; it is the best evidence of a distorted market. For Saudi Arabia, the ability to attract FDI has been in a decade-long lull. It is not attributable solely to the project of Vision 2030 or the leadership style of Crown Prince Mohamed bin Salman. The lack of FDI is more of a structural feature of the Saudi economy and the problem of state investment crowding out opportunity for others.

Figure 5.2 illustrates the profound challenge of the last decade, between the global financial crisis of 2009 and late 2019. There are dips that we can attribute to the political climate, particularly in 2017 with the corruption purge and investor scare concerning the possible vindictiveness of Saudi foreign policy. But the general trend is beyond leadership politics. The recent upward trend in outflows between 2017 and 2019 (declining slightly between 2018 and 2019) demonstrates the capacity of the PIF and state outward investments. As we have seen, this is a kind of sovereign gamble, directing funds away from the domestic economy in the hope of generating a return on investment to spend at home. Private outflows have also been significant, signalling that domestic investors and wealthy businesspeople are not optimistic about the prospects of growth at home. The government's reaction, especially informally imposing import controls during 2017–18, only heightened the sense of risk in domestic investing.[83]

According to research by JPMorgan, capital outflows of residents in Saudi Arabia were projected at $65 billion in 2018, or 8.4 per cent of GDP. This is less than the $80 billion lost in 2017, but the sign of a continuing trend.[84] This

[83] A. Carey, 'Wealthy Saudis Trying to Move 9-Figure Sums out of the Country Are Being Intimidated by the Government', Business Insider (10 February 2019), https://www.businessinsider.com/alaco-wealthy-saudis-moving-nine-figure-sums-out-intimidated-2019-2.

[84] K. E. Young, 'Saudi Arabia's Problem Isn't the Canada Fight, It's Capital Flight', Bloomberg (17 August 2018), https://www.bloomberg.com/opinion/articles/2018-08-17/saudi-arabia-s-problem-not-the-canada-fight-but-capital-flight.

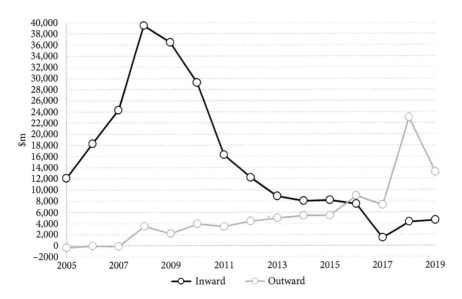

Figure 5.2 Saudi foreign direct investment flows, 2005–19
Source: UNCTAD.

flight signalled a dimming optimism surrounding Crown Prince Mohammed
bin Salman's Vision 2030. Many of the institutional reforms outlined in the
plan—designed to diversify the Saudi economy, attract foreign investment,
and create jobs—are needed to liberalize the state-led, resource-dependent
economy. Investors had hoped Riyadh would follow through on economic
reforms, but they have been cautioned by the lack of parallel reforms in the
social sphere and a persistent inclination towards repression of any form of
opposition, perceived or real. Such high-profile actions as the arrest of prominent businessmen and members of the ruling family continued from 2017
into 2020.[85] Arrests and accusations of terrorism against women activists are
an especially alarming signal of the limits to the state's pace and management of social liberalization.[86] These measures indicate that the state favours
regime stability and consolidation over the rule of law and the creation of
institutions and regulations that can check the state. Drawing direct causa-
tion to the ability of the Saudi economy to attract FDI is difficult, but there has
clearly been a difficult public relations battle for the Kingdom simultaneously
to celebrate new opportunities and cases of domestic repression.

[85] K. Knipp and T. Allinson, 'High-Profile Arrests in Saudi Arabia Shore Up Crown Prince's Power', Deutsche Welle (9 March 2020), https://www.dw.com/en/mohammed-bin-salman-saudi-arabia-crown-prince/a-54804532.
[86] L. Doucet, 'Loujain al-Hathloul: Saudi Activist's Trial "Moved to Terrorism Court"', BBC News (25 November 2020), https://www.bbc.com/news/world-middle-east-55069863.

Most striking is that the capital flight that occurred between 2017 and 2019 took place during a period of relative recovery in global oil prices after the sharp decline that began in late 2014. Since 2020, the economic situation has only reinforced the Kingdom's need for FDI, while painful austerity measures (including the imposition of 15 per cent VAT in July 2020) have proved a risk to domestic growth.[87] The period between 2016 and 2019 may now look more like an opportunity lost.

While efforts at privatization and encouraging private sector investment have lagged, government spending continues to focus on large, state-funded development and infrastructure projects. Neom is a $500 billion project to develop 10,000 square miles in the north-western corner of Saudi Arabia, on the shores of the Red Sea.[88] It is far from major population centres, where people are looking for work, and there is a mismatch between planned high-tech industrial projects and the Saudi labour force's available skill set. The insistence on moving forward with such 'giga projects', despite declining revenues and a challenging FDI outlook, again shows the dependency of such projects on funding from the PIF. In turn, the PIF depends on debt or other state entities as a source of leverage or cash, as it did in the cases of both Aramco and SABIC discussed above.

Conclusion

Saudi state capitalism is indeed distinct from its Chinese contemporary and its earlier East Asian or South American predecessors. It is personalistic, driven by the aspirations and at the direction of the Kingdom's new leadership under Crown Prince Mohamed bin Salman. But it also has structural roots, based in a rentier political economy and a history of natural resource dependency and pro-cyclical fiscal policy. Diversification efforts tend to repeat old patterns of state-led intervention in the economy, despite some real efforts at liberalization in financial markets and the expansion of investment and ownership opportunities. The externalities of the reform period since 2016 have proven extremely difficult, especially the impact on tourism and entertainment in the wake of the COVID-19 pandemic. There may yet be an opportunity for significant FDI in tourism within the Kingdom, but it will

[87] Z. Sabah and V. Nereim, 'Saudi Arabia Plans $26.6 Billion Austerity Cuts, Triples VAT', BNN Bloomberg (10 May 2020), https://www.bnnbloomberg.ca/saudi-arabia-plans-26-6-billion-austerity-cuts-triples-vat-1.1434283.
[88] K. E. Young, 'Saudi Arabia's Neom: State-Led Growth Meets New Global Capitalism', Arab Gulf States Institute in Washington (26 October 2017), https://agsiw.org/saudi-arabias-neom-state-led-growth-meets-new-global-capitalism/.

most certainly be in partnership with state entities. Where state-led development agendas in other countries have tried to create ecosystems guided by state industrial policy, those ecosystems have usually deployed investments in human capital and an array of supporting institutions from universities to business groups to multiple supporting ministries, while the Saudi case seems to rely on a central institution, the PIF, for its diversification and revenue generation plans.

This chapter has argued that the Saudi state developmental model relies on some old structural features and some predatory new ones. The old structural features are related to the nature of an oil-dependent national economy, fed by revenues of a state-owned oil company. The PIF dominates the new Saudi state capitalism. The four interlinked examples in this chapter have demonstrated how state intervention in the economy functions in Saudi Arabia, precisely through the institutions and forces meant to forward diversification and liberalization. The examination of the Saudi domestic stock market, the Tadāwul, suggests that despite efforts such as index inclusion for institutional investors abroad, the exchange remains dominated by state investor activity and incentives. The chapter has dissected the role of the PIF and the government's efforts to feed it with capital intended for both domestic investment and outward acquisition, showing that it has ended up with a fund that takes risks with citizens' shared wealth and often crowds out private investment. The example of 'captured unicorns' demonstrates this crowding-out effect. Finally, the discussion of the problem of FDI has revealed how the Saudi market is viewed by free capital. Saudi state capitalism has historical institutional roots, but its manifestation since 2016 reveals new patterns of state intervention and an appetite for risk that may have distinct social and political effects in the future.

PART 2
ECONOMIC THEMES

6

Decolonizing the GCC

The Case of the Labour Market in Saudi Arabia

Zafiris Tzannatos and John Sfakianakis

Introduction

This chapter examines the functioning and outcomes of the labour market in the context of the development model Saudi Arabia has pursued since the 1970s. It notes the historical failure of policies to provide decent employment to Saudis outside the public sector, to increase productivity, and to accelerate economic growth despite massive revenues from the oil sector. The reasons for these less than satisfactory outcomes can be associated politically with a social contract that has been based on an authoritarian bargain between the political leaders and the citizens, and economically with the patronage of the private sector in such a way that its proceeds have mainly been appropriated by the establishment's elite. Both have resulted in the poor use of the oil revenues.

The end result has been problematic for both segments of the labour market. On the one hand, the public sector lacks *fiscal* discipline by acting as the employer of last resort. On the other hand, the private sector lacks *domestic* market discipline as the migration policy allows employers to hire workers at the low levels of wages that prevail in the sending countries. Public sector employment has not been a vehicle for providing valuable goods and services but instead has served as a mechanism for redistributing the national patrimony. This political and economic configuration combined with an excessive reliance on low-wage migrant labour has had a direct adverse effect on the employment outcomes for nationals.

The findings of this chapter can be summarized in two terms. The first is an 'illusion of political permanence': that is, a belief that the country can be modernized and became a dynamic market economy without accommodating

Zafiris Tzannatos and John Sfakianakis, *Decolonizing the GCC*. In: *The Economy of Saudi Arabia in the 21st Century*.
Edited by: John Sfakianakis, Oxford University Press. © Zafiris Tzannatos and John Sfakianakis (2024).
DOI: 10.1093/oso/9780198863878.003.0007

changes in governance that would create productive, not rentier, economic opportunities and empower citizens to choose freely between them.

The second term is 'reverse colonization', whereby the numbers of migrants have not only shaped labour market outcomes but also acted as a population Ponzi scheme, leading to the growth of the domestic economy based on non-tradables (for example, housing, transport, utilities, private consumption, and so on). The production of non-tradables has attracted few Saudi job-seekers while it has benefited a relative small class of Saudis who sponsor migrant workers.

Vision 2030 aims to address these areas, among others, by eliminating corruption, energizing the economy through the private sector, reducing the number of migrants, and increasing the employment of nationals. Its likely prospects are discussed at the end of this chapter after a presentation of the characteristics and outcomes of the labour market for Saudi workers and a discussion of their likely causes.

The Bird's-Eye View of Employment and Wages

Real gross domestic product (GDP) in the Kingdom of Saudi Arabia (henceforth Saudi Arabia) increased by 5.4 times between 1970 and 2019, amounting to a reputable annual rate of growth 3.5 per cent.[1] However, between these two dates the resident population had increased by 5.9 times, from 5.8 million to 34 million, which corresponds to an annual growth of 4 per cent. Combining the changes in these two variables implies that real GDP per capita declined at an annual rate of 0.2 per cent, from $22,133 in 1970 to $20,542 by 2019.[2] Hidden in this comparison are, first, the high volatility of the economic growth rate due to fluctuations in the international price of oil, and second, the growth in the non-Saudi population from 357,000 to 10.2 million—a thirty-fold increase.[3] In addition, the first reliable estimates of population came only in 1974 when the first census was conducted and, if the starting period of the comparison is set to 1974, real GDP grew at an annual rate of 2.1 per cent until 2019 and employment at 4.7 per cent.[4] This is disheartening as

---

[1] From SAR303 billion in 1970 to SAR1,649 billion in 2019 in constant 2017 national prices. https://fred.stlouisfed.org/series/RGDPNASAA666NRUG.

[2] In constant 2010 US dollars. See https://data.worldbank.org/indicator/NY.GDP.PCAP.KD?locations=SA.

[3] See 'Saudi Arabia Immigration Statistics 1960–2021', *Macrotrends*, https://www.macrotrends.net/countries/SAU/saudi-arabia/immigration-statistics.

[4] The first census in 1974 estimated the population at 6.7 million people of whom 800,000 were foreigners and 5.9 million (88 per cent) were nationals. Notably, the working age at the time started at the age of 12 (not the more conventional age of 15 years) and according to this definition there were

it implies an employment/output elasticity that is significantly higher than 1 (in fact, 2.2), clearly indicating negative productivity growth. The reasons for this macro outcome are discussed below and summarized at the end of this section.

A Four-Way Segmented Labour Market: The Employment Side

By 2019, total, national and migrant, employment stood at 12.5 million. The employment growth by sex and nationality is shown in Figure 6.1. This translates to a total dependency rate of 170 per cent that is reputable but driven by the high numbers of non-Saudis. The dependency rate among Saudis is double that figure, standing at 330 per cent due to their low labour force participation rates, which for men stand at 67 per cent and for women only 23 per cent. As will be argued below, the low labour force participation rate of nationals and the high number of migrant workers have important implications for the economy in terms productivity growth, and for society in terms of the ability of labour earnings alone to sustain the welfare of citizens in the absence of generous social benefits.

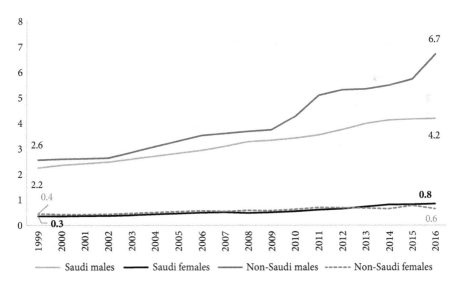

Figure 6.1 Employment (15+) by sex and nationality, 1999–2016 (millions)

Source: Official Labour Force Survey results.

1.536 million workers of whom 1,286 thousand (84 per cent) were Saudis. See https://digitalcommons. uri.edu/cgi/viewcontent.cgi?article=2118&context=theses; https://population.un.org/wpp/Download/ Standard/Population/.

The confluence of the above three factors (the national/migrant population composition, the low propensity of Saudis to work, and gender differences) is reflected in the employment distribution shown in Table 6.1.

The significant employment differentials are accompanied by equally big differences in wages (Table 6.2).[5] The wages of Saudi workers are a multiple of those for non-Saudis (2.7 times in the case of men and 3.0 times in the case of women).

This aggregate view of the labour market is already adequate to establish the much-noted threefold segmentation of the labour market, which is also commonly found in the other Gulf Cooperation Council (GCC) economies: The labour market is divided between nationals and migrant workers, between the public sector and the private sector, and between women and men.

Table 6.1 Employment (000s) and its composition (%), by sector, sex, and nationality, 2018

	Saudi			Non-Saudi			Saudization rate
	Male	Female	Total (*n*)	Male	Female	Total (*n*)	
Public	28.3%	17.0%	1,407	0.7%	0.4%	79	95%
Private*	37.3%	17.4%	1,704	95.8%	3.1%	6,896	20%
Total (*n*)	2,041	1,070	3,111	6,729	246	6,975	31%

Note: * Excludes 3.7 million domestic workers, all of whom are non-Saudi, and those in the security and military sectors and the non-registered in the records of GOSI; figures are subject to rounding.
Source: General Organization for Social Insurance (GOSI).

Table 6.2 Comparison of wages by nationality and sex, 2018 (Index 100 = average wage in the economy)*

Nationality	Male	Female	Total
Saudi	167	150	164
Non-Saudi	61	50	60
Ratio of Saudi/non-Saudi	2.8	3.0	2.8
Total	99	106	100

Note: * The average wage was SAR6,277 ($1,695); see also notes to Table 6.1.
Source: General Organization for Social Insurance (GOSI).

[5] The average wage for citizens is about $2,800 in the public sector and $2,000 in the private sector. The average wage for migrants in the private sector is $1,000. S. Hertog, 'Making Wealth Sharing More Efficient in High-Rent Countries: The Citizens' Income' (2017), Springer Open Access paper at https://link.springer.com/article/10.1007/s41825-017-0007-2.

The result is that labour productivity in Saudi Arabia has remained low (Figure 6.2). This also applies to total factor productivity growth. Labour contribution to non-oil growth has been in decline since 2011 and capital accumulation has followed in the same downward pattern.[6] Saudi Arabia, like other oil exporters, experienced a slowing down in non-oil growth after the oil price shock in 2014. The delinkage between oil, productivity, and non-oil growth has yet to happen structurally, though it may if the outcomes of Vision 2023 materialize as originally envisaged.

A fourth divide in the labour market has received less attention in the literature. The labour market also is segmented *within* the private sector. The tell-tale sign of this is that there are practically no self-employed Saudis, especially women. In fact, not only has the share of the self-employed in employment been low; it has also been declining over time from more than 8 per cent in 1991 to less than 5 per cent by 2020.[7] This compares to 15 per cent in high-income economies, reaching 25 per cent in South Korea.[8] The low rate in Saudi Arabia seems unexpected on the face of it, as small and

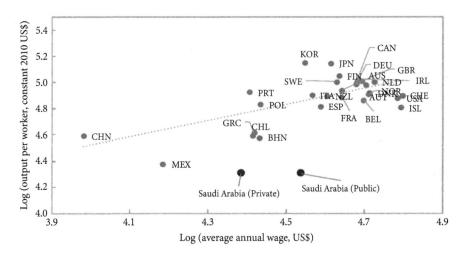

Figure 6.2 Average wages and labour productivity, 2010

Note: Productivity for Saudi Arabia and Bahrain is estimated using the relationship between the quality of human capital (based on the World Bank's Human Capital Index) and productivity in the sample of countries shown, as direct data on productivity of nationals in Saudi Arabia and Bahrain are not available.

Sources: International Labour Organization; World Bank; country authorities; IMF staff calculations.

---

[6] Saudi Arabia, Article IV Consultation (2021). IMF Country Report No. 2021/149 (2021), p. 62.

[7] United Nations, Department of Economic and Social Affairs, Population Division, 'International Migrant Stock 2019', United Nations database, POP/DB/MIG/Stock/Rev.2019.

[8] https://data.worldbank.org/indicator/SL.EMP.SELF.ZS?locations=SA, reporting ILO modelled estimate from ILOSTAT database. Data retrieved 20 September 2020.

medium-sized enterprises (SMEs) contribute 20 per cent to non-oil GDP,[9] though the total contribution of the private sector to non-oil/non-financial GDP is only 30 per cent.[10]

The virtual absence of self-employment has been attributed to 'the many Pakistani store owners, Egyptian engineers and Indian restaurateurs who work in SMEs under Saudi sponsors.'[11] The sponsorship system described below has given rise to hundreds of thousands of business ventures (*tasattur*) that are effectively conducted by expatriates but are registered in the name of some Saudi sponsor. Nearly all (more than 95 per cent) are small-scale undertakings in the form of retail shops, restaurants, car/appliance/repair workshops, and vegetable markets, among others, and are operated by migrants.[12] Under this system, which is officially illegal, Saudi sponsored foreigners invest in such ventures and pay the sponsor a portion of the profits.[13] This arrangement leaves the vast majority of the private sector in the hands of migrants and benefits a few Saudi sponsors with obvious adverse effects on other nationals.

The Labour Supply Side

Education

The outsourcing of a large part of the private labour market to migrants is not just a numerical issue but has behavioural implications for Saudis. It creates an incentive to invest in their education for the sake of credentialism, so they can get a job in the public sector. In addition to offering low wages and poor employment conditions, the private sector does not require sophisticated skills. The education levels of migrants are low by any standard for a high-income economy: the share of non-Saudi workers who can 'read and write' is 27 per cent and a further 42 per cent (nearly 70 per cent) are

---

[9] Contribution of SMEs to the non-oil GDP in 2016 when Vision 2030 was announced and set the goal of raising that percentage to 35 per cent by 2030.

[10] The non-oil private sector contribution to GDP has been below 40 per cent and that from the financial sector has been around 10 per cent. SAMA, *Forty-Sixth Annual Report* (Riyadh: Saudi Arabian Monetary Authority, 2019). Available online: http://www.sama.gov.sa/en-US/EconomicReports/Pages/YearlyStatistics.aspx; https://www.mdpi.com/2227-7099/8/2/39/htm; https://www.gib.com.sa/sites/default/files/saudi_-_non-oil_-_draft_28_spread_-_for_web_0.pdf.

[11] Atlantic Council, 2020 June.

[12] http://www.coastaldigest.com/labour-drive-fails-eliminate-tasattur?page=7.

[13] According to a study by the Riyadh Chamber of Commerce and Industry, there are an estimated 200,000 such businesses and over 120,000 in Jeddah alone. *Tasattur* business transactions in the Kingdom are estimated at more than SAR230 billion (nearly 10 per cent of GDP) annually. The end result is that 60 per cent of remittances come from *tasattur* activities carried out by an estimated 30 per cent of migrant workers working in SMEs whose monthly revenue ranges between SAR50,000 and SAR1 million. See https://www.arabnews.com/saudi-arabia/news/686836; https://www.hindustantimes.com/world/saudi-arabia-may-close-expat-run-service-stores-report/story-WEsVDELN7LQRh2G6cHu84K.html.

educated only up to the intermediate level.[14] This means that more than 7 million migrants (or 5 million migrants excluding domestic workers) have less than secondary education. This should have made their replacement by nationals straightforward, if the labour market had not been segmented and if wages in the private sector had not been affected by the reservation wage and qualifications of nationals. Compared to the aforementioned 70 per cent of migrants, 98 per cent of 18-year-old Saudis still are in education. This is highest rate of all Organization for Economic Cooperation and Development (OECD) countries, where the average is 76 per cent.[15]

In plain terms, Saudis do not lack the education to replace migrants but are justifiably reluctant to work at wage levels and under employment conditions that are found in low-income countries. The main problem with the *economic* system in Saudi Arabia is that nationals do not see the private sector as an attractive employer.[16] Notice that the problem relates to the economic system, not to the education system. The domestic education system is largely irrelevant when the majority of jobs are filled by workers from abroad. In short, the equilibrium of the Saudi labour market has historically been determined more by the abundant supply of low-educated migrants than by the labour supply of the Kingdom's own citizens.

At higher education levels (especially tertiary education), a misplaced charge is that humanities and social sciences account for a significant share of enrolments, and that this renders Saudi job-seekers ill equipped for work in the private sector. In conventional labour markets, this should not have a serious adverse effect in service-based economies where the great majority of jobs are managerial, administrative, and clerical.[17] For such occupations, the important skills tend to be generic ones. It is the function of the humanities and social sciences to provide an opportunity for the development of precisely these generic skills, including the capacity for critical thinking and independent thought, problem-solving skills, the ability to undertake written assignments, and intellectual discipline.

In Saudi Arabia, the employment prospects of the more educated nationals, including those who have studied soft subjects, are less favourable. Given the public/private divide, even those with 'hard core' degrees, such as in

---

[14] Ninth Plan, p. 170, table 10.1.

[15] https://www.oecd-ilibrary.org/docserver/eag-2017-82-en.pdf?expires=1615676096&id=id&acc name=guest&checksum=72E49907DCED5109EC23EA705CDE5F39.

[16] I. Diwan, 'Fiscal Sustainability, the Labour Market and Growth in Saudi Arabia', in G. Luciani and T. Moerenhout (eds.), *When Can Oil Economies Be Deemed Sustainable?* (Singapore: Palgrave Macmillan, 2021), p. 32. Open access at https://link.springer.com/book/10.1007/978-981-15-5728-6.

[17] As Table 1.1 in Chapter 1 shows, the employment share of services in Saudi Arabia is higher than that in Norway.

engineering, prefer to work and are in fact employed in the public sector in managerial and senior administrative jobs. In conventional labour markets, humanities and social sciences graduates generally tend to enter the larger enterprises. However, in Saudi Arabia there are few large private sector enterprises as the sector is dominated by a myriad of poorly paying SMEs offering low-quality jobs. In fact, it has been noted since the mid-1980s that even larger enterprises, many of which are in the construction sector, are 'foreign firms which bring their own countrymen to fill skilled labor needs, rather than try to employ skilled Saudi workers ... [thus preventing] the transfer of skills and knowledge from the foreign firms to the Saudi labor force.'[18]

Three Labour Market Options for Saudis

Under these conditions, the demands of citizens for a job in the public sector are driven principally by the perception that the government has an obligation to employ them together with a limitless ability to pay. These conditions give rise to the (justified) general feeling among citizens that, if someone with few qualifications gets a public sector job, then another person who is equally inadequately qualified should also get such a job. In such an environment, Saudi job-seekers have three options.

The first option is to remain unemployed or even economically inactive. Both cases are shown below. The male unemployment rate has historically been kept stable at around 6–7 per cent through employment in the public sector, various measures imposed on the private sector to hire Saudis, and social pressure for men to work. The female unemployment rate has been increasing over time and has reached nearly 35 per cent (Figure 6.3). The youth inactivity rate is the highest in the GCC (Figure 6.4).[19]

A second option is to emigrate. Arab countries with tight domestic labour markets, such as Lebanon, Jordan, and Tunisia, have better-performing students and high emigration rates. However, job-seekers in countries where the school-to-work transition is made easier through opportunities offered by public sector jobs have low academic performance. This is the case in Saudi Arabia and generally among its neighbours (Figure 6.5), including among the skilled nationals (Figure 6.6). The reason for the low desire to emigrate is that Saudi job-seekers have largely chosen the third option, discussed next.

---

[18] S. S. Alsaleh, 'Saudi Arabian Industrial Development and Manpower Requirement: Problems and Prospects'. University of Rhode Island (1984) p. 52 at https://digitalcommons.uri.edu/theses/1112/.
[19] The youth inactivity rate after excluding students is also highest in Saudi Arabia, apart from in the UAE. Sources: ILO, Key Indicators of the Labour Market (KILM), 7th edn. (2011); and UNESCO, UNESCO, World Data on Education 2010/2011 (2012), Paris: International Bureau of Education.

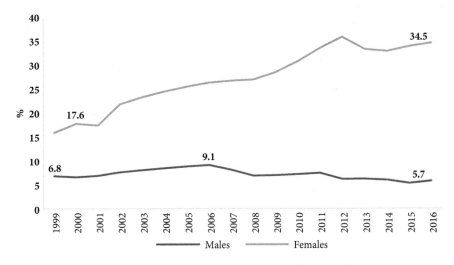

Figure 6.3 Saudi unemployment rates, 1999–2016 (%)

Source: Labour Force Surveys 1999 and 2016.

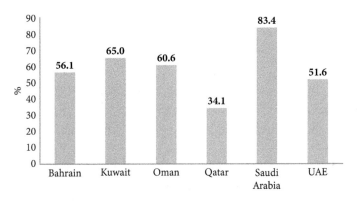

Figure 6.4 Youth (15–24) inactivity rates in the GCC, 2012 (%)

Sources: ILO, Key Indicators of the Labour Market (KILM), 7th edn. (2011) and UNESCO, World Data on Education 2010/2011 (2012), Paris: International Bureau of Education.

The third and most commonly chosen option is to put pressure on the government to provide employment. This pressure has generally been successful with the problem of unemployment among nationals traditionally being 'solved' by the public sector acting as the employer of last resort. This also explains the low learning outcomes of nationals. The percentage of primary school children not actually learning in Saudi Arabia has been found to be 40 per cent. In an international context, Saudi Arabia was ranked 45th in mathematics and 42nd in science among the fifty countries participating in the TIMSS comparative study in 2011. Similarly, Saudi Arabia was ranked

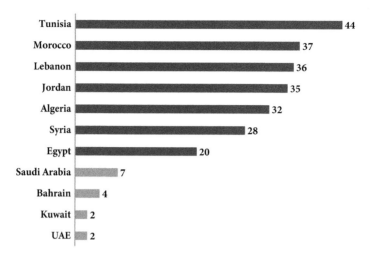

Figure 6.5 Proportion of young people who desire to emigrate permanently

Note: Emigration rate is measured as the percentage of emigrants to total domestic population. Skilled emigration rate is measured as the percentage of tertiary education graduates who have emigrated compared to their counterparts at home. In logs of numbers of emigrants out of 100 persons.
Source: 'The Silatech Index: Voices of Young Arabs: November 2010', Silatech (Qatar).

41st (of forty-five countries) in reading ability in the PIRLS comparative study in the same year.[20] The low learning outcomes in these specific subjects may have something to do with the content of the curriculum and pedagogic methods. Saudi Arabia allocates nine weekly sessions for the study of Islamic Education and the Qur'ān.[21] This is more than double the average in the other GCC countries (four sessions) and almost three times more than among the remaining sixteen Arab countries (3.2 sessions).[22]

Still, low academic achievement does not necessarily lead to unemployability. Given that nearly 70 per cent of migrant workers are educated only up to intermediate level, this should not be the case. Relatedly, the impact of education on earnings is low in Saudi Arabia. This is driven only in part by the low wages in the private sector, where few Saudis are employed, notwithstanding the fact that, under various waves of the Saudization policy, the private

---

[20] Trends in International Mathematics and Science Study (TIMSS) is an internationally comparable assessment of the knowledge students have acquired of mathematics and science by Grade 4. Similarly, Progress in International Reading Literacy Study (PIRLS) is an internationally comparable assessment of students' literacy when they reach Grade 4.

[21] The sessions on Islamic Education and the Qur'ān are five in Oman and Qatar; four in Kuwait and the UAE; and two in Bahrain (International Association for the Evaluation of Educational Achievement).

[22] 'World Data on Education 2010/2011', International Bureau of Education, UNESCO (2011).

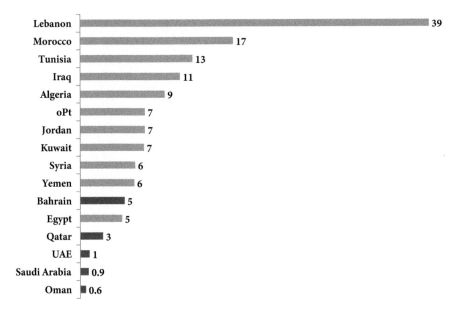

Figure 6.6 Emigration rates and skilled emigration rates

Note: Emigration rate is measured as the percentage of emigrants to total domestic population. Skilled emigration rate is measured as the percentage of tertiary education graduates who have emigrated compared to their counterparts at home. In logs of numbers of emigrants out of 100 persons.
Source: Constructed from World Bank, *Migration and Remittances Fact Book* (2011).

sector has increased the wage for nationals over time while the wages for migrant workers have remained the same or even declined.[23] The low rates of return on education for Saudi nationals are mainly driven by wage compression in the public sector, where wages of the less educated are relatively high due to social considerations, while those for the better educated are relatively low. An econometric study of the effect of an additional year of education on earnings estimated that the impact is lowest for both Saudi males and Saudi females among the GCC economies and also compared to both the average of the other sixteen Arab countries and the global average (Table 6.3).

Gender Differences in Education Achievement

The gender differences in learning outcomes are significant. At primary education level, the percentage of Saudi boys not actually learning is around 50 per cent compared to 30 per cent for girls—a 40 per cent difference. At secondary level, the difference stands at 23 per cent in mathematics and rises

[23] I. Diwan, 'Fiscal Sustainability, the Labour Market and Growth in Saudi Arabia', in G. Luciani and T. Moerenhout (eds.), *When Can Oil Economies Be Deemed Sustainable?* (Singapore: Palgrave Macmillan, 2021). Open access at https://link.springer.com/book/10.1007/978-981-15-5728-6.

Table 6.3 Effect of education on earnings, early 2010s (%)

	Males	Females
Saudi Arabia	**2.1**	**1.4**
Kuwait	2.5	3.1
UAE	3.2	4.9
Qatar	4.6	5.5
Bahrain	7.8	6.7
Oman	8.8	4.5
GCC	**4.8**	**4.4**
16 other Arab countries	5.4	6.4
World average	5.8	6.2

Source: Z. Tzannatos, I. Diwan, and J. Abdul-Ahad, 'Rates of Return to Education in Twenty Two Arab Countries: An Update and Comparison between MENA and the Rest of the World' (Cairo: Economic Research Forum, 2016), Working Paper No. 1007.

to 43 per cent in sciences. Worldwide the gender differences generally vary around 5 per cent.[24]

There is no evidence or reason to believe that Saudi boys are innately different from their counterparts in other parts of the world. More valid explanations can be sought in the incentives that males and females face. When male unemployment is kept low, the incentive for males to excel in education is also low. When female employment is kept low, for cultural reasons or to make room for male employment, females try to make inroads into the economy and society by staying on and excelling in education, in the expectation that this can also increase their agency and delay marriage. In fact, most of the unemployed women are educated to university level, pushing the graduate total unemployment rate among 25–34-year-olds to 20 per cent compared to the OECD average of 7 per cent. Conversely, the unemployment rate among those with less than secondary education is 2 per cent in Saudi Arabia compared to an average of 17 per cent in the OECD.[25]

Skills

A popular claim in various development plans, policy documents, and project objectives is that the reason for the low employment rate of Saudis in the private sector 'is the mismatch between the skills and experience

[24] Trends in International Mathematics and Science Study (2007). Amsterdam: International Association for the Evaluation of Educational Achievement (IEA).

[25] https://www.oecd-ilibrary.org/docserver/eag-2017-82-en.pdf?expires=1615678426&id=id&accname=guest&checksum=8F7E8A8B434C6C929DD7647DE5829413.

of Saudi nationals and those required by the private sector.[26] This chimes in with the claim that across the Middle East many young people 'are not just unemployed but unemployable'[27] as well as various international assessments that repeat the need 'for the education system in Saudi Arabia to provide appropriately trained individual who meet the requirements of the labour market.'[28] Such claims miss three points. First, there is a difference between 'markets' and 'competitive markets'. Second, the competition in Saudi Arabia is not among nationals but between nationals and migrants from low-income countries. And third, while the Saudis can replace the millions of lower-educated migrants, the incentives for doing so are lacking given the duality between the wages and conditions of employment offered in the private sector and the public sector.

In fact, the skills of half of those employed in Saudi Arabia have been found to match the requirements of the jobs that workers are expected to do, and another quarter of workers have been found to be overqualified for what they are doing.[29] No mismatches were reported for higher-level clerical jobs or certified occupations in professional, technical, and humanitarian areas that are largely performed by Saudis. And 56 per cent of those employed in these three areas but at a lower level (technicians) were deemed to be overqualified. Similarly, the share of overqualified workers in basic engineering was also found to be more than half (52 per cent). The highest rates of underqualified workers were found to be in jobs in agriculture, animal husbandry and fishing (70 per cent), the industrial/chemical and food sectors (42 per cent), and in services (34 per cent) that have relatively high numbers of non-Saudis or employ less qualified Saudis who have not secured a job in the public sector.

Another survey solicited the views of Arab employers about the constraints they face.[30] Private sector employers outside the GCC listed among their top constraints macroeconomic instability, corruption, tax rates and tax administration, political instability, anti-competitive or informal practices, cost of finance, and access to land and electricity. For them, skill shortages were

---

[26] 'Saudi Labor Market Update—Q1 2018', Saudi General Authority for Statistics (GaStat) (July 2018).

[27] M. Adeel, 'The Economics of The Arab Spring: The Region's Dependence on Natural Resources Has Prevented the Emergence of a Strong Private Sector', Al Jazeera (13 October 2011), https://www.aljazeera.com/indepth/opinion/2011/10/20111010142425419849.html.

[28] https://www.oecd-ilibrary.org/docserver/eag-2017-82-en.pdf?expires=1615678426&id=id&acc name=guest&checksum=8F7E8A8B434C6C929DD7647DE5829413.

[29] Based on an ILO survey conducted by Bayt.com Poll between June and August 2015 as reported in Z. Tzannatos, 'Employment and Skills in the Middle East since 2010: A Statistical Analysis and Review of Challenges' (2016) (mimeo). Beirut: ILO Regional Office for the Arab States.

[30] World Bank, 'Form Privilege to Competition: Unlocking Private-Led Growth in the Middle East and North Africa' (Washington, DC: World Bank, 2009).

among the least concerns.[31] However, the two GCC countries surveyed, namely Oman and Saudi Arabia, listed their priority constraints as labour regulations and the low education and skills of workers. This is paradoxical given the presence of large numbers of ready-made low-wage migrant workers but effectively refers to the forceful regulations that the two countries have adopted in order to promote the nationalization in their labour force, which are the most stringent among the other GCC countries. We will return to this in the section on post-2010 policies later in the chapter.

These findings suggest that it is the dominance of low-educated migrants in the private sector and the Saudization policies of the government that are responsible for the largely misplaced belief that skill shortages and mismatches are inhibiting the employment prospects of Saudis. In other words, had the labour market been determined by the reservation wage of nationals and a reasonable use of migrant labour, the education and skills composition of employment would have been higher and would also reflect better the social preferences of Saudis. The key issue here is whether the job requirements are higher than the low academic achievements of nationals. If the above analysis is broadly correct, this is not the case in the Saudi private sector.

Labour Market Outcomes and Economic Performance

High Dependency Rates among Saudi Workers

The large number of migrant workers, most of whom are young, has prevented Saudi Arabia from taking advantage of its own demographic dividend: that is, the increasing share of the working age population in the labour force arising from high rates of fertility. The median age of the Saudi population is around 30 years—a level comparable to that in high-income countries in the 1950s, which have since seen the median age climbing to more than 40 years, averaging 43 years in Europe and reaching 49 years in Japan.[32] The artificial high total employment rate (compared to population) and the resulting economy-wide low dependency rate arises from the massive presence of migrant workers. This mask the fact that the Saudi dependency rate is 330 per cent. Thus, a Saudi salary has to support 4.3 persons: that is, the person him- or herself and 3.3 additional persons.

---

[31] World Bank (2009), Z. Tzannatos, 'Labour Demand and Social Dialogue: Two Binding Constraints for Decent Work for Youth in the Arab Region' (Geneva: ILO, Employment Policy Department, 2016), Employment Working Paper No. 164.
[32] United Nations, 'World Population Prospects 2019', Department of Economic and Social Affairs, Population Division, online edn. rev. 1 (2019).

This in part explains the high salaries granted to government workers and the pressure the government puts on the private sector to offer higher wages to Saudis employed therein. The economy-wide average annual wage in Saudi Arabia is 10 per cent lower than the per capita GDP, but for nationals it is higher by more than 50 per cent. The latter compares with a difference of less than 20 per cent in favour of wages, for example, in the European Union.[33]

Sizeable Welfare Loss from Missing Nearly Half of the Potential Labour Force

In 2016, at 23 per cent the female labour force participation rate used to be among the lowest in the world. Among those in the labour force, one in three women were unemployed, although most have a university education, whereas unemployed men mostly have secondary education or less.[34] When employed, few women were working side by side with men as legislation, societal attitudes, and religion exercised a strong negative effect on the size of women's employment and what kind of jobs they can do.[35] On the labour supply side, female job-seekers (and their families) have certain views of what is acceptable employment for women, especially as regards working along-side men to whom they are not related in the private sector. On the labour demand side, employers also have certain views on what kind of jobs and at what seniority level women should be employed. It is therefore not surprising that employment segregation used to be acute. Until the 2000s, a relevant measure of employment segregation, the Duncan Index,[36] had the value of 0.55 for occupational segregation, reaching 0.77 for industrial segregation. Both values were the highest in the world, whose global averages for both industrial and occupational segregation are typically between 0.2 and 0.4.[37]

---

[33] Average annual wages in the European Union were $42,500 compared to the average annual per capita GDP of $35,623. https://ec.europa.eu/eurostat/web/labour-market/earnings/database; IMF, 'World Economic Outlook Database', October 2019.

[34] Labour Force Survey 2016.

[35] G. Psacharopoulos and Z. Tzannatos, 'Female Labor Force Participation and Education', in G. Psacharopoulos (ed.), *Essays on Poverty, Equity and Growth* (Oxford: Pergamon Press, 1991); however, others have claimed that the role of religion is subordinate to the part that oil rents are playing. For example, oil production may reduce the number of women in the labour force and also their political influence, thereby perpetuating patriarchal norms and restrictive laws. See M. L. Ross 'Oil, Islam, and Women', *American Political Science Review* 102 (2008), pp. 107–23, doi.org/10.1017/S0003055408080040.

[36] The value of the Duncan Index ranges from 0 (women and men do exactly the same jobs) to 1 (no woman works where men work). See O. D. Duncan and B. Duncan, 'A Methodological Analysis of Segregation Indexes', *American Sociological Review* 20, no. 2 (Apr., 1955), pp. 210–17. https://doi.org/10.2307/2088328; Z. Tzannatos, 'Employment Segregation: Can We Measure It and What Does the Measure Mean?', *British Journal of Industrial Relations* 28 (1990), pp. 105–11.

[37] Z. Tzannatos, 'Monitoring Progress in Gender Equality in the Labour Market', in M. Buvenic, A. Morrison, A. W. Ofosu-Amaah, and M. Sjöblom (eds.), *Equality for Women: Where Do We Stand on Millennium Development Goal 3?* (Washington, DC: World Bank, 2008), pp. 150–51.

The sharp gender differences observed in the Saudi labour market are not unexpected. Saudi women face more legal constraints than any other women in the world. According to a global survey in the mid-2010s, Saudi women faced twenty-nine explicit restrictions that did not apply to men, compared to fewer than twenty restrictions on average in the GCC and a global average of only four restrictions.[38] Financial exclusion of women is highest in Saudi Arabia, even among the Middle East and North Africa (MENA) economies.[39] Under 60 per cent of Saudi women have bank accounts and only 15 per cent have access to online banking.[40]

The past approach to women's position in the labour market is well captured in the following passage:

> The country cannot afford to waste approximately half of its most valuable resource. However, this must not be taken to suggest that Saudi Arabia should move away from its conservative Islamic way of life in order to achieve the full participation of its female labor force. … Female participation in the labor force must be increased without endangering religious and traditional beliefs and attitudes. … New ways and innovations to help achieve this objective without changing the social structure will be the best way to achieve higher female participation. The success of the women's branch of the civil service bureau should indicate that women can perform many jobs without necessitating integration with men.[41]

The total income loss due to the low female labour force participation rate of Saudi women has been estimated to be as high as 45 per cent of GDP, of which 9 per cent arises from gender differences in the employment distribution. This loss is five times more than in high-income countries, the group of

---

[38] Such restrictions arise from guardianship laws whereby a woman is not allowed to work outside the home without the permission of her legal guardian (her husband or another male relative), and is not free to decide where to live or travel, or to get a passport, or until recently even to drive. See International Finance Corporation/World Bank, 'Women, Business and the Law 2016: Removing Barriers to Economic Inclusion, 2011', http://wbl.worldbank.org/~/media/FPDKM/WBL/Documents/Reports/2012/Women-Business-and-the-Law-2012.pdf. However, Saudi Arabia is among the top ten countries in the world that have had the greatest improvements in legislation since then, including making progress towards addressing domestic violence. Of course, this relatively fast progress relates to the high number of restrictions that previously applied, but nevertheless its significance cannot be overlooked. McKinsey & Company, 'Women at Work: Job opportunities in the Middle East set to double with the Fourth Industrial Revolution', 2020, at https://www.mckinsey.com/~/media/mckinsey/featured%20insights/middle%20east%20and%20africa/women%20at%20work%20in%20the%20middle%20east/women-at-work-in-the-middle-east.pdf.
[39] Female-to-male ratio; composite indicator of the rate of account holders at a financial institution, borrowing from a financial institution in the previous twelve months, and use of mobile phones to send money, extracted from the Global Findex database, World Bank.
[40] McKinsey op. cit.
[41] S. S. Alsaleh, 'Saudi Arabian Industrial Development and Manpower Requirement: Problems and Prospects', Open Access master's theses, Paper 1112 (1984), https://digitalcommons.uri.edu/theses/1112, pp. 107, 109.

countries to which Saudi Arabia belongs. In fact, it is the highest loss globally and more than double the average for MENA countries (20 per cent), most of which also have severely gender-segregated labour markets (Figure 6.7).[42]

Lack of Productivity Gains and Wealth Creation

Measuring labour productivity as well as total factor productivity over a short period of time can be misleading in Saudi Arabia, as both are heavily influenced by widely fluctuating oil prices. It is therefore more appropriate to take a longer-term perspective. As the period between the early 1970s and the late 2010s, discussed earlier, includes the extraordinary increase in GDP during the 1970s, it is more appropriate to focus on more recent changes in output and employment. For example, between 1990 and 2018 the economy grew at an annual rate of 3.1 per cent and employment at an annual rate of 3.7 per cent.[43] The resulting value of employment/output elasticity is more than 1, implying negative productivity growth. By comparison, a value of this elasticity between 0.3 and 0.5 is usually the norm, and it is much lower than that, even close to zero, in high-income economies. In fact, had it not been for oil

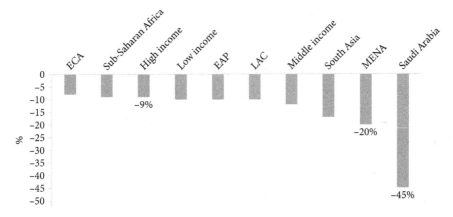

Figure 6.7 GDP loss (%) due to the gender gap in the labour force

Note: ECA = East Europe and Central Asia; EAP = East Asia and the Pacific; LAC = Latin Maerica and the Caribbean; MENA = Middle East and North Africa.
Source: D. Cuberes and M. Teignier, 'Aggregate Effects of Gender Gaps in the Labor Market: A Quantitative Estimate', University of Barcelona (2015).

[42] D. Cuberes and M. Teignier, 'Aggregate Effects of Gender Gaps in the Labor Market: A Quantitative Estimate', University of Barcelona (2015) at http://www.ub.edu/ubeconomics/wp-content/uploads/2014/02/308-Web.pdf. In an earlier study, the authors find that the loss arising from not fully utilizing female entrepreneurship is generally much lower than that from lower female labour force participation. See. D. Cuberes & M. Teignier, 'Gender Gaps in the Labor Market and Aggregate Productivity'. Working Papers 2012017 (2012), The University of Sheffield, Department of Economics at https://ideas.repec.org/p/shf/wpaper/2012017.html.
[43] https://data.worldbank.org/indicator/SL.TLF.TOTL.IN?locations=SA.

revenues also increasing by 1.9 per cent during this period, the value of the elasticity would have been even higher.[44]

In more sophisticated terms, a study examined what contributed to the increase in real per capita income in Saudi Arabia between 2001 and 2009.[45] It used the Shapley decomposition[46] and found that changes in the share of the working age population and the employment rate contributed to a net increase in per capita incomes of almost SAR2,500. However, changes in productivity growth took nearly all this increase away. The study further decomposed changes in productivity between those within sectors and those between sectors. The within-sector positive effect was significant (SAR1,800) but came almost exclusively from the mining sector as oil prices had increased significantly during the decade under study. The intersectoral effect was negative and had the highest impact among all other factors: had it been the only effect, then per capita incomes would have declined by SAR4,000. In other words, investment and production had been switching from higher- to lower-value-added sectors.[47]

The persistent reliance on low-wage, low-skill migrant workers is another factor that has held back productivity growth. The large number of migrants and the type of their contracts are affecting the level and growth of skills in two ways: first, directly by recruiting migrants who have low skills; and second, indirectly through the high labour turnover of migrants—they are aptly called 'contractual temporary workers' in Saudi Arabia, as most of them are employed under contracts of limited duration with no long-term prospects.

The resulting high labour turnover hinders the progressive acquisition of skills as migrant workers are often dismissed at the same level of skills which they had when they were first recruited. What is acquired through learning by doing is eventually appropriated by the sending country when the migrant leaves Saudi Arabia. Then, when a migrant leaves, his or her replacement is generally hired at the same low level of skills. This results in keeping production processes basic, and limits productivity-enhancing investment. Moreover, given the relatively high employment agency fees, and transport and related costs associated with recruitment from abroad, employers may practise labour hoarding in case a migrant deserts for another employer

---

[44] During this period the correlation between the increase in the oil revenues and GDP growth was 0.84.

[45] A. Jaafar and Z. Tzannatos, *An Analysis of Economic Growth, Employment, Productivity and Incomes: Saudi Arabia in 2001–2009* (Beirut: International Labour Organization, 2015).

[46] A. F. Shorrocks, 'Decomposition Procedures for Distributional Analysis: A Unified Framework Based on the Shapley Value', *Journal of Economic Inequality* 11 (2013), pp. 99–126.

[47] Similar results and conclusions are found in IMF, Saudi Arabia Article IV Consultation (2019) and Country Report No. 2019/290 (2019).

or returns home before their contract expires.[48] This can lead to excess employment of migrant workers in the private sector. Overemployment, and therefore low productivity, can be further intensified if Saudi workers are employed in the private sector as a result of forcefully imposed 'Saudization quotas' (see the later section on labor market policies post-2010).

All in all, economic growth has largely been driven by factor accumulation in the form of oil-financed investments and large-scale utilization of unskilled and semi-skilled migrants. A study estimated the opportunity cost of this approach. If the labour force participation rates of Saudis increased from 40 per cent to 60 per cent, and if unemployment were reduced to its natural rate, non-oil national income would more than double if the additional workers joined the non-oil sector even at current productivity levels. Moreover, if labour productivity increased, then 'the national wealth could become comparable to the kingdom's current oil wealth'.[49]

The Adverse Social Impact

By granting employers access to low-wage migrants, the profits of such employers increase at the expense of the labour earnings of national job-seekers. And as more Saudis join the private sector, voluntarily or not, inequality increases. The Gini coefficient is 0.459 in Saudi Arabia compared with the world median of 0.318, while the average up to the world median is 0.318 and above it is 0.439.[50] Inequality has many ill effects. The empirical links between inequality and social outcomes are well known and several of them apply to Saudi Arabia. Greater inequality is associated with obesity, lower health outcomes, shorter lives, and more marginalization of the lower classes, leading to civil unrest, more crime and, in fact, less innovation.[51] More broadly, a recent study by the International Monetary Fund (IMF) estimated that a 1 per cent increase in the income share of the bottom quintile

---

[48] G. Luciani, 'Framing the Economic Sustainability of Oil Economies', in G. Luciani and T. Moerenhout (eds.), *When Can Oil Economies Be Deemed Sustainable?* (Singapore: Palgrave Macmillan, 2021); open access at https://link.springer.com/book/10.1007/978-981-15-5728-6. Another study has found that employer-tied workers had equal to worse employment outcomes than migrants working on no visa at all: https://www.cgdev.org/end-of-kafala-labor-mobility.

[49] I. Diwan, 'Fiscal Sustainability, the Labour Market and Growth in Saudi Arabia', in G. Luciani and T. Moerenhout (eds.), *When Can Oil Economies Be Deemed Sustainable?* (Singapore: Palgrave Macmillan, 2021); open access at https://link.springer.com/book/10.1007/978-981-15-5728-6.

[50] https://worldpopulationreview.com/country-rankings/gini-coefficient-by-country.

[51] R. Wilkinson and K. Pickett, *The Spirit Level: Why More Equal Societies Almost Always Do Better* (Harmondsworth: Penguin, 2010). Despite the adverse impact of migration polices on national workers in the GCC, for the sake of completeness one can add that, ironically, these policies have resulted in a dramatic reduction in global inequality, although wages for migrants are lower than those for nationals. These policies have been found to have done much more to reduce global inequality than all the welfare states and transfers in the more egalitarian OECD countries. This suggests a disturbing trade-off between openness to global inequality-reducing migration and internal equality. See E. G. Weyl, 'The Openness–Equality Trade-Off in Global Redistribution', *Economic Journal* 128, no. 612 (2018), pp. F1–F36.

results in a 0.38 per cent increase in GDP, while a 1 per cent increase in the income share of the top 20 per cent results in a 0.08 per cent decrease in GDP growth.[52] Similarly, an OECD study found that an increase in inequality on the Gini scale of 2 points corresponded to a 4.7 per cent drop in GDP.[53]

In addition, in Saudi Arabia there is significant pre-entry to the labour market inequality. Although family background universally plays a role in education outcomes, the test scores of students are more closely related to their socio-economic status in Saudi Arabia than in other parts of the world. The share of inequality in test scores accounted for by family background and community characteristics (inequality of opportunity) was higher in Lebanon, Egypt, Qatar, and Saudi Arabia than in the other nine Arab countries it covered, and approached the level of education inequality in Latin America where inequality generally is higher than in the Arab region. The high level of inequality in Saudi Arabia (and in the GCC) is puzzling given that, first, public education is provided free and even attracts scholarships and, second, the poverty rate is low and there is no pressure for child labour that would result in a premature withdrawal of children from schools. However, while there is no evidence that inequality of opportunity in educational achievement in the Arab countries has changed much over time, in the case of Saudi Arabia inequality seems to have increased.[54]

If not checked, inequality can give rise to social tensions. The authorities are aware of this and their comprehensive reaction to the impact of the Global Financial Crisis in 2008 and the Arab uprisings is suggestive.[55] In 2011, Saudi Arabia increased spending on infrastructure (a demand-side intervention); it raised wages, launched an unemployment assistance programme, and expanded public sector employment, including 60,000 military jobs (all labour market interventions); and it provided grants, bonuses, and benefits to students, charities, and pensioners (social policy interventions).[56]

---

[52] https://qz.com/429487/a-new-imf-study-debunks-trickle-down-economics/.

[53] https://www.oecd.org/social/income-distribution-database.htm.

[54] R. Assaad, C. Krafft, and D. Salehi-Isfahani, 'Inequality of Opportunity in the Labor Market for Higher Education Graduates in Egypt and Jordan', mimeo (2013). Education inequality accentuates the effects of other forms of inequality, such as inequality of opportunity in child health. R. Assaad, C. Krafft, N. Belhaj Hassine, and D. Salehi-Isfahani, 'Inequality of Opportunity in Child Health in the Arab World and Turkey', ERF Working Paper 665 (Giza: Economic Research Forum, 2012).

[55] For the response to the Global Financial Crisis, see Z. Tzannatos, *The Global Financial, Economic and Social Crisis and the Arab Countries: A Review of the Evidence and Policies for Employment Creation and Social Protection* (Beirut: ILO Regional Office for the Arab States, 2009), Annex 2, at https://www.ilo.org/wcmsp5/groups/public/---arabstates/---ro-beirut/documents/meetingdocument/wcms_208696.pdf.

[56] It increased the minimum wage for government employees by 19 per cent to SAR3,000 ($800). Teachers working in the private sector had their minimum wages increased to SAR5,000 ($1,333) in 2011. In Saudi Arabia, there was creation of 60,000 military jobs in the Interior Ministry, 500 jobs to assist the Ministry of Trade and Industry in monitoring the jobs market, and 300 more jobs for the administration of scientific research. The minimum pension of retired civil servants increased to SAR4,000 ($1,067), more than double the minimum salary for levying social security contributions. A bonus worth two months' salary was given to all public sector employees, another reward of two months to state university students,

This massive increase in spending came on top of a plethora of other labour market and social protection measures that had previously been introduced or expanded after the global financial crisis in 2008.[57]

In this way, the reaction adopted 'the more or less habitual response to increase spending on subsidies, public sector workers and support for the private sector.'[58] The measures effectively amounted to a 'peace bill' that was deemed to be worth paying politically. In a sense, they aimed to create decent employment with 'indecent' (from an economic perspective) fiscal implications. However, they may have negated any progress towards changing job-seekers' expectations based on repeated proclamations by the government that it would no longer act as the employer of last resort. They reignited expectations that the social contract driven by an 'authoritarian bargain' would continue as in the past.[59] Under such a contract, citizens (at least, a critical mass of them) exchange political freedom and moderate their voices in return for state handouts, generously provided public services and goods, low taxes, and public sector employment largely irrespective of effort and the business needs of the administration. It is this political approach that has created the undesirable symptoms found in the labour market. At the heart of this approach lies the migration policy, to which we will turn next.

Migration Policy Has Resulted in the 'Colonization' of the Labour Market

By now it should be clear that a major determinant of labour market outcomes in Saudi Arabia (and other GCC countries) has been migration policy. Though this policy has been reconsidered in the 2010s, it has shaped the structure of the economy and many of its effects persist to the present day.

---

and a total of $300 million in grants to charities and the needy. Saudi Arabia launched an unemployment assistance programme that pays a monthly unemployment benefit of SAR2,000 ($533) to job-seekers aged between 20 and 35 years for a period up to twelve months. Author's compilation based on ILO/UNDP, 'Rethinking Economic Growth: Towards Productive and Inclusive Arab Societies' (Beirut: ILO Regional Office for the Arab States, 2012), Table 1.3 at https://www.ilo.org/wcmsp5/groups/public/---arabstates/---ro-beirut/documents/publication/wcms_208346.pdf and official publications.

[57] See Z. Tzannatos, 'The Global Financial, Economic and Social Crisis and the Arab Countries: A Review of the Evidence and Policies for Employment Creation and Social Protection' (Beirut: International Labour Organization, 2009).

[58] V. Neriem, 'Saudi Arabia's Quarterly Budget Deficit Widens to $8.9 Billion', Bloomberg (31 July 2019), https://www.bloomberg.com/news/articles/2019-07-30/saudi-arabia-s-quarterly-budget-deficit-widens-to-8-9-billion.

[59] R. Desai, A. Olofsgard, and T. Yousef, 'The Logic of Authoritarian Bargain: A Test of Structural Model', Brookings Global Economy and Development Working Paper 3 (Washington, DC: Brookings Institution, 2007); ILO/UNDP, 'Rethinking Economic Growth: Towards Productive and Inclusive Arab Societies' (Beirut: ILO Regional Office for the Arab States, 2012), p. 102, at https://www.ilo.org/wcmsp5/groups/public/---arabstates/---ro-beirut/documents/publication/wcms_208346.pdf.

The Saudi migration policy pursued since the 1970s has been based on the system of *kafala* (meaning 'to take care of').[60] Under this system, migrant workers must be sponsored by a citizen and, after the sponsorship expires or is terminated for some reason, the migrant worker is deported. During their stay, workers are covered only by the terms of their individual contracts, which are outside the jurisdiction of the local labour laws regarding working hours, leave, overtime, freedom of association, abuses, or at times health and safety regulations. The police or inspectors from the Ministry of Human Resources and Social Development (MHRSD) often ignore allegations made by the migrants. The *kafala* system has been described as a form of modern slavery in effectively treating migrant workers as objects.[61] The use of the *kafala* system has been extensive in Saudi Arabia, to the point that it places the Kingdom among the top destination countries in the world in terms of the number of non-native residents, whose share is 37 per cent of the total population. This is more than double that in the United States of America (USA), where immigrants make up 15 per cent of the population.

The effects of the *kafala* system are straightforward. An increase in labour supply depresses wages at a given level of labour demand. This is, however, only one channel via which the effects of migration operate. Another channel is the contractual treatment of migrant workers in terms of lower pay, longer hours, inferior employment conditions, and the ease with which they can be dismissed compared to nationals. This would migrant workers more productive and cost effective than nationals, even if the wages were the same between the two groups. Moreover, the migrants are already qualified for what they are expected to do, and do not require training.

The adverse effect of the *kafala* system is well documented.[62] More specifically, the dynamics of more or less open migration policies lead to a vicious circle that can be described as follows:

- Immigration at low wages for migrant workers induces the use of labour-intensive techniques in the private sector, leading to low productivity.

---

[60] The *kafala* system is also practised in other GCC countries as well as in other Arab countries, such as Lebanon and Jordan. For a historical review see https://www.researchgate.net/publication/326749671_Global_Governance_and_Labour_Migration_in_the_GCC.

[61] P. Rak, 'Modern Day Slavery: The Kafala System in Lebanon', *Harvard International Review* (21 December 2020), https://hir.harvard.edu/modern-day-slavery-the-kafala-system-in-lebanon/.

[62] S. Hertog, 'A Comparative Assessment of Labor Market Nationalization Policies in the GCC', in S. Hertog (ed.), *Labour Market, Unemployment, and Migration in the GCC* (Geneva: Gulf Research Center, 2011); M. Baldwin-Edwards, *Labour Immigration and Labour Markets in the GCC Countries: National Patterns and Trends* (London: LSE Kuwait Programme, 2011); I. Forstenlechner and E. Rutledge, 'Unemployment in the Gulf: Time to Update the "Social Contract"', *Middle East Policy* 17 (2010), pp. 38–51; I. Forstenlechner and E. Rutledge, 'The GCC's "Demographic Imbalance": Perceptions, Realities and Policy Options', *Middle East Policy* 18 (2011), pp. 25–43.

- Low wages in the private sector are not attractive to nationals and encourage them to seek employment in the public sector.
- The government tries to accommodate the concerns of the nationals and increases employment in the public sector in the short term and, with it, the expectations of job-seekers for getting a job in the public sector in the medium and longer terms.
- In such an environment, there are few incentives for nationals to invest in their own human capital—beyond credentialism.
- This results in low productivity in the public sector too, due to over-supply and under-employment of workers combined with the low education attainment of nationals.
- As a result, the economy is locked into a low-productivity equilibrium.
- Low productivity means that low wages prevail—and the attractiveness of immigration increases.
- And the vicious circle continues.

Despite the repeatedly stated intention since the 1980s to replace migrant workers by Saudi workers, the *kafala* system has survived more or less intact over time. If the law allows it, Saudi employers see it as their right to make use of migrant labour and minimize labour costs. If migrant workers are employed under pay and employment conditions that reflect the situation in their country of origin, then Saudi job-seekers have a right to demand that they are employed under conditions commensurate with their own country's level of income and development. Citizens therefore see a job in the public sector not as a privilege to be earned through service, but as an entitlement to be awarded on the basis of national identity.[63]

The resulting labour market segmentation between citizens and migrant workers resembles that between colonizers who keep the high-end jobs for themselves, and locals who carry out the precarious ones. If colonialism means to use the labour of people in foreign lands to amass wealth in your own country, then the development model in the Saudi Arabia, and more generally in the GCC since the 1970s, can in some sense be labelled 'reverse colonialism'. Though in Saudi Arabia the system is not associated with invasions, the imposition of religion, cultural practices, and language, or directly pursuing political and military objectives, from an economic perspective the political and business leaders have enriched their fortunes by employing

---

[63] Z. Tzannatos, 'Youth Employment in the GCC States: Is It the Youth (and Schools), Employment (and Migrants) or the Gulf (and Oil)?' Paper presented at the 2012 Gulf Research Meeting, Gulf Research Centre, University of Cambridge (11–14 July 2012).

foreigners under conditions inferior to those deemed to be acceptable in their own land.

While all countries have migrant workers and practically all control their numbers, once accepted they are generally employed on the same terms as nationals. Saudi Arabia, like other GCC countries, has not effectively controlled the numbers of migrants and has also allowed their employment conditions to be different. These conditions can be said to be closer to 'sharecropping' than to the more economically efficient systems based on 'land-to-the-tiller' or wage-based competitive labour markets.[64]

Another implication is that such a system discourages entrepreneurial activities and limits employment opportunities among nationals. The migration policy and the *tasattur* have created obstacles for business start-ups and as a result 'many small- and medium-sized business owners start and then relocate and operate their businesses in a different country, notably in the United Arab Emirates',[65] while 'the complicated governmental requirements and procedures for new businesses have cost young Saudis a significant number of jobs'.[66]

Furthermore, migration is dividing nationals between the ordinary citizens who have to compete for low-wage private sector jobs and the wealthier rentiers (the sponsors). The wealthy residents benefit from the historically increasing numbers of migrants, who have fuelled a 'population Ponzi' scheme by boosting aggregate domestic demand in the form of additional accommodation, transport, food and other consumption requirements, of which little, if any, is supplied by ordinary citizens.

A numerical example highlights the impact of the presence of migrants on the sponsors' incomes. Paying migrants low wages is one thing. Another thing is their large numbers. The ratio of international migrants to nationals in the GCC has generally been more than 45 per cent, compared to the world average (excluding the GCC) of only 3 per cent.[67] While the nearly 30 million nationals in the GCC account for 0.4 per cent of the world population, the GCC countries host over 10 per cent of all migrants globally.[68]

---

[64] J. Stiglitz, 'Incentives and Risk Sharing in Sharecropping', *Review of Economic Studies* 41, no. 2 (1974), pp. 219–55, doi: 10.2307/2296714.

[65] T. Al Maeena, 'Dynamics of the "Moving" Trend from Saudi Arabia' (15 February 2014), retrieved from http://gulfnews.com/opinions/columnists/dynamics-of-the-moving-trendfrom-saudi-arabia-1. 1291311.

[66] A. Alghamedi, 'Enhancing Employment Opportunities in the Saudi Arabian Private Sector University' (2016), ProQuest Dissertations Publishing, https://search.proquest.com/openview/a5fa75401ad9f5a5426dea9a8b059b6d/1?pq-origsite=gscholar&cbl=18750&diss=y.

[67] According to the UN International Trends in Migration Stock (June 2020), this figure is up from 248 million in 2015, 220 million in 2010, 191 million in 2005, and 173 million in 2000 (New York: United Nations Department for Economic and Social Affairs, 2019).

[68] https://www.ilo.org/beirut/areasofwork/labour-migration/lang—en/index.htm.

Saudi Arabia alone hosts nearly 13 million migrants, the third highest globally after the USA and Russia, whose populations are 330 million and 150
million respectively.[69]

The combined large number of migrants and their low costs create a size-
able surplus value that is appropriated by their sponsors. For example, if the
net payback to a national from sponsoring a migrant is $10/day and Saudi
Arabia has 10 million migrants, this would amount to $36.5 billion/year.
Among the 20 million or so nationals, this corresponds to a per capita
income of $1,800/year or, if an average household has six members, nearly
US$10,800/year per household. To start with, this is not a small amount.
However, not all nationals are sponsors. If 10 per cent of households are sponsors, then the resulting income from sponsorship for each such household
would be more than $108,000.

Labour Market Policies, the Development Plans, and Vision 2030

Before 2010

Saudi Arabia and Oman have been rigorous in applying policies for the
nationalization of their labour forces, to the point where employers in the
two countries not only complain about labour regulations but, as mentioned
earlier, list them as their top constraints. By the mid-2000s, Saudi Arabia
already had in place a long list of measures placing restrictions on employers regarding the use of migrant workers. It also enforced these restrictions
rigorously while providing incentives for the employment of nationals in the
private sector.[70] The restrictions included exclusion from certain sectors or
jobs, imposed work permit fees and quotas, and limited mobility for migrants
across employers or sectors. Enforcement of these restrictions took place
through inspections, fines, and sanctions against private sector employers

---

[69] This twenty-five-fold discrepancy (10/0.4) is even greater since migrants in the GCC are primarily
workers (for example, compared with asylum-seekers) and migrant workers constitute less than 60 per
cent of the global stock of migrants The migrant/national population balance is even more impressive in
the labour markets in the GCC due to the low employment rates of nationals: the working migrants are
more than twice the number of employed Saudis, whose labour force participation rate is just over 40 per
cent. United Nations, Department of Economic and Social Affairs, Population Division, 'International
Migrant Stock 2019', United Nations database, POP/DB/MIG/Stock/Rev.2019 (2019). The calculated
estimates are rounded.

[70] N. Kabbani, 'Facilitating the School-to-Work Transition: Labor and Youth in the Middle East and
North Africa Region', mimeo (2005, in Vol. III); U. Fasano and R. Goyal, 'Emerging Strains in GCC Labor
Markets', *Topics in Middle Eastern and North African Economics: Proceedings of the Middle East Economic
Association* 6 (September 2004).

who did not comply or only partially met specific targets. At the same time, the promotion of the employment of nationals was attempted through reserving certain jobs and sectors for them, giving priority to hiring nationals, incentives for substituting migrant workers, training programmes, support for self-employment, and various benefits.

The targets these labour market policies aimed to achieve were included in successive five-year development plans prepared by the Ministry of Economy and Planning. Each plan summarized the achievements of the previous five years and set new targets for the following five years. The discussion below focuses on how the Ministry incorporated labor issues and policies into the plans while the broader macro and industrial aspects of the plan can be seen in Chapter 1.

The First Development Plan (1970–5) was drafted prior to the sudden increase in the price of oil when nearly half (46 per cent) of the total workforce were still engaged in agriculture. In addition to envisaging a prominent development role for the state, it called for 'the expansion of social programs and the development of Saudi human resources'.[71] It did not fail to mention that there would be 'a gradual increase of women in the labor force'.[72] It made some vague references to 'possible replacement of some [sic] foreigners currently working in the Kingdom'[73] and 'encouragement of the replacement of foreigners by Saudis with the required training or experience',[74] but nothing hinted at the Saudization of employment. On the contrary, and this was the difference compared to subsequent plans, a predicted shortfall of 170,000 in 'manpower requirements' was to be covered by non-Saudis.[75]

The Second Development Plan (1975–80) was prepared after the increase in oil prices, government revenues having increased sixteen-fold since the previous plan (from SAR6 billion in 1970 to SAR93 billion in 1975).[76] During that plan an increase in the size of the state was set in motion that could not be sustained by the domestically available labour. The government started employing foreign workers 'to perform quickly the jobs needed to establish the development of the infrastructure in both the public and private sectors'.[77]

---

[71] Employment in the other sectors was 17 per cent in industry and 37 per cent in services, p. 75 https://www.mof.gov.sa/en/about/OldStratigy/First%20Development%20Plan%20-%20Chapter%201%20-%20Introduction-%D9%85%D8%AF%D9%85%D8%AC.pdf.

[72] Ibid., p. 67.

[73] Ibid., p. 86.

[74] Ibid., p. 93.

[75] Ibid., p. 87.

[76] Saudi Arabia Monetary Agency (SAMA), *Annual Report* (1981).

[77] S. A. Ewain, 'Perceptions of Employers and Job Seekers toward Obstacles to Saudization of the Workforce in the Saudi Private Sector' (1999), ProQuest Dissertations & Theses database, UMI No. 304517094.

At the same time, there was limited administrative capacity and expertise to manage a largely illiterate society. The combination of these factors together with political considerations gave rise to a rentier state whereby the regime's elites appropriated much of the oil wealth while ordinary citizens were coopted by being granted 'generous social benefits in exchange for political quiescence'.[78]

It was also during this plan that the term 'Saudization' was introduced.[79] The seeds for the migration policy, an authoritarian bargain, and private sector patronage were sown in a way that would serve the interest of a relatively small number of sponsors at the expense of a large number of Saudi job-seekers and also at a high cost to the economy from the high volume of migrant workers' remittances to their countries of origin. By 2017, remittances from Saudi Arabia stood at more than $35 billion (5.1 per cent of GDP), second only to the USA where GDP was $20 trillion—nearly thirty times more than Saudi Arabia's $700 billion (Figure 6.8). Interestingly, 60 per cent of remittances come from *tasattur* activities.[80]

The Third Plan (1980–5) was prepared when oil revenues had peaked by the end of the 1970s and government revenues had increased further to

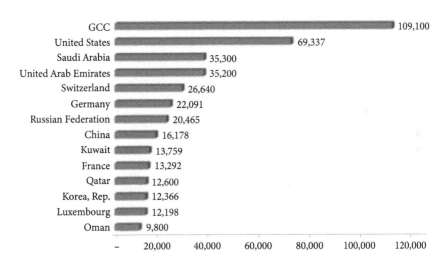

Figure 6.8 Remittances in 2017 (US$bn)

Sources: Author's calculations from World Bank's KNOMAD data base.

[78] S. Hertog, *Princes, Brokers, and Bureaucrats: Oil and the State in Saudi Arabia* (Ithaca: Cornell University Press, 2010).

[79] H. O. Alogla, 'Obstacles to Saudization in the Private Sector of the Saudi Arabian Labor Force' (1990), ProQuest Dissertations & Theses database, UMI No. 303856243.

[80] https://www.arabnews.com/saudi-arabia/news/686836; https://www.hindustantimes.com/world/saudi-arabia-may-close-expat-run-service-stores-report/story-WEsVDELN7LQRh2G6cHu84K.html.

SAR320 billion by 1980.[81] It reflected all the optimism that came with this situation but also acknowledged the sharp increase in migrant workers and explicitly called for 'a more efficient use of non-Saudi labor'. This observation was correct and was repeated in all subsequent plans without visible success until the mid-2010s. However, oil prices collapsed in 1981 and in the four decades since then there have been budget surpluses in only thirteen years.[82]

The Fourth Development Plan (1985–90) emphasized the need for 'restructuring the economy with the private sector playing a leading role', noted the decline in productivity, and acknowledged once more that women could contribute to productivity gains 'as they were becoming more educated'.[83] It set the Saudization target at 51 per cent by the end of the plan (up from 40 per cent), to be achieved by a 600,000 reduction in non-Saudi employment (which did not happen).

The Fifth Development Plan (1990–4) again encouraged private sector participation in areas where the government had traditionally provided services (such as public utilities and transportation). It called for a decline in the number of non-Saudi workers by 220,400 but their numbers kept increasing.

The Sixth Development Plan (1995–9) lamented that no progress had been made regarding the employment of non-Saudis, 'regardless of the calls in the Fourth and Fifth Development Plans'. The expected creation of 489,000 jobs for Saudis 'through replacement' had again fallen short as 'the influx of foreign workers ... has put further pressure on the ability of Saudi nationals to compete for new jobs or to replace non-Saudis'. It allocated SAR277 billion to develop the skills of Saudi workers.

The Seventh Plan (2000–4) was the last one to be completed during the long hiatus of oil prices, by which time the lesson had been learnt. Though total employment increased at the same annual rate as the economy, suggesting no productivity gains, most of the increase in employment (56 per cent) came from Saudis.[84] Yet by the end of this plan the number of non-Saudi workers was still nearly double that of Saudi workers.[85] Another SAR480 billion was allocated for training, this time to target employment in SMEs as compared to previous efforts that had focused on large organizations.

[81] SAMA, op. cit.
[82] https://journals.sagepub.com/doi/full/10.1177/0046958020984682; IMF, Article IV Consultation (2020).
[83] https://www.mof.gov.sa/en/about/OldStratigy/Fifth%20Development%20Plan%20-%20Chapter%201%20-%20Planning%20And%20Development%20In%20Saudi%20Arabia-%D9%85%D8%AF%D9%85%D8%AC.pdf, p. 6.
[84] https://www.mep.gov.sa/en/AdditionalDocuments/PlansEN/8th/Eighth%20Development%20Plan%20-%20Chapter%201-8%20.pdf, pp. 157–8.
[85] 'Proportional Distribution', Ministry of Labor database.

The Eight Development Plan (2004–9) benefited from a substantial increase in the price of oil, from just under \$38/barrel in 2004 to \$62/barrel in 2009, having peaked at \$97/barrel in 2008. Yet the average annual GDP growth of 3.5 during the plan was below the expected target of 4.6 per cent. Similarly, the employment target was missed by 20 per cent as only 10 per cent of the increase in private sector jobs was taken up by nationals. Unemployment increased to more than 410,000 compared to an expected decline from 268,000 to 139,000.[86]

Despite the experience with Saudization in the previous plans, the targets set by the Ninth Development Plan (2009–14) were again optimistic. Prepared at a time of high oil prices, it forecast that Saudi employment would increase by 1.2 million and unemployment would be reduced by 300,000. In terms of unemployment rates, the overall reduction was expected to be from 9.6 per cent to 5.5 per cent—from 6.5 per cent to 3.8 per cent for males, and from 26 per cent to an impressive 13 per cent for females. Neither was achieved, however, as the unemployment rate for men remained practically the same, while that for females increased to 33 per cent by 2014 compared to 28 per cent in 2009 (and 16 per cent in 1999).[87]

The outcomes of the plans are summarized in Table 6.4 with reference to the Seventh, Eighth, and Ninth Plans.[88] The figures are interesting in several ways. First, setting the Saudization target as a rate misses the point that the rate also depends on how much migrant employment has increased. So even if all Saudi job-seekers find a job and unemployment declines, a bigger increase in the number of migrant workers will still miss the point that

Table 6.4 Saudization rates and employment growth, 2000–14

2000	47.3%
2014	44.8%
Change in Saudi employment (000s)	2,185
Change in non-Saudi employment (000s)	3,002

Source: Saudi General Authority for Statistics: Labour Force Surveys 2000 and 2014.

[86] J. Sfakianakis, 'Saudi Arabia's Upcoming 10th Economic Development Plan Is of Critical Importance', Saudi–US Trade Group (27 May 2014).

[87] If unemployment is adjusted to include what the official statistics separately classify as 'job seekers', the unemployment rate for men is practically equal to its long-term average (7.7 per cent) but for women it increases to 43 per cent (Labour Force Survey, 2014).

[88] The Tenth Development Pan coincided with the introduction of Vision 2030; both are discussed later.

Saudi workers are doing well (though this may not necessarily be the case for productivity and the economy).

Second, the rate ignores whether there are sufficient numbers of Saudis to fill the opportunities that arise from economic growth and/or substitution of migrant jobs. For example, between 2000 and 2014 it would have been fully satisfactory if Saudi employment had increased by 2,754, 000 instead of 2,300,000: that is, if there had not been an increase in unemployment by 454,000. If so, the increase in the number of migrant workers would have more or less been justified as there would not have been any Saudis to be added to employment.

All in all, the plans have adopted a 'manpower planning' methodology and consistently misdiagnosed what has been holding back the increase in Saudi employment. The focus of policies has been on the alleged lack of skills among Saudis rather than their lack of motivation to join the low-wage private sector, which had been fuelled by the failure to control the increase in migrant workers. The failures of one plan do not seem to have provided guidance to the plan that followed. As for the labour market: 'The Saudization policy did not achieve the goals of increasing the skilled-job opportunities for Saudis. As a result of the failure of the Saudization policy, the Government has introduced a series of labor market programs of which the Nitaqat is the most prominent.'[89] Nitaqat and other recent labour market policies as well as Vision 2030 are discussed next.

Labour Market Policies Post-2010

Since the early 2010s, Saudi Arabia has intensified the previous Saudization policies and announced new ones. In 2011, it introduced Hafiz which offers cash assistance and supports training to the unemployed 'to find suitable jobs in the private sector'. Another programme, Nitaqat, was introduced in 2011 and has now become part of Vision 2030. Nitaqat prescribes Saudization targets in the form of quotas to be observed (one Saudi worker for every ten non-Saudi workers for companies employing ten or more workers) and imposes penalties for failing to achieve them. It also provides subsidies for on-the-job training costs (the Tamheer programme); offers childcare and transportation to female workers in the private sector (the Qurrah and Wusool programmes); offers opportunities for online training (the Doroob

---

[89] https://core.ac.uk/download/pdf/288854162.pdf, p. 48.

programme); and provides labour market information, employment services for skills assessment, counselling, and placement.[90]

In 2015, the Labor Law included thirty-eight amendments that made the employment of migrants more expensive by introducing prohibitions on confiscating migrant workers' passports, and penalties for failing to pay salaries on time and provide copies of contracts to employees. It strengthened enforcement and imposed higher or new fines for transgressors reaching up to SAR100,000 ($26,665)—an increase from the previous SAR70,000 ($18,667).[91] In 2017, nearly seventy new measures for job-seekers and employers were announced, aiming to increase the Saudization rate in the private sector and to expand the employment of women. In 2018, the annual fee for the dependants of expatriates was doubled to SAR2,400 and it has since been doubled again to SAR4,800 while that for migrants workers was set to SAR7,200.[92]

Additional initiatives included the expansion of vocational and technical education, aiming to provide 400,000 places over the next decade. The measures aiming to increase Saudization were amplified and consolidated in the Labor Reform Initiative launched in November 2020, although they do not apply to all categories of workers (such as domestic and agricultural workers).[93] Overall, Saudi Arabia can be said to have the strictest Saudization laws in the GCC.[94] In addition, there has been a loosening of the *kafala* system and migrants can change employers without prior approval.

However, against the aspirational goal to create a knowledge economy,[95] reality has prevailed. The focus is now 'on the retail sector, because retail is labour-intensive, a sector that requires medium skills which is aligned with the unemployment supply [*sic*], so it means we are not pushing the private sector where they cannot find demand'. Accordingly, a dozen retail sectors were reserved for Saudis, including furniture, car spare parts, watches, spectacles, and sweetshops.[96]

---

[90] See Chapter 7 on social protection.

[91] https://www.hrw.org/news/2015/11/15/saudi-arabia-steps-toward-migrant-workers-rights.

[92] Moody's Investor Service (2019) at https://www.asifma.org/sponsors/moodys-investors-service-2019-annual/.

[93] S. L. Shadmand, B. K. Biesenthal, J. S. Beaumont, and O. Gidalevitz, 'Saudi Arabia Introduces Significant Labor Reforms' (11 December 2020), https://www.shrm.org/resourcesandtools/hr-topics/global-hr/pages/saudi-arabia-labor-reform-initiative.aspx; https://www.business-humanrights.org/en/latest-news/saudi-arabia-reforms-to-allow-migrant-workers-to-change-jobs-leave-country-without-employer-permission-cautiously-welcomed-by-civil-society/; https://www.iom.int/news/iom-welcomes-launch-labour-reforms-kingdom-saudi-arabia; https://www.bbc.com/news/world-middle-east-54813515.

[94] M. Malik and T. Nagesh, 'GCC Fiscal reforms and Labor Market Policies', in G. Luciani and T. Moerenhout (eds.), *When Can Oil Economies Be Deemed Sustainable?*, table 10.2 (Palgrave Macmillan, 2021); open access at https://link.springer.com/book/10.1007/978-981-15-5728-6.

[95] https://oxfordbusinessgroup.com/analysis/long-game-new-development-plan-shows-clear-commitment-education-and-private-sector.

[96] https://www.reuters.com/article/us-saudi-labour-jobs-idUSKBN1HW1CO.

In terms of its effects, the loosening of the *kafala* system may add to the costs of migrant labour, thus indirectly contributing to the objective of Saudization. This is because when migrant workers decide to change employers, this is most likely in order to obtain higher wages. One study estimated that the wage increase in such cases can be more than 10 per cent of the previously paid wage.[97]

According to the MHRSD, Hafiz 'has benefitted more than 2.3 million individuals since [its] launch in 2011', while Nitaqat 'has helped to bring 750,000 Saudis into the private sector in four years, a 100 per cent increase'.[98] The National Transformation Program—one of the Vision-affiliated programmes—expected in 2016 that Saudi employment would increase by 1.2 million between 2017 and 2022. This would amount to an unprecedented annual increase in Saudi employment by 240,000 with a view to accommodating an increase in the female labour force participation rate to 28 per cent. However, these numbers are rather high compared to the historical data presented in Table 6.4. In fact, Saudi employment increased only by 650,000 between the beginning of 2017 to the end of 2022, and this was mainly because of the increase in women's employment by 400,000.[99]

Still the Saudization target may somewhat unexpectedly be achieved due to a massive exodus of migrant workers.[100] The doubling of dependants' fee has led to 1.1 million expatriates leaving the country.[101] Another 180,000 migrants have registered in the Awdah ('Return') initiative, which facilitates the return of workers to their home countries.[102] The impact of subdued oil prices conflated by the recession after the COVID-19 pandemic is estimated to have resulted in a loss of 1.7 million jobs and a population decline of 4 per cent.[103]

The departure of migrants on long-term contracts may lead to a reduction in skills as well as in the activities of *tasattur*. These are generally migrants who were living with their families and had higher-paying jobs. A study of the

---

[97] https://www.nber.org/papers/w20388.

[98] https://oxfordbusinessgroup.com/interview/building-workforce-obg-talks-mofarrej-al-haqbani-minister-labour. In parallel, the Ministry of Manpower introduced measures to increase the mobility of migrant workers from 'low-ranked to higher-ranked' companies without seeking permission from their current employer; started a wage protection system; enacted a Domestic Labour Law (2013) that regulates working hours, time off, sick pay, worker accommodation, and means of payment; and entered into bilateral agreements with Indonesia, the Philippines, and Sri Lanka regarding the protection of domestic workers.

[99] https://gulfmigration.grc.net/sa-emp-1-1-saudi-arabia-employed-population-by-nationality-saudi-non-saudi-and-sex-q1-2017-q3-2022/.

[100] Ibid. During this period the number of foreign workers remained the same at around 11 million.

[101] 'Saudi Labor Market Update', Q1 2018.

[102] https://www.arab-reform.net/publication/covid-19-and-the-intensification-of-the-gcc-workforce-nationalization-policies/.

[103] https://www.bloomberg.com/news/articles/2020-05-22/oxford-economics-sees-exodus-of-expat-workers-from-across-gcc.

effects of the Nitaqat programme during the first sixteen months of its implementation found that 11,000 firms had closed down through being unable to
satisfy the quotas or unwilling to pay the fines. According to another report,
more than 200,000 private firms had closed down two years later, having also
failed to meet the conditions set by the Nitaqat programme.[104] Nitaqat has
been successful in reducing the number of migrant workers by 904,000. However, it has been less successful in creating more jobs for Saudi citizens. The
number of such jobs has increased only by 93,000 and probably not all of that
increase was due to the programme.[105]

These early estimates of the impact of the post-2010 policies do not negate
their potential usefulness, particularly when combined with recent reforms
introduced by Vision 2030. The case of Saudi women in the labour market is
telling. By the first half of 2022, the female labour force participation rate had
increased from 23 per cent to 35 per cent, surpassing the 2030 target of 30 per
cent. Specifically for Saudi women in the 25–54 age group, the labour force
participation rate reached 48 per cent by mid-2023. Despite more women
joining the labour market, the female unemployment rate declined from 35
per cent in 2016 to 15 per cent in 2023.[106]

The increasing presence of Saudi women in the labour market has been
encouraged by allowing women to drive together with changes in the
guardianship law, labour law, and family law. It may have also been influenced by changing employers' hiring practices so that they could gain political acceptance. Over the course of two years, the employment gains of Saudi
women have been substantial, especially in the accommodation and food sectors, administrative and support services, and the health and social sectors,
followed by manufacturing (Figure 6.9).

It is therefore important to see Nitaqat in the context of Vision 2030 and
the emerging 'new social contract' that emphasizes the employment of the
young and of women together with the empowerment of these two groups.
Nitaqat has forced private sector employers to hire more Saudis to some
extent regardless of the impact on their firms and the private sector at large. If
young Saudis replace migrant workers without the same level of motivation
and at higher wages, and Saudi women are also employed at higher wages
than migrants previously doing the same work, productivity targets and the

[104] '200,000 firms closed down', *Arab News* (5 August 2014).
[105] J. R. Peck, 'Can Hiring Quotas Work? The Effect of the Nitaqat Program on the Saudi Private Sector', *American Economic Journal: Economic Policy* 9, no. 2 (2017), pp. 316–47; R. Smith, 'Saudi Arabia Could Rewrite Its Record on Labor Mobility by Ending Kafala', Centre for Global Development (3 March 2020), https://www.cgdev.org/end-of-kafala-labor-mobility.
[106] Labour Force Survey 2016 and for 2023, see https://www.stats.gov.sa/sites/default/files/LMS%20Q2_2023_PR_EN%20Press%20Release_0.pdf.

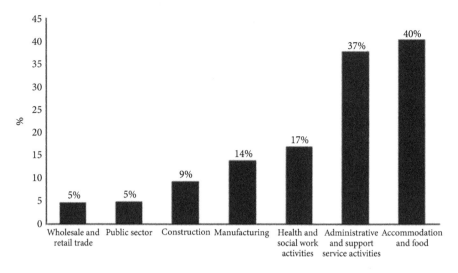

Figure 6.9 Employment increase of Saudi women (% growth between Q1, 2019 and Q4, 2020)

Source: Saudi General Authority for Statistics (GASTAT).

growth of the non-oil sector will be compromised in the short run. The likely longer-run trajectory of the Saudi economy and of the labour market until 2030 is examined next.

Vision 2030

Vision 2030 was announced soon after the Tenth Development Plan (2015–19) was published. Like its predecessors, the Tenth Plan had upbeat expectations.[107] The annual economic growth rate was expected to average 5 per cent, the share of the private sector in GDP to increase to 51 per cent from 45 per cent in 2014, and employment of Saudis to increase annually by around 250,000 (compared to 160,000 in the decade before the plan).[108] Vision 2030 was based on similarly aspiring targets and also included ambitious legal, structural, institutional, economic, social, and cultural reforms, although no political reforms appear to be on the horizon.[109] Still, progress has been made in the sense that the programmes under the Vision have been established and

---

[107] Unlike all previous plans, the Tenth Development Plan has not been posted on the government's website.

[108] http://g20.org.tr/wp-content/uploads/2014/12/g20_comprehensive_growth_strategy_saudi_arabia.pdf.

[109] J. Kinninmont, 'Vision 2030 and Saudi Arabia's Social Contract' (2017), https://www.chathamhouse.org/sites/default/files/publications/research/2017-07-20-vision-2030-saudi-kinninmont.pdf.

most have been posted online, although little information has so far been made public to assess their evolution.[110] From the available documentation, six issues stand out.

First, the Vision nowhere includes the term 'Saudization' or the achievement of any targets associated with it by 2030.

Second, there is no reference to public sector rationalization of employment or new regulations for future recruitment. Instead there is a target to train 'through distance learning, 500,000 government employees', apparently with the intention not to make any retrenchments.

Third, the not-for-profit sector, which employs only 11,000 workers but contributes a probably debatable 1 per cent of GDP, is expected to employ 1 million workers and contribute 5 per cent of GDP by 2030. This is a small addition to GDP relative to the employment increase from 11,000 to 1 million, while the 1 million is debatable in itself as it implies that nearly one-quarter of Saudi workers will be employed in the non-profit sector. Moreover, if this sector's contribution to GDP by 2030 is added to the expected growth of the private sector, it would reduce the oil sector's share in GDP ambitiously from 60 per cent to 30 per cent.[111]

Fourth, GDP is expected to double between the late 2010s and 2030, reaching $1.3 trillion and making Saudi Arabia the fifteenth largest economy in the world, surpassing Mexico and Spain. Assuming oil prices remain high, this may be a reasonable target: Saudi Arabia's nominal GDP reached $1 trillion in 2022 following high oil prices and producing 11 million barrels of output per day. To increase by another 40 per cent by 2030 would require a consistent annual growth rate of 4.5 per cent, something that would be largely dependent on oil prices and oil production. Raising the share of SMEs from 20 per cent to 35 per cent of GDP would require an annual growth rate of more than 10 per cent. Reaching a 50 per cent share of non-oil exports to GDP from 16 per cent would require an annual growth rate of 17 per cent. All this would require the private sector to sustain an annual growth rate of more than 9 per cent.[112]

---

[110] https://www.atlanticcouncil.org/wp-content/uploads/2020/06/Assessing-Saudi-Vision-2030-A-2020-review.pdf.

[111] Council of Economic and Development Affairs of Saudi Arabia, 'Saudi Vision 2030' (April 2016); A. Amirat and M. Zaidi, 'Estimating GDP Growth in Saudi Arabia under the Government's Vision 2030: A Knowledge-Based Economy Approach', *Journal of the Knowledge Economy* 11, no. 3, pp. 1145–70, doi: 10.1007/s13132-019-00596-2; http://vision2030.gov.sa/en (accessed 16 November 2016).

[112] A promising development is the private sector reforms that have been introduced in line with Vision 2030, which encompasses a variety of legal and structural reforms. Between 2018 and 2019 Saudi Arabia introduced eight reforms in the areas measured by the World Bank's *Doing Business* report, which ranked it as the top global performer. In terms of specific reforms, it overhauled the previous insolvency framework and strengthened minority investor protections; established a one-stop shop for company registration procedures; made issuing construction permits easier by launching an online platform;

Fifth, even if these rates are achieved, they will not be enough to reduce unemployment by nearly half (from 12 per cent to 7 per cent), to absorb the projected overall increase in the Saudi workforce. By 2030, the number of Saudis reaching the working age population will likely increase by about 6 million compared to 2015, of whom as many as 4.5 million may join the labour force.[113] This would employment to be created around three times faster than in the ten years or so preceding the Vision.[114] Recall from Table 6.4 that since 2000, despite oil prices being high, the annual growth of Saudi employment has averaged 160,000 and unemployment more than 30,000.

Sixth, the many targets included in Vision 2030 (more than 300) are to be coordinated by as many as twenty-five ministries and agencies that will oversee more than 150 planned initial public offerings.[115] Streamlining and becoming a more efficient and effective government is something to which the Vision aspires; however, the more than ninety new institutions of government have over-complicated and over-bureaucratized the affairs of the state. If anything, public sector hiring, in absolute and relative terms, has increased and more Saudis work in government than ever before. Most of the new hires have been attracted from the private sector on very high salaries compared to permanent civil service employees as part of a drive to attract talent and private sector experience. Many of these executives, however, worked in a private sector that was mainly rent seeking and benefited from insulated activities of property development, finance, and agency representation.

Much will depend on the oversight authority of Crown Prince Mohammed bin Salman and his ability to reduce corruption in a 'society where family, tribal, and regional ties are stronger than the nebulous conception of state identity'[116]. Such informal relationships can create coordination problems at

streamlined getting electricity connections; strengthened access to credit; introduced a value added tax; reduced red tape for trading across borders; reduced the paid-in minimum capital requirement as percentage of per capita income to zero; and eliminated the requirement for married women to provide additional documents when applying for a national identity card. See https://documents1.worldbank. org/curated/en/688761571934946384/pdf/Doing-Business-2020-Comparing-Business-Regulation-in-190-Economies.pdf, p. 8. http://documents1.worldbank.org/curated/en/688761571934946384/pdf/ Doing-Business-2020-Comparing-Business-Regulation-in-190-Economies.pdf. The two areas in which there were no reforms were 'registering property' and 'paying taxes'.

[113] https://www.mckinsey.com/~/media/McKinsey/Featured%20Insights/ Employment%20and%20Growth/Moving%20Saudi%20Arabias%20economy%20beyond%20oil/ MGI%20Saudi%20Arabia_Full%20report_December%202015.pdf.

[114] The Vision also envisages an increase of 1 million volunteers per year (compared to the currently estimated stock of 11,000). It is not clear what their salary and terms of employment would be and what they would contribute to private sector growth and exports. This can further tilt the balance from tradable to non-tradable goods and services.

[115] R. Bhatia, 'Assessment of the National Transformation Program (NTP)', Gulf International Bank (June 2016), https://www.gib.com/sites/default/files/ntp_ebook_-_website_1.pdf.

[116] H. Khashan, 'Saudi Arabia's Flawed "Vision 2030"', *Middle East Quarterly* (1 January 2017), https:// www.meforum.org/middle-east-quarterly/pdfs/6397.pdf.

a macro level that calls for greater harmonization in policy making so the pursue of national objectives is not diluted by specific group interests. Some of the gains achieved in several social and labour market areas may work against themselves. For example, the religious police are reported to have now been consigned to desk duties, and this raises the prospect that at some point citizens' demands may get ahead of how far the political leaders are prepared to go.[117]

What is more certain is that Saudi Arabia needs high rates of investment. However, they may be slow to come (see Chapter 1 on the overview of the economy over time). If they do come, the cost per job created may be high. For example, since the inception of Vision 2030 the Kingdom's sovereign wealth fund, the Public Investment Fund (PIF), and its subsidiary companies have invested SAR170 billion ($45 billion) and claimed to have created 331,000 direct and indirect jobs by the end of the third quarter of 2020. This amounts to a cost per job created of $346,000. In January 2021, the PIF announced that it plans an additional contribution to non-oil GDP of SAR1.2 trillion ($320 billion), expected to create 1.8 million jobs. This implies a lower, though still relatively high, cost per job created of $178,000.[118] Neom, the flagship project to build from scratch a zero-carbon city in the north-west of the country, is projected to require investments of between $500 billion and $1 trillion that would create 380,000 jobs. If so, the cost per job would be between $1.3 million and $2.6 million.[119] Mega projects typically provide employment to construction workers who are mostly foreigners from South Asia, with some Saudis holding executive positions. Historically, half of all jobs held by foreign workers were in construction.

Thus, mega projects cannot be relied upon to create much employment among Saudis, while other initiatives may still produce limited results as they have done in the past. For example, in addition to reducing the number of its own migrant workers,[120] Aramco launched an ambitious In-Kingdom Total Value Add programme in 2015 that prioritizes contracts among domestic companies, which are in turn expected to employ nationals for locally produced goods and services and to enhance the transfer of technology,

[117] https://edition.cnn.com/travel/article/saudi-arabia-fun-tourists/index.html.
[118] The investments are to cover sectors such as real-estate development, infrastructure, tourism, hospitality, entertainment, transportation, recycling, renewable energy, and some unspecified others. https://english.aawsat.com/home/article/2768136/pif-seeks-invest-66-bln-annually-new-saudi-projects.
[119] https://www.reuters.com/article/us-saudi-neom-project/saudi-crown-prince-launches-zero-carbon-city-in-neom-business-zone-idUSKBN29F0L8; https://www.wsj.com/articles/inside-saudi-arabias-plan-to-build-a-skyscraper-that-stretches-for-75-miles-11658581201.
[120] 'Saudi Aramco Cuts Hundreds of Jobs Amid Oil Market Downturn, Sources Say', Reuters (18 June 2020), https://www.reuters.com/article/us-saudi-aramco-jobs-idUSKBN23P2PN.

expertise, and skills.[121] Despite being supported by the biggest company in the world and having the involvement of twenty-five countries, it had only attracted an estimated capital expenditure of $7 billion over the six-year period to 2021.[122] This is a small amount in relation to the Saudization objectives and the apparent high cost of creating Saudi jobs.

Whether the above numerical analysis is in line with historical trends of investment, employment creation, policy coherence, and consistent implementation is perhaps irrelevant, as much depends on what happens in the future, especially with respect to global demand for Saudi oil and whether oil prices stay above the $110/barrel deemed necessary to balance the fiscal accounts if considering all its mega projects. If Saudi Arabia plays the role of price leader in the oil market and cuts production, this will lower exports and its revenues, upon which much of domestic economic development depends. Even if oil prices increase and stay at a high level, they could have indirect adverse effects by making shale production profitable and Iran's reaction unpredictable. In the meantime, the rest of the world is moving ahead with greening their economies, which could have dire implications for Saudi Arabia's main export commodity. Thus, the benefits from oil could be compromised. This raises doubts about whether the planned mega projects will be completed, at least on time, and whether payments for social benefits and grants to compensate citizens for the reforms included in Vision 2030 can go ahead without aggravating the fiscal situation.[123]

In the year Vision 2030 was announced, the IMF's assessment was that Saudi Arabia was facing the risk of running out of foreign reserves to fund imports given the rate of deficit spending, to the point that the targets of the Vision 'will be challenging to meet and will require considerable political follow-through to implement'.[124] The fact that the Vision is silent on political reforms may perpetuate the 'illusion of political permanence', which

---

[121] D. Olawuyi, 'Local content and procurement requirements in oil and gas contracts: Regional trends in the Middle East and North Africa'. MEP 18. Oxford: Oxford Institute for Energy Studies, 2017 at https://www.oxfordenergy.org/wpcms/wp-content/uploads/2017/11/Local-content-and-procurementrequirements-in-oil-and-gas-contracts-regional-trends-in-the-Middle-East-and-North-Africa-MEP18.pdf.

[122] https://www.arabianbusiness.com/politics-economics/saudi-aramcos-iktva-programme-to-support-kingdoms-localisation-initiatives.

[123] See vision2030.gov.sa/sites/default/files/attachments/BB2020_EN.pdf. Saudi Arabia had the highest fiscal allocation to energy subsidies, estimated at 10 per cent of GDP, among the oil producers and not only in the GCC included in the study by the IMF: *Energy Subsidy Reform: Lessons and Implications* (Washington, DC: International Monetary Fund, 2013). This pessimistic view has been reiterated ever since to the point that by 2020 the Vision was considered by some to be 'more or less over'. See Ian Leclerc, 'Saudi Arabia's Vision 2030 Is Going to Fail' (16 May 2016), https://www.theodysseyonline.com/saudi-arabias-vision-2030-is-going-to-fail.

[124] IMF, Saudi Arabia 2016 article IV consultation—press release; staff report; and informational annex. Country Report No. 16/326 at https://www.imf.org/external/pubs/ft/scr/2016/cr16326.pdf, p. 14.

economically may preserve at least a significant part of the rentier private sector through patronage. This can forestall the creation of a productive state, and which socially may perpetuate the need for the 'authoritarian bargain' that has compensated citizens through overemployment in the public sector.

Policy Directions

In a sense, the economy of Saudi Arabia can be said to have been characterized by 'entropic' growth, whereby the revenues from (oil) energy have not created a sustainable economy and a prosperous society based on a well-functioning labour market. What has been built in the past needs now to be re-examined and changed.

This is what Vision 2030 aims to address and as such it is a positive development. Its results remain to be seen, but 'change is always possible, if only because necessity makes it inescapable'.[125] The issue to be addressed is the balance between creating a 'shared economy' and the desire for political stability that has been a challenging goal for authoritarian elites.[126] What Saudi Arabia needs to address is a problem that Western democracies also face: that is, to curb the ability of economic elites and organized groups to substantially influence government policy. Ordinary citizens and their mass-based interest groups have little, and at times no, independent influence. Such an environment gives rise to 'elite domination' or 'biased pluralism' where even elected governments do not matter much for the majority of citizens.[127]

It is unfortunate that the beginnings of Vision 2030 coincided with a decrease in the price of oil and that this was followed by the onset of the COVID-19 pandemic. The targets originally set for 2020 have already been pushed back, including postponing the very ambitious target of a balanced budget from 2020 to 2023. The response to these crises has been to increase spending, for example by granting yet more allowances to public sector employees, while savings, for example from the introduction of value added tax, are being compromised.[128] Still, irrespective of whether all or some of the goals of the Vision are achieved, there are several employment and social

[125] K. Elliott House, 'Saudi Arabia in Transition: From Defense to Offense, but How to Score?', Harvard Kennedy School Belfer Center for Science and International Affairs, Senior Fellow Paper (June 2017).

[126] I. Elbadawi, 'Thresholds Matters: Resource Abundance, Development and Democratic Transitions in the Arab World', in I. I. Diwan and A. A. Galal (eds.), *The Middle East in Times of Transitions* (London: Palgrave Macmillan, 2016).

[127] M. Gilens and B. I. Page, 'Testing Theories of American Politics: Elites, Interest Groups, and Average Citizens', *Perspectives on Politics* 12, no. 3 (2014), pp. 564–81.

[128] M. Malik and T. Nagesh, 'GCC Fiscal reforms and Labor Market Policies' in G. Luciani and T. Moerenhout (eds.), *When Can Oil Economies Be Deemed Sustainable?* (Singapore: Palgrave Macmillan, 2021); open access at https://link.springer.com/book/10.1007/978-981-15-5728-6.

policies that could be considered in order to improve the functioning of the labour market. As the proverb goes, 'The best time to plant a tree was twenty years ago. The second best time is now.' The earlier these policies can be considered and introduced, the better.

Future policies can be grouped into: those that apply to employment in the public sector; those that affect employment in the private sector; and the benefit structure that affects both the reservation wage of workers and fiscal affordability. Obviously, not all policies fall under the responsibility of the MHRSD as it has narrowly been seen in the past.

First, the blades of employment in the public sector and those in the private sector must converge. This should not rely on administrative measures, which have been found to have limited and short-lived effects, while incurring dire budgetary costs and creating incentives to evade them. A more desirable and certain approach is to increase the professionalism of the public sector and reduce its function as a means of social protection. This approach might include the following actions:

1. Announce and implement zero public sector employment growth for x years but in a way that would allow the growth of demographically driven positions (such as teachers and medical personnel). This will give an incentive to citizens to increase their educational attainment.
2. Design and administer competitive exams with clear minimum requirements for entry into public sector employment, whose results would be used for hiring those applicants who achieved the highest performance. This would again encourage prospective job-seekers to invest in their human capital.
3. Promote public sector workers on the basis of merit and results, and only when there are vacancies at the next grade rather than according to years of service. This would increase effort.
4. Freeze public sector salaries and benefits for x years, taking into account existing or new social protection benefits (see below). This will start closing the public/private wage gap and increase the incentives of nationals to join the private sector.

Second, policy initiatives for the private sector should address the concerns of both employers and Saudi workers therein. The following are some relevant actions:

5. Amend the migration policy gradually by announcing that in each year there will be a certain number of renewals and a certain reduction in new permits. This should be a gradual process to avoid disruptions in production (as the experience with Nitaqat has shown).

6. As mentioned earlier, define Saudization targets in terms of numbers, not rates.

7. Set minimum wages and social security contributions in consultation with employers and apply both of them in the same way to all workers, Saudi and migrants. This will eliminate the labour market duality that arises from the labour costs for migrant workers being lower than those for employing Saudis.

8. Similarly, ensure that labour legislation applies equally to national workers and migrant workers.

9. Support the private sector in the transition from migrant workers to Saudi workers: for example, through wage subsidies and training allowances. This is being done already but Such measures should have a clear timeline and sunset clauses as well as penalties for slow transition.

10. Modernize the training system to become more demand driven and reliant on employer-based training. Training before entry to the labour market will be needed and much can and should be supported by public funds, but this training should be led, managed, and co-financed by employers to ensure the need for training and ownership by the private sector.

Third, as the previous proposals are bound to affect the welfare of citizens by changing the nature of social protection, they should be accompanied by actions that will cushion the cost of adjustment, such as:

11. Assess the social impact of moving away from the established social contract based on public sector employment and adjust the benefits/subsidies structure to initially preserve the level of the current 'social wage'.[129] Eventually let the labour market set the level of wages in line with productivity on the labour demand side and the reservation wage of nationals on the labour supply side.

12. Create a unified pension system between the public sector and the private sector, and rationalize it. For example, introduce penalties for early retirement and set the level of pensions after an independent actuarial review. The pension system could include a non-contributory pension to be paid to all persons above the age of 65 irrespective of their employment history.[130]

[129] The social wage is the nominal wage plus all subsidies/benefits that ensure minimum levels of real income and, one can add, fairness.

[130] Such a pension is called 'social pension', 'demogrant', 'categorical pension', and 'citizen's pension'. Its merits are increasingly acknowledged in the literature.

Two final remarks relate to social policy. One relates to the treatment of women in public and privates spheres. In fact, promoting gender equality and increasing the labour force participation of women may turn out to be one of the most reachable targets.[131]

The other is drawn from international experience, which shows that efforts to transform the economy can stall because of their social costs, of which the employment impact is the most dominant. It also shows that initial attempts can be followed by 'policy reversals': that is, policy-makers water down or even abandon what they started as soon as the first results appear (resulting in lower pressure to continue) and when political opposition reaches some critical level.[132]

If the public sector is rationalized, until the rewards from working in the private sector improve and unemployment is reduced, citizen resentment could increase. A new way of distributing the oil revenues to the broader population should be sought, replacing the social protection role of public sector employment. One such measure could take the form of an 'oil dividend' paid to citizens as a cash transfer, also taking into account the future structure and levels of other benefits.

The oil divided should be set at a flat rate for all of its recipients, who could be either all Saudis or adults only. A flat rate would not be distortionary in the economic sense of affecting choices. Its level could be set in relation to the (changing) price of a certain number of barrels of oil per year and therefore be variable over time.[133] This would reduce the perception that the government has unlimited resources and can pay salaries to public sector employers and benefits to the broader population no matter what the level of oil revenues. It would constitute a transparent way of distributing the oil wealth and cannot but be considered transparent and fair. Finally, the dividend should replace

---

[131] Vision 2030 aspires that 30 per cent of women will be at work by 2030, something that has been said to be 'almost surely one of the easiest—and yet one of the most significant' targets to be achieved (Elliott House, 'Saudi Arabia in Transition'). This may indeed turn out to be the case as the agency of Saudi women increases. Fertility, especially adolescent fertility, has declined significantly from almost seven births per woman in the 1970s to 2.5. Saudi women now account for 60 per cent of university graduates and are less inclined to marry or will do so at an older age: *The Little Data Book on Gender* (Washington, DC: World Bank, 2019). Data on marriage reveal a trend towards delaying the marriage age, with its average rising from 25.3 years for young men and 20 years for young women in 1979 to 27.2 years and 24.6 years respectively by the late 2000s (Ninth Plan, p. 321). Because of the discrimination they may have faced, women could be more willing to nurture younger female employees and provide them with role models. The international experience suggests that women can also be more productive employees than their male colleagues although they are typically, and sadly, paid less. The increased participation of women can only boost productivity and thus provide support to the achievement of other targets included in Vision 2030.

[132] In the case of Saudi Arabia, additional opposition could arise from the private sector, which has systematically been found in various surveys to oppose the reduction in the number of migrant workers and the resulting disruption of production and reduction in profits. The policies proposed in this chapter can go some way towards containing employers' opposition.

[133] In this respect, it differs from the universal basic income.

many other benefits whose fiscal costs are high and their targeting doubtful (such as energy subsidies, housing or other social allowances, family benefits tied to employment, no cost recovery of selected public services, and so on).

Addressing these effects might be more difficult than funding and implementing the Vision. Institutional reforms require transformative policies on the part of the government, and the mindset and expectations of citizens are not easily changed. The former requires clear leadership. The latter requires that citizens are faced with opportunities that are credible and fair. The road to be travelled is long, as it takes at least a generation for the labour market to change: that is, until all those workers who are about to join or are currently in the labour market retire.

7
Social Protection in Saudi Arabia

Jumana Alaref

Introduction

A lot has been written in the political science literature about the authoritarian bargain between citizens and the state, and its implications for the welfare system, in both rentier and non-rentier[1] economies of the Middle East and North Africa (MENA) region.[2] In Saudi Arabia's rentier economy, citizens have been guaranteed varying degrees of free education, free health care, employment in the public sector, and cash benefits. In the absence of an income taxation system, investments in social sectors have been financed by oil wealth. In the 1970s and 1980s, economic booms were fuelled by enormous revenues from state oil exports, resulting in a steep increase in government total expenditures, mostly driven by high capital spending (Figure 7.1). Aided by an unrestricted supply of low-skilled migrant workers, the government increased its investment in social services, the provision of health, education, and housing services, and the development of economic sectors such as transportation and telecommunications.[3]

Substantial investment in social sectors in the Kingdom has since resulted in material standards of living that are on a par with other high-income countries. Life expectancy rose from 53 years in 1970 to 75 years in 2018, and between 1990 and 2015, Saudi Arabia experienced significant declines in

---

[1] Rentier economies in MENA commonly refer to oil-exporting countries, namely the Gulf Cooperation Council (GCC) countries, Iraq, Libya, and Algeria. Non-rentier economies refer to oil-importing countries, such as Egypt, Jordan, Morocco, and Tunisia.

[2] The chapter and its findings, interpretations, and conclusions should not be attributed in any manner to the World Bank, to its affiliated organizations, or to the members of its Board of Executive Directors or the countries they represent. I am thankful to Johannes Koettl, Montserrat Pallares-Miralles, Samik Adhikari, and Anush Bezhanyan for their helpful comments on an earlier draft of the chapter. I would also like to thank the broader team at the World Bank Social Protection and Jobs Department that has worked on Saudi Arabia. The chapter benefited hugely from their previous and ongoing work. The chapter was written in 2020 and reflects the state of affairs at that time.

[3] S. A. Alshahrani and A. J. Alsadiq, 'Economic Growth and Government Spending in Saudi Arabia: An Empirical Investigation', IMF Working Paper WP/14/13 (Washington, DC: International Monetary Fund, 2014), https://www.imf.org/external/pubs/ft/wp/2014/wp1403.pdf.

Jumana Alaref, *Social Protection in Saudi Arabia*. In: *The Economy of Saudi Arabia in the 21st Century*. Edited by: John Sfakianakis, Oxford University Press. © Jumana Alaref (2024). DOI: 10.1093/oso/9780198863878.003.0008

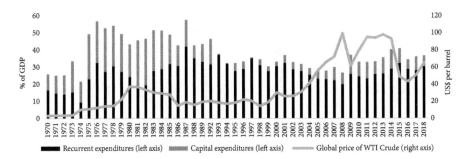

Figure 7.1 Saudi government expenditure on recurrent and capital expenditures and global price of WTI Crude, 1970–2018

Sources: Saudi expenditures from SAMA; WTI price from Federal Reserve Bank of St Louis.

maternal mortality, infant mortality, under-5s mortality, malnutrition, and deaths from communicable diseases. Investment in education has also led to an increase in the average years of schooling. As a result, Saudi Arabia's score on the Human Development Index[4] increased from 0.70 in 1990 to 0.85 in 2017, resulting in a ranking of thirty-nine out of 189 countries. Extreme and moderate absolute poverty, defined by the World Bank as living on less than $1.90 and $3.10 per day in Power Purchasing Parity terms, respectively, are virtually non-existent in the Kingdom.

In recent years, fiscal concerns and limited economic outcomes have prompted the government to examine the effectiveness and efficiency of government spending on social sectors. Previous levels of government spending became fiscally unsustainable as the decline in oil prices after 2011 reduced government revenues and resulted in a fiscal deficit that stood at 5.9 per cent of gross domestic product (GDP) in 2018 (Figure 7.2). The fiscal deficit widened in 2020 to 11.3 per cent of GDP after the outbreak of the COVID-19 pandemic.[5] The concern for fiscal sustainability has been compounded by a weak economy-wide productivity performance (Figure 7.3). Total factor productivity (TFP) steadily declined between 2000 and 2009, and has not substantially increased in recent years.[6] Saudi Arabia has also done less well than other high-income countries in transforming its overall wealth into

---

[4] The Human Development Index is a summary measure developed by the United Nations to assess long-term progress on three basic dimensions of human development: (i) a long and healthy life, (ii) access to knowledge, and (iii) a decent standard of living.

[5] IMF, 'Saudi Arabia: 2021 Article IV Consultation', IMF Country Report 21/149 (Washington, DC: International Monetary Fund, 2021), https://www.imf.org/-/media/Files/Publications/CR/2021/English/1SAUEA2021001.ashx.

[6] Labour productivity and TFP for Saudi Arabia are heavily influenced by oil prices. Despite these difficulties in measurement, however, the results are quite striking (and mostly consistent with the literature).

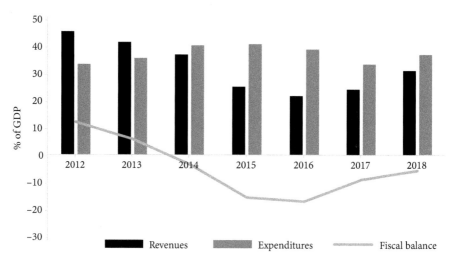

Figure 7.2 Government finances, 2012–18

Sources: IMF, 'Saudi Arabia: 2017 Article IV Consultation', IMF Country Report 17/316 (Washington, DC: International Monetary Fund, 2017); IMF, 'Saudi Arabia: 2018 Article IV Consultation', IMF Country Report 18/263 (Washington, DC: International Monetary Fund, 2018); IMF, 'Saudi Arabia: 2019 Article IV Consultation' IMF Country Report 19/290 (Washington, DC: International Monetary Fund, 2019).

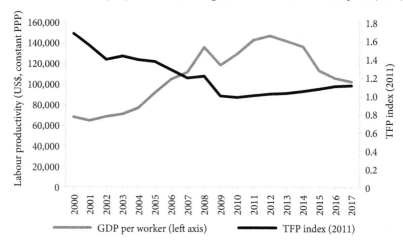

Figure 7.3 Labour productivity and total factor productivity, 2000–17

Source: Penn World Tables 9.1.

human capital wealth—measured as the present value of the expected earnings of the labour force.[7] For example, human capital wealth as a share of total wealth was 31 per cent in 2014, compared to a share of 78 per cent in the United States.

---

[7] This measure factors in not only the number of years of schooling completed by workers, but also the earnings gains associated with schooling (which implicitly factor in the quality of the learning taking place in school) and how long workers can work (which implicitly accounts for health conditions

Finally, relative vulnerability and inequality are believed to have increased among Saudi households in recent years, despite the lack of public government statistics.[8] According to the Household Income and Expenditure Survey 2018, disparities appear to be particularly pronounced across regions, in female-headed households, and in households with lower-educated heads (Figures 7.4 and 7.5).

Cognizant of this situation, in 2016, Saudi Arabia adopted Vision 2030, a strategic plan to build a vibrant society, diversify the economy while reducing oil dependence, and modernize the public sector. Under Vision 2030, the government is implementing a fiscal consolidation programme and wide-ranging economic and social reforms structured under thirteen Vision Realization Programs, with important consequences for Saudi citizens.

The remainder of this chapter will examine the extent to which social welfare programmes currently play a role in improving welfare, productivity, and human capital among Saudis, and how social spending can become more

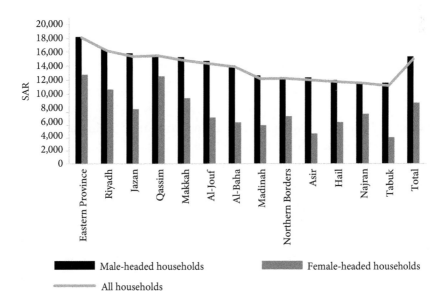

Figure 7.4 Average Saudi household monthly income by gender of household head, 2018

Source: GASTAT.

through life expectancy, among other parameters). G.-M. Lange, Q. Wodon, and K. Carey, 'The Changing Wealth of Nations 2018: Building a Sustainable Future' (Washington, DC: World Bank, 2018), https://openknowledge.worldbank.org/handle/10986/29001.

[8] Press reports and private estimates suggest that between 2 million and 4 million Saudis live on less than about $530 a month—about $17 a day—considered the poverty line in Saudi Arabia. See, e.g., https://www.theguardian.com/world/2013/jan/01/saudi-arabia-riyadh-poverty-inequality.

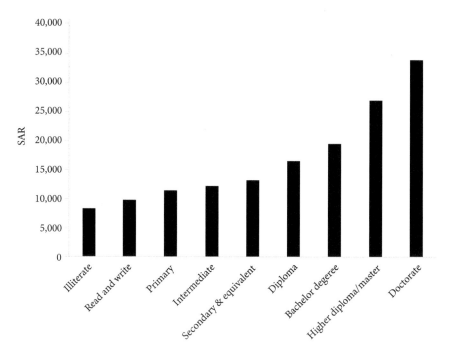

Figure 7.5 Average Saudi household monthly income by education of household head, 2018

Source: GASTAT.

efficient and effective. It will place welfare programmes within the landscape of social protection, defined by the World Bank as follows: systems, policies, and programmes that aim to protect against poverty, to insure against (prevent) drops in well-being from a range of shocks, and to promote opportunity for all through human capital and access to productive work.[9] Based on these objectives, social protection programmes are generally grouped into the following core components: social assistance programmes (also known as social safety net programmes—including cash transfers and in-kind transfers); social insurance programmes, such as unemployment insurance, health and disability insurance, and old-age pensions; and active labour market policies and programmes, such as skills-building programmes and job search and matching programmes.

The chapter is organized as follows. The first section presents an overview of social protection programmes in Saudi Arabia and summarizes the main arguments made in the chapter. The second section delves into social

---

[9] World Bank, 'Resilience, Equity, and Opportunity: The World Bank's Social Protection and Labor Strategy 2012–2022 (English)' (Washington, DC: World Bank, 2012), http://documents.worldbank.org/curated/en/443791468157506768/Resilience-equity-and-opportunity-the-World-Banks-social-protection-and-labor-strategy-2012-2022/.

assistance, by presenting an overview of key programmes, challenges, and the way forward. The third section examines social insurance programmes and discusses challenges and opportunities for reform. The fourth section looks into active labour market programmes and their impact on promoting productive employment among Saudi nationals, given the structure of Saudi Arabia's economy. A final section concludes.

Overview of Social Protection Programmes

The rationale for government intervention to address failures in labour and insurance markets is well documented in the literature.[10] In the case of Saudi Arabia, there are various risks facing different populations that social protection programmes aim to address. Figure 7.6 highlights the major programmes that Saudi Arabia currently has, mapped against the three objectives of social protection programmes. For example, to protect against the risk of poverty, the Ministry of Human Resources and Social Development (MHRSD) administers cash transfer programmes, social care services for orphans and persons with disabilities (PwDs), fee waivers, and other social services like food subsidies, housing subsidies, and electricity and water subsidies.

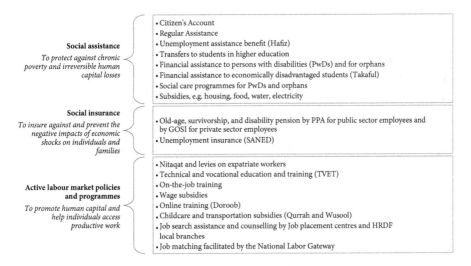

Figure 7.6 Social protection programmes in Saudi Arabia

Note: Programme classification and social protection terminology draws on World Bank, 'Resilience, Equity, and Opportunity: The World Bank's Social Protection and Labor Strategy 2012–2022 (English)' (Washington, DC: World Bank, 2012).

[10] N. Barr, 'Economic Theory and the Welfare State: A Survey and Interpretation', *Journal of Economic Literature* 30, no. 2 (1992), pp. 741–803.

To prevent against shocks, Saudi Arabia has two separate pension systems—one for public sector employees (run by the Public Pension Agency, PPA) and the other for private sector employees (run by the General Organization for Social Insurance, GOSI)—to address the risk of old-age poverty and provide for consumption smoothing over the life cycle. Saudi Arabia also has an unemployment insurance scheme (SANED) for private sector workers to protect against income shocks during spells of unemployment. There is currently no social health insurance in Saudi Arabia, but public health care services are provided free to Saudi nationals.

To promote human capital and productive employment, the MHRSD has implemented quota- and price-based interventions to increase the proportion of Saudis working in the private sector. In addition, its public employment agency—the Human Resource Development Fund (HRDF)—implements a set of active labour market programmes, such as training schemes, wage subsidies, and job search assistance and counselling. Saudi Arabia also spends on publicly provided vocational education and training programmes.

The argument of this chapter is that social protection policies and programmes in Saudi Arabia are heavily influenced by two distinct features that—while very commonly found across all GCC countries—remain divergent from other high-income countries. First, citizens have long been provided with access to lifelong employment in the public sector on a large scale, with generous wages and employment conditions. Figure 7.7 shows the wage bill as a percentage of GDP, estimated at 16 per cent in 2018. This share has increased in recent years and remains on an upward trajectory. This has contributed to Saudis overwhelmingly preferring employment in the public sector, limiting their labour market mobility within and across sectors. The wage bill also effectively crowds out other forms of social protection spending that are less distortive and, if well targeted, can support sustainable and inclusive growth (Figure 7.8).

The second feature is the dominance of foreign workers in the labour market, which Saudi Arabia utilizes to meet the increasingly high demand for goods and services generated by higher government investment and expenditure, as well as private consumption. At the heart of this challenge is that foreign labour is not on a level playing field with Saudi labour, as foreign nationals are willing to work at much lower wage levels than Saudi citizens and enjoy far more limited social and employment protection, which until recently included not being able to switch employers easily. Many Saudis do not compete with non-Saudis directly, especially for semi- and low-skilled positions, due to Saudis' high reservation wages. This reality has for many years shaped citizens' preferences and attitudes towards meritocracy, competition, and human capital investment.

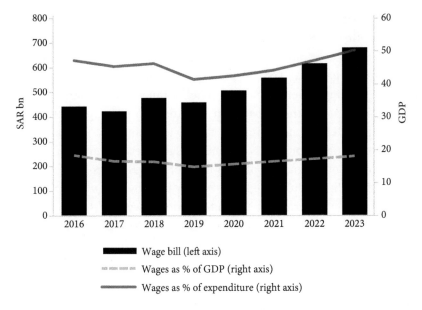

Figure 7.7 Saudi Arabia's wage bill, 2016–23

Note: Numbers from 2019 onwards are projections.
Source: IMF 'Saudi Arabia: 2018 Article IV Consultation'.

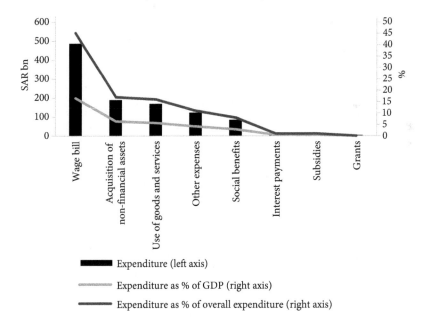

Figure 7.8 Breakdown of expenditure items, 2018

Notes: Subsidies include those for social and sports clubs, private education, private hospitals, and other agricultural subsidies. Social benefits include *zakat* charity transfers, social welfare payments, the Cost of Living Allowance Program (estimated at 0.1 per cent of GDP, suspended as of June 2020), and Hafiz (unemployment assistance scheme).
Source: IMF, 'Saudi Arabia: 2018 Article IV Consultation'.

The impact of social protection policies and programmes has often been limited by these two key distortions, and the design of the programmes may at times have contributed to existing distortions. The design of most social protection programmes appears to reflect the objective of channelling wealth to citizens through overly generous benefits, but with weak targeting and little attention paid to the impacts on incentives to participate in the labour market, productivity, and human capital accumulation. Social assistance remains dominated primarily by energy subsidies. Other social assistance programmes consist mainly of cash transfer programmes that reach a large proportion of the population. However, because they are uncoordinated and fragmented, their overall impact on households' welfare is unclear. Furthermore, the system might induce work disincentives, given the absence of activation measures among its work-capable beneficiaries and the preference to remain on benefit instead of participating in training and accepting low-paid jobs in the private sector.

Social insurance, namely the old-age pension, is generous and induces many Saudis to stop working years before the official retirement ages of 58 for public employees and 58 and 53, respectively, for men and women working in the private sector. While the pension system has a favourable ratio of contributors to retirees, given Saudi Arabia's young population, the generosity of the benefit is driving an imbalance between contributors and recipients in the system, which is becoming unsustainable financially. Moreover, the design of social insurance may contribute to mobility barriers in the labour market, leading to the inefficient allocation of resources. For example, the public pension scheme is considered more generous than the private scheme, with different qualifying conditions, and this might discourage labour mobility between sectors and further exacerbate the differential in compensation between the public and private sectors. The pension system also excludes foreign workers, which contributes to their unequal employment conditions when compared to Saudi workers. Furthermore, the unemployment insurance scheme in the private sector (SANED) has been ineffective in supporting job mobility for Saudis in light of onerous labour regulations, such as expensive severance pay upon dismissal. The costs of other forms of entitlement, such as maternity and sick leave, are fully borne by employers and further contribute to reduced labour demand and movement of workers. In the case of maternity leave, the absence of a financing arrangement in the form of a social insurance fund to share social costs translates into women remaining largely excluded from private sector employment.

Finally, the impact of active labour market programmes to promote skills among Saudi workers and increase their productive employment may be ineffective given limited coordination with other social protection programmes. For example, social assistance beneficiaries are not benefiting from labour market programmes to improve their skills, and the pension system provides disincentives to keep working and contributing. In addition, labour policies to increase the proportion of Saudis in the private sector likely produce suboptimal outcomes without addressing the underlying reasons why firms prefer to hire foreign workers and the generous wage-setting policies in the public sector that shape Saudis' preferences and decisions to invest in skills and education. Present weaknesses in education and training systems add to the challenge of skilling and reskilling Saudi workers. For example, enrolment in early childhood education is low and the quality of learning in the formal education system appears to be weak. Adult training programmes, such as vocational training, still cover only a small proportion of the workforce. Labour intermediation and job matching do not work well enough due to a lack of good-quality vacancy collection, weak service provision for employers, and limited case management for job-seekers.

Aware of such challenges, Saudi Arabia has embarked recently on a series of landmark reforms to strengthen targeting and improve the performance of many of its social protection programmes. Moving forward, there are important reform directions for the government to consider in each of the three social protection components. For social assistance, it is important to strengthen targeting, reduce programme fragmentation, and integrate able-bodied beneficiaries within existing labour market programmes. For social insurance, addressing fiscal sustainability and affordability, as well as improving incentives to work and contribute, require, at a minimum, substantial parametric reforms or even more fundamental systematic reforms of the old-age pension schemes. Other forms of social insurance, such as strengthened unemployment insurance in lieu of costly labour regulations, could help improve worker mobility in the labour market. For active labour market programmes, targeting services towards job-seekers with multiple employability barriers could yield the highest impact, while strengthening training and education systems is required to prepare the Saudi workforce for the labour market. Finally, there are important cross-cutting reform areas that need to be tackled in parallel, such as reforming distortive wage-setting policies and employment in the public sector and reducing the existing segmentation between Saudi and non-Saudi workers in the labour market.

Social Assistance

Saudi Arabia currently administers two large cash transfer programmes that are targeted towards different groups, with some overlap. The oldest programme under the MHRSD is Regular Assistance, which was initiated under the Social Security Law by Royal Decree in 1963 to guarantee a minimum income to select vulnerable groups. The programme is funded through *zakat* collection (60 per cent) and by the government (40 per cent). The programme uses a combination of an income and asset checks, as well as categorical targeting, to reach Saudi poor and vulnerable households. Eligible categories include orphans, PwDs, elderly, women without providers (widows or divorcees), families without providers, and single women over the age of 35. The benefit is also available to low-income households, but beneficiaries are required to be without active employment, without any commercial licences, without assets that exceed one residential home, and below an income threshold which depends on family size.[11] In 2017, the number of beneficiaries receiving financial assistance reached 1,134,629 individuals.[12] The benefit amount for each beneficiary was estimated at SAR862 per month, with an additional SAR284 for each additional family member. In 2018, spending on Regular Assistance reached 0.8 per cent of GDP (Table 7.1).

The second cash transfer programme, which is significantly bigger than the Regular Assistance programme in terms of expenditure and number of beneficiaries, is the Citizen's Account. The programme was announced

Table 7.1 Spending on social assistance programmes, 2018

Programme	Spending in 2018 (% of GDP)
Regular Assistance	0.8
Citizen's Account	1.0
Social care programmes for persons with disabilities and orphans	0.2
School programmes (*takaful*)	0.2
Other programmes (including Hafiz)	0.6
Total	2.8

Source: IMF, 'Saudi Arabia: 2019 Article IV Consultation'.

[11] The threshold increases from SAR2,000 for a family size of one to SAR10,000 for a family size of fifteen members.
[12] https://mlsd.gov.sa/sites/default/files/uploads/%D8%A7%D9%84%D9%83%D8%AA%D8%A7%D8%A8%20%D8%A7%D9%84%D8%A7%D8%AD%D8%B5%D8%A7%D8%A6%D9%8A%201434%20-%20S1435_0.pdf.

in 2017 to compensate Saudi families for the cost of higher energy prices, value added tax (VAT), and levies imposed on expatriate workers. Unlike Regular Assistance, the Citizen's Account targets in principle both low- and middle-income families. Households in the bottom 50 per cent of the income distribution receive a full entitlement, while households between 50 and 80 per cent of the income distribution receive a partial entitlement that is tapered in a linear fashion, and there is no transfer to households in the top 20 per cent of the income distribution. The individual full entitlement amount is SAR382 per month, and the household transfer can be computed as a multiple of this individual amount, given an equivalence scale.[13] In April 2018, 3.7 million households —that is, 83 per cent of all those registered—received a cash transfer, for a monthly fiscal cost of SAR2.2 billion. Of these, 57 per cent received a full compensation that averaged SAR933 per month.[14]

Saudi Arabia also implements other cash transfer schemes, some of which are targeted while others are universal. In response to social pressures created by persistent unemployment, the government implemented in 2011 an unemployment assistance scheme (Hafiz) that benefited as of 2018 a total of 537,717 job-seekers.[15] Other programmes include financial assistance for PwDs and for orphans, financial assistance to economically disadvantaged students (*takaful*), as well as transfers to students in higher education. In addition to cash transfers, in-kind benefits are available to vulnerable populations. For example, beneficiaries from Regular Assistance can also benefit from subsidized housing. Social care services and rehabilitation centres are also provided to PwDs and families in distress. Table 7.1 presents the breakdown of spending on cash transfers and social care services by the MHRSD. In 2018, these transfers made up 2.8 per cent of GDP.

Cost, System Overlap, and Fragmentation

Despite a series of reform measures that the government started as part of its economic transformation plan in 2015 to improve the government's fiscal

---

[13] The equivalence scale used is the OECD-modified one, which assigns a value of 1 to the household head, of 0.5 to each additional adult member (above 18), and of 0.3 to each child (below 18).

[14] IMF, 'Saudi Arabia: 2019 Article IV Consultation', IMF Country Report 19/290 (Washington, DC: International Monetary Fund, 2019), https://www.imf.org/en/Publications/CR/Issues/2019/09/09/Saudi-Arabia-2019-Article-IV-Consultation-Press-Release-and-Staff-Report-48659.

[15] The benefit is divided into two phases. Phase I is intended for job-seekers aged 20–35. Monthly financial support in the amount of SAR2,000 is provided for one year. Phase II is intended for job-seekers who have already completed phase I but are still searching for employment, or are between the ages of 36 and 60. HRDF, *Annual Report* (2018), https://www.hrdf.org.sa/media/Annual%20report/HRDF_Annual_Report_2018_(Arabic).pdf.

position and reduce domestic energy consumption, social assistance in Saudi Arabia is mostly dominated by energy subsidies. In 2018, energy subsidies made up 5.2 per cent of GDP.[16] Aside from being regressive and encouraging excessive consumption by citizens and inefficient investment by the private sector, subsidies are costly and present a large opportunity cost in terms of forgone revenue that could have been used for other purposes.

The existing cash transfer schemes suffer from overlap, fragmentation, and little coordination. It is possible that beneficiaries may benefit from multiple cash transfer programmes at the same time, given overlapping eligibility requirements. For example, PwDs are eligible for assistance from both Regular Assistance and from a separate programme that provides financial assistance specifically to PwDs. In the absence of coordination and with rising political economy pressures, social assistance has at times been used as a vehicle to channel wealth back to civil servants. In 2018, Saudi Arabia introduced another cash transfer programme, the Cost of Living Allowance, as a compensation for rising domestic energy prices and VAT, even though the Citizen's Account was already in place. It provided monthly cash transfers of SAR1,000 to public sector employees and military personnel. Other beneficiaries included students and individuals on social benefits, the majority of whom were already benefiting from existing transfers. The programme was in contradiction to the ongoing civil service reform intended to contain the wage bill and align public and private sector wages. Targeted mainly to civil servants, it did not reach the least well-off segments of the population either. The programme was eventually discontinued in June 2020.[17]

In recent years, the MHRSD has consolidated many small initiatives into several large cash transfer programmes as part of its efforts to rationalize and reorient social assistance programmes. For example, in 2017, several social assistance programmes were terminated and their funding incorporated into Regular Assistance.[18] However, the absence of an official definition of a household and of a national registry that maps every individual to a household, as verified by a residential address, presents a critical hurdle to the rationalization of Saudi Arabia's social assistance programmes, which could in turn lead to considerable improvement in targeting accuracy (a reduction

---

[16] In 2018, energy subsidies to Saudi Aramco totalled SAR152.6 billion (5.2 per cent of GDP). See the Saudi Aramco bond prospectus at https://www.rns-pdf.londonstockexchange.com/rns/6727U_1-2019-4-1.pdf

[17] https://thearabweekly.com/saudi-arabia-adopts-its-largest-budget-yet-continues-cost-living-allowances.

[18] These programmes included a cash programme for the purchase of school bags, a cash assistance programme to subsidize electricity costs, a food assistance programme, a temporary assistance programme, and other small cash-support programmes provided by the MHRSD.

in inclusion and exclusion errors) and a higher poverty impact. For example, the household definition adopted by the Citizen's Account differs from that used by Regular Assistance in that the former sets no age limit for dependants, whereas the latter counts dependants up to the age of 26. Students who are studying far away from their families are not accounted for as part of the household in the Citizen's Account, unlike Regular Assistance. The definition used by the Citizen's Account also differs from the definition offered by the General Authority for Statistics (GASTAT). The definition of a household, according to GASTAT, includes all those living in the dwelling who are not related to the household head (e.g. domestic workers), whereas family relation is needed for eligible beneficiaries within the Citizen's Account.

Without a national registry, instances may occur of benefit duplication and multiple payments from the same programme accruing to families residing within the same household. This is one potential explanation of the discrepancy between the number of household beneficiaries in the Citizen's Account database (counted at 3.7 million in 2018) and the total number of 'heads of households' derived from the GASTAT 2010 census (2.9 million).[19] Incorrect construction of households may also lead to benefit leakage to higher income quintiles and inefficient targeting, given that families may have the incentive to split up to qualify for benefits if appropriate oversight mechanisms are not in place. As a result, total coverage of all social assistance programmes among the population and their impacts on welfare cannot be determined from administrative data.

Countries' national registries of households are often linked to and harmonized with other ministries' databases, forming a management information system (MIS).[20] A well-functioning MIS would facilitate tracking of beneficiaries of multiple programmes, detect benefit duplication and/or fraud, and strengthen referral mechanisms between programmes after identifying synergies or gaps in benefit provision. While the Citizen's Account was initially set up with that objective, technical difficulties with the platform and the absence of data protection regulations ultimately discouraged data sharing across ministries. In the absence of an MIS, the cumulative impact of not only cash transfer programmes but also other social assistance and labour programmes on each household cannot be assessed.

[19] https://www.stats.gov.sa/sites/default/files/en-census2010-dtl-result_2_1.pdf.
[20] P. Pereira Guimaraes Leite, T. G. George, C. Sun, T. Jones, and K. Lindert, 'Social Registries for Social Assistance and Beyond: A Guidance Note and Assessment Tool (English)', Social Protection and Labor Discussion Paper 1704 (Washington, DC: World Bank, 2017), http://documents.worldbank.org/curated/en/698441502095248081/Social-registries-for-social-assistance-and-beyond-a-guidance-note-and-assessment-tool.

Lack of a Unified Targeting Mechanism and Exclusion and Inclusion Errors

Across the multiple social assistance programmes in Saudi Arabia, there is no unified definition of what constitutes low-income or vulnerable households and mechanisms to target them accordingly. For example, Regular Assistance and the Citizen's Account adopt varying definitions of low-income households. The former does not count wage income (as, by definition, beneficiaries have to be unemployed), uses some asset filters for the eligibility criteria, and does not count non-wage income such as student allowances, while the latter counts wage income and includes other student allowances in its calculation of income. The equivalence scale that is used to account for each family member varies between the two programmes. Such inconsistencies would render the cumulative impact of these programmes on low-income households uncertain and could potentially result in exclusion errors. For example, Regular Assistance does not cover low-income working Saudi families, who are generally found among the self-employed and those working in the private sector. According to the GASTAT Labor Force Survey, 2.6 million Saudis worked outside the generally well-paid jobs in the public sector in 2019.

Moreover, the definition of vulnerability in many social assistance programmes extends to the cases of individual persons, who may not reside in low-income households. For example, Regular Assistance relies primarily on categorical targeting and extends benefits to various cases of female beneficiaries, such as divorcees, widows, or single women above the age of 35, who may be capable of work and who may reside in a household that is not in need of monetary support. In the same vein, programmes do not count the income that belongs to wives as part of the overall family income when determining eligibility and benefit calculation. Transfers to students in higher education are not targeted and could end up disproportionately benefiting higher-income families. The unemployment assistance scheme (Hafiz) is open to all job-seekers. It is not means-tested nor is it explicitly focused on individuals with a history of longer distance from the labour market, such as first-time job-seekers. Lack of targeting could ultimately lead to significant inclusion errors and efficiency losses.

Weak Work Incentives

The principle of the 'work-first approach' that is often attached to social assistance in the Organization for Economic Cooperation and Development

(OECD) countries[21] is admittedly hard to enforce fully in Saudi Arabia, where benefits have been considered for so long an entitlement and part of the government's obligation towards its citizens. Indeed, most of the social assistance support that beneficiaries receive is not conditional on job search efforts and there is virtually no connection between Regular Assistance beneficiaries and active labour market programmes. This presents a missed opportunity in the country's efforts to improve labour market outcomes for vulnerable individuals, especially among women, who may make up a large proportion of social assistance beneficiaries. The requirements on Hafiz beneficiaries to fulfil certain obligations intended to help them find employment as well as signal commitment to a serious job search were not enforced when Hafiz was originally implemented and the programme was eventually perceived as another unconditional transfer made from the government to its citizens. This resulted in adverse incentives among beneficiaries, encouraging them to consider looking for employment only towards the end of the benefit eligibility period.[22]

Furthermore, the design of cash transfers that results in steep withdrawal of benefits in response to increasing wage income may lead to a negative labour supply response. Work disincentives may be particularly pronounced among Regular Assistance beneficiaries, given that the programme displays a 100 per cent implicit marginal tax rate because the full benefit is immediately withdrawn as soon as beneficiaries find work. On the other hand, work disincentives caused by the Citizen's Account may not be a concern, given that the literature on the negative impact of universal basic income schemes on work incentives is generally weak.[23]

The Way Forward for Social Assistance in Saudi Arabia

The challenges with social assistance systems highlighted here have been recognized within Vision 2030, which calls for modernizing the social welfare system, redirecting price subsidies towards those in need, preparing and

[21] OECD, 'Labour Market Programmes and Activation Strategies: Evaluating the Impacts', OECD Employment Outlook 2005 (Paris: Organization for Economic Cooperation and Development, 2005), pp. 173–208, https://www.oecd.org/els/emp/36780874.pdf.
[22] R. Hanna, R. Pande, M. Abel, H. Esper, and Z. Ali, 'Searching for Jobs while Receiving Hafiz Unemployment Benefit: Early Searches Earn More', Harvard Kennedy School: Evidence for Policy Design (April 2019), https://epod.cid.harvard.edu/sites/default/files/2019-06/Employability.pdf.
[23] U. Gentilini, M. Grosh, J. Rigolini, and R. Yemtsov, 'Exploring Universal Basic Income: A Guide to Navigating Concepts, Evidence, and Practices' (Washington, DC: World Bank, 2020), https://openknowledge.worldbank.org/handle/10986/32677.

training those unable to find employment, and providing tailored care and support to the most vulnerable citizens.

In 2020, the Social Security Law for Regular Assistance was revised accordingly,[24] with three primary objectives: to guarantee a minimum income to low-income Saudis; to implement social assistance programmes for less-well-off segments of society; and to provide job search assistance and sustained work-based income. This presents the first milestone in a series of reforms that the government is currently in the process of undertaking to move from a fragmented social assistance system towards a unified and well-targeted system.

The new system could consolidate existing cash transfer programmes into one guaranteed minimum income (GMI) benefit, where households falling below a threshold minimum income could be provided with assistance. Assistance would then phase out as income reaches closer to the threshold. The threshold could be calculated based on standards of living and relative poverty rates among Saudi households. Additionally, the method for defining and targeting low-income households across programmes requires eliminating categorical targeting. Instead, it should be unified and set according to scientific measures that best predict economic well-being at the household level, which could be based on a combination of the wage incomes of working members within the household, together with other proxies of actual expenditure or consumption, such as owned assets.[25] GMI schemes are concentrated in central Asian and eastern European countries and they have been recently introduced in several emerging economies, such as Brazil, India, and China. Experience demonstrates that they are flexible tools as the threshold can be raised or lowered depending on the specific objective of the programme or in times of economic shock. For example, the threshold for a poverty targeted programme, such as Regular Assistance, would be lower than for the Citizen's Account. GMI-type programmes can include income disregards or moderated withdrawal of benefits to reduce disincentives to work, particularly around threshold values.[26]

---

[24] https://www.mubasher.info/news/3647826/.

[25] This method of targeting is referred to as a hybrid means test. It can be considered an intermediate targeting method between the means test and the proxy means test. It is most commonly used in formal economies, where more than half of income is in the formal sector and there are good asset and business registries in the country.

[26] E. Tesliuc, L. Pop, M. Grosh, and R. Yemtsov, 'Income Support for the Poorest: A Review of Experience in Eastern Europe and Central Asia (English)', Directions in Development: Human Development (Washington, DC: World Bank, 2014), https://documents.worldbank.org/en/publication/documents-reports/documentdetail/527851468029956890/income-support-for-the-poorest-a-review-of-experience-in-eastern-europe-and-central-asia.

A well-targeted GMI system could then become the basis on which other benefits are designed and added, such as social pensions for the elderly, disability benefits, student transfers, as well as other allowances for special vulnerable categories. It could also support the government in introducing other politically sensitive reforms. For example, a well-targeted platform such as the Citizen's Account could be used to compensate households and individuals in exchange for scaling back on generous wages in the public sector.

A key principle of a well-targeted system is the correct construction of a household registry in the country and its interoperability with beneficiary registries across all programmes. In this regard, the Turkish experience offers a good example in modernizing information systems by moving from separate beneficiary registries to a dynamic and interoperable Integrated Social Assistance Information System (ISAS). Key success factors in ISAS include strong political will, efficient coordination across several public entities, creation of data-sharing protocols between various ministries, and high human capacity in the implementing agency.[27]

Social Insurance

Like most countries around the world, Saudi Arabia has a mandatory and publicly provided pension system that covers old age, survivorship, and disability. The system is composed of two separate funds. GOSI serves the private sector and employees who work on a contractual basis with the public sector, while PPA governs pensions for civil servants.[28] Both schemes are contributory, earnings-related, pay-as-you-go (PAYG), and defined-benefit schemes.[29] The social insurance system administered by GOSI also includes a mandatory unemployment insurance scheme, SANED, offered to Saudi workers in the private sector in cases of involuntary termination (Table 7.2).[30]

---

[27] https://documents1.worldbank.org/curated/en/099010011072245762/pdf/P17316601c8b0401b0 ab340214079f623b6.pdf.

[28] PPA also covers the armed forces and the police.

[29] *Contributory* means that participating employees in the pension scheme are required to support the scheme with contributions (often through payroll taxes). *Earnings related* means that pensions are based on the beneficiary's earnings. *PAYG*, in its strictest sense, is a method of financing whereby current pensions are paid out of current revenues from contributions. When revenues are higher than expenditures, some reserves can be accumulated, hence PAYG can be fully or partially funded. *Defined benefit* means the pensions are calculated based on a prescribed formula that usually considers several factors—mostly length of employment and salary history.

[30] The pension system also includes compensation for work-related injury, and other lump-sum payments that are not included in this analysis.

Table 7.2 Main parameters and rules of the old-age pension and unemployment schemes

Parameter	PPA	GOSI	SANED
1. Contribution rate			
	Employer: 9% Employee: 9%	Employer: 9% Employee: 9%	Employer:1% Employee: 1%
2. Qualifying conditions			
Retirement age (years)	58 (men and women)	58 (men), 53 (women)	N/A
Minimum months of service required for benefit eligibility	120	120	1st compensation: 12 months within the 36-month period preceding the first claim
3. Benefit			
Earnings base for benefit calculation	Last year base salary	Average base salary over the last 2 years	The average of wages contributed in the 24 months prior to unemployment
Net replacement rate	The pension is based on 2.5% of the insured's average monthly earnings during the last 2 years for each year of contributions, up to 100%		In the first 3 months, the benefit is equal to 60 per cent of the average monthly contributory wages. For every month that follows, the benefit is equal to 50% of the average monthly contributory wage
Minimum benefit (SAR/month)	1,984	1,984	2,000
Maximum benefit (SAR/month)	N/A	N/A	9,000 for each of the first 3 months and 7,500 for each additional month
Benefit duration	N/A	N/A	12 consecutive or non-consecutive months
Benefit indexation	Ad hoc	Ad hoc	Not subject to indexation

Sources: GOSI, OECD.

Unsustainability of the Pension System

The pension system is fiscally unsustainable due to its small number of contributors and parametric inconsistencies that exist in the current design between retirement ages, contribution rates, and pension benefit levels. In 2018, the total amount of pension benefit payments in GOSI and PPA represented 3.6 per cent of GDP. When considering revenues from both contributions and returns to investment, both schemes currently have surpluses, given the current demographics of a young Saudi population. However, the financial situation of both schemes is deteriorating, particularly in the PPA, which is already in deficit when considering revenues from contributions only (Table 7.3).

The number of contributors in both pension schemes is insufficient to generate enough resource to finance the current and future level of benefits. In 2018, GOSI had 1,929,096 contributors[31] and 375,580 beneficiaries in its old-age, disability, and survivorship schemes.[32] This means a support ratio of roughly 5.1 contributors for each beneficiary in GOSI. However, this is much lower than the national population support ratio of around sixteen Saudis between the ages of 15 and 64 for every Saudi aged 65 and above.[33]

The number of contributors in Saudi Arabia is low for various reasons. While the overall labour force participation rates among Saudis have risen considerably in the last few years (estimated at 51.5 per cent in 2021, according to GASTAT), women and young people still participate in lower numbers.[34] Among young people, in 2021, 26.7 per cent of Saudis between the ages of 15 and 24 participated in the labour market. Among women, 36 per cent participated in the labour market in 2021. The current efforts that the government is making to increase female labour force participation rates and improve the percentage of Saudi workers in the private sector (see the next section on active labour market programmes) will likely improve the financial situation of both schemes.

Table 7.3 Revenues and expenditures for PPA and GOSI (% of GDP), 2011–18

		2011	2012	2013	2014	2015	2016	2017	2018
PPA	Revenue	1.4	3.2	3.3	2.0	1.3	2.9	3.3	1.9
	Expenditure	1.5	1.6	1.6	1.8	2.2	2.7	2.6	2.7
	Overall balance	−0.2	1.6	1.6	0.2	−0.9	0.2	0.6	−0.8
GOSI	Revenue	1.0	1.0	1.3	1.7	2.0	2.1	2.4	2.2
	Expenditure	0.4	0.5	0.7	0.6	0.8	0.9	1.0	0.9
	Overall balance	0.6	0.5	0.7	1.1	1.2	1.2	1.4	1.3

Note: 2015–18 do not include data from the Public Investment Fund.
Sources: IMF, 'Saudi Arabia: 2018 Article IV Consultation', 'Saudi Arabia: 2019 Article IV Consultation'.

[31] There are more than 10 million people contributing to GOSI, but the non-Saudi population is not covered by the pension scheme.
[32] https://www.gosi.gov.sa/GOSIOnline/Open_Data_Library&locale=en_US.
[33] Saudi population data are available at https://www.stats.gov.sa/sites/default/files/en-demographic-research-2016_2.pdf.
[34] https://www.stats.gov.sa/en/814.

However, there are various design elements in the pension system that make it particularly generous, and which distort incentives to work and further contribute to the fiscal unsustainability of the system. Addressing them ultimately becomes necessary as the increasing flow of old-age entrants into the system will produce longer-term amplified effects. The legal retirement ages of 58 for men (age 60 in the Hijri calendar) and 53 for women (age 55 in the Hijri calendar) are generally lower than in other countries—particularly within the OECD, where the majority of countries require today's workers to carry on beyond the age of 65. The system implicitly encourages early retirement rather than working to the normal pension age, since there are easy conditions for early retirement and pensions are not reduced accordingly.[35] In contrast, it is common policy in many countries to reduce pension benefits for early retirees, which are often called 'actuarial' deductions. Moreover, workers at any age are allowed to retire if they have reached twenty-five years of contributions or, in the case of PPA, twenty years with employers' approval. This, in turn, involves a significant economic cost from lost labour supply, given the large negative disincentives to keep working and contributing. The

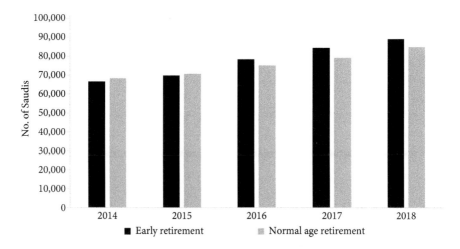

Figure 7.9 GOSI beneficiaries by retirement type, 2014–18

Source: GOSI, *Statistical Report* (2018).

---

[35] Early pensions in Saudi Arabia are calculated according to the same benefit formula as benefits at normal retirement age. The only difference is the requirement of a minimum length of service. An individual cannot retire before the normal retirement age if he or she has less than twenty-five years of service. If an individual does not have twenty-five years but reaches the normal retirement age, he or she needs to have contributed for at least ten years in order to have an annuity pension, which is calculated according to the formula: years of service × 2.5 per cent × average of two years of wages in GOSI or the last wage in PPA.

incentives for early retirement are evident in the data. In 2018, 173,218 beneficiaries received old-age retirement benefits, of whom 49 per cent were early
retirement cases (Figure 7.9).

Around the world, early retirement has been one of the most active areas
for pension reform over the past two decades. Within the OECD, countries
have significantly tightened access to early retirement, through increasing the
eligibility age, extending the contribution requirement, and/or increasing the
actuarial deductions for early retirement.

An additional generous design element in the Saudi system is that the pension accrues at a rate of 2.5 per cent of individual earnings for each year
of contributions. With forty years' contributions as a baseline case, the
replacement rate—pension relative to individual earnings—is 100 per cent.
Moreover, the benefit is estimated based on the last two years in GOSI, and
the last year in PPA, instead of a lifetime average. Such a policy is considered
unfair among people with different patterns of pay over their careers and
may cause distortions to people's work decisions. In contrast, most advanced
economies consider the earnings of the entire working life of an employee for
the pension calculation.

Aside from producing adverse incentives, these generous design elements
mean that the system treats workers differently at different earning levels,
stages of career, and retirement ages. This could contribute to loss of the
economic equity and 'fairness' principle that is an important objective of a
pension scheme: namely, that each riyal of contributions should produce
the same amount of benefits to all individuals. The fragmentation of the
PPA and GOSI schemes may further contribute to inequities, given that the
PPA is considered more generous in its qualifying conditions and earnings
base for benefit calculation. Fragmentation also adds administrative costs
and may discourage labour mobility between sectors and further exacerbate
the documented differential in compensation between the public and private
sectors.

Exclusive coverage to Saudi salaried workers also reduces the system's
contribution base and may perpetuate social inequities. For example, the
self-employed are currently not covered in either pension scheme and the
non-Saudi population remains excluded. Further challenges relate to data
administration and tax collection. In the absence of universal and mandatory wage protection systems, there might be concerns of tax evasion as
well as lack of data reliability, given instances of wage underreporting by
employers.[36]

[36] https://www.arabnews.com/news/462406.

The generosity of the pension system extends to survivorship and disability pension programmes. Family members of a passing old-age/disability pensioner can qualify for a survivorship pension and are entitled to half or more of a deceased person's pension from both of the public and private pension agencies, with a minimum benefit of SAR1,985.[37] Family members who qualify do not just include widows and dependent children. Benefits are also extended to other family members such as grandchildren, parents, and grandparents, as well as brothers and sisters. Some of the characteristics of the survivorship pension programme discourage women from working. Both widows and daughters are entitled to the benefit (regardless of their age) unless they get married, whereas sons receive the benefit only until the age of 21, or 26 if they are students. In 2018, there were around 188,000 survivorship pension beneficiaries in GOSI, the majority of whom (80 per cent) were women. These beneficiaries represented half of the total beneficiaries of the pension scheme, and benefits represented 11 per cent of overall pension expenditures in GOSI (Figure 7.10).

In a marked shift to promote longer working lives for all amid the prospects of an ageing population, many countries worldwide have reformed their survivorship pensions. In many OECD countries, widowed survivors need to be at or above retirement age to receive permanent survivorship pensions. Before beneficiaries reach the eligibility age, many countries grant survivor benefits for a limited period to help survivors adjust to their new situation.

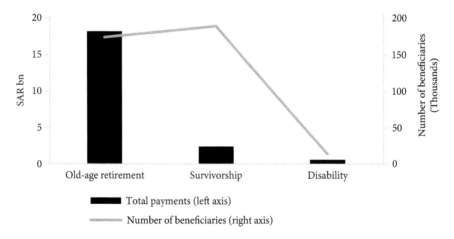

Figure 7.10 GOSI benefits and beneficiaries, 2018

Source: GOSI, *Statistical Report* (2018).

---

[37] If there are three or more survivors, 100 per cent of the old-age or disability pension that the deceased received or was entitled to receive is paid; 75 per cent of this amount for two dependants; 50 per cent for one dependant. The pension is split equally among all eligible survivors.

Those with a disability or who have to care for dependent children are exempted from this rule. Children (daughters and sons) are not eligible for survivorship pensions once they reach 18. Some OECD countries also implement other measures that tighten benefits, such as lowering replacement rates as well as means-testing them against individual income (as was done in France in 2003).[38]

Rare Utilization of SANED

Set up with the objective of supporting workers during transition between jobs, SANED had 46,056 beneficiaries in 2018. However, it is a rarely utilized scheme given that a large proportion of Saudis work in lifelong public employment, and in the private sector, mobility between jobs is limited due to coercive firing regulations and expensive severance pay upon dismissal. On average, Saudi workers are entitled to 15.2 weeks of full salary upon redundancy. Workers with a tenure of ten years or more are entitled to 32.5 weeks, considered among the highest in the world (Figure 7.11). Following the outbreak of COVID-19, the government tapped into the scheme's surplus to

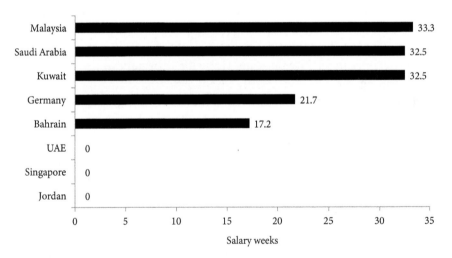

Figure 7.11 Severance pay for redundancy dismissal for a worker with ten years of tenure, 2019

Source: World Bank, 'Doing Business' database.

[38] OECD, 'Are Survivor Pensions Still Needed?', Policy Brief on Pensions (Paris: Organization for Economic Cooperation and Development, 2018), https://www.oecd.org/els/public-pensions/OECD-Policy-Brief-Survivor-Pensions-2018.pdf.

cover 60 per cent of the salaries of Saudi employees in the private sector for a period of three months.[39]

Among those who benefit from SANED, there is weak job search conditionality attached to it. Building on the documented empirical literature that supports the existence of moral hazard in an unemployment insurance scheme,[40] OECD countries impose, on average, 5–9 weeks of suspension of the benefit for the refusal of the first training offer and 10–14 weeks for subsequent refusals. In contrast, a beneficiary in Saudi Arabia is allowed to reject two proposals for training without any benefit suspension.

The Way Forward for Social Insurance in Saudi Arabia

The demographic situation in Saudi Arabia provides an important opportunity to reform pension design elements that contribute to its financial unsustainability. The current population support ratio indicates that the national population in Saudi Arabia has around twenty-four people (including expatriates) between the ages of 15 and 64 for every person aged 65 and above. However, as shown in Figure 7.12, support ratios are expected to decrease considerably in the near future, highlighting the urgent need for reform, given the prospects facing Saudi Arabia of a shrinking working-age population to support a growing retirement-age population in the near future. Population support ratios are directly affected by current and projected declines in fertility rates and rising life expectancy.

Reforming the pension system to adapt to the changing demographic realities requires, at a minimum, comprehensive and long-term *parametric* reform measures that focus on increasing retirement ages, introducing penalties for early retirement, reducing the accrual rate, expanding the earnings base for pension calculation, and increasing coverage rates—or even more systematic reforms, such as introducing a multi-pillar approach with defined contribution and voluntary saving schemes. The latter would help improve the efficiency of the system by relying more on private savings and individual investment accounts to compensate for the lower pension amounts offered by the PAYG system. Most of these reforms are undoubtedly politically difficult, and experiences from other countries demonstrate that they can be phased in gradually so that workers closer to retirement are affected less than

---

[39] https://www.al-monitor.com/pulse/originals/2020/04/saudi-arabia-pay-private-sector-coronavirus-fallout.html.

[40] J. F. Schmieder and T. von Wachter, 'The Effects of Unemployment Insurance Benefits: New Evidence and Interpretation', *Annual Review of Economics* 8 (2016), pp. 547–81.

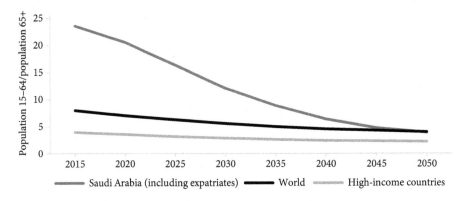

Figure 7.12   Population support ratios, 2015–50

Source: UN Population Projection.

younger workers. To preserve the pension system's fiscal balance, the survivorship pension programmes would also need to be considered, in a way that provides the right balance between enhancing protection for dependent survivors and promoting their labour force participation.

Moreover, reforming social insurance constitutes an important step in improving job mobility in the labour market. In a rapidly expanding economy, workers can move quickly to more productive firms, thus increasing labour productivity in aggregate. Reducing the fragmentation between the PPA and GOSI requires a unified contributory system to realign employment benefits between the public and private sectors, and improve the labour mobility of Saudis between them. An interesting emerging idea is the use of 'mobility savings accounts' to cover the non-Saudi population and improve their mobility in the domestic market. These accounts could replace the employer-mandated end-of-service benefit and would consist of an employee- and employer-funded mandatory saving mechanism to enable foreign workers' job search in the country for a given period after the initial fixed-term work contract ends.[41] Additionally, social insurance could be designed to provide adequate protection to workers, in lieu of rigid and costly labour regulations that further hinder labour mobility. For example, SANED could be further strengthened by replacing expensive severance pay upon dismissal. This is consistent with policies to shift the focus from protection

[41] R. Gatti, M. Morgandi, R. Grun, S. Brodmann, D. Angel-Urdinola, J. Manuel Moreno, D. Marotta, M. Schiffbauer, and E. Mata Lorenzo, 'Jobs for Shared Prosperity: Time for Action in the Middle East and North Africa' (Washington, DC: World Bank, 2013), https://openknowledge.worldbank.org/handle/10986/13284.

of jobs to protection of transitions, so that the individual risk of unemployment and income loss is reduced, while the potentially negative effects of job protection are avoided.[42] Other entitlements in current labour legislation that increase labour costs on private sector firms, such as maternity and sick leave entitlements, could be covered using social insurance funds as a means of sharing the social costs between workers, employers, and/or the government.

Active Labour Market Programmes

The Saudi Arabian labour market is characterized by heavy segmentation along three main dimensions: public and private sector employment; national and expatriate workers; and male and female labour force participation. Figure 7.13 demonstrates the high dependence on foreign labour in the private sector[43] and the high share of national public sector workers in Saudi Arabia. Figure 7.14 presents divergent labour force participation rates between Saudi men and women. However, the gap has been narrowing in the last few years, as more Saudi women have joined the labour market.

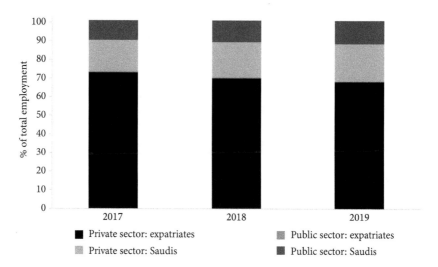

Figure 7.13 Employment shares of nationals and expatriates, 2017–19
Source: GASTAT.

[42] European Commission, 'Modernising Labour Law to Meet the Challenges of the 21st Century', Commission Green Paper (22 November 2006).
[43] The number of expatriate workers as a proportion of total employment in the private sector has gone down due to COVID-19. Between the first quarter of 2019 and the fourth quarter of 2020, the employment of non-Saudis in the private sector is estimated to have decreased by 5 per cent (GASTAT) due to the departure of many workers back to their home countries.

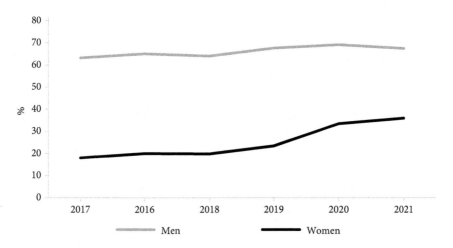

Figure 7.14 Saudi labour force participation rates, 2017–21
Source: GASTAT.

In recent years, Saudi Arabia has continued to grapple with unemployment challenges as it has faced a young and growing population. Labour force participation rates have risen since the early 2000s and are projected to increase further, given rising participation rates among women. Meanwhile, in 2016, 64 per cent of Saudi women aged 15+ were neither in training nor in employment, and unemployment among Saudis had reached 12.6 by 2020 (Figure 7.15). In 2021, the unemployment rate fell by 1.6 percentage

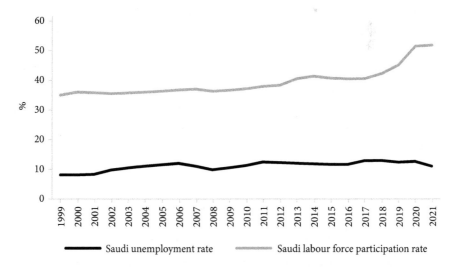

Figure 7.15 Labour market outcomes among Saudis, 1999–2021
Source: GASTAT.

points to 11 per cent, mainly owing to higher employment of Saudi women in the private sector, offsetting expatriates' departure in the wake of the COVID-19 pandemic.[44]

The government has implemented a series of labour policies and programmes to expand job opportunities for Saudis in the private sector. The signature labour policy of the MHRSD is the Nitaqat programme, a quota-based programme introduced in 2011 that is part of a wider strategy to increase Saudi employment in the private sector, while reducing the country's dependence on foreign labour. Nitaqat has two distinct features: quotas are assigned differentially across sectors and firm sizes, and the programme relies on a novel enforcement mechanism that ties firms' access to expatriate labour to Saudization ratios.

In parallel, several other programmes have also been implemented to improve the skills of Saudis to work in the private sector and to support firms in hiring Saudi workers. HRDF oversees a series of active labour market programmes,[45] such as wage subsidies to young workers to cover their on-the-job training costs (Tamheer programme) and to firms for employing Saudis (Employment Subsidy programme). It also provides subsidies for childcare and transport costs to low-wage women in the private sector as a means of improving female labour force participation rates (Qurrah and Wusool programmes). And HRDF helps workers find a job through online training (Doroob programme), a database that helps match job-seekers with jobs (the National Labor Gateway—NLG), and job search counselling and placement through local placement branches, as well as through privately contracted job placement centres (JPCs). The Technical Vocational Training Corporation is the leading agency in the country that provides post-secondary educated graduates with vocational education.

Finally, in recognition of the importance of women's economic inclusion, the government has implemented important reforms to its labour laws. According to the 2020 World Bank *Women, Business, and the Law* (*WBL*) report,[46] Saudi Arabia had made the biggest improvement worldwide since 2017 in its legal reforms to encourage higher female participation and employment, increasing its score in the *WBL* database by 38.8 points. In 2021, the country implemented more historic reforms, which led its score

[44] IMF, 'Saudi Arabia: Staff Concluding Statement of the 2022 Article IV Mission' (Washington, DC: International Monetary Fund, 2022), https://www.imf.org/en/News/Articles/2022/06/17/saudi-arabia-staff-concluding-statement-of-the-2022-article-iv-mission.

[45] Active labour market programmes listed in this chapter are a summary of HRDF's programmes. For a complete list, see HRDF's *Annual Report* (2018) at https://www.hrdf.org.sa/media/Annual%20report/HRDF_Annual_Report_2018_(Arabic).pdf.

[46] World Bank, *Women, Business and the Law 2020* (Washington, DC: World Bank, 2020), https://openknowledge.worldbank.org/handle/10986/32639.

to increase by an additional 10 points from the previous year. Encouraging improvements in laws include: abolishing the guardianship law; removing restrictions on women's mobility and ability to obtain documents without permission from a male guardian; equalizing women's right to choose a place of residency to that of men; allowing women to drive; forbidding gender-based discrimination in employment; abolishing the requirement of segregation in the workplace; eliminating restrictions on women's employment in industrial jobs, jobs deemed dangerous, and jobs that require a night shift; forbidding the dismissal of women from jobs for maternity- or pregnancy-related reasons; equalizing the retirement age between men and women; and prohibiting gender-based discrimination in accessing financial services. To provide a safe working environment, Saudi Arabia has criminalized sexual harassment in public and private sector workplaces.

Increasing Saudi Employment in the Private Sector

Since its inception, the Nitaqat programme has undergone several adjustments to fine tune its policies. The programme operates by classifying firms into industry-by-size categories and firms are subsequently assigned to four colour bands based on their current Saudization ratios: Red (non-compliant), Yellow, Green, and Platinum (most compliant). Firms with the lowest Saudization ratios face the largest restrictions on hiring foreign workers. By improving their Saudization ratios, whether by increasing employment of Saudis, reducing employment of expatriates, or both, firms can improve their colour band rating and subsequently their ability to hire and retain foreign workers.

Several studies have evaluated the impact of Nitaqat on labour market outcomes and found that the programme has increased reported Saudi employment dramatically in the private sector, especially for women, who increased from just 56,000 workers in 2010 to 606,000 by the end of 2017, raising the female share of the Saudi private sector workforce from 8 per cent to 32 per cent.[47] At the same time, the programme has produced significant unintended effects, including an increase in the likelihood of firm exit and a reduction of firm growth. Jennifer Peck estimated that in the initial sixteen-month period (between July 2011 and October 2012), Nitaqat caused 11,000 firms to shut down, raising exit rates from 19 per cent to 28 per

[47] J. R. Peck, C. Miller, and M. Seflek, 'Increasing Female Employment by Investing in Up-front Costs: The Critical Lesson in Nitaqat's Success', Harvard University Policy Brief (2017), https://epod.cid.harvard.edu/sites/default/files/2018-06/Nitaqat.pdf.

cent. Peck also found that surviving firms reduced the total number of their workers. She attributed 948,000 reductions to Nitaqat.[48] Maha Al Abdulkarim studied longer-term effects of Nitaqat. She found that high exit rates among private sector firms were sustained after 2012, reaching 17 per cent in 2013, while declining slightly in 2014 and 2015 to around 15 per cent.[49] Other studies of Nitaqat effects include the analysis by Mohamed Ramady, who warned that Saudization may reduce firms' competitiveness and force them to reallocate to more business-friendly environments.[50] Finally, Rita Koyame-Marsh pointed out that Nitaqat has been unable to curb unemployment and has contributed to 'ghost Saudization' through fake employment registrations.[51]

At the heart of the challenge that Nitaqat did not address is the labour cost differential between Saudi and foreign workers, which causes employers overwhelmingly to prefer hiring foreign workers. In 2019, the average Saudi wage was SAR10,273, compared to an average expatriate wage of SAR3,866. Saudi workers are paid on average 1.7 times the amount paid to foreign workers in the private sector (Figure 7.16). The wage premia exist across all education levels, but are particularly pronounced at lower levels (Figure 7.17). The economics of most parts of the private sector are far out of line with the cost of Saudi labour, particularly as investment and growth have been geared for years towards low-skilled occupations and sectors. For example, between 2010 and 2016, employment grew most strongly in sectors that heavily depend on low-skilled foreign labour: namely, construction and retail.[52] From an employer's perspective, high Saudi wages and likely weak elasticity between skills and wages mean that the demand for Saudi workers when there is an alternative of non-Saudi workers will be low. From a Saudi worker's perspective, the combination of an increasingly educated Saudi workforce (when compared to the aggregate foreign labour force) and attractive public pay and working conditions have raised their reservation wages against private sector market wages. In 2019, Saudi workers in the public sector were paid 1.6 times the amount paid to Saudi workers in the private sector (Figure 7.16).

[48] J. R. Peck, 'Can Hiring Quotas Work? The Effect of the Nitaqat Program on the Saudi Private Sector', *American Economic Journal: Economic Policy* 9, no. 2 (2017), pp. 316–47.

[49] M. K. Al Abdulkarim, 'Labour Demand, Firm Survival, and Productivity in Dual Labor Markets: The Case of the Nitaqat Policy in Saudi Arabia', Doctoral thesis, King's College London Business School (2018), https://kclpure.kcl.ac.uk/portal/files/96987505/2018_Alabdulkarim_Maha_1148473_ethesis.pdf.

[50] M. Ramady, 'Gulf Unemployment and Government Policies: Prospects for the Saudi Labour Quota or Nitaqat System', *International Journal of Economics and Business Research* 5, no. 4 (2013), pp. 476–98.

[51] R. O. Koyame-Marsh, 'Saudization and the Nitaqat Programs: Overview and Performance', *Journal of Accounting, Finance and Economics* 6, no. 2 (2016), pp. 36–48.

[52] GASTAT, *Establishment Survey 2017*, https://www.stats.gov.sa/sites/default/files/annual_economic_survey_2017en.pdf.

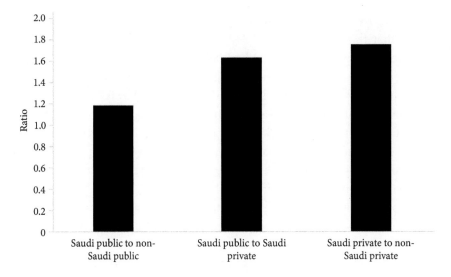

Figure 7.16 Comparison of wage premia, 2019

Source: GASTAT.

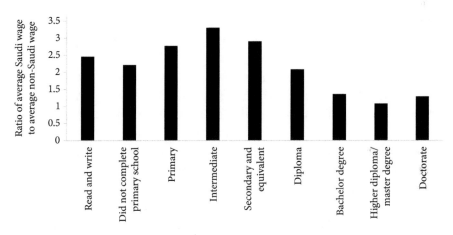

Figure 7.17 Wage premia by education level, 2019

Source: GASTAT.

In an attempt to raise the cost of foreign labour, Nitaqat was complemented by several price-oriented interventions, such as imposing an expatriate levy in 2017 on companies employing more foreign workers than Saudi workers, as well as an additional dependant levy.[53] However, in the absence of a minimum wage law for foreign workers, employers likely passed the extra

---

[53] The fee on dependants was SAR300 per month for each dependant in 2019. On the workers' levy, the government charged companies SAR500–600 in 2019 for each foreign worker they hired (https://gulfbusiness.com/expat-fees-will-continue-increase-2020-planned-saudi-finance-ministry/).

costs onto foreign workers by reducing their wages.[54] Several reports suggested that this resulted in the departure of many foreign workers, given that their newly adjusted wages had fallen below their reservation wages.[55] Between 2017 and 2019, the foreign labour force shrank from 10.6 million to 9.8 million workers. Meanwhile, real GDP contracted by 0.7 per cent in 2017 and the IMF estimates that the departure of expatriates could have reduced real GDP growth by 0.5–0.75 percentage points in 2018. Even policies that helped subsidize the cost of Saudi labour for employers, such as wage subsidies provided by HRDF, proved largely unsuccessful given that most workers were let go upon subsidy expiration.

The assumption that many policy-makers may have made when designing these policies is that there is a very close substitution between foreign and Saudi workers. However, Saudi unemployment rates persisted at 12 per cent in 2019 and many of the vacant positions were not filled by Saudi workers. Improving the job opportunities for Saudis in the private sector will require substituting a large proportion of low-value-added jobs with technology-intensive production, which in turn will create higher-value-added jobs that many Saudis are willing to work in. What is therefore needed is a strategy to steer firms' production function away from reliance on cheap labour and subsidies.

Reaching this new equilibrium requires political will combined with important reforms, some of which the government is already embarking on. Perhaps the most important is to commit to removing factor market distortions in the Saudi labour market. The lack of social and employment protection for foreign workers reduces the costs and wage payments involved in hiring foreigners, thus increasing the attractiveness of foreign compared to Saudi workers. Partly to address this, in November 2020,[56] Saudi Arabia announced major reforms to increase the mobility of foreign workers in the domestic labour market, by allowing workers to change their jobs without their current employer's consent after completing one year of their contract or once their contract expires. This key reform is expected to push up prices for non-Saudi labour.[57] It is also likely to improve productivity, given that workers will be able to move quickly to more productive firms,

[54] The question of who bears the burden of the expatriate levies depends crucially on supply elasticities and labour demand. The expatriate labour supply is presumably perfectly inelastic above the reservation wage but perfectly elastic below it.

[55] https://www.middleeasteye.net/news/saudi-levy-foreign-workers-pushes-thousands-leave-country.

[56] https://english.alarabiya.net/News/gulf/2021/03/14/Saudi-Arabia-s-labor-reforms-to-kafala-sponsorship-system-comes-into-effect-Sunday.

[57] Improving labour mobility in the United Arab Emirates was found to increase incumbent workers' wages by 10 per cent. S. Naidu, Y. Nyarko, and S.-Y. Wang, 'Monopsony Power in Migrant Labor Markets: Evidence from the United Arab Emirates', *Journal of Political Economy* 124, no. 6 (2016), pp. 1735–92.

and it will increase their incentives to acquire human capital. Going further, to eliminate fully the labour market segmentation between Saudi and foreign labour, Saudi Arabia should consider a national minimum wage in the long run. Removing these distortions will likely manage the entry of foreign workers, in contrast to only using quota- or price-oriented interventions, as Saudi Arabia has already done. Furthermore, investing in higher-value-added sectors with comparative advantage and high potential for Saudi employment requires a shift from broad utility subsidies to targeted firm subsidies for technology adoption to promote capital deepening.

Arriving at this new equilibrium requires complementary reforms in other areas, such as reforming the business environment to improve firm dynamism. Typically, productivity is increased as firms with new ideas and innovative technology enter the market, while older firms with low levels of efficiency exit the market so that labour and capital can be reallocated to more efficient firms. In Saudi Arabia, however, regulatory requirements, slow administrative processes, high fees, and rigid labour regulations make it costly to start a new firm and for existing firms to expand.[58] Additional key reforms to contribute to the creation of high-value-added jobs include the areas of investment and trade, as well as competition. Finally, skills policies are critical to improve human capital availability and contribute to a more skilled and diverse workforce comprising Saudis and foreign workers of both genders.

Skilling and Reskilling the Saudi Workforce

Improving the skills of workers is critical to transitioning to a higher productivity equilibrium in the labour market and to coping with rapid changes in technology. However, the composition of skills among Saudi workers poses a strong challenge to productivity and innovation. Many Saudi workers lack the skills needed for the labour market. The World Bank's Human Capital Index (HCI) confirms this finding. The HCI is an index between 0 and 1. A country in which all children born today can expect to achieve both full health (no stunting and 100 per cent survival into adulthood) and full education potential (fourteen years of high-quality schooling by the age of 18) will score a value of 1 on the index. Therefore, a score of 0.60, as seen in Saudi Arabia in 2020, signals that the future productivity of

---

[58] World Bank, 'Doing Business 2019: Training for Reform—Saudi Arabia (English)' (Washington, DC: World Bank, 2019), http://documents.worldbank.org/curated/en/403891541167454278/Doing-Business-2019-Training-for-Reform-Saudi-Arabia.

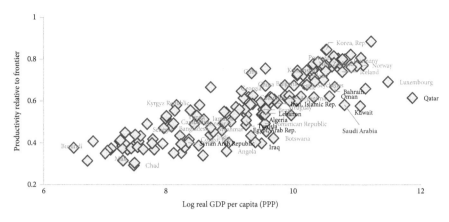

Figure 7.18 Overall Human Capital Index (HCI)

Source: World Bank, Human Capital Project.

a child born today is 40 per cent below what could have been achieved with complete education and full health (Figure 7.18). Saudi Arabia has a lower level of skills than any other country with equal or higher income, and many countries with lower levels of income have higher levels of skills.

Low skills reflect problems at various levels of the education and training system. Pre-primary education enrolment is low. Enrolment rates in early childhood education for 3- and 4-year-old children are 3 per cent and 12 per cent, respectively.[59] And while educational attainment has increased substantially in recent years, the quality of education appears to be low. The share of eighth graders in Saudi Arabia passing the low international benchmark of the Trends in International Mathematics and Science Study (TIMSS) test in 2015 was 34 per cent in mathematics and 49 per cent in science.[60] Another perspective on quality is that Saudis between 25 and 29 years old have, on average, more than ten years of schooling. However, if the number of years of schooling is adjusted for the amount actually learned (based on results of TIMSS tests), then young Saudis have the equivalent of fewer than eight years of schooling.[61]

The training system faces challenges with regard to upskilling and reskilling of workers. There is low coverage, given that 96.2 per cent of Saudi job-seekers report that they have never received any type of training.[62] Technical and vocation education and training (TVET) graduates make up

[59] https://data.oecd.org/students/enrolment-rate-in-early-childhood-education.htm.
[60] World Bank, Education Statistics Database (from TIMSS), 2015.
[61] World Bank, Human Capital Project.
[62] https://www.stats.gov.sa/en/34.

a small proportion of the workforce.[63] Some of the training programmes offered by HRDF attract a low number of beneficiaries. For example, only 3,377 job-seekers participated in the Tamheer (on-the-job training) programme in 2018.[64] Furthermore, wage and on-the-job training subsidy programmes may not be well targeted, given that they do not explicitly focus on disadvantaged job-seekers who remain unemployed after a certain period. This might generate significant deadweight losses. In other words, firms may hire subsidized workers whom they would have hired even in the absence of the subsidy.[65]

Improving adulting training programmes requires increasing access and coverage: for example, through on-line courses. Making courses more flexible and modular, as well as providing certification, could increase their appeal. Outreach and targeting efforts could focus on inactive people, the long-term unemployed, and workers in changing industries. Strengthening employer engagement in designing and delivering TVET programmes could increase the quality of training courses and make them more responsive to labour market demand. Sector skills boards could be established to assess skills needs, identify challenges in recruiting and retaining qualified workers, and design and implement employer-driven training programmes. Greater efforts are also required at pre-school. Improved access to quality pre-schools would improve learning outcomes and increase the participation of women in the labour market.[66]

Targeting Vulnerable Job-Seekers

The quality and frequency of coaching and counselling at HRDF, especially for job-seekers at risk of long-term unemployment, appears not to be effective. There is no referral system to JPCs, and in the absence of monitoring through performance-based payment mechanisms, it is most likely that only the best—most motivated and highly qualified—candidates are placed

---

[63] Slightly more than 8 per cent of upper-secondary students attended technical vocational programmes in 2017. The Ministry of Education in 2020 reported that 170,000 students were enrolled in the TVET sector (https://wenr.wes.org/2020/04/education-in-saudi-arabia#:~:text=Only%20slightly%20more%20than%208,enrolled%20in%20the%20TVET%20sector).

[64] HRDF, *Annual Report* (2018), https://www.hrdf.org.sa/media/Annual%20report/HRDF_Annual_Report_2018_(Arabic).pdf.

[65] OECD, 'Policies Targeted at Specific Workforce Groups or Labour Market Segments', OECD Employment Outlook 2006 (Paris: Organization for Economic Cooperation and Development, 2006), pp. 127–56, https://www.oecd.org/employment/emp/38569405.pdf.

[66] N. M. Shafiq, A. Devercelli, and A. Valerio, 'Are There Long-Term Benefits from Early Childhood Education in Low- and Middle-Income Countries?', *Education Policy Analysis Archives* 26, no. 122 (2018), http://dx.doi.org/10.14507/epaa.26.3239.

in jobs by private providers. Coverage gaps in accessing employment services persist. For example, accessibility of JPCs to cover all job-seekers, especially females in outer cities, appears to be limited.

Improvement in the management of job search assistance and counselling requires more effective targeting and better use of resources. In many OECD countries with developed job intermediation systems, job-seekers go through comprehensive assessment and profiling, considering each job-seeker's circumstances and barriers to employment. The approach relies on using profiling to identify those at risk of falling into long-term unemployment as early as possible and offering them intense treatment.[67] This could include individual action plans, tailor-made counselling, and more intense follow-up on the job search process. The employability of vulnerable job-seekers could be increased through their participation in active labour market programmes that provide training or subsidized employment following a period of unsuccessful job search. And greater resources could be devoted to reach the many women who are unemployed or not looking for a job. For example, Qurrah and Wusool programmes could be expanded to improve outreach to women in smaller cities.

Matching Firms and Job-Seekers

Job matching can help improve the efficiency of the labour market by overcoming information and search frictions. Job matching that serves both employers and firms does not work well enough in Saudi Arabia due to the absence of employer services. While HRDF currently maintains NLG as some form of a job-opening database, many employers resort to other private or informal recruitment channels. HRDF does not maintain frequent employer outreach and does not actively conduct vacancy intake and registration to support a high-quality list of vacancies.

Enhancing matching services remains essential for small and medium-sized enterprises (SMEs), especially now that labour mobility has recently been granted to expatriates in the domestic labour market, and given that SMEs face high search and information costs when hiring. This also entails considering expanding HRDF services to non-Saudi workers. As is done in many countries, services to employers could include vacancy intake and registration, informing employers about available active labour market programmes (wage subsidies, employment training), organizing information

[67] M. Vodopivec, D. Finn, S. Laporsek, M. Vodopivec, and N. Cvornjek, 'Combating Long Term Unemployment in Slovenia', *IB Magazine* 52, no. 1 (2018), pp. 32–56, https://www.umar.gov.si/fileadmin/user_upload/publikacije/ib/2018/IB_1_18_splet.pdf#page=32.

sessions or job fairs where employers and job-seekers can meet, and pre-selecting job-seekers for employer interviews by screening candidates, vetting their quality, and testing them on certain skills and language proficiency. This will enable public employment services to be both more efficient and more effective in achieving quality job placements, which will attract more employers and generate more and higher-skilled job listings at the NLG.

The Way Forward for Active Labour Market Policies and Programmes

Active labour market policies and programmes in Saudi Arabia will likely continue to produce suboptimal outcomes and have limited impact unless the key distortions that are causing a heavily segmented labour market are reformed. Differences in social and employment protection between foreign and Saudi workers mean that firms will resist hiring Saudi workers and it will be hard to steer their production function away from low-skilled sectors and towards higher-value-added activities that can support Saudi wages. In the meantime, quota- or price-based interventions to limit the entry of foreign workers without addressing the underlying cost differential between workers may continue the status quo of a low-productivity economy and could produce significant unintended consequences in terms of reduced output, firm exits, and other negative phenomena such as ghost employment in the private sector. A second important distortion relates to the dominance of the public sector as a proportion of Saudi employment. Wages in the public sector play a significant role in setting the market wage for Saudis in the private sector, and may induce incentives to acquire skills and educational qualifications that are largely relevant for the public sector but not demanded by employers in the private sector.

Removing these two main distortions to arrive at a high-productivity equilibrium requires in parallel strong investment in education and training systems. Building a strong foundation for learning is an important priority, beginning with pre-school education. Important programmes like Qurrah could be expanded and improved, with a long-term plan for providing affordable access to quality childcare. These services would also make it easier for women, who typically have the major responsibility for childcare, to participate in the labour market. This would in turn help the country sustain further gains in women's economic participation. Another important priority is investing in improving the quality of general education. In addition to strengthening cognitive skills, investing in other skills at a young age, such as soft and behavioural skills, is important, given their well-documented linkage with labour market outcomes.[68] Technical education can be further aligned with labour market needs.

Arriving at the new equilibrium also requires strengthening the current system of labour intermediation services. Considerable work is necessary to strengthen existing active labour market programmes to enhance skills among workers. If well designed, one-the-job training programmes can help vulnerable workers signal their productivity and acquire work experience to support their transition to full-time employment. Vulnerable workers, including those unemployed for at least a year or previously out of the labour force, could be provided with personalized, intensive, and tailor-made training programmes. The programmes could include skills training, career guidance, and placement support.

Finally, improving efficiency in the labour market and removing mobility barriers faced by firms and workers necessitates a strong job-matching system that is open to both Saudi and foreign workers. A key principle is to empower job counsellors to focus on clients—job-seekers and employers—and their core functions of finding the best possible employment opportunities for job-seekers and finding qualified pools of workers for employers. Efficient matching can improve the quality of matches between firms and workers, which is key to limiting the skills mismatch in the labour market and ultimately reducing structural unemployment. It will also undoubtedly accelerate the recovery from current economic and health shocks.

Conclusion

Under Vision 2030, the government of Saudi Arabia has taken commendable steps to reform its social protection policies and programmes. However, the efficiency and effectiveness of the current system can be significantly improved. Benefits are generous, targeting is weak, there is no coordination between different social protection programmes, and impacts on welfare, employment, and productivity are limited. At times, the impact of programmes has been undermined by the distortions existing in the labour market. For instance, policies to promote skills development and productive employment in the private sector are unlikely to work effectively in light of a labour market segmented between foreign and Saudi workers, and between public and private sector workers.

[68] J. J. Heckman and T. Kautz, 'Hard Evidence on Soft Skills', *Labour Economics* 19, no. 4 (2012), pp. 451–64.

If well reformed, social protection can become a powerful tool to correct existing distortions and to promote a transition to a high-productivity economy as set out by Vision 2030. For example, a programme such as the Citizen's Account, if well targeted and correctly administered, could become the platform for boosting the welfare of many vulnerable Saudi households, as well as for reforming distortive wage-setting policies in the public sector. The social insurance system could reward longer working lives and become a powerful instrument to promote worker mobility and stimulate labour demand. Active labour market programmes could target reforms that touch on the root causes of the wage differential between Saudi and foreign labour and on the ways through which foreign labour recruitment has encouraged rent seeking by employers from the lowest-skilled workers. They could play a key role in improving the efficiency of the labour market by strengthening job intermediation services and investing in stronger education and training systems.

Social protection is not the responsibility of one ministry or one actor. It is a web of interconnected policies and programmes. In order for social protection to work well and achieve a positive cumulative impact, a coherent strategy is required, underlined by strong collaboration across all relevant stakeholders, together with a well-thought-out implementation arrangement and a focus on measuring results and impacts.

8

Environment and Climate Change

Do They Synchronize with Saudi Arabia's Economy?

Aisha Al-Sarihi

Introduction

Saudi Arabia holds around 18 per cent of the world's proven petroleum reserves, the export of which accounted for about 70 per cent of total government export earnings and about 50 per cent of gross domestic product (GDP), as of 2019.[1] Since the discovery of oil and gas in the 1930s, the wealth generated from their export has contributed significantly to Saudi Arabia's socio-economic development, having turned the Kingdom within a few decades into one of the wealthiest nations (in per capita terms) in the world.[2] Oil wealth has boosted spending on infrastructure including health, education, and welfare, and has contributed to the general expansion of industries, manufacturing, urbanization, and transport. The Kingdom's GDP increased by 382 per cent over the last four decades, between 1980 and 2019.[3] Simultaneously, the population of Saudi Arabia increased by 161 per cent in the same period, from about 9 million in 1980 to over 34 million in 2019.[4] With the present population, Saudi Arabia is the 41st most populous country in the world.[5] The population is predicted to grow to 50 million by 2060.[6]

The Kingdom's economic development, together with its population growth and improving standards of living, has put pressure on the country's

---

[1] Organization of the Petroleum Exporting Countries, 'Saudi Arabia Facts and Figures' (2020), https://www.opec.org/opec_web/en/about_us/169.htm. These statistics and all other data and information in the chapter are correct up to 2019/2020, when this chapter was written.
[2] M. Al-Moneef, The Contribution of the Oil Sector to Arab Economic Development', OFID Pamphlet Series 34 (Vienna: OPEC Fund for International Development, 2006).
[3] World Bank, 'GDP (current US$)' (2019), https://data.worldbank.org/indicator/NY.GDP.MKTP.CD.
[4] General Authority for Statistics, 'Population Estimates' (2019), https://www.stats.gov.sa/en/43.
[5] Worldometer (2020), https://www.worldometers.info/world-population/population-by-country/.
[6] US Census Bureau, 'Saudi Arabia Demographic data as of July 1, 2020' (2020), https://www.census.gov/popclock/world/sa#world-footer.

Aisha Al-Sarihi, *Environment and Climate Change*. In: *The Economy of Saudi Arabia in the 21st Century*.
Edited by: John Sfakianakis, Oxford University Press. © Aisha Al-Sarihi (2024).
DOI: 10.1093/oso/9780198863878.003.0009

natural environment, the degradation of which could impose unintended economic losses. In 2014, for example, the economic costs associated with environmental degradation accounted for 3 per cent of the Kingdom's GDP.[7] Water resources, air quality, biodiversity, agricultural lands, and the marine environment have all come under pressure due to the expansion of industries, manufacturing, urbanization, and transport. In fact, the Kingdom has been ranked at 90 out of 180 countries in terms of its overall environmental performance.[8] Climate change furthermore brings additional pressure on Saudi Arabia's natural environment and its economy, presenting challenges to both non-oil and oil-based economic sectors. Non-oil economic sectors such as agriculture, food security, water, fisheries, tourism, and infrastructure have already been already negatively affected by the physical impacts of climate change, including rising temperatures, falling annual rainfall, sea level rise, and increased exposure to extreme events like intense rainfall.[9] Climate change also imposes risks to the economic sustainability of oil-based economic sectors, especially due to international climate mitigation policies aiming to reduce fossil fuel consumption, which could impose direct economic losses on the Kingdom.[10]

While great attention has been paid to the Kingdom's economic development and social transformation by analysts and researchers alike, little is known about the interaction between the Kingdom's economic development and its natural environment, or to what extent it has considered protecting its natural environment and addressing the issues of climate change while progressing in socio-economic development. This chapter investigates whether the Kingdom's natural resources, such as its air quality, water resources, biodiversity, marine and coastal environments, and arable land, have been positively or negatively impacted by its seven decades of

---

[7] Ministry of Environment, Water and Agriculture, الملخص التنفيذي للاستراتيجية الوطنية للبيئة (Riyadh: MEWA, 2018).

[8] Z. A. Wendling, J. W., Emerson, A. de Sherbinin, D. C. Esty, et al. '2020 Environmental Performance Index' (New Haven, CT: Yale Center for Environmental Law and Policy, 2020), epi.yale.edu.

[9] M. Komurcu, C. A. Schlosser, I. Alshehri, T. Alshahrani, W. Alhayaza, A. AlSaati, and K. Strzepek, 'Mid-Century Changes in the Mean and Extreme Climate in the Kingdom of Saudi Arabia and Implications for Water Harvesting and Climate Adaptation', *Atmosphere* 11 (2020), p. 1068, doi: 10.3390/atmos11101068.; T. Kompas, V. H. Pham, and T. N. Che, 'The Effects of Climate Change on GDP by Country and the Global Economic Gains from Complying with the Paris Climate Accord', *Earth's Future* 6, no. 8 (2018), pp. 1153–73.

[10] A. Al-Sarihi, 'Prospects for Climate Change Integration into the GCC Economic Diversification Strategies', LSE Kuwait Programme Paper 20 (London: London School of Economics, 2018); A. Al-Sarihi, 'Climate Change and Economic Diversification in Saudi Arabia: Integrity, Challenges, and Opportunities', Arab Gulf States Institute Policy Paper 1 (Washington, DC: Arab Gulf States Institute, 2019); D. Manley, J. Cust, and G. Cecchinato, 'Stranded Nations? The Climate Policy Implications for Fossil Fuel-Rich Developing Countries', Oxford Centre for the Analysis of Resource Rich Economies Working Paper 34 (Oxford: Oxford University, 2017); International Energy Agency, *Net Zero by 2050* (Paris: IEA, 2021), https://www.iea.org/reports/net-zero-by-2050.

economic development. It furthermore examines the Kingdom's efforts to enhance environmental protection and address climate change in line with its economic development.

Drawing from the main governmental documents of Vision 2030, the National Transformation Program (NTP) 2020, Saudi Arabia's nationally determined contributions (NDCs), the Kingdom's national communications to the United Nations Framework Convention on Climate Change (UNFCCC), reports on the country's Sustainable Development Goals (SDGs), and the National Environmental Strategy (2018), this chapter reveals that Saudi Arabia has made some progress in addressing environmental sustainability and climate change in line with its economic development. Notably, Vision 2030 and the NTP explicitly mention the main environmental challenges facing the Kingdom, including water and food security, biodiversity, environmental pollutants, desertification, and coastal and marine environments. However, this chapter also reveals that the Kingdom still faces challenges that, without proper intervention, could hinder its progress in addressing environmental sustainability and climate change. These issues include gaps in monitoring and observational data and measurements, fragmentation of leadership, weaknesses in implementing environmental protection regulations, the absence of a climate action plan, and fragmentated environment- and climate-related policies and efforts. Furthermore, tangible alignment between economic development, the environment, and climate change requires the enhancement of human, technical, and financial resources.

Saudi Arabia's Natural Environment

The wealth generated from oil and gas export revenues has contributed significantly to Saudi Arabia's socio-economic development, having turned the Kingdom within a few decades into one of the wealthiest nations (in per capita terms) in the world.[11] The Kingdom's GDP increased by 382 per cent between 1980 ($164,541.66 million at current prices) and 2019 ($792,966.84 million at current prices).[12] Simultaneously, the population of Saudi Arabia increased by 161 per cent over the same period, from about 9 million in 1980 to over 34 million in 2019.[13] The Kingdom's economic development,

---

[11] Al-Moneef, 'The Contribution of the Oil Sector to Arab Economic Development'.
[12] World Bank, 'Imports of Goods and Services (% of GDP)' (2019), https://data.worldbank.org/indicator/NE.IMP.GNFS.ZS.
[13] General Authority for Statistics, 'Population Estimates'.

population growth, and increasing standards of living have put pressure on the country's natural environment including its air quality, water resources, biodiversity, marine and coastal environment, and agricultural lands. This section provides an overview of how these natural resources have been influenced by the country's decades of socio-economic development.

Air Quality and Greenhouse Gas Emissions

In Saudi Arabia, dust plays a primary role in causing air pollution because more than 90 per cent of the land area is desert. The World Health Organization asserts that the air quality in Saudi Arabia is considered unsafe as the country's annual mean concentration of PM2.5 is 88 μg/m^3, exceeding the recommended maximum of 10 μg/m^3.[14] Seasonal variations in pollution exist, with the highest levels in spring (March to May) due to an increase in dust storms.

Furthermore, the growth of energy-intensive industries (even those that support economic diversification), rapid urbanization, the expansion of desalinations units, and the development of transport—all of which are currently reliant on oil and gas for their operation—have contributed to deteriorating air quality across the Kingdom. Available data indicate that Riyadh, Dammam, Jubail, Yanbu, and Jeddah are cities with consistently high levels of air pollution, specifically NOx, O_3, PM10, SO_2, and volatile organic compounds.[15]

Additionally, the annual surge in energy demand of 5 per cent per year between 2010 and 2018[16] and the fact that almost 99 per cent of primary energy consumption is sourced from oil and natural gas means that the Kingdom's greenhouse gas (GHG) emissions are continuously growing (Figure 8.1). While Saudi Arabia's contribution to total global GHG emissions is relatively small, accounting for nearly 1.44 per cent of the total, the Kingdom's per capita carbon emissions are among the highest in the world. According to the World Resources Institute, the electricity and heat (41 per cent), transportation (20 per cent), manufacturing and construction

---

[14] IQAir, 'World's Most Polluted Countries', 'World Air Quality Index' (2019), https://www.iqair.com/us/world-most-polluted-countries.

[15] T. Husain, and A. Abdulwahab Khalil, 'Environment and Sustainable Development in the Kingdom of Saudi Arabia: Current Status and Future Strategy', *Journal of Sustainable Development* 6, no. 12 (2013), pp. 14–30. Data as of 2013. While air quality data are available, they are inconsistent or inaccurate. Therefore, it was impossible to provide accurate analysis of the Kingdom's air quality, and associate the type of pollutants with their sources.

[16] S. Soummane, 'Saudi Electricity Demand for 2018–2019 based on Saudi Electricity Company Data', Data Insight (Riyadh: King Abdullah Petroleum Studies and Research Center, 2020).

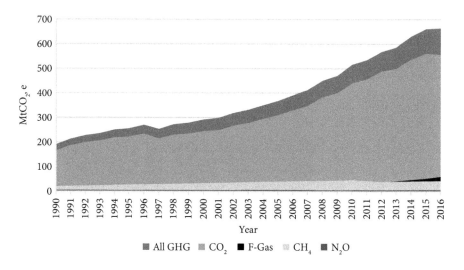

Figure 8.1 Saudi Arabia greenhouse gas emissions, 1990–2016

Source: CAIT Climate Data Explorer (Washington, DC: World Resources Institute, 2019), available online at http://cait.wri.org.

(16 per cent), and industrial (13 per cent) sectors are the major GHG emitters in Saudi Arabia, followed by the waste (4 per cent), agriculture (0.97 per cent), and building (0.70 per cent) sectors.[17]

Natural Water Resources

Like other Gulf Arab states, Saudi Arabia has experienced a rapid (140 per cent) rise in water demand over the past decade. The total water withdrawals are more than 80 per cent of the available renewable water supplies on average every year, so the Kingdom faces extremely high levels of baseline water stress.[18] Renewable freshwater per person per year stood at 73 m³ on average in 2017.[19]

Characterized by low rainfall and high evaporation rates, Saudi Arabia is one of the driest areas in the world. There are no surface water resources like rivers or lakes, and most of the Kingdom's water is sourced from its

[17] World Resources Institute, 'CAIT Climate Data Explorer' (Washington, DC: World Resources Institute, 2019), https://www.wri.org/blog/2020/02/greenhouse-gas-emissions-by-country-sector.
[18] Luo, R. Young, and P. Reig, 'Aqueduct Projected Water Stress Rankings, Technical Note' (Washington, DC: World Resources Institute, 2015), http://www.wri.org/publication/aqueduct-projected-water-stress-country-rankings.
[19] World Bank, 'Renewable Internal Freshwater Resources Per Capita (Cubic Meters)' (2021), https://data.worldbank.org/indicator/ER.H2O.INTR.PC.

limited underground reserves.[20] Between 2010 and 2016, 91 per cent of the Kingdom's water was sourced from underground, followed by desalination (8 per cent), and surface and waste-water treatment, both accounting for 1 per cent.[21]

Despite being one of the driest countries in the world, the Kingdom has the third highest per capita freshwater consumption in the world. The per capita average daily use of water in Saudi Arabia has been increasing since 2009 when it hit 227 litres/day, recording a gradual increase to touch 270 litres/day in 2016,[22] twice the world average.[23] The Kingdom withdrew nearly 23 billion cubic metres of water yearly, as of 2013–17.[24]

The growing demand for water has been associated with the Kingdom's population growth, urbanization, and industrialization, along with the expansion of agricultural programmes aiming to enhance self-sufficiency to meet the growing food requirements. During the oil boom years that followed the rise of crude prices in 1973, Saudi Arabia addressed the rising food demand by resorting to a policy of self-sufficiency.[25] In the 1980s, the Kingdom introduced ambitious agricultural programmes, which have led to achieving self-sufficiency in many food commodities and the country becoming the sixth largest wheat exporter. Such self-sufficiency in food, however, was achieved at the expense of its water resources.[26] According to a 2013 study conducted by the World Resources Institute,[27] more than 80 per cent of Saudi Arabia's usable water for agriculture, industry, and domestic consumption has been withdrawn annually, putting Saudi Arabia among the countries that face the highest pressure on renewable water resources. Extensive groundwater extractions from non-renewable aquifers over the last few decades have resulted in substantial declines in groundwater levels and the deterioration of groundwater quality. Population growth, inefficient water

[20] Chowdhury and Al-Zahrani, 'Implications of climate change on water resources in Saudi Arabia'. *Arabian Journal for Science and Engineering* 38 (2013), pp.1959–71.

[21] GSA, General Authority for Statistics (2018). https://www.stats.gov.sa/en/search?search_api_views_fulltext=water&Site-search-form-btn=nd.

[22] M. B. Baig, Y. Alotibi, G. S. Straquadine, and A. Alataway, 'Water Resources in the Kingdom of Saudi Arabia: Challenges and Strategies for Improvement', in S. Zekri (ed.), *Water Policies in MENA Countries*, Global Issues in Water Policy, vol. 23 (Cham: Springer, 2020), pp. 135–60, doi: 10.1007/978-3-030-29274-4_7

[23] Baig et al., 'Water Resources in the Kingdom of Saudi Arabia'

[24] Food and Agriculture Organization of the United Nations, 'AQUASTAT—FAO's Global Information System on Water and Agriculture' (2021), http://www.fao.org/aquastat/statistics/query/index.html.

[25] R. Khrais, 'What Saudi Arabia Is Doing to Save Water', Al-Monitor (2016), https://www.al-monitor.com/pulse/originals/2016/04/saudi-arabia-self-sufficiency-water-policy.html.

[26] Baig et al., 'Water Resources in the Kingdom of Saudi Arabia'.

[27] WRI, World's 36 Most Water-Stressed Countries (2013). World Resources Institute. https://www.wri.org/insights/worlds-36-most-water-stressed-countries.

use practices, limited water supply management, and lax agricultural policies have led to an unsustainable culture of water usage in Saudi Arabia.[28]

While groundwater is the main source of water used in Saudi Arabia, the production of desalinated water increased by up to 126 per cent between 2010 and 2019 in response to the Kingdom's increasing water needs.[29] Water desalination, however, is an energy-intensive process and relies on oil and gas for its operation. The production of desalinated water uses up to eight times more energy than using groundwater and accounts for 10–20 per cent of the energy consumption in Saudi Arabia.[30] The water desalination process, without proper management, is associated with environmental challenges including the release of air and water pollutants like brine, as well as GHG emissions that contribute to climate change.

Biodiversity

According to the Ministry of Environment, Water and Agriculture (MEWA), Saudi Arabia is home to 79 species of mammal, 99 reptiles, 432 local and migratory birds, and 3,099 invertebrates.[31] To date, fifteen protected areas, covering almost 4 per cent of the country's surface, conserve all of the country's major habitats, key wetlands, marine and mountain habitats, and viable populations of endemic, endangered, and key plant and animal species.[32] The vitality of these species, however, has come under natural and human-induced pressures including from habitat destruction and fragmentation, over-grazing, illegal hunting, the change to intensive modern agricultural practices, pollution, recreational activities, littering, introduction of exotic and invasive species, expansion of urban areas, and road construction.[33] For instance, MEWA has reported that 111 species have become endangered

[28] Ibid.; T. W. Lippman, 'Biggest Mideast crisis: Growing water scarcity'. *Business Mirror* (2014). Available at: http://www.ipsnews.net/2014/05/biggest-mideast-crisis-probably-dontknow-enough/.

[29] General Authority for Statistics, 'About Kingdom' (2021), https://www.stats.gov.sa/en/%D8%B5% D9%81%D8%AD%D8%A9/about-kingdom#:~:text=Saudi%20Arabia's%20Red%20Sea%20coastline, 560%20kilometers%20(350%20miles).&text=The%20total%20Saudi%20population%20as%202010%20 amounted%2029%2C195%2C895%20million; Saline Water Conversion Corporation, *Annual Report*, No. 37 (2010), https://www.swcc.gov.sa/english/MediaCenter/SWCCPublications/Pages/default.aspx.

[30] Baig et al., 'Water Resources in the Kingdom of Saudi Arabia'.

[31] MEWA, الملخص التنفيذي للاستراتيجية الوطنية للبيئة.

[32] National Center for Wildlife, 'Protected Areas' (2020), https://www.ncw.gov.sa/Ar/Wildlife/ ProtectedAreas/Pages/default.aspx.

[33] Convention on Biological Diversity, 'Saudi Arabia—Main Details. Status and Trends of Biodiversity' (2020), https://www.cbd.int/countries/profile/?country=sa#:~:text=The%20varied%20biodiversity%20 of%20Saudi,amphibians%20found%20in%20Saudi%20Arabia.

or extinct, and nearly 12 million birds are hunted every year.[34] Saudi Arabia has pursued a number of efforts to protect its biodiversity. It has put forward two relevant policy documents—the National Biodiversity Strategy and Action Plan, and the Protected Area System Plan—which set national targets and a vision for protected areas in the Kingdom. It established the Saudi Wildlife Authority in 1986 to oversee the protection of the country's wildlife.

Marine Pollution and Coastal Environments

The coastline of Saudi Arabia stretches for about 2,640 kilometres, with the Red Sea coastline accounting for about 1,760 kilometres and the Arabian Gulf coastline roughly 560 kilometres.[35] Coastal areas provides various habitats for diverse communities of corals and sponges. As one of the largest countries bordering the Red Sea, Saudi Arabia has undergone rapid transformation into a modern industrial country. A significant part of the coast has been subjected to extensive exploitation, and metal pollution is becoming a threat to the coastal ecosystem. Incidents of damaged oil wells, oil pipeline leaks, and domestic sewage from coastal cities are contributing significantly to coastal pollution.[36]

The marine and coastal zone environments are under pressure from unsustainable expansion of urban areas and the development of ports, industrial activities, and desalination plants along the coastline. Expansion of shipping and trade, overfishing, discharge of solid and chemical waste, and, on some occasions, oil spills present a challenge for the marine environment. Climate change exacerbates these challenges by contributing to an increase in oceans' temperature, while the high absorption of CO_2 emissions has negative effects on mangrove ecosystems and marine life in general. It is estimated that mangrove cover in the Kingdom's seas declined by 70 per cent between 1985 and 2013.[37]

---

[34] MEWA, الملخص التنفيذي للاستراتيجية الوطنية للبيئة.
[35] General Authority for Statistics, 'About Kingdom'.
[36] M. S. Hariri, M. Kh. Khalil, and A. E. Rifaat, Assessment of the Present Status of the Red Sea Coastal Zone Between Haql and Yanbu, Saudi Arabia', *JKAU* 24, no. 2 (2013), pp. 115–31, https://marz.kau.edu.sa/Files/1001002/Researches/65211_36546.pdf.
[37] MEWA, الملخص التنفيذي للاستراتيجية الوطنية للبيئة.

Waste Management

Saudi Arabia, like its neighbours in the Gulf region, has high per capita waste generation values. It produces almost 53 million tons of waste annually, and its per capita waste generation is estimated at 1.5 to 1.8 kg per person per day.[38] Nearly half of the total waste comes from three major cities in the Kingdom: 21 per cent from Riyadh, 14 per cent from Jeddah, and 8 per cent from Dammam.[39]

Despite progress in dealing with municipal and industrial waste, more than 75 per cent of the Kingdom's waste still ends up in dumpsites and sanitary landfills that do not meet environmental standards. Waste recycling is still nascent, as only 10–15 per cent of waste gets recycled and that is mainly due to the presence of the informal sector,[40] which extracts paper, metals, and plastics from municipal waste. Inappropriate waste management forms a threat to groundwater, soil, and the marine environment.

The Saudi government is aware of the critical demand for waste management solutions and is investing heavily in solving this problem. The 2017 national budget allocated SAR54 billion for the municipal services sector, which includes water drainage and waste disposal. The government is making concerted efforts to improve recycling and waste disposal activities. Recently it approved new regulations to ensure an integrated framework for the management of municipal wastes. The Ministry of Municipal and Rural Affairs will be responsible for overseeing the tasks and responsibilities of the solid waste management system.[41]

Desertification and Land Degradation

Arable land in the Saudi Arabia accounts for only 1.7 per cent (3.42 million hectares) of the total land area, and only 0.6 per cent (1.81 million hectares) is used for agriculture. Forests, on the other hand, account for only 1.1 per cent (2.1 million hectares) of the Kingdom's total land. The

[38] S. Zafar, 'Solid Waste Management in Saudi Arabia', EcoMENA (2020), https://www.ecomena.org/solid-waste-management-in-saudi-arabia/.

[39] A. Bashraheel, 'Saudi Arabia Seeks to Vitalize Waste Management Sector', *Arab News* (9 November 2020), https://www.arabnews.com/node/1760736/saudi-arabia.

[40] Informal sector, as per OECD/ILO, refers to all economic activities by workers and economic units that are—in law or in practice—not covered or insufficiently covered by formal arrangements. Organization for Economic Cooperation and Development/International Labour Organization, 'Definitions of Informal Economy, Informal Sector and Informal Employment', in *Tackling Vulnerability in the Informal Economy* (Paris: OECD Publishing, 2019), pp. 155–157, doi: 10.1787/103bf23e-en.

[41] Zafar, 'Solid Waste Management in Saudi Arabia'.

arid climate, which is characterized by elongated periods of drought, exacerbated by climate change and human-induced pressures such as unsustainable agricultural practices, overgrazing, expansion of mining, manufacturing, and infrastructure, and unsustainable use of water present challenges to the Kingdom's arable and agricultural areas. MEWA reported that 10 per cent of Baha's forest cover had been lost between 1984 and 2014, and 565 plant species are currently endangered. The increase in soil salinity due to unsustainable irrigation practices has rendered 40 per cent of agricultural areas unsuitable for agriculture.[42]

Climate Change Impacts on Saudi Arabia's Economy

Climate change poses threats both to Saudi Arabia's oil-based economic sectors and to its non-oil based sectors.[43] The sustainability and resilience of Saudi Arabia's non-oil economic sectors such as agriculture and food security, water, fisheries, tourism, and infrastructure are already being affected by the physical impacts of climate change due to increases in the Earth's average surface temperature, decreases in annual total precipitation, sea-level rise, and, in some cases, extreme events like intense rainfall.[44] A 2018 study suggested that the impact of 3 °C warming could cause Saudi Arabia large annual losses in GDP of 0.4 per cent from 2027 and 2 per cent from 2067. GDP losses stem from sea-level rise, loss in work productivity due to heat/humidity exposure, and proliferation of infectious disease.[45] These estimates, however, do not factor in the costs of extreme weather events such as storms, flooding, and wildfires. Examples of extreme rainfall events in Saudi Arabia include the flash floods that hit Jeddah in November 2009 and most recently in October 2018. The 2009 flash flood was described as the worst in the region in thirty years, causing the deaths of more than 150 people and resulting in great economic losses, with damage to more than 7,000 vehicles and 8,000 homes. Over 3.5 inches of rain fell in four hours over an area that normally receives

[42] MEWA, الملخص التنفيذي للاستراتيجية الوطنية للبيئة.

[43] Al-Sarihi, 'Prospects for Climate Change Integration into the GCC Economic Diversification Strategies'.

[44] United Nations Economic and Social Commission for Western Asia et al., 'Arab Climate Change Assessment Report—Main Report' (Beirut: RICCAR, 2017); B. O. Elasha, 'Mapping of Climate Change Threats and Human Development Impacts in the Arab Region' (New York: United Nations Development Programme/Regional Bureau for Arab States, 2010).

[45] Kompas et al., 'The Effects of Climate Change on GDP by Country'.

1.8 inches per year.[46] The flash flood in 2018 caused the deaths of at least thirty people.[47]

Climate change also poses risks to the sustainability and resilience of oil-based economic sectors. Since fossil fuels represent more than 70 per cent of global GHG emissions,[48] future access to fossil fuel-based energy will need to be constrained to keep climate change at a (relatively) safe level, meaning a rise in global mean surface temperatures well below 1.5 °C compared to pre-industrial levels. These are the objectives of the Paris Agreement. Such constraints on fossil fuels present a challenge for Saudi Arabia's economy because, being a home for around 18 per cent of the world's proven petroleum reserves, oil makes a significant contribution to the Saudi economy, accounting for about 70 per cent of total export earnings, 64 per cent of government revenue, and about 50 per cent of its GDP in 2019.[49] Global constraints on fossil fuels could affect both the demand and production outlook.

On the demand side, different international organizations, such as BP and International Energy Agency (IEA) have published projections about energy demand that are consistent with the objectives of the Paris Agreement. BP Energy Outlook 2020 released two energy pathways that are consistent with the Paris Agreement emission reduction targets: rapid (a 70 per cent decline in emissions by 2050, consistent with 2 °C by 2100) and net-zero (a 15 per cent decline in emissions by 2050, consistent with 1 °C). In both scenarios, while primary energy demand is expected to rise by 10 per cent, the share of hydrocarbon will decline from 80 per cent in 2018 to between 20 and 70 per cent by 2050.[50] The IEA net-zero scenario suggests that oil demand will have to fall by almost 75 per cent between 2020 and 2050, a decline from 88 million barrels per day (mb/d) in 2020 to 72 mb/d in 2030 and to 24 mb/d in 2050, in order to bring global energy-related carbon emissions to net-zero by 2050 and to keep global warming within 1.5 °C.[51]

On the production side, a recent study by Oil Change International also suggests that for a likely chance of keeping warming below 2 °C, 68 per cent of reserves must remain in the ground, and 85 per cent of fossil fuels should

[46] M. Mahmoud, 'Weathering Climate Change in the Gulf' (Washington, DC: Arab Gulf States Institute, 2017).

[47] A. Nagraj, 'Saudi Officials Form Committee in Qassim to Investigate Flood-Related Incidents', *Gulf Business* (19 November 2018), https://gulfbusiness.com/saudi-officials-qassim-form-committee-investigate-flood-related-issues.

[48] B. Metz et al. (eds.), *Intergovernmental Panel on Climate Change*, 'Technical Summary: Contribution of Working Group III to the Fourth Assessment Report of the Intergovernmental Panel on Climate Change' (Cambridge: Cambridge University Press, 2007).

[49] General Authority for Statistics, 'Population Estimates'; OPEC, 'Saudi Arabia Facts and Figures'.

[50] BP, *Energy Outlook 2020* (London: BP, 2020).

[51] IEA, *Net Zero by 2050*.

remain unburned in order to keep global warming below 1.5 °C.[52] In this context, the Middle East would need to leave about 40 per cent of its oil and 60 per cent of its gas underground.[53] In this context, if Saudi reserves are fully extracted and burned, the resulting emissions would amount to an estimated 112 gigatons of carbon dioxide, one-seventh of total global emissions in a 2 °C carbon budget, or one-third of total global emissions in a 1.5 °C carbon budget.[54] Similarly, a 2020 Production Gap Report finds that to follow a 1.5 °C-consistent pathway, the world would need to decrease fossil fuel production by roughly 6 per cent per year between 2020 and 2030. Specifically, between 2020 and 2030, global coal, oil, and gas production would have to decline annually by 11 per cent, 4 per cent, and 3 per cent respectively, to be consistent with the 15.5 °C pathway.[55]

While acknowledging that there is no single story for the future of global energy, the implications of such future scenarios translate into direct economic losses for Saudi Arabia due to the decline in future oil export revenues, especially if no proper mitigation measures are implemented and crude petroleum and downstream oil products continue to dominate Saudi Arabia's export profile. At present, many of the Kingdom's importers, such as European countries, China, and India, are pursuing ambitious programmes to cut GHG emissions and improve energy efficiency. India aims for at least 15 per cent of the vehicles on its roads to be electric within five years, and more than 30 per cent by 2030.[56] Similarly, China is targeting a complete ban on internal combustion engines by 2040.[57]

Environment and Climate Change Governance in Saudi Arabia

In Saudi Arabia, MEWA is the dedicated entity that oversees the country's protection of the natural environment, including in the areas of air quality,

---

[52] G. Muttitt, 'The Sky's Limit: Why the Paris Climate Goals Require a Managed Decline of Fossil Fuel Production', Oil Change International (September 2016).
[53] C. McGlade and P. Ekins, 'The Geographical Distribution of Fossil Fuels Unused When Limiting Global Warming to 2C', Nature 517 (2015), pp. 187–90.
[54] G. Muttitt, and H. McKinnon, 'Overheated Expectations: Valuing Saudi Aramco's IPO in Light of Climate Change', Oil Change International (August 2017).
[55] SEI, IISD, ODI, E3G, and UNEP. (2020). The Production Gap Report: 2020 Special Report. http://productiongap.org/2020report
[56] A. Kotoky, P. R. Sanjai, and A. Upadhyay, 'India Proposes a Goal of 15% Electric Vehicles in Five Years', Bloomberg (6 September 2018).
[57] C. Busch, 'China's All In On Electric Vehicles: Here's How that Will Accelerate Sales in Other Nations', Forbes (30 May 2018).

water and food security, biodiversity, the marine and coastal environment, waste management, and desertification.

The governance of most climate-related issues, especially those related to reducing GHG emissions, on the other hand, is led by the Ministry of Energy with participation from different entities such as the King Abdullah Petroleum Studies and Research Center (KAPSARC), King Abdullah City for Atomic and Renewable Energy (KACARE), Saudi Energy Efficiency Center (SEEC), the Designated National Authority (DNA), the Electricity and Cogeneration Regulatory Authority (ECRA), the Nuclear and Radiological Regulatory Commission (NRRC), and the Executive Committee for Governance of Price Adjustment of Energy and Water Products.

While the Ministry of Economy and Planning (MEP) could play a significant role in ensuring that economic development does not happen at the expense of the Kingdom's long-term environmental sustainability, its current role in addressing environmental issues is restricted to reporting on the country's progress in achieving its SDGs.

Governance of the Environment

The government's initial interest towards the environment goes back to 1927. It was mainly driven by the need to boost the development of agriculture and enhance food security. In 1932, King AbdulAziz ratified the first decision of the Shura Council to support farmers in the Kingdom by importing some agricultural machinery and equipment, which was distributed among farmers by the Ministry of Finance at affordable prices. In 1947, the first environment governance institution (i.e. the Directorate-General for Agriculture) was established and linked to the Ministry of Finance. The main mandates of the Directorate-General for Agriculture were reforming lands, improving irrigation, distributing water pumps, building dams and canals, digging springs and artesian wells, providing loans to farmers, and assisting with the development of technical training for farmers and guiding them towards modern agricultural methods. In 1953, the Directorate-General for Agriculture was transformed into the Ministry of Agriculture and Water. Agriculture remained the main focus of the new ministry, which then had six agricultural units located in several cities: Riyadh, Kharj, Ahsaa, Madinah, Jazan, and Buraidah. To oversee the issues of water, in 1961, the Agricultural Affairs Agency and the Water Affairs Agency were established. In 2002, the water sector was separated from the Ministry of Agriculture, and became an independent ministerial body, the Ministry of Water and Electricity. In

2016, the Ministry of Water and Electricity was abolished, and the Ministry of Agriculture was renamed as the Ministry of Environment, Water, and Agriculture, assigned tasks and responsibilities related to water and environmental affairs. The ministry now consists of seven directorates: the Directorate of Environment, the Directorate of Water Affairs, the Directorate of Water Services, the Directorate of Agriculture, the Directorate of Land and Survey, the Directorate of Animal Resources, and the Directorate of Planning and Development.

The ministry is also associated with public institutions and companies, including: the National Water Company, the Saudi Grain Organization, the Saline Water Conversion Corporation, the Saudi Wildlife Authority, the General Authority for Meteorology and Environmental Protection, the Saudi Irrigation Organization, the Agricultural Development Fund, SALIC Company, and the Water and Electricity Company.

Governance of Climate Change

Climate change governance in Saudi Arabia is pursued at international and national levels. At the international level, the Saudi delegation to international climate change negotiations has been dominated by the Energy Ministry (now the Ministry of Energy, Industry, and Mineral Resources). The centrality of the Energy Ministry reflects the early focus of Saudi Arabian climate change policy on its economic, rather than its environmental, dimension. The Ministry of Energy, Industry, and Mineral Resources also dominates Saudi Arabia's climate change governance at the national level.

At the international level, Saudi Arabia ratified the UNFCCC, the international environmental treaty (adopted on 9 May 1992 and coming into force on 21 March 1994), by accession on 28 December 1994. In 2005, when the Kyoto Protocol[58] emerged from the UNFCCC to strengthen the global response to climate change by mandating individual countries' GHG reductions, including non-Annex I countries, Saudi Arabia acceded to the protocol on 31 January 2005. In response to the protocol, the Kingdom submitted its

---

[58] The Kyoto Protocol recognizes that developed countries (i.e. Annex I countries) are primarily responsible for the high levels of GHG emissions into the atmosphere due to more than 150 years of industrial activity. Thus, it imposes a greater burden on developed countries under the principle of 'common but differentiated responsibilities'. To demonstrate all parties' compliance with the Kyoto Protocol, non-Annex I countries are also required to submit National Communication reports providing a vulnerability and adaptation assessment and relevant information on national circumstances; GHG inventories; financial resources and transfer of technology; and education, training, and public awareness. Non-Annex I parties are required to submit their first National Communication within three years of entering the convention and every four years thereafter.

first, second, and third National Communications in 2005, 2011, and 2016, respectively. In December 2015, parties to the UNFCCC reached a landmark agreement to combat climate change and accelerate and intensify the actions and investments needed for a sustainable low-carbon future. The Paris Agreement builds upon the convention and—for the first time—brings all countries, including developing countries, into a common cause to undertake ambitious efforts to combat climate change and adapt to its effects, with enhanced support to assist developing countries to do so. Entering into force on 4 November 2016, the Paris Agreement requires all parties to make their best efforts through NDCs and to strengthen these efforts in the years ahead. This includes requirements that all parties report regularly on their emissions and implementation efforts. Saudi Arabia ratified the Paris Agreement on 3 November 2016 and submitted its first NDC ahead of the Conference of Parties held in December 2015.

At the national level, the Kingdom has established different initiatives to address the impacts of climate change. These include the National Committee for the Clean Development Mechanism and the DNA, which were established in 2009. The DNA oversees the development process of Clean Development Mechanism projects, preparation and submission of National Communications, Biennial Update Reports, and preparation and updating of intended NDCs.[59]

Other climate-related initiatives include the launch of the first National Energy Efficiency Program in 2003, as a three-year programme to improve the management and efficiency of electricity generation and consumption in the Kingdom. Building on the experiences gained during that period, a Council of Ministers' decree established the SEEC in 2010. The centre is managed by a Board of Directors representing twenty-six ministries, government departments, and private sector organizations. Its main tasks have included the development of a National Energy Efficiency Program, promoting awareness about energy efficiency, participating in the implementation of pilot projects, proposing energy efficiency policies and regulations, and monitoring their implementation. In 2012, the SEEC launched the Energy Efficiency Program to improve the Kingdom's energy efficiency by designing and implementing energy efficiency initiatives. To establish the programme, an Executive Committee was created by the SEEC board, chaired by Prince Abdulaziz bin Salman, Vice Minister of Petroleum and Mineral Resources

---

[59] See home page of Clean Development Mechanism Designated National Authority at: https://www. cdmdna.gov.sa.

(now the Ministry of Energy, Industry, and Mineral Resources), and composed of members from fourteen government and semi-government entities. The Executive Committee targeted more than 90 per cent of the Kingdom's energy consumption by creating specialized teams that focused on the building, transportation, and industrial sectors. The Energy Efficiency Program is currently focusing on the design of the first energy conservation law and national and regional regulations, preparation of a new national database on energy supply and demand, capacity development of energy efficiency managers, and public awareness. Furthermore, in 2010, the Saudi Green Building Forum was launched to promote the construction of energy- and resource-efficient and environmentally responsible buildings. By the end of 2014, the Kingdom had more than 300 green building projects, investing approximately $53 billion.

Additionally, as part of its G20 Presidency in 2020, Saudi Arabia, led by the Ministry of Energy, put forward the concept of the Circular Carbon Economy (CCE) and plans to put it at the centre of its climate mitigation plan.[60] A key insight from CCE is to achieve a pathway towards net-zero emissions. This is based around 'four Rs': Reduce, focusing on energy efficiency, renewable energy, and other low-carbon energy sources such as nuclear power; Reuse, concerned with carbon capture and utilization, and emissions to value; Recycle, addressing natural sinks such as forests and oceans, bio-energy, and hydrogen; and Remove, focusing on carbon capture and storage, and direct air capture. CCE builds on the Kingdom's earlier efforts to reduce its carbon emissions, including the Kingdom's first CO_2 enhanced oil recovery demonstration project which commenced its operation in 2015. The Uthmaniyah CO_2 enhanced oil recovery demonstration compresses and dehydrates CO_2 from the Hawiyah natural gas liquid recovery plant in Saudi Arabia's Eastern Province.[61] The captured CO_2 is transported via pipeline to the injection site at the Ghawar oil field (a small flooded area in the Uthmaniyah production unit) for enhanced oil recovery. In addition, in 2017 a Renewable Energy Project Development Office was established at the Ministry of Energy to increase the Kingdom's generation of renewable energy to 30 per cent by 2030.[62] At the centre of this ambitious CCE approach are the Ministry of Energy and the Energy Ecosystem, consisting

---

[60] Williams, Achieving Climate Goals by Closing the Loop in a Circular Carbon Economy (2019). King Abdullah Petroleum Studies and Research Center.

[61] Global CCS Institute, 'The Global Status of CCS' (2018), https://adobeindd.com/view/publications/2dab1be7-edd0-447d-b020-06242ea2cf3b/qhqw/publication-web-resources/pdf/CCS_Global_Status_Report_2018_Interactive.pdf.

[62] International Renewable Energy Agency, 'Renewable Energy Market Analysis: GCC 2019' (Abu Dhabi: International Renewable Energy Agency, 2019).

of KAPSARC, KACARE, the SEEC, the DNA, the ECRA, the NRRC, and the Executive Committee for Governance of Price Adjustment of Energy and Water Products.

Alignment of the Environment and Climate Change with Economic Development

In 2015, the United Nations (UN) member states adopted two agreements to ensure a global drive towards long-term sustainable and climate-resilient economic growth: the Paris Climate Agreement and Sustainable Development Agenda and seventeen related SDGs. As a UN member state and having ratified the Paris Agreement, Saudi Arabia submitted its 'Intended NDCs' report to the UNFCCC in 2015 and its updated NDCs in October 2021, detailing its aspirations to contribute towards mitigation of and adaptation to climate change. In 2018, the Kingdom submitted its First Voluntary National Review covering the seventeen SDGs.

The operationalization of NDCs and SDGs implies that climate-related activities and environmental protection need to be aligned with economic planning and development to ensure that economic development does not happen at the expense of the natural environment, and that the degradation of natural resources does not stand in the face of economic development.[63]

Vision 2030 and related implementation programmes, such as the NTP, provide the foundations underpinning the integration of climate-related activities and SDGs into the national planning process. This section provides an assessment of the extent to which the NDCs and SDGs, and the different environment- and climate-related issues discussed earlier, have been aligned to the Kingdom's Vision 2030 goals and its 2020 implementation programme, the NTP. It does so by using content analysis applied to selected governmental documents: Vision 2030; the NTP; the Kingdom's NDCs; its National Communications to UNFCCC; its SDG reports; and the National Environmental Strategy (2018).

---

[63] Swedish International Development Cooperation Agency, 'Integrating Climate Action into National Development Planning: Coherent Implementation of the Paris Agreement and Agenda 2030—A Guide to Support Implementation of the Paris Agreement' (Stockholm: Sida, 2017); United Nations Environment Programme, 'Aligning Nationally Determined Contributions and Sustainable Development Goals: Lessons Learned and Practical Guidance' (2017), file://kapsarc.org/UP/U3$/Sarihias/Downloads/FINAL_NDC-SDG-9Nov.pdf.

Vision 2030, Environmental Sustainability, and Climate Change

Vision 2030 is built around three themes: a vibrant society, a thriving econ-omy, and an ambitious nation. The Vision makes reference to environmental sustainability under its first theme, a vibrant society, aiming to increase waste management efficiency, build comprehensive recycling projects, reduce all forms of pollution, and protect biodiversity and coastal and marine environ-ments:

> By preserving our environment and natural resources, we fulfill our Islamic, human and moral duties. Preservation is also our responsibility to future generations and essential to the quality of our daily lives. We will seek to safeguard our environment by increasing the efficiency of waste management, establishing comprehensive recycling projects, reducing all types of pollution and fighting desertification. We will also promote the optimal use of our water resources by reducing consump-tion and utilizing treated and renewable water. We will direct our efforts towards protecting and rehabilitating our beautiful beaches, natural reserves and islands, making them open to everyone.[64]

The Vision also refers to renewable energy under the vibrant economy theme, aiming to expand the scale of renewable energy technological development and deployment:

> Even though we have an impressive natural potential for solar and wind power, and our local energy consumption will increase threefold by 2030, we still lack a competitive renewable energy sector at present. To build up the sector, we have set ourselves an initial target of generating 9.5 gigawatts of renewable energy. We will also seek to localize a significant portion of the renewable energy value chain in the Saudi economy, including research and development, and manufacturing, among other stages.[65]

The NTP, Environmental Sustainability, and Climate Change

To operationalize the ambitions outlined in Vision 2030, the NTP was estab-lished in 2020 as an implementation programme and was designed under

[64] Saudi Arabia Vision 2030. https://www.vision2030.gov.sa/media/rc0b5oy1/saudi_vision203.pdf.
[65] Saudi Arabia Vision 2030. https://www.vision2030.gov.sa/media/rc0b5oy1/saudi_vision203.pdf.

eight themes. Theme 2, improving living standards and safety, and Theme 3, ensuring the sustainability of vital resources, are the main two themes relating to climate change and environmental sustainability. Theme 2 puts forward strategies and initiatives to improve living standards and safety through reducing all types of pollution, waste management, tree planting, natural disaster management, and protection of marine and coastal environments. Theme 3 puts forward strategies and initiatives aiming to ensure sustainability and safeguard vital resources by protecting natural environments and wildlife, combating desertification, and ensuring food and water security.

Food and water security has received the highest attention in the NTP's environment-related programmes and initiatives, with fifteen programmes and initiatives dedicated to enhancing water supply and twenty to enhancing food security. At the end of 2020, the NTP targeted improving the Kingdom's food security index from a baseline of 71.1 (in 2016) to 72, increasing the rate of treated waste water from 13.6 per cent (in 2015) to 35 per cent, increasing the proportion of renewable water consumption in the agricultural sector from 16 per cent (in 2016) to 35 per cent, and enhancing water access from 87 per cent (in 2015) to 92 per cent. Protection of biodiversity was the third area that received priority in the NTP. Under its third theme, the NTP provided an explicit commitment to ensuring the sustainability of vital resources. It proposed seven strategies aiming to enhance maintenance and rehabilitation of wildlife and biodiversity, expand natural reserves, and regulate hunting activities. The key indicator for measuring achievement is to improve the Kingdom's ranking in the Biodiversity and Habitats Index from 82 (in 2016) to 70 by the end of 2020. The NTP also sought to improve the liveability of Saudi cities, making a healthy local urban environment a priority. It is committed to the development of efficient municipal waste management systems, aiming to reducing disease and food poisoning, increase waste recycling and treatment, and enhance the Population Satisfaction Index through a pest-free environment, cleanliness of cities, and food safety. To improve living conditions in cities, the NTP also proposed establishing specialized centres around the Kingdom to monitor and control all types of environmental pollution resulting from human and industrial activities, including: air pollution (toxic emissions sourced from transport and industrial waste), noise pollution, water pollution, soil pollution (caused by non-biodegradable materials), and visual, thermal, and light pollution. The objective was to raise the Environmental Performance Index from 68.63 (in 2016) to 77.28 by 2020.

The NTP also gave attention to the importance of combating desertification by setting a target to increase the area covered by rehabilitated natural vegetation from 18,000 (only 0.06 per cent of the total forest area in 2017) to 80,000 hectares (0.11 per cent of the total forest area) by the end of 2020. To achieve this objective, the Kingdom aims to cultivate 12 million trees, while ensuring that 60 per cent of the water utilized to achieve the objectives of this initiative is sourced from the treated waste water. To increase the vegetation cover, the Kingdom also aims to rehabilitate and invest in national parks. The NTP mentions only one initiative targeting the protection of the marine and coastal environment. The aim of this initiative is to increase the level of environmental control in coastal areas and the marine environment through an integrated system that enables the protection and utilization of coastal and marine areas, while achieving environmental compliance.

While climate change presents an additional challenge to the environmental issues acknowledged by the NTP, the impact of climate change is yet to be linked to these environmental issues. In its first NDC, the Kingdom made an explicit commitment 'to achieve mitigation co-benefits ambitions of up to 130 million tons of carbon dioxide equivalent avoided by 2030 annually through contributions to economic diversification and adaptation', which was revised in the updated NDC to 'reduce, avoid, and remove 278 MtCO2e of emissions annually by 2030'. While the most important goal of Vision 2030 is to diversify the economy by substantially reducing its reliance on oil, and this might imply a reduction in CO_2 emissions, the NTP makes no explicit mention of climate change. Under its fifth strategic objective of ensuring development and food security, the NTP does suggest the importance of ensuring the sustainability of vital resources like energy by, for example, enabling renewable energy to sustain energy supply. Yet the NTP suggests no strategies or initiatives to achieve this objective or to achieve the renewable energy goal mentioned in Vision 2030.

Environment, Climate Change, and Economic Development: Do They Synchronize?

The assessment presented above suggests that the Kingdom's main environmental challenges—water and food security, biodiversity, environmental pollutants, desertification, and coastal and marine environments—have been considered as integral elements of Vision 2030 and its implementation programme, the NTP. Furthermore, the environment- and climate-related objectives presented in Vision 2030 and the NTP can be linked to eight SDGs. These are: SDG2 (zero hunger), which links to food security programmes; SDG6 (clean water and sanitation), which links with water security programmes; SDG7 (affordable and clean energy), which links to clean energy programmes; SDG11 (sustainable cities and communities), which links to environmental pollution programmes; SDG12 (responsible consumption and production), which links to waste management; SDG 13 (climate action), which links to natural disaster management programmes; SDG 14 (life below water), which links to the protection of marine and coastal environments; and SDG15 (life on land), which links with biodiversity, desertification, and tree-planting programmes (Table 8.1). While these linkages exist, adapting the SDGs to the realities of Saudi Arabia is still work in progress, and further alignment and integration needs to be achieved through incorporating the SDG targets and indicators into the government's detailed action plans and programmes, which are being developed in Vision 2030 and refined under the NTP framework.[66] To put this into perspective, Saudi Arabia is still ranked twelfth (out of twenty-one countries regionally) in terms of its performance in achieving its SDGs.[67] The 2019 Arab Region SDG Index and Dashboards, which is a tool for governments and other stakeholders to measure progress on the SDGs, suggests that none of Saudi Arabia's SDG targets have been achieved and the Kingdom is still faced with 'major challenges' in implementing SDG6, SDG7, SDG12, and SDG13, 'significant challenges' in implementing SDG11 and SDG14, while only SDG15 is moderately improving (Table 8.2).[68] Another widely cited index, the 2020 Environmental Performance Index, which uses thirty-two performance indicators across eleven issue categories on environmental health (air quality, sanitation, drinking water, and waste management) and ecosystem vitality (biodiversity, fisheries, climate change, and pollution) to assess the state of sustainability of 180 countries around the world, ranks Saudi Arabia in ninetieth position.[69] According to this index, the Kingdom performs below the world average in terms of air quality, pollution emissions, biodiversity and habitats, water resources, and climate action.[70]

Furthermore, the Kingdom's NDCs, which express the country's main climate change mitigation and adaptation objectives, make linkages to five SDGs (and hence five NTP programmes). In terms of adaptation to climate

[66] Ministry of Economy and Planning, 'Sustainable Development Goals 1st Voluntary National Review Kingdom of Saudi Arabia, UN High-Level Political Forum 2018' (Riyadh: MEP, 2018), https://sustainabledevelopment.un.org/content/documents/20230SDGs_English_Report972018_FINAL.pdf.

[67] M. Luomi, G. Fuller, L. Dahan, K. Lisboa Båsund, E. de la Mothe Karoubi, and G. Lafortune, 'Arab Region SDG Index and Dashboards Report 2019' (Abu Dhabi and New York: SDG Centre of Excellence for the Arab Region/Emirates Diplomatic Academy and Sustainable Development Solutions Network, 2019).

[68] Ibid.

[69] Wendling et al., '2020 Environmental Performance Index'.

[70] Ibid.

change, the NDCs link to five SDGs, and five NTP programmes and initiatives. These are as follows: the water and waste-water management NDC links to SDG6 and the NTP's water resources; the urban planning NDC links to SDG12 and the NTP's waste management; the reduce desertification NDC links to SDG15 and the NTP's desertification and tree planting; the marine protection and integrated coastal zone management NDC links to SDG14 and the NTP's protection of marine and coastal environments; and the early warning system NDC links to SDG13 and the NTP's natural disaster management. In terms of mitigating the emissions that contribute to climate change, the NDCs refer to energy efficiency, renewable energy, carbon capture and utilization, utilization of gas, and methane recovery and flare minimization, which are linked with SDG13. While the Vision itself makes reference to renewable energy, the NTP refers to renewables only once and proposes no programmes that can help achieve renewable energy aspirations (see Table 8.1).

Despite the existing linkages between NDCs and national economic development programmes, climate change mitigation and adaptation objectives are yet to be translated into reality in the government's detailed economic development plans and programmes. This is mainly because there is a lack of national strategy for climate change mitigation and adaptation. Despite the Kingdom's intention to address climate change in line with economic diversification, these two policies will continue to be viewed separately unless clear targets, plans, and strategies are set out, not only progressing towards economic diversification but also factoring climate action into economic planning and development.[71] Moreover, while MEWA is responsible for addressing the sustainability of environmental issues like food and water security, agriculture, and marine and coastal environments, these environmental issues are yet to be linked to climate change. It is also worth mentioning that the NDCs still have gaps in terms of providing an exhaustive list of areas that need to be considered as vulnerable to the impacts of climate change, and hence the need for adaptation in these areas. For example, agriculture and health are not mentioned in the NDCs' contribution to climate change adaptation.[72]

[71] Al-Sarihi, 'Climate Change and Economic Diversification in Saudi Arabia'.
[72] W. P. Pauw, D. Cassanmagnano, K. Mbeva, J. Hein, A. Guarin, C. Brandi, A. Dzebo, N. Canales, K. M. Adams, A. Atteridge, T. Bock, J. Helms, A. Zalewski, E. Frommé, A. Lindener, and D. Muhammad, 'NDC Explorer' (Bonn: German Development Institute, African Centre for Technology Studies, and Stockholm Environment Institute), doi: 10.23661/ndc_explorer_2017_2.0; J. F. Braun, 'Climate Change in the Gulf Cooperation Council: Vulnerability and Readiness', in S. Kasten-Lechtenberg and A. Arora (eds.), *Resilient Cities in the Gulf Cooperation Council* (London: Routledge, forthcoming).

Table 8.1 The alignment of environment and climate SDGs and climate change NDCs with the Kingdom's NTP

Environment- and climate-focused SDGs	NTP 2020 Environment and climate areas	No. of programmes	Names of programmes	NDCs: climate change mitigation and adaptation areas
SDG2: zero hunger	Food	20	Program for Prevention and Control of Red Palm Weevil; Develop and Apply Agricultural Best Practices; Develop an Effective Food Strategic-Reserve Program that Includes an Early Warning and Information System for Agricultural Markets; Strengthen Applied Agricultural Research; Develop Fishing Harbors; Support and Improve the Performance of Agricultural Cooperative Societies; Transform the Delivery of Agricultural Services; Establishment of Marketing Service Centers Targeting Small Farmers and Producers; Development of an Integrated Management System for Controlling Plants Epidemics; Development of an Agricultural Records System; Improvement of Sustainable Livestock Production; Study the Establishment of Agricultural Quarantine City; establish the National Center for Marketing and Promoting Fish Products Consumption; Establish a National Portal for the Palm and Dates Sector; Establish an Entity to Develop and Manage Public Benefit Markets (Wholesale); Develop a Strategy and Implementation Plan for Responsible Saudi Agricultural Investment Abroad; Develop a Structure, Coordination Mechanism and Governance System for Food Security Institutions, Policies, and Legislation; Establish a New Company for Aquaculture in Partnership with the Private Sector; Increase the Utilization of Dam Water for Agricultural Purposes	
SDG6: clean water and sanitation	Water resources	15	Rehabilitate Agricultural Terraces and Apply Rainwater Harvesting Techniques in the Kingdom's Southern Region; Enhance Desalinated Water Resources; Deliver Drinking Water to Consumers; Enhance Surface Water Sources from Dams and Rainwater Harvesting; Reduce Water Losses in Water Networks; Reinforce Groundwater Sources from Wells; Increase Efficiency and Performance to enable capacity of the Saline Water Conversion Corporation; Develop Badia Irrigation; Expand Programs to Rationalize Individual Daily Water Consumption; Increase the Capacity of Strategic Water Reserves; Integrate Linkages Among all Desalinated Water Distribution Systems; Increase the Utilization of Dam Water for Agricultural Purposes; Develop Groundwater Resources; Reduce Water Consumption for Agricultural Purposes	Water and Waste-water management

SDG	Category	No.	Description	Notes
SDG11: sustainable cities and communities	Environmental pollution	4	Establish a Central Air Quality Control Unit; Establish an Environmental Inspection Program (inspection of industrial establishments); activate a National Program for Chemical Safety; Activate an Environmental Periodic Inspection for Fuel Stations and Service Centers	Urban planning
SDG12: responsible consumption and production	Waste management	6	Develop a Municipal Waste Management System; Upgrading Environmental Sanitation System; Monitoring Sewage from the Source; Activate Supervision of Proper Management of Solid Municipal Waste and the Regulation of Waste Recycling; Activate the Integrated Management of Industrial and Hazardous Waste; Establish a Regulatory Framework for Waste Management in the Kingdom	
SDG 13: climate action	Natural disaster management	2	Development of Numerical Modelling Systems to Improve the Accuracy of Forecasts of Weather and Natural Hazards; Establishment of a Climate Change Center to Implement the National Strategy for Adaptation to Climate Change and Manage Climate Data and Information	**Mitigation:** Energy efficiency, renewable energy, carbon capture and utilization, utilization of gas, methane recovery and flare minimization **Adaptation:** Early warning system
SDG 14: life below water	Protection of marine and coastal environments	1	Increase the Level of Environmental Control in Coastal Areas and the Marine Environment through an Integrated System that Enables the Protection and Utilization of Coastal and Marine Areas	Marine protection, integrated coastal zone management planning
SDG15: life on land	Biodiversity	7	Conservation of Plant Genetic Resources; Expand Natural Reserves and Integrate Their Management; Integrated Management of Trading Fungal Organisms; Develop Wildlife Research Centers; Facilitate Biodiversity-Based Investments; Regulate Hunting Activities; Develop an Integrated Program for Animal Disease Investigation and Control	
	Desertification and tree planting	2	Cultivate 12 Million Trees, while Ensuring that 60% of the Water Utilized to Achieve the Objectives of This Initiative Is Sourced from the Treated Waste Water; Rehabilitate and Invest in National Parks	Reduced desertification

Table 8.2 Saudi Arabia's environment and climate performance, as per Environmental Performance Index and SDG performance by Indicator

SDG	NTP environment and climate areas	Environmental Performance Index[a]	SDG performance by indicator[b]	Performance
SDG2: zero hunger	Food	N/A	Poverty headcount ratio at $1.90/day: 0.3% of population Poverty headcount ratio at $3.20/day: 2.0% of population Working poor at PPP$3.10 a day: 9.7% of total employment	Major challenges remain
SDG6: clean water and sanitation	Water resources	11.8	Population using at least basic drinking water services: 93.5% Population using at least basic sanitation services: 87.5% Freshwater withdrawal: 88.0% of total renewable water resources Imported groundwater depletion: 7.5 m³/year/capita Anthropogenic waste water that receives treatment: 46.1% Degree of implementation of integrated water resources management: 48% Mortality rate attributed to unsafe water, unsafe sanitation, and lack of hygiene: 1.9 per 100,000 population	Major challenges remain
SDG11: sustainable cities and communities	Environmental pollution	Air quality: 37.4 Pollution emissions: 34.7	Annual mean concentration of particulate matter <2.5 microns in diameter (PM2.5): 38.9 μg/m³ Satisfaction with public transport: 57.7%	Significant challenges remain
SDG12: responsible consumption and production	Waste management	61.4	E-waste generated: 6.2 kg/capita Production-based SO₂ emissions: 8.5 kg/capita Imported SO₂ emissions: 0.7 kg/capita Nitrogen production footprint: 10.8 kg/capita Total municipal solid waste generated: 304.8 kg/year/capita Value realization score (Resource Governance Index): 40 Fossil-fuel pre-tax subsidies (consumption and production): $222.6 per capita (current US$) Compliance with multilateral environmental agreements on hazardous waste and other chemicals: 54.2%	Major challenges remain

SDG				Status
SDG 13: climate action	Natural disaster management	Climate change: 37.5	Energy-related CO_2 emissions: 3.4 tCO_2/capita Imported CO_2 emissions, technology-adjusted: −0.1 tCO_2/capita People affected by climate-related disasters: 195.2 per 100,000 population CO_2 emissions embodied in fossil fuel exports: 3,194.1 kg/capita	Major challenges remain
SDG 14: life below water	Protection of marine and coastal environments	Fisheries: 18.5	Mean area that is protected in marine sites important to biodiversity: 54.9% Ocean Health Index Goal–Clean Waters (0–100): 40.5 Ocean Health Index Goal–Fisheries: (0–100): 61.2 Fish caught by trawling: 29.6%	Significant challenges remain
SDG15: life on land	Biodiversity Desertification and tree planting	38.8 Agriculture: 64.3	Mean area that is protected in terrestrial sites important to biodiversity: 38.8% Red List Index of species survival (0–1): 0.9 Imported biodiversity threats: 0.7 threats per million population	Challenges remain

---

[a] Z. A. Wendling, J. W., Emerson, A.de Sherbinin, D. C. Esty, et al. '2020 Environmental Performance Index' (New Haven, CT: Yale Center for Environmental Law and Policy, 2020), epi.yale.edu.

[b] M. Luomi, G. Fuller, L. Dahan, K. Lisboa Bäsund, E. de la Mothe Karoubi, and G. Lafortune, 'Arab Region SDG Index and Dashboards Report 2019' (Abu Dhabi and New York: SDG Centre of Excellence for the Arab Region/Emirates Diplomatic Academy and Sustainable Development Solutions Network, 2019).

Why Is There Limited Alignment between the Environment, Climate Change, and the Economy?

A content analysis of the main government documents (Vision 2030, the NTP, the Kingdom's NDCs, its National Communications to UNFCCC, its SDG reports, and the National Environmental Strategy) suggests that the alignment of environment and climate change with Saudi Arabia's economic development is still hindered by fundamental challenges that contribute to low environmental performance. These are: the low profile of data and research, limitations in institutional capacity, human skills and cadre number, as well as technical capacities.

Availability of Data and Research

Limitations in country-specific data and research, and gaps in knowledge and awareness, have played a crucial role in delaying action towards addressing issues relating to the environment and climate change, let alone aligning them with the country's economic development.

Environment- and climate-related data, if available, is inconsistent and of a high level of uncertainty. Data uncertainty and unavailability are demonstrated by many organizations, such as MEWA and the MEP, and in many reports such as 'The Kingdom's First Voluntary National Review of Sustainable Development Goals' and 'The Kingdom's National Communications'.[73] The Kingdom's third National Communication, for instance, addressed data uncertainty and unavailability:

> Due to the unavailability of certain source specific input data including emission factors, uncertainties are unavoidable when any estimate of national emissions or removals is made. It is therefore important to establish and express uncertainties quantitatively and/or with the acceptable confidence interval or range. …
>
> Uncertainties related to input data depend mainly on the size and quality of data collection and record keeping. …
>
> Uncertainties also appear when the unavailability of input data compels the use of extrapolated and/or averaged values for a particular set of data. Uncertainty of extrapolated or averaged data cannot be quantified precisely because the

---

[73] Saudi Arabia's National Communications provide relevant information on the Kingdom's national circumstances, GHG inventories, and their sources and sinks—or reservoirs—as well as the impacts of climate change on water resources, desertification, health, agriculture, and food security.

uncertainties associated with the interpolation and/or averaging procedures also depend on the quality of the relevant data including accuracy.[74]

Similarly, the unavailability of data inputs was addressed in 'The Kingdom's First Voluntary National Review of Sustainable Development Goals':

> Major challenges highlighted in the review are the availability of data and identifying measures to enhance the capacity of statistical bodies to collect and disseminate SDG-related statistics; achieving more effective coordination among government and non-government institutions to ensure synergies rather than duplication of efforts.[75]

The inconsistency of available data can be attributed to the lack of a focal point for collecting, monitoring, and validating environment- and climate-related data. Indeed, the Saudi Open Data Portal, the General Authority for Statistics, the King Abdulaziz City for Science and Technology (KACST), KACARE, KAPSARC, and the King Abdullah University of Science and Technology, as well as industry entities, are important sources of environment- and climate-related data and information. Yet the lack of a central mechanism to coordinate the efforts between these different entities and communicate their research outcomes to end users, including policy-makers, have contributed to delays in the effective management of environment- and climate-related issues in the Kingdom. Importantly, fragmentation and uncoordinated efforts to collect data have led to ineffective communication of information between environment and climate change experts and economic decision-makers, and thus hindered the integration of science into economic policy.

Furthermore, the environment and climate research needed to guide strategies, plans, and decision-making processes, although growing, is still limited. This includes the implications of environmental degradation and physical impacts of climate change—such as increased average temperatures, changes in precipitation, and sea-level rise—on the growth of Saudi Arabia's oil and non-oil economic sectors, such as agriculture, fisheries, tourism, water, and infrastructure (to guide adaptation plans), as well as the potential co-benefits resulting from addressing environment and climate issues in line with general economic development. The need for research was addressed in the Kingdom's 'Intended Nationally Determined Contributions' report:

---

[74] United Nations Framework Convention on Climate Change, 'Third National Communication of the Kingdom of Saudi Arabia' (2016), p. 16. https://unfccc.int/documents/81607.

[75] First Voluntary National Review (VNR) for Saudi Arabia. 2018. https://sustainabledevelopment.un.org/memberstates/saudiarabia.

Saudi Arabia will take the necessary actions to understand international policy measures to response to climate change, ... these include i. socio-economic
research studies to assess the impacts of mitigation measures implemented outside Saudi Arabia, ii. research and development activities to provide technologies
that enhance economic competitiveness.[76]

In addition, Saudi Arabia's updated NDCs call for enhanced international
cooperation to enhance climate change studies, including through 'socio-
economic research studies that assess the impacts of mitigation policy measures implemented outside Saudi Arabia on the Saudi economy, including
data and modelling tools'.[77]

Additionally, the limited communicationchannels and coordination
between research institutes and policy-makers has been a barrier to
the knowledge transfer important to raising awareness among stakeholders regarding environment- and climate-related issues. Awareness and
knowledge of environmental sustainability and climate change is vital both
at a decision-making level and at a consumer levels, and should be addressed
at cross-sectoral and multi-levels of governance. In Saudi Arabia, there is a
gap in knowledge and understanding of environmental sustainability and
climate issues beyond, for example, MEWA, the MEP, and the Ministry of
Energy, Industry, and Mineral Resources. For instance, the third National
Communication indicates that

The public and health care professionals are not fully aware about the issue of
climate change and its adverse health impacts. There is also a lack of [a] comprehensive research programme on climate change and health impacts across
the kingdom. As a result, there [are] scarce statistics on climate related health
problems and other environment related health events ...[78]

Institutional Capacity

Successful planning for aligning environment- and climate-related issues
with economic development is about leadership, coordination, and collective
action. In Saudi Arabia, the political will to enhance environmental

[76] United Nations Framework Convention on Climate Change, 'The Intended Nationally Determined
Contribution of the Kingdom of Saudi Arabia under the UNFCCC' (2015), https://www4.unfccc.int/
sites/ndcstaging/PublishedDocuments/Saudi%20Arabia%20First/KSA-INDCs%20English.pdf.

[77] United Nations Framework Convention on Climate Change, 'Updated First Nationally Determined
Contribution' (2021), https://www4.unfccc.int/sites/ndcstaging/PublishedDocuments/Saudi%20
Arabia%20First/KSA%20NDC%202021%20FINAL%20v24%20Submitted%20to%20UNFCCC.pdf.

[78] United Nations Framework Convention on Climate Change, 'Third National Communication of the
Kingdom of Saudi Arabia' (2016). https://unfccc.int/documents/81607.

protection and address climate change does exist. Yet fragmentation of leadership, lack of clarity of responsibilities, limited coordination (or duplication of efforts), and lack of monitoring programmes to assess the performance of implementation are the main institutional factors that hinder effective alignment between the Kingdom's environment, climate change, and economy.[79]

Fragmentation of Leadership

The Ministry of Energy, Industry, and Mineral Resources leads the country's efforts in addressing climate change at both national and international levels. At the international level, the ministry has dominated Saudi delegations to international climate change negotiations. At the national level, the ministry, under the oversight of its DNA, is also responsible for developing climate mitigation polices that target cutting the country's GHG emissions. Most notably, as part of Saudi Arabia's Presidency of the G20, the ministry has put forward the concept of the CCE and plans to put it at the centre of the country's climate change mitigation strategy.[80] While MEWA leads the country's effort to protecting its natural environment in terms of environmental pollution, water and food security, marine and coastal environments, desertification and afforestation, waste management and biodiversity, the Ministry of Environment, Water and Agriculture also oversees the country's adaptation to climate change. Furthermore, climate affairs are also under the oversight of the General Authority of Meteorology and Environmental Protection, with a focus on meteorology and weather forecasting.

Evolving but Limited Coordination

The fragmentation in environment and climate leadership has led to diminishing clarity and an overlap of responsibilities. In particular, there are multiple entities responsible for issuing environment and climate regulations.[81] This is challenging as the implementation of regulations requires coordination between not only environment- and climate-leading entities but also other bodies like the MEP. The practice of coordination between relevant entities is evolving. For instance, the Ministry of Energy, which leads the country's efforts in climate mitigation, formed the National Committee on Climate Change, which consists of: the Ministry of Energy, Industry and Mineral Resources, the Ministry of Transportation, the Ministry of Municipal and Rural Affairs, the Ministry of Health, the Royal Commission for Jubail and Yanbu, the Saline Water Conversion Corporation, Saudi Aramco, Saudi Basic Industries Corporation, the Saudi Electricity Company, the General

---

[79] MEWA, الملخص التنفيذي للاستراتيجية الوطنية للبيئة.
[80] Williams, Achieving Climate Goals by Closing the Loop in a Circular Carbon Economy (2019). King Abdullah Petroleum Studies and Research Center.
[81] MEWA, الملخص التنفيذي للاستراتيجية الوطنية للبيئة.

Authority of Meteorology and Environmental Protection, MEWA, KACST, KACARE, ECRA, Ma'aden, and Modon.[82] This is, indeed, useful. However, most of the coordination in the area of environment and climate change has been limited to preparing and delivering reports for international organizations, such as the delivery of NDCs and National Communication reports to the UNFCCC.

Weakness in Policy Implementation and Lack of Monitoring and Reporting

Both environmental protection and climate change mitigation have been hindered by either the lack of policies and regulations or weaknesses in implementing existing policies and regulations. At present, there are twenty-two environmental laws and regulations covering issues such as chemical waste management, aquaculture, agriculture, water management, and biodiversity.[83] However, as stated by MEWA's National Strategy for the Environment (2018), the implementation of these policies and regulations is hindered by the complexities and lack of clarity of regulations as well and by limitations in the technologies and technical capacities needed to monitor and evaluate the implementation of regulations.[84] As to climate policies, in its NDCs, Saudi Arabia listed its climate change ambitions in terms of mitigation (such as promoting energy efficiency, renewable energy, carbon capture and storage or utilization, methane recovery, and flare minimization) and adaptation (such as water and waste-water management, urban planning, marine protection, desertification reduction, early warning system establishment, and coastal zone management). At the time of writing, however, Saudi Arabia does not have a national climate action plan, which is essential for translating these ambitions into action.

Financial, Human, and Technical Capacities

Financial Capacity

The availability of financial resources is not an impediment to addressing environment and climate change issues; rather, it is the allocation of finances

---

[82] Ministry of Energy, 'Clean Development Mechanism, Designated National Authority' (Riyadh: Ministry of Energy, 2021), https://www.cdmdna.gov.sa/p/structure-of-dna/11.

[83] Ministry of Environment, Water and Agriculture, 'The Current Budget of the Ministry of Environment, Water and Agriculture (Budget 2018/2019)' (Riyadh: MEWA, 2021), https://mewa.gov.sa/en/Ministry/AboutMinistry/Pages/Budgets.aspx; Ministry of Environment, Water and Agriculture, 'Laws and Regulations' (Riyadh: MEWA, 2021), https://mewa.gov.sa/en/InformationCenter/DocsCenter/RulesLibrary/Pages/default.aspx.

[84] MEWA, الملخص التنفيذي للاستراتيجية الوطنية للبيئة.

that is the challenge. MEWA suggests that the annual cost of environmental degradation was SAR86 billion in 2014, which is around 3 per cent of the Kingdom's GDP.[85] Yet, according to MEWA analysis, the Kingdom's environment sector receives some of the lowest finance in the world[86]—in 2019, only 0.0013 per cent of the total governmental budget.[87] An important factor in the limited finance allocated to the environment sector is the lack of environmental financial incentives such as environmental fines, tax credits, licensing fees, and low-interest loans. Additionally, there has been limited engagement in environmental activities from the private sector, which can be a source of finance. The lack of necessary information about the costs of climate change impacts and environmental degradation, and the potential co-benefits associated with aligning climate action and environmental protection with economic development, are further challenges in allocating available funding towards addressing environment and climate-related issues. Moreover, the weaknesses associated with implementing environmental regulations and the lack of a national climate action plan create no clear signs as to whether to invest in clean technology or divestment from fossil fuels. 'Green finance', or 'climate finance', which is a mechanism aimed at funding sustainable projects and enabling green economic growth,[88] is yet to be adopted in the Gulf Arab states except in the United Arab Emirates. In Saudi Arabia, oil and gas export revenue continues to account for over 70 per cent of government revenue. Saudi Arabia's sovereign wealth fund, the Public Investment Fund (PIF), has shifted attention towards investing in green technologies only recently. For example, the PIF has agreed to invest more than $1 billion in the electric car start-up Lucid Motors.[89]

Human Capacity

Human capacity, on the other hand, offers a mixture of challenge and opportunity for Saudi Arabia to support its efforts in aligning the environment

[85] Ibid.

[86] Ibid.

[87] Ministry of Environment, Water and Agriculture, 'The Current Budget of the Ministry of Environment, Water and Agriculture (Budget 2018/2019)' (Riyadh: MEWA, 2021), https://mewa.gov.sa/en/Ministry/AboutMinistry/Pages/Budgets.aspx; Ministry of Finance, 'Budget Statement 2019' (Riyadh: Ministry of Finance, 2021), https://mof.gov.sa/en/financialreport/budget2019/Pages/default.aspx.

[88] United Nations Environment Programme, 'Green Financing' (2019), https://www.unenvironment.org/regions/asia-and-pacific/regional-initiatives/supporting-resource-efficiency/green-financing; Climate Mundial, 'Report: Defining Green Finance for Climate Change (2017), https://climatemundial.com/2017/12/green-finance-for-climate-change/.

[89] T. Arnold, 'Saudi's PIF Invests More Than $1 Billion in Electric Carmaker Lucid Motors', Reuters (17 September 2018), https://www.reuters.com/article/us-saudi-investment-auto/saudis-pif-invests-more-than-1-billion-in-electric-carmaker-lucid-motors-idUSKCN1LX1IG.

and climate change with the country's economic development. Saudi Arabia's NDC suggests that there is a need for sustained capacity-building efforts and upgrading of skills at the individual and systemic level to support the implementation of the country's climate ambitions.[90] MEWA, furthermore, emphasized that limitations in the skills and number of skilled workforce have been a barrier to enhancing environmental protection. For instance, while there are ten of thousands of facilities that require environmental auditing, the number of employees responsible for environmental auditing did not exceed 241 in 2018.[91] Insufficient knowledge of links between the environment, climate change, and economic development poses a barrier to specifying the need for capacity building, and the financial support for the upgrading of skills.

Technical Capacity

Like its neighbours, Saudi Arabia is highly dependent on technology imports rather than in-house technology innovation and research and development (R&D). In 2013, R&D investment in Saudi Arabia averaged 0.82 per cent of GDP, compared with 2–3 per cent in industrialized countries. The 0.82 per cent figure is far less than the minimum percentage (1 per cent) needed for an effective science and technology base specified by United Nations Educational, Scientific and Cultural Organization. As indicated by the Kingdom's NDC report:

> The implementation of Saudi Arabia's INDC [intended nationally determined contribution] is not contingent on receiving international financial support, but the Kingdom sees an important role for technology cooperation and transfer as well as building for INDC implementation.[92]

Conclusions

This chapter has explored the extent to which natural environment, climate change, and the sustainability of natural resources have been properly

---

[90] United Nations Framework Convention on Climate Change, 'The Intended Nationally Determined Contribution of the Kingdom of Saudi Arabia under the UNFCCC' (2015), https://www4.unfccc.int/sites/ndcstaging/PublishedDocuments/Saudi%20Arabia%20First/KSA-INDCs%20English.pdf.
[91] MEWA, الملخص التنفيذي للاستراتيجية الوطنية للبيئة.
[92] United Nations Framework Convention on Climate Change, 'The Intended Nationally Determined Contribution of the Kingdom of Saudi Arabia under the UNFCCC' (2015), https://www4.unfccc.int/sites/ndcstaging/PublishedDocuments/Saudi%20Arabia%20First/KSA-INDCs%20English.pdf.

addressed alongside Saudi Arabia's economic development. It has, first, investigated the effects of industrial expansion, rapid urbanization, the expansion of desalinations units, and the growth of transport on the Kingdom's natural environment and resources, including air quality, water resources, biodiversity, marine and coastal environments, and arable lands, as well as the country's involvement in waste management. Second, it has examined whether environmental sustainability and climate change have been considered as integral elements of Saudi Arabia's economic development vision and strategies. Third, it has identified the challenges that have assisted or delayed the Kingdom's alignment of environmental sustainability and climate change with its economic development.

The Saudi economy has advanced significantly since the discovery of oil in 1930s. While the Kingdom's interest in protecting its natural environment goes back to 1927, years before the discovery of oil, the early stages of environmental protection were mainly focused on enhancing agricultural production and water management. Other environmental issues like biodiversity, marine environment, and air quality, as well as the side-effects of unsustainable agricultural practices, have been left unchecked until recently, with the establishment of the MEWA in 2016. Furthermore, economic advancement, increasing standards of living, and the low prices of electricity, water and fuel products have resulted in the unintended consequences of unsustainable patterns of energy consumption, making the Kingdom not only affected by the impacts of climate change but a contributor to them, as one of the world's top emitters of carbon emissions on a per capita basis.

The Kingdom has in place an institutional architecture which is in principle conducive to environmental protection, with twenty-two environmental regulations covering a range of environmental issues such as agriculture, water, biodiversity, the marine environment, and air quality. Importantly, such environmental concerns have been made an integral part of the Kingdom's Vision 2030 and its operationalization plan, the NTP. The latter dedicated fifty-seven programmes and initiatives to enhancing the sustainability of water, food, biodiversity, urban spaces, and marine environments, while aiming to reduce all types of environmental pollution and waste, and to combat desertification. Despite the ongoing efforts, however, the Kingdom still performs below the world average in terms of air quality, pollution emissions, biodiversity and habitats, water resources, and climate action, and is still facing substantial challenges in implementing its environment- and climate-related SDGs.

This chapter has revealed that an effective alignment of environmental sustainability and climate change in Saudi Arabia is still hindered by a low data and information profile; fragmentation of leadership; weaknesses in implementing environmental protection regulations; the absence of a climate action plan; and fragmentated environment- and climate-related policies and efforts. Furthermore, it has shown that tangible alignment between economic development, the environment, and climate change requires an enhancement of human, technical, and financial resources.

9

The New Industries

Tourism and Entertainment in a Changing Saudi Arabia

Kristin Diwan and Larry Fallin

Introduction

Within the ambitious strategic framework envisioning Saudi Arabia's future, Saudi Vision 2030, tourism and entertainment loom large. Tourism figures prominently in the portfolio of giga projects slated for the capital region and the western shoreline. And the myriad entertainment initiatives, once unthinkable in the austere Kingdom, have played a leading role in announcing globally the new direction of Saudi Arabia: youthful and open to the world.

The priority of these industries in Saudi Arabia's diversification plans is striking due to their previous absence. The nine five-year plans covering the periods from 1970 to 2010 make no mention of entertainment or tourism, except of course the important sector of religious tourism encompassing the Hajj pilgrimage. Only in the Ninth Development Plan of 2010–14 is there a specific reference to the tourism sector as a means to diversify the economy.[1] The Ministry of Tourism, responsible for both tourism and entertainment within the Kingdom, was formally established as a full authoritative body by Royal Decree only in February 2020.[2]

However, with the change in leadership to King Salman and his son, the Crown Prince Mohammed bin Salman, entertainment and tourism have become central: to the expansive economic diversification program, to the social liberalization championed by the Crown Prince, and to his political

[1] Ministry of Economy and Planning, *Ninth Development Plan* (2017), pp. 34, 211. https://www.mep.gov.sa/en/AdditionalDocuments/PlansEN/9th/Ninth%20Development%20Plan%20-%20Chapter%204%20-%20National%20Economy%20Under%20The%20Ninth%20Development%20Plan%20.pdf.

[2] 'Saudi Royal Decree Forms 3 New Ministries, Merges 2 Others', *Asharq Al-Awsat* (25 February 2020), https://english.aawsat.com//home/article/2149016/saudi-royal-decree-forms-3-new-ministries-merges-2-others.

Kristin Diwan and Larry Fallin, *The New Industries*. In: *The Economy of Saudi Arabia in the 21st Century*. Edited by: John Sfakianakis, Oxford University Press. © Kristin Diwan and Larry Fallin (2024).
DOI: 10.1093/oso/9780198863878.003.0010

positioning of building a supportive constituency among urban youth eager for a cultural opening.

This chapter seeks to analyse the rise of these new industries and to assess their importance and potential within Saudi Arabia's transformation plans. First, it will situate entertainment and tourism within the intertwined goals of social change, youth empowerment, and an economic diversification that can attract foreign investment and visitors. It will then trace the evolution of tourism from one focused on religious pilgrimage to something much more expansive. The scope of these ambitions will be captured through a cursory review of many of the new capital projects being executed by administrative bodies close to the leadership within the centralizing state apparatus. While the coronavirus pandemic which emerged in 2020 has forestalled their rapid advance, there are few signs that a fundamental rethink is under way that would downgrade the premier position these new industries hold under the leadership of Mohammed bin Salman and in the reign of King Salman. Indeed, tourism and entertainment remain at the head of Saudi diversification plans and global branding.

Tourism and Entertainment at the Nexus of Economic, Social, and Political Change

In many ways, Saudi Arabia is facing the same challenge posed to all the Arab Gulf states: how to transition from a welfare state based on oil exports to a more diversified economy with a workforce prepared and empowered to contribute. Year to year the Saudi budget is buffeted by the combination of oil price volatility and a growing population placing increasing demands on both employment and government services.[3] Today the imperative to diversify the economy is mounting as the global energy transition—from hydrocarbon fuels to those based on renewables and low-carbon alternatives— accelerates, shortening the time horizon to exploit oil reserves.[4] These same trends also place a premium on green initiatives that better position the Kingdom within shifting global expectations from consumers, investors, and governments.[5]

---

[3] S. Hertog, 'Challenges to the Saudi Distributional State in an Age of Austerity', in *Saudi Arabia: Domestic, Regional, and International Challenges*, LSE research online (December 2016), http://eprints.lse.ac.uk/id/eprint/68625.

[4] E. Hinckley, 'Historic Moment: Saudi Arabia Sees End of Oil Age Coming and Opens Valves on the Carbon Bubble', *Energy Post* (22 January 2015), https://energypost.eu/historic-moment-saudi-arabia-sees-end-oil-age-coming-opens-valves-carbon-bubble/.

[5] C. Bianco, 'Power Play: Europe's Climate Diplomacy in the Gulf', European Council on Foreign Relations (October 2021), https://ecfr.eu/wp-content/uploads/Power-play-Europes-climate-diplomacy-in-the-Gulf.pdf.

Previous Saudi administrations started this economic restructuring, primarily through strategic investments into petrochemicals, gas exploration, and power generation: all areas where Saudi Arabia has some comparative advantage.[6] Now the emphasis is on expanding diversification into new technologies and creative fields, as well as investing in heritage and leisure sites able to attract both Saudis and foreign visitors. Unlike the investments in petrochemicals, this expansion into tourism and entertainment, as well as the broader knowledge economy and creative fields, cannot be successfully pursued without a fundamental sociocultural shift.[7] To compete internationally in attracting foreign investment, foreign talent, and foreign visitors, as well as to benefit from the full participation of Saudi citizens, the Saudi leadership must cultivate a new work culture and a more open social environment.

Here Saudi Arabia has faced a challenge unlike its Gulf neighbours: the tight social control imposed by religious officials and the informal Islamic networks which long dominated civic life, both empowered by the state itself. Gender segregation and social prohibitions have blocked diversity in the workplace and desiccated public life. Religious constraints on economic activity, exemplified by the closure of shops during the call to prayer, have hindered growth. This is especially true for tourism and entertainment which have faced explicit religious barriers, preventing many cultural activities such as music concerts, prohibiting mixed gatherings, forestalling the development of pre-Islamic antiquities, and decrying the memorialization of heritage sites.[8]

Today that cultural and political re-engineering is well under way.[9] The reasons for the move away from the distinctive religious political economy and pan-Islamic global positioning previously pursued by the Saudi state are complex and variable. In addition to the clear economic imperatives, they encompass new calculations for regime survival and global acceptance following the attacks of 11 September 2001 and the ensuing global war on terrorism, as well as the driver of generational change. Initial political reforms were evident in the years of King Abdullah's reign and have accelerated

[6] J. F. Seznec, 'The End of Saudi Arabia's Addiction to Oil: Downstream Industrial Development', Atlantic Council (January 2017), https://www.atlanticcouncil.org/wp-content/uploads/2017/01/The_End_of_Saudi_Arabias_Addiction_to_Oil_web_0106.pdf.

[7] M. Nurunnabi, 'Transformation from an Oil-Based Economy to a Knowledge-Based Economy in Saudi Arabia: The Direction of Saudi Vision 2030', *Journal of Knowledge Economy* 8 (2017), pp. 536–64, https://link.springer.com/article/10.1007/s13132-017-0479-8.

[8] R. Bsheer, *Archive Wars: The Politics of History in Saudi Arabia* (Stanford, CA: Stanford University Press, 2020), p. 185.

[9] E. AlHussein, 'Vision 2030 in Saudi Peripheries: Modeling Local Identities', Italian Institute for International Political Studies (10 September 2020), https://www.ispionline.it/en/pubblicazione/vision-2030-saudi-peripheries-modelling-local-identities-27327.

decisively under King Salman and his son and ruling heir Muhammed bin Salman. Since 2015, and in rapid succession, the Saudi leadership has shackled the religious police, ended commercial closings during prayer time, and curbed public calls to prayer. Concrete steps have been taken to end strict gender segregation and male guardianship, including ending the longstanding ban on women driving. All of this has allowed for increased women's participation in the economy and presence in public life, while fundamentally shifting public interactions towards greater social liberalization.[10]

That these changes could even be contemplated reflects a new urban youth demographic in the Kingdom. Through the 2000s, Saudi millennials demonstrated, through online activism, a desire for sociopolitical change, and through new creative enterprises, the economic potential of ventures in media, comedy, and the arts.[11] Under Muhammed bin Salman, this youth constituency for change has been courted with entertainment and cultural openings, while their political demands have been checked through arrests and intimidation.[12]

The new industries of entertainment and tourism come at the nexus of these changes: enabled by the political shift from Wahhabi austerity and positioned to tap the energy and talents of the new generation. The new Saudi state is placing a big bet on these industries, with ambitions to make it the second most important sector after hydrocarbons.[13] It is wagering that massive state investment can attract international capital and visitors, spurring growth that will create profits and employment opportunities attractive to young Saudis. Tourism and entertainment, along with new investment in the arts, are seen as complementary, generating festivals and events to attract visitors to the new tourist and heritage sites. All are key to solidifying a more youthful and dynamic national identity, supplanting the austere image of the Kingdom globally.

These changes find resonance in some earlier Arab efforts at tourism-led diversification and growth, most notably in nearby Dubai, but also further afield in the Tunisian experience. The political economist Waleed Hazbun

---

[10] S. Gomez Tamayo, J. Koettl, and N. Rivera, 'The Spectacular Surge of the Saudi Female Labor Force', Brookings (21 April 2021), https://www.brookings.edu/blog/future-development/2021/04/21/the-spectacular-surge-of-the-saudi-female-labor-force/.

[11] C. Montagu, 'Civil Society and the Voluntary Sector in Saudi Arabia', Middle East Journal 64, no. 1 (Winter 2010), pp. 67–83, https://www.jstor.org/stable/20622983; S. Foley, Changing Saudi Arabia: Art, Culture, and Society in the Kingdom (Boulder, CO: Lynne Rienner, 2019).

[12] K. S. Diwan, 'Mohammed bin Salman's Media Obsession—and What It Means for Dissent', Arab Gulf States Institute in Washington (30 October 2018), https://agsiw.org/mohammed-bin-salmans-media-obsessed-and-what-it-means-for-dissent/.

[13] H. Ellyatt, 'Tourism to Replace Oil Economy in Saudi Arabia?', CNBC Online (1 October 2015), https://www.cnbc.com/2015/10/01/tourism-to-replace-oil-economy-in-saudi-arabia.html.

has referred to this development approach as 'paradoxical globalization', which he defines as 'a highly filtered form of openness in which expanded state control over domestic space is achieved through global economic integration'.[14] As will be demonstrated, the centralization of state control and expansion of state investment through the Saudi sovereign wealth fund, the Public Investment Fund (PIF), certainly characterizes the current Saudi experience of launching into the global tourism market. It will be important to reflect on the contradictions this yields and the implications of this simultaneous embrace of greater cultural pluralism and openness within the Saudi context, while maintaining and even strengthening an authoritarian form of political control.[15]

Beyond Pilgrimage: The Evolution of Tourism in Saudi Arabia

Up until now, the face of Saudi tourism has been almost exclusively religious. Tourism has provided an economic stimulus to the Hejaz region since biblical times when the Prophet Ibrahim declared a pilgrimage to all mankind.[16] As Islam spread as a religion and the Prophet Muhammad formalized the Hajj pilgrimage, the level of trade and commerce grew along with it. Merchants saw an opportunity for trade and the Bedouins saw an opportunity to extract a 'tax' on the pilgrims passing through their areas. After King Abdul-Aziz joined the Kingdoms of Hejaz and Nejd to form the Kingdom of Saudi Arabia in 1932 and up until the start of the oil economy, religious tourism formed a primary pillar of the Saudi economy.

Yet even as the discovery of oil and the expansion of its exploitation fundamentally remade the Saudi state, shifting the focus of the economy eastwards to the capital and to the new oil cities of Dharan, Dammam, and Khobar, religious tourism remained important to the Saudi leadership. This was for reasons of political legitimacy, the able custodianship of the holy sites promoting domestic standing and global leadership of the Islamic community. But religious tourism also continued to be a key sector anchoring the non-oil economy and development in the west of the country. Thus, as oil revenues flowed into the country in the 1950s and then skyrocketed in the 1970s these

---

[14] W. Hazbun, *Beaches, Ruins, Resorts: The Politics of Tourism in the Arab World* (Minneapolis: University of Minnesota Press, 2008), p. 38.
[15] Ibid., pp. 71–2.
[16] F. E. Peters, *The Hajj: The Muslim Pilgrimage to Mecca and the Holy Places* (Princeton, NJ: Princeton University Press, 1994).

Figure 9.1   Mecca, *c.*1910: camel caravan of pilgrims to Mecca

Source: American Colony (Jerusalem), 'Mecca, ca. 1910. Camel caravan of pilgrims to Mecca', Library of Congress (1910), http://hdl.loc.gov/loc.pnp/matpc.04654.

resources were invested in expanding both the prophet's mosque in Medina and the grand mosque complex in Mecca to accommodate more pilgrims.

While significant, these infrastructure projects in the 1950s and again under King Fahd in the 1980s have been dwarfed by the wholesale remaking of central Mecca which occurred in the last two decades, deftly analysed by the scholar Rosie Bsheer in her work *Archive Wars* and captured in the photographic study by artist Ahmed Mater in *Desert of Pharan: Unofficial Histories behind the Mass Expansion of Mecca*.[17] Here the difficult mountain topography of Mecca itself was razed along with historic neighbourhoods and much of early Islam's material heritage in the relentless pursuit of real estate and commercial development. These multibillion-dollar enterprises—the King Abdulaziz Endowment development project to the south, the Jabal Omar development project to the west, the Al-Shammiya development project to the north—represent some of the earliest tourism megaprojects in the Kingdom. This and earlier construction, spearheaded by the Saudi leadership and executed by the Saudi Bin Laden Group partnered with other

[17] Bsheer, *Archive Wars*, pp. 177–207; A. Mater, *Desert of Pharan: Unofficial Histories behind the Mass Expansion of Mecca* (Zurich: Lars Muller, 2016).

construction firms, provided upscale investment opportunities to local and international investors, and introduced what has been described as the 'privatization of prayer space', allowing for distinct new services and religious tourism packages for pilgrims.[18] The inequalities of these developments—the mass displacement of at least 100,000 residents and catering to high-end users in addition to the mass expansion of services—were incongruous in this central site of religious pilgrimage. But they nonetheless characterize the new logic of neoliberal capitalist development and marketing taking hold in the Kingdom in the post-Gulf War era.

This post-war era also introduced the first attempts to expand and diversify tourism. First, the strict quota system regulating Hajj participation was eased, and repeat visits for religious pilgrims during non-Hajj times, or Umrah, were encouraged.[19] Later Saudi Arabia's strict limits on foreign visitors through restrictive visas began to relax. For the first time, in the period 2013–16, Saudi Arabia began offering extended Umrah tourist visas, permitting pilgrims to join organized travel packages to parts of the Kingdom outside of Mecca and Medina.[20] This presaged the more dramatic expansion of non-religious tourism and the welcoming of foreign tourists to the Kingdom initiated under King Salman and Muhammed bin Salman.

Under the Saudi Vision 2030 programme, the Kingdom is looking to build upon its intrinsic strengths as custodian of the holy sites. The ongoing importance of religious tourism is underlined through its inclusion as one of the eleven transformation programmes that translate the vision into action.[21] The *Dayouf al-Rahman* programme seeks to enhance the experience of pilgrims through big investments in both transportation and technology. These upgrades include the launch of the Haramain high-speed rail connecting Mecca and Medina to King Abdullah Economic City, Jeddah, and the King Abdelaziz International Airport (KAIA) in 2018, as well as a new airport terminal at KAIA which had a soft opening in 2019. In 2021, the 'Hajj smart card' or *Shaaer* was introduced, controlling the entry of pilgrims into various facilities, and managing personal, medical, and residential information.[22]

[18] Bsheer, *Archive Wars*, pp. 186, 194.
[19] 'Grand Plans: Sustained Focus on Raising Pilgrim Numbers and Expanding beyond Religion-Oriented Tourism', in *The Report: Saudi Arabia 2018* (London: Oxford Business Group, 2018), pp. 1–2, https://oxfordbusinessgroup.com/overview/grand-plans-sustained-focus-raising-pilgrim-numbers-and-expanding-beyond-religion-oriented-tourism.
[20] Bsheer, *Archive Wars*, p. 190; 'Grand Plans'.
[21] '*Doyof Al Rahman* Program', *Vision 2030* (accessed 14 October 2021), https://www.vision2030.gov.sa/v2030/vrps/darp/.
[22] 'Ministry of Hajj and Umrah Launches Hajj Smart Card to Enhance Technical Services for Pilgrims', Saudi Press Agency (13 July 2021), https://www.spa.gov.sa/viewfullstory.php?lang=en&newsid=2258250.

Religious tourism forms 20 per cent of non-oil gross domestic product (GDP), so ambitions to increase non-oil GDP from 16 to 50 per cent of the economy take that into account.[23] Direct government revenues from religious tourism are being generated by the introduction of pilgrimage visa fees of over $500 for return pilgrims. Pre-Covid, the Kingdom hosted 2.5 million pilgrims during the Hajj season and approximately 1 million Umrah pilgrims per month.[24] Any additional spending by these visitors to the Kingdom will result in significant economic growth for the hospitality and tourism sector. The last stage of the *Doyof Al Rahman* programme, then, looks to introduce new interactive experiences and museums along the Hajj journey, and to link religious tourists with the new secular tourist sites being developed in the Kingdom.[25] As described by Minister of Hajj and Umrah Dr Mohammed Saleh Bentin, the Saudi government seeks to enhance the pilgrim experience 'by managing the archaeological and cultural sites in our country so that pilgrims can experience a spiritual, religious and cultural journey full of faith.'[26]

The confirmation of a more fundamental shift occurred in September 2019, with the introduction, for the first time, of a tourist visa independent of either business sponsorship or pilgrimage. These new visas, permitting multiple entries and valid for a year, greatly eased travel to the Kingdom, which had long been inaccessible to most visitors. They were promoted with great fanfare as the opening of the new Saudi Arabia to the outside world, through advertising campaigns in traditional media, and notably, via the cultivation of social media influencers and entertainment personalities.[27]

The shift in visa regimen accompanied, of course, the inauguration of new tourism and heritage sites. It is hard to overstate the importance of these new tourist sites in the reign of King Salman and their centrality to the Saudi Vision 2030. Fully 50 per cent of the new 'giga projects' being developed by the PIF are in non-religious tourism, with the goal to make the overall

[23] 'Thriving Economy', Vision 2030 (accessed 4 October 2021), https://www.vision2030.gov.sa/v2030/overview/thriving-economy/.
[24] General Authority for Statistics, 'Hajj Statistics 2019' (August 2019), https://www.stats.gov.sa/sites/default/files/Hajj_40_en.pdf. Calculated from Ministry of Hajj and Umrah, 'News' (accessed 29 October 2021), https://www.Hajj.gov.sa/en/News/Details/12324.
[25] The Spiritual Journey Enrichment Program is undertaking projects such as the restoration of the Hejaz Railway, which facilitated pilgrim travel from 1908 to 1920. 'King Salman launches new program to "enrich" pilgrimage experience', *Argaam* (29 May 2019), https://www.argaam.com/en/article/articledetail/id/611794.
[26] 'Inaugurates King Salman "Guests of God Service Program"', *Arab News* (29 May 2019), https://www.arabnews.com/node/1503666/saudi-arabia.
[27] E. Gillespie, 'The Instagram Influencers Hired to Rehabilitate Saudi Arabia's Image', *The Guardian* (11 October 2019), https://www.theguardian.com/world/2019/oct/12/the-instagram-influencers-hired-to-rehabilitate-saudi-arabias-image.

tourism sector the second most important one following the hydrocarbon economy.[28] The next section will outline the major tourism projects, many along the Red Sea, presenting a new western face of Saudi development as economic diversification shifts the Kingdom's focus away from the eastern oil-producing regions.

Reimagining the Kingdom: The New Tourism Giga Projects

In her book, *Archive Wars*, Rosie Bsheer characterizes the new Saudi economic and political order that has emerged since the Gulf War: more globally engaged, less tied to traditional religious foundations, and assertively capitalizing on land as resource.[29] This new political orientation has freed the Saudi leadership to pursue touristic projects once frowned upon by religious authorities—among them heritage sites venerating the Al Saud, pre-Islamic sites, and beach resorts—all enhanced by new arts and entertainment events once unthinkable in the Kingdom. These include United Nations Educational, Scientific and Cultural Organization (UNESCO) world heritage sites, such as the location of the first Saudi state in Diriyah, and the pre-Islamic archaeological site of Mada'in Salih, or Hejra, which anchors the AlUla touristic region. The touristic giga projects, so named due to their enormous size and comprehensive development, include the new luxury beach developments along the Red Sea coast, and the planned entertainment city south of Riyadh, Qiddiya.

In addition to these UNESCO sites and giga projects, there are numerous other prominent tourism initiatives occurring in almost every region of the Kingdom. Some capitalize on sites of historical significance such as the controversial restoration of Lawrence of Arabia's house in Yanbu.[30] Others playfully subvert the image of the Saudi oil state, like the Rig, a project to convert an offshore oil platform in the Persian Gulf into an adventure amusement destination.[31] Another state-owned company, Soudah Development,

[28] Public Investment Fund, 'Our Investments—Giga Projects' (accessed 29 October 2021), https://www.pif.gov.sa/en/Pages/OurInvestments-GigaProjects.aspx.

[29] Bsheer, p. 142.

[30] S. Salama, 'Saudi Arabia: Lawrence of Arabia's Home Restored as Tourist Attraction after Decades of Neglect', *Gulf News* (8 September 2020), https://gulfnews.com/world/gulf/saudi/saudi-arabia-lawrence-of-arabias-home-restored-as-tourist-attraction-after-decades-of-neglect-1.73691299.

[31] Public Investment Fund, 'PIF Announces "THE RIG" Project, the World's First Tourism Destination on Offshore Platforms' (accessed 15 October 2021), https://www.pif.gov.sa/en/Pages/NewsDetails.aspx?NewsId=203.

has been established to coordinate the tourism initiatives in the mountainous Asir region, capitalizing on its natural beauty and distinct culture.[32]

Overall, these projects are the main engine for expanding the tourism sector. Saudi investments to initiate them and to prepare the infrastructure are proposed to pass $1 trillion over the next ten years: an astounding figure and a measure of the emphasis placed on this sector.[33] As one can see in the descriptions that follow, many of these new tourism sites are akin to new cities, with multi-use development plans incorporating hotels, restaurants, entertainment and arts venues, as well as housing. When taken altogether, and especially in consideration with the futuristic city of Neom to be built in the upper reaches of the Red Sea closer to Jordanian, Israeli, and Egyptian tourist developments, they project an image of a post-oil future for the Kingdom.

As we will see, the existing sites and projects are animated through the scheduling of entertainment festivals and sports and art events, often drawing from the nascent cultural movements that once operated at the margins in the Kingdom. The marketing of these tourism opportunities leans heavily on local character and new media images, providing opportunities to project a more youthful and nationalist Saudi Arabia.

Figure 9.2 The restored Hejaz train

Source: Crystal Eye Studio (date unknown)

---

[32] Soudah Development, 'Home' (accessed 2 November 2021), https://soudah.sa/?lang=en.

[33] This figure was proposed by the Saudi Tourism Minister, Ahmed al-Khateeb, at the 2021 Saudi Foreign Investment Initiative in Riyadh. M. Nahal, 'FII: Saudi Arabia Plans to Invest $1tn in Tourism over 10 Years', *The National* (26 October 2021), https://www.thenationalnews.com/business/2021/10/26/saudi-arabia-plans-to-invest-1tn-in-tourism-over-10-years/.

Diriyah: The 'Home of Kings'

Situated to the north-west of Riyadh along the Wadi Hanifa ravine, Diriyah played an essential role in the early history of the Kingdom. It was the capital of the first Saudi state established in 1744, and the site of the historic pact between the political leader Muhammed ibn Saud and the religious revivalist Muhammed ibn Abd al-Wahhab that secured the future state's royal and religious character.

One would assume that a site so foundational to its early history would have been preserved by the Saudi leadership. But this is not the case. Indeed, Diriyah was utterly neglected, its adobe buildings and alleyways allowed to fall into almost complete collapse. The first stage of its restoration was begun only in the 1990s under the watchful eyes of Riyadh's then governor, the current King Salman.[34] The historic Turaif district was inscribed as a UNESCO world heritage site in 2010 and partially opened to the public in 2017.[35] The main tourist infrastructure of parking, restaurants, parks, and public spaces is situated in its sister district across the Wadi Hanifa, al-Bujairi, which was given an emotional public opening by King Salman months after coming to power in 2015.[36]

Domestically, the revival of Diriyah alongside other historical sites in Riyadh associated with the monarchy stands to elevate the Al Saud within a new nationalist narrative, now notably free of its Wahhabi associations. This was made explicit in January 2022 through the inauguration of a new national holiday, Saudi Founding Day, which shifts the foundational moment of the Saudi state from the traditional date of 1744, the year of the pact established between Al Saud and the religious revivalist Muhammed ibn Abd al-Wahhab, to 1727, the beginning of the reign of Mohammed ibn Saud, the progenitor of the Saudi dynasty.[37] Internationally, this 'Home of Kings' is central to the rebranding of the nation's capital, the iconic image of its partially restored adobe palaces compared by the Diriyah Gate Development Authority (DGDA) chief executive officer (CEO) Jerry Inzerillo to other must-see historic tourist destinations: 'It is to Saudi Arabia what the Acropolis is to the Greeks, what the Colosseum is to Rome, what Machu Picchu is to Peruvians.

---

[34] Bsheer, p. 156.

[35] UNESCO, 'At-Turaif District in ad-Dir'iyah' (accessed 2 November 2021), https://whc.unesco.org/en/list/1329/.

[36] B. al-Shareeda, 'King Salman Opens the Bujairi Development within the Historic Diriya Project', *Asharq al-Awsat* (10 April 2015), https://aawsat.com/home/article/332931/الدرعية-التاريخيةالملك-سلمان-يفتتح-مشروع-تطوير-«البجيري»-ضمن-برنامج.

[37] S. Alamer, 'The Saudi "Founding Day" and the Death of Wahhabism', AGSIW (23 February 2022), https://agsiw.org/the-saudi-founding-day-and-the-death-of-wahhabism/.

So when people come to the Gulf, they're going to want to see where it all started—the home of the House of Saud.'[38]

The DGDA, established in 2017, marks a second stage of development of Diriyah beyond its heritage status.[39] CEO Inzerillo's background—launching his career in Las Vegas; heading the luxury resort developer Kerzner International, which operates destinations such as Atlantis Dubai; CEO of IMG Artists and later of the Forbes travel guide—is indicative of the new direction towards high-end property development, entertainment, and global tourism. Upon completion, Diriyah is expected to feature numerous art and historical museums, more than twenty hotels, retail, over 100 places to dine, as well as offices and residential housing for a permanent population of 100,000.[40] The commitment of the Saudi leadership to this project has not wavered, its starting budget of $27 billion nearly doubled to $40 billion in June 2021 to expand the vision and attract more tourists in a shorter period.[41]

In addition to being anchored as a heritage site, Diriyah epitomizes the new role that art and culture is playing within the Kingdom. This district on the outskirts of Riyadh is set to house offices of the Ministry of Culture, which has recently established eleven specialized commissions to promote the expansion of the creative fields, from film to architecture to design. In addition to a dedicated arts district, Diriyah has been flagged as host of the Saudi Museum of Contemporary Art (SAMoCA).[42] In this new capacity, it hosts international events such as the Diriyah Contemporary Arts Biennale to be held on alternate years to the Islamic Arts Bienanale in the warehouses of the new arts district south of Diriyah known as JAX.[43]

---

[38] 'Saudi Arabia Wants to Move from Oil to Tourism with Series of "Giga Projects"', *Globetrender* (3 December 2020), https://globetrender.com/2020/12/03/saudi-arabia-tourism-giga-projects/; Frank Kane, 'Saudi Arabia Doubling Down on Diriyah Gate Project, Says DGDA CEO', *Zaywa* (13 June 2021), https://www.zawya.com/mena/en/business/story/Saudi_Arabia_doubling_down_on_Diriyah_Gate_project_says_DGDA_CEO-SNG_216932421/.

[39] 'Cornerstone for Iconic Diriyah Gate Project to Be Laid Today', *Saudi Gazette* (19 November 2019), https://saudigazette.com.sa/article/582949.

[40] The property development extends into the surrounding environs with plans to plant a million date trees in the Wadi Hanifah and to transform the nearby Safar Valley into 'Riyadh's own Beverly Hills'.

[41] Kane, 'Saudi Arabia Doubling Down'; Gavin Gibbon, 'Saudi's $20bn Diriyah Gate on Schedule to Attract "Millions" of Visitors', *Arabian Business* (19 November 2020), https://www.arabianbusiness.com/travel-hospitality/454865-saudis-20bn-diriyah-gate-on-schedule-to-attract-millions-of-visitors. According to CEO Inzerillo, the completion of the first phase of DGDA is scheduled for late 2021, with estimates that it will create up to 55,000 job opportunities and contribute SAR27 billion ($7.2 billion) to Saudi GDP by 2030.

[42] D. Dudley, 'Saudi Arabia Joins the Gulf's Culture Race with Plans for Modern Art Museum', *Forbes* (22 October 2019), https://www.forbes.com/sites/dominicdudley/2019/10/22/saudi-modern-art-museum/?sh=2eead6ed5790. These plans have been in flux, as have those for a new Islamic museum.

[43] G. Harris, 'Artists Announced for Saudi Arabia's First Ever Contemporary Art Biennial', *Art Newspaper* (24 September 2021), https://www.theartnewspaper.com/2021/09/24/artists-announced-for-saudi-arabias-first-ever-contemporary-art-biennial.

Also flagged as an educational district, there are plans for a new university in Diriyah, named after King Salman and focused on tourism and hospitality, as well as several new academies teaching arts including calligraphy and Islamic arts, Najdi architecture, Najdi cuisine, theatre, and Arab music.[44] Diriyah has also become a premier location for the Saudi hosting of international sports events, including Formula E racing on a track built within sight of the Salwa palace ruins, a men's tennis tournament, an international World Cup equestrian event which for the first time allowed the participation of women, and a world heavyweight boxing title fight, marketed as 'The Clash on the Dunes'. These sporting events were matched by music concerts of international artists such as Pitbull, Future, Akon, Calvin Harris, and the Swedish House Mafia.[45] All of this is a striking departure from Diriyah's conservative patrimony as the historic centre of Wahhabi propagation, now effectively erased.[46]

AlUla: A Pre-Islamic History Revived

A second UNESCO world heritage site, the ancient city of Mada'in Salih or Hegra, anchors the new touristic region of AlUla. This region in the northwest of the Kingdom north of Medina boasts a spectacular natural setting of desert and oasis landscapes with striking geological formations. The impressive archaeological site of Hegra, the southernmost city of the Nabatean civilization, is similar to its sister city in Petra, Jordan, bearing over 100 tombs with elaborate façades carved in stone. Though inscribed by UNESCO in 2008, it long remained inaccessible to visitors, in part due to the disapproval of religious authorities for pre-Islamic sites. That is now changing dramatically, with Hegra and the wider region of AlUla being prioritized as a second cultural capital of the Kingdom and postcard for the new Saudi touristic aspirations.

The development objectives for touristic offerings in the AlUla governate are many: from the archaeological and cultural, to adventure and wellness. To develop the AlUla region and deepen its cultural positioning, the Royal Commission of AlUla (RCU) signed a partnership agreement with the French government, establishing the French Agency for AlUla (Afalula) in Paris in

---

[44] 'Diriya Gate Concept', presentation of the DGDA authority, 2020.
[45] Diriyah Season, 'Sports & Entertainment' (accessed 2 November 2021), https://diriyahseason.sa/en/events.html.
[46] K. Diwan, 'Rethinking Diriyah: Heritage and Entertainment in the New Saudi Nationalism', paper presented to the Gulf Research Meeting, Cambridge, UK, 23–4 July 2021.

July 2018.[47] This partnership is working to develop AlUla into an 'open air living museum' preserving its cultural and natural resources, drawing upon French expertise and industry in culture, archaeology, tourism, and environment.[48] Some early indications of this collaboration and its direction can be seen not only in the ongoing archaeological work but also in the partnership between the RCU and French architect Jean Nouvel to build a luxury resort within the newly established Sharaan nature reserve near Hegra.[49] The innovative design, sculpted within the stone landscape, will present a landmark wellness destination for high-end clientele, and an international summit centre, complementing the early construction of the mirrored Maraya concert hall which has already hosted musical events as well as state visits. This and other high-end hotel projects are in the works and not scheduled for opening before 2024.

Early marketing of the region also draws upon its attraction for nature and adventure tourists, promoting hiking trails, climbing routes, and dune buggy rides.[50] These promotions have also been supported through collaborations and attention-grabbing events such as serving as a stop for the 2021 Dakar rally and hosting the first ever EXTREME X Desert X Prix race featuring electric sport utility vehicles in extreme environments.[51] Other international partnerships have advanced its cultural agenda, such as the launch of a site-responsive art exhibition with the California-based Desert X organization in 2020, representing an important collaboration between international and Saudi artists.[52]

Despite the clear appeal of the landscape and archaeological attractions, the challenge of executing a project on this scale in a remote region covering some 23,000 square kilometres and without much pre-existing tourism infrastructure is formidable. At this early stage, tourism has been concentrated in a defined season—the Winter at Tantoura—a nearly three-month

[47] Afalula, 'The Journey Through Time Masterplan Marks a Major Step in Protecting and Sharing the AlUla Cultural and Heritage Site with the World' (7 April 2021), https://www.afalula.com/en/journey-through-time-masterplan/.

[48] Afalula, 'French Agency for AlUla Development' (2 November 2021), https://www.afalula.com/en/french-agency-for-alula-development/.

[49] M. Benmansour and R. Jalabi, 'Archaeologists in Saudi Arabia Excavate Forgotten Kingdoms', Reuters (2 November 2021), https://www.reuters.com/world/middle-east/archaeologists-saudi-arabia-excavate-forgotten-kingdoms-2021-11-02/; Royal Commission for AlUla, Royal Commission for AlUla, 'Sharaan Resort' (accessed 2 November 2021), https://www.rcu.gov.sa/en/fact-sheets/sharaan-resort/.

[50] Visit Saudi, 'Exploring AlUla' (accessed 2 November 2021), https://www.visitsaudi.com/en/see-do/destinations/alula.

[51] Extreme E, 'Desert X Prix' (accessed 2 November 2021), https://www.extreme-e.com/en/events/desert-xprix.

[52] Desert X, 'Desert X AlUla' (accessed 2 November 2021), https://desertx.org/dx/desert-x-alula.

festival held in December 2018 and 2019.[53] Here the paucity of beds and services was managed by bringing in tents and restaurant pop-ups to meet the temporary demand.

Another pathway to increase capital investment beyond that being deployed by the state is to encourage buy-in and investment from existing property owners in AlUla. This can be seen in phase 1 for residential and commercial permits announced in 2020, which requires adherence to extensive design principles and regulations established by the RCU.[54] Another important step was taken in 2021 to increase the capacity of the existing Prince Abdul Majeed Bin Abdulaziz Airport by 400 per cent and to begin receiving international flights.

Though relatively remote, AlUla could be complementary to the range of other tourist destinations and urban projects being developed along the Red Sea coast of Saudi Arabia. One could imagine synergies developing among these massive state infrastructure projects, with the newly planned technology city of Neom as well as the religious pilgrimage cities of Mecca and Medina, also in the west.

Amaala and the Red Sea Project: Bringing Beach Tourism to the Kingdom

In addition to the cultural capitals of Diriyah and AlUla, the Saudi government is pursuing two new tourism 'giga projects' along the western coast: the Red Sea Project and Amaala. These massive developmental areas occupy the coastline between Neom and King Abdullah Economic City and will introduce a form of beach and ecotourism once taboo to the Kingdom.[55] These are being promoted as 'green projects' with a focus on environmental sustainability and preservation, renewable energy use, and water conservation, albeit still within a luxury tourism package.[56]

The area placed under the auspices of the Red Sea Project Development Company encompasses 28,000 square kilometres—an area the size of Belgium—composed of beaches, over ninety islands, mountains, canyons,

---

[53] Experience AlUla, 'Events & Festivals' (accessed 2 November 2021), https://www.experiencealula.com/en/past-events-festivals.

[54] 'Saudi's RCU Announces Details on Phase 1 of South Al-Ula Development', *Construction Week* (8 March 2020), https://www.constructionweekonline.com/projects-tenders/263485-saudis-rcu-reveals-details-on-phase-1-of-south-al-ula-development.

[55] Saudi Center for International Communication, 'Public Investment Fund Unveils Amaala, a New Global Leading Destination for Wellness Tourism' (26 September 2018), https://cic.org.sa/2018/09/public-investment-fund-unveils-amaala-a-new-global-leading-destination-for-wellness-tourism/.

[56] D. Barbuscia and S. Azhar, 'Saudi Red Sea Tourism Project to Raise up to $2.7bln "Green" Loan Next Year', Reuters (21 September 2021), https://www.reuters.com/world/middle-east/saudi-red-sea-tourism-project-raise-up-27-bln-green-loan-next-year-2021-09-21/.

dormant volcanoes, and the world's fourth largest barrier reef system.[57] Current plans call for twenty-two of the islands to be developed for tourism, while around 75 per cent of them will be untouched and nine will be designated as special conservation sites. Indeed, the Red Sea Project is being marketed as 'the world's most ambitious regenerative tourism project', highlighting plans to preserve and enhance the environment within the site including its coral reefs.[58]

According to the masterplan, the Red Sea Project will eventually include fifty hotels and resorts offering up to 8,000 hotel rooms and around 1,300 residential properties, in addition to retail, entertainment, and leisure spaces to include golf courses and marinas.[59] The first phase of the project is already under way with plans to deliver sixteen hotels along with a new international airport that will serve the region, with the potential to welcome guests by the end of 2023.[60] In this first phase, the site hopes to attract around 300,000 visitors a year, with contracts already awarded for hotels on Shrayah and Ummahat AlShaykh islands, as well as the southern dunes and an inland location nearer to the airport.[61] There are also infrastructural sub-projects within the Red Sea Project, such as the 100-hectare Landscape Nursery, which is already operational and will provide more that 15 million plants for the project site, a waste management facility, and an accommodation village for construction staff with a medical facility.[62] So far, over 80 kilometres of roads have been paved, including the airport road, and the construction village, set to house 10,000 employees, is complete.[63]

[57] Red Sea Development Company, 'Destination' (accessed 21 October 2021), https://www.theredsea.sa/en/destination.

[58] Red Sea Development Company, 'The Red Sea Development Company Commences Hotel Construction with Award of Two Key Contracts' (3 February 2021), https://www.theredsea.sa/en/media-center/news/trsdc-commences-hotel-construction-with-award-of-two-key-contracts.

[59] Red Sea Development Company, 'The Red Sea Development Company Commences Hotel Construction'.

[60] S. Azhar and M. Rashad, 'Saudi Red Sea Project Plans 16 Hotels by 2023, Finalizing $3.7bln Loan—CEO', Reuters (12 November 2020), https://www.reuters.com/article/saudi-redsea-tourism/saudi-red-sea-project-plans-16-hotels-by-2023-finalising-3-7-bln-loan-ceo-idUSL4N2HW36W.

[61] T. Ravenscroft, 'Foster + Partners Designs Coral Bloom Resort on Saudi Arabian Island', Dezeen (11 February 2021), https://www.dezeen.com/2021/02/11/coral-bloom-resort-foster-partners-red-sea-development-company-saudi-arabia/; A. Williams, 'Luxury Resort Will Sleep Hotel Guests Inside an Arabian Mountain', New Atlas (29 September 2021), https://newatlas.com/architecture/oppenheim-desert-rock-hotel-resort/; T. Ravenscroft, 'Foster & Partners' Hotel to Be Built amongst Saudi Arabian Sand Dunes', Dezeen (23 February 2021), https://www.dezeen.com/2021/02/23/foster-partners-southern-dunes-hotel-saudi-arabia-the-red-sea-project/.

C. Carlson, 'Kengo Kuma and Foster + Partners Designing "World's Most Ambitious Tourism Development" in Saudi Arabia', Dezeen (4 November 2020), https://www.dezeen.com/2020/11/04/red-sea-project-kengo-kuma-foster-partners-tourism-saudi-arabia/.

[62] 'SAU: Contracts Signed for a 100-Hectare Landscape Nursery', Floral Daily (10 September 2019), https://www.floraldaily.com/article/9142248/sau-contracts-signed-for-a-100-hectare-landscape-nursery/.

[63] Red Sea Development Company, 'Development Progress' (21 October 2021), https://www.theredsea.sa/en/project/development-progress.

Though similar in many ways, Amaala promises a more refined experience, promising a 'transformative personal journey inspired by the arts, wellness and the purity of the Red Sea'.[64] The Amaala site spans 4,155 square kilometres within the Prince Mohammad bin Salman Natural Reserve, making it much smaller than its southern neighbour.[65]

The first phase of Amaala is set to open in mid-2024, with six hotels and around 1,000 rooms, while the entire project—comprising 3,000 hotel rooms in approximately twenty-five hotels—is expected to be ready by 2027.[66] The plans call for three distinct developments. The Island, located right off the coast, will comprise gardens, private villas, beach-front resorts, an artist village with studios and exhibition spaces, and plenty of outdoor facilities (equestrian, golf, and eco-diving).[67] Triple Bay, on the southern edge of Amaala, will feature mountains and seascapes, and will be more centred on its coral reefs with a state-funded Marine Life Institute partnering with the Monaco Foundation to study the impact of human activity on the marine environment.[68] Lastly, the Coastal Development aims to become yet another centre for arts in the Middle East and will feature a contemporary art museum, a cultural village, hotels, villas, and a golf course.[69]

The project aims to operate with a zero-carbon footprint, though Foster + Partners, the firm behind the Red Sea Project and Amaala airports, came under fire for violating the terms of the Architects Declare movement, which aims to demand more sustainable architectural practices. Though Foster + Partners chose to leave the movement and to continue with its plans to build the airport, this episode sheds light on the tension inherent in developing touristic sites from scratch in remote areas while aiming to be sustainable.[70]

Qiddiya: Riyadh's New Entertainment City

Perhaps more than any other tourism project, Qiddiya epitomizes the new intent of Vision 2030 to provide two things long neglected in the Kingdom: entertainment and an improvement in quality of life. Situated just 40 kilometres south of the capital city, the opening of this family-oriented resort

---

[64] Amaala, 'Home' (accessed 21 October 2021), https://www.amaala.com/en/home.

[65] 'Royal Reserves to Be New Tourist Attractions', *Saudi Gazette* (2 June 2018), https://saudigazette.com.sa/article/536138.

[66] Amaala, 'About Us' (accessed 21 October 2021), https://www.amaala.com/en/about-us.

[67] Amaala, 'The Island' (accessed 21 October 2021), https://www.amaala.com/en/master-plans/theisland.

[68] 'Amaala Partners with Monaco Foundation to Protect and Preserve Marine Environment', *Saudi Gazette* (4 October 2019), https://saudigazette.com.sa/article/578986; Amaala, 'Triple Bay' (accessed 21 October 2021), https://www.amaala.com/en/master-plans/triplebay.

[69] Amaala, 'The Coastal Development' (accessed on 21 October 2021), https://www.amaala.com/en/master-plans/coastal-development.

[70] S. Pires, 'Architects Worldwide Declare a Climate + Biodiversity Emergency and Are Doing Something About It', My Modern Met (3 January 2021), https://mymodernmet.com/architects-declare/.

and sports complex is seeking to encourage Saudis to spend more of their money on sports and entertainment, and to spend it at home.

The masterplan for Qiddiya, approved in 2019, covers some 334 square kilometres, an area almost three times larger than Disney World Florida, which would make it the world's largest entertainment city.[71] Of the total area, one-third is designated for development, leaving the rest for natural conservation. Qiddiya is to be another integrated mixed-use development offering immersive experiences under five themes: Parks & Attractions, Sports & Wellness, Motion & Mobility, Art & Culture, and Nature & Environment. The heart of Qiddiya entertainment city will be the largest Six Flags Parks to date, featuring twenty-nine rides and attractions spread over six different themed areas.[72]

Like most of the giga projects in the Kingdom, the expectations for the project's economic impact are ambitious. The Saudi government targets for the number of annual visitors to Qiddiya by 2030 are 17 million visitors for the entertainment sector, 12 million for the shopping sector, and 2 million for the hospitality sector. If the project proceeds as planned, it is expected to contribute to up to $4.5 billion of GDP by 2030 and to create 57,000 jobs.[73]

Reimagining the State: The New Tourism Administration

As demonstrated, the new tourism giga projects and initiatives mark an expansive—and expensive—push for land and touristic development that seeks to reimagine vast areas of the Kingdom. All of this is being executed by an array of new governmental institutions that reflect an equivalent reimagining of the Saudi state. Consonant with other political changes within the Kingdom, this reorganization places decision making and financial directives under the ultimate control of Crown Prince Muhammed bin Salman.

The tourism strategy being envisioned from the top is state designed and, at this early stage, state funded. Its planning and implementation are being executed by newly established ministries and authorities, with some projects delegated to developmental companies and royal commissions. Other equally new authorities charged with invigorating arts and culture and planning entertainment are playing an important supportive role. The once-passive sovereign wealth fund, flush with funds from the initial public offering of

---

[71] Qiddiya, 'About Qiddiya' (accessed 2 November 2021), https://qiddiya.com/en/about-qiddiya/what-is-qiddiya/.

[72] O. Ralph, 'Six Flags Qiddiya to Bring Year-Round Thrills to Saudi Arabia', Blooloop (30 January 2020), https://blooloop.com/features/six-flags-qiddiya/; Qiddiya, 'About Qiddiya'.

[73] Public Investment Fund, 'Al Qiddiya Fact Sheet' (accessed on 2 November 2021), https://www.pif.gov.sa/en/MediaCenter/NewsAttachments/Al-Qiddiya_Factsheet_EN.pdf. For comparison, Walt Disney World, including all of its constituent parks, employs 77,000.

Aramco and the acquisition of Saudi Arabia's Basic Industries Corporation, is the vehicle for driving most of these new projects and investments. The fact that the PIF, sometimes directly or through companies it owns, often oversees and finances construction raises questions about the initial—and perhaps future—(im)balance between state and private sector involvement.

Tourism within Vision 2030

The overall place of tourism within the state transformation project is defined and contextualized in Vision 2030.[74] This strategic blueprint for the Kingdom's future is built on three pillars identified as Saudi Arabia's comparative advantage: its place in the heartland of Arab and Islamic worlds, its economic positioning as a hub among three continents, and its prodigious investment capability, now pledged to diversifying the economy. These strengths are to be drawn upon in advancing the vision for the Kingdom's future, which is itself organized around three themes: a vibrant society, a thriving economy, and an ambitious nation.

Tourism and entertainment are woven within all of these, drawing upon the pillars of identity, global connectivity, and state investment, and underlying many of the concrete targets enumerated to advance the Vision themes by the year 2030. Examples within the Vision 2030 document abound: targets to increase the capacity of Umrah visitors, double the number of UNESCO heritage sites, and more than double household spending on cultural and entertainment activities. Other targets—increasing women's participation in the workforce, attracting more foreign direct investment (FDI), and increasing non-oil government revenue—are to be advanced in part through the tourism sector. Tourism is also a primary or secondary target of several of the eleven established Vision Realization Programs designed to translate the Vision into action.[75] Examples include the previously discussed *Dayof Al Rahman* programme to upgrade and expand religious tourism, and the Quality of Life programme to improve individual lifestyles by developing an ecosystem to enhance participation in cultural, environment, and sports activities.

The centrality of tourism within this strategic blueprint becomes even more apparent when examining the portfolio of investments of the PIF, the

---

[74] Vision 2030, 'Vision 2030—Kingdom of Saudi Arabia' (accessed 29 November 2021), https://www.vision2030.gov.sa/media/rc0b5oy1/saudi_vision203.pdf.
[75] Vision 2030, 'Vision Realization Programs' (accessed 29 November 2021), https://www.vision2030.gov.sa/v2030/vrps/.

sovereign wealth fund tasked with 'leading the charge to create new sectors, companies and jobs, and achieve Vision 2030's objectives'.[76] Here, as mentioned before, two of the four PIF giga projects—the Red Sea Project and Qiddiya—are focused on tourism and entertainment, while the third, Neom city, has several tourism components. Beyond the giga projects, the PIF is advancing diversification by establishing companies which it fully owns. Many of these are directed towards strategic tourism projects, including the already discussed Qiddiya investment company, the Red Sea Development Company, and Amaala, as well as two newer companies in the southern Abha region and the eastern Gulf respectively: the Al Soudah Development Company and the Rig. In addition, the PIF has recently established Cruise Saudi, which has already begun offering cruises in the Red Sea. These connect Jeddah with the Red Sea port being positioned as the gateway to AlUla, AlWajh, and on to stops in Jordan and Egypt, realizing the Saudi ambition to connect its Red Sea coast with the other tourist hubs in the region.[77] Plans are in the works to expand cruise options to other ports, including Dammam in the Persian Gulf.

Royal Commissions and Royal Reserves

Another institutional vehicle for advancing tourism objectives is the royal commissions. The Kingdom of Saudi Arabia has a long history of establishing these commissions to focus on economic development and industrialization for a special purpose. For example, the Royal Commission for Jubail and Yanbu and the Royal Commission for Riyadh City were created for urban development and economic expansion. In July 2017, the Saudi government formed the RCU, charged with both protecting and reinvigorating the AlUla region into a world-class tourist destination that highlights Saudi Arabia's diverse history and culture.[78] At the same time, the royal order to establish the DGDA was issued, delegating to it the task of extensive development plans to expand the cultural and tourism districts abutting the al-Turaif heritage site outside Riyadh. While all the tourism development companies fall under the management of the PIF chaired by the Crown Prince, this assignment holds

[76] Public Investment Fund, 'About PIF' (accessed 29 November 2021), https://www.pif.gov.sa/en/Pages/AboutPIF.aspx.
[77] Cruise Saudi, 'Home' (accessed 29 November 2021), https://www.cruisesaudi.com.
[78] 'King Salman Appoints Commissions to Develop Al-Ola and Diriyah Gate into Major Tourist Attractions', Business Wire (25 July 2017), https://www.businesswire.com/news/home/20170725005989/en/King-Salman-Appoints-Commissions-to-Develop-Al-Ola-and-Diriyah-Gate-into-Major-Tourist-Attractions.

these two areas—central to the overall tourism project and encompassing more sensitive political and heritage sites—closer to royal authority. Another royal commission has been established for Mecca City and the holy sites.

Other lands have been placed under conservation and royal authority through the Council of Royal Reserves which was established in 2018, again under the chairmanship of Crown Prince Mohammed bin Salman.[79] This new council manages both existing land reserves and others that are newly established, such as the Mohammed bin Salman reserve near Amaala. Other nature reserves, such as the Sharaan nature reserve near Mada'in Salah and the Wadi Safar near Diriyah, abut new tourist sites and will be drawn into tourism plans, such as the luxury hotel by Jean Nouvel planned for the Sharaan nature reserve.

In a much quieter effort, a Heritage Commission within the Ministry of Culture is evaluating smaller but culturally significant heritage locations and archaeological sites across the Kingdom. Rather than relying on direct government funding, the Heritage Commission is attempting to revive, restore, and operate these sites through public–private partnership mechanisms. As of early 2021 the commission had identified nineteen potential sites that could be attractive to investors.[80] The Heritage Commission faces a difficult challenge in competing with giga projects such as Diriyah Gate and AlUla, and, as is often the case with large projects in the Kingdom, there are conflicts of interest, overlapping goals, and duplication of efforts.

The Governmental Infrastructure for Tourism

The new prominence of tourism within the economy and the more comprehensive approach to the sector have been met by both an elevation and an overhaul of the governmental bodies dealing with it. The state agency overseeing tourism had already seen a number of evolutions since the establishment in 2000 of the Supreme Commission for Tourism, placed under the leadership of Salman bin Abdelaziz's son, Prince Sultan. In 2008, antiquities were added to its portfolio, and then in 2015 it underwent another reorganization, being renamed the Saudi Commission for Tourism and National Heritage. These authorities were reshuffled only a few years later, when in

[79] Ministry of Interior, 'Royal Orders Issued' (3 June 2018), https://www.moi.gov.sa/wps/portal/Home/sectors/moidiwan/contents/!ut/p/z0/tY49D4IwEIb_CgsjuSttCoxo_CYx4iB2IQ02WmNLQIL-fC kuRmeXy93zvrk8IOBIkHLEOE44FCCs7PVZdrq28jbcR8FLXDG2JCzcxHTKMOX5LtpmC4JRCHtlYQ3 is7Sl6WwozbMkT5CsCLov-to0IgVR1bZTzw4KU2vvpB_S-ujWS22UN4a282TrowM-WvW4v-cAq4vu1 VgvHSlDGiANQiT8VMr2W-PX9U8agwNypxFLp2HE5NabQ_oCf_d4VQ!!/.
[80] Ministry of Culture, internal document (February 2021).

2018 the King established a new Ministry of Culture which brought heritage under its authority. At this time, Prince Sultan ended his long association with heritage and tourism. Instead, a close confidant from Prince Mohammed bin Salman's inner circle, Prince Badr ibn Farhan Al Saud, was appointed the country's first Minister of Culture. In the next two years, Saudi Arabia would elevate tourism even higher in importance, creating a new Ministry of Tourism in 2020 and launching a National Tourism Strategy, seeking to increase the GDP contribution of the sector from 3 per cent to 10 per cent, and to create a million new jobs by 2030.[81]

The Ministry of Tourism is responsible for overall strategy, planning, and regulation, and coordinates with other public and private sector institutions. An intergovernmental body, the Tourism Development Council, aligns policies among relevant ministries such as Planning, Labor, Transport, Culture, Hajj, and Environment as well as municipal bodies. A Tourism Development Fund, established in June 2020 and endowed with an initial capital base of $4 billion, aims to attract and support tourism investment in partnership with the private sector. Finally, a separate Saudi Tourism Authority is the more public face of tourism promotion, dealing with branding and marketing, and interfacing with international destination management companies.

The Arts and Entertainment

As mentioned previously, the rise in tourism as a priority has been accompanied by the elevation of the arts and entertainment within the Kingdom. Indeed, one should consider these fields holistically, as key elements of public life that were not only neglected but shunned in the previous order.

To understand the evolution of entertainment in the Kingdom and how dramatic this new opening is one could consider the history of cinema within the Kingdom. The first movie theatre in the Gulf Cooperation Council (GCC) was opened in Bahrain in 1926. While other Gulf countries slowly introduced cinemas, in the Kingdom cinemas were restricted primarily to supporting the entertainment needs of the growing oil industry and its Western workers. Prior to 1983 there were many makeshift cinemas in Saudi Arabia.[82] These were improvised and served mostly the construction camps

[81] 'Saudi Arabia Hires Former WTTC Chief to Help Drive Tourism Ambitions', *Arabian Business* (21 May 2021), https://www.arabianbusiness.com/travel-hospitality/463626-saudi-arabia-hires-former-wttc-ceo-to-help-drive-tourism-ambitions.
[82] Y. Admon, 'Revival of Cinema Sparks Debate in Saudi Arabia', Middle East Media Research Institute (11 March 2010), https://www.memri.org/reports/revival-cinema-sparks-debate-saudi-arabia.

involved in the major infrastructure programmes under way at the time, usually held outdoors and screening movie releases catering to the country of origin of the residents.[83] While they were often attended by Saudi families living on the compound, there was little economic benefit from these cinematic adventures.

On 20 November 1979, Islamist militants seized control of the Grand Mosque in Mecca.[84] The government response to appease the cultural unease expressed by this event set back the advancement of entertainment in the Kingdom for the next thirty-five years. In the aftermath, all cinemas were closed, pictures of women were banned in print, and further gender segregation was imposed on society. Materials were censored by the authorities and edited to conform with strict Islamic values. By 1983, all public showing of movies was banned. Entertainment was confined to small gatherings and in-home video watching. During this period live entertainment consisted of traditional dancing, singing, Koran recitals, and poetry readings. Within the borders of Saudi Arabia these events were segregated along gender lines and had very little, if any, economic impact as most were held at private venues.

This began to change slowly under the reign of King Abdullah. A small film festival in July 2006 opened in Jeddah, under the title of the Jeddah Visual Shows Festival.[85] Such efforts were met with resistance from the religious clerics and others. Proposals at the Shoura Council and other forums to open cinemas were quickly defeated. After that there were a number of film festivals and in 2009 the first official screening of a Saudi-made movie, *Menahi*. Below the surface, however, a new generation was active, making entertainment and commentary online. The Telfaz 11 and U-Turn collectives, specializing in short skit comedy and based in Riyadh and Jeddah respectively, were finding vast audiences through YouTube and other media, demonstrating the talent, appetite, and commercial viability of this new entertainment percolating below the official bans. Informal arts salons headed by prominent artists such as Abdelnasser Algharam and Ahmed Mater were also attracting attention and nurturing creative communities.[86]

Today there is a recognition that arts and entertainment must flourish as animators of the new Saudi opening and presentation to the world and as

[83] L. Fallin, personal diary, 1979–85, Jeddah, Saudi Arabia. For example, during the period 1978–83 the Hochtief AG compound on the site of the King Abdul-Aziz International Airport typically showed movies on Thursday night (the weekend was Thursday–Friday at that time) of German or American origin.

[84] R. Lacey, *Inside the Kingdom: Kings, Clerics, Modernists, Terrorists, and the Struggle for Saudi Arabia* (London: Hutchinson, 2009).

[85] Admon, 'Revival of Cinema'.

[86] S. Foley, *Changing Saudi Arabia: Art, Culture, and Society in the Kingdom* (Boulder, CO: Lynne Rienner, 2021).

attractions for tourism offerings. These areas are being promoted by two new governmental bodies—the Ministry of Culture and the General Entertainment Authority (GEA)—whose priority is signalled by individuals from the Crown Prince's innermost circle being tapped for their leadership.

The Ministry of Culture is taking a comprehensive approach to invigorating the arts in the Kingdom, running an inventory of the resources and talent already present and then looking to build upon this base through the establishment of eleven new commissions. These span the creative fields including film, theatre, visual arts, literature, fashion, architecture and design, as well as heritage and the culinary arts. These commissions are working both to develop new talent through scholarships and educational programmes and to promote Saudi participation in the arts through events both in the Kingdom and abroad, such as the now permanent Saudi pavilion on art and architecture at the Venice Biennale. The link to tourism is clear through the holding of international events which draw cultural communities into the Kingdom. In 2021, these included the first Red Sea International Film Festival held in Jeddah, and the Contemporary Arts Biennale in Diriyah.[87] These are to be regular events on the international cultural calendar, with the arts biennale alternating between contemporary and Islamic art. Many of the new tourist zones, including Diriyah, are being planned with dedicated arts districts in addition to already noteworthy heritage sites and newly planned museums. Arts and culture also feature in the tourist seasons which structure the annual calendar of entertainment across the Kingdom.

Until Vision 2030, the promotion of entertainment within the country was practically non-existent. The GEA was established in 2017 as the main body to organize and develop the entertainment sector in the Kingdom. The GEA is also responsible for developing recreational options and opportunities for all segments of society in all regions of the Kingdom plus stimulating the role of investment from the private sector in the construction and development of recreational activities. The GEA has taken the lead in the development and promotion of live events including World Wrestling Entertainment (WWE), music concerts, National Day celebrations, and the Saudi Seasons among others.

Saudi Seasons was launched by the GEA in March 2019. This programme encompasses year-round entertainment festivals, which are held across multiple locations and feature a wide variety of entertainment and cultural experiences for both domestic and international audiences. The Seasons

[87] G. Harris, 'Artists Announced for Saudi Arabia's First Ever Contemporary Art Biennial', *Art Newspaper* (24 September 2021), https://www.theartnewspaper.com/2021/09/24/artists-announced-for-saudi-arabias-first-ever-contemporary-art-biennial.

Figure 9.3 Ferris wheel at the Riyadh Season, 2019
Source: photograph by Larry Fallin.

consist of eleven different festival periods taking place in a different province each period. This event-based festival relies heavily on 'transformation in-place', by activating historical sites, vacant land, and existing real estate assets. Furthermore, the Seasons have developed both temporary and permanent revenue-generating entertainment assets, which serve to enhance the attractiveness and footfall of the environs close to festival locations beyond the Seasons period.[88]

The Seasons are also vehicles for social and economic transformation. They have been structured to promote cultural interaction among everybody with minimum segregation of genders in restaurants, entertainment venues, and other activities. Regional differences have sometimes altered these general rules but for the most part this experiment has had positive social and economic benefits. The fact that the Seasons are year long smooths out seasonality impacts to a certain extent. However, the Seasons in major cities like Riyadh and Jeddah are currently significantly larger than the other regions.

The potential for this new tourism and entertainment nexus can be gauged by the outcome of the first Riyadh Season held in 2019, and among the biggest

---

[88] Ministry of Tourism, 'Home' (accessed 29 November 2021), https://mt.gov.sa/en/Pages/default.aspx; General Entertainment Authority, 'Home' (accessed 29 November 2021), www.gea.gov.sa/en/.

events to have been hosted by the Kingdom. Over 12 million people from all parts of the Kingdom, the GCC, and beyond attended two months of events. These included over 100 musical, theatrical, sports and arts events and hosted some thirty international pop-up restaurants. The median seasonal spending was between $130 and $200 per attendee.

For its short duration, the economic impact was significant.[89] The Saudi government estimates that $4.6 billion was generated, with a contribution of 0.6 per cent to GDP. For every riyal the GEA invested there were approximately 8.8 riyals of economic activity returned. The promise of entertainment as an employment generator was also confirmed. The events generated seasonal employment equivalent to 75,000 full-time employment (FTE) hours.[90] Every seasonal job at the GEA had a multiplier effect of approximately nine indirect and induced jobs for the economy. The Seasons also offered many opportunities for youth development in the areas of job skills and work experience. Volunteerism was high as many wanted to gain experience through internships and exposure to a new industry.

The legacy of the Seasons in terms of FDI and partnering with international entertainment companies should also be positive, contributing to the emergent entertainment industry and reputation of Riyadh as a place for artists and performing arts. The belief that the leadership places in the Seasons model can be seen by the decision to extend the Riyadh Season post-pandemic in 2021 to nearly six months, double the length of the previous season.

The Kingdom has established other state vehicles for activating entertainment within the country. Saudi Entertainment Ventures (SEVEN) started as a subsidiary company of the GEA, initially named the Development and Investment Entertainment Company and launched by the PIF in January 2018 with initial capital of $2.6 billion. It provides an investment arm to the entertainment industry in Saudi Arabia, acting as a developer and operator of entertainment centres across the Kingdom. One of its first agreements was with United States-based AMC Theaters in April 2018 to operate AMC cinemas in the Kingdom.[91] The Kingdom opened the doors to this new cinematic era with the showing of the movie *Black Panther* in Riyadh, at the first of a planned 300 cinemas with more than 2,000 screens by 2030. To date over fifty cinemas have opened across the Kingdom, catering to mixed gender

---

[89] Riyadh Season Final Report, April 2020 (unpublished), authors' analysis. Economic impact was calculated using traditional Leontief I/O model by authors.

[90] FTE calculations are about hours worked rather than number of employees. We annualized the hours by dividing the total hours worked by 2,080 hours (40 hours per week × 52 weeks) to estimate FTE.

[91] US International Trade Administration, 'Saudi Arabia—Travel, Tourism, and Entertainment' (22 January 2020), https://www.export.gov/apex/article2?id=Saudi-Arabia-Travel-Tourism-and-Entertainment.

and age-appropriate audiences. Ultimately, the government hopes the industry will contribute more than $24 billion to the economy and create 30,000 permanent jobs over the same period.[92]

The Saudi Conventions and Exhibition General Authority (SCEGA) was established to promote the Saudi exhibitions and conferences industry, increasing its efficiency and establishing the Kingdom as a meeting destination of choice. SCEGA is responsible for developing a regulatory infrastructure to attract investment, meetings, and visitors. As in other arenas, SCEGA has ambitious targets for 2030: to attract 2.2–2.4 million meetings, conference, and exhibition tourists, generate $7 billion, and create 43,000 additional jobs.

The Promise and the Perils of the New Industries

When assessing the potential of these new industries of tourism and entertainment for Saudi Arabia, it is important to approach the subject holistically. These sectors are emerging as a central focus for economic diversification and attraction of FDI. They are also multibillion-dollar government projects deploying state funds towards land development. Their significance does not stop at the economic, however, as they are also serving as vehicles for sociocultural transformation and national identity formation. Any assessment should consider this multifaceted reach.

The promise of these new industries is built from their previous neglect; both non-religious tourism and entertainment were discouraged under Saudi Arabia's earlier religious-sanctioned order. Consequently, Saudis often sought entertainment and leisure abroad, most proximately in Bahrain and Dubai. There is clear potential for growth in recapturing some of these entertainment dollars at home even before attracting foreign visitors to the Kingdom.

The risks come in the big bets and huge investments being placed in tourism, especially at a time of rising economic competition. Every state in the Gulf is making a similar move to diversify into tourism, and it is unclear whether these offerings will be complementary. The appeal of Saudi Arabia is unproven apart from in religious tourism. Will foreign visitors appreciate the novelty of the Kingdom newly opening to visitors and offering unique

---

[92] K. Paul, 'Saudi Arabia Lifts Cinema Ban, Directors and Movie Chains Rejoice', Reuters (11 December 2017), www.reuters.com/article/us-saudi-film/saudi-arabia-says-cinemas-will-be-allowed-from-early-2018-idUSKBN1E50N1. General Entertainment Authority, 'Enjoy' (accessed 29 November 2021), www.gea.gov.sa/en/.

heritage and archaeological sites beyond those offered in neighbouring countries? Or will the sociocultural barriers and as-yet deficient infrastructure deter them? The Ministry of Tourism itself recognized these challenge in its annual report, which noted 'the local population's lack of mixing with other cultures' and concerns about the lack of private sector interest.[93] Such concerns can explain both the expense being stomached by the state to rapidly increase tourism and entertainment infrastructure as well as the legal efforts to make society more welcoming of foreigners. These include new regulations to punish the harassment of women and tourists, as well as hinting at the creation of specialized regulations in some tourist zones to allow alcohol consumption. However, every step to accommodate global norms brings not only the threat of a backlash at home but also the risk of contravening Saudi Arabia's Islamic appeal and leadership abroad. The challenge of catering to two distinct tourist customer bases is driving plans to segregate these markets: for instance, through the creation of an entirely new Saudi airline based in Riyadh while dedicating the existing Saudia airlines more to religious travellers.

The Ministry of Tourism also noted in its annual report the lack of skills in the labour force to address the needs of the sector. To that end, through the Takamul programme it has instituted a series of training programmes to encourage Saudis to join the tourism professions.[94] There are also plans to establish a new university in Diriyah named after King Salman and focused on tourism and hospitality. It is hoped that as Saudis enter the tourism profession, the quality of services will improve at the same time as the need to employ expatriates in these areas is reduced.

Other risks of tourism are shared throughout the Gulf region. The COVID-19 pandemic punished travel and tourism more than almost any other sector, with global tourist arrivals declining by 73 and 76 per cent over 2020 and 2021 respectively. The Middle East was one of the hardest-hit regions, recording the second highest regional decline in both tourist arrivals and income over this period behind the Asia and Pacific region. While was a modest recovery in summer 2021 compared to summer 2020, for instance, at the time of writing things are nowhere near 2019 levels.[95]

---

[93] A. AlBalawi, السياحة تحديات أكبر الخارجية بالثقافات الاختلاط (Mixing with Foreign Cultures Is the Biggest Tourism Challenge), *Al Riyadh* (19 September 2020), http://www.alriyadh.com/1843008.

[94] Ministry of Tourism, 'Takamul' (accessed on 4 December 2021), https://mt.gov.sa/en/Programs-Activities/Programs/Pages/Takamul.aspx.

[95] All tourism data are from the United Nations World Tourism Organization. For comparison, international arrivals in July 2021 rose to 54 million from 34 million in 2020. July 2019 arrivals were 163 million. https://www.unwto.org/unwto-tourism-recovery-tracker (accessed 2 December 2021).

Religious tourism was not spared in this collapse. For the first time in its modern history, the Hajj in 2020 was practically cancelled altogether. Only 1,000 local pilgrims were allowed permits, although local news sources suggested that closer to 10,000 performed the religious rites.[96] Though expanded, the 2021 Hajj marked the second year foreign pilgrims were banned, with only 60,000 vaccinated citizens and residents granted permits. Religious tourism was reopened to Umrah visitors in the third quarter of 2021, which could mark the beginning of an uptick in tourism-driven economic activity.[97]

The timing of the pandemic could not have been worse for Saudi Arabia's grand opening to foreign visitors, following closely on the unveiling of the Kingdom's new e-tourist visa regime in September 2019. Yet while the pandemic unquestionably delayed the Kingdom's opening, it has not appeared to weaken its commitment to the overall tourism project. Even with the travel restrictions preventing tourist visitors and the oil price plunge of 2020 leading to budget cuts and higher tax levies, state investment in the new tourism sites has remained robust.[98] For example, the DGDA budgetary plans were doubled from $20 billion to $40 billion between 2019 and 2021.[99]

The negative impact of the pandemic slowed touristic development in other ways. It accelerated the departure of many expatriates who were already exiting the Kingdom due to onerous expat levy fees and increasing value added tax. Although giga project managers claim there has been no slowdown, non-Saudi employment decreased by approximately 2 per cent per month with over 50 per cent of the decline located in the construction industry.[100] Even with the government's generous budgets, the lack of cheap labour put some of the contractors in financial difficulty as schedules slip due to a labour shortage.

The complications posed by the nearly eighteen-month restriction on international travel did not end with the pandemic. Even with the infrastructure improvements and new attractions, it will be difficult to compete with the more traditional tourist hotspots as international travel resumes. This may include the penchant of Saudi nationals for international travel now that there is a pent-up demand to leave the Kingdom. That represents an outflow

---

[96] 'Pilgrims Head to Mina as Hajj 2021 Officially Begins', Al Jazeera (18 July 2021), https://www.aljazeera.com/news/2021/7/18/saudi-arabia-stages-second-scaled-down-Hajj-of-coronavirus-era.

[97] The Saudi General Authority for Statistics shows Umrah visitors declining from 19 million to under 6 million between 2019 to the partially affected pandemic year of 2020. General Authority for Statistics, 'Umrah Statistics Bulletin, 2019' (April 2020), https://www.stats.gov.sa/sites/default/files/umrah_2019_e-15-3_kp.pdf.

[98] A. England, 'Saudi Prince Powers Ahead with Futuristic City and Sports Giga-Projects', *Financial Times* (16 August 2020), https://www.ft.com/content/c0c47647-4fc3-4b67-901e-3d4438f42ada.

[99] Kane, 'Saudi Arabia Doubling Down'.

[100] L. Fallin, 'Report on Saudi Labor Market, Q4 2020' to Ministry of Human Resources and Social Development, unpublished.

of tourist and entertainment dollars if citizens look to travel abroad rather than look to unfinished projects for vacations. Global industry restructuring could also impact entertainment offerings. For example, the expansion of cinemas through the partnership of PIF-funded SEVEN and AMC Theaters saw a slowdown in its plans to open fifty cinemas by 2024 due to changes wrought by the global collapse of movie theatre attendance.

Still, the Saudi leadership quickly resumed both entertainment events and tourism events as soon as health conditions permitted, restarting the issuance of international tourist visas in August 2021. While the Saudi Seasons festivals were cancelled in 2020, the leadership doubled down on them in the recovery, doubling the length of the premier Riyadh Season in 2021 to six months, as we have seen. The commitment to live events appears undeterred, as are efforts to promote international headliners and integrate the Kingdom as a fixture on concert tours. The PIF's $500 million investment in Live Nation Entertainment in 2020 is an indication of its ongoing interest in this sector. Another example is the resumption of premier events including WWE, which committed to a long-term relationship with the Kingdom.[101] In 2018, WWE and the General Sports Authority (now the Ministry of Sports) signed a ten-year multi-level deal to provide live events and broadcasting rights for WWE trademarked events. Although the deal is very lucrative to the WWE (approximately $50 million per show), it has been met with controversy including several shareholder lawsuits regarding potentially fraudulent activities and a bizarre delay in performers flying out of the Kingdom, allegedly due to a payments dispute.[102] Nonetheless, the partnership resumed for the 2021 Riyadh Season.

Such alleged contract disputes are not the only reputational challenges Saudi Arabia has to manage in attracting both international talent and foreign tourists. Other controversies centring on human rights issues regarding lesbian, gay, bisexual, and transgender people, women, and ongoing political repression speak to the ongoing reputational risk which has dogged the Kingdom, especially since the murder of *Washington Post* contributor Jamal Khashoggi. Human rights campaigns have at times successfully achieved the cancellation of talent, as in the case of the American rapper Nicki Minhaj, but they have not resulted in a full boycott of the Kingdom.[103] Other concerns regarding the business environment, especially stemming from the round-up and imprisonment of prominent businessmen in 2017, in a stated

---

[101] J. Currier, 'Preview and Predictions for WWE's "Crown Jewel" in Saudi Arabia', *Sports Illustrated* (20 October 2021), https://www.si.com/wrestling/2021/10/20/wwe-crown-jewel-saudi-arabia-preview.

[102] A. Konuwa, 'New WWE–Saudi Lawsuit Features Shocking Testimony from Anonymous Former Star (Updated)', *Forbes* (15 June 2020), https://www.forbes.com/sites/alfredkonuwa/2020/06/15/new-wwe-saudi-lawsuit-features-shocking-testimony-from-anonymous-former-star/#25fed9187790.

[103] 'Nicki Minaj Pulls Out of Saudi Arabia Festival after Backlash', *BBC Online* (9 July 2019), https://www.bbc.com/news/world-middle-east-48930029.

anti-corruption campaign which took capital and ownership rights away from some, may have had an even greater impact on the appetite for foreign investment.

Tourism within the Kingdom also faces risks from the security environment. It is not coincidental that Saudi Arabia's increased interest in Red Sea security, including the establishment of a Red Sea Council, has expanded alongside planned tourist and urban investments along that coastline.[104] To this end, ongoing military conflicts in Yemen and unresolved tensions with Iran will narrow the tourist appeal for a more general clientele. It is noteworthy that the United States of America maintained the highest 'do not travel' advisory on the Kingdom in 2021, not only due to risks from COVID-19 but also 'due to the threat of missile and drone attacks on civilian facilities'.[105] Such attacks on Saudi Arabia's south has repeatedly halted flights into the Abha airport. Concerns not only about security but about its drag on economic development are probably contributing to the Saudi leadership's mounting efforts to negotiate an end to the Yemen war and to forge an agreement with the Iranian leadership.

Despite these challenges, the Saudi leadership has had extraordinary success in attracting mega-events that may supercharge the tourism and entertainment agenda. In the past year, the Kingdom has presented the winning bid to host the 2030 World Expo, a global event expected to attract millions of visitors. It also has a near lock on the hosting of the 2034 World Cup soccer tournament, the world's premier sporting event. It is clear that the Saudi leadership under the direction of the young Prince Mohammed bin Salman is pressing ahead, if not accelerating its ambitions in tourism, the arts, and entertainment, viewing difficulties in pursuing tourism within the conservative Kingdom as opportunities for socioeconomic reform.

Indeed it is difficult to discern if such social and cultural changes are a necessary consequence of pursuing this line of economic diversification, or if these particular industries have been selected for their service to the end of sociocultural opening and land development. Clearly the new leadership is embracing the opportunity to leave its mark on the Kingdom by remaking law, culture, vast landscapes, and Saudi Arabia's orientation in the world. This is a younger and more globally oriented Kingdom, and tourism, accompanied by entertainment and other creative ventures, is central to its new national presentation.

---

[104] L. Alfaisal, 'Saudi Arabia Announces Establishment of Red Sea, Gulf of Aden Council', Al Arabiya English (6 January 2020), https://english.alarabiya.net/News/gulf/2020/01/06/Saudi-Arabia-announces-establishment-of-Red-Sea-Gulf-of-Aden-council-.

[105] US Department of State—Bureau of Consular Affairs, https://travel.state.gov/content/travel/en/international-travel/International-Travel-Country-Information-Pages/SaudiArabia.html (accessed 6 December 2021).

PART 3
THE FUTURE

10
Saudi Vision 2030

Repurposing Ministries and Creating New Institutions

Mark C. Thompson and Neil Quilliam

Introduction

The unveiling of Saudi Vision 2030 in April 2016 coincided with the high-profile 'launch' of Crown Prince Mohammed bin Salman as a new-generation leader intent on driving Saudi Arabia towards a new future—one envisioned and desired by the Kingdom's young, aspirational, interconnected Saudis of both genders.[1] Although ambitious in scope and magnitude, in many ways Vision 2030 drew together the strands of earlier plans to break the Kingdom's dependency on hydrocarbons.[2] However, on this occasion, not only was the Vision being pushed hard by a young leader willing to break the mould of consensus politics, but also it enjoys the support of young nationals. In truth, young Saudis are a natural constituency for the Kingdom's transformation initiative, and not surprisingly, as Diwan notes, there have been concerted efforts by the government to reach out to them.[3]

Yet the principal challenge, among many others, was the limited capacity of state institutions to break with the past and respond to the demands that Vision 2030, and the accompanying National Transformation Program (NTP),[4] placed upon the existing bureaucratic system. This chapter therefore discusses how, in order to deliver Vision 2030, it has been necessary to introduce new methods of policy and decision making. These include the repurposing of existing ministries and/or creating new institutions

---

[1] For up-to-date statistics on Saudi demographics, see www.stats.gov.sa/en/820.

[2] Government of Kingdom of Saudi Arabia, *Saudi Vision 2030*, available to download at: https://www.vision2030.gov.sa/

[3] K. Smith Diwan, 'Youth Appeal of Saudi Vision 2030', Arab Gulf States Institute in Washington (6 May 2016), www.agsiw.org/youth-appeal-of-saudi-vision-2030/.

[4] See, for example: M. C. Thompson, 'Saudi Vision 2030: A Viable Response to Youth Aspirations and Concerns?', *Asian Affairs* 48, no. 2 (2017), pp. 205–21, doi: 10.1080/03068374.2017.1313598.

Mark C. Thompson and Neil Quilliam, *Saudi Vision 2030*. In: *The Economy of Saudi Arabia in the 21st Century*. Edited by: John Sfakianakis, Oxford University Press. © Mark C. Thompson and Neil Quilliam (2024).
DOI: 10.1093/oso/9780198863878.003.0011

that can short-circuit lengthy bureaucratic processes. In addition, foreign management consultancy firms such as McKinsey have been allowed access to the highest policy-making circles with, it appears, significant input into Vision 2030 projects.

First, the chapter outlines the domestic context assessing Vision 2030 and related mega projects such as Neom and Qiddiya.[5] Secondly, it discusses the controversial role of foreign management consultancy firms and the increasing importance of the capital, Riyadh. The chapter then moves on to examine the changing role of existing government and hybrid institutions in post-Vision 2030 Saudi Arabia, as well as those institutions that were created specifically to implement some of the Vision's goals, such as the General Authority for Entertainment (GEA). The chapter considers whether these institutions are of the kind that the Kingdom needs and if the capacity of the new and/or reconfigured institutions is sufficient to achieve the overall goals of Vision 2030.

The final discussion revisits the debate on institutions and assesses whether the reconfigured and newly created post-2016 institutions have been effective in delivering the Vision. It addresses several questions. Have these institutions helped the Saudi government to become more efficient, and if this is the case, how is this efficiency measured? To what extent have Saudi management consulting firms contributed towards Vision 2030 and what proportion continues to be carried out by foreign management consultancies? Finally, to what extent have foreign consultancy firms helped Saudi Arabia—or have they, in fact, inhibited its development?

Assessing Saudi Vision 2030

As a Chatham House report on Saudi Vision 2030 stresses, diversification has been an economic policy priority since the 1970s, but the implementation of successive initiatives, including a series of five-year development plans first introduced in 1970 as well as the creation of six new 'economic cities' formulated in the 2000s, have usually fallen short of their targets.[6] More astute Saudis are aware of this issue and, therefore, are sometimes jaded by government reform announcements and/or concerned that extremely

---

[5] https://www.neom.com; https://qiddiya.com.
[6] J. Kinninmont, 'Vision 2030 and Saudi Arabia's Social Contract: Austerity and Transformation', Chatham House (July 2017), p. 3, www.chathamhouse.org/sites/default/files/publications/research/2017-07-20-vision-2030-saudi-kinninmont.pdf.

high-profile ones such as Vision 2030 are in danger of overpromising and underdelivering.

Certainly, scepticism about Vision 2030 abounds in the West, but as Fahad Nazer observes, although the package of reforms is as ambitious in its goals as it is broad in its scope, there is also a significant segment of Saudis who value Vision 2030 as a much-needed effort to wean the Kingdom off its dependence on oil revenue.[7] Despite setbacks such as the COVID-19 pandemic of 2020–2 and the impact of fluctuating oil prices on government expenditure, as well as an accompanying rise in value added tax and fuel prices young Saudis continue to support the Vision. This is because the 'idea' of the Vision matches the expectations and aspirations of most young nationals. Yet the problem for the government is that by launching Vision 2030 with great fanfare, it unwittingly raised youthful expectations to a level that it might not be able to equal, and therein lies the problem.[8]

According to a special report by the Atlantic Council, *Assessing Saudi Vision 2030: A 2020 Review*, Saudi Arabia has the luxury of wealth that it can channel towards revamping its economy.[9] The report's authors argue that the Saudi government should not shy away from doing so, but it should avoid large public mega projects, which have a dubious track record of success and only augment rather than diminish the role of the state in the economy.[10] Indeed, mega projects such as Neom,[11] The Line,[12] and Coral Bloom[13] may be eye catching and generate headlines, but to date, their track record in generating jobs for Saudis has been limited, despite the fact that the crux of Vision 2030 is creating jobs for nationals today and into the future.[14] There appears to be a degree of scepticism among many of the Kingdom's diverse communities about the sustainability of these mega projects, especially in times of economic uncertainty. In addition, it is not always evident how projects such as Neom are going to benefit wider Saudi society: for instance, how is a robot city in the north-west of the Kingdom going to provide jobs for nationals in

---

[7] F. Nazer, 'Saudi Vision 2030 and "A Day in Riyadh"', Arab Gulf States Institute in Washington (25 October 2016), www.agsiw.org/saudi-vision-2030-day-riyadh/.

[8] Thompson's research and observations across Saudi Arabia, 2016–21.

[9] See: www.atlanticcouncil.org/in-depth-research-reports/report/assessing-saudi-vision-2030-a-2020-review/.

[10] Ibid.; see, for example, King Abdullah Economic City: www.kaec.net/.

[11] https://www.neom.com.

[12] R. Taha and I. Naar, 'Saudi Arabia's Crown Prince reveals project "THE LINE" in futuristic city of NEOM', Al Arabiya English (10 January 2021), https://english.alarabiya.net/News/gulf/2021/01/10/Vision-2030-Saudi-Arabia-s-Crown-Prince-reveals-project-The-Line-in-futuristic-city-of-NEOM.

[13] Anon., 'Saudi Arabia's Crown Prince Launches "Coral Bloom" Luxury Red Sea Project', *Arab News* (10 February 2021), https://www.arabnews.com/node/1807111/saudi-arabia.

[14] See: www.atlanticcouncil.org/in-depth-research-reports/report/assessing-saudi-vision-2030-a-2020-review/.

line with Vision 2030's goals? Hence, as Saudi Arabia moves towards 2030, one of the most important questions centres on whether the government is likely to reorient its policies—in other words, execute a 'course correction'—and lessen the focus on some of its mega projects and high-cost items in order to avoid their becoming 'white elephants'. Indeed, the danger is that mega projects such as Neom could begin to feel a little 'pre-pandemic'.[15]

The Role of Foreign Management Consultancy Firms

The position of foreign consultancy firms in the wider Gulf Cooperation Council states, especially Saudi Arabia, is considered by many political economists to be unique, although not necessarily in a positive way. Riyadh is home to the Saudi headquarters of foreign management consultancies such as McKinsey and Boston Consultancy Group, to name just two, even though the role they play in the Kingdom's transformation remains contentious.[16] A necessary question related to the role of foreign consultancy firms in Saudi Arabia is whether these firms perceive important issues such as unemployment among nationals as problems for which optimal solutions need to be delivered, or whether they see their involvement rather as an opportunity to raise revenue for themselves. In other words, have they assisted the Kingdom's development or inhibited it?

The role of foreign management consultants in Saudi public sector policy making and governance is particularly pervasive by international standards. As David B. Jones documents, consultants are contracted in traditional projects to occupy strategic, public relations, human resources, financial, and technical roles, as well as being embedded as expert 'advisers' in the provision of basic social and civil services, military capability, technological and information resources, and in a wide range of other government functions.[17] Nonetheless, Calvert W. Jones argues that the evidence collectively suggests that, while bringing some important benefits, 'experts' such as foreign

[15] In May 2020, Finance Minister Mohammed Al Jadaan stressed that everything, including some of the high-profile Vision 2030 projects, was under consideration in a bid to get government costs under control. See, for example, F. Kane, 'Al-Jadaan Reveals Full Extent of Saudi Arabia's Pandemic Challenge', *Arab News* (4 May 2020), https://www.arabnews.com/node/1669151.

[16] There is also a 'home-grown' consultancy, Strategic Gears, established by a former King Fahd University of Petroleum and Minerals (KFUPM) graduate and staffed mainly by other KFUPM graduates. See: www.strategicgears.com.

[17] D. B. Jones, 'King-Makers or Knaves? The Role of Consultants in Domestic Policy Making and Governance in Saudi Arabia', in M. C. Thompson and N. Quilliam (eds.), *Governance and Domestic Policy Making in Saudi Arabia: Transforming Society, Economics, Politics and Culture* (London: IB Tauris Bloomsbury, 2022), p. 65.

management consultants neither rationalize governance nor provide legitimacy in any consistent way for the leaders who enlist them. Jones maintains that many expert advisers add knowledge and data, and bring experience 'to bear in potentially rationalizing ways, especially in the early stages of a reform effort', but that after a time 'they also engage in the art of not speaking truth to power'. In other words, foreign management consultancies can be guilty of self-censorship, exaggerating successes while at the same time they 'downplay their own misgivings in response to the incentive structures they face'. Jones argues that this is 'a response in keeping with more critical perspectives on expert actors'.[18] This exaggeration of success and embellishing of potential benefits was witnessed first-hand by one of the authors, when prominent foreign management consultants overstressed the 'benefits to all parties' (while disregarding obvious problems) during pitches for high-profile Vision-related projects to Saudi governmental institutions or hybrid public–private sector entities.[19]

Critics of foreign consultancy firms also believe that they are guilty of convincing policy-makers in the various Saudi ministries that complicated solutions to longstanding problems can be achieved in a very short time, when in fact the consultancy's stated goals and accompanying timelines are unrealistic and unreachable. Indeed, we should question whether it is really in the interests of foreign consultancy firms to solve Saudi national problems when this would bring to an end their flow of invoices to the various Saudi ministries. The situation is frequently exacerbated by multiple consultancies being hired by the client to work on the same project simultaneously. Hence, it becomes unclear to everyone who actually 'owns what' and the situation becomes confused. In consequence, some Vision projects are in danger of becoming overly expensive and ultimately ineffective.[20]

An important question is the extent to which foreign management consultancies have influenced nascent and/or existing policies.[21] David B. Jones points out that using consultants, particularly in designing and implementing rapid reform programmes and far-reaching policy reviews, 'means that government clients within the Kingdom can benefit from the flexibility, rapid outputs and bandwidth offered by consultants'.[22] In fact, one Saudi Riyadh-based consultant maintains that foreign management consultancies have filled a gap, as they can be hired for specific projects regardless of whether

---

[18] C. W. Jones, 'Adviser to the King: Experts, Rationalization, and Legitimacy', *World Politics* 71, no. 1 (2019), pp. 1–43, doi: 10.1017/S0043887118000217.

[19] Thompson's observations, Riyadh, 2019 and 2021.

[20] Thompson's observations while advising a major consultancy firm, Riyadh, 2019.

[21] Thompson's interviews, Riyadh, 2021.

[22] Jones, 'King-Makers or Knaves?'

the scope is broad or narrow.[23] Indeed, due to limited scientific data as well as data-gathering problems, frequently exacerbated by a 'silo mentality'—that is, a lack of horizontal coordination—among government institutions, the demand for foreign management consultancies became high demand precisely because they were able to fill existing information gaps quickly. Yet ultimately it is the role of the hiring institution that is vital. Success can only be achieved if the parent institution takes ownership of the project from the outset. Those institutions which farm out the problem to a foreign consultancy, taking no accountability for the project and simply thinking that 'the problem will go away', are likely to fail.[24]

Could it be said that the existing cadre of civil servants was inept in pushing forward reformist agendas, or did not have the original ideas needed to facilitate the Vision's goals, and that was why the government was obliged to bring in foreign consultancies? This is untrue, according to one young Saudi high-flyer. In the past, the talent gravitated towards Saudi Aramco or Saudi Basic Industries Corporation (SABIC) rather than government positions. However, the situation changed post-2016 with the arrival of foreign management consultancy opportunities and prestigious Vision 2030 projects.[25] Indeed, nowadays, at first sight many Saudi institutions appear to be staffed by people in their twenties and thirties, with a significant female presence in specific ministries. Still, in certain quarters, there is a degree of recognition that some government decisions have gone awry due to a lack of experience and a disregard for the 'accepted and trusted' way of doing things, including the importance of consensus building. For example, a young well-educated national concedes that mistakes have sometimes been caused by 'inexperience due to age and lack of maturity in the last few years'.[26]

Another issue is whether the current high profile of foreign management consultancies is an acknowledgement that local talent does not exist yet in sufficient quantity or quality to implement the Vision's projects effectively; or rather, whether the reliance on foreign consultancies reveals a lack of confidence in the skills and abilities of Saudis. As an example, in January 2021, the Misk Foundation published a report called *The Impact of Covid-19 on Saudi Youth*, compiled and written by Kearney Management Consultancy in conjunction with Misk.[27] The report draws on insights from Saudi youth in a survey conducted by another foreign company, Phronesis Partners. As

---

[23] Thompson's interviews, Riyadh, 2021.
[24] Ibid.
[25] Ibid.
[26] Thompson's interviews, Riyadh, 2019.
[27] https://misk.org.sa/en/files/17246/.

Misk's stated mission is to provide various means for the Kingdom's youth to 'foster, empower, and create a healthy environment for young creative talents to grow and see the light',[28] it seems odd that the report was undertaken by Kearney. Even if young Saudis worked on the report, no individual Saudi names are mentioned, and it is Kearney's name on the report's cover rather than those of individual young Saudis.

Certainly, Saudi Arabia's overly bureaucratic and often leisurely decision-making processes have been shaken up seriously in recent years, but while some things have improved, others have not. According to an economic consultant who works on several NTP initiatives, there are definite pros and cons to the current decision-making process. He says that these days it is possible for a consultant to pitch an idea to a vice-minister, or even a minister directly, and if it is approved then it can be activated quickly. However, a major issue is that such individuals are rarely in a meeting for the full duration, and even if they are, they are frequently working on something else on their laptops:

Everyone is rushing in and out of meetings and sometimes very influential decision-makers, who should attend the whole meeting, are only there for five minutes (usually on their mobiles throughout). It makes things very confusing, to say the least. And this is where you get mixed messages and ultimately mistakes.[29]

In consequence, there sometimes appears to be little understanding that it is better to do (and complete) one thing well rather than several things badly. This situation is often complicated further by ministerial concern about international ratings, but as one prominent Saudi policy-maker points out, there is frequently 'nothing beyond the tick in the box'. This can create a credibility gap between government and society because, whereas on paper a problem has been 'solved', in reality it has not.[30]

Additionally, the foreign management consultants are sometimes at odds with Saudi decision-makers—not because either lacks intelligence or does not know what they are doing, but rather because they are 'on different pages', especially with regard to the sociocultural context. Consequently, you get foreign consultants telling their Saudi counterparts that the Kingdom's decision-making processes should follow the 'circular paradigm' to be effective, whereas nearly everything in Saudi Arabia (especially decision

[28] https://misk.org.sa/en/about-misk/.
[29] Thompson's interview, October 2020.
[30] Thompson's interview, February 2022.

making) is based on a vertical model. As a result, the two sides are looking at a problem in two entirely different ways, which simply confuses the issue.[31]

Another increasingly important issue is the 'brain drain' away from other parts of Saudi Arabia to Riyadh—to the detriment of the former. This is particularly pertinent when considering the lure of public sector jobs: for instance, in certain ministries such as Investment, Culture or Energy, or positions in the royal court (Diwan), or, most significantly post-pandemic, the prestigious Public Investment Fund (PIF), which has become the favoured destination for well-qualified and ambitious young Saudis. Since 2016, the royal court has made a concerted effort to recruit young Saudi graduates (both male and female) to join its committees focused on Vision 2030 policy, either from local universities or returning from overseas scholarship programmes. However, it is difficult to measure whether the royal court is yet hiring the 'best and brightest', or if, in reality, positions are being taken by the most ambitious who have an eye on proximity to the centre and/or want to work on some of the most prestigious, high-salary Vision 2030 projects. According to a former Saudi consultant, around 60 per cent of those offered positions are well educated and motivated, but as the recruitment process is usually rapid, there are others who 'slip through the net'. These very highly paid individuals resemble '1980s managers' who attend a few 'breakfast meetings', but that is the sum of their work.[32] At the same time, there are reservations about joining the royal court among other talented young Saudis. These young nationals believe they are better off working for the PIF (or similar) or in more lucrative private sector positions where there are more relaxed and open environments. Of course, working for the royal court can increase a person's personal *wasta* (connections), especially if they work for a committee that is close to the centre of power. However, the problem is that once 'inside', an individual can become cut off from other important institutions because of supposed confidentiality issues, and ultimately get trapped inside the royal court's 'echo-chamber'.[33]

What is not in doubt, however, is that intelligent and ambitious young Saudis, many of them graduates from prestigious institutions such as KFUPM in Dhahran, are often drawn to certain public sector positions, such as those in the PIF, or to foreign management consultancies due to higher salaries and 'fashionable' connotations associated with them. Moreover, a position with an important foreign management consultancy firm such as McKinsey is seen as an effective way to 'kickstart' a career immediately following

[31] Thompson's observations while advising a major consultancy firm, Riyadh, 2019.
[32] Thompson's interviews, Riyadh, 2021.
[33] Thompson's interviews, Riyadh, 2019.

graduation. Former Saudi consultants point out that, while a job with one of the major Riyadh-based foreign consultancy firms has a definite 'shelf life', usually a couple of years, an individual can use it to gain experience and the necessary connections to transfer afterwards to a prestigious position in the public sector, often in a ministry.[34] A former Saudi consultant concurs, saying that government institutions are 'bending over backwards' to recruit young nationals with two or more years' experience with foreign management consultancies.[35]

Centralization in Riyadh

It has been customary for the King and the royal court to leave Riyadh every summer for Jeddah (and nearby Makkah for the end of Ramadan and Eid), although more recently, due to the pandemic, King Salman decamped to his new palace in Neom.[36] That said, the annual move does not in any way negate the growing dominance of the capital Riyadh in all aspects of Saudi life. This concerns some astute Saudis who perceive the ascendency of the capital, in terms of concentration of wealth, power, and employment opportunities, as having a detrimental socio-economic impact on other areas of the Kingdom.

Indeed, since the launch of Saudi Vision 2030, the importance of the capital has increased. Vision 2030 is a decidedly 'top-down' project that exemplifies Crown Prince Mohammed bin Salman's drive to centralize all decision-making processes.[37] Therefore, Riyadh is where everything happens and most Saudis, especially the young and ambitious, comprehend that if an individual wants to get ahead, he or she needs to be in Riyadh. As a result, the capital's population has ballooned to approximately 7.5 million[38] with, according to Fahd Al Rasheed, President of the Royal Commission for Riyadh, plans to double the population by 2030 and turn the capital 'into a mega-metropolis'.[39] Furthermore, Hosam Alqurashi, chief marketing officer at the commission, which oversees $800 billion of spending plans, says the Kingdom's leadership saw the 2020 pandemic period as an opportunity

---

[34] Thompson's interviews, Riyadh, 2021.
[35] Ibid.
[36] See, for example: https://gulfbusiness.com/saudi-king-heads-to-500bn-mega-city-neom-for-holiday/.
[37] See, for example: H. Fathallah, 'Failure of Regional Governance in Saudi Arabia', Carnegie Endowment for International Peace (26 July 2018), https://carnegieendowment.org/sada/76928.
[38] See: https://populationstat.com/saudi-arabia/riyadh. The other main urban centres of Jeddah and the Dammam-Khobar-Dhahran conurbation have also grown considerably.
[39] F. Kane, 'Plan Afoot to Make Riyadh the Middle East's Mega-Metropolis', *Arab News* (23 January 2020), https://www.arabnews.com/node/1616341/business-economy.

to accelerate Vision 2030 projects related to the capital.[40] For instance, the Riyadh-based government is implementing massive projects to 'beautify' the capital and improve the overall quality of life for residents. Fahd Al Rasheed said that the government has already committed some $266.6 billion for ongoing and new projects over the next ten years to transform the capital in collaboration with the private sector. According to Al Rasheed, 'Riyadh is already the epicentre of economic development in the country and the region. We have now the ambitious plan under Vision 2030 of doubling both our economy and population over the next ten years.'[41] These initiatives and policies were underscored further by plans unveiled by Crown Prince Mohammed at the January 2021 Future Investment Initiative. The Crown Prince announced that the government aims to make Riyadh one of the ten largest city economies in the world (it is the fortieth largest city economy worldwide), with an increase in residents from 7.5 million in 2021 to around 15–20 million in 2030.[42]

However, research conducted outside Riyadh, particularly in the northern and southern regions, documents a sense of marginalization, a feeling that it is necessary to migrate to the capital, or other urban centres, in order to find a job and 'get on in life'.[43] This trend has also started to affect Jeddah and Dammam-Khobar-Dhahran, with residents who already have jobs in these cities, even with state-owned enterprises such as Saudi Aramco, trying to relocate to the capital in search of higher salaries and jobs on prestigious government projects.[44] The danger is that this internal migration could create a gulf between Riyadh and the rest of the Kingdom.[45] Moreover, it appears that the traditional geographic core–periphery polarization (between urban centres and the provinces) is being replaced by a social core–periphery

---

[40] S. Kalin, 'Saudi Crown Prince Barrels Ahead with Big Projects to Boost Economy', *Wall Street Journal* (26 August 2020), www.wsj.com/articles/saudi-crown-prince-barrels-ahead-with-big-projects-to-boost-economy-11598434201.

[41] Rasheed first disclosed plans to turn the city of some 7 million people into what he then described as a mega-metropolis in an interview with the *Arab News* daily in January, before COVID-19 swept the world and oil prices collapsed in April. 'Despite Downturn, Saudi Arabia Pursues Goal of Doubling Size of Capital City', Reuters (7 July 2020), https://uk.reuters.com/article/uk-saudi-investment-riyadh/despite-downturn-saudi-arabia-pursues-goal-of-doubling-size-of-capital-city-idUKKBN2481HA.

[42] F. Kane, 'Saudi Crown Prince Unveils Plan to Make Riyadh One of World's 10 Largest City Economies', *Arab News* (29 January 2021), https://www.arabnews.com/node/1800231/business-economy.

[43] Views expressed by multiple focus groups across Saudi Arabia, 2016–18.

[44] Multiple interviews, 2021.

[45] Menoret documents how waves of migrants moved to Riyadh from the steppes and highlands of central Arabia. In addition, a large share of the capital's population moves back and forth between the capital and their home villages, where they spend weekends and holidays. This makes Riyadh 'an extension of the patch of scorched earth on which they were born and where they were entrenched in dense social networks'. P. Menoret, *Joyriding in Riyadh: Oil, Urbanism, and Road Revolt* (Cambridge: Cambridge University Press, 2014), p. 26.

polarization based on economic stratification, driving a perception that there is a policy of exclusion.[46] This could prove politically problematic if dangerous disconnects are created between the urbanized, often cosmopolitan, population of the capital and more marginalized provincial populations. This issue should be of concern to the Saudi government as the sense of provincial marginalization (and sometimes disregard from urban elites) is reminiscent of the anger and disempowerment that Donald Trump and the Brexit Leave campaigns tapped into successfully in 2016, thereby disrupting the political systems in both the United States of America and the United Kingdom.[47] The November 2018 visit by King Salman, accompanied by Crown Prince Mohammed, to Qassim, Hail, and Tabuk was interpreted as the government recognizing the importance of regional economies and interests.

Clearly, the convergence of the launch of Vision 2030, the increased input from large-scale foreign management consultancy firms into policy formulation, and the growing importance of the capital Riyadh has highlighted limitations in the Kingdom's institutional capacity, as well as impacting on, and sometimes straining, existing bureaucratic processes. What the above has revealed is the limited capacity of state institutions to break with the past and respond to the demands that Saudi Vision 2030 has placed upon the creaking bureaucratic system.

Government and Hybrid Institutions

The single biggest challenge to the Saudi leadership lies in implementing Vision 2030. As documented, previously the Kingdom lacked the institutional capacity to fulfil its ambiguous goals and meet its key performance indicators (KPIs). Furthermore, there was a large institutional gap between the concept and its realization, even though post-COVID-19 a growing pool of young talent has been more than willing to bridge that gap.

Circumnavigating Established Processes

Saudi Vision 2030 has placed additional strain on a the existing bureaucratic system. Not only was the old system not fit for purpose; it was also part of the problem—there is an inbuilt resistance to change within most bureaucracies,

---

[46] A. Hoogvelt, *Globalization and the Postcolonial World*, 2nd edn. (Basingstoke: Palgrave Macmillan, 2001), pp. 64–5.
[47] Others wonder, as the population of the provinces is small in comparison to the 84 per cent of the population who reside in the main urban centres (especially Riyadh), is this really a problem?

especially those that are partly designed to provide employment as part of a social contract between state and citizens. Therefore, in order to deliver Vision 2030, it has been necessary to repurpose existing ministries and create new institutions that can short-circuit lengthy bureaucratic processes. At the same time, given the emphasis on achieving KPIs and pushing through reforms at a rapid pace, the Crown Prince has sought not only to circumvent many layers of bureaucratic resistance, but also to put in place trusted individuals whom he believes can fulfil mandates to advance the Vision. In almost every way possible, this has challenged the very essence of traditional Saudi decision making, from the royal court down to the smallest administrative unit. Of course, this approach is not unique to Saudi Arabia or new to any country wishing to bring about far-reaching change.

It is commonplace for new Gulf Arab leaders—as they succeed—to establish new institutions with mandates that often overlap with existing institutions; and, by doing so, to create redundancy. For example, King Abdullah founded several new institutes, such as the King Abdullah City for Atomic and Renewable Energy, which closely resembled the Atomic Energy Institute. The only major difference is that the newly established entities tend to be fully funded, while the older ones struggle to raise funds, operate, and add value. Yet existing institutions are rarely, if ever, closed down: for example, the moribund King Abdulaziz Center for National Dialogue continues to hang on. In most, if not all, cases, these incidences lead to unnecessary duplication.

This approach to policy making is not confined to the Gulf Arab states and is prevalent among many countries: for example, in the United Kingdom, quasi-autonomous non-governmental organizations (quangos) proliferated under UK Prime Minister Margaret Thatcher, when she set about reforming the country.[48] As such, it is a tried-and-tested means of ushering in new policies by circumnavigating established processes, which are more inclined towards frustrating innovative policy approaches. The question that needs to be addressed in Saudi Arabia, therefore, is whether and to what extent the 'new' institutions can deliver on Vision 2030 projects.

Before one can address this question, however, it is important to consider the implications of the previous analysis of how foreign management consultancies have shaped the Vision and influenced its implementation.

Without doubt, the Saudi chequebook attracts a lot of interest from international consultancies and former high-profile Western politicians, in particular. Although foreign management consultancies tend to cherry-pick

---

[48] M. White, 'Coalition Beware: Bonfires of Quangos Usually Burn Themselves Out', *The Guardian* (24 September 2010), https://www.theguardian.com/politics/blog/2010/sep/24/coalition-bonfire-of-quangos.

national talent, as mentioned above, and corral dynamic young Saudis into their stables, their outputs and recommendations often accord with 'cookie-cutter' solutions proffered in other jurisdictions with little consideration of local context. A common criticism levelled at consultancies by Saudi decision-makers is that they import philosophies, values, and practices that ill suit the local environment and are rolled out as universal panacea. In this way, local talent brought into the process often finds itself unable to influence the introduction of new measures before running up against local customs. In other words, when new institutional policies, procedures, and processes are introduced, they are often frustrated by local context factors—even though local Saudi talent has been engaged in the process.

The following section maps out the institutional architecture and specific bodies mandated to deliver Vision 2030. As noted already, these include newly created entities at the heart of decision making, repurposed ministries, and recently formed authorities, which have all been given far-reaching autonomy to pursue their goals. We then present two case studies of key institutions to assess their efficacy and contribution towards realizing the Crown Prince's vision.

New Institutional Arrangements

What follows is an outline of the new institutional arrangements that have emerged since 2016 (see Figure 10.1). We will then look in greater detail at a number of institutions—traditional and hybrid—to better understand how they fit within Saudi Arabia's decision-making ecosystem.

The new institutional framework set to deliver Vision 2030 can best be described as 'hybrid'. It is built upon traditional institutions, in the forms of ministries; newly formed and purpose-built agencies; and repurposed institutions. What all of these institutions have in common is that they are led by a cohort of the Crown Prince's allies drawn from the technocracy, security apparatus, and preferred branches of the ruling family. Each and every one owes its position and allegiance directly to Crown Prince Mohammed bin Salman. It is notable that the Crown Prince has placed at the helm of so many projects—both old and new—just a handful of inner circle confidants, which carries some advantages, but also serves as a constraint.

To date, multiple newly created institutions have been established, including the Council of Economic and Development Affairs (CEDA), the Strategic Management Committee (SMC), the Strategic Management Office (SMO), the Project Management Office (PMO), the Delivery Unit

Newly established entities	Establishment date
CEDA PMO	29/01/2015
Strategic Management Committee and Strategic Management Office (SMO)	30/05/2016
Delivery Unit (DU)	09/10/2015
National Center for Performance Management (Adaa)	19/10/2015
Decision Support Center (DSC)	16/05/2016
Corporate Communication Unit at CEDA (CCU)	28/01/2016
General Authority for Culture (GAC)	07/05/2016
General Entertainment Authority (GEA)	07/05/2016

Previous entity	Current entity
Ministry of Commerce and Industry	Ministry of Commerce and Investment
Ministry of Labor	Ministry of Labor and Social Development
Ministry of Social Affairs	
Ministry of Petroleum and Mineral Resources	Ministry of Energy
Ministry of Water and Electricity	Ministry of Industry and Mineral Resources
Ministry of Agriculture	Ministry of Environment, Water and Agriculture
Ministry of Hajj	Ministry of Hajj and Umrah
Saudi Arabian General Investment Authority (SAGIA)	Ministry of Investment
Public Education Evaluation Commission	Education Evaluation Commission

New government entities established

Existing entities merged and/or restructured

Figure 10.1 The ecosystem to drive the implementation of Vision 2030

Source: developed by the authors based on the 'Governance Model for Achieving Saudi Arabia's Vision 2030', https://www.spa.gov.sa/viewstory.php?lang=en&newsid=1507337.

(DU), the Corporate Communication Unit (CCU), the National Center for Performance Management (Adaa), the General Authority for Culture (GAC), the General Entertainment Authority (GEA), and the Decision Support Center (DSC).

The Council of Economic and Development Affairs (CEDA), a policy advisory body, was established by royal decree in January 2015 and replaced the Supreme Economic Council. Crown Prince Mohammed presides over CEDA, and its members include leading ministers and prominent royals.[49] It is best described as the core decision-making institution and has oversight over all reporting agencies and institutions. It has the authority to define the roles and responsibilities of relevant government agencies and mechanisms, including the SMC and SMO, as well as the authority to override bureaucratic obstacles that might prevent agencies and programmes from achieving their goals. Former UK Prime Minister Tony Blair's success in centralizing decision making around No. 10 appears to have influenced the structure and functions of CEDA, which has come to resemble the UK Cabinet Office. As such, the SMC, SMO, PMO, DU, CCU and Adaa—described below—serve as support units to CEDA.

[49] Shearman & Sterling LLP in association with Dr Sultan Al-Masoud & Partners, 'Understanding the Key Government Institutions and Ministries in the Kingdom of Saudi Arabia' (September 2019).

The SMC was established in November 2017 and provides strategic guidance to CEDA and is, in turn, served by an executive body, the SMO. The primary function of the SMC is to translate Vision 2030 into action plans and implementation programmes. This includes providing oversight to all major projects, supervising and monitoring progress, and problem solving. The SMC has the authority to 'cascade' major projects down to constituent agencies and to escalate matters up to CEDA when programmes or initiatives face insurmountable delays.[50]

The PMO serves as a critical communications hub between CEDA and its subordinate bodies. It is charged with following up on decisions taken by CEDA, as well as monitoring progress made by other agencies towards realizing goals and commitments. It reports to the SMO.[51]

The DU was established in 2016 and is chaired by a technocrat, the acting Minister of Economy and Planning, Faisal bin Fadhil Al Ibrahim. The DU's model is based on the delivery unit approach developed in the UK under Tony Blair. It is mandated is to monitor all of CEDA's economic and development programmes, as well as manage and implement unassigned programmes and initiatives.

The CCU at CEDA is mandated to strengthen the image of Vision 2030, and essentially performs a strategic communications function. It serves to unify messages directed towards the Saudi public and address 'misperceptions' about the Vision.

All the bodies mentioned above are an integral part of a highly centralized system whose collective function is to conceive of, design, mandate, and monitor Vision 2030. They are not, of themselves, implementing agencies, but a complex of units situated between CEDA and those institutions tasked with actually delivering programmes. Although the reporting structures are clear and each unit has a specific mandate, there are natural overlaps, which lead to a duplication of efforts and competition too, but these are features of any governing system. The following institutions exist outside of the centralized decision-making process.

The Adaa, which is an 'independent' organization led by the technocrat Fahd bin Abdullah Toonsi, has the specific aim to assess the performance of government agencies by measuring the performance of public bodies in meeting their targets and gauging satisfaction with government services among end-users. To this end, Adaa established citizen feedback tools in April

---

[50] 'Vision 2030 Operations Framework Set Up', *Arab News* (4 June 2016), https://www.arabnews.com/node/933976/saudi-arabia.

[51] 'CEDA Unveils Integrated Governance Regulation for Vision 2030', *Saudi Gazette* (3 June 2016), https://saudigazette.com.sa/article/156369.

2018, known as the Beneficiary Experience Program (BEX), which seek to assess satisfaction felt by citizens, residents, visitors, and investors in their interactions with government agencies.[52]

The GAC was established in May 2016 and is tasked with supervising, preserving, and developing the Kingdom's cultural sectors. Its overall objective is to reverse decades of policies that pushed against the promotion of its diverse cultural, intellectual, and artistic heritage, in a bid to foster and disseminate common values that deepen the population's sense of national belonging. It is led by the Minister of Culture and Information, Awwad bin Saleh Al-Awwad. A new Board of Directors was formed in April 2018 and includes three women, two of whom are theatre and film directors. The authority has developed sectors—including literature; film and media content; theatre and performing arts; music; and visual arts—with the aim of supporting creativity and talent in the Kingdom.[53]

The GEA, which was created at the same time as the GAC, is responsible for developing and expanding Saudi Arabia's entertainment sector. Crown Prince Mohammed has invested considerable political capital in the GEA, considering it to be not only an engine of growth and employment, but also a vehicle to mobilize and sustain popular support among the Kingdom's young population. Prior to the pandemic, estimates suggested that the Saudi population spent on average $20 billion annually on tourism and entertainment outside the country. Vision 2030 aims to increase household spending on cultural and entertainment events inside the Kingdom from 2.9 per cent to 6 per cent by 2030.[54] The GEA, therefore, was established to develop a tourism sector to appeal not only to foreign visitors, notably religious travellers, but also to Saudi nationals and expatriates with the goal of retaining at least 25 per cent of financial outflows currently going towards international tourism. The Crown Prince has placed this responsibility in the hands of a trusted close aide, Turki bin Abdulmohsen Al Sheikh[55] and a Board of Directors that includes both national and international members.

The DSC was established in May 2016 with the objective of developing evidence-based policy making. It is best described a think tank and reports directly to the royal court. It is dedicated to monitoring and analysing developments and trends at the domestic, regional, and international levels. It is

[52] https://www.adaa.gov.sa/en/BEX.

[53] 'Three Saudi Women Appointed in Newly Formed General Authority for Culture', Al-Arabiya (6 April 2018), https://english.alarabiya.net/en/life-style/art-and-culture/2018/04/06/Three-Saudi-women-become-part-of-newly-formed-General-Authority-for-Culture.html.

[54] S. Dadouch, 'Saudis Promised Double the Fun in 2018 Drive to Lure Back Tourist Dollars', Reuters (22 February 2018), https://www.reuters.com/article/us-saudi-entertainment-idUSKCN1G622T.

[55] The GEA was first chaired by Ahmed al-Khatib, who was later appointed as Minister of Tourism. 'Ahmed Al-Khatib, Saudi Minister of Tourism', Arab News (27 February 2020), https://www.arabnews.com/node/1633776/saudi-arabia.

also tasked with developing scenarios across a range of disciplines, preparing forecasts, and outlining policy pathways and choices to decision-makers in the Council of Ministers, the Committee for Political and Security Affairs, and CEDA. Additionally, it assists in educating the public around governmental decisions.[56] The DSC is led by the Chair of Aramco and Governor of the PIF, Yasir Al-Rumayyan, who has a technocratic background and is now a trusted aide of Crown Prince Mohammed.

The Crown Prince is highly invested in the new institutions, especially as they are purpose built to deliver his vision. However, he is also dependent upon the more formal structures of governance—namely, key ministries—to manage the country. The complex of formal and informal institutions, which can best be described as a mixture of government and hybrid institutions, forms a network of bodies invested with the direct authority of the Crown Prince to pursue the 'big' policy items, including those referenced above. On the other hand, those aspects of the Vision that fit with the more traditional sectors of governance, such as energy, environment, education, and religion, sit within ministries. Nevertheless, the division of labour is far less clear than it might appear, given the overlap between key areas such as housing and employment, and as often happens when authorities overlap, this results in competition among agencies not only for resources, but also for access to the highest decision-maker.

The undertaking to repurpose the technocratic ministries has followed a particular pattern, which highlights both the Crown Prince's overriding goal of bringing about rapid change and his impatience with outer circle advisers and willingness to dispense with them at will. This pattern can be seen in the ministries of Human Resources and Social Development; Industry and Mineral Resources; Environment, Water and Agriculture; and Hajj and Umrah. The following section reviews the principal ministries that Crown Prince Mohammed has come to rely upon—it is notable that they have been redesigned as 'new' ministries.

New Ministries

Since coming to prominence, Crown Prince Mohammed has repurposed some of the Kingdom's key ministries and, in some instances, created super-ministries and brought them under aegis of his 'champions'. Again, the Crown Prince has appointed ministers who can be considered to be part of his inner and outer circle, in whom he has placed considerable trust.

---

[56] https://www.mondaq.com/saudiarabia/constitutional-administrative-law/498732/the-new-saudi-arabian-decision-making-support-center.

Ministries such as the Ministry of Industry and Mineral Resources, the Ministry of Tourism, and the Ministry of Investment are considered to be instrumental in marshalling the country's resources into serving Vision 2030. As such, they form an integral part of the institutional architecture purposed with transforming the Kingdom.

Six 'new' ministries emerged to complement and, in fact, compete with the newly created institutions. They initially comprised: the Ministry of Human Resources and Social Development; the Ministry of Energy, Industry and Mineral Resources; the Ministry of Investment; the Ministry of Tourism; the Ministry of Environment, Water and Agriculture; and the Ministry of Hajj and Umrah.

The Ministry of Human Resources and Social Development was established in 2019 after merging the ministries of Labor and Social Development and Civil Service. It is responsible for formulating government policy on social and labour affairs and undertakes to guide social development in a way that balances the goal of improving living standards with upholding the Kingdom's spiritual and moral framework. The current minister, Ahmed Al Rajhi, a technocrat from a well-known business family, was appointed in June 2018.[57]

The Ministry of Petroleum and Mineral Resources was reorganized as the Ministry of Energy, Industry and Mineral Resources in May 2016 with Khalid Al Falih, a technocrat and internationally respected energy leader, appointed as minister. In August 2019, however, the ministry was split into the Ministry of Energy and the Ministry of Industry and Mineral Resources. In September 2019, Crown Prince Mohammed's half-brother, Prince Abdulaziz bin Salman, replaced Al Falih, who remained without office until February 2020 when he became Minister of Investment (see below). At the time, the move appeared aimed at diminishing the influence of Saudi Arabia's 'Mr Energy', as well as instilling some momentum into stalled policy initiatives in the industrial and mining sectors.

While independent from the ministries of Energy and of Industry and Mineral Resources, Saudi Aramco is directly overseen by a board that comprises Ministers of Finance, the former Minister of Foreign Affairs and Finance, the adviser to the royal court, a member of CEDA, a board member of the PIF and Chairman of its Investment Committee, five overseas representatives, and Saudi Aramco's President and Chief Executive Officer (CEO). The national oil company has increasingly sought to model itself on the lines of an international oil company but remains wedded to its national obligations, with

---

[57] https://hrsd.gov.sa/.

incremental politicization—counterintuitive given the initial public offering in 2019—having been under way for some time. Crown Prince Mohammed and those around him are relying on the national champion to help the Kingdom push forward with Vision 2030, and transition to a post-oil era.

The Ministry of Industry and Mineral Resources, which is led by private sector investor Bandar Al Khorayef, aims to increase the value of mining operations from $21.3 billion to $69.3 billion per annum. Saudi Arabia's central and northern regions contain large amounts of bauxite, as well as silver, zinc, copper, magnesite, and kaolin deposits. The country is also host to some of the world's largest reserves of phosphate and tantalum, and up to 20 million ounces of gold in known deposits. The Kingdom aims to attract foreign investors to explore such deposits, as part of the mandate of the new ministry—which oversees the Saudi Industrial Property Authority.[58]

The Ministry of Investment of Saudi Arabia was set up in February 2020 and replaced the Saudi Arabian General Investment Authority. It is headed by Khalid Al Falih, former Minister of Energy, Minister of Health, and CEO of Aramco. Since February 2020, Al Falih has been building the new ministry and appointing a new team, which complements the activities of the PIF. The ministry is responsible for drawing investment into the Kingdom and has been tasked with encouraging global businesses to relocate their headquarters from neighbouring states to Riyadh.

The Ministry of Tourism was established by a royal decree in February 2020, upgrading the former Saudi Commission for Tourism and National Heritage, which had been led by Crown Prince Mohammed's half-brother, Prince Sultan bin Salman Abdulaziz. Its goal is to revolutionize the tourist sector in the Kingdom, encouraging domestic, religious, and high-end international tourism. It is led by Crown Prince Mohammed's trusted aide, Ahmed Al Khatib, who is also responsible for developing the country's local defence industry.

The Ministry of Environment, Water and Agriculture was established in 2016 after the Ministry of Water and Electricity was abolished. It is led by the technocrat Abdulrahman Abdulmohsen Al Fadley.[59] The new ministry's ambitious but crucial remit includes supporting agriculture in the pursuit of water and food security, while achieving sustainability of the environment and natural resources.

[58] V. R. Leotaud, 'Saudi Arabia Creates New Ministry of Industry and Mining', *Mining Intelligence* (1 September 2019), https://www.mining.com/saudi-arabia-creates-new-ministry-of-industry-and-mineral-resources/.

[59] https://www.mewa.gov.sa/en/Ministry/AboutMinistry/Pages/MinistryBrief.aspx.

Finally, the Ministry of Hajj and Umrah handles all issues related to pilgrimage and Umrah. The ministry is headed by Tawfiq bin Fawzan Al-Rabiah, a technocrat.[60] The ministry coordinates between different sectors catering to Hajj and Umrah operations as well as between different Hajj-related agencies in countries all over the world. It is responsible for developing plans as well as implementing and supervising the services provided to pilgrims and visitors of the two holy mosques. The ministry also launched an application to issue e-visas for Umrah visitors and pilgrims.[61]

So far, this chapter has depicted the institutional architecture designed to deliver Vision 2030. It has alluded to the core constituent agencies that comprise the 'nerve centre' of the operation: namely, CEDA and its subordinate units, newly created authorities tasked with creating and enhancing underdeveloped parts of the economy, and, finally, repurposed ministries. Of course, putting in place such an architecture is no guarantee of success, and in any case the task of realizing Vision 2030—in its entirety—is a monumental project. The challenge is made even greater as previous efforts to transform the economy have ultimately failed. Although it is not possible or indeed within the ambit of this chapter to evaluate all of the institutions listed above, we next consider the efficacy of four institutions in the form of case studies.

Case Studies

In any system, there are stresses and strains, as well as constraints and restraints on the units that make up the system. These often come in the form of poor governance, limited capacity, over-ambition alongside financial constraints, redundancy, intra-unit competition, and poor integration in the system itself, among other factors. Such stresses and strains are multiplied when transforming an existing system or creating a subsystem intended to complement or subvert it. The institutional architecture described above, naturally, suffers from all of these factors, especially as the existing system is being repurposed to deliver against the goals set out in Vision 2030 alongside newly created service institutions established to achieve the same goal. In many cases, as detailed below, key institutions have similar or overlapping remits, share the same set of leaders, and compete for resources. At the same time, they draw upon and compete for a limited pool of human resources,

---

[60] https://www.haj.gov.sa/en.
[61] 'E-service for Umrah Expanded', *Arab News* (7 January 2013), https://www.arabnews.com/e-service-umrah-expanded.

which amounts to a cadre of Saudi elite who have for the most part studied outside the Kingdom and are versed in approaches, methodologies, and pedagogies of Western educational and business systems and practices.

As a result, many of the institutions currently undergoing change, or those that have been newly created, lack depth or capacity to sustain early successes or achieve the KPIs set out for them. In many cases, it is still early days to evaluate the true success of these institutions, as so much rests in the hands of their leaders and their ability not only to give direction and mobilize resources, but also to recruit staff, inspire confidence in them, and, at the same time, to empower them and, by doing so, retain them. Furthermore, a full understanding of the culture of each institution requires primary research in the form of access to decision-makers, personnel, and documentation. Circumstances have not permitted this, so we focus here more on the mandates and challenges that these institutions face, rather than providing an in-depth analysis of their capacities and capabilities. The following case studies highlight some of these issues faced by the DSC, Adaa, the GEA, the Ministry of Tourism, and the PIF.

Decision Support Center

Despite the royal court sometimes being accused of being 'cut off' from other Saudi institutions and bodies, one arm of the royal court, the DSC, has made efforts to engage, both nationally and internationally, with a wide range of expert opinion across a broad range of issues that are of direct concern to the Saudi government and society. The DSC occupies a unique space within the Saudi system and can serve as a semi-independent policy and research centre dedicated to supporting a wide pool of decision-makers with evidence-based analysis. Since being established, it has gone to considerable lengths to develop in-house capacity and learn from and benchmark itself against similar institutions in North America, Europe, and Asia. However, its capacity cannot be developed overnight and will take many years, although it has attracted a strong pool of national talent, which will drive it towards that goal.

Unlike other policy research centres in the Kingdom, the DSC is vertically linked from the royal court to grassroots level, rather than horizontally linked to similar institutions. According to a DSC official, the centre understands that major domestic issues, such as unemployment among nationals, cannot be solved unless the DSC consults relevant parties outside the confines of the royal court. Furthermore, it is insufficient to focus solely on high-profile, 'glamorous' issues, such as future cities and entertainment options. The DSC and other governmental bodies have a duty to address real problems that citizens face, such as unemployment. For example, the DSC was tasked with considering ways to make private sector jobs in sectors such as defence, food production, and construction more attractive to young Saudis. The DSC is also trying to focus on the demand side by finding out what employers in these sectors require from Saudi employees. It is important to consider both sides of the coin—the employee and the employer—in order to attempt to solve the structural problems associated with unemployment among nationals.[62]

As previously argued, high-profile projects such as Neom and the Red Sea Resort are not going to help the Saudization of jobs. A frequent complaint is that the people who run these projects are only interested in achieving their set objectives within budget and on time—Saudization is irrelevant to them, even though young nationals could be employed on the ground in these areas.

As a newly formed institution, the DSC benefits from being invested with a clear mandate, having leadership that is directly connected to the royal court and the capacity to attract national talent. It also benefits from occupying a unique space within the decision-making institutional structure and faces no real domestic competitor. Its real challenge comes from favoured consultancies, which have dominated the space since 2016.

National Center for Performance Management

Adaa was set up as independent organization and exists outside of the established governing structures, reporting directly into the office of the Prime Minister, formerly King Salman bin Abdulaziz Al Saud and, since September 2022, Crown Prince Mohammed. It is neither a government ministry nor an agency tasked with delivering Vision 2030, but it is mandated to monitor government performance. It works closely with public agencies to measure progress and create a culture of transparency and accountability, which has often been lacking in the past. As such, it measures the performance of public bodies against targets and KPIs, and surveys end-user satisfaction with government services. In 2018, Adaa established a citizen feedback tool as part of the BEX, which targets the experiences of citizens, residents, visitors, and investors.[63] It has also launched the International Performance Hub, which

[62] Author's interviews, Riyadh, 2019.
[63] 'Adaa Officially Launches Watani App to Measure People's Satisfaction', *Saudi Gazette* (16 February 2019), https://saudigazette.com.sa/article/559309.

benchmarks more than 200 countries in relation to over 700 KPIs under twelve main pillars.[64]

Adaa faces the same challenges as other agencies in competing for and retaining qualified staff and developing its own capacity to perform. However, given that it reports directly into the Prime Minister's office it appears well resourced and supported. In fact, one consequence of its success has been the broadening of its scope, which in many ways is a double-edged sword, as it now not only monitors and evaluates government agencies, but also crafts interventions to improve both performance and customer satisfaction.

Adaa performs a hybrid function of assessor and consultancy, as it helps the subjects of its enquiries enhance capability, improve performance, and further develop services. In doing so, Adaa has borrowed heavily from the international consultants' 'playbook' by standardizing relevant tools, methods, and approaches, and raising the performance measurement of public bodies by identifying issues through a process of consultation and communication.[65] Its methods also include a package of training provided by domestic and international teams to build capabilities through continuous training based on international best practices.[66]

General Entertainment Authority

The GEA is the cornerstone of Vision 2030 and has been placed in the trusted hands of Turki Al Sheikh, one of Crown Prince Mohammed's closest aides and the former President of the General Sports Authority.

As noted above, GEA is tasked with transforming and developing the Kingdom's entertainment industry. It is arguably the most prominent of the new agencies and it has certainly grabbed the headlines both domestically and internationally. To that end, it has sought not only to capitalize upon the Kingdom's natural resources and create a new industry, which can compete with all its neighbours, but also, by doing so, to change outside perceptions of Saudi Arabia. Certainly, pre-COVID-19, it struggled to change those perceptions, however, given the negative attention that the Kingdom drew

[64] 'Adaa, the Saudi National Center for Performance Measurement, Introduces Tool to Improve Data-Led Policy-Making to DC Audiences', PR Newswire (21 March 2018), https://www.prnewswire.com/news-releases/adaa-the-saudi-national-center-for-performance-measurement-introduces-tool-to-improve-data-led-policy-making-to-dc-audiences-300617170.html.
[65] World Bank, 'How to Set Up a Government-Wide Monitoring Framework: Learning from Saudi Arabia' (25 May 2018), https://www.worldbank.org/en/news/feature/2018/05/25/how-to-set-up-a-government-wide-monitoring-framework-learning-from-saudi-arabia.
[66] 'Saudi: Adaa Center Qualifies 5,700 Employees from 28 State Agencies', Asharq al-Awsat (1 February 2019), https://english.aawsat.com//home/article/1571971/saudi-adaa-center-qualifies-5700-employees-28-state-agencies.

from a number of high-profile issues, including the war in Yemen, the Jamal Khashoggi affair, and the temporary detention of then serving Lebanese Prime Minister Rafiq Hariri, among other things. However, post pandemic, it has begun to change perceptions in the Middle East region (and beyond) breaking down older tropes and stereotypes of the country.

The GEA has hosted a wide array of high-profile events, ranging from wrestling to comic cons (conventions) to multiple festivals held in different regions across the country;[67] it also organized more than 5,000 shows, events, and concerts in 2018.[68] In March 2019, the GEA in collaboration with the General Sports Authority, the Saudi Commission for Tourism, and National Heritage organized a seventeen-day 'Sharqiah Season' in the eastern region, which was very successful and was later repeated in Riyadh, lasting for seventy days and more than 100 events during the period October 2019–January 2020. The events were organized by 280 Saudi companies with a manpower of 24,000 seasonal workers in addition to more than 22,000 part-timers.[69] This was an impressive endeavour, clearly enjoyed much success, and, at the same time, showed the public appetite for such occasions. Because of its success, Riyadh Season has become an annual event, attracting large numbers of visitors from inside the Kingdom as well as many others from the neighbouring Gulf states. In this way, the GEA has been able to tap into a reservoir of widespread public interest, although interviewees for this chapter remained critical of some major events, given that they fall outside of the Kingdom's cultural norms and have been enjoyed by a small, affluent elite. Of course, the advent of the COVID-19 throughout 2020 curtailed the activities of the GEA; however, the Kingdom resumed its entertainment activities in 2021: for example, AlUla region celebrates Winter at Tantora, a four-month programme of events, running from December to March annually; the region also offers other experiences such as Hegra After Dark, and art events such as Desert X AlUla 2022, available to book via the Experience AlUla website.[70]

The GEA partners with both public and private actors to reduce government spending on entertainment and this has included working closely with international businesses, such as Six Flags Entertainment Corporation, which has plans to open at least three theme parks in the country from 2022 onwards. Furthermore, the Development and Investment Entertainment Company, a subsidiary of the PIF, signed, in April 2018, an agreement

---

[67] The Kingdom hosts eleven festivals, known as Saudi Seasons: namely, Riyadh Season; Jeddah Season; Eastern Province Season; Taif Season; Al Soudah Season; National Day Season; Al-Diriyah Season; AlUla Season; Hail Season; Ramadan Season; and Eid Al-Fitr Season.

[68] Dadouch, 'Saudis Promised Double the Fun'.

[69] 'Riyadh Season Extended Till End of Jan 2020', *Saudi Gazette* (18 November 2019), https://saudigazette.com.sa/article/582890.

[70] https://www.experiencealula.com/.

with AMC Theaters to operate AMC cinemas in the Kingdom. According to the agreement, AMC will initially open between thirty and forty cinemas in about fifteen cities in Saudi Arabia, and a total of fifty to a hundred cinemas in around twenty-five Saudi cities by 2030.[71]

To date, the GEA's projects have been 'hit and miss', however, and have been criticized by many Saudi business leaders, as they remain predominantly driven by the state rather than by the domestic private sector. There is considerable debate among business, trade, and diplomatic communities about the merits of state-driven major projects. On the one hand, some argue that because the new entertainment sector requires social norm-defying measures, it rests upon the government to forge ahead and take bold initiatives. Additionally, the state has the resources, capacity, and risk appetite to take the lead, and can eventually step back and leave the private sector to fill that space. On the other hand, critics of the approach believe that the state has every intention of marginalizing the domestic private sector: first, as it has very little faith in its ability to deliver; and secondly, because it wants to continue in its capacity as 'rentier' state, marshal all available reserves, and manage diversification from above. What is clear, however, is that the domestic private sector has neither the capacity nor the means for the time being to take forward major initiatives, and, therefore, the task rests with the state to do so.

Many of those interviewed for this chapter argued that the choice and high cost of many events to date has tended to serve the interests of urban elites. While breaking down social customs and norms has been at the forefront of Vision 2030 and hosting celebrity entertainers from North America may be popular with a proportion of Saudi youth, they argued, it largely caters for urbanites and the intelligentsia, and that has become a point of contention for those residing outside urban centres. Of course, this approach is symptomatic of a system managed predominantly by Western-educated elites, even though the Crown Prince does not share that particular background. Having said that, the 'Seasons' have enjoyed popular appeal and appear to be better suited to the tastes and interests of the wider population.

Former GEA Chairman, Ahmed Al Khatib, stated in 2016 that the organization had been created to boost citizen participation and opportunities for young people,[72] and it has, to some extent, worked towards that goal. It launched in 2019 a scholarship programme intended to train and educate young Saudis in the entertainment field at foreign universities, undertaken in partnership with the Qiddiya Investment Company. The programme should

[71] https://www.pif.gov.sa/en/MediaCenter/Pages/NewsDetails.aspx?NewsID=39.
[72] 'General Authority for Entertainment Chief Seeks Citizen Participation', *Arab News* (27 December 2016), https://www.arabnews.com/node/1030206/saudi-arabia.

support students in finding employment in the Qiddiya mega project as well as in the many other entertainment projects taking place in Saudi Arabia.[73]

The GEA has sought to balance the range of interventions and activities that it and its partners have introduced to the Kingdom. While the penchant appears to be more towards garnering Western or international artists and activities, it has also sought to align some events more with the Kingdom's traditions. In 2019, for example, it helped organize the largest Qur'ān competition and the first Adhan competition.[74] The goal was to highlight cultural diversity within the Islamic world and affirm Saudi Arabia's position within it.

Ministry of Tourism

The Ministry of Tourism is another institution invested with resources to achieve the goals of Vision 2030. It is led by Ahmed Al Khatib, one of Crown Prince Mohammed's closest aides. Al Khatib holds a number of prominent portfolios in the Vision 2030 canon, including Chair of Saudi Arabian Military Industries, and is entrusted with transforming the Kingdom into a major tourist destination.

As a key tenet of Vision 2030, tourism is at the forefront of political and policy priorities. It forms a crucial part of diversifying the economy and its development from a practically standing start should bring many positive effects. However, as they stand the plans appear too ambitious to be realized within the timeframe allocated, especially considering the focus on foreign tourism.

Saudi Arabia's plans to open up the country to tourism were advancing prior to COVID-19 and have, to a large degree, continued. In spite of Covid, the ministry has gone to considerable lengths to promote the Kingdom's diverse heritage sites and landscapes in a bid to transform traditional images of the Kingdom. This forms part of a wider campaign to change subconscious associations with Saudi Arabia.

With the aim of securing a 70:30 ratio of non-religious to religious foreign visitors by 2030, the Kingdom has developed a tourism plan which is mainly focused on leisure. The relaxation of social norms and increase in domestic-led investments in the entertainment sector, as noted above, are

---

[73] 'Saudi GEA, Qiddiya Initiate Scholarship Program for Entertainment Disciplines', Al-Arabiya (4 July 2019), https://english.alarabiya.net/en/life-style/entertainment/2019/07/04/Saudi-GEA-Qiddiya-announce-scholarship-program-for-entertainment-disciplines.

[74] 'GEA to Shortlist 42,000 Applications for Qur'an and Adhan Competitions', Saudi Gazette (25 August 2019), https://saudigazette.com.sa/article/575430.

aligned with plans to grow the domestic tourism market. These ventures are also likely to make local businesses thrive. Such opportunities lie not only in entertainment-related ventures, such as cinemas, but also in family-friendly, lower-budget accommodation, given that domestic tourists spend an estimated three times less per day than foreign tourists, and they travel with extended family members for longer time periods.

To this end, substantial investment has been earmarked for expanding and diversifying offerings, such as hosting international events as well as providing 'high-end' tourists with luxury destinations, access to heritage sites, and eco-tourism experiences. Government agencies have also announced major agreements with travel agencies, real-estate, and retail companies as well as major hotel groups. This, in effect, has created movement in the construction sector, where approximately 48,000 new rooms—almost 40 per cent of construction projects in the Middle East—are expected to be added to the supply of tourist accommodation over the next decade.[75] Furthermore, the Ministry of Tourism announced in June 2020 plans to establish a Tourism Development Fund with an initial capital investment of $4 billion, which will launch equity and debt investment vehicles to develop the tourism sector in collaboration with the private sector and investment banks.[76]

In addition to obvious geopolitical risks in the region and the generally negative press surrounding Saudi Arabia, more specific hurdles facing the sector include logistical under-capacity, labour shortages, and social issues. Strong government commitment to mega projects does not protect investors against exposure to inefficient bureaucracy, public fiscal pressures, or red tape. The payments system is known to be particularly cumbersome and instances of companies not being paid and suffering damaging cashflow problems are well documented. Therefore, the ministry will need to develop a better system, supported by regulatory powers, which not only compels government agencies and associated businesses to pay vendors on time, but also penalizes those that do not comply. Such actions cannot simply rest with the minister, to whom the issue is finally passed as others in the chain of command are not authorized to act.

Although the plans look impressive on paper and the directives from the ministry are clear, it remains to be seen whether the ministry has the capacity to manage such a large, complex undertaking. Government-led projects in the region—notably, in Egypt, Jordan, and (in the past) Syria—have often led

[75] J. Arnold, M. Hickey, and S. Pillai, 'Spotlight: Saudi Arabia Hotel Market', Savills (21 January 2019), https://www.savills.com.eg/research_articles/243971/274275-0.
[76] 'Saudi Arabia to Launch $4 Billion Tourism Development Fund', Amwal al-Ghad (21 June 2020), https://en.amwalalghad.com/saudi-arabia-to-launch-4-billion-tourism-development-fund/.

to suboptimal results, not only because regional events have affected tourist numbers, but also because the provision of services has fallen well below international standards. Servicing the tourism sector at a standard demanded by international tourists will, therefore, constitute a significant challenge for the Kingdom. Notwithstanding private and public initiatives to train human capital for hospitality—for example, the OYO Skills Institute and Takamul—the dual aims of tripling the number of tourism-related jobs and increasing the percentage of Saudis in them will run counter to each other, as an increase in foreign workers will be required.[77]

The degree to which the Ministry of Tourism tries to manage development of the sector will have a direct impact upon its success and, more importantly, the sector's longevity and sustainability. The early signs are positive that it will seek to play a more regulatory and supportive role, rather than one that micromanages the sector.

Public Investment Fund

The PIF is Saudi Arabia's primary sovereign wealth fund (SWF), established in 1971 with the objective of funding the economic development of the Kingdom. While originally intended to act as an 'angel investor', providing financial support to companies in the start-up phase, it remained a silent partner in numerous Saudi state-owned companies, such as the chemicals and metals group SABIC.[78] The PIF only became more prominent on the global stage in 2015 when it was brought under the chairmanship of Crown Prince Mohammed and its mandate was broadened. In fact, between December 2015 and September 2017, the PIF's assets had already increased by almost 50 per cent, from $152 billion to $224 billion, reaching around $360 billion in 2018. The current assets under management are estimated at $620 billion,[79] making it one of the largest SWFs globally, but still significantly smaller than its regional neighbours, the Abu Dhabi Investment Authority (ADIA) and the Kuwait Investment Authority (KIA), both of which are much older as well as more globally engaged.

[77] D. Moshashai and R. Uppal, 'Tourism as a Pillar of the New Saudi Arabia?', *Gulf Monitor* (3 December 2019), https://castlereagh.net/tourism-as-a-pillar-of-the-new-saudi-arabia/.

[78] S. Hall, 'A Sovereign Wealth Fund for the Prince: Economic Reforms and Power Consolidation in Saudi Arabia', SWP Research Paper 8 (Berlin: German Institute for International and Security Affairs, 2019).

[79] H. El-Sayegh, 'Saudi PIF Buys Shares in Alphabet, Zoom and Microsoft in US Shopping Spree', Reuters (16 August 2022), https://www.reuters.com/markets/europe/saudi-pif-buys-shares-alphabet-zoom-microsoft-us-shopping-spree-2022-08-16/.

Vision 2030 plans to develop the PIF into the largest SWF in the world, managing financial assets worth $2 trillion. It is intended that the PIF will help diversify state revenues, opening up new economic sectors—especially for private sector involvement—and directing foreign direct investment to the Kingdom, hopefully leading to knowledge and technology transfer. To this end, rather than acting as a passive investor, the PIF is set to invest actively in (1) existing Saudi companies, (2) Saudi companies to be established, (3) real estate and infrastructure in Saudi Arabia, (4) 'giga' development projects, (5) international strategic partnerships with funds and companies, and (6) international capital investments with a long-term profit orientation.

In terms of strategy, there has always been a sense that the PIF is constantly trying to play catch-up with regional peers but wants to fast-track the kind of returns that investments by ADIA or KIA and even the Qatar Investment Authority (QIA) have generated over many years. Although the PIF has a well-defined strategy and a mandate to achieve the objectives of that strategy, this has not so far played out in its international investments.[80] To a large extent, the PIF missed out on the heyday of the 1990s and beyond, and then, more recently, it was not able to capitalize on the spending spree unleashed by the 2008–9 financial crisis, which proved particularly fruitful for the QIA, until the Qatar Stock Exchange stepped in. Starting from a solid base, the United Arab Emirates is now in a position where it has two major SWFs—ADIA and Mubadala—which serve different state interests, in terms of domestic economic development objectives as well as economic diversification through a sophisticated global investment portfolio.

To the extent that any SWF can be really be independent, the PIF would feature towards the lower end of the spectrum. One criticism often levelled is that it is managed like a personal investment vehicle of the Crown Prince, and he is ultimately responsible for all major investment decisions—with little regard for bankers and advisers. Crown Prince Mohammed has been known to rely on his gut instinct and rapport with people more often than on financial arguments. This was especially seen to be the case with a $45 billion investment in SoftBank's Vision Fund 1, compared to Mubadala's $15 billion. The technology fund has suffered a massive depreciation in value in 2019 and plans to launch a second Vision Fund remain on hold as both Saudi Arabia and Abu Dhabi await a turn in market conditions. This top-down decision-making strategy provides little motivation for bankers/financiers

---

[80] https://vision2030.gov.sa/sites/default/files/attachments/PIF%20Program_EN_0.pdf.

and risk teams to work in the Kingdom, due to their limited contribution and the perception that it is necessary be part of the inner circle to be heard.

The predominantly Saudi-led and Saudi-based operational structure at the PIF, and the fact it has only been more active recently, has led to a lack of strong, established relationships globally, much as ADIA and KIA have developed over many years. The Saudi SWF has also been constrained by a lack of in-house expertise, although this is certainly changing with a raft of new hires in key senior positions in more recent times. Despite the expected high salaries on offer, the lure of relocating to Riyadh for expatriates is not as strong as it is to other cities in the region, such as Dubai, Abu Dhabi, and Doha. An international presence may change that view among some top finance executives.

Conclusion: Creating Solutions or Adding Bureaucratic Layers?

This chapter has argued that Crown Prince Mohammed understood early on that Saudi Arabia's institutions were not fit for purpose if they were to deliver against the ambitious targets of Vision 2030. This realization has given rise to repurposed and new institutions tasked with helping transform the Kingdom as it journeys towards a post-hydrocarbon (and post-pandemic) future. We have discussed the pathway followed by Crown Prince Mohammed and his trusted inner circle in not only changing the Kingdom's institutional infrastructure, but also developing its capacity by drawing on Saudi Arabia's youth dividend. At the same time, we have addressed the thorny issue of foreign management consultancies and the role they have played in the Kingdom's transition, which has often divided opinion within Saudi Arabia.[81]

We have attempted to assess whether the reconfigured and newly created post-2016 institutions have been effective to date in delivering Vision 2030. In truth, it is too early to make a robust assessment and it requires access to decision-makers, personnel, and documentation in each institution which was unavailable for this research. Nevertheless, there are features within the institutional landscape and characteristics embedded within the early cultures of each institution which allow for analysis. Our research, which has drawn upon primary and secondary sources, set out to answer three key questions in assessing the efficacy of the institutions examined:

---

[81] And at the time of writing in 2022 it continues to do so.

- Have changes to government and hybrid institutions helped the Saudi government to become more efficient, and if this is the case, how is this efficiency measured?
- To what extent have Saudi management consulting firms contributed towards Vision 2030 and what proportion of this work continues to be carried out by foreign management consultancies?
- To what extent have foreign consultancy firms helped Saudi Arabia or, in fact, inhibited its development?

First, foreign management consultancies continue to play a dominant role in contributing towards Vision 2030 and are given a higher priority than Saudi management consultancies. Although criticism has grown over the past few years and an aversion to 'cookie-cutter' solutions has developed among decision-makers, foreign management consultancies continue to be revered and admired by the Kingdom's most senior leaders. The balance is likely to shift in the coming years as more and more young Saudis pass through the foreign management consultancy machine and look to apply their newly acquired skills and experience in better-situated Saudi-led consultancies. From our own observations, this process is already happening.

Secondly, Vision 2030 was largely informed and shaped by international consultancies, which put together a package aimed at transforming the Kingdom and kickstarting its journey towards the post-hydrocarbon era. In that sense, they were instrumental in filling the significant capacity gaps found in state institutions and also recruiting young Saudis into the Vision 2030 process, which helped with achieving efficiencies and ensuring popular buy-in of the overall project among Saudi youth. Foreign management consultancies, therefore, helped the Saudi government clear the route for Vision 2030. However, by doing so, they also made themselves an indispensable part of the process, and instead of enabling institutions to develop their own capacities and pursue an independent pathway, they have tended to create a culture of dependency, especially among senior decision-makers, many of whom continue to rely upon external expert advice. As such, the contribution that foreign management consultancies now offer is finely balanced between help and hindrance with an increasing tendency towards the latter.

There are other issues all too familiar in Saudi Arabia's longstanding institutions. They include an intense competition for resources among peer institutions—not only financial, but also in terms of securing time and access to the Kingdom's most senior leaders—and a still limited, although growing rapidly, pool of available human capital. At times, there remains some unproductive redundancy, as the newly established and reconfigured institutions and agencies coexist with their predecessors and, in some cases, pursue overlapping mandates. Finally, the manner in which these institutions have been established—with guidance from foreign management consultancies—has set in store a number of problems they will need to overcome, if they are to meet their objectives.

Yet there can be little doubt that repurposing key ministries, creating new agencies, and forming hybrid institutions tasked specifically with meeting Vision 2030 targets has been a positive move. It has not only empowered decision-makers with the authority to overcome bureaucratic inertia, but also opened doors to a new generation of young Saudis to push forward a national project. In the final analysis, Saudi Arabia is a country with its sights set firmly on the future, to 2030 and beyond.

11
The Political Economy of Reforms under Vision 2030

Steffen Hertog

Introduction

Although Saudi plans for economic diversification are almost as old as the Saudi oil age itself, the economic reform agenda that started with Vision 2030 in 2016 is unprecedented in reach and ambition. Within just a few years, key taboos have been broken regarding taxation, subsidy reform, high-profile deployment of sovereign wealth, and opening of new sectors like tourism and entertainment. At the same time, the new reform drive has not yet tackled many of the basic structural constraints that have held back non-oil growth in past decades, most notably dependence on low-cost foreign labour and, closely related, a wealth distribution system that disincentivizes skills acquisition and entrepreneurial efforts among citizens while increasing their reservation wages.

This chapter analyses the structure of the Saudi social contract and how it relates to the Kingdom's traditional 'growth model', focusing specifically on how wealth distribution has been used to grow consumer markets. It examines attempts to adjust the social contract since 2015, how they have affected growth, and how the persistence of the old social contract is holding back the economic diversification process under the Vision.

The Saudi Social Contract

The Saudi social contract, like that of other Gulf Cooperation Council (GCC) countries, relies on broad-based wealth distribution through several channels. These include energy subsidies, housing aid, free education and health care, and, most importantly, an implicit government employment guarantee for (at least male) citizens. The only other country in the world that

Steffen Hertog, *The Political Economy of Reforms under Vision 2030*. In: *The Economy of Saudi Arabia in the 21st Century*. Edited by: John Sfakianakis, Oxford University Press. © Steffen Hertog (2024). DOI: 10.1093/oso/9780198863878.003.0012

shares its wealth with its citizens as generously as the GCC countries is tiny oil-rich Brunei. Decades of rent sharing have led to the emergence of a broad, state-dependent middle class with its own material expectations and vested interests across the GCC.[1]

It is worth remembering that the origins of the Saudi social contract are political, if only to underline that any adjustment to it is an essentially political process facing potential political constraints. The emergence of large-scale oil rents after the Second World War did not automatically lead to wealth distribution.[2] Instead, the Saudi leadership pursued the rapid expansion of public employment and public goods provision to an important extent as a counter-revolutionary measure at a time when Arab nationalism and other leftist ideologies appeared to threaten the Saudi monarchy in the late 1950s and 1960s. Then Prime Minister Prince Faisal's ten-point programme in 1962 took up many of the economic demands of the nationalist opposition and the archival record shows that Faisal saw economic development and wealth distribution as tools to counteract republican opposition.[3]

To understand the political economy of this mass co-optation process, it is important to emphasize that it has not happened primarily through conventional 'welfare state' mechanisms; calling Saudi Arabia a welfare state is a misnomer. While social safety and security mechanisms like publicly supported pensions, unemployment benefits, and income supplements for poor families and widows exist in the Kingdom, they constitute only a small share of the overall patronage system. Instead, wealth sharing relies on an essentially Nasserist model of state employment. Social benefits amounted to only SAR77 billion of SAR1,048 billion of total state spending in 2019, compared to SAR504 billion of expenditure on public sector employee compensation (the official subsidy tally reached SAR22 billion, which, however, undercounts implicit energy subsidies of perhaps SAR100 billion or more).[4]

The share of public sector salaries in the national budget in Saudi Arabia is about twice as high as the typical share for advanced countries. It is the budget item that has grown the most consistently over the years, even during episodes of relative austerity like the years of low oil prices from the

[1] M. Herb, *The Wages of Oil: Parliaments and Economic Development in Kuwait and the UAE* (Ithaca, NY: Cornell University Press, 2014).
[2] G. Okruhlik, 'Rentier Wealth, Unruly Law, and the Rise of Opposition: The Political Economy of Oil States', *Comparative Politics* 31, no. 3 (1999), pp. 295–315.
[3] S. Hertog, 'Challenges to the Saudi Distributional State in the Age of Austerity', in M. Al-Rasheed (ed.), *Salman's Legacy* (Oxford: Oxford University Press, 2018), pp. 73–96.
[4] Ministry of Finance, 'Budget Statement', 2020.

mid-1980s to the late 1990s and the post-2014 period until 2020. In short, the Saudi social contract revolves primarily around public employment.

The majority of Saudis in dependent employment continue to work for the government. The exact number of public employees is not known as many of them work in the security sector and other areas that do not fall under published civil service statistics, which only indicate 1.48 million Saudi government employees. We know from official labour force survey data, however, that average public sector salaries reached SAR116,000/month in early 2020, while total official wage spending in 2019 reached SAR504 billion. Combining the two figures results in an estimated number of 3.6 million citizens holding public jobs. This also roughly aligns with Crown Prince Mohammad bin Salman's own public statements, in which he has mentioned about 3 million government employees.[5]

The total number of Saudi private sector employees, by contrast, was only 1.7 million in early 2020, with their total wage income only reaching SAR150 billion due to lower average wages of SAR7,300/month.[6] The public sector is not only a lot larger than the private labour market for Saudis, it also pays considerably better on average. This contrasts with the situation in non-rentier countries—both rich and poor—where public employees seldom exceed a third of the total labour force and the vast majority of wages are generated in the private economy.

Figure 11.1 shows that Saudi labour markets continue to be deeply segmented, with private employment dominated by foreign workers and sheltered government employment largely reserved for Saudis. This structure has remained largely unchanged since 2015. While the expansion of public employment has slowed down due to fiscal constraints, private sector employment of Saudis has barely budged since 2015. Saudis' labour market participation continues to be very low, moreover, with only 46.7 per cent of working-age Saudis active as (employed or unemployed) participants in the labour market.

In many ways, the Saudi labour market and the country's wider benefits systems are an extreme version of a general Arab social contract that also exists in less affluent countries in the Middle East and North Africa (MENA) region and which relies excessively on public employment and subsidies as quasi-welfare tools. This type of wealth distribution system

[5] https://www.pbs.org/wgbh/frontline/article/mohammed-bin-salman-speaks-about-role-khashoggis-murder-first-time/.
[6] General Authority for Statistics (GASTAT), *Labor Force Survey Bulletin*, Q1, 2020.

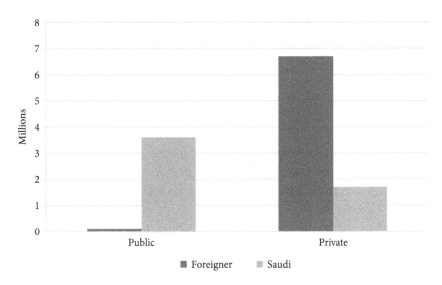

Figure 11.1 Segmentation of labor markets in Saudi Arabia, Q1, 2020 (millions)
Sources: GASTAT; Ministry of Finance; author's calculations.

disproportionately benefits relatively privileged 'insiders' who have access to government employment or who derive larger benefits from subsidy systems due to their higher income and therefore consumption levels.[7] Sharing wealth through public employment rather than other welfare mechanisms gives the government stronger discretion in choosing whom to share rents with, but it also divorces recipients from the market in a particularly profound way.

What makes Saudi Arabia and GCC political economies different from other Arab countries is, first, that the insider group is relatively large (albeit gradually shrinking due to fiscal constraints). Perhaps more important from an economic development perspective, in the GCC there is an additional, large group of outsiders in the shape of non-nationals who hold the majority of private sector jobs, often at very low wages. This extra labour segment makes cheap and convenient services available to state-supported nationals. The practically unlimited supply of foreign labour has allowed GCC economies to expand rapidly without facing the acute labour bottlenecks that

---

[7] T. M. Yousef, 'Development, Growth and Policy Reform in the Middle East and North Africa since 1950', *Journal of Economic Perspectives* 18, no. 3 (2004), pp. 91–115; R. Assaad, 'Making Sense of Arab Labor Markets: The Enduring Legacy of Dualism', *IZA Journal of Labor & Development* 3, no. 1 (2014), p. 6; S. Hertog, 'Segmented Market Economies in the Arab World: The Political Economy of Insider-Outsider Divisions', *Socio-Economic Review* (forthcoming); World Bank, 'Corrosive Subsidies', *MENA Economic Monitor* (Washington, DC: World Bank, 2014).

tend to lead to inflationary shocks in oil-rich countries with limited labour migration, sometimes called the 'Dutch disease'.[8] The availability of a large foreign workforce has also, however, further contributed to the distancing of nationals from the private labour market.

While public employment has been the main channel of wealth sharing with the broader citizenry, since the onset of the oil age the Saudi state has also developed a well-documented partnership with the local merchant class, which in return has abjured its political ambitions[9]—a co-optation process that has also happened in other GCC countries.[10] Merchants have benefited handsomely from state contracts, even if they have on occasion been expected to cut members of the royal family into their transactions.[11] Other traditional elites like tribal leaders, ulama, and urban notables have been similarly co-opted or side-lined by the Saudi rentier state through targeted patronage.[12]

While there is some rivalry between spending on citizen benefits and spending on economic development that directly benefits the merchant class,[13] mass patronage for citizens also has benefits for the merchants: salary income and other transfers from government are the main source of consumer demand in Saudi Arabia, which in turn benefits private investors operating in real estate, retail, and other consumer services. Due to the central role of government in recycling oil rents and generating demand, the size of total state spending is closely correlated with that of the private sector.[14] This remains the case also in the era of Vision 2030.

---

[8] B. Razgallah, 'The Macroeconomics of Workers' Remittances in GCC Countries', Economic Research Forum Working Paper (2008), https://erf.org.eg/publications/the-macroeconomics-of-workers-remittances-in-gcc-countries/?tab=undefined&c=undefined; M. Beine, S. Coulombe, and W. N. Vermeulen, 'Dutch Disease and the Mitigation Effect of Migration: Evidence from Canadian Provinces', Economic Journal 125, no. 589 (2015), pp. 1574–615.

[9] S. Hertog, Princes, Brokers, and Bureaucrats: Oil and the State in Saudi Arabia (Ithaca, NY: Cornell University Press, 2010).

[10] J. Crystal, Oil and Politics in the Gulf: Rulers and Merchants in Kuwait and Qatar (Cambridge: Cambridge University Press, 1995); P. W. Moore, Doing Business in the Middle East: Politics and Economic Crisis in Jordan and Kuwait, 1st edn. (Cambridge: Cambridge University Press 2009); F. G. Gause, Oil Monarchies (New York: Council on Foreign Relations Press, 1994); S. Hertog, 'The Post-WWII Consolidation of Gulf Nation-States: Oil and Nation-Building', in J. Peterson (ed.), The Emergence of the Gulf States (London: Bloomsbury, 2016), pp. 323–51.

[11] M. Field, The Merchants (New York: Overlook Press, 1986).

[12] M. Al-Rasheed and L. Al-Rasheed, 'The Politics of Encapsulation: Saudi Policy towards Tribal and Religious Opposition', Middle Eastern Studies 32, no. 1 (1996), pp. 96–119, doi: 10.2307/4283777; Gause, Oil Monarchies.

[13] Herb, The Wages of Oil.

[14] S. Hertog, 'The Evolution of Rent Recycling during Two Booms in the Gulf: Business Dynamism and Societal Stagnation', in M. Legrenzi and B. Momani, Shifting Geo-Economic Power of the Gulf (Farnham, UK: Ashgate, 2011), pp. 55–74.

The Saudi Social Contract and the Saudi Growth Model

Comparative political economists have come to realize that different capitalist systems can generate growth in very different ways, be it through export competitiveness or stimulating domestic consumption, laissez-faire approaches or deep state intervention and coordination.[15]

More recently, comparative political economy has particularly focused on different 'growth models', analysing the varied ways in which demand is generated in different types of capitalist economies and probing the different political coalitions that underlie these demand generation processes.[16]

Saudi Arabia and the GCC arguably have developed their own, unique growth model in the period since the Second World War; economic expansion is generated through very different mechanisms than in tax-based 'production states'. As Giacomo Luciani argued more than three decades ago, the size of the economy in rentier states is mostly a function of state spending rather than the other way around.[17] More specifically, in GCC countries, consumer markets primarily depend on government employment and transfers rather than privately generated income derived from the market. Government spending in turn is independent of the local business cycle, as none or only a small share of it is financed through local taxes.[18] Different from 'production states' with mature tax systems, the causal link between state spending and the private economy runs in only one direction.[19]

Rapid growth has been further facilitated by the availability of low-cost foreign workers, the numbers of whom can be quickly increased when the government stimulates the local economy through spending growth. Facing a flat international labour supply curve, there are no conventional supply constraints on GCC labour markets, as a result of which a large increase in demand does not necessarily trigger an inflationary spiral. The absence of collective wage bargaining mechanisms and the fragmentation of the labour force through the labour sponsorship system leads to further

---

[15] J. R. Hollingsworth and R. Boyer, *Contemporary Capitalism: The Embeddedness of Institutions* (Cambridge: Cambridge University Press, 1997); P. A. Hall and D. W. Soskice (eds.), *Varieties of Capitalism: The Institutional Foundations of Comparative Advantage* (Oxford: Oxford University Press, 2001); B.-Å. Lundvall, B. Johnson, E. Sloth Andersen, and B. Dalum, 'National Systems of Production, Innovation and Competence Building', *Research Policy* 31, no. 2 (2002), pp. 213–31, doi: 10.1016/S0048-7333(01)00137-8.

[16] L. Baccaro and J. Pontusson, 'Rethinking Comparative Political Economy: The Growth Model Perspective', *Politics and Society* 44, no. 2 (2016), pp. 175–207, doi: 10.1177/0032329216638053.

[17] G. Luciani, 'Allocation vs. Production States', in H. Beblawi and G. Luciani (eds.), *The Rentier State* (London: Croom Helm, 1987), pp. 63–82.

[18] H. Mahdavy, 'Patterns and Problems of Economic Development in Rentier States', in M. A. Cook (ed.), *Studies in the Economic History of the Middle East* (Oxford: Oxford University Press, 1970), pp. 428–67.

[19] Hertog, 'The Evolution of Rent Recycling'.

wage suppression in the foreign workforce.[20] This set-up has allowed rapid growth with limited inflation during oil boom periods—an attractive model for GCC governments as long as national populations remain small and can be sheltered through public employment, while reaping the benefits of infrastructural modernization and cheap markets for private services.

State dependence of most economic activity lies at the core of this model, however. Privately generated consumer demand is limited: as mentioned above, Saudi private sector wages of SAR150 billion per year are less than a third of public sector wages. The total wage income of foreign workers in 2019 was higher at SAR350 billion, but more than a third of this was remitted out of the country, contributing nothing to local consumption.[21] Moreover, even wage income and capital returns from the private economy are often generated through activities that themselves depend on state spending.

Dependence on foreign labour has also depressed productivity, as employers tend to rely on low-skilled expatriate workers, who are easier to control and for whom labour cost arbitrage is most attractive, given the large wage differentials in low-skilled labour across international labour markets. As foreign workers can often be imported with at least some on-the-job experience, local investment in skills formation has traditionally been limited. Figure 11.2 reflects how the low-skill bias of the Saudi economy has led to stagnating productivity over the decades.[22]

Low productivity has limited economic diversification. While non-oil gross domestic product (GDP) has grown considerably since the 1970s, it is deeply affected by state spending, so is not very useful as a measure of sustainable diversification. A more meaningful indicator that is relatively independent of state stimulus is the scale of non-oil exports, which have to compete on international markets. On this account, the Saudi economy—like all other GCC economies bar Dubai—remains quite undiversified. Despite some non-oil export growth in the early 2010s, the vast majority of goods sold internationally remain oil and refined products. Exports of petrochemicals, the Kingdom's biggest export success, which is at least one step removed from the oil and gas sector, stagnated after the 2014 oil price collapse and have only

---

[20] M. Baldwin-Edwards, 'Labour Immigration and Labour Markets in the GCC Countries: National Patterns and Trends' (London: LSE Kuwait Programme, 2011); S. Hertog, 'A Comparative Assessment of Labor Market Nationalization Policies in the GCC', in S. Hertog (ed.), *Labour Market, Unemployment, and Migration in the GCC* (Geneva: Gulf Research Center, 2011a), pp. 75–116.

[21] Data from the Saudi Arabian Monetary Authority (SAMA) and GASTAT.

[22] Some of the stagnant aggregate productivity is due to compositional effects: the oil sector in GCC countries is particularly productive, so relative growth in non-oil activities tends to pull down average productivity numbers. Within-sector productivity trends in recent decades have also been stagnant, however.

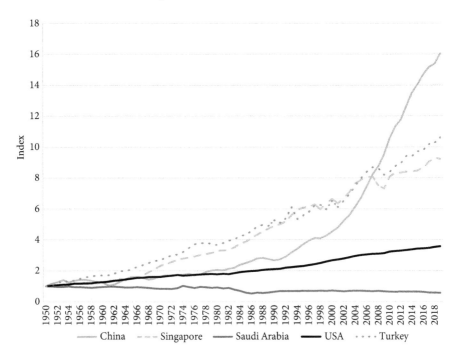

Figure 11.2 Relative productivity trends, 1950–2019 (index of output per worker, 1950 = 1)

Source: Conference Board.

recently picked up again, indicating their relative dependence on global oil markets (see Figure 11.3).

In sum, the Saudi/GCC growth model represents a crude kind of Keynesianism without either significant taxes or a conventional macroeconomic cycle. It relies on an oversized state that generates consumer demand through (over-)employment in the public sector and uses a flexible, low-skilled foreign labour force in the private sector to cater to this demand. Despite growing sophistication of the Saudi private sector over time,[23] private economic activity remains largely state-dependent.

As the size of the domestic economy largely remains a function of state spending, and because much state spending goes towards broad wealth sharing, the Saudi growth model itself is based on the social contract. Changing the growth model *ipso facto* implies changing the social contract.

---

[23] G. Luciani, 'From Private Sector to National Bourgeoisie: Saudi Arabian Business', in P. Aarts and G. Nonneman (eds.), *Saudi Arabia in the Balance: Political Economy, Society, Foreign Affairs* (New York: New York University Press, 2006), pp. 144–81.

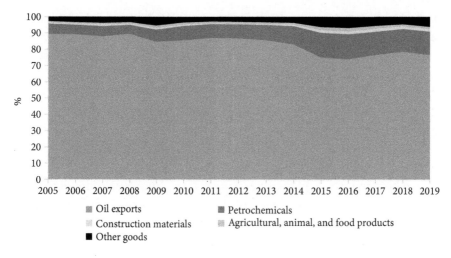

Figure 11.3 Composition of Saudi exports, 2005–19 (%)
Source: SAMA, Annual Report.

Attempts to Adjust the Social Contract

While the broad foundations of the social contract remain the same at the time of writing (2021), since 2016 Saudi Arabia has witnessed measures to curtail wealth sharing that have cut deeper than any previous fiscal adjustments, even during the fiscal crises of the late 1980s and late 1990s. The economic driver has been the decline in oil prices since 2014, which has led to double-digit deficits in several years. The surprising outcome is not austerity per se, however, but the fact that since 2020 more of it has been borne by regular households than ever before. This stands in contrast to previous lean periods, when fiscal adjustment happened almost exclusively through cuts in capital expenditure and state contract spending, which primarily affected large local construction and service companies rather than average citizens.[24]

Fiscal adjustment since 2015 has followed a meandering learning curve. The first iteration of the Kingdom's 'Fiscal Balance Program' issued in 2016 aimed to reduce the government's net spending—total expenditure minus fees and taxes—from SAR921 billion in 2015 to SAR634 billion by 2020, a shrinkage of 35 per cent. The aim was a balanced budget by 2020, which, however, would have meant taking away about a third of the primary source of economic demand in Saudi Arabia within five years. The leadership quickly abandoned the plans when the formal abolition of a number of (mostly

---

[24] Hertog, *Princes, Brokers, and Bureaucrats.*

smaller) public sector allowances in autumn 2016 led to social backlash as well as a consumer recession. The allowances were reinstated in spring 2017.

The government instead took a more cautious approach to fiscal reform in which subsidy cuts and new taxes were at least partially compensated with other forms of welfare spending. As a result, while some spending has been rationalized and the revenue apparatus modernized, net fiscal savings have been limited.

Most notably, since 2016 the Saudi leadership has made significant adjustments to state-controlled domestic gas, electricity, and fuel prices that have affected both industry and household consumers. Energy subsidies have historically been seen as a key plank of the GCC social contract,[25] and while prices remain below international benchmarks, the increases have had a significant effect on Saudi citizens' purchasing power.

In January 2018, the government also introduced a 5 per cent value added tax (VAT), following a GCC agreement on the matter which, however, only Saudi Arabia and the United Arab Emirates acted upon at the time. Again, the absence of taxation was generally seen as a key plank of the rentier social contract in the GCC,[26] giving even a modest tax an outsize symbolic importance for local citizens and Gulf experts alike.

Energy price increases and VAT were partially compensated through the introduction of a Citizen's Account in December 2017. This programme provides means-tested cash payments to Saudi households below specific income thresholds; these were reported to average SAR930 (about $250) per month in July 2020.[27] Despite some targeting issues and carping on social media, the programme appears to have been a success: while continuing to provide income supplements to deserving households, its cost is below the opportunity cost of previous energy subsidies and different from the latter, in that it does not distort consumption decisions or disproportionately benefit richer households. It represents an attempt to maintain the social contract while modernizing it and trimming it around the edges—and it broadly follows the reform prescriptions of international organizations like World Bank and International Monetary Fund.[28]

---

[25] B. Fattouh and L. El-Katiri, 'A Brief Political Economy of Energy Subsidies in the Middle East and North Africa' (2015), https://ora.ox.ac.uk/objects/uuid:dcbbe09e-8d29-4a11-bcef-0d809bc79d3a; J. Krane, 'Stability versus Sustainability: Energy Policy in the Gulf Monarchies', Ph.D. dissertation, Judge Business School, University of Cambridge (2013).
[26] Luciani, 'Allocation Vs. Production States'.
[27] 'Two Million Saudis Lose Cash Aid When They Can Least Afford It', Bloomberg (15 July 2020), https://www.bloomberg.com/news/articles/2020-07-15/two-million-saudis-lose-cash-aid-when-they-can-least-afford-it.
[28] World Bank, 'Corrosive Subsidies'.

As a result of the leadership's relative caution until 2020, government net spending has remained roughly constant since 2016 as tax and subsidy reforms have gone hand in hand with higher spending. Net spending in 2020 reached SAR868 billion, only 6 per cent less than in 2015. Fiscal deficits have therefore continued until 2021, although declining over time.

A more disruptive, historically unprecedented adjustment to the social contract happened in summer 2020, after the collapse of oil prices that was induced by the Saudi–Russian war for market share in March of the same year. Starting on 1 July, the VAT rate was tripled to 15 per cent, while a SAR1,000/month 'cost of living allowance' for public sector employees—created as recently as January 2018 in the wake of the introduction of the 5 per cent VAT—was abolished from 1 June.

Critically, this time the government made no attempt to compensate for these more significant cuts. Instead of modernizing the social contract, it opted simply to shrink its material basis. As the VAT increase hit private sector employees as much as public sector ones—and arguably hit lower-income households harder—it has done little to address the existing distortions of the Saudi wealth-sharing system: wage gaps between public and private employment persist and many higher-income 'insiders' were less hit by the adjustment than lower-income households.

The abolition of the cost of living allowance, by contrast, has contributed somewhat to narrowing the public–private wage gap, but only on the margin (recall that the average wage differential between the two sectors is more than SAR4,000/month). Its suppression has moreover affected lower-income public employees disproportionately, as it constituted a proportionately larger share of their take-home pay.

The abolition of the allowance is particularly politically significant in light of the failed previous attempt to suppress a range of (mostly smaller) public sector allowances in 2016–17. The leadership was clearly more willing to inflict pain this time around.

The total annualized reduction in the fiscal deficit resulting from the two measures of summer 2020 could amount to SAR150 billion or more than 5 per cent of GDP. Assuming that expatriate households and private businesses will absorb some of the hit, the resulting reduction in Saudi households' purchasing power could reach between SAR100 billion and SAR120 billion. In light of total Saudi wage income of less than SAR700 billion per year, this is a significant blow to household finances.

The uncompensated fiscal cuts directly affect a key source of economic growth in the Kingdom: state-supported household consumption. While the effect of the global COVID-19 crisis on the Saudi economy has somewhat masked the specific impact of the cuts, their effect will become clearer once Covid restrictions are fully lifted and is likely be reflected in sluggish growth of key consumer markets. While the large deficit that the Kingdom was facing in 2020 arguably required fiscal action, the targets—primarily households rather than large-scale capital expenditure—and the lack of accompany-ing compensation measures reflect a structural break in the leadership's approach to the social contract.

The measures reflect a level of political confidence vis-à-vis Saudi citi-zens that was lacking in the earlier phase of Prince Mohammad bin Salman's economic reign. While the government intends to stimulate the local econ-omy increasingly through off-balance-sheet project expenditure by the Public Investment Fund (PIF), such spending does less to maintain consumer demand and the traditional social contract undergirding it. Remarkably, even after the substantial recovery of oil prices from late 2021 onwards, the King-dom has seen barely any fiscal loosening in the central government budget devoted to salaries.

An arguably even more drastic adjustment to the social contract at the elite level happened with the anti-corruption crackdown in November 2017, dur-ing which hundreds of members of the Saudi merchant, technocratic, and princely elite were detained at the Ritz-Carlton hotel in Riyadh. While the growth impact of the crackdown was less immediate, the elite disenfranchise-ment that it symbolized was more profound: it signalled to leading merchant families that their cosy relationship with government was essentially over. Internally, some advisers to the Crown Prince even spoke of the need to create a 'new private sector' that would replace the old rentier class.

Emblematic of the new order were the bankruptcy and partial nationaliza-tion respectively of what were arguably the Kingdom's two largest contracting firms, Saudi Oger and Saudi Binladin Group. Other members of the busi-ness elite survived but lost assets and much of their privileged access to government and their roles as intermediaries with international business. More openly than before, moreover, private firms are now expected to adjust their investment decisions to government priorities. At the same time, the leadership signalled a preference for foreign investors through the organiza-tion of high-profile investor events (one held in the same Ritz-Carton just ten days before the crackdown) and the construction of new mega projects that explicitly target foreign direct investment (FDI), foreign technology, and foreign residents.

The new private sector that Vision 2030 is implicitly built on has been slow in emerging, however, given the private economy's historical dependence on state spending and relatively low productivity rates. FDI similarly has plummeted due to lower growth, policy uncertainty and the fact that 'quick wins' in the fields of heavy industry and telecoms had mostly been reaped by the early 2010s (see Figure 11.4). A recent peak of FDI inflows in 2021 at an estimated $19.3 billion was mostly due to one-off proceeds from the partial sale of Saudi Aramco's oil pipeline network.

Closely related, few new sources of private household income have emerged to replace state-orchestrated mass wealth sharing. Saudi employment in the private sector remained stagnant until recently (see Chapter 6): in Q1, 2020, 1.87 million Saudis held jobs under private social security regulations. At 1.86 million, the number was almost the same in Q1, 2017, despite continuing growth of the Saudi population and of working-age individuals in particular, which would require the creation of perhaps 200,000 new jobs annually (see Figure 11.5).[29] Since then, the number of privately employed Saudi workers has increased more quickly, but for the most part in the low-wage segment, creating limited private purchasing power.

The number of actual Saudi private sector workers has probably improved somewhat in recent years due to the decline of 'phantom employees' who are

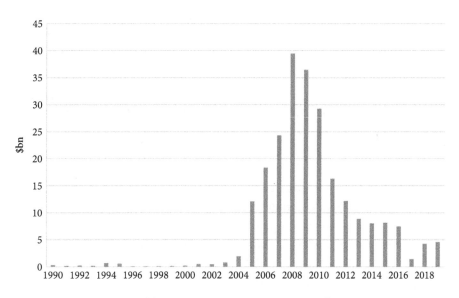

Figure 11.4 Annual FDI inflows into Saudi Arabia, 1990–2019 ($ billion)

Source: United Nations Conference on Trade and Development.

---

[29] Employees under social security also include workers in quasi-public entities that do not fall under civil service regulations. Unfortunately, the number of individuals employed in truly private establishments (1.7 million in Q1, 2020) is only reported in the most recent labour force bulletins.

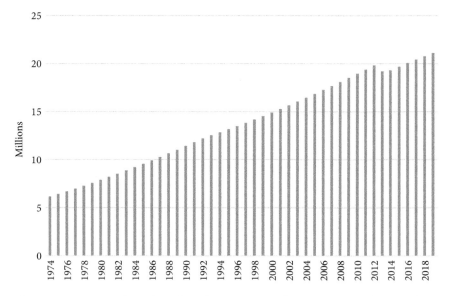

Figure 11.5 Estimated number of Saudi citizens in mid-year, 1974–2019 (millions)
Source: SAMA.

only put on companies' payroll to fulfil Saudization quota requirements.[30] Yet the aggregate size of the private Saudi wage bill—whether resulting from real or phantom employment—has not moved much and continues to be about a third of aggregate public sector wage payments due to substantially lower private salaries. The relative stagnation of private employment is unsurprising, given that most private production directly or indirectly caters to state-generated demand, which has not grown substantially since 2015. Public and private employment in Saudi Arabia tend to be complements, not substitutes.

In principle, the Saudi state retains enough fiscal and administrative resources for a more fundamental revision, rather than just curtailment, of the social contract: It could gradually replace excess public sector employment with mechanisms to support private employment of Saudis at socially acceptable income levels: for example, through a universal basic income[31] or a negative income tax that would make lower- to mid-skilled nationals more competitive with low-income foreigners.

There has, however, not been any clear sign that such more fundamental revisions are being considered. 'Saudization' of labour markets continues to rely on prescriptive quota rules which are costly for business and encourage

---

[30] This is not least suggested by the clearly increased visibility of Saudis rather than foreigners in customer service jobs in recent years.

[31] S. Hertog, 'Making Wealth Sharing More Efficient in High-Rent Countries: The Citizens' Income', *Energy Transitions* 1, no. 2 (2017), p. 7.

evasion without addressing the large labour cost gap between nationals and foreigners. While the quotas of the *Nitaqat* Saudization system have been periodically adjusted, the system remains essentially the same as it was before 2015. Government employment, while much less easily available, remains more attractive for most Saudis,[32] and foreigners by and large more competitive in the private labour market.[33]

Change in the social contract has therefore mostly happened through erosion, accelerated by continued population growth and a period of depressed oil prices, which has increasingly pushed younger Saudis into low-wage jobs in the private sector. While oil prices have recovered at the time of writing, the erosion is likely to continue in the long run given that average per capita oil rents in the Kingdom are likely to drop further as the working-age citizen population continues to grow.

The only adjustments to the wealth-sharing regime that pointed in the direction of a proactive reform were the 2017–18 energy subsidy reforms and the introduction of the Citizen's Account. These were significant steps forward but they pale in terms of scale and complexity compared to the challenge of reforming public employment. Moving from a growth model based on surplus public job creation to one that is at least in part driven by private demand generation is not impossible. It is, however, both technocratically and politically more challenging and cannot easily draw on existing prescriptions from international organizations and consultants like the subsidy reform process could.

Vision 2030 and the Social Contract

Political and economic constraints created by the Saudi social contract are key to understanding both the potential and limits of Vision 2030. This is even though the wealth-sharing and welfare regimes underlying the Saudi growth model are not a core concern of the Vision document and its attendant 'Vision Realization Programs'. The Vision focuses more on top-down diversification through state-owned enterprises and related mega projects, accompanied by broader support for entrepreneurship and opening new sectors and, perhaps most dramatically, a set of fundamental lifestyle changes and a broad social opening of the Kingdom. The basic incentive environment for citizens in the labour market is not the focus of the Vision process.

---

[32] S. Hertog, 'The "Rentier Mentality", 30 Years On: Evidence from Survey Data', *British Journal of Middle Eastern Studies* 47, no. 1 (2020), pp. 1–18.
[33] Baldwin-Edwards, 'Labour Immigration and Labour Markets in the GCC Countries'.

To the extent that the Vision proposes a new social contract, it is based around new social freedoms for a younger generation of Saudis who are meant to seize new, private economic opportunities. What these opportunities will be has not yet become clear, however. Tourism and entertainment alone, while important new fields of investment, will not provide sufficient jobs for young Saudis and under current labour market structures run the danger of once more providing more opportunities for foreigners than for locals.

To be fair, the social liberalization component of the Vision seems to have paid considerable political dividends. While independent polls are not available, anecdotal evidence suggests that the process has been popular, especially among young Saudis. This is true even though much of the investment in entertainment has consisted of government-organized 'loss leaders' in the shape of high-profile sports events, concerts, and city festivals, the logistical and security costs of which have been very high.[34]

The economic diversification component of the Vision process has moved more slowly than the social one. Due to the post-2014 fiscal slowdown, GDP growth in recent years has barely exceeded the growth rate of the citizen population of close to 2 per cent, including in the non-oil sector (see Figure 11.6).

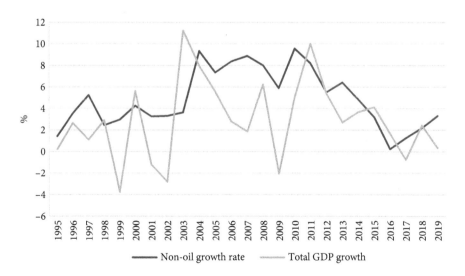

Figure 11.6 Annual real GDP growth rates, 1995–2019 (%)
Source: SAMA.

[34] Interviews in Riyadh, 2018 and 2019.

As Figure 11.7 shows, the share of the private sector in GDP—which had been expanding significantly in the 2000s—has stagnated since the early 2010s, mostly due to the slowdown in state spending growth from 2014. While it can be argued that much of the previous expansion was not really autonomous diversification, it is clear that the private sector has not found an autonomous growth path after 2014 either.

For the time being, due to the post-2014 fiscal slowdown, Saudi citizens face narrower opportunities in the public sector that are at best partially compensated through private opportunities. Many of the new Vision-related projects have remained enclave investments that exist in parallel to the rest of the economy. They have not yet involved the wider Saudi population— few of whom are employed in structures like Neom or the Red Sea Tourism Project—or the local merchant class, which has yet to invest significantly in the new projects. Some local observers expect the latter to change as the government uses its post-Ritz Carlton powers of political suasion to extract commitments of private capital to its flagship projects.

Implementation of the Vision has often moved slowly because of inherited institutional constraints that are in turn rooted in the Kingdom's social contract. While some public job benefits have been cut, the government employment structures that the Saudi social contract is based on have remained largely the same. This has made improving accountability and performance of the bureaucracy below the top level difficult, explaining the

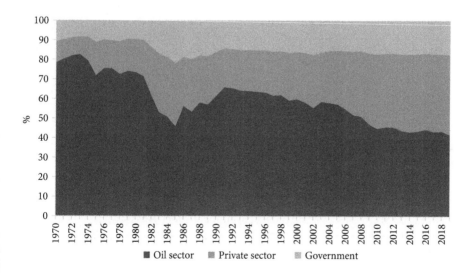

Figure 11.7 Composition of Saudi GDP, 1970–2019 (constant prices)

Source: SAMA.

relative stagnation in Saudi Arabia's scores on the World Bank's 'government effectiveness' indicator (see Figure 11.8).

Lingering bureaucratic ineffectiveness in turn affects the speed at which reforms are implemented and the general administrative environment for investors—even if there have been significant improvements in individual areas like bankruptcy legislation and the introduction of e-government in the slow-moving judicial system. Many processes still rely on the discretion of flesh-and-blood bureaucrats; investors report that just opening a bank account in the country can still take nine months even with government support.[35]

One arena in which the constraints that the social contract imposes on reform are particularly visible is that of privatization. In 2017, the government announced that it would raise about $200 billion (or SAR750 billion) through privatization in the coming years as part of the Vision 2030 reforms. It has since turned out, however, that many of the entities slated for sale or private participation were in no state to generate commercial returns. Many of them did not have separate balance sheets or corporate structures and, most importantly in the context of the social contract, even potentially profitable entities are weighed down by their employment obligations. The

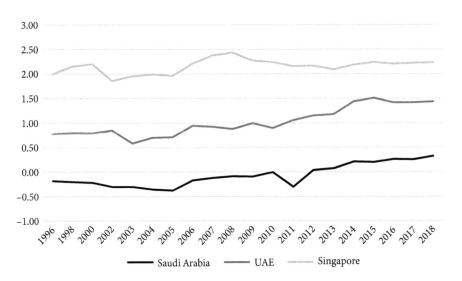

Figure 11.8 Scores on the World Bank's government effectiveness indicator of Saudi Arabia and benchmark countries, 1996–2018 (minimum –2.5, maximum 2.5)

Source: World Bank, World Governance Indicators.

[35] https://www.reuters.com/article/us-saudi-reforms/factbox-saudi-arabias-main-economic-and-social-reforms-investor-concerns-idUSKBN2AG1V5.

new National Center for Privatization often had insufficient control over the government entities historically in charge of specific assets.[36]

As early as 2018, drastically reduced targets were announced, with the government aiming for SAR35–40 billion of proceeds by 2020. Even this target has not been achieved, as by 2020 the government's main asset sales were two flour mills formerly operated by the General Silos and Flour Mills Organization (privatization of desalination assets was ongoing at the time of writing). Little has been heard of the ambitious initial plans to privatize health and education assets, which are particularly deeply tied up with the social contract through the mass employment—and often over-employment—of nationals. This might change in the future, but for now the government has been reluctant to risk mass redundancies in the public sector. It has instead in many cases grown the public sector through the creation of new state-owned companies under the PIF.

The struggle to reform existing government structures is also reflected in the Vision planning process itself, which has been relatively insular, relying heavily on foreign consultants and rapidly growing new bodies around the royal court, while both the wider ruling family and local merchant elites have had only a limited say in it. Vision Realization Programs have been bolted on top of existing administrative structures, sometimes adding to the complexity of an already fragmented and multilayered government apparatus.[37]

As a sign of the new attitude to the old social contract, investment in key mega projects like Neom, entertainment city Qiddiya, and the Red Sea Tourism Project continued apace in 2020 at the same time that the VAT rate was tripled and the public sector cost of living allowance suppressed. This has led to some guarded criticism on social media. Some locals have taken to privately calling the increased VAT the 'Neom tax'—but there has been no sign of organized political resistance within government or outside, reflecting the newly centralized power of the leadership.

Some top-down force and risk taking is clearly needed to modernize the Saudi economic system. There is, however, a danger that change is planned without taking relevant social constituencies on board, both reducing their 'buy-in' into the process and insufficiently taking their needs and capabilities into account. In some cases, this marginalization has improved policy outcomes: the post-2015 diminution of the status of traditional religious forces,

---

[36] The only large asset sale that has happened since was the partial initial public offering of Saudi Aramco in 2019, which struggled to attract international investors and which was conducted separately from the main privatization process.

[37] Hertog, Princes, Brokers, and Bureaucrats; Hertog, 'Challenges to the Saudi Distributional State'.

including in the judicial system, has removed a veto player that previously undermined legal modernization and social opening.

The much more centralized decision making in the Vision era does, however, also reduce the political integration of local capitalist interests. While many of them are indeed rentiers who have lived off the state's generosity for decades, they still control local private capital and need to be brought on board if new diversification initiatives are to result in private investment. While there are occasional consultations, these appear mostly ad hoc and are a far cry from the close state–business coordination known from successful East Asian industrializers.[38] There is considerable potential in new service sectors like entertainment and tourism, especially for Muslim visitors, but many local stakeholders would want to see a more decentralized development model with more input from the private sector.

The new era in Saudi Arabia has brought with it a centralization and personalization of power that is much closer to the typical pattern across the Arab world than the Kingdom's previous collective, consensus-oriented governance. After decades of rent distribution and coalition building had reduced the Saudi leadership's independent room for manoeuvre, the Vision-era Saudi state is characterized by a fairly high level of independence from social interests—bringing it back, forcefully, to the position of political autonomy predicted by classical rentier state theory.[39]

Yet many of the Vision's components are deployed only slowly, not only because of limited buy-in from stakeholders but also because they are in tension with the structural foundations of the established social contract and growth model. The privatization programme has struggled to get off the ground not least because many of the entities slated for sell-off serve a job creation function for Saudi citizens. The ambitions of the cross-sectoral National Transformation Program had to be revised downwards because the overstaffed bureaucracy has often failed to deliver change at lower levels. The National Companies Promotion Program has had trouble finding top-performing private companies to support, given the orientation of local firms towards government and the protected local market (as well as distrust of new government initiatives on the part of some company owners).

---

[38] P. B. Evans, *Embedded Autonomy* (Princeton, NJ: Princeton University Press, 1995); R. Wade, *Governing the Market: Economic Theory and the Role of Government in East Asian Industrialization* (Princeton, NJ: Princeton University Press, 2003); D. Rodrik, *One Economics, Many Recipes: Globalization, Institutions, and Economic Growth* (Princeton, NJ: Princeton University Press, 2008).

[39] Luciani, 'Allocation vs. Production States'; Mahdavy, 'Patterns and Problems of Economic Development in Rentier States'.

The Fiscal Balance Program needed to be slowed down as the government realized how heavy the contractionary impact of spending cuts and new revenue measures was in the state-dependent Saudi economy; the specific aim to shrink the public payroll was postponed several times. The National Industrial Development and Logistics Program has struggled finding sectors to support that are not dependent on state-provided subsidized energy. Finally, the Human Capability Development Program, which focuses on Saudi skill formation, was only issued in 2021 after substantial delays; it will face a difficult battle reforming the teaching profession, which historically has been used as a job creation tool and has often attracted lower-calibre candidates.

These tensions are inevitable and not the fault of the new programmes. Yet they have not been addressed in a systematic manner through a fundamental reform of the existing wealth distribution system that underlies many of the performance issues in the Saudi economy. While government programmes have undergone numerous internal revisions, an overarching analytical framework that would address the binding constraints to Saudi growth is yet to emerge.

Conclusion and Outlook

This chapter has shown that the old Saudi social contract is eroding, and with it the old growth model based on state spending and in particular state employment. Some of the components of Vision 2030 have politically compensated for this, especially the social opening of the Kingdom. Yet the new era has not yet brought about new sources of private demand generation, as most economic activity continues to rely on fiscal stimulus from the state. The government is currently working on the introduction means-tested welfare tools. Yet a comprehensive reform of the social contract towards a less distortive and more market-conforming welfare system—one that would scale down government employment and help bridge the labour cost gap with foreigners in the private sector—is not yet in sight.

The re-established political autonomy of government under Vision 2030 has allowed the government to marginalize veto players that undermined previous reform efforts. Yet increased autonomy also means that constituencies that need to contribute to Vision 2030, notably the local private sector, have not been fully integrated into the project, which does not always take their interests and capacities into account.

Economic diversification is hard and takes a long time under the best of circumstances. Saudi Arabia has not yet moved to a new growth model. It has few non-oil goods to export as Saudi labour by and large remains far from cost competitive and no significant non-government sources of demand are in sight for now.

That said, the relative austerity of recent years has led to some necessary adjustment: as government has stopped hiring freely, labour market attitudes have gradually been changing and reservation wages have fallen, with Saudis taking on more service sector jobs that they would have shunned just a few years ago. Gradual erosion of Saudi wages could lead to better competitiveness—not unlike what happened in Egypt after the forced devaluation of the Egyptian pound in 2016—but the road to such competitiveness is long. The adjustment process will not be finished by 2030 and much pain could be inflicted along the way, with living standards dropping for a younger generation of labour market entrants.

The transition could be smoothed through more proactive reforms of current wealth distribution structures, reorienting some of the rent sharing towards market-conforming welfare mechanisms rather than simply dismantling the old social contract through a reactive policy of austerity. For the time being, the Vision has focused more on large projects than on addressing structural constraints to economic development—although in the end, it will very likely be these constraints which determine the Kingdom's growth and diversification trajectory.

12

Saudi Arabia—Beyond the Rentier State?

Giacomo Luciani

Introduction

The collapse of global oil prices in 2015, and again in 2020 due to the COVID-19 pandemic, has brought the issue of the sustainability of major oil-exporting economies sharply into focus. The preoccupation with the future of these economies beyond oil is, however, certainly not new. In the case of Saudi Arabia, the first of the five-year development plans was launched in 1970, motivated by the need to develop the economy—that is, to diversify and establish various activities unrelated to oil—but also by a more general need to advance the well-being and prosperity of the country. The fact that, sooner or later, oil would run out, and a future beyond it needed to be secured, was always explicitly envisaged.

It is only logical that initially the emphasis was laid on meeting the most immediate necessities of a population which, at the time, was extremely poor; but very soon the goal of economic diversification emerged and began to be pursued vigorously, and also imaginatively. The implementation of the gas gathering system, which curbed the flaring of natural gas produced in association with crude oil (a malpractice that is still rampant in Iraq, Iran, and other major oil-producing countries); the creation of the Royal Commission for Jubail and Yanbu, which led to the founding of these two extremely successful industrial cities; the establishment of Saudi Arabia's Basic Industries Corporation (SABIC), which initiated the development of the petrochemical industry; the acquisition of Aramco from its original four United States (US) partner companies, and consolidation of all petroleum-related activities under Saudi Aramco—these are all milestones in a process of economic diversification, shaped by a long-term strategy to reduce the Kingdom's exclusive dependence on oil exports.

Giacomo Luciani, *Saudi Arabia—Beyond the Rentier State?* In: *The Economy of Saudi Arabia in the 21st Century*. Edited by: John Sfakianakis, Oxford University Press. © Giacomo Luciani (2024). DOI: 10.1093/oso/9780198863878.003.0013

This process is not completed, and cannot be wholly completed for as long as the rest of the world expresses a demand for oil, which underpins Saudi exports at prices well above the cost of production. For as long as oil is highly valued—as is the case still today—it will generate value added, exports, and a stream of revenue which will inevitably appear prominently in gross domestic product (GDP), foreign trade, and government finance statistics, projecting an image of dependency. It is only when oil ceases to have any commercial value (if ever), or runs out completely, that diversification will per force be complete. But if the process is not completed, it would also not be correct to portray it as having just started: in fact, the further pursuance of sustainability must take into account the heritage of past decisions, which is in many cases positive, but also in some cases problematic.

The Arab Gulf exporters (as well as Iran, in fact) have since the start of the oil era opted for leveraging oil revenue to pursue the transformation of their economies. This objective has been pursued through a combination of direct engagement by the state in the economy, as investor in multiple sectors and purveyor of critical services, accompanied by reliance on a private sector to whose formation the state has frequently directly contributed, creating opportunities for the accumulation of private fortunes. This combined public–private strategy was accompanied by an open-door rather than protectionist foreign trade policy, and orthodox monetary management, anchored to a fixed exchange rate peg to the US dollar. Finally, the strategy relied on opening the door widely to the temporary inflow of foreign labour, accompanied by strict (if not always effective) security control of expatriate labourers.

We may call the cocktail of strategies described above the 'Gulf consensus' to differentiate it from the well-known Washington consensus.[1] The main differences between the two were: the prominent role of the state, which the Washington consensus condemned; the fixed peg exchange rate, to which the Washington consensus preferred a floating peg; and the extensive reliance on expatriate labour, coupled with wage discrimination and labour market segmentation, which was not contemplated in the vision of the Washington consensus. The latter aimed at maximizing the exchange of good and services, but assumed that movement of labour would be limited.

The Gulf consensus is now being seriously challenged by the increasingly accepted conclusion that the world cannot go on emitting greenhouse gases into the atmosphere, and containment of global warming necessitates

---

[1] G. Luciani (ed.), *Resource Blessed: Diversification and the Gulf Development Model* (Berlin: Gerlach, 2012).

accelerated decarbonization. What adaptations, economic and political, are necessary for the Gulf Cooperation Council (GCC) countries to remain sustainable? This is the central question that is discussed in this chapter, further building on another recent publication of mine.[2] The thrust of my argument is that economic adaptation is possible, but more of the reduced rent that will be received in the coming years and decades must be allocated to domestic investment, and the state needs to rely on taxation of income and wealth to cover current expenditure.

Financial Diversification versus National Development

The decision to leverage oil revenue to promote economic transformation may appear obvious or unavoidable, but this is not the case. The alternative for the Gulf oil exporters would have been to accumulate all revenue in a sovereign wealth fund, and limit the use of it in support of the government budget to a small share of the accumulated fund, in line with the fund's expected revenue yield. This has been Norway's solution, which is frequently presented as a model of best practice. The implication of such a strategy is that mineral wealth is transformed into financial wealth, generating a potentially perpetual stream of income; but over time the impact on the economy is minimized and extremely diluted. From the point of view of sustainability, it may be viewed as the most reliable solution because it is vulnerable only to either a catastrophic financial crisis or massive mismanagement of funds. It is also a strategy for maximizing the rentier nature of the state, strengthening and perpetuating its economic independence from society, and essentially denying any form of sharing of the oil rent.

Soon after the first major oil price increase in 1973–4, this strategy, which we may call one of financial diversification, was advocated by many, who considered that the Gulf countries could never succeed in truly diversifying their economies. The reasoning underlying the strategy is simple: major oil producers enjoy huge wealth in the form of oil in the ground, which is not recognized because oil-yet-to-be-extracted is not a liquid asset with a well-recognized value. The process of oil production is in fact only minimally a true process of production; mostly it is a form of liquidation of an inherited, or God-given, asset. The 'income' which is obtained by selling the oil should not be viewed as proper income from value-adding activities,

[2] G. Luciani and T. Moerenhout (eds.), *When Can Oil Economies Be Deemed Sustainable?* (London: Palgrave Macmillan 2020), open access, https://link.springer.com/book/10.1007/978-981-15-5728-6.

but as divestment of existing assets, a capital transaction rather than current earnings. Thus, it is widely, and correctly, maintained that the part of oil revenue exceeding the remuneration of the capital and labour needed for extraction—that is, the oil rent—should be devoted exclusively to capital accumulation because if it is devoted to current expenditure, the original wealth base will be progressively eroded and eventually disappear.[3]

Viewing oil production as essentially a capital transaction encourages a financial understanding of the management of the oil wealth. From the point of view of a prudent investor, holding all of one's wealth in the form of a single asset—oil in the ground—is extremely risky and also possibly allows only a very low yield. You must be convinced that the price of oil extracted and sold in the future will be higher than that of oil extracted and sold today, to conclude that holding oil in the ground may have a positive yield. Indeed, this has been a frequently held conviction in the oil-producing countries ever since the 1960s, when the Organization of Petroleum Exporting Countries first articulated a preference for conservation. And it is the reversal of expectations in this respect that is influencing current oil production policies, in the face of the possibility of a peak and gradual decline of global oil demand.

A prudent investor would then normally decide to reduce their exposure to the one predominant asset and diversify their portfolio by purchasing alternative assets (preferably with different and uncorrelated risk profiles). This means devoting the oil rent to investment, either in real productive assets at home (i.e. opting for national economic development) or abroad, or in financial placements in various international financial instruments. The latter was the inspiration of the original discussion about the 'recycling of petrodollars' that was very popular in the 1970s. It also seems to have been the original inspiration of the decision to formally create a Saudi sovereign wealth fund, recycling the existing Public Investment Fund (PIF) to perform this role.[4]

Mixed strategies are of course possible, with some of the rent devoted to domestic investment in real assets and the rest devoted to international financial placements—it is a matter of proportions. Generally, the argument against maximizing domestic investment has been that the absorption capacity of the domestic economy is limited, and the return on marginal investment is bound to decline very rapidly. Hence the appeal of pursuing financial rather than productive diversification, and devoting the bulk of the

---

[3] J. Beutel, 'Conceptual Problems of Measuring Economic Diversification, as Applied to the GCC Economies', in Luciani, *Resource Blessed*, pp. 29–70; J. Beutel, 'Economic Diversification and Sustainable Development of GCC Countries', in Luciani and Moerenhout (eds.), *When Can Oil Economies Be Deemed Sustainable?*, pp. 99–151, open access, https://link.springer.com/chapter/10.1007/978-981-15-5728-6_6.

[4] G. Luciani, 'The Durability of the Rentier State', paper presented at the Rahmania Annual Seminar, 'Post-Rentierism: Is the Wolf Really Here This Time?', Malta (5–7 May 2018).

rent to international financial investment, as Norway has done, in search of better yield but also less exposure to domestic political risk—if one is permitted to say so, when speaking of the state (or power incumbents, to whom the state literally belongs). The latter may not be a relevant consideration in the case of Norway, but it certainly is for rentier states, whose survival is less linked to support from the people than to being the direct recipient of a stream of income from the rest of the world.[5] It is also a relevant consideration for states like Kuwait that have seen their very existence challenged by hostile neighbours.

Thus, it is certainly true that a strategy of pure financial diversification is more functional to the eternalization of the rentier state than one of national economic development, fraught as the latter is with complex and potentially unsettling social and cultural change. Yet this path was not taken. Thanks also to pressure from society,[6] and notwithstanding opposition from everyone who saw economic transformation in any form as a threat to social, cultural, and political stability, the path of 'modernization' was taken, which meant spending oil revenue domestically and providing for key services such as education and health, infrastructure, housing, and industry.

Taking the Option of Development

But the moment that oil revenue is spent domestically, the so-called Dutch disease, which is manifested by an increase in the prices of non-tradables relative to the prices of internationally traded goods and services, sets in.

Openness to foreign trade helped in keeping the Dutch disease in check, maximizing the number of goods and services that are freely tradable with respect to those that are necessarily procured locally. It also discouraged the subsidization of internationally non-competitive import substitution projects: some were pursued anyhow—like the production of wheat based on irrigation with fossil water—but were eventually abandoned, or at least limited.

The fixed peg to the dollar has prevented the Gulf currencies from appreciating in nominal terms, also thanks to the fact that oil is traded and paid for in dollars. But avoiding real appreciation—that is, domestic inflation exceeding that of the rest of the world—was not automatic. In the end, the result

[5] G. Luciani, 'Allocation vs. Production States: A Theoretical Framework', in H. Beblawi and G.Luciani (eds.) *The Rentier State* (Beckenham, Croom Helm, 1988) pp. 63–82.
[6] S. Hertog and E. Ferdinand, 'When Do Oil Dictators Share the Wealth? Evidence from the Gulf Monarchies', unpublished manuscript (n.d.).

was obtained through an emphasis on increasing the supply of key non-tradables, such as housing and real estate in general; through openness to imports; and through the open door to expatriate labour. The latter was crucially important and took various successive forms, aiming at minimizing the cost of labour: first, foreign enterprises were called to implement projects by bringing machinery, staff, and labourers from their own countries; then workers were invited from other Arab countries; and finally preference was given to the cheapest labour available, mostly from South or South-East Asia.

Reliance on Cheap Immigration

The decision to thrust the door wide open to the importation of foreign expatriate labour is a path that was taken by all the Arab Gulf economies, in most cases to an extent even more extreme than in Saudi Arabia. Had the door not been opened to expatriate labour, wages—the price of labour—would have exploded and frustrated any attempt at containing the Dutch disease.

Thus, reliance on expatriate labour was initially inevitable, but it evolved progressively into structural reliance on low-paid and largely unskilled foreign workers, viewed as a policy to support the birth of new activities, especially those promoted by the private sector; and it led to a widening gap between the pay of the vast majority of foreign nationals and the wages that nationals were willing to accept. As is well known, this in turn led to nationals predominantly seeking employment with the public sector, and expatriates constituting the bulk of the labour force in the private sector. Hence also the paradoxical phenomenon of unemployment among nationals while millions of expatriates are employed.

In international experience, many countries have relied on workers coming from abroad. Although in some cases (e.g. Germany or Switzerland) the original intention was that foreign workers would be only temporary residents (*Gastarbeiter*, or guest workers), in fact unions obtained a situation where the wages of expatriates would not be significantly lower than those of nationals, to prevent foreigners from competing and displacing nationals in the workforce. Eventually, large numbers of foreigners were naturalized; even before that, they paid taxes and contributed to social security schemes. This was made possible by the fact that the difference between the wages they earned, net of taxes, and the wages that they would have earned in their countries of origin was still sufficiently large. In other words, in countries outside the Gulf region, a model of 'expensive immigration' has been followed.

This has created social tensions that periodically become more acute, then are contained. But the model has been a clear success for both the economy and government finances.

In contrast, the model of 'cheap immigration' followed by the Arab Gulf countries, aiming to minimize the cost of foreign workers and insisting on their temporary presence, has progressively led to a number of distortions, such as excessive reliance on labour-intensive solutions, declining product-ivity, and wage segmentation by nationality. It is clear that if workers are paid the bare minimum that is needed to convince them to move from their home country (and sometimes less than that), any attempt to raise taxes from them will result in their departure and/or further deterioration in the quality of the available workforce (because only workers that cannot find a better solution are left or attracted).

This policy also creates incentives to invest in activities that are profitable only because very cheap labour is available, but which could not survive economically if wages were to increase. At the same time, the technologic-ally advanced solutions that allow reductions in the cost of labour through increased productivity are not viewed as attractive, because wages are so low. This state of affairs has been going on for a very long time, so that any attempt at redressing the course and shifting to a model of reliance on foreign workers based on wages closer to, or in line with, wages paid to nationals would neces-sarily entail significant industrial restructuring, and is resisted by incumbents who have an interest in the continuation of the present pattern.

Different Patterns of Diversification

Why is this discussion central for the future of the rentier state? The answer is that, while diversification of the economy based on the wealth of avail-able natural resources (not just hydrocarbons) has been quite successful and may be expected to continue to be so, fiscal diversification—that is, reduced dependence of the state on oil revenue—has not happened, and must overcome some very steep obstacles. The Gulf economies are, I submit, sus-tainable today, and will continue to be, in the sense that their economies can adapt to the progressive loss in the commercial value of oil. But the rent available to the state will progressively shrink, and fiscal sustainability will be severely challenged. It is this fiscal crisis that will eventually force the trans-formation of the rentier state, necessitating increasing reliance on taxation of all sectors of the economy, which in turn will have profound effects on the structure of the same economy.

Diversification of the major oil-exporting economies can broadly be said to follow one of two alternatives: either diversification *based on* available natural resources—that is, pursuing backward and forward integration into related activities and services functional to the natural resources sector—or diversification *away from* the natural resources sector, aiming at acquiring a competitive advantage and promoting investment in activities that are unrelated to the extraction of minerals, and constituting a departure from them. The two strategies may be pursued as alternatives or in parallel, but the issue is that neither is likely to generate a surplus that might be taxed sufficiently to support the state, substituting for the rent component of oil revenue.

The oil-exporting countries are not the only ones relying on exploitation of natural resources. Several advanced economies specialize in the production and export of minerals or agricultural products, and the question of their sustainability is rarely posed.[7] For the oil- and gas-exporting countries the question was posed in the past because of fear of exhaustion of resources (peak oil supply), which in any case would likely be a slow and progressive process. At any rate, this preoccupation has now given way to the opposite preoccupation of a peak in oil demand in connection with global warming and the need to decarbonize our energy supply. Can oil rentier states survive?

In the aftermath of the COVID-19 crisis and the attendant sharp decline in energy demand, several sources have proposed scenarios featuring considerably closer dates for the expected plateau or peak.[8] However, a sharp decline is only envisaged in so-called back-casting scenarios: that is, those where the shape of the final state is predetermined on the basis of politically defined goals, and the scenario serves the purpose of illustrating how those goals can be reached.

More realistically, in a world in which policies are still far from being able to deliver the desired outcome, and multiple paths are possible to reach that outcome, demand for oil may be expected to decline gradually. In this context, oil prices are likely to remain relatively low, and supply to be reduced especially from those sources that feature the highest production costs. Low-cost Arab producers may thus look forward to maintaining or progressively increasing their share of an overall declining market. Therefore, as Bassam Fattouh and Anupama Sen state, 'even in a world where oil demand growth is expected to slow down, the oil sector will continue to play the dominant role in these economies for the foreseeable future'. But, as the same authors

---

[7] Luciani and Moerenhout, *When Can Oil Economies Be Deemed Sustainable?*
[8] International Energy Agency *World Energy Outlook* 2023, Paris

argue, 'rather than treating the oil industry as sunset industry in a world of heightened uncertainty about the prospects of oil demand, these countries will need to be much more strategic in terms of how the oil sector can further contribute to economic diversification.'[9] This means taking a range of initiatives to defend the role and value of oil and gas, even in a decarbonizing world.

The required initiatives are discussed in the following pages, and have been clearly identified also by some Saudi institutions, but it is not clear that they have been fully internalized or adopted by mainstream policy making. In other words, what needs to be done to preserve a future for the Saudi economy is largely known, and some steps are being taken that point in the right direction, but competing goals are being simultaneously pursued, threatening the prospects of success.

The Future of Oil in a Decarbonizing World

Pursuing diversification *based on* natural resources is possible for an oil exporter like Saudi Arabia on condition that the use of oil is rendered compatible with the objectives of decarbonization and avoidance of climate change. Decarbonizing hydrocarbon production and use entails the systematic, if progressive, elimination of emissions from oil and gas:

- scope 1 emissions, connected to the extraction of hydrocarbons and their transformation into final products;
- scope 2 emissions, connected to the generation of electricity used in the hydrocarbon industry; and
- scope 3 emissions, related to the final use of the products derived from hydrocarbons.

This is technically and economically possible, if the appropriate international institutional framework is put in place. Both Saudi Aramco and the King Abdullah Petroleum Studies and Research Center (KAPSARC) have been arguing and researching in this direction, the former also taking initial steps

[9] B. Fattouh and A. Sen, 'Economic Diversification in Arab Oil-Exporting Countries in the Context of Peak Oil and the Energy Transition', in Luciani and Moerenhout (eds.), *When Can Oil Economies Be Deemed Sustainable?*, open access, https://link.springer.com/chapter/10.1007/978-981-15-5728-6_5, pp. 73–97; see also A. Al-Saffar, 'Outlook for Producer Economies', in Luciani and Moerenhout (eds.), *When Can Oil Economies Be Deemed Sustainable?*, open access, https://link.springer.com/chapter/10.1007/978-981-15-5728-6_4, pp. 55–71; *International Energy Agency, The Oil and Gas Industry in Energy Transitions* (Paris: IEA, 2020), open access, https://www.iea.org/reports/the-oil-and-gas-industry-in-energy-transitions

to launch investment projects, although not as courageously as would be needed. The Saudi government has officially promoted the concept of the Circular Carbon Economy (CCE) and succeeded in having it included in the final Leaders' Declaration of the 2020 (Riyadh) G20: 'We endorse the Circular Carbon Economy (CCE) Platform, with its 4Rs framework (Reduce, Reuse, Recycle and Remove).'[10] Unfortunately in subsequent years very little concrete effort has been made to translate the concept in reality, and credibility has been affected.

Scope 1 Emissions

With respect to scope 1 emissions, it is a well-recognized fact that not all oil and gas streams are the same, depending on conditions for extraction and leakage of gases into the atmosphere. It has been shown that the carbon intensity of the extraction process varies greatly between fields, and is much higher in fields producing heavy oil and/or flaring or venting associated gas.[11] The GCC oil and gas producers are in a favourable position by international comparison because of the prolific nature of their fields and the vast investments made in containing gas flaring or venting. Extracting oil from the majority of Gulf fields does not require energy-intensive technology such as steam injection, fracking, or heating of the extracted oil. Flaring and venting have been minimized in all GCC countries (in contrast to Iraq or Iran). Recent analysis conducted on the basis of satellite data found that Saudi Arabia showed only one visible methane leak in 2019.[12] This is a methane intensity 100 times less than the Permian Basin in the United States, and 1,000 times smaller than Turkmenistan, the authors concluded.

Further decarbonization is possible through the use of renewable energy (primarily solar power) for heat (as pioneered in the Miraah project in Oman)[13] and/or electricity, and more systematic use of electricity (if from clean sources) as a substitute for hydrocarbons in all operations. Finally, systematic use of carbon capture and utilization or sequestration (CCUS) of the CO_2 generated in the extraction, transportation, and refining processes is a major possibility. Oil and gas producers enjoy ideal conditions for the

---

[10] G20, 'Riyadh Summit Leaders Declaration' (2020), https://www.g20riyadhsummit.org/pressroom/g20-riyadh-summit-leaders-declaration/.

[11] M. A. Masnadi and others, 'Global Carbon Intensity of Crude Oil Production', *Science* 361, no. 6405 (2018), pp. 851–3.

[12] Kayrros, 'Eliminating Methane Super Emitters', white paper (November 2020).

[13] Petroleum Development Oman, 'Miraah Solar Project' (n.d.), https://www.pdo.co.om/en/technical-expertise/solar-project-miraah/.

sequestration of CO_2, which can be injected in the same fields that contain hydrocarbons, with the added advantage of facilitating the recovery of the latter.[14] The CO_2 to be injected can also be captured from power plants or other energy-intensive industrial transformations.

Carbon Capture and Utilization or Sequestration

CCUS is indeed likely to be a key component of any decarbonization strategy in the long run because complete elimination of fossil fuels is difficult to envisage, even by the end of the century.[15] In a world in which a universally accepted (if not necessarily uniform) carbon price is imposed, sequestering carbon can become a source of revenue, in addition to the benefit of enhanced oil recovery.

Researchers at KAPSARC have proposed the creation of Carbon Sequestration Units;[16] the immediate proposal is that a group of countries (or 'club'), with a common interest in pursuing cleaner fossil fuels, backs a new CCUS-specific technology mechanism set up under Article 6 of the Paris Agreement. This is an interesting proposal but the first step to make it credible would be for Saudi Arabia to establish a large-scale CCUS project, capturing and sequestering CO_2 from its own emissions, certifying the quantities captured and sequestered in an internationally recognized way, and on this basis promoting the creation of the 'club'.

In this respect, Saudi Aramco concluded in 2022 an agreement with Schlumberger and Linde to establish a CCUS hub in Jubail.[17] The Jubail hub aims to capture and store 9 MtCO2 emissions per year by 2027, a part of Saudi Arabia's interim sequestration target of 44 MtCO2 per year by 2035. This is a good first step, but, considering that Saudi Arabia's CO_2 emissions from fossil fuels and industry were 608 million tons in 2022, a reduction of

[14] KAPSARC and International Energy Agency, *Decarbonizing Oil: The Role of CO2-Enhanced Oil Recovery (CO2-EOR)*, conference report (April 2018), open access, https://www.kapsarc.org/research/publications/decarbonizing-oil-the-role-of-co2-enhanced-oil-recovery-co2-%E2%80%90eor/.

[15] International Energy Agency, *CCUS in Clean Energy Transitions - Special Report on Carbon Capture Utilisation and Storage* September open access https://www.iea.org/reports/ccus-in-clean-energy-transitions.

[16] P. Zakkour and W. Heidug, 'A Mechanism for CCS in the Post-Paris Era: Piloting Results-Based Finance and Supply Side Policy under Article 6' (April 2019), open access, https://www.kapsarc.org/research/publications/a-mechanism-for-ccs-in-the-post-paris-era/; KAPSARC, Paris Agreement CCS Policy and Mechanisms, conference report (July 2019), open access, https://www.kapsarc.org/research/publications/paris-agreement-ccs-policy-and-mechanisms/; P. Mollet, W. Heidug, P. Zakkour, and E. Williams, 'Carbon Sequestration Units (CSUs): A New Tool to Mitigate Carbon Emissions' (January 2020), open access, https://www.kapsarc.org/research/publications/carbon-sequestration-units-csus-a-new-tool-to-mitigate-carbon-emissions/.

[17] Reuters 11.11.2022 https://www.reuters.com/business/energy/saudi-aramco-energy-ministry-sign-agreement-establish-carbon-capture-storage-hub-2022-11-10/, last accessed 25.11.2023.

barely 1.5 per cent. It is unlikely that the envisaged 'club' will see the light of day until projects of an order of magnitude larger size are implemented, and the feasibility, credibility, and advantages of the proposed scheme have been tested in practice.

The CCE strategy,[18] based on the 'four Rs' of reduction, reuse, removal, and recycling of carbon, says all the right things in principle, but, at least at the time of writing, lacks an implementation plan to make it truly credible.

Scope 2 Emissions

Electricity generation (scope 2) in the GCC countries is today almost entirely based on oil or gas. The opportunity to develop renewable or nuclear sources has been discussed for years, and ambitious plans have been announced, but implementation is lagging. The United Arab Emirates (UAE) is leading the way, but even there, more could be done. It is unrealistic to think that oil and gas in power generation will be phased out anytime soon, but CCUS could be systematically implemented, especially in newer plants, to reduce emissions progressively.

In Saudi Arabia, greater reliance on renewable energy sources, notably solar and wind, to produce electricity for export has also been on the agenda since at least 2010, when the King Abdullah City for Atomic and Renewable Energy (KACARE) was founded. This institution suffered from an unclear mission, combining elements of a policy-making body, a regulatory authority, an investment fund, and an implementation agency with attributions conflicting with several other existing institutions. Whether for this or other reasons, it has been largely ineffective, publishing ambitious plans, but failing to make any real progress.[19] It was only in November 2019 that a first utility-scale (300 MW) photovoltaic plant was inaugurated at Sakaka. A wind project at Dumat al Jandal was launched in 2019 with total capacity of 400 MW. According to the International Renewable Energies Agency (IRENA), as of 2021 wind and solar accounted for 0.065% of total power generation (less than one tenth of one per cent!)[20]

---

[18] N. B. Alqahtani, 'Circular Carbon Economy Research & Development' (n.d.), https://unfccc.int/sites/default/files/resource/RD%20Poster%20T1%20Saudi%20Arabia.pdf.

[19] G. Luciani and R. Ferroukhi (eds.), *Political Economy of Energy Reform: The Clean Energy–Fossil Fuel Balance in the Gulf* (Berlin: Gerlach, 2014).

[20] IRENA Energy Profile *Saudi Arabia* available at https://www.irena.org/-/media/Files/IRENA/Agency/Statistics/Statistical_Profiles/Middle%20East/Saudi%20Arabia_Middle%20East_RE_SP.pdf, last accessed on 25.11.2023

In addition to renewables, the Kingdom has also been targeting a nuclear power component, which of course would contribute to cleaning up electricity production. In contrast to the UAE, where the Al Baraka nuclear power park of four reactors, each with 1.4 GW capacity, is completed, with three reactors in operation in 2023 and the fourth to start operating very soon, in Saudi Arabia no similar project has yet been launched.

Unless a drastic acceleration is given to this programme, the prospects of exporting renewable or clean electricity, as frequently touted, remain pie in the sky. Reducing the role of fossil fuels in domestic power generation must certainly take priority over any notion of exporting clean electricity or decarbonized fuels. And development of CCUS is a prerequisite even for the possibility of exporting blue hydrogen (i.e. hydrogen from steam reforming of methane). Nevertheless, just as with the empty promises of KACARE, the official line is now that Saudi Arabia will be producing and exporting green hydrogen, produced from electrolysis of water with clean electricity, in a $5 billion project at Neom, announced in July 2020—a project that would make sense only if the country had already achieved clean domestic electricity, plus capture and sequestration of all emissions, and decarbonization of heavy industry. Saudi Arabia should invest massively in green electricity, but electrolysing water is not the most urgent utilization of such electricity. In the Saudi context, hydrogen is much more conveniently produced out of natural gas with carbon capture and sequestration, and renewable electricity targeted to reduce reliance on fossil-fuel burning. Furthermore, there is currently no proven technology to electrolyse seawater (several research projects are under way),[21] so the envisaged huge plant at Neom would need to rely on desalinated water, which would require further energy use.

But leaving aside Neom's fantasy land, the conclusion is that what needs to be done with respect to the cleaning of electricity generation is known, and also clearly understood by Saudi authorities, except that implementation is just embryonic.

Scope 3 Emissions

Scope 3 emissions are the most important size-wise, but also the most difficult to tackle. Oil-producing countries can follow three strategies to be able to eliminate scope 3 emissions.

---

[21] T. Schley, 'Generating Renewable Hydrogen Fuel from the Sea' (2020), https://news.psu.edu/story/633345/2020/09/29/research/generating-renewable-hydrogen-fuel-sea.

The first strategy consists in turning hydrocarbons into intermediate products that are not destined to be burned as fuel, by integrating downstream into the value chain, towards an increasingly diversified and sophisticated array of advanced intermediary or final consumer products, while at the same time capturing and sequestering the CO_2 emitted in the process. This means aiming to refine more of the crude oil produced and to export final products. Since the beginning of the current century, Saudi Arabia has made a determined effort to increase the share of its crude oil production that is refined domestically, or in Saudi Aramco-owned refineries abroad. The two solutions are not equivalent, however, as in the former value is added at home and enters the calculation of GDP, while in the latter value is added abroad. Furthermore, refineries mostly produce CO_2-emitting fuels; it is only through the further transformation of refinery products into petrochemicals that production of non-fuel derivatives is maximized, and this is possible mostly if refineries are available domestically. Saudi Aramco and SABIC, which is now a fully owned subsidiary of the former, are working together to develop a crude-to-petrochemicals refinery in Ras al Khair.[22]

The second strategy for eliminating scope 3 emissions consists in using hydrocarbons locally in energy-intensive transformations coupled with CO_2 CCUS. Key target industries are steel, cement, and aluminium—which, together with chemicals, are by far the most carbon-intensive industrial transformation processes.

- Saudi Arabia's steel production has been oscillating between 5 and 6.3 million tons per annum in the past ten years, accounting for less than 0.3 per cent of global production. From the perspective of decarbonizing steel, which entails reducing reliance on blast furnaces and increasing the role of direct reduction iron using natural gas or, in the future, hydrogen, Saudi Arabia clearly has the potential to expand its role in global steel production.
- Aluminium smelting is a highly electricity-intensive process, which may ideally be coupled with clean electricity from renewable or nuclear sources. Ma'aden has developed a fully integrated aluminium project stretching from the mining of bauxite to the production of aluminium sheets. This line of industrial activity could first of all be rendered zero-emission with the use of clean electricity, then possibly expanded using the advantage of availability of clean electricity.

---

[22] Reuters   23.11.2022   https://www.reuters.com/business/energy/saudis-sabic-aramco-plan-start-project-convert-crude-into-petrochemicals-2022-11-23/, last accessed 25.11.2023.

- Finally, cement production is also a very emission-intensive industrial process, which can be 'cleaned' primarily through CCUS. Reutilization of CO_2 in cement production is possible and is being actively researched by the industry.

In summary, the strategy focusing on carbon-intensive industrial transformations is based on a combination of CCUS and availability of clean electricity, both of which Saudi Arabia may enjoy well beyond the end of the hydrocarbon era.

The third strategy for eliminating scope 3 emissions consists in turning hydrocarbons into non-carbon, clean-burning fuels—which basically means hydrogen and its non-carbon composites, while also engaging in systematic CCUS. The concept of exporting 'blue' hydrogen (produced from hydrocarbons with carbon capture and sequestration) or 'green' hydrogen (produced from clean electricity via electrolysis of water) is an interesting diversification possibility per se, but is less promising than the previous two strategies. This is because hydrogen is difficult and expensive to transport, and turning it into a more easily transportable non-carbon fuel, such as ammonia, entails further costs. Therefore, it will always be more convenient to utilize renewable energy or blue or green hydrogen locally, for the production of otherwise carbon-intensive intermediate or final products, rather than exporting it for utilization elsewhere. It is not clear at all that exporting hydrogen or ammonia will create value for Saudi Arabia, and many alternatives exist which are likely to create more value.

Diversification based on natural resources is, in summary, a very concrete possibility for Saudi Arabia. It is sometimes objected that these industries are very capital intensive and offer few job opportunities. This is certainly true, and the investment effort required to implement a vision of diversification based on hydrocarbons is certainly very large. But the jobs created are more likely to attract Saudi nationals, and be able to pay higher wages than most other jobs in manufacturing.

Impact of Oil-Based Diversification Strategies on Government Finance

The impact of these complementary policies on government finance is likely to be important. They all entail considerable investment in projects whose rate of return is likely to be much lower than in simple oil production with no abatement of emissions. This has long been a source of resistance towards pursuing backward or forward linkages, as locally procured inputs are likely to be somewhat more expensive than imported ones, and investment in refining and petrochemicals has much lower returns than investment in the production of crude oil. CCUS is an added cost whose only potential benefit is as a method for enhanced oil recovery.

Recently launched reform of the electricity sector and an increase in electricity tariffs may pave the way to a change in decision making, highlighting the true opportunity cost of burning crude oil and natural gas in power plants.[23] If this plays out as hoped, it is clear that Saudi Arabia has huge potential for developing clean energy, and for shifting progressively from exporting hydrocarbons to exporting decarbonized petrochemicals and other energy-intensive products embodying clean electricity and/or hydrogen. The direction in this case is clear, but the required investment effort is colossal, and can only credibly be undertaken if financial resources from the private sector and foreign investors can be mobilized.

It should be stressed that Saudi Arabia has numerous valuable natural resources besides hydrocarbons, sunshine, and wind. There is considerable competitive value added that can be developed through the decarbonized exploitation of other mineral resources, to produce a potentially very diversified array of intermediates for industry. Notwithstanding all that has been done so far, it is fair to say that the country has barely scratched the surface of the potential for diversification based on natural resources. But taking full advantage of this potential requires huge investment.

Albeit probably reduced relative to the past, because the shift to decarbonized from carbon-intensive products has added costs that will inevitably erode the margin, the rent available over the coming years and decades remains substantial, and is a huge opportunity to finance investment and leverage additional funds accruing from abroad. But if the rent is devoted to pay for the government's current expenditures or investment unrelated to diversification, it will not be available to finance investment for diversification.

The challenge for the state is, then, to move progressively away from fiscal reliance on the oil rent, towards reliance on taxation of industry or private incomes and wealth, at least for supporting current expenditure.[24] This can

---

[23] T. Moerenhout, 'Fuel and Electricity Reform for Economic Sustainability in the Gulf', in Luciani and Moerenhout (eds.), *When Can Oil Economies Be Deemed Sustainable?*, pp. 191–213, open access, https://link.springer.com/chapter/10.1007/978-981-15-5728-6_8.

[24] I. Diwan, 'Fiscal Sustainability, the Labor Market, and Growth in Saudi Arabia', in Luciani and Moerenhout (eds.), *When Can Oil Economies Be Deemed Sustainable?*, pp. 191–213, open access, https://link.springer.com/chapter/10.1007/978-981-15-5728-6_3; M. Malik and T. Nagesh, 'Fiscal Sustainability and Hydrocarbon Endowment Per Capita in the GCC', in Luciani and Moerenhout (eds.), *When Can Oil*

only be achieved progressively, by allocating a growing share of the rent to domestic investment by institutions that largely already exist, such as Saudi Aramco, SABIC, Ma'aden, the Saudi Electricity Company, and others; and by finding alternative sources to cover the government's current expenditure. But raising taxes on industry, at a time when its rapid expansion is sought, is a challenge.[25] Any investment strategy requires time to come to fruition, and while successful investment will, after a time, generate added income, which can then be taxed, the initial effect will inevitably be lower availability of financial resources for current expenditure.

Diversification away from Natural Resources

Diversification *away from* natural resources may also be a valid strategy, provided that the right projects are selected. But finding the right projects—that is, investments that will yield internationally competitive products and will be commercially viable in the long term—is easier said than done.

We may distinguish between investment geared to the production of non-tradables and investment for the production of internationally traded goods and services. Historically, attention has focused on investment in non-tradables because of the assumption that they might be in short supply domestically, and in any case because they are not subject to international competition. Hence the common emphasis on real-estate or retail trade investment (shopping centres), which are viewed as attractive and may be a significant form of diversification, at least for as long as domestic competition does not become so acute that margins are seriously eroded. In the Gulf economies, this type of investment has for decades been supported by rapid population growth and the importation of cheap labour. By definition, however, it is a kind of investment that cannot improve the international competitiveness of the economy, except in the limited sense of preventing the Dutch disease from deploying its negative effects.

The risk involved in diversification away from natural resources is much higher when it comes to internationally traded goods and services. The most frequently quoted possibilities are international tourism, travel, logistics, and financial services. The common characteristic of these sectors is that they are all very open to international competition and extremely vulnerable to shocks. For many years, some of the ventures launched by some of the Gulf

Economies Be Deemed Sustainable?, pp. 215–53, open access, https://link.springer.com/chapter/10.1007/978-981-15-5728-6_9.
[25] Diwan, 'Fiscal Sustainability, the Labor Market, and Growth in Saudi Arabia'.

Arab states—especially first movers—have been very successful. For example, Emirates has certainly been a successful airline, but Etihad and Qatar Airways never quite managed to match the success of the pioneer. Similarly, tourism can be severely affected by the global crises, but is also vulnerable to location-specific threats, such as political instability or insecurity in the region, if not in the country itself. Specialization in tourism is therefore also very vulnerable.

As for financial services, the region has done a good job in improving its governance and the credibility of regional institutions, and it is not impossible that progressively the Gulf might consolidate its role as a regional financial hub. However, in this case as for airlines, regional competition has prevented the emergence of a single leading financial centre, and dispersion of assets and know-how damages all competitors, preventing the formation of the critical mass needed to enter the premier league.

The intense competitive environment also means that it may be difficult to turn these sectors into sources of income for the state. On the contrary, not only do they generally require support in the form of subsidies and other privileges in the early stages of development, but also they rarely become truly independent of continuing support.

With the exception of financial services, all sectors offering hospitality, logistics, travel, or retail trade are labour intensive and rely heavily on low-paid expatriates, although an effort is being made to encourage employment of nationals. Minimizing the cost of labour is an important consideration for these sectors, and opposition to a policy of progressively bringing the remuneration of expatriates in line with that of nationals, to avoid labour market segmentation and distortions, is likely to be intense.

Hence a strategy of diversification away from natural resources is very much an uphill battle. All sectors in which the Gulf countries may hope to make inroads are highly competitive, fragile, and dependent on low-cost labour. As such, they offer only a weak tax base, and are more likely to require continuing support from the state rather than providing support to the state. To avoid nurturing uncompetitive parasite activities, it is crucially important to rely on market discipline to make sure that failed ventures are abandoned and only well-managed ones prosper. The main implication is that in a strategy of moving away from natural resources the role of state-owned companies must be limited or altogether absent, and the field must be left open for private entrepreneurs. The state may devote a share of the oil rent to special credit institutions tasked with offering long-term credit (in Saudi Arabia this has been done by the Saudi Industrial Development Fund) or even acquiring equity participations on a temporary basis to facilitate capitalization, but such tools should not be abused to the point of keeping zombie enterprises running. The latter is a well-known problem for all countries, not just oil exporters.

Fiscal and Investment Discipline

Our main argument so far has been that it is possible to continue successfully diversifying the Saudi economy, and the main direction of further development should be the continuation of past efforts and the decisive intensification of solutions that have long been identified but only minimally implemented. The investment effort required necessitates mobilizing domestic as well as international capital, and simultaneously devoting a progressively larger share of the oil rent to productive investment rather than current expenditure.

It is frequently asserted that the Saudi government 'needs' a high oil price in order to balance its budget. This would indicate that there is no room for manoeuvre to shift funds from current expenditure to investment, but fortunately this is probably not the case at all. The Saudi government devotes large sums to expenses whose social, political, or economic benefit is dubious at best. Military expenditure and conflictual regional relations cannot be considered positive or even neutral for the development prospects and future stability of the state: they are either destructive or wasteful. In the new global environment, serious fiscal and investment discipline is required.

It is also possible to revise the modalities of the provision of key services, especially in education and health care, but the temptation to move in the direction of imposing fees and favouring privatization should be resisted as it would affect the well-being of nationals and the accumulation of human capital directly.

Investment discipline is especially necessary. Only investment projects that have sound commercial and economic justification should be undertaken, carefully avoiding white elephants.

Thus, the state should certainly aim at drastically reducing current expenditure, while avoiding a reduction of investment in human capital (education and health). But it is not clear that this will liberate sufficient resources to sustain the investment required for the very fundamental transformation sketched in the previous paragraphs. Inevitably, the state must accept a growing role for the private sector, as both an essential contributor to the required investment effort and also, down the road, as a potential source of revenue through taxation.

In the early years of the current century, the fiscal position of the Saudi government was very weak, while the private sector had accumulated substantial financial, technological, and managerial capabilities. At that time, the state explicitly solicited a more independent role for the private sector in support of the continuing diversification of the Saudi economy. This represented a logical continuation of a policy of support and incubation of the private sector that had been in place since the beginning of the oil era. This policy initially enriched a number of merchant companies, which were little more than opportunistic intermediaries of foreign providers. But progressively, these merchants, or at least some of them, became proper entrepreneurs much less dependent on oil rent redistribution through government expenditure. In other words, a national bourgeoisie emerged at this time,[26] which enjoyed very considerable financial means, was very well integrated in the global business environment, was frequently well educated and capable, and was keen to play a role in the development of the country in association with, yet independently of, and in a dialectical relationship with the state.[27]

At that stage, the state should have devised a new set of policies to facilitate the transformation of family conglomerates into proper corporations, encouraging their listing on the stock exchange and the emergence of national champions through the rationalization of several sectors. It should also have implemented privatization of key companies such as SABIC and those in power generation, which had been envisaged by successive development plans for the previous twenty years at least. It should have inaugurated a new way of managing the rent, focusing on creating endowments and institutional investors in support of the private sector.[28] In contrast, the state went back to the old expenditure pattern focusing on subsidies and infrastructure investment, whose marginal benefit was rapidly decreasing. Not surprisingly, the private sector went back to the old habit of just profiting from the bonanza of public expenditure projects.

---

[26] G. Luciani, 'Saudi Arabian Business: From Private Sector to National Bourgeoisie', in P. Aarts and G. Nonnemann (eds.), *Saudi Arabia in the Balance: Politics, Economics and International Relations between 9/11, the Iraq Crisis and the Future* (London: Hurst Publishers and New York University Press, 2005), pp. 144–81.

[27] G. Luciani, 'Linking Economic and Political Reform in the Middle East: The Role of the Bourgeoisie', in O. Schlumberger (ed.), *Debating Arab Authoritarianism: Dynamics and Durability in Nondemocratic Regimes* (Stanford, CA: Stanford University Press, 2007), pp. 161–76.

[28] G. Luciani, 'Beyond Sovereign Funds: Transforming a Rentier Economy and Improving Governance through the Creation of Autonomous Endowments', Rahmania Occasional Paper 01 (Riyadh: Al-Rahmania Cultural Center, 2010), open access, https://www.researchgate.net/publication/273619932_Beyond_Sovereign_Funds_Transforming_a_Rentier_Economy_and_Improving_Governance_through_the_Creation_of_Autonomous_Endowments_Rahmania_Occasional_Paper_01_Riyadh_2010.

When prices collapsed again in 2014–15, the new leadership continued to speak of growing reliance on the private sector, but acted in the diametrically opposite direction. The imprisonment of numerous prominent business leaders at the Ritz-Carlton Hotel in Riyadh based on unsubstantiated accusations of corruption led to the 'recovery' of an officially estimated $100 billion, never properly accounted for. While it is not difficult to believe that some of this money had been accumulated with less than orthodox methods, the modalities of this shake-down, conducted with total disregard for due process, certainly sent a clear signal to the entire Saudi business community. The state has in this way made it very clear that no independent bourgeoisie will be permitted: wealthy private individuals will be requested, enticed, or pressured to invest in ways and in projects that the ruler will designate. In the process, a number of formerly entirely private companies were partially or completely acquired by the state, which henceforward controls their investment decisions.

The opportunity of fostering the transformation of the private sector from opportunistic client to independent partner of the government in the envisaged investment effort has been lost, and will be very difficult to recover. It is only to be expected that private entrepreneurs will be keen to provide their services to the government in the implementation of projects, without asking themselves whether the same projects are viable, for as long as they are not expected truly to invest in them. The major benefit of requesting private entrepreneurs to invest alongside the government is to have their critical understanding of the viability of the project in question. Corralling private investors through political pressure or the offer of side benefits (e.g. the allocation of large implementation contracts), which may outweigh the perceived risk of the investment, is not a successful strategy in the longer term. In other words, the state must impose market discipline on the private sector but also accept the discipline that private investors will inevitably impose on the selection of investment projects.

Privatization has been on the agenda since at least the Fourth Development Plan (1985–9), but has been implemented only minimally. In recent times, the state has increased its direct participation in the equity of several formerly entirely private corporate entities, and the initial public offering of Saudi Aramco with the flotation of a minuscule 5 per cent share of the equity does not really empower the private sector much. The takeover of SABIC on the part of Saudi Aramco with the sole purpose of allowing the PIF to improve its liquidity is very clearly a step in the wrong direction. The state must accept that it needs a prosperous and independent private sector: it is legitimate to steer private business towards maximizing the benefit from the point of view of national development, but subjecting it to political control undermines the contribution that is needed from it.

In the absence of an autonomous national bourgeoisie, the burden of economic diversification will fall exclusively on the shoulders of a state that has demonstrated its inability to evaluate investment projects critically. The latest manifestation of the lack of investment discipline is, of course, the pet project of the ruler, a new city called Neom whose only clearly specified characteristic is that it will cost $500 billion. Does anyone dare to ask what the internal rate of return is expected to be?

Developing a Domestic Taxable Base

In the end, the state must aim at reducing its dependence on the oil rent as its main source of revenue, and develop alternative sources through various forms of taxation. For that, it is necessary to create a taxable base and taxation system.[29]

The first and easiest step in this direction is to reduce consumption subsidies and impose consumption taxes. The May 2020 decision to triple the rate of value added tax to 15 per cent (which is relatively high by international comparison: the average rate of indirect tax in the Organization for Economic Cooperation and Development was 19.23 per cent in 2020, the Asian average 11.79 per cent)[30] clearly and dramatically demonstrates the urgency of the challenge. It also demonstrates the limits of consumption taxation, which is almost inevitably regressive, weighing on the poor more than on the rich; and inflationary, as it is added to previously set prices.

Thus, the imposition of direct taxes on income and wealth can hardly be further postponed. The state may in theory attempt to limit the political impact by privileging taxes on corporate rather than individual incomes, especially if measures are taken to encourage corporatization of family businesses—with the implementation of proper accounting, this may allow better understanding of the results effectively obtained by the private sector.

Income taxes are the rule in most countries, while wealth taxes are relatively rare, primarily because of the difficulty of assessing the wealth of private individuals. But in the case of Saudi Arabia, where two-thirds of nationals are employed by the government, the option of introducing a wealth tax, built

---

[29] Diwan, 'Fiscal Sustainability, the Labor Market, and Growth in Saudi Arabia'.
[30] KPMG, Indirect Tax Rates Table 2020), https://home.kpmg/xx/en/home/services/tax/tax-tools-and-resources/tax-rates-online/indirect-tax-rates-table.html.

and legitimized on the precedent of *zakat*, is probably more promising than taxing income. There is more of a taxable base in accumulated wealth than in incomes being currently earned by the vast majority of the population.

Direct income taxes may be introduced for all, nationals and expatriates; or for expatriates only (as has been repeatedly proposed). Direct income taxes on expatriates are likely either to have to be absorbed by their employer or to lead to the departure of employees, who might conclude that employment in the Kingdom is no longer sufficiently attractive. Both results may be viewed as positive, in the context of the needed transition from a strategy of cheap immigration to one of equal pay for expatriates and nationals alike. Thus, it may be sensible to exclude most nationals from an income tax (e.g. establishing an adequately high threshold for the minimum taxable income, with progressive rates above that level); or even, as has been proposed for Kuwait,[31] to envisage a universal basic income (UBI) for all nationals who are not employed in the public sector to narrow further the difference between nationals' and expatriates' reservation wages. So far, the Citizen's Account programme has been implemented, which, however, is neither universal nor unconditional.

Steffen Hertog believes that a UBI can be funded through the elimination of energy subsidies, which is an attractive way of presenting the proposal. However, the two policies are not necessarily coupled, and each has its own independent rationale. The elimination of energy subsidies should certainly be pursued to improve the fiscal equilibrium of the state (but it should be noted that declining oil prices also automatically reduce subsidies, in the definition of the latter which is adopted by the International Monetary Fund and the International Energy Agency), and it is quite possible that this may be made politically more palatable through the introduction of monetary compensation for poorer citizens. The latter may be viewed as a form of negative income tax in the context of introducing a progressive personal income tax scheme, further accentuating the redistributive features that should characterize the latter.

---

[31] S. Hertog, 'Reforming Wealth Distribution in Kuwait: Estimating Costs and Impacts', LSE Middle East Centre Kuwait Programme, Paper Series 5 (London: London School of Economics, 2020), open access, http://eprints.lse.ac.uk/105564/2/Reforming_Wealth_Distribution_in_Kuwait_New.pdf.

The Importance of the Regional Environment

A final set of considerations concerning the possible future transformation of the rentier state is related to the regional environment. Economists are accustomed to discussing national economies while paying little attention to their size and regional integration prospects, but in reality, successful economies are either, on the one hand, very large (i.e. have large domestic markets) and/or part of a regional integration scheme; or, on the other, small, highly specialized, and globally orientated. Saudi Arabia does not have a significantly large domestic market, and its international specialization is under threat, hence further diversification requires a credible strategy of regional integration.

Although value chains have stretched internationally, there are properly only relatively few globally traded goods, mostly in the category of intermediate products. For most products, be they intermediate or finished, proximity to the market is an important consideration in determining the location of productive activities, either because of the high cost of transportation relative to value added, or because of the need to be close to the final customer and able to adapt to their needs and tastes. What this means is that there is a lot of trade that is geared towards a geographically proximate market. A country trading with the world at large but isolated from its proximate regional market loses attraction and competitiveness, and eventually misses opportunities.

This is a key obstacle for Arab and specifically Saudi economic diversification and sustainability.[32] Until 2017, there was hope that the GCC might develop a viable regional integration project, notwithstanding repeated delays in the effective implementation of decisions such as complete trade liberalization within the group and adoption of a common external tariff. But since the decision on the part of Saudi Arabia and the UAE to implement a radical boycott of Qatar in June 2017, cutting not only all trade, but also all movements of people and communications, including closure of air space, the credibility of the GCC has collapsed. In 2021, an official reconciliation was staged, thanks to an almost complete climbdown on the part of Saudi Arabia and the UAE, but it would be disingenuous to believe that this episode will simply be forgotten. Since then, the rivalry between Saudi Arabia and the United Arab Emirates has resurfaced.

---

[32] G. Luciani, 'Oil Rent and Regional Economic Development in MENA', in G. Luciani (ed.), *Combining Economic and Political Development: The Experience of MENA*, International Development Policy Series 7 (Geneva: Graduate Institute Publications; Boston, MA: Brill-Nijhoff, 2017), pp. 211–30, open access, https://journals.openedition.org/poldev/2239.

But even if the GCC were to find a new life, the group as a whole still does not constitute a sufficiently large and diversified market to have a truly promising prospect of attracting manufacturing investment and limiting extreme dependence on imports from the rest of the world. For that, the borders of the regional integration strategy must be wider, and encompass countries extending from the Fertile Crescent to the other side of the Red Sea—not to speak of the benefits that might be derived from closer integration with Iran.

But the reality is that the Middle East and North Africa region is in the midst of a regional civil war[33] which does not show much sign of heading towards a resolution. Saudi Arabia, in particular, has intervened in Yemen, and after many years of a bloody civil war obtained little or nothing, except being trapped with no exit option in sight. Once this war comes to an end, what prospects may exist? Yemen is a country of 35 million extremely poor people who have profound historical ties with the Saudi population. Before 1990, Yemenis could enter and work in Saudi Arabia without a visa. But after the then Yemeni President Ali Abdullah Saleh sided with Saddam Hussein and supported the annexation of Kuwait, Saudi Arabia expelled all Yemenis en masse, and it has not been able to re-establish a win–win relationship ever since. Is the solution a tall wall across the desert? How can a project of shared prosperity, capable of underpinning peace and reconciliation, be envisaged?

In a world that is increasingly organizing into large trading blocs, a regionally isolated Saudi Arabia, constantly on the verge of armed conflict with its neighbours, and in some cases actively implicated in it, will continue to waste resources in massive weapons purchases and forfeit a large number of otherwise promising economic diversification opportunities.

The Twilight of the Rentier State

In a decarbonizing world, major oil- and gas-producing countries may successfully adapt their economies, and prosper by leveraging their comparative advantage; for that they need to engage in a massive investment effort. Therefore, oil economies can be sustainable, although it remains to be seen whether they will be sustained: that is, whether the necessary policies will be implemented. In any case, the oil states' access to a rent accruing from the rest of

---

[33] G. Luciani, 'The Political Economy of Change in MENA', in C. Jones (ed.), *The Politics of Change in the Middle East*, Durham University Middle East Papers 78 (Durham: Institute for Middle Eastern and Islamic Studies, 2017), pp. 54–71, open access, https://www.dur.ac.uk/resources/imeis/HIGH-DMEP78-ThePoliticsofChangeintheMiddleEast.pdf; G. Luciani, 'Oil and the Arab Civil War', *Aspenia* 77–8 (2018), pp. 132–40.

the world will be eroded because of the added costs of eliminating carbon emissions.

The required diversification is first and foremost in the fiscal foundations of the state. The equilibrium of government budgets must to be adapted to revenues that will likely be both lower in absolute terms and differently composed, with oil rents playing a progressively reduced role.

By definition, this means that the state will progressively lose its rentier nature. The transformation may be slow and major discontinuities may be avoided, but the direction of the process must be firmly established and the pace accelerated. It is highly likely that institutions will also need to be adapted and broader political participation allowed; however, there is nothing mechanical about the link between taxation and democracy, and there may be many shades of democracy. Regional conflicts must give way to regional economic integration. Transitions do not need to be revolutionary, but it is difficult to envisage economic adaptation in the absence of parallel political adaptation.

Conclusion

John Sfakianakis

Since 2016, Saudi Arabia has undergone a sea change that is arguably irreversible. Sweeping reforms have awakened the economy, politics, and society. It is still uncertain if these reforms will be sufficient to bring the necessary income in a post-hydrocarbon world. Yet Saudi Arabia is trying to direct change to its economy, as this is the key piece of the puzzle it has the power to control.

Saudi Arabia is making whopping and eager bets. Similar bets were made in the past; however, this time, they are greater in magnitude and have galvanized the support of the entire state machine to support its pledges financially. No doubt, these wagers are leveraging the balance sheet of the state in unique and profound ways. However, there are genuine attempts to diversify the sources of revenue and to use different mechanisms to increase the state's coffers: fees, value added tax, budget rationalization, and efficiency procurement measures. At the same time, Saudi Arabia must direct and optimize its hydrocarbon revenues to drive its transformation. In some ways, the country's openness to reform is a recognition that oil revenues are both volatile and perilous, and will not last forever. The task will be to find and sustain new sources of income in the coming years in order to replace the $250–350 billion of oil export revenues which are set to gradually dwindle. If adjusted for inflation, real revenues are in continuous decline for many years and have been accentuated as a result of the global inflationary pressures of 2022–23. Time affects the value of cash flows, and the future will require additional expenditures as the country's population ages and there is an implicit discount rate on everyone. The wager being made today is that many of these projects can be financially self-sustaining, generating a positive cash flow in the medium term, and will not require the state to support off-budget costs in perpetuity from on-budget activities. For this ambition to be realized, the price of oil is as crucial as ever, dovetailing with the economic choices that the country's leadership makes.

The role of the private sector is paramount. Over the next few years, a balance between the state and business will have to be devised. By and large,

John Sfakianakis, *Conclusion*. In: *The Economy of Saudi Arabia in the 21st Century*. Edited by: John Sfakianakis, Oxford University Press. © John Sfakianakis (2024). DOI: 10.1093/oso/9780198863878.003.0014

employment can only be generated in a sustainable way by the private sector and, more importantly, small and medium-sized actors. Over the last few years, employment was generated by the state and the myriad of newly created government bodies. Employment for Saudis in the private sector has been generated, but not fast enough, and the impetus came from political and economic considerations of compliance and private sector conformity. Productivity must be tackled meaningfully. The state's role in the economy is partly derived from the private sector's rent-seeking performance of the pre-2016 period and its conviction about the country's economic development project. The state's perception of the private sector and the size and timing of its own 'giga projects' led it to press ahead with a state capitalist project that crowded out potential participants. As the state grows its edifice in the economy, it will be interesting to watch how it exits from its current, centrist role. Policy-makers are embedded in managing the economic affairs of the state. Restraining private sector oligopolies from participating in the economy is positive, but preventing the state from becoming a giant near-monopoly over time requires careful calibration. Casting a wider net and crowding in local and foreign businesses is essential to address the equity injections required to provide know-how and diversify the credit pool away from local banks and capital markets. There is no one-size-fits-all model, but the private sector is essential in helping to generate ideas, enhance market confidence, and meet the country's targets.

As the government embarked on revenue-generating policies, it had to provide something in return, in the form of employment, inclusion, social reforms, and a general opening of the country's social norms. Whether this is part of a new social contract, a way to provide legitimacy for the new ruler, or, more appropriately, a combination of both, it is a boon for the economy. Social reforms have also provided hope for a young generation that has long remained idle and on the fringes.

Saudi Arabia's external environment will equally determine the country's economic future. Even as Saudi Arabia introduces reforms and tries to establish its primacy, so do others in the wider region. As the rest of the world becomes more inward looking and the region finds its bearings and develops its alliances, the Kingdom's regional competitors will not stay aloof. Saudi Arabia is trying to make up for lost time and catch up with the rest of the region. In some areas, a second-mover effect may be enough, as many lessons can be learned; but in others, it will be a tough battle. The wisdom of the country's leadership will be measured and tested. Moreover, Saudi Arabia understands that peace and stability in the wider region is a prerequisite for its ability to attract investments and place the country on the world map.

For a long time, Saudi Arabia has stayed within the Western mix of political and military alliances. This was a suitable arrangement as both its exports and its assets were broadly located in the same hemisphere. Today more than two-thirds of Saudi Arabia's oil exports are destined for Asia and around one-fifth end up between Europe and the United States of America. The Kingdom's currency is pegged against the greenback, which has served the country well for decades. But at some point, this will have to end, due to a combination of endogenous and unforeseen exogenous forces. Its military is dependent on the West for its inter-operability and equipment, while the country's main exports are all in the East. Its foreign policy will have a bearing on its allies as well as its investors. Foreign investors will have to be cajoled and incentivized while the country's business environment is improved. Foreign investments remain a critical part of the puzzle, but regional competition is increasing. Attracting foreign talent is essential if Saudi Arabia is to shift to more complex modes of production, and the interplay of culture and tradition will have to be balanced. What happens to Asia's decarbonization efforts is as essential for Saudi Arabia as what happens in the rest of the world. Saudi Arabia is attempting to make inroads in developing its renewables capacity in this new era of climate change, at a time when technology is progressing fast. One advantage that Saudi Arabia possesses is its vast sources of capital, which it is able to use to make its decarbonization wagers. The balance is not easy, as now it is being called upon to address external economic prospects as well as domestic considerations. It will become important to prioritize the state's economic affairs as it transitions over time to a paradigm of lower oil revenues.

Saudi Arabia's brand recognition has reached new heights over years be it due to attracting football stars, golf tournaments, hosting the grand prix formula 1 contest or others athletic, cultural and hospitality events. Saudi Arabia is seeking notoriety in the hopes that it becomes a destination—for business or pleasure—in peoples minds. This is a long-term dividend policy, and it remains to be seen how it is done in tandem with the country's more conservative norms whilst the world is changing. Also, Saudi Arabia is encountering a world that is becoming increasingly concerned about climate change. And as it attempts to promote its softer power elements through sports, culture and entertainment, criticism will unavoidably rise for sportswashing and greenwashing. Since 2016, Saudi Arabia has spent a lot to promote its brand and image both as an investment hub and more recently as a leisure and tourist destination. Massive projects have captured the imagination, welcomed by some, while others among a climate-conscious global citizenry have raised questions about sustainability. These projects have exposed Saudi

Arabia to the world and its ability to deliver is essential. Perhaps many of the projects are so intertwined with the country's leadership that they are too big to fail, or will fail because they are too big. Although the jury is still out on what will fail and what will not, in many ways Saudi Arabia has very few options available. The counterfactual reality of doing nothing and continuing with business as usual does not offer a wide range of options or choices, as the external changes are likely to be revolutionary. If the pace of decarbonization is expedited, a demand shock in oil prices will begin to be felt by 2030, and deepen thereafter. This does not confer Saudi Arabia with much time.

Picking the right sectors to provide significant economic growth is not easy. The reform period could perhaps best be described as a massive trial-and-error campaign, albeit a very costly one that will generate winners and losers. Perhaps this is the only way Saudi Arabia can have a shot at catching up in a Gerschenkronian way, turning its latecomer effect into an advantage. Saudi Arabia has limited low-hanging fruit in the world of technology and innovation. Localizing cutting-edge technologies and knowledge through international strategic investments is a way forward. Partnering with foreign firms and sharing much-coveted intellectual properties is not easy, as the world is becoming more introverted and protective. Saudi Arabia has diversified into chemicals, plastics, and various manufacturing materials. Countries tend to diversify by moving into a product ecosystem that requires similar competences to their existing abilities and building complex high valued products for local and export markets. A challenge for many economies is that automation is advancing apace, as jobs—especially in manufacturing—are being replaced by robotization. Saudi Arabia has a young population, which is a mixed blessing as it needs to create high-skilled employment opportunities for its citizens. Aligning educational programmes with employer needs is crucial. Improving the quality of education, including vocational training, would also help boost productivity. High economic growth of the kind mandated in Vision 2030 also requires stability, which the country has maintained since redrawing its political map.

Looking forward, the economy requires a rigorous and continuous process of severe competition among its private sector participants, strong institutions, and a willingness to allow creative destruction to run its course within the wider economy. To date, the economic reform experiment undertaken by Saudi Arabia remains among the most sweeping ever seen among the emerging market economies. The changes are all encompassing and involve a complex redrawing of the political, economic, religious, and social maps. Saudi Arabia's grand reform experiment is a lesson in the fine balancing act required of one of the world's largest economies and most significant energy providers. Although predicting a country's future economic trajectory is a near impossible task, Saudi Arabia has been taking all the right steps after decades of dormancy to transition to a more secure and remunerative post-oil economy. The right government policies, private sector development, and intelligent regulations will be needed to turn Saudi Arabia's ambitions into reality and make it one of the world's best-performing economies.

Index

For the benefit of digital users, indexed terms that span two pages (e.g., 52–53) may, on occasion, appear on only one of those pages.

Tables and figures are indicated by an italic *t* and *f*, following the paragraph number; 'n.' after a paragraph number indicates the footnote number.